The All England Law Reports Annual Review 1989

UNITED KINGDOM   Butterworth & Co (Publishers) Ltd,
                 88 Kingsway, **London** WC2B 6AB and
                 4 Hill Street, **Edinburgh** EH2 3JZ

AUSTRALIA   Butterworths Pty Ltd, **Sydney, Melbourne,
                 Brisbane, Adelaide, Perth, Canberra**
                 and **Hobart**

CANADA   Butterworths Canada Ltd, **Toronto** and **Vancouver**

IRELAND   Butterworth (Ireland) Ltd, **Dublin**

MALAYSIA   Malayan Law Journal Pte Ltd, **Kuala Lumpur**

NEW ZEALAND   Butterworths of New Zealand Ltd, **Wellington** and **Auckland**

PUERTO RICO   Equity de Puerto Rico Inc, **Hato Rey**

SINGAPORE   Malayan Law Journal Pte Ltd, **Singapore**

USA   Butterworth Legal Publishers,
                 Austin, Texas, **Boston**, Massachusetts,
                 Clearwater, Florida (D & S Publishers),
                 Orford, New Hampshire (Equity Publishing),
                 St Pau, Minnesota, **Seattle**, Washington

General Editor
Paul Brown, MA

ISBN 0 406 86309 1

Typeset by Phoenix Photosetting, Chatham, Kent
Printed and bound in Great Britain by
Mackays of Chatham PLC, Chatham, Kent

THE
ALL ENGLAND
LAW REPORTS
ANNUAL REVIEW
1989

London
BUTTERWORTHS
1990

Contributors

Administrative Law
Keith Davies, JP, MA, LLM
Barrister, Professor of Law,
University of Reading

Arbitration
J E Adams LLB, FCIArb
Solicitor, Emeritus Professor of Law,
Queen Mary and Westfield College,
University of London

Commercial Law
N E Palmer, BCL, MA
Barrister, Professor of Law,
University of Southampton and
Robert Merkin, LLB, LLM
Professor of Law, University of Sussex

Company Law
D D Prentice, MA, LLB, JD
Barrister, Reader in Company Law,
Fellow of Pembroke College,
Oxford

Conflict of Laws
J G Collier, MA, LLB
Barrister, Vice-Master of Trinity Hall,
Cambridge

Consumer Law and *Contempt of Court*
C J Miller, BA, LLM
Barrister, Professor of Law,
University of Birmingham

Contract
Michael P Furmston, TD, BCL, MA, LLM
Bencher of Gray's Inn,
Professor of Law,
University of Bristol

Criminal Law, Criminal Procedure and Sentencing
G J Bennett, MA
Barrister, Lecturer in Law,
University of Leeds and
Brian Hogan, LLB
Barrister, Professor of Common Law,
University of Leeds

Employment Law
Ian Smith, MA, LLB
Barrister, Senior Lecturer in Law,
University of East Anglia

European Community Law and *Public International Law*
C J Greenwood, MA, LLB
Barrister, Fellow of Magdalene College,
Cambridge

Evidence and *Practice and Procedure*
Adrian A S Zuckerman, LLM, MA
Fellow of University College,
Oxford

Extradition
Ian M Yeats, BCL, MA
Barrister, Senior Lecturer in Law,
Queen Mary and Westfield College,
University of London

Family Law
S M Cretney, DCL, FBA
Solicitor, Professor of Law,
University of Bristol

Land Law and Trusts
P J Clarke, BCL, MA
Barrister, Fellow of Jesus College,
Oxford

Landlord and Tenant
Philip H Pettit, MA
Barrister, Professor of Equity,
University of Reading

Medical Law
Andrew Grubb, MA
Barrister, Senior Lecturer in Law,
King's College,
University of London

Shipping Law
R P Grime, BA, BCL
Professor of Law,
University of Southampton

Solicitors
Brian Harvey, MA, LLM
Solicitor, Professor of Property Law,
University of Birmingham

Sport and the Law
Edward Grayson, MA
Barrister

Statute Law
Francis Bennion, MA
Barrister, Research Associate of the
University of Oxford Centre for
Socio-Legal Studies

Succession
C H Sherrin, LLM, PHD
Barrister, Reader in Law,
University of Bristol

Taxation
John Tiley, MA, BCL
Reader in the Law of Taxation,
Fellow of Queen's College, Cambridge

Tort
B A Hepple, MA, LLB
Barrister, Professor of English Law,
University College, University of London

Town and Country Planning
Paul B Fairest, MA, LLM
Professor of Law, University of Hull

Publishers' Note

This is the eighth All England Law Report Annual Review and as in previous years it is designed as a companion to the All England Law Reports. A number of academic lawyers have been invited to contribute articles evaluating the decisions of the courts relevant to their particular speciality and reported in that series in 1989. Not all of the cases, of course, fall neatly into one or other of the categories of conventional legal classification. The authors have tried to avoid duplication in their discussion of cases and there are a number of cross-references to be found in the articles. Some cases, however, are examined in more than one article because different aspects are of importance in different contexts.

Amongst the topics covered in the 1989 Review Christopher Greenwood in the article on Public International Law deals with the litigation spawned by the International Tin Council which appears to be drawing to a close, and in the article on European Community Law he discusses two decisions of the House of Lords relating to the important question of the supremacy of Community law over national legislation. Once again the issue of Mareva injunctions has generated several reported cases, dealt with by Adrian Zuckerman in the article on Practice and Procedure. Andrew Grubb discusses in the article on Medical Law the difficult legal and moral questions raised by *F v West Berkshire Health Authority* [1989] 2 All ER 545 in the House of Lords concerning sterilisation and adult women.

Cases from the 1989 All England Law Reports, Simon's Tax Cases and Butterworths Company Law Cases are printed in bold type in the Table of Cases. A bold page number indicates where discussion of the case is to be found.

This volume should be cited as All ER Rev 1989.

BUTTERWORTH LAW PUBLISHERS LTD

Contents

Contents

Table of Cases

Abbreviations

ACT	Advance Corporation Tax
BCLC	Butterworths Company Law Cases
BTR	British Tax Review
CGTA	Capital Gains Tax Act 1979
CLJ	Cambridge Law Journal
CLR	Commonwealth Law Reports
Conv	The Conveyancer
Cr App R	Criminal Appeal Reports
Crim LR	Criminal Law Review
DLR	Dominion Law Reports
DLT	Development Land Tax
ECR	European Court Reports
EG	Estates Gazette
EHRR	European Human Rights Reports
FA	Finance Act
Fam Law	Family Law
FLR	Family Law Reports
FSR	Fleet Street Reports
ICR	Industrial Cases Reports
ILM	International Legal Materials
ILR	International Law Reports
Imm AR	Immigration Appeals Reports
IRLR	Industrial Relations Law Reports
JP	Justice of the Peace Reports
LGR	Local Government Review
LPA	Law of Property Act 1925
LQR	Law Quarterly Review
LRA	Land Registration Act 1925
LS	Legal Studies
LSG	Law Society Gazette
MLJ	Malayan Law Journal
MLR	Modern Law Review
NLJ	New Law Journal
NLJR	New Law Journal Law Reports
Ox Jo LS	Oxford Journal of Legal Studies
P & CR	Property and Compensation Reports
RTR	Road Traffic Reports
SC	Session Cases
SJ	Solicitors' Journal
STC	Simon's Tax Cases
TA	Income and Corporations Taxes Act 1970 and 1988
TC	Tax Cases
TMA	Tax Management Act 1970

Administrative Law

KEITH DAVIES, JP, MA, LLM
Barrister, Professor of Law, University of Reading

Judicial review and statutory challenges—a confusion

Early in 1989 the All England Law Reports included a Court of Appeal decision (actually arrived at in July 1988) which reveals a strange situation which may perhaps require the clearing up of a muddle. The case is *R v Secretary of State for Transport, ex p de Rothschild* [1989] 1 All ER 933.

As this title shows, the case seems unquestionably one of judicial review. The substantive dispute, concerning compulsory purchase, is not of special importance. The landowner objected to the acquisition of particular land for a new by-pass at Leighton Linslade in Bedfordshire (formerly Leighton Buzzard). He offered an alternative site. The inspector reported that the alternative site was much less convenient for the purposes of locating the by-pass, from the standpoint of the public interest. The Court of Appeal upheld the decision of Mann J that the Secretary of State's confirmation of the compulsory purchase order (CPO) had been arrived at fairly and reasonably, and so judicial review was refused. A distinction was drawn between these facts and those of *Prest v Secretary of State for Wales* (1982) 81 LGR 193, in which the Court of Appeal quashed a compulsory purchase order because of a blatant failure to weigh fairly and reasonably the advantages and disadvantages of two different sites.

The report of the *Rothschild* case in the Estates Gazette of the decision of Mann J at first instance refers to it as 'an application under section 23 of the Acquisition of Land Act 1981'. Mann J expressly described s 23 as 'the source of the court's jurisdiction'. This Act, replacing earlier legislation, sets out the standard procedure for making and confirming compulsory purchase orders. That decision, like ministerial decisions in planning matters, housing matters, highway matters etc is final, except for a statutory challenge on purely legal grounds in the High Court, which follows the same pattern in all these cases.

The pattern is this. A provision in the relevant Act expressly states that the validity of the ministerial decision can be questioned by the statutory challenge and in no other way. This is a matter of some importance, because it must inevitably rule out judicial review. The time-limit for making an application for judicial review is three months. The standard time-limit for these standard-form statutory challenges is only six weeks.

The Acquisition of Land Act 1981, in accordance with this pattern, in s 25 forbids any challenge to the legal validity of a compulsory purchase order other than by procedure specified in s 23. That as in similar statutes is an application to the High Court to quash or suspend on the basis that the confirmation of the CPO is not within the powers specified by the relevant statute or that there has been a procedural default to the prejudice of the applicant. In this way judicial review is ruled out, just as it is in the comparable statutory provisions relating to planning: see ss 242 and 245 of the Town and Country Planning Act 1971.

We thus have the puzzling situation in the *Rothschild* case that under the Act of 1981, ss 23 and 25, judicial review is excluded, yet judicial review proceedings took place. The fact that these proceedings failed has nothing to do with the fact that they should not have been brought.

An earlier case, *R v Secretary of State for the Environment, ex p Ostler* [1976] 3 All ER 90, was also concerned with challenging the validity of a CPO. As its title shows, it too was brought in the form of judicial review proceedings. But its ratio decidendi is confined to one issue, the time-limit for bringing proceedings. The Court of Appeal unanimously rejected the claimant's argument that the standard-form 6-weeks' limit for challenging the vires of a ministerial decision in the High Court could be extended if it would be unjust not to do so. An attempt to pray in aid the decision of the House of Lords in *Anisminic v Foreign Compensation Commission* [1969] 1 All ER 208, failed to move the Court of Appeal from the view that the 6-week time-limit is absolute.

There are two separate but closely connected issues here: (i) whether the legal validity of a ministerial decision of the relevant kind should or should not be contested by judicial review or by specific statutory challenge; (ii) whether the time-limit for challenge is six weeks, three months, or neither of those periods.

In the *Ostler* case the two issues were treated as one. The complainant challenged a compulsory purchase order confirmed on 17 May 1974, the challenge being an application made on 18 December 1975 for an order of certiorari. The Acquisition of Land (Authorisation Procedure) Act 1946, Sch I, paras 15 and 16, stated that challenge must be by statutory procedure under those paragraphs and in no other proceedings whatsoever. This fact alone should have ensured that the application for certiorari was rejected. In fact the decision was based on the question of time-limits. At that time the time-limit for certiorari was six months, not three months as it is now, but even so that limit was long past. The real dispute was whether the time-limit (whichever it was) could be extended in a proper case, by virtue of *Anisminic*. The answer was, again, 'no'; but even if it had been 'yes' certiorari is discretionary, and the Court of Appeal pointed out that the work in constructing road improvements on the land compulsorily purchased was already far advanced. For this reason alone (a very practical reason, relevant to the question of public interest) the discretion would have been exercised against the claimant. It is true that Lord Denning MR did say: 'It is quite clear that if Mr Ostler had come within six weeks his complaint could and would have been considered by the court'. But it is equally clear that such consideration might not have led to the claimant being granted certiorari by the court in the exercise of its discretion.

When we come back to the *Rothschild* case we see a similar conflation of the issues. The relevant provisions of the Acquisition of Land (Authorisation Procedure) Act 1946 have now been re-enacted in the Acquisition of Land Act 1981, ss 23 and 25. That being so, the complainants' challenge, like that of Mr Ostler, ought to have failed in limine, especially as Mann J at first instance referred to s 23 of the 1981 Act as the source of the court's jurisdiction. This is reinforced by the undoubted fact that whereas the procedure for judicial review is prescribed in Order 53 of the Rules of the Supreme Court, the statutory procedure for challenging ministerial decisions under the standardised 6-weeks time-limit is prescribed in Order 94. Yet the decision in the *Rothschild* case is reported as being made on an application by way of judicial review for certiorari. Behind all these procedural conundrums the real justification for the failure of the challenge in the *Rothschild* case, as in the *Ostler* case, is a practical one—the Department of Transport had made its choice on the basis of which route and which land was the best, and the most sensible, and had done so reasonably and fairly with due regard for the public interest and no undue disregard for the claimants' private interest.

Before leaving this question it is worth remembering that 'the public interest' is of paramount importance in public law, though all too easily played down especially by people who (like one of the appeal judges in the *Rothschild* case) use words such as 'draconian' to describe compulsory purchase. Public powers and private rights can be abused, and frequently are, which is why we have both public and private law. But when they are not abused they should be upheld and respected fully. Lord Diplock's words in *Bushell v Secretary of State for the Environment* [1980] 2 All ER 608, [1981] AC 75, remind us of this uncompromisingly:

> 'There is a third party' [ie one distinct from the acquiring authority and the objectors] 'who was not represented at the inquiry, the general public as a whole whose interests it is the minister's duty to treat as paramount.'

'Illegality', 'irrationality' and 'procedural impropriety'

On the general question of public law and judicial review, further interesting light is shed on their basic principles by the Court of Appeal in *R v Panel on Take-Overs and Mergers, ex p Guinness plc* [1989] 1 All ER 509. This is more or less a re-run of the unsuccessful proceedings for judicial review brought against the panel by Datafin plc (see [1987] 1 All ER 564). In the instant case the action of the panel which was being challenged was a refusal to adjourn proceedings in the investigation of a 'concert party' allegation in relation to a contested take-over. The application for judicial review failed, because although in the Court of Appeal's view the panel's refusal to adjourn was conceivably 'open to criticism', its investigation viewed as a whole had been conducted fairly and there had been no real injustice to the claimants.

The interest of this case lies in various observations on the principles of public law made by the members of the Court of Appeal. Lord Donaldson of Lymington MR once again, much as in the *Datafin* case, described the panel as

> 'a truly remarkable body . . . its self-imposed task is to regulate and police the conduct of take-overs and mergers . . .'

though he lamented that some of his statements in the *Datafin* case had 'been misunderstood, at least by academic writers.' Judicial review 'is a supervisory or "longstop" jurisdiction. It also has a large discretionary content, which contributes to its value.' Furthermore,

> 'if Parliament . . . has provided for an appeals procedure it is not for the court to usurp the functions of the appellate body.'

And

> 'the public interest normally dictates that, if the judicial review jurisdiction is to be exercised, it should be exercised very speedily . . .'

As for the panel's refusal to adjourn proceedings at the claimant's request, which was that they should be held up for a long period or even indefinitely, although the refusal was reasonable it should not have ruled out the possibility of imposing, on the panel's own initiative, a shorter adjournment of perhaps three months.

> 'Parties who open their mouths far too wide may still be entitled to a cut off the joint, even if they are clearly not entitled to the joint itself.'

But the evident decision of the panel that the claimant did not deserve even to be given 'a cut off the joint' was not objectively unreasonable (in what is often called the *Wednesbury* sense of that word) so as to be ultra vires, irrespective of what the judges' private opinions might be.

As to the underlying question whether in this kind of case the court is 'entitled to intervene at all', Lloyd LJ said that this 'is not to be answered . . . by reference to *Wednesbury* unreasonableness' (or to use Lord Diplock's terminology, 'irrationality') but

> 'in accordance with the principles of fair procedure which have been developed over the years, and of which the courts are the author and sole judge. These principles, which apply as well to administrative as to judicial tribunals, are known compendiously (if misleadingly) as the rules of natural justice.'

(Breach of them, to use Lord Diplock's terminology, is 'procedural impropriety'.) Lloyd LJ went on to distinguish once more between the supervising procedure of judicial review and (which is very different) an appeal on the merits. He said:

> 'When the substance of a decision is attacked by judicial review, on the ground of *Wednesbury* unreasonableness or any other ground, the court will be very reluctant indeed to intervene, if there is an immediate appeal open on the merits. However, the court will be less reluctant to intervene where the attack is based on procedural irregularity, and the substantive appeal has to be postponed for some reason or is limited in scope.'

In the event the claimant had not shown 'that there has been any real injustice, or even any real risk of injustice, in this case' i e no effective breach of the rules of natural justice to set against

> 'the public interest in the panel getting on with, and being seen to get on with, its self-appointed task. I have applied the penetrating oil of natural justice to the facts before us. I conclude that the procedure adopted by the panel in the instant case was not unfair.'

Woolf LJ said:

> 'The closest analogy to the panel is to be found in bodies set up by the Crown under its prerogative powers, such as the Criminal Injuries Compensation Board. . . In the words of its then own chief executive . . . the object of the panel's procedures is to produce the right answer in code terms in the circumstances. If it goes about this role in a manner which manifestly creates a real and not theoretical risk of injustice, then it would be abusing its power and,

because it is performing a public function, on an application of judicial review the courts could intervene on behalf of the public to protect those liable to be adversely affected by the exercise of the power. . . . Nowadays it is more common to test decisions of the sort reached by the panel in this case by a standard of what is called "fairness". I venture to suggest that in the present circumstances . . . it is more appropriate to use the term . . . "natural justice". In particular in considering whether something has gone wrong the court is concerned whether what has happened has resulted in real injustice. If it has, then the court has to intervene, since the panel is not entitled to confer on itself the power to inflict injustice on those who operate in the market which it supervises.'

But, in the instant case, although

'many of the criticisms counsel makes of the panel's conduct are well-founded . . . intervention would not be justified because no injustice has been caused, and what was wrong was not of the nature or gravity which required the intervention of the court.'

The prerogative of the Crown, referred to above by Woolf LJ, featured in another Court of Appeal decision, *R v Secretary of State for Foreign and Commonwealth Affairs, ex p Everett* [1989] 1 All ER 655. The claimant, who lived abroad, held a British passport. When it expired the Foreign Office refused to renew it because there was a warrant out for his arrest. This policy decision was alleged to be ultra vires. The Court of Appeal held that although the policy decision was proper in itself it was vitiated in this case because, before refusing renewal, the Foreign Office should have notified the claimant of the reasons for the refusal and particulars of the warrant, and should have given him an opportunity to make (if he could) a special case for justifying exceptional treatment. On the facts, however, it emerged that no special case could be shown. He had been given the relevant information, and there was no injustice. Therefore although the decision was ultra vires for what would seem to be 'procedural impropriety', the court held that in the circumstances a remedy in judicial review ought not to be given, and the decision at first instance to grant certiorari and mandamus was reversed. Taylor LJ said:

'The House of Lords in *Council of Civil Service Unions v Minister for the Civil Service* [1984] 3 All ER 935, [1985] AC 374, made it clear that the powers of the court cannot be ousted merely by invoking the word "prerogative" [and] that whether judicial review of the exercise of prerogative power is open depends on the subject matter and in particular on whether it is justiciable . . . the ready issue of a passport is a normal expectation of every citizen unless there is good reason for making him an exception.'

Here we have a 'normal'—ie 'legitimate'—expectation, which does not give the citizen in question a 'right' as in private law but does give him 'sufficient interest' or locus standi in public law: he is not a 'busybody or crank' and should be given leave to apply for judicial review. Whether he succeeds is quite another matter. It depends first on proof of ultra vires conduct by the public authority that he is challenging ('illegality', 'irrationality' or 'procedural impropriety'). If he succeeds on that substantive issue he still needs a decision of the court that justice as between the public interest and his private interest requires that discretion to grant a remedy ought to be exercised in his favour. Arbitrary conduct by public authorities, of whatever kind, is ultra vires; but not every ultra vires act ought to be overturned.

There is also the word 'justiciable', used not only by Taylor LJ but by Lord Scarman in the *Civil Service Unions* (GCHQ) case. An alternative word is 'remediable', used by Lord Bridge of Harwich in *Leech v Parkhurst Prison Deputy Governor* [1988] 1 All ER 485. Any public authority decision is 'justiciable' ('remediable') except, at one end of the scale, certain 'matters of high policy' under the prerogative—such as foreign policy, national security and the operation of constitutional conventions—and mere administrative or executive routine decisions at the other end of the scale.

A case where the latter kind of decision was said to be in issue was *R v Norfolk County Council, ex p M* [1989] 2 All ER 359. The social services department of the local authority had been notified that a 13-year-old girl had made an allegation of sexual abuse by the claimant in the case, and his name was placed on the authority's confidential register of child abusers. He was not told of this and not given an opportunity to defend himself against the allegation which was the basis of the decision. His employers, however, were notified, confidentially, 'behind his back' as Waite J put it. Soon afterwards he was sent a direct notification, and applied for judicial review of the authority's decision by way of certiorari to quash it. Counsel for the local authority coolly argued that their action consisted of nothing more than 'purely clerical or ministerial acts, internal to the council's own administrative procedures' (a 'courageous' submission!) and moreover that no wrong in private law had been done to the claimant. Without pursuing the private aspect, which raises the question separately from judicial review of whether an actionable injury to reputation had occurred, the judge rejected the argument that there had been no wrong in public law.

> 'I am satisfied . . . that it is not the law that local authorities are free to exercise arbitrary control over the entry of names of alleged abusers on a child abuse register with total immunity from supervision by the courts. Any such immunity would seriously erode the rights of the citizen.'

Two key words here are 'arbitrary' and 'supervision', both central to the whole rationale of judicial review. The judge held that the decision itself was 'unreasonable . . . within the *Wednesbury* principle' (ie 'irrationality') and also that 'the council's case conference acted . . . in manifest breach' of what he termed the council's 'legal duty to act fairly towards' the claimant (ie 'procedural impropriety'). But:

> 'I accept that a case conference' [acting in this way] 'is not acting judicially so as to make the rules of natural justice automatically applicable to its procedures as though it had been functioning as a tribunal.'

If we put this statement beside those of Woolf LJ in the *Guinness* case we can see that 'fairness' and 'natural justice', though closely related, are not synonymous; but both are aspects of procedure for the purposes of public law and the ultra vires principle. Thus the claimant justified his claim to judicial review. Certiorari was granted.

Three other decisions shed further light on the fundamental principles which govern the nature and extent of judicial review. In *Lonrho plc v Secretary of State for Trade and Industry* [1989] 2 All ER 609, the fuliginous saga of the Fraser take-over surfaced in the form of a claim for judicial review of the Secretary of State's refusal to publish the report of inspectors appointed to examine certain matters relevant thereto. This is of course a matter of public knowledge, not to say general fascination. The claim succeeded in the Divisional Court but failed in the Court of Appeal and the House of Lords. The underlying point of law is simple. The relevant statutory provisions give discretion to the Secretary of State: but was his decision the result of an intra vires or an ultra vires exercise of that discretion? Was it 'rational' or 'irrational' in the late Lord Diplock's terminology—was it reasonable or unreasonable in the *Wednesbury* sense? Given that the Director of the Serious Fraud Office had advised against publication, Lord Keith of Kinkel had no difficulty in holding that 'the attack on the rationality of the decision of the Secretary of State cannot be sustained.' He added: 'Judicial review is a protection and not a weapon'. An attempt to argue that the situation was virtually the same as in *Padfield v Minister of Agriculture, Fisheries and Food* [1968] 1 All ER 694, [1968] AC 997, on the ground that there was a lack of reasons in support of the decision, failed also. Lord Keith said:

> 'The only significance of the absence of reasons is that if all other known facts and circumstances appear to point overwhelmingly in favour of a different decision, the decision-maker who has given no reasons cannot complain if the court draws the inference that he had no rational reason for his decision.'

True of *Padfield's* case; not true here.

Again, in *R v Secretary of State for Transport, ex p Pegasus Holidays (London) Ltd* [1989] 2 All ER 481, judicial review was refused, by Schiemann J at first instance (actually on 7 August 1987), in regard to a decision made by the Secretary of State under the Air Navigation Order 1985 (SI 1985/1643), summarily but provisionally to suspend certain permits relating to the operation by certain Romanian pilots of charter aircraft on behalf of certain British airlines. The reason for the suspension was alarm caused by doubts about the competence of those pilots. The challenge to it was mounted on the basis of both 'irrationality' and 'procedural impropriety'. The former—*Wednesbury* unreasonableness—was alleged because the suspension was said to be disproportionately severe in relation to the problem (sometimes regarded as a separate principle known as 'proportionality', though as the judge pointed out it is still at bottom 'irrationality'). This argument failed, because suspension of permission is the very least safeguard applicable in the circumstances, given the risk to passengers' lives if planes are being flown by 'duff' pilots. It is true that this reaction was based on a prima facie opinion; but obviously if fuller investigation showed it to be unfounded then, though only then, the suspension could be lifted. As for 'procedural impropriety', it was alleged that the suspension was so quickly applied that the applicants had no chance to be heard in their own defence, and were thus denied natural justice and fairness; but the same answer applied, since subsequent representations, capable of being made promptly with the object of persuading the authorities to lift the suspension, were in no way precluded.

'Procedural impropriety' was yet again put forward as a basis for judicial review, and again failed, in *Al-Mehdawi v Secretary of State for the Home Department* [1989] 3 All ER 843. The claimant, an immigrant with temporary leave to stay in the UK, overstayed his leave and the Home Secretary ordered his deportation. He appealed, but the adjudicator dismissed his appeal because neither he nor his solicitors appeared at the hearing. The solicitors knew of the date of the hearing, but the letter they sent to the claimant was wrongly sent to his previous address. He alleged that the decision against him was ultra vires because it was brought about by a procedural fault which denied him natural justice. The House of Lords rejected this claim. Negligence might well be alleged in a private law action in contract or tort against those responsible, but the public authority was not at fault on these facts. A similar dispute arose in *R v Diggines, ex p Rahmani* [1985] 1 All ER 1073, [1985] QB 1109. The Court of Appeal in judicial review proceedings quashed the decision of an adjudicator because of a blunder by the claimant's advisers. The House of Lords upheld the Court of Appeal's decision but on an altogether different aspect of ultra vires. The House of Lords in this case now over-ruled the Court of Appeal's decision in that case. It is difficult, however, to be altogether happy about the decision. Clearly the public authority—the adjudicator—was not to blame, and private proceedings might well be available against the claimant's advisers if they were at fault (and they may not have been). Yet the official procedure did result in the outcome that the claimant was deprived of a hearing of which he ought not to have been deprived, in circumstances which make it appear, prima facie, that he was not responsible for the blunder. Judicial review should be more flexible than this.

Judicial Review, the Crown, and interim relief

Is there jurisdiction to grant interim injunctions against the Crown in judicial review cases? In *R v Secretary of State for the Home Department, ex p Herbage* [1986] 3 All ER 209, [1987] QB 872, the High Court held that there was. In *R v Licensing Authority, ex p Smith Kline & French Laboratories Ltd* [1989] 2 All ER 113, the Court of Appeal agreed. The House of Lords has now overruled those decisions.

In *Factortame Ltd v Secretary of State for Transport* [1989] 2 All ER 692, certain companies which controlled deep-sea fishing vessels were in dispute with the Secretary of State about registration of those vessels under the Merchant Shipping (Registration of Fishing Vessels) Regulations 1988. They challenged the validity of this legislation on the ground that it deprived them of certain rights under EEC law. The Divisional Court requested a preliminary ruling from the European Court of Justice and granted interim relief in the form of injunctions disapplying the 1988 Regulations in regard to the applicants pending the European Court's decision on the substantive issue. The House of Lords held that the courts have no power to grant such injunctions in judicial review or in public law generally. The Supreme Court Act 1981, the Rules of the Supreme Court (Ord 53) and the Crown Proceedings Act 1947 should all be interpreted in context—ie against the background of the earlier common law whose rules they amended. The Law Commission had recommended that there should be a form of interim injunctive relief available against the Crown; but this was not taken up in the reform of RSC Ord 53 in 1977, nor in s 31 of the Supreme Court Act 1981. The revised law on judicial review under that Act relates to *final* relief. As Lord Bridge said:

'The form of final relief available against the Crown has never presented any problem. A declaration of right made in proceedings against the Crown is invariably respected and no injunction is required. If the legislature intended to give the court jurisdiction to grant interim injunctions against the Crown, it is difficult to think of any reason why the jurisdiction should be available only in judicial review proceedings and not in civil proceedings as defined in the 1947 Act. Hence, an enactment which in terms applies only to the forms of final relief available in judicial review proceedings cannot possibly have been so intended.'

But the question whether such an interlocutory remedy is available under Community law was referred by their Lordships to the European Court of Justice, requesting a quick interim decision thereon.

Time limits

The hurdles over which applicants for judicial review have to leap when challenging public authorities include: (i) the need to obtain leave; (ii) the need to prove the substantive claim of ultra vires action; (iii) the need to persuade the court to exercise its discretion to grant relief even when the substantive argument succeeds; (iv) the need to bring proceedings promptly; (v) the need to bring proceedings within three months. What if it is not possible to bring proceedings within three months?

In *R v Dairy Produce Quota Tribunal for England and Wales, ex p Caswell* [1989] 3 All ER 205 this last point arose. The Dairy Produce Quota Tribunal in 1985 misled the applicants, who were dairy farmers, so that they lost the chance to increase their quota of dairy cows and were financially penalised. The applicants did not realise this until 1987. They then sought, and were granted, an extension of time for bringing judicial review proceedings. The Court of Appeal, which upheld the judge's decision not to grant judicial review, held that there is 'undue delay' after three months even if an extension of time is fairly granted, and this is a factor to be taken into account when exercising the court's discretion. The Supreme Court Act 1981, s 31(6), provides that, in the event of 'undue delay', the court has discretion to refuse relief if (inter alia) 'it would be detrimental to good administration' to grant it.

The applicants had undoubtedly been misled and had suffered. But (it was said) to quash the offending decision would either open the way to untold numbers of other challenges or would be unjust to other potential challengers if they were not allowed to proceed. Either way the consequence would be 'detrimental to good administration'. Here we seem to have the 'floodgates' argument raising its head once again. Whether this approach is really desirable is far from certain.

Arbitration

J E ADAMS LLB FCIArb
Solicitor, Director of Training, Titmuss Sainer & Webb; Emeritus Professor of Law, Queen Mary and Westfield College, University of London

Only four arbitration cases featured in the All England Reports for 1989. One of them (*Ipswich Borough Council v Fisons plc* [1989] 2 All ER 737) was a further example of a judge departing from the *Nema/Antaios* guidelines, but was reversed by the Court of Appeal before the year was out (too late for the 1989 Reports). A second, *Home and Overseas Insurance Co Ltd v Mentor Insurance Co (UK) Ltd (in liq)* [1989] 3 All ER 74, saw a substantial move to acceptance of an honourable engagement arbitration clause. In *Richco International Ltd v International Industrial Food Co SAL* [1989] 1 All ER 613 a party in default of an order for payment in was visited with a stay of the arbitration. The fourth case, *Tate & Lyle Industries Ltd v Davy McKee (London) Ltd* [1989] 2 All ER 641, settled a challenge to the validity of reference of an application for leave to appeal to an Official Referee.

No model law for now

Outside the courts, the year saw the publication of the Report of the Committee chaired by Mustill LJ on the UNCITRAL Model Law. Adoption of that measure is firmly rejected, although there is a plea for a new Arbitration Act to consolidate existing statutes and some aspects of the common law of arbitration. A start has been made, in early 1990, on drafting such a Bill; perhaps a major but non-partisan measure of this sort would prove quite attractive, as a General Election comes nearer, to the managers of parliamentary time.

Leave to appeal

The worries of those concerned with arbitrations in the property field at the rigidity of *The Nema/Antaios* guidelines on leave to appeal, stilled by the decision of the Vice-Chancellor in *Lucas Industries plc v Welsh Development Agency* [1986] 2 All ER 858 (discussed at [1986] All ER Rev 12–13), were further quietened when he reiterated his views in *Ipswich Borough Council v Fisons plc* [1989] 2 All ER 737 and applied them in circumstances lacking many of the features of the earlier case. He noted that his earlier decision had been followed in other first instance cases. Instead of just the two tests of 'obviously wrong', for cases in the one-off category, and 'prima facie wrong', for standard clauses, a third of 'left in real doubt' applied where the arbitration award regulated the future property rights of the parties. However, this third class did not survive the appeal in this case, so it is not proposed to discuss it further, and full treatment of the issues must await the next edition of this work.

Honourable engagement clauses

The facts of *Home and Overseas Insurance Co Ltd v Mentor Insurance Co (UK) Ltd (in liq)* [1989] 3 All ER 74 are, as Parker LJ remarked (at 76c), 'few and simple'. Between 1973 and 1981 Mentor had obtained re-insurance from Home under which the latter provided re-insurance of Mentor's ultimate nett loss in excess of £60,000 with a limit of £60,000 (both for each and every loss). 'Ultimate nett loss' was defined as 'the sum actually paid' by Mentor in respect of certain defined policies. Mentor went into liquidation in August 1985, and in June 1988 Home issued a summons for a declaration that the only recovery permitted was of sums ultimately paid by Mentor, a construction very much to Home's advantage if the level of dividend payable in the liquidation reduced the total payment below the £60,000 threshold and possibly to its advantage to a lesser extent if the dividend paid reduced the excess over £60,000 from what it might otherwise have been. On 28 July 1988 Hirst J dismissed that application in RSC Ord 14 proceedings on Home's claim, and ordered a stay of Home's action, begun by writ in May 1988, under s 4 of the Arbitration Act 1950. Home appealed.

This note will not deal with the Order 14 point at length. Parker LJ (at 77j) makes it clear that such proceedings 'should not . . . be allowed to become a means for obtaining, in effect, an immediate trial'. This would be the result if the court permitted determination of 'points of law which may take hours or even days and the citation of many authorities' on Ord 14 summonses; the force of these strictures is greater when the parties had concluded an arbitration agreement, especially a commercial arbitration involving implied terms or trade practices (78a–c). Parker LJ concludes this part of his judgment by explaining his view of certain earlier and apparently contrary statements. Lloyd LJ merely stated his agreement with this aspect of the judgment. Balcombe LJ agreed with the two other judgments without giving a judgment of his own.

Parker LJ then turned to a statement of the main issues raised, namely (i) whether actual payment might mean only established liability to pay, (ii) whether the arbitration clause allowed the arbitrators to depart from the ordinary and natural meaning of the words used, and (iii) whether s 597 of the Companies Act 1985 over-rode any requirement for payment by the reinsured before it could recover.

He then stated (79g–80b) seven factors that had led him to the conclusion that the matter should be fully tried, but expressed no opinion on the merits. Comment on these factors is not relevant to the present discussion.

The arbitration clause used provided that the arbitrators (one nominated by each party) and the umpire were to 'interpret this Reinsurance as an honourable engagement' and to make an award 'with a view to effecting the general purpose of this Reinsurance in a reasonable manner rather than in accordance with a literal interpretation of the language'.

Counsel for Mentor argued that this clause was valid and permitted the arbitrators to interpret the contract more leniently than could a court; his opponent argued that it made no difference but, if it did, the clause was invalid. Parker LJ found the cases relied on by the former—*Eagle Star Insurance Co Ltd v Yuval Insurance Co Ltd* [1978] 1 Lloyd's Rep 357 and *Home Insurance Co v Administratia Asigurarilor de Stat* [1983] 2 Lloyd's Rep 674—not 'directly applicable'; he agreed with Home's counsel that a clause allowing arbitrators to decide a dispute wholly without regard to the law and, say, on their own notion of fairness would not be a valid arbitration clause. However, he found that the present clause 'does not do any such thing' (80e); it permitted adoption of what was approved in *The Antaios* [1984] 3 All ER 229, [1985] AC 191 and was characterised there by Lord Diplock, with some distaste, as 'purposive construction'. The clause permitted departure from the literal or ordinary meaning (81d); if the arbitrators went too far that could be dealt with on appeal, if leave to appeal were given at the relevant time.

Finally, Parker LJ briefly considered whether Hirst J had wrongly exercised his discretion in granting a stay but found that he had not. Mentor had the right for the validity of its case to be decided by its chosen tribunal.

Lloyd LJ dealt mainly with the validity of the arbitration clause. He referred to the decisions in *Orion Cia Espanola de Seguros v Belfort Maatschappij voor Algemene Verzekgringeen* [1962] 2 Lloyd's Rep 257 and *Eagle Star Insurance v Yuval Insurance* (above) which dealt, he said, with 'similar' clauses, the former finding the clause invalid but the latter upholding it. The Court of Appeal, in the second case, accepted the validity of a clause allowing a decision 'on equitable grounds rather than a strict legal interpretation' or 'more leniently and having regard more generally to commercial considerations'.

He continues that 'if. . . the *Eagle Star* case was correctly decided . . . there is [here] a dispute . . . which ought to go to arbitration' (83c). Counsel for Home argued that it was not correctly decided, being inconsistent with *Czarnikow v Roth Schmidt & Co* [1922] 2 KB 478, [1922] All ER Rep 45, *Pilgrim Shipping Co Ltd v State Trading Corp of India, The Hadjitsakos* [1975] 1 Lloyd's Rep 356 and *Ashville Investments Ltd v Elmer Contractors Ltd* [1988] 2 All ER 577, [1988] 3 WLR 867 (a case later than *Eagle Star*). That line of attack is rejected. Indeed, Lloyd LJ finds *Eagle Star* as foreshadowing a later consistent trend apart from just being followed in the 1983 *Home Insurance* case. He also refers to the speech of Lord Diplock in *The Antaios* supporting an arbitral 'purposive' approach. He cites several non-arbitration cases demonstrating that concept.

Finally, Lloyd LJ cites *DST v Raknoc* [1987] 2 All ER 769, [1987] 3 WLR 1023, a case already discussed in the review of 1987 cases at [1987] All ER Rev 12–14, as showing a new flexibility in the judicial approach to commercial arbitration. If the English court will permit enforcement of a foreign award not governed by any state law why would it not enforce an English award similarly based? If it would enforce, then why not stay litigation to allow arbitration to proceed? (85a).

Counsel for Home pointed to the alleged problems of supervising awards not conducted under a fixed and recognisable system of law and claimed the arbitration agreement here fell outside the Acts of 1950 and 1979. The Lord Justice brusquely disagreed (85b). As an aside, he comments that the result if counsel was right would be to destroy the attraction of ICC arbitrations in this country.

'Equity' and 'honourable engagement' arbitration clauses are commonplace and routine in re-insurance contracts. The court was told there were some eighty arbitrations based on points similar to those in the Home-Mentor dispute and asked the court accordingly to give a decision. Lloyd LJ found those facts, in contrast, to justify the court in not 'usurp[ing] the decision which rightly belongs . . . to the tribunal chosen by the parties', although accepting that the issues might eventually come back to the courts. So he, too, upheld the decision of Hirst J.

Comment

The decision is one more example of the liberalisation of the judicial attitudes to arbitration in allowing the parties to give the arbitrators a measure of discretion denied to the courts. There are limits to that freedom and the final stage of allowing full disregard of the law will exceed what is permitted. How far the relaxation may go before the court calls a halt may well occupy the judges (and law reporters) of the years ahead, but certainly *Home Insurance v Mentor Insurance* has moved the marker posts to give a wider circle of flexibility than existed before. The present writer, moreover, finds each of the judgments entirely convincing in their reasons for allowing such an advance, given that no-one needs even to agree to arbitrate unless he wishes to, although it would be a determined would-be reinsured which declined that choice.

Stay of arbitration for non-compliance with payment in order

Richco International Ltd, a Bermudian company, sold wheat to International Industrial Food Co SAL, a Lebanese company, for some $US2.3m. Disputes erupted shortly after shipment and the buyers rejected the cargo, then en route to Syria. They confirmed later that the sub-buyers, a Syrian state purchasing body, had also rejected the goods. The buyer's bank rejected the documents when presented. Attempts at negotiating a compromise failed and a GAFTA arbitration was initiated. Whilst unfortunate, this sequence of events was not abnormal. The next steps were, however, extraordinary, to adopt the epithet chosen by Hirst J in the ensuing litigation, for the buyers presented the documents to the sub-buyer's bank and obtained payment of $US3.02m, representing a price to allow for the alleged defects and about $US1m for freight and insurance, as the sub-contracts were cif. An injunction was obtained by the sellers to prevent the ship from entering the Syrian port of discharge, but the Syrian authorities placed it under restraint. A Syrian court then ordered it to discharge and armed Syrian officers supervised that operation. The sellers, unaware of the payment by the sub-buyers, had asked the buyers to confirm the seller's continuing ownership.

So Richco and International Food came to court when, on an inter partes summons, the judge ordered the buyers to lodge $US1.8m 'being a fund in dispute' in court within 14 days, the buyer's claims in the arbitration to be stayed in default. Subsequent stages, heard in chambers but with judgment in open court, are now reported in *Richco International Ltd v International Industrial Food Co SAL, The Fayrouz III* [1989] 1 All ER 613. The sellers' claims in the arbitration included a claim to the amount received by the buyers on a fiduciary basis, as the sellers' wheat had been sold. That claim to a fund had been conceded for present purposes. The sellers were seeking an extension of the earlier order so that non-compliance would lead to a bar on the buyers defending any of the sellers' claims, and not only on pursuing their own.

The judge identified the relevant statutory provision as para (f) of s 12(6) of the 1950 Act, giving the court power to make orders for 'securing the amount in dispute in the reference' with a close parallel in para (a) relating to security for costs. He pointed out that the court's powers in respect of the first was dealt with in RSC Ord 29 and the second in Ord 23, which has identical provisions. In *Dorval Tankers Pty Ltd v Two Arrows Maritime and Port Services Ltd, The Argenpuma* [1984] 2 Lloyd's Rep 563 the Court of Appeal had ruled that default in giving security for costs when so ordered permitted a permanent stay on claims in an arbitration. The court had distinguished *Bremer Vulkan Schiffbau Und Maschinenfabrik v South India Shipping Corp* [1981] 1 All ER 289, [1981] AC 909, because the power to order the stay was statutory; the problems of the absence of an inherent power, as established by the House of Lords' decision, did not thus arise.

Counsel for the sellers had contended for a statutory power to order the stay sought, because of the comparability of the two paragraphs of s 12(6); counsel for the buyers denied that proposition and argued, alternatively, that imposition of a stay would be unjust. The remedies against the defaulter should be confined, he argued, to enforcement of the order by appointment of a receiver, committal or sequestration. Hirst J preferred the sellers' arguments. *The Argenpuma* decision was 'so close as to provide all but binding authority' (619c).

Thus having jurisdiction, Hirst J had little hesitation on the facts in making the order sought. He gave a further four weeks for compliance with his earlier order failing which the buyers would be debarred from defending the sellers' claims in the arbitration.

Given the dismay at the situation disclosed by the *Bremer Vulkan* and allied decisions (which the new statute advocated by the Mustill Committee might well alleviate), the present decision is welcome. It will not necessarily provide an easy way to circumvent *Bremer Vulkan* because the circumstances of a fund to be preserved may not often be present, but, where it can be shown, the decision enhances a claimant's remedies significantly.

Official Referees can rule, OK?

Under RSC Ord 73 applications for leave to appeal are made to a judge of the Commercial Court, but under r 6 the powers of the commercial judge can be exercised by any judge of the High Court. Applications in rent review cases have routinely been referred to Chancery judges and construction cases to Official Referees. That practice was challenged in *Tate & Lyle Industries Ltd v Davy McKee (London) Ltd* [1989] 2 All ER 641. Leave to appeal had been refused by the Official Referee; thereupon the plaintiff applied for a rehearing on two grounds, namely that the Official Referee had lacked jurisdiction, being neither a Commercial Court judge nor a High Court judge and, secondly, that the application was not Official Referee business as defined in the Rules. Hirst J heard the summons in chambers, but gave judgment in open court, dismissing the application.

He examined the definition of Official Referee business and the powers of the Official Referees, specified in Ord 36, rr 1 and 4 respectively, and a commentary upon it in *The Supreme Court Practice 1988*. Counsel for the plaintiff asserted that applications for leave fell within neither branch of r 1; the first branch covered matters involving prolonged examination of documents or accounts, or a technical, scientific or local investigation, and the second referred to trial by an Official Referee. On the latter, he argued that no trial was involved in an application under s 1 of the 1979 Act. His opponent countered by calling for a broad construction and asserted that 'trial' covered any determination deciding a point at issue.

Hirst J rejected the narrow construction, and held trial to equate with determination. The desirability of leaving such applications to the Official Referees lay partly in the fact that it would further the growth of the Official Referees as a construction industry court as advocated by the Master of the Rolls in *Northern Regional Health Authority v Derek Crouch Construction Co Ltd* [1984] 2 All ER 175, [1984] QB 644. So the practice of referring these applications in construction industry or building cases can continue.

Commercial Law

N E PALMER, BCL, MA
Barrister, Professor of Law, Univeristy of Southampton

ROBERT MERKIN, LLB, LLM
Professor of Law, University of Sussex

Banking

Hongkong and Shanghai Banking Corp v Kloeckner & Co AG [1989] 3 All ER 513 is authority for two important principles. First, it is open to a debtor to contract out of a right of set off which he would otherwise have enjoyed against his creditor, and thus to disable himself from reducing the amount payable to that creditor by the amount owed by the creditor to him. Thus, where a bank's contract for the provision of financing facilities to a trading organisation made the relevant payment undertakings independent of any 'discount, deduction, offset, or counterclaim' on the trader's part, that express exclusion prevented the trader from off-setting the amount of its counterclaim against the bank, notwithstanding earlier authority indicating that the right of set off was not displaceable by agreement: *Lechmere v Hawkins* (1798) 2 Esp 626; *Taylor v Okey* (1806) 13 Ves 180. Hirst J preferred to follow the hint given by Lord Denning MR in *Halesowen Presswork and Assemblies Ltd v Westminster Bank Ltd* [1970] 3 All ER 473, at 477, that a banker has a right to combine the two accounts of a single customer (one in credit and one in debit) whenever he pleases, *'unless he had made some agreement, express or implied, to keep them separate'*; there was no justification, in Hirst J's opinion, for inferring that this caveat was confined to bank accounts as opposed to other aspects of the banker–customer relationship. Secondly, the principle that a bank's obligation under a letter of credit or a performance bond is unaffected by disputes arising between their customer (buyer) and the beneficiary (seller), and thus that disputes concerning the underlying sale transaction should not impair the beneficiary's right to draw on a letter of credit, does not apply where a claim to exercise a right of set off arises not as between the customer (buyer) and the beneficiary (seller) but as between the beneficiary and the bank itself. In such a case, there is no reason in principle why the bank should not enjoy a right of set off, and no attendant threat to 'the lifeblood of commerce', at least where (as in the instant case) the claim to set off arises out of the same transaction as the liability arising under the letter of credit, and where the set off is claimed in respect of a liquidated as opposed to an unliquidated sum (the latter restriction following a parallel with the law on bills of exchange). As Hirst J remarked, the identity of the bank as a party to whom the beneficiary is indebted will almost invariably be a fortuitous circumstance from the beneficiary's point of view, and the incidence of debts entitling the bank to set off will thus be very small; moreover, the beneficiary can always eliminate a particular bank by prior stipulation, thereby avoiding the risk that his entitlement to draw on the letter of credit will be diminished in this way. No contrary conclusion was therefore justified by reference to those authorities which have repeatedly stressed the need to preserve the integrity of letters of credit (eg, *Edward Owen Engineering Ltd v Barclays Bank International Ltd* [1978]] 1 All ER 976, at 981, per Lord Denning MR; *Power Curber International Ltd v National Bank of Kuwait SAK* [1981] 3 All ER 607, at 612–613; *Intraco Ltd v Notis Shipping Corp, The Bhoja Trader* [1981] 2 Lloyd's Rep 256, at 257, per Donaldson LJ), or indeed by reference to arts 10(a) and 46 of the UCP. Hirst J seems to have been prepared to accept in principle that the right of set off was capable of assertion independently of the two factual limitations stated above, but the instant circumstances rendered the statement of any wider principle technically unnecessary.

In several further decisions, the courts have refused to incorporate or to imply particular terms into the banker–client relationship. In each case, the court has rejected the contention that the term in question was imported into the contract by a market usage or course of dealing between the parties, or was essential to lend efficacy to that relationship. In *Elawadi v Bank of Credit and Commerce International SA* [1989] 1 All ER 242, Hutchinson J refused to imply a term into a contract for the sale of travellers' cheques that the purchaser's entitlement to a refund should be conditional upon his having refrained from carelessness or recklessness in his custody of the cheques (see further below). In *Libyan Arab Foreign Bank v Bankers Trust Co* [1989] 3 All ER 252, at 275–276 (a decision discussed in detail under the title 'Conflict of Laws', post p 49) the rejected term was one to the effect that only CHIPS or Fedwire forms of transfer would be permitted in transferring funds from the relevant London account. Staughton J observed (at 277):

> 'I find difficulty in seeing how course of dealing by itself could support a negative implied term of the kind alleged. The phrase is often used to elucidate a contract or to add a term to it. But, if course of dealing is to eliminate some right which the contract would otherwise confer, I would require evidence to show, not merely that the right had never been exercised, but also that the parties recognised that as between themselves no such right existed. In other words, there must be evidence establishing as between the parties what would be a usage if it applied to the market as a whole. But, whether that be so or not, I find no implied term such as Bankers Trust allege to be established either by usage or by course of dealing or both.'

In *Barclays Bank plc v Taylor* [1989] 3 All ER 563, the asserted obligation was one whereunder the bank should contest an application by the police for an access order under s 9(1) of the Police and Criminal Evidence Act 1984. The Court of Appeal first held that disclosure of the accounts in compliance with the order was not a breach of the bank's duty of confidence, because it fell within the first exception stated by Bankes LJ in *Tournier v National Provincial and Union Bank of England* [1924] 1 KB 461, at 473, [1923] All ER Rep 550, at 554, viz, that disclosure was made under compulsion of law. It was irrelevant for this purpose that the legal conditions for issue of the order might not have been met; all that was necessary was a court order valid on its face, for such an order demanded compliance till set aside by due process of law. Secondly, the court held that the bank owed no supplementary contractual obligation to 'preserve the . . . confidence', ie to use its best endeavours to ensure that no relevant exception under the *Tournier* principles should become applicable, thereby destroying the confidence. The accountholders alleged four distinct categories of breach of this term: the failure by the bank to notify them of the making of the application, the failure to consider the terms of the application or to obtain advice about it, the failure to oppose the application and the failure to make representations to the police. But the court was unanimous that there was (in the words of Lord Donaldson MR at 568) no duty on the part of the bank to do everything possible to prevent the *Tournier* exceptions from being activated:

> 'The duty to maintain confidentiality is not all-embracing, subject to exceptions. It does not exist in the four exceptional circumstances and it is no part of the duty of confidentiality to seek to avoid disclosure under compulsion by law.'

The only possible situation in which a bank might become obliged to contest the application in a case like the present would arise where the bank

> 'knew something relevant to [*the application*] which was not likely to be apparent on the face of the application or of the notice relating to it or might not be known to the police' (at 569).

As Croom-Johnson LJ remarked, a contractual obligation of the kind alleged could not have been confined to the 1984 Act but would necessarily have applied to those other statutes which authorise the inspection of confidential information in the possession of banks; further, there was nothing in Sch I to the 1984 Act to support an obligation of this kind.

In *National Bank of Greece SA v Pinios Shipping Co No 1 and another, The Maira* [1989] 1 All ER 213 (see also our Titles on 'Contract' (post, p 78) and 'Tort' (post, p 329)) the Court of Appeal refused to discover an obligation on the part of the guarantor bank to ensure that a management agent who had been appointed in relation to the mortgaged ship could carry out its obligation to maintain a full insurance on the vessel. The court also held that, in the particular circumstances, the bank was entitled to recover only simple (and not compound) interest over the period from the date of demand for repayment until the date of judgment. This latter aspect of the decision has since been reversed by the House of Lords, which (while accepting the absence of any express term justifying the exaction of compound interest in this case) rejected the asserted rule of law that a banker–customer relationship necessarily came to an end when the bank demanded payment of sums outstanding on the customer's account, and held that the usage of bankers to charge compound interest was not confined to 'a mercantile account current for mutual transactions': see [1990] 1 All ER 78. We are therefore deferring a full discussion of the right to charge compound interest until our 1990 issue.

Two decisions in 1989 dealt with the obligation of an issuer of travellers' cheques to reimburse the purchaser in the event of their loss or theft. Both turned on the wording of the particular agreement but contain more general observations. In *Braithwaite v Thomas Cook Travellers Cheques Ltd* [1989] 1 All ER 235 the purchaser's entitlement to a refund was expressed to be conditional (inter alia) upon his having 'properly safeguarded each cheque against loss or theft'. A purchaser who rose at 4 am on the day in question and bought £50,000 worth of travellers' cheques in Jersey, drank steadily throughout the ensuing fourteen hours or so, travelled back to England and around London with the cheques visible in a plastic carrier bag along with a carton of cigarettes, visited public houses with the cheques still in his possession instead of going straight home on his arrival in London, mentioned in one of the public houses that he had the cheques in his possession, travelled home and fell asleep on the London underground after 'closing time' (during which journey the cheques disappeared), and failed to notice that the bag was missing until he was out of the underground station, was held not to have discharged the burden of proving that he had exercised proper care. The question required the court to consider the purchaser's conduct as a whole, rather than each specific episode individually:

> 'It may well be that some of these factors can be present without the plaintiff failing properly to safeguard. But in the present case they were all present and . . . all contributed to the ultimate loss and, between them, were causative of it. The reason he fell asleep and did not notice the loss was because he was dead tired and not sober. Falling asleep, and the subsequent loss or theft, could and should have been foreseen as the not unlikely conclusion to that evening following that day.'

In a concise summary of general principles affecting travellers' cheques, Schiemann J observed that a term requiring the purchaser to have taken proper care did not technically impose a duty upon him, but merely stipulated a condition precedent to his entitlement to recovery in the stated events: an entitlement which, in the judge's view, would not exist without some express contractual undertaking to that effect. The judge was prepared to read into the contract an enduring right of recovery if any failure of proper care was causally unconnected with the loss, and did not consider that the word 'loss' in the issuer's conditions should be construed as excluding cases where the disappearance of the cheques was a certainty, or was brought about by the purchaser's own act. Further, a mere momentary inadvertence should not per se debar the right to a refund: see *Fellus v National Westminster Bank plc* (1983) 133 NLJ 766. But the burden of establishing proper care resides with the purchaser because the relevant facts are within his knowledge; and the obligation of rebutting any causal connection between his lack of proper care and the ensuing loss or theft should likewise fall upon him.

Hutchison J's judgment in *Elawadi v Bank of Credit and Commerce International SA* [1989] 1 All ER 242 differs in at least one significant respect from that of Schiemann J. In *Elawadi*, Hutchison J held that an obligation to refund the value of lost or stolen travellers' cheques might arise by implication irrespective of any express undertaking to that effect. The observation was made obiter, however, and the principal point of interest probably lies in the judge's conclusion that, in the absence of an express term to that effect, the issuer was not entitled to refuse reimbursement simply on the ground of the purchaser's lack of care. In this case, £50,000 worth of cheques was stolen from the purchaser's car in circumstances indicating substantial inadvertence on his part: having originally kept the cheques in his safe, he took them out and left them in a plastic bag in the car from a Friday evening until some time around six o'clock on the Saturday. During that period, the car was parked unattended in public streets while the purchaser made business calls, and in an open parking space beside his house overnight. The judge considered that, on a balance of probabilities, the car would have been unlocked when the theft took place, and he had little difficulty in finding that (in so far as the question was relevant) the purchaser was guilty of the most serious negligence, In his opinion, the burden of proof lay on the bank in this respect (cf *Braithwaite*, above), although the onus was of little significance on the present facts.

The bank defended the claim for a refund on two principal grounds: first, that the terms of the contract gave them an unfettered discretion as to whether to refund, and secondly that the contract was subject to an implied term whereby reimbursement might be denied if no proper care had been taken. The judge rejected these defences and held that the bank had expressly undertaken to reimburse. That undertaking was supportable both by reference to a contractual statement at the time of issue by the bank's deputy manager (who warned that if the purchaser took the cheques away unsigned he would be unable to claim for loss), and by reference to para 3 of the contract (whereunder 'Any claim for a refund . . . shall be subject to approval by the Issuer'). In Hutchison J's view, that provision did not confer on the bank an absolute discretion as to whether to reimburse; any discretion not to pay must be limited to occasions on which the purchaser had broken one of the contractual obligations imposed on him by the agreement. Here no such breach had occurred and the express obligation therefore survived unimpaired. Moreover, even in the absence of any explicit obligation an implied undertaking to like effect would be discovered, subject again to the issuer's discretion in the event of a breach of the contract by the purchaser: the commercial features of the normal transaction were such as to render 'an obligation of some sort . . . to refund the value of lost or stolen cheques' a necessary incident of that transaction.

Adopting, in particular, a long statement on the nature of implied terms by Lloyd LJ in *National Bank of Greece SA v Pinios Shipping Co No 1, the Maira* [1989] 1 All ER 213, at 218–220 (post, pp 81, 332), Hutchison J declined to discover a further implied term to the effect that the issuers would be relieved of their obligation to reimburse if the relevant loss or theft resulted from some carelessness or recklessness on the purchaser's part. Although it might not be unreasonable to expect some such qualification to be implied, it was difficult to devise any formulation of the qualification which would command the assent of both issuer and purchaser; and 'Such deficiencies on the part of the traveller do not determine whether he or the issuer is out of pocket' (at 255).

Finally, Hutchison J considered it 'distinctly arguable' that the issuers were guilty of the tort of conversion in relation to those stolen cheques which it had honoured, but on which the signatures and countersignatures did not compare favourably. Such cheques continued to be the property of the purchaser (cf *Australian Guarantee Corpn Ltd v Commissioners of the State Bank of Victoria* [1989] VR 617), and the payments evidently constituted a breach of the issuer–purchaser agreement. Hutchison J also toyed with the notion that the reimbursement obligation itself might be qualified by reference to factors of this kind, but found it unnecessary to express a concluded opinion on the point.

The system of law governing a performance bond was considered by the Court of Appeal in *Attock Cement Co Ltd v Romanian Bank for Foreign Trade* [1989] 1 All ER 1189. It emerges from this decision that, failing some special agreement to such effect, a performance bond issued by a bank in support of the contractor's obligations under a building contract cannot be assumed to be governed by the same system of law as that governing the building contract itself. A performance bond, like a letter of credit, is prima facie governed by the law of the place in which payment under it is to be made; it is a separate transaction and should not be approached in the same manner as a guarantee. Parties who intend a different applicable law from that of the proposed place of payment must stipulate for it, or make their choice apparent from the general contractual circumstances. See further the title on 'Conflict of Laws' (post, p 49).

Carriers

Important points of interpretation of the Warsaw Convention as amended at the Hague 1955 arose in two cases reported in 1989. While the first of these, *Holmes v Bangladesh Biman Corp* [1989] 1 All ER 852 was concerned with the carriage of passengers, the principles enunciated therein by the House of Lords are equally applicable to the carriage of goods.

In *Holmes* the respondent's husband was killed when the aircraft in which he was a passenger crashed as it approached Zia International Airport in Bangladesh. The plane was on a purely internal Bangladesh flight from Chittagong to Dhaka, and the widow sued the airline for damages under the Fatal Accidents Act 1976 and the Law Reform (Miscellaneous Provisions) Act 1934. Liability was admitted, but there was dispute as to the level of damages to be awarded. The Bangladesh legislation relating to carriage by air imposed a ceiling of £913 on the damages recoverable; under the relevant UK legislation (Sch 1 to the Carriage by Air Acts (Application of Provisions) Order 1967, SI 1967/480) damages would be recoverable up to a maximum of £83,763.

Although the contract of carriage was stated to be governed by Bangladesh law, the respondent argued that, upon a correct interpretation of Sch 1 to the Carriage by Air Acts the much higher UK limit was applicable. This argument was accepted by both the trial judge and the Court of Appeal, but was rejected by the House of Lords.

The Warsaw Convention of 1929 and the Warsaw Convention as amended at the Hague in 1955 apply to international carriage as defined in art 1(2) of both Conventions. The Warsaw Convention was enacted into United Kingdom law by the Carriage by Air Act 1932 and the Hague Convention by the Carriage by Air Act 1961. Under s 1 of the 1961 Act the provisions of the 1932 Act ceased to have effect. However, as certain states which had ratified the original Warsaw Convention had failed to ratify the Hague rules it was necessary to give continuing force in the United Kingdom to the provisions of the original Convention. Section 10(1) of the 1961 Act therefore provides:

> 'Her Majesty may by Order in Council apply the First Schedule to this Act, together with any other provisions of this Act, to carriage by air, not being carriage by air to which the Convention applies, of such descriptions as may be specified in the Order . . .'

This enabling power was exercised by the Carriage by Air Acts (Application of Provisions) Order 1967, SI 1967/480 both in order to give continuing force to the original Convention (Sch 2 to the 1967 Order) and to provide a set of rules governing carriage which did not fall within the definition of 'international' as contained in either Convention (Sch 1 to the 1967 Order). Article 3 of the Order provides that 'This Order shall apply to all carriage by air, not being carriage to which the amended Convention applies. The question which fell to be decided in *Holmes* was whether the United Kingdom rules apply to carriage by air which is to be performed wholly within the territory of a foreign state, ie to what extent should the Order be considered to have extra-territorial effect. Lord Bridge and Lord Jauncey each considered the so-called 'presumption against extra-territorial legislation', Lord Bridge emphasising that legislation enacted to implement international conventions is of necessity extra-territorial in effect. The 'presumption' in question is against illegitimate usurpation of another state's power to legislate for its own nationals. The judgment of Dr Lushington in considering the applicability of the Merchant Shipping Act 1854 to a foreign ship in *The Zollverein* (1856) Sw 96 at 98 was cited by both Lord Bridge and Lord Jauncey:

> 'In endeavouring to put a construction on a statute, it must be borne in mind how far the power of the British legislature extends, for unless the words are so clear that a contrary construction can in no way be avoided, I must presume that the legislature did not intend to go beyond this power. The laws of Great Britain affect her own subjects everywhere – foreigners only when within her own jurisdiction.'

It had been argued by the respondent that the doctrine of forum non conveniens could provide an effective counterweight to the presumption of non extra-territoriality since in the overwhelming majority of cases the carrier would be able to avoid the applicability of the Order by obtaining a stay of execution on the ground that the foreign state constituted the only convenient forum for the litigation. This argument was roundly rejected by Lord Bridge on the ground that a foreigner who has been duly served in a British court should not be forced to rely on the doctrine of forum non conveniens rather than stating simply that the Order is inapplicable.

Lord Jauncey, after considering a number of authorities, stated that

> 'it is clear . . . that the presumption proceeds on the basis that Parliament is unlikely to seek to interfere and has no interest to interfere in matters which are properly the concern of the legislature of another state.'

To what extent, then, should the 1967 Order be interpreted as having such extra-territorial effect? In the 4th edition of Shawcross and Beaumont *Air Law* published in 1977 it was stated (at p 389) that the normal presumption against giving a statute extra-territorial effect does not apply since some of the provisions of the Order (ie those relating to carriage under the original Warsaw Convention) expressly apply to international carriage and are not limited to carriage linked in some way to England. This view was also adopted in the 10th edition of *Dicey and Morris on the Conflict of Laws* (at p 844). However, in order to construe the 1967 Order it is essential to have regard to the purpose and provisions of the 1961 Act since it is this which determines the scope of the Order. The underlying rationale for the Warsaw Convention was the adoption of a uniform code governing international air carriage in order to remove the difficulties created by the different laws which could be applicable where an accident took place either in the country of departure or the country of destination or an intermediate country. Such difficulties do not arise in the case of purely internal carriage and it is therefore difficult to see why United Kingdom law should seek to apply United Kingdom law to such contracts of carriage whose proper law is not in doubt and in relation to which no question of conflict of laws could otherwise arise.

The second carriage by air case concerned the right of action under the Warsaw Convention of the owner of goods who is neither the consignor nor the consignee named in the air waybill. In *Gatewhite Ltd v Iberia Lineas Aereas de España SA* [1989] 1 All ER 944 a consignment of chrysanthemums belonging to the first plaintiff (ownership having passed from the grower upon delivery of the consignment to the defendant) arrived at Heathrow some four or five days late and in a damaged condition. The defendant contended that the plaintiff was precluded by the Warsaw Convention as amended at the Hague and as implemented by the Carriage by Air Act 1961 from bringing an action since he was neither the consignor nor the consignee of the goods. It is clear that at common law the plaintiff would have had a cause of action as the owner of the damaged goods; the question was therefore whether the effect of the Act and the Convention is to deprive the owner of his common law right of action or whether the provisions of the Act and the Convention should be regarded as supplementary to the common law.

The plaintiff relied strongly on section 1(1) of the 1961 Act which provides that:

> 'Subject to this section, the provision of the Convention known as "The Warsaw Convention as amended at the Hague 1955" . . . shall, so far as they relate to the rights and liabilities of carriers, carriers' servants and agents, passengers, consignors, consignees and *other persons* . . .'

have the force of law in the United Kingdom in relation to international air carriage.

The defendant however, relied on Ch III of the Convention as providing an implied limitation of the right to bring an action to the consignor and the consignee. Article 17 (relating to death or personal injury suffered by a passenger) is expressly stated in art 24(2) to apply 'without prejudice to the questions as to who are the persons who have the right to bring suit and what are their respective rights'. However, in relation to damages arising out of the destruction or loss of or damage to baggage or cargo (art 18) or delay (art 19), art 24(1) provides that 'any action for damages, however founded, can only be brought subject to the conditions and limits set out in this Convention'. In addition, art 30(3) sets out the various circumstances in which the consignor and the consignee, and they alone, have a right of action in the case of carriage performed by successive carriers.

Gatehouse J considered a number of authorities from other jurisdictions concerning the question of whether the right to sue should be limited to the consignor and the consignee. In most of these, the restrictive view is taken (see particularly *Manhattan Novelty Corp v Seaboard and Western Airlines Inc* 5 Avi Cas 17229, *Pan American World Airways Inc v SA Fire and Accident Insurance Co Ltd* 1965 (3) SA 150 and *Bart v British West Indian Airways Ltd* [1967] 1 Lloyd's Rep 239); however, in many of the restrictive authorities, either the report is brief or the decision turned on a particular provision of the local statute adopting the Convention. The most recent decision in this area is that of Prichard J in the New Zealand High Court in *Tasman Pulp and Paper Co Ltd v Brambles J B O'Loghlen Ltd* [1981] 2 NZLR 225 where the restrictive approach was rejected. While recognising that the decision of the judge was not final, in that the case before the court was an application by the carrier to strike out the statement of claim against it, which application was refused on the ground that the owner of the goods had an arguable case against the carrier under the Convention, Gatehouse J considered that comments of Prichard J taken together with the dissenting judgments of Stoby C in *Bart* and of Steyn CJ in the *Pan American* case and the silence of the Convention itself where it could easily have made provision lead to the conclusion that it was not intended to exclude the right of the owner or goods to bring an action. It should be recognised that in practice the consignee will often be a forwarding agent or the buyer's bank; it would be undesirable that the buyer's remedy should depend upon the ability and willingness of the actual consignee to bring an action against the carrier.

We shall pass briefly over the two remaining cases in this category. As we observed in last year's issue, the Court of Appeal's decision in *The Dominique* [1988] 3 All ER 233 has now been reversed by the House of Lords: see *Bank of Boston Connecticut v European Grain and Shipping Ltd, The Dominique* [1989] 1 All ER 545, and the discussion in our title on 'Shipping' (post, p 253). This authority may have implications within the law of carriage by road, as well as within its immediate context of sea carriages. In *Chloride Industrial Batteries Ltd v F & W Freight Ltd* [1989] 3 All ER 86, the Court of Appeal held that the Convention on the Contract for the International Carriage of Goods by Road 1956 (the CMR), as set out in the Schedule to the Carriage of Goods by Road Act 1965, does not apply to road transport between England and Jersey even though the convention is not part of the law of Jersey and the United Kingdom's accession to it does not extend to Jersey. The reason is that Jersey does not qualify as a 'country' within the English version of para 1 of the Convention, which requires that, in order for the convention to apply, the place of taking over of the goods and the place designated for delivery should be situated in two different countries, of which at least one is a contracting country. Dillon LJ acknowledged that s 9 of the 1965 Act gives Her Majesty the power to direct by Order in Council that the Act shall extend (inter alia) to the Isle of Man and to any of the Channel Islands; that no such extension had been made with regard to Jersey; and that the exercise of the power in relation (for example) to the Isle of Man rendered it unarguable that the Isle of Man fell to be treated as part of the United Kingdom for the purposes of the convention. (A similar power had been exercised in relation to Guernsey and Gibraltar). But this did not mean that, until such extension, the jurisdiction in question qualified as a separate country for Convention purposes. If that were the case, no power akin to that contained in s 9 would have been necessary in the first place, for, as Dillon LJ observed,

'. . . before the Act was extended to the Isle of Man, the Isle of Man could not have been regarded as a different country for the purposes of art 1 because, if it was a different country, it would be a country which could itself apply independently to accede to the convention and it would not have been necessary to reserve a power of extension in the United Kingdom's accession to the convention, or in s 9 of the 1965 Act.'

Insurance

Life insurance

Davitt v Titcumb [1989] 3 All ER 417 raised in a complex form the question of how the proceeds of a life policy are to be allocated where the beneficiary is precluded by public policy from making any claim for them. The policy in question was an endowment taken out by T and G on their joint lives, proceeds payable to the survivor, and was assigned to their mortgagee building society on terms that in the event of the death of either party the building society would use the insurance proceeds to pay off the mortgage. T later murdered G. The insurer paid the building society (which it was bound to do, as the building society was the assignee of the policy and as such unaffected by the circumstances giving rise to the loss), and the building society used the proceeds to pay off the mortgage. The dispute in question arose subsequently when the house previously subject to the mortgage was sold: T claimed that he was entitled to share the proceeds of sale with G's estate.

Had T succeeded, he would clearly have derived some indirect benefit from his original unlawful act, a result which Scott J sought to avoid. The reasoning leading to Scott J's ultimate conclusion that G's estate was entitled to the entirety of the proceeds was, perhaps inevitably, somewhat strained. In the view of Scott J, everything turned upon the decision of the building society to pay off the mortgage with the insurance proceeds for, while G's estate could have compelled it to do so, T could not, by reason of ex turpi causa. It followed that the sums applied by the building society belonged in their entirety to G's estate, with the result that G's estate was to be regarded as having paid off a debt owed jointly by G and T. This left T as the debtor of G's estate. Consequently, when the house was sold, G's estate was entitled to claim against the proceeds both G's share and, by way of contribution, the amount owed by T to G's estate; the figures were such that, after the contribution claim, no proceeds remained.

Purists might like to question whether the fact that T was unable, by virtue of a personal bar imposed by public policy, to require the building society to discharge the mortgage, meant that the moneys in question necessarily belonged to T. The result itself is, however, beyond reproach.

Property insurance

A number of cases determining the meaning of property policies were decided in the period under review. Perhaps the most important and, it would seem, the most widely misunderstood, is *Kelly v Norwich Union Fire Insurance Society Ltd* [1989] 2 All ER 888, which concerns the meaning of the word 'event' in a householders' policy. The policy, which was in force between 1977 and 1981, covered loss caused by 'events' occurring during its currency. Prior to the inception of the policy a pipe had burst under the property, but had been repaired. In 1980 a further burst occurred and was similarly repaired. In 1981 while the property was still in force, cracks appeared in the walls of the assured's property, and while the evidence demonstrated that these had been caused by one or other of the pipe bursts, it could not be established which of the bursts had caused the damage. The assured argued that the 'event' insured against was the occurrence of damage, ie the cracking, and that as this had occurred during the currency of the policy the insurers were liable. The insurers argued that the relevant 'event' was not the cracking but rather the incident which had given rise to the cracking; as the assured had not been able to demonstrate that the incident had occurred during the policy period, he could not recover. The Court of Appeal preferred the argument of the insurers and ruled that the assured could not recover. The unfortunate consequence of this case has been that at least some insurers have taken the view that they are *never* liable for property damage occurring during the currency of a policy where the causes of that damage cannot be shown to have occurred during the currency of the policy. That is only true, however, where the insurer's liability is expressed in terms of loss caused by events occurring during the policy period: a different result may be reached where, for example, the policy insures against 'damage occurring' or where it is plain from the wording that the event is intended to be the damage itself and not the *cause* of the damage.

In *Dino Services Ltd v Prudential Assurance Co Ltd* [1989] 1 All ER 422 the keys to the assured's business premises were stolen from his car, and the keys were later used to effect entry into the assured's premises from which various items of property were stolen. The assured claimed against his insurers for the loss of the property, the policy providing that cover attached in respect of 'theft involving . . . entry to the premises by forcible and violent means'. The question for the Court of Appeal was, therefore, did the use of stolen keys amount to 'forcible and violent' entry? The Court of Appeal was constrained, and not a little surprised, by previous authority, to hold that entry to premises was 'forcible' even if the only force used was the turning of a doorknob (see *Re George and Goldsmiths and General Burglary Insurance Association Ltd* [1899] 1 QB 595). The plaintiff failed, however, on the additional requirement that entry be violent: the Court of Appeal refused to accept that the word 'violent' could properly be applied to the mere turning of a key in the lock or to any entry which was unlawful, and held that what was required was 'some physical act which can properly be described as violent in its nature of character' in accordance with the popular understanding of the word. It might be added that the Court of Appeal expressed great sympathy with the assured, as his expectation of cover in these circumstances was perfectly reasonable, and also deprecated the continuing use of a phrase dating back nearly 100 years.

The phrase before the Court of Appeal in *Dobson v General Accident Fire and Life Assurance Corp plc* [1989] 3 All ER 927, 'loss by theft', led the Court of Appeal into detailed analysis of the intricacies of the criminal law. The assured advertised two items of jewellery for sale, and was telephoned by an interested purchaser who soon afterwards came to the assured's house and agreed to buy the jewellery at the asking price. The purchaser paid by cheque. The cheque subsequently proved to have been stolen and the jewellery could not be traced. The assured thus claimed against his insurers, asserting that he had suffered 'loss by theft' in accordance with the insuring clause of his householders policy. It should be said from the outset that, had the assured's policy covered simply 'loss', he would have failed, for it is settled law that in circumstances such as those occurring in *Dobson* the loss is not of the property itself but rather of the proceeds of the sale (see *Eisinger v General Accident Fire and Life Assurance Corp Ltd* [1955] 2 All ER 897). The insurers did not rely upon *Eisinger*, and thus would appear to have made the curious concession that the expression 'loss by theft' bears a broader meaning than the expression 'loss'. That point aside, it was apparently conceded that the only issue in the case was whether there had been 'theft' of the jewellery within the meaning of s 1 of the Theft Act 1968, ie whether there had been a dishonest appropriation of property belonging to the assured.

Each of these aspects of the definition of 'theft' gave rise to dispute, although ultimately both issues were resolved in the assured's favour. First, as to the question whether the property had 'belonged' to the assured when the appropriation had taken place, the Court of Appeal ruled that, in accordance with the intentions of the parties, property had passed to the purchaser only on payment by him, so that the assured had been the owner of the property throughout and in particular at the time of the appropriation. A commercial lawyer could be forgiven for thinking that a strong case could be made for the proposition that property had passed on agreement rather than on payment, although it is easy to sympathise with the Court of Appeal's unwillingness to allow the case to turn on the *scintilla temporis* between agreement and the acceptance of the cheque. More seriously disputed was the question of appropriation itself, for the Court of Appeal was faced with conflicting House of Lords authority as to whether there could be an appropriation where property is handed over with consent: their Lordships in *Lawrence v Commissioner of Police for the Metropolis* [1971] 2 All ER 1253, [1972] AC 626 held that the taking of possession was appropriation whether or not accompanied by consent, whereas in *R v Morris* [1983] 3 All ER 288, [1984] AC 320 the House contrived to reach precisely the opposite conclusion as regards consent. The Court of Appeal, plainly in some difficulty, preferred *Lawrence* and held that there had been an appropriation and thus loss by theft.

Dobson provides an interesting lesson. While the civil courts continually stress that words in insurance policies are to be given their narrow legal meaning, where the word in question is a term of art in the criminal law those courts are generally less obsessed with the precise technicalities of the law than their criminal counterparts.

Reinsurance

The House of Lords in *Forsikringsaktieselskapet Vesta v Butcher* [1989] 1 All ER 402 has upheld the decision of the Court of Appeal, noted in last year's Annual Review, in essence for the same reasons. It will be recalled that the case arose out of the insurance of a Norwegian fish farm by a Norwegian insurer. The policy contained a warranty by virtue of which the assured promised to keep a 24-hour watch over the fish farm. Loss was caused by a storm, and while at the time of the loss the warranty was not being complied with, the insurers were nevertheless liable in accordance with Norwegian insurance law which does not allow the insurer to plead a warranty unless its breach was causative of the loss. The Norwegian insurer's liability had been reinsured on the London market under standard reinsurance wording (Form J1) whereby the reinsuring underwriters accepted liability in the following terms: 'being a reinsurance of and warranted same gross rate, terms and conditions as and to follow the settlements'. It was conceded before Hobhouse J that the effect of this clause was to incorporate the terms of the original insurance policy into the reinsurance agreement. The reinsurers argued that, because the effect of a breach of warranty in English law is to permit the insurers to deny liability whether or not the breach was causative of the loss, and because the reinsurance agreement was governed by English law (England being the contract's 'centre of gravity'), they were entitled to plead the assured's breach of warranty as a defence against the reinsured.

All nine judges who heard this case came to the conclusion that the plain object of the reinsurance agreement was to provide the insurer with reinsurance cover matching that of its own liability to the original assured. Achieving this result proved to be problematical. Hobhouse J had found for the reinsured by relying on a novel conflict of laws approach. The learned judge ruled, flying in the face of the facts, that the reinsurance agreement was either governed by Norwegian law in its entirety or at least that its construction and interpretation were to be governed by Norwegian law. The Court of Appeal found the first of these approaches to be unrealistic and the second to be unduly complex; its own view was that the warranty was to be given the meaning that it would have received had the case been heard by a Norwegian court. The House of Lords affirmed the reasoning of the Court of Appeal. In the view of Lords Bridge, Templeman, Ackner and Lowry, the warranties in the two policies were intended to have the same effect, so that if the warranty could not be pleaded by the insurer against the assured it could not be pleaded against him by the reinsurers. Lord Griffiths, agreeing with the ultimate conclusion, preferred to challenge the assumption that the reinsuring clause had had the effect of incorporating the warranty in the original policy into the reinsurance agreement; in his Lordship's view the reinsurance agreement provided only that the assured would be indemnified if it faced liability in Norway.

The practices and wordings adopted by the English reinsurance market came in for a good deal of criticism in their Lordships' judgments. Lord Templeman described the wording as 'insurance jargon . . . which is ungrammatical and contradictory' (at p 405), while Lord Griffiths advised the market to redraft its standard forms to avoid the situation in which inappropriate terms might arguably be incorporated into reinsurance agreements (at p 409).

The Court of Appeal in *Home and Overseas Insurance Co Ltd v Mentor Insurance Co (UK) Ltd (in liq)* [1989] 3 All ER 74 was required to consider standard reinsurance wording of a different nature but of equal obscurity and pedigree to that in *Vesta*. Under the reinsurance agreement Home as reinsurer was bound to meet Mentor's 'ultimate nett loss', a term defined as the 'sum actually paid' by Mentor to its policyholders. Any dispute between the parties was to be referred to arbitrators under an arbitration clause in 'honourable engagement' form, ie that the arbitrators were to make their award with a view to effecting the general purpose of the reinsurance rather than in accordance with a literal interpretation of its terms. Mentor went into liquidation prior to having made payment on a number of claims against it, but Mentor's liquidator nevertheless sought to recover from Home sums representing liabilities which Mentor had yet to meet. The attitude of the Court of Appeal to the arbitration clause has been discussed in the 'Arbitration' section of this work, and it will be recalled that the court was prepared to leave to the arbitrators the meaning of the ultimate nett loss clause. Given that, it was not necessary for the Court of Appeal to determine whether the words 'actually paid' meant what they said or whether they could be construed as meaning that Home was liable in the absence of actual payment by Mentor as long as its liability to pay its assureds had been established. It is sufficient here to note that the Court of Appeal felt that there was a sufficient issue to be left to the arbitrators, and that in his unreported first instance judgment Hirst J had gone further and had indicated that actual payment by Mentor was not required despite the apparently clear wording to the contrary, as such a condition would confer windfall benefits on Home.

Utmost good faith

Two first instance decisions in 1988 determined that the duty of utmost good faith is reciprocal, and is thus also owed by the insurer to the assured. Both of those decisions went to the Court of Appeal in 1989, and the limitations of the insurer's duty were in that court exposed.

The first decision was *Banque Finacière de la Cité v Westgate Insurance Co Ltd* [1989] 2 All ER 982, other aspects of which are discussed in the 'Tort' section of this volume. The dispute arose through an independent series of frauds perpetrated by different persons. The plaintiff bank was one of a syndicate of banks which had agreed to lend some £30 million to B and his companies. By way of security, B offered gemstones and credit insurance policies. The banks were not prepared to release any money until the securities were in place. A valuation of the gemstones was arranged. B subsequently disappeared with the loans, and the gemstones, despite apparently independent valuation, proved to be worth little. The banks thereupon sought to rely upon the credit insurance policies. The policies had been broked by a major firm of brokers, acting through L, a senior employee. L had not in fact been able to obtain full cover, and had issued a series of false cover notes; this fact was known to D, a senior representative of one of the insurers involved, but nothing had been said to the banks. On making claims under the policies, the banks discovered the severe shortfall in cover, and commenced proceedings against the insurers for damages for the insurers' failure to disclose to the banks what they had— through D—known about the insufficiency of cover.

The Court of Appeal held that, as a matter of principle, an insurer owes a duty of utmost good faith to its assureds, extending to least to

> 'disclosing all facts known to him which are material either to the nature of the risk sought to be covered or the recoverability of a claim under the policy which a prudent insured would take into account in deciding whether or not to place the risk for which he seeks cover with that insurer' (at p 990).

Given that the information not disclosed by the insurers was material within the meaning of this test, the crucial question became whether damages could be awarded against the banks for breach of this duty. There was no authority on this matter, which was hardly surprising, for in all previous cases the party in breach of duty had been the assured, and it is plainly a sufficient remedy for the insurer to avoid the policy and thus its liability; the argument for the assured in *Banque Financière* was that a duty of disclosure owed to the assured is of little use if the assured's sole remedy is avoidance of the contract and recovery of the premium. The Court of Appeal, unlike Steyn J, was not persuaded by this argument. The Court of Appeal classified the duty of disclosure, in common with misrepresentation and duress, as a matter *ex contractu* and thus not one whose breach sounds in damages. Two further considerations justified this conclusion: first, given that the duty of utmost good faith is tested on objective grounds, it would be wrong to award damages to a plaintiff who might subjectively not have been misled by the insurer's silence; and, secondly, given that non-disclosure may be innocent (in that the significance of the information was not appreciated by the person failing to disclose), it would become possible to award damages against an innocent party.

Banque Financière thus produces the result whereby the insurer owes a duty of utmost good faith, but whereby in the majority of cases—where avoidance and return of premium are of little value to the assured—no effective remedy is conferred. Further, as noted in the 'Tort' section of this volume, the Court of Appeal went on to hold that the mere fact that the insurer owes a duty of utmost good faith to the assured is insufficient to create the necessary relationship between them to allow the assured to found an action in tort against the insurer.

Bank of Nova Scotia v Hellenic Mutual War Risks Association (Bermuda) Ltd, The Good Luck [1989] 3 All ER 628 concerned the ambit of an insurer's duty of disclosure to the assured's assignee. The assured in this case insured its vessel 'The Good Luck' under a policy which contained a warranty against the vessel trading in specified war zones. The vessel had been purchased by means of a loan from the bank, secured by a mortgage on the vessel and an assignment of the proceeds of the policy. In addition, the insurers had given to the bank a letter of undertaking which provided, inter alia, that the bank would be informed by the insurers in the event that the insurance cover should cease. The vessel was lost while trading in a war zone. The insurers did not immediately plead breach of warranty, and while they were considering their position the bank, not realising that the policy was liable to be terminated for breach, made further advances to the assured on the assumed security of the policy proceeds. The insurers subsequently repudiated liability. The bank, having found that its further advances were irrecoverable from the assured, claimed damages from the insurers for failing to disclose the existence of their defence to it. The Court of Appeal denied the existence of any tortious duty on the insurers to speak (see the 'Tort' section of this volume) and of any implied term in the letter of undertaking whereby the insurers were obliged to reveal the existence of defences open to them (see the 'Contract' section of this volume). Two insurance questions did arise, however: did the letter of undertaking by its express terms require the insurers to disclose the situation; and did the insurers owe a duty of utmost good faith to the bank thereby requiring them to make disclosure of their defence?

The first of these issues raised the question of the nature of an insurance warranty. The bank's contention was that breach of warranty by an assured had the effect of automatically terminating the policy; on this basis the policy had ceased to exist by the time of the further advance and the insurers were thus in breach of their express duty of disclosure to the bank in the letter of undertaking. The Court of Appeal accepted that the wording of s 33(3) of the Marine Insurance Act 1906—'the insurer is discharged from liability as from the date of the breach'—supported that contention, but it ultimately held that the section did not provide for automatic termination. This conclusion was based upon pre-1906 cases, which the 1906 Act had sought to codify, and upon the undesirability of laying down different rules for marine and non-marine insurance.

The bank's reliance on utmost good faith was not its greatest hope, and indeed was doomed to failure. The Court of Appeal was prepared to accept that an insurer does owe a duty of utmost good faith to its assureds and, further, that the duty might persist for certain purposes beyond the stage of contract formation. This did not assist the bank here, for two reasons. First, the assured under the policy was not the bank but the owner of the vessel, as the bank was merely the assignee of the proceeds of the policy rather than the policy itself. To put the matter a rather different way, the bank was not the assured and thus could not owe any duty of utmost good faith to the insurers, and the principle of reciprocity demanded that the insurers were themselves similarly exempt from such a duty. Secondly, even if the bank had established a duty of utmost good faith, the Court of Appeal was constrained by its own decision in *Banque Finacière* to hold that damages were not available to the bank.

Contribution between insurers

Equity has long recognised that, subject to various qualifications, where two or more insurers are liable for the same loss, payment by any one of them to the assured entitles that insurer to seek proportionate contribution from the other insurers. The right of contribution is a corollary of the assured's right to overinsure as many times as he wishes, and in recovering his indemnity to choose which of the insurers he wishes to make payment to him.

An interesting question arose in *Legal and General Assurance Society Ltd v Drake Insurance Co Ltd* [1989] 3 All ER 923. Here the assured had two motor policies and, following a motor accident in June 1976, made a claim against the plaintiff company. In the course of the following year the plaintiff discovered that the assured possessed a further policy issued by the defendant company, and the plaintiff informed the defendant of the accident late in 1977. The plaintiff finally reached a settlement of the assured's claim—for £65,000—in 1982, and sought 50% contribution from the defendant. The defendant, relying on the principle that contribution can only be claimed from an insurer who would have been liable to the assured, argued that by failing to give notice of loss in accordance with the policy, the assured was in breach of condition and unable to recover from the defendant; given that the defendant was not liable to the assured, it could not be liable to make contribution to the plaintiff.

A defence of this nature had succeeded before Judge Graham Rogers in *Monksfield v Vehicle and General Insurance Co Ltd* [1971] 1 Lloyd's Rep 139, but closer perusal indicates its fundamental inconsitency with the very concept of contribution, for if contribution depends upon the assured making a claim against the insurer from whom contribution is subsequently sought, it becomes immediately apparent that in the nature of things very few cases of contribution could ever succeed. This was recognised by Roger Buckley QC in *Legal and General*, who refused to follow *Monksfield* and held that any notice provisions in the policy with the defendant could not affect the plaintiff's claim, as this was based in equity and not on contract. The only qualification on this principle to be recognised by Roger Buckley QC, and this did not give rise to difficulty in the instant case, was that the insurer seeking contribution must act equitably and in particular must alert other insurers as soon as possible after he becomes aware of their existence that they are likely to face contribution claims by him.

Third parties

In *Bradley v Eagle Star Insurance Co Ltd* [1989] 1 All ER 961 the House of Lords, Lord Templeman dissenting, confirmed that the Third Parties (Rights against Insurers) Act 1930 cannot operate in favour of a claimant who seeks a direct claim against the liability insurers of an assured company which has ceased to exist. It will be recalled that the 1930 Act permits the victim of an insolvent assured to bring a direct action against the assured's liability insurers. In *Bradley* the plaintiff did not appreciate that she had a claim against her corporate ex-employer until long after it had been dissolved by removal from the register of companies. Their Lordships ruled that the dissolution of the company prevented it from being sued and thus prevented its liability to her from being established; given that its liability could not be established, there was no basis for an action against its liability insurers under the 1930 Act, in accordance with the principle espoused by the Court of Appeal in *Post Office v Norwich Union Fire Insurance Society Ltd* [1967] 2 QB 363.

This decision produced an immediate outcry, for it affected a large number of pending similar cases involving ex-employees and their families. Fortuitously, at the time of the decision the Companies Bill 1989 was proceeding through Parliament, and the government took the opportunity to amend section 651 of the Companies Act 1985 to provide some relief. Under the section in its original form, application could be made to the court for the revival of a company to allow it to be sued, but such application could be made only within two years of dissolution; this section was of no comfort in *Bradley*. The 1989 amendments remove the two-year limitation where the applicant is seeking damages for death or personal injury and, moreover, are retroactive for twenty years. Consequently, claims such as those in *Bradley* are now possible, assuming of course that the applicant can overcome issues of limitation and of evidence as to the cause of the loss.

Procedural matters

Two important procedural matters were discussed in cases reported in 1989. In *Ricci Burns Ltd v Toole* [1989] 3 All ER 478 the plaintiff's business premises were burgled, and an insurance claim was made in respect of the loss. The insurers denied liability, claiming that the brokers who had arranged the policy had exceeded their authority by failing to alert the assured to the fact that the policy would not be binding unless certain security measures were first taken by him. It was obvious to the plaintiff that either the insurers or the brokers were liable to him, and he issued proceedings against them both. The plaintiff then sought an interim payment under Ord 29, r 11(1) of the Rules of the Supreme Court. This provides, so far as is relevant, that a plaintiff is entitled to seek an interim award where 'if the action proceeded to trial, the plaintiff would obtain judgment for substantial damages against the respondent or, where there are two or more defendants, against any of them . . .' The Rules of the Supreme Court go on to allow for post-judgment adjustment of payments made under Ord 29, r 11. The plaintiff's action prima facie fell directly within the wording of Ord 29, r 11, but the Court of Appeal held that the power to make interim payments did not apply to this type of case. Before the court could make an interim award against any defendant, it would have to be satisfied that the plaintiff would at trial obtain judgment against that defendant even though there might be other defendants in a similar position.

The scope of representative actions was at stake in *Irish Shipping Ltd v Commercial Union Assurance Co plc, The Irish Rowan* [1989] 3 All ER 853, [1989] 2 Lloyd's Rep 144. The plaintiffs in this case, the owners of a vessel, had obtained arbitration awards against the vessel's charterers. The charterers went into liquidation leaving the awards unsatisfied, and the plaintiffs thus sought to invoke the Third Parties (Rights against Insurers) Act 1930 against the charterers' insurers. The insurance cover procured by the charterers had been broked in Antwerp and was under 12 separate policies which had been subscribed to by 77 insurers located in various parts of the world. The defendant, an English company, had been nominated as the 'leading underwriter', with authority to bind all of the insurers with regard to matters such as extensions, amendments and settlements. The plaintiff sought to bring a representative action against the plaintiff under Ord 15, r 12 of the Rules of the Supreme Court. That rule provides that proceedings may be commenced against any one of a group of persons who 'have the same interest in any proceedings'. A number of the following insurers raised objections to the use of this procedure. All of their arguments were dismissed by the Court of Appeal.

It was suggested by the insurers, first, that they did not have the 'same interest' in the proceedings as each insurer was liable for a specific part of the risk rather than each being jointly liable for the whole. The Court of Appeal held that this did not prevent the rule from operating. Secondly, it was pointed out that each of the insurers might have a separate defence distinct to himself under the policies, so that once again the interests of the parties could not be said to be the same. The Court of Appeal held that the correct approach to this point was not to deny the possibility of a representative action but rather for the court to set aside judgment against any insurer who could demonstrate that he had a defence; the Court of Appeal added that the 'leading underwriter' clause in any event rendered small the likelihood of the availability of separate defences. Thirdly, the insurers objected that the use of a representative action sidestepped the need for service outside the jurisdiction under Ord 11 of the Rules of the Supreme Court; the Court of Appeal denied this, and stressed the convenience of the representative procedure. The Court of Appeal did concede, however, that the discretion of the court to allow a representative action against parties outside the jurisdiction should be exercised on grounds similar to those applicable to Ord 11 itself; applying this test, the Court of Appeal ruled that the plaintiff would derive a legitimate jurdical advantage from proceedings in England rather than Belgium, as English proceedings would confer the ability to rely upon the 1930 Act, so that it was appropriate to permit the representative action to proceed.

Intellectual property

Only two cases involving intellectual property rights were reported in the period under consideration. In *Thetford Corporation v Fiamma SpA* (case 35/87) [1989] 2 All ER 801 the European Court of Justice held, on a preliminary reference from the English Court of Appeal, that the enforcement of non-discriminatory domestic patent laws (in this case, s 50 of the Patents Act 1949) against unlicensed goods made in Italy and imported into England, did not contravene the free movement of goods rules in arts 30 to 36 of the Treaty of Rome. The European Court of Justice further held that the English court was entitled to grant any remedy available under domestic legislation—here, an injunction—and was not required by the free movement rules to permit importation subject to the payment of a royalty; art 30 did not introduce compulsory licensing.

Re Dee Corporation plc [1989] 3 All ER 948 was an important test case on the service mark amendments to the Trade Marks Act 1938, introduced with effect from 1986 by the Trade Marks (Amendment) Act 1984. A service mark is defined by s 1(7) of the 1938 Act as including a mark 'used or proposed to be used in relation to services for the purpose of indicating . . . that a particular person is connected, in the course of a business, with the provision of those services'; the word 'provision' is itself defined by s 68(1) as meaning 'provision for money or money's worth'.

The applicants, all retailers, sought to register as service marks their distinctive name logos. Registration was refused by the registry on the basis that a mark is registrable only if used in relation to a business of providing services for money or money's worth; retailing, by contrast, amounted to trading in goods and not to the provision of any independent service as such. This approach was upheld by Falconer J and, on appeal in the instant proceedings, by the Court of Appeal. In the view of the Court of Appeal, a mark is registrable in respect of a service only if that service is charged for as such; arguments by the applicants to the effect that the price of their services was included in the price of the goods sold by them were held to be misconceived. Stocker LJ, at p 958, perhaps put the matter most clearly:

> 'The "business" of a retailer of goods is not the provision of the services by which the sale may be induced or rendered easier or more agreeable. The "business" of the retailer is the sale itself.'

Sale of goods

Mitsui & Co Ltd and another v Flota Mercante Grancolombiana SA, The Ciudad de Pasto, The Ciudad de Neiva [1989] 1 All ER 951 provides yet another contribution to the vexed question of title to sue in relation to goods in transit. In this case, the second plaintiffs were buyers of prawns which had been shipped fob on the defendants' vessels. The prawns were damaged and the second plaintiffs were paid by their insurers, who now sought to recover from the shipowners. The second plaintiffs had no express or implied contractual relationship with the shipowners and were neither consignees named in, nor indorsees of, the bills of lading. It followed that any action brought by the second plaintiffs (or on their behalf) would have to be in tort. This, according to Staughton LJ, necessitated proof of ownership on their part.

The Court of Appeal, reversing Hobhouse J, held that no such title had been made out. Whereas payment of 80% of the purchase price had been made by letter of credit before shipment, there was no evidence to suggest that the residue of the price was not outstanding when the damage occurred. Moreover, the bills of lading made the prawns deliverable to the order of the sellers. In the court's view, these considerations activated s 19 of the Sale of Goods Act 1979 and prevented property from passing to the second plaintiffs until the residual 20% had been paid. The seller must be deemed to have reserved a right of disposal in the goods within the contemplation of s 19(2), and by s 19(1) the property would not then pass until the relevant condition was fulfilled. That condition must be presumed to have been the full payment of the price. Staughton LJ rejected the argument that the sellers might well have been content to surrender their property in the goods upon payment of the original 80% of the price, and to look exclusively to the letter of credit as security for the outstanding 80%. The normal assumption in international sales is that the seller does not part with property until he has either received, or been given an adequate assurance of, payment. Even the most 'copper-bottomed' letter of credit might fail to produce payment for some reason or another, and the difference between a seller who has received 80% of the price and one who has merely received (say) 40% or 20% is simply one of degree rather than of substance. Conversely, there was no substantial reason to suppose that the buyers, having already paid 80% of the price as 'a matter of trust', would have required or expected the transmission of title to them before payment of the remaining 20%. This conclusion need cause no substantial hardship to parties in the position of the buyers, because such parties could simply require in future that they be inserted as consignees in the bills of lading.

A few final remarks should be made. First, Staughton LJ approved (at 956) the second plaintiffs' concession that it would not be a breach of contract for an fob seller to reserve the right of disposal when the goods are shipped: see further *Benjamin's Sale of Goods* (3rd edn, 1987) para 1861. Secondly, the shipowners reserved for future proceedings the point that the second plaintiffs in this action had already been paid by the first plaintiffs (their own buyers) and had accordingly suffered no loss. Such considerations would not, however, appear to have affected the second plaintiffs' entitlement to sue had they been capable of establishing property in themselves: see *The Sanix Ace* [1987] 1 Lloyd's Rep 465, esp at 468, per Hobhouse J; *The Aramis* [1989] 1 Lloyd's Rep 213, CA; *R G & T J Anderson Pty Ltd v Chamberlain John Deere Pty Ltd* (1988) 15 NSWLR 363. Thirdly, it is not in fact entirely accurate to say (as did Staughton LJ at 953) that *Leigh & Sillivan Ltd v Aliakmon Shipping Co Ltd, The Aliakmon* [1986] 2 All ER 145 prevents a plaintiff 'who is not the owner at the time that the damage occurred' from suing in tort for damage to goods; such a claim might also be grounded on the plaintiff's 'possessory title': see All ER Rev 1986 p 25. But in the present case, of course, nothing turned upon the point.

Company Law

D D PRENTICE, MA, LLB, JD
Barrister, Reader in Company Law, University of Oxford,
Fellow of Pembroke College, Oxford

Proceedings for the appointment of an administrator

When the procedure for the appointment of an administrator under Part II of the Insolvency Act 1986 was first introduced, it was expected that it would not be invoked with any great frequency because of the ability of a floating charge holder to block the procedure by appointing an administrative receiver to enforce his charge (s 9(3)). This appears to have materialised to the extent expected and a number of cases have been reported which deal with various aspects of the procedure.

An application for an administration order can be sought by among others 'the directors' of the company (s 9(1) of the 1986 Act). In *Re Equiticorp International plc* [1989] BCLC 597 Millett J had to determine whether a petition had been properly presented where a meeting of directors, from which two directors were absent, had resolved that an administration order should be sought and that any one of their number was authorised to take the necessary proceedings to have the appointment made. The doubts about the propriety of this procedure were attributable to the decision of Mervyn Davies J in *Re Instrumentation Electrical Services Ltd* [1988] BCLC 550 who had held that the phrase 'the directors' in s 124(1) of the 1986 Act (setting out who could present a winding up petition) required the petition be presented 'by all the directors'. Millett J avoided the difficulties raised by that decision by holding that (at 599)—

> 'Once a proper resolution of the board has been passed . . . it becomes the duty of all the directors, including those who took no part in the deliberations of the board and those who voted against the resolution, to implement it; and even in the absence of a specific authorisation to any and every director to take such steps as are necessary to implement it . . . that remains the legal position.'

This decision while sensible must throw into question the judgment of Mervyn Davies J in the *Re Instrumentation* decision.

In *Re Consumer and Industrial Press Ltd* [1988] BCLC 177 Peter Gibson J stated that the court should only make an administration order if it was satisfied that it was 'more probable than not' that one or more of the purposes set out in s 8(3) of the 1986 Act would be achieved. Hoffmann J in *Re Harris Simons Construction Ltd* [1989] BCLC 202 considered that this set too high a standard of probability and that the court make an order where it was satisfied that there was a 'real prospect' where one of the purposes could be achieved. Even where this more relaxed standard is satisfied, it still remains a matter of judicial discretion whether an order will ultimately be made and the court can still decline to make one where it would be inappropriate to do so. Also, as Vinelott J pointed out in *Re Primlaks (UK) Ltd* [1989] BCLC 734 at 742 (in which he adopted the views of Hoffmann J in the *Harris Simons* case), s 18(2)(*a*) obliges an administrator to apply to the court where there is no real prospect that the purposes stated in the administration could be achieved, and this will reduce the extent to which hopeless administrations are continued.

One of the essential features of the administration procedure is that it can only operate effectively if proceedings against the company are suspended since otherwise the administrator will not have an opportunity to assess whether he can carry out any of the purposes for which he was appointed: administration is a collective procedure for dealing with the company's problems which precludes the piecemeal dismemberment of the company. This aspect of the procedure is brought out by the recent decision of Harman J in *Re a company (No 001992 of 1988)* [1989] BCLC 9. The question before the court was whether it could restrain the advertisement of a winding up petition which had been followed about three weeks after it had been presented by a petition for the appointment of an administrator. Harman J held that it was a central feature of the administration procedure that nothing should be done to continue legal proceedings where a petition for the appointment of an administrator had been presented (see Insolvency Act 1986, s 10(1)(*c*)) and therefore such a restriction on the advertisement of the winding up petition should be granted.

The order of Harman J in the above case did not significantly interfere with the rights of the creditor who presented the winding up petition. However, in order for the administration provisions to operate effectively it is necessary to curtail significantly the rights of creditors as otherwise a creditor could thwart the procedure by enforcing his rights against the company outside the administration. A number of cases deal with the extent of the restrictions on the rights of creditors to take proceedings to enforce their security. Where an administrator has been appointed, the holder of a charge over the company's assets cannot take steps to enforce it without the leave of the court. In *Royal Trust Bank v Buchler* [1989] BCLC 130 such leave was sought (Insolvency Act 1986, s 11(3)). Peter Gibson J held that the onus was on the secured creditor to persuade the court to grant leave to enforce its charge but it was not necessary to show that there was something improper in the conduct of the administrator before it would be granted. On the facts of the case he declined to grant the secured creditor leave to enforce its charge even though the administration had continued for nearly ten months. But so as to protect the interests of the secured creditor he ordered the administrator to come back to the court in two months' time if he had not disposed of the property of the company which was subject to the administration order.

Re ARV Aviation Ltd [1989] BCLC 664 dealt with the right of the administrator to obtain an order under s 15 of the 1986 Act to sell property of the company which was subject to a fixed charge. Knox J rejected the argument put forward in that case that the 'sacrosanct' rights of the secured creditor should be protected and no order for sale should be made unless there was a bona fide dispute as to the value of the property subject to the security. In exercising its discretion under s 15 the court had to balance the prejudice to the secured creditor against those interests promoted by the carrying out of the administration order—in many situations (if not most) this would be the interests of the unsecured creditors. Where the court orders a sale under s 15, the proceeds of sale must be applied in discharging the 'sums secured by the security' (s 15(5)). In *Re ARV Aviation Ltd* Knox J held that this covered not only the principal and interest due but also 'costs involved in proceedings in relation to the realisation or otherwise in connection with the security' (at 669e–f). These latter costs could include costs associated with s 15 proceedings. In exercising its jurisdiction to order a sale under the section, the order had to be final, but the court could make such an order and at the same time order an inquiry to determine whether there was a deficiency within the meaning of s 15(5)(b) which would have to be made up to protect the interests of the security holder. (See also *Re Cloverbay Ltd* [1989] BCLC 724 dealing with the power of the administrator to obtain documents under s 234 of the Act.)

Charges and the powers of an administrative receiver

Edwin Hill & Partners (a firm) v First National Finance Corp plc [1989] BCLC 89 throws light on a difficult and important aspect of the law relating to administrative receivership. Where an administrative receiver is appointed, it will often transpire that his management of the affairs of the company involves the company failing to fulfil its contracts. Why, where this occurs, is the receiver not liable in damages for the tort of inducing a breach of contract? It is clear that the receiver does enjoy a wider right than the company in not having to fulfil contracts that the company has entered into, but the justification for this has never been clear. A neat answer to this problem is suggested by the *Edwin Hill* decision. In that case a property company financed its project through a bank loan which was secured on the property which was being developed. It retained the services of the plaintiffs, a firm of architects. When the company ran into financial difficulties the bank successfully insisted that the plaintiffs be dismissed as the company's architects and another more prestigious firm be maintained. The plaintiffs brought an action against the bank for damages for inducing a breach of contract and were unsuccessful; the court reasoned that the bank, pursuant to its charge, had a superior right to the contractual right of the architects and this entitled them with impunity to seek the termination of the plaintiffs' contract with the company. This of course supplies also a justification for why an administrative receiver is not liable for inducing a breach of contract, something which was implicitly, if not explicitly, recognised by the court in the *Edwin Hill* decision (at 96g–j, 99b–d). If such an action lay, it would have the effect of standing priorities on their head since an unsecured creditor could always sue an administrative receiver for damages for inducing a breach of contract and this would make it impossible for him to enforce the security—it is for this reason (the preservation of priorities and the protection of the chargee's interests) that such an action does not lie.

A number of cases illustrate the novel nature of the agency of the administrative receiver (Insolvency Act 1986, s 44(1)(a)). In *Gomba Holdings UK Ltd v Minories Finance Ltd* [1989] BCLC 115 the Court of Appeal upheld the judgment of Hoffmann J that the debtor company was only entitled to obtain those documents in possession of the administrative receiver which were brought into existence to enable the receiver to discharge his duties to the mortgagor company. The somewhat artificial nature of the administrative receiver's agency was also illustrated in *Re Aveling Barford Ltd* [1989] BCLC 122 which involved the right of a receiver to demand under s 236 of the Insolvency Act 1986 documents of the company from the company's solicitors who claimed to have a lien over them. Hoffmann J held that the administrative receiver had a statutory right to inspect the documents even though the solicitors had a right as against the company to exercise its lien. This of course is the result of s 236 which confers greater powers on the administrative receiver than on the company to demand information. Nevertheless it illustrates the unique nature of the receiver's agency since it results in wider powers being conferred on an agent than on his principal.

However, that the agency of the administrative receiver has some real content is illustrated by *Rhodes v Allied Dunbar Pension Services Ltd* [1989] BCLC 318. One of questions before the court in that case was whether a mortgagor company with respect to which the mortgagee had appointed an administrative receiver was nevertheless entitled to receive rents from tenants to whom the mortgaged property had been leased. The court held that if a mortgagee permitted a mortgagor to remain in possession then the mortgagor remained entitled to the rents of the property without any obligation to account to the mortgagee; this right continued even on the appointment of an administrative receiver since the receiver was the agent of the mortgagor company. The effect of this was that the mortgagor company's lessor could serve a notice on subtenants under s 6 of the Law of Distress Amendment Act 1906 and defeat the entitlement of the charge holder.

Wrongful trading

Section 214 of the Insovlency Act 1986 is unquestionably one of the most important modifications to the principle of limited liability this century. Where a company is insolvent, the principle of limited liability provides a perverse incentive for the company to continue trading as the members of the company have everything to gain and nothing to lose: if the company is successful they benefit while any additional losses will be borne by its creditors. The fraudulent trading provisions were designed to reduce the incentive for insolvent companies to continue to trade but these were not completely successful. However, s 214, involving as it does potential personal liability on the part of the directors for continuing to trade when there was no reasonable prospect that the company could pay its debts, is a different matter. *Re Produce Marketing Consortium Ltd (No 2)* [1989] BCLC 520 is the first case to deal with the section at any lenght and it indicates that the section should provide a powerful deterrent against the misuse of the corporate form. In that case the company had traded at a loss and had relied on overdraft facilities and trade credit to finance its activities. It had regularly prepared its accounts late. One of the directors had guaranteed the overdraft of the company with the company's bank. In early 1987 the auditors of the company had warned the directors of the company that they might be liable for fraudulent trading. Eventually the company went into liquidation and the liquidator sought an order under s 214 against the directors of the company. The court found the directors liable and ordered them to pay £75,000. A number of important points emerge from the judgment:

(a) first, in determining the degree of knowledge required of a director by s 214(4), Knox J held that the requirement to have 'regard to the functions to be carried out by the director in question, in relation to the company in question' involved a consideration of the 'particular company and its business' (at 550b–c). From this it follows that the knowledge and skill required form a director of a company in a modest line of business will be different from that of a company which possesses more elaborate procedures.

(b) The relativity of standards set out in (a) is subject to one important qualification. Directors will be presumed to possess a certain minimum standard of competence and, more importantly, will be presumed to possess the knowledge that they would have acquired had the company complied with the financial reporting provisions of the Companies Act 1985. On the facts of *Produce Marketing*, Knox J held that had the company produced its accounts on time then the directors would have appreciated in July 1986 that there was no reasonable prospect that the company would avoid going into insolvent liquidation and it was from this date that the liability of the directors under s 214 was to be measured.

(c) Having found liability under s 214(1), the next question the court had to determine was the amount the directors (there were two of them) had to contribute to the assets of the company. Section 214(1) gives the court power to make such order as the court 'thinks proper'. In exercising this discretion, Knox J considered that the court's jurisdiction under s 214 was compensatory rather than penal and that prima facie

> 'the appropriate amount that a director is declared to be liable to contribute is the amount by which the company's assets can be discerned to have been depleted by the director's conduct which caused the discretion under sub-s (1) to arise' (at 553).

The manner in which the court should approach its jurisdiction under the section is to treat the extent of liability as being a question of causation—to what extent has the conduct of the director caused loss to the company's creditors. In making this evaluation, the upper limit of a director's liability was not to be determined by fraudulent intent as this would introduce the standard relating to fraudulent trading which s 214 was designed to replace. Fraud, however, was not a factor to be completely ignored.

(d) Knox J did not award the full amount sought by the liquidator but the basis on which he reduced is not clear but it was probably the absence of fraud—'[This] was a case of failure to appreciate what should have been clear rather than a deliberate course of wrongdoing' (at 553g). As between the directors themselves, he ordered that one should be liable for £50,000 and the other for the remaining £25,000. The reason for this was that the former director had been more responsible for the management of the company's affairs than the other and also that director would benefit from the s 214(1) contribution since his liability on his guarantee to the company's bank would be proportionately reduced.

(e) It is an assumption of Knox J's judgment that the money paid under s 214 would feed the bank's charge. This is open to question: the right to bring the action is one vested in the liquidator and it is difficult to see how a company could execute a charge over it (cf *Re Yagerphone Ltd* [1935] Ch 392; for a fuller discussion of this see Prentice 'Creditor's Interests and Director's Duties' (1990) 10 OJLS 265).

(f) Interest was payable on the sums awarded on the grounds that the creditors had been kept out of their money and therefore it was proper that the creditors should be compensated for this loss.

(g) The costs of the liquidator had to be paid by the two directors against whom the order was made.

The other cases on s 214 merit a brief note. First, in *Re Produce Marketing Consortium Ltd* [1989] BCLC 513 Knox J held that s 727 of the Companies Act 1985 did not apply to s 214. Given the breadth of the court's discretion under s 214, it is to be doubted if this makes a great deal of difference to the powers that can be exercised by the court. The second case of interest is *Re a company (No 005009 of 1987), ex p Copp* [1989] BCLC 13 where Knox J refused to strike out as disclosing no cause of action a claim against the company's bank under s 214 that it was a shadow director and therefore potentially liable under s 214 (s 214(7)). Obviously too much should not be read into an unsuccessful summons to strike out a cause of action but the case does demonstrate that involvement in the affairs of a company opens up the risk of liability under s 214. Because of this potential liability, banks may be more disposed to put a company in difficulties into liquidation rather than enter into negotiation to try to find a way to enable it to trade out of its problems.

Third Party (Rights against Insurers) Act 1930

In *Bradley v Eagle Star Insurance Co Ltd* [1989] BCLC 469 the House of Lords by a majority held that the above Act had no application where the insured was a company which had been dissolved before its liability to a third person had been determined. Accordingly, one of the dissolved company's employees who suffered from an industrial illness in circumstances where it was not possible to invoke s 651 of the Companies Act 1985 could not make use of the Act. Section 141 of the Companies Act 1989 is designed substantially to reverse the effects of this decision. It does so by altering s 651 of the 1985 Act by allowing an application to be made at any time to declare a dissolution void where the application is made to enable an action for personal injuries to be brought. No order can be made where the proceedings with respect to which the application is being sought would fail because they are statute-barred (s 141(3)). Special provision is made for companies dissolved before the commencement of s 141 (see s 141(4)).

Take-over bids

Dawson International plc v Coats Paton plc [1989] BCLC 233 involves the important question as to whether directors owe fiduciary duties to the shareholders of a company. In that case the directors of the defendant company had allegedly agreed with the plaintiff company that they would recommend the plaintiffs' bid and that they would discourage any rival bids for the company. After the announcement of the bid had been made, the defendant company entered into negotiations with another company which eventually took it over. An action by the plaintiffs for breach of contract on the part of the defendant company in not recommending the bid was met in part with the defence that the directors could not make the commitment that they did to recommend the bid since this constituted a breach of their fiduciary duty to the defendant company's shareholders. It was argued that this duty imposed on the directors an obligation to be free at all times to act in the best interests of shareholders and, where appropriate, recommend any higher bid. The court rejected this proposition. In line with what is the orthodox position, the court held that the directors did not owe shareholders 'as sellers of shares' any direct fiduciary duties; the only duty that the directors owed to the shareholders was to consider their interests in so far as they were involved in the discharge of the duty that the directors undoubtedly owed to the company. The merit of this approach is that it prevents possibly two fiduciary duties being owed on the same set of facts—one to the company and one to the shareholders—but at the same time the shareholders' interests are not completely ignored. It does, however, enable the shareholders' interests to be ignored where they have no significant role to play, for example, where the company is insolvent (*West Mercia Safetywear Ltd (in liq) v Dodd* [1988] BCLC 250). Of course, if the directors do decide to advise the shareholders as regards the merits of a take-over then they will be subject to the duty to do so honestly and competently; this, however, flows from the fact that they have proffered advice and not because they owe any special duty as directors to shareholders.

The regulation of take-overs has been an area of business activity that has been left predominantly to self-regulation. However, as *Lonhro plc v Fayed* [1989] BCLC 485 indicates, it is inevitable that the civil law will at least impinge (if not more) in this area; the principle of complete and unadulterated self-regulation in this area is a chimera. In *Lonhro* the plaintiffs had been interested in taking over a company. The defendants had taken it over and the plaintiffs claimed that this had in part been due to the fraudulent statements made to the Secretary of State by the defendants about themselves. The plaintiffs claimed that the fraudulent statements of the defendants about themselves entitled the plaintiffs to damages for wrongfully interfering with their right to bid for the company which the defendants had acquired. The Court of Appeal reversed Pill J ([1988] BCLC 75) who had held that the statement of claim disclosed no cause of action. (See also *R v Panel on Take-overs and Mergers, ex p Guinness plc* [1989] BCLC 255, which confirms if such were needed that the panel is subject to judicial review.)

Director's duties

Dorchester Finance Co Ltd v Stebbing [1989] BCLC 498 was decided in 1977. In that case an action was commenced against directors alleging that the directors had been negligent in the discharge of their duties. Two of the directors were accountants and the other had considerable accounting experience. Since directors in the discharge of their duties have to display 'such a degree of skill as may reasonably be expected of a person with [their] knowledge and experience', the court held that it could take into consideration the respective financial expertise of the directors. This aspect of the judgment is unexceptionable and follows from *Re City Equitable Fire Insurance Co Ltd* [1925] Ch 407. Of slightly greater interest is that aspect of the judgment dealing with the failure of some directors to exercise any supervision over a fellow director who was given a free hand in the running of the affairs of the company. It was claimed that they could not be liable since it was the other director who had mismanaged the affairs of the company. The court held that by failing to perform any duty in the conduct of the affairs of the company the directors had been negligent and this applied to a non-executive director on the grounds that the 'duties of a director whether executive or not are the same' (at 505). Old cases such as the *Marquis of Bute's Case* [1892] 2 Ch 100, dealing with the liability in negligence of the president of a trustee savings bank, appear to be authority for the proposition that a failure to do anything could not constitute negligence (there were, however, special factors in that case, for example, the size of the board). In the context of the modern role of a director this doctrine has little to recommend it and the position put forward in *Dorchester Finance* is to be preferred. It has also been brought about indirectly by s 214(5) of the Insolvency Act 1986.

Disqualification of directors

Re Tasabian Ltd [1989] BCLC 720 reveals what was probably a not intended consequence of s 7(2) of the Company Directors Disqualification Act 1986. This subsection provides that the Secretary of State cannot make an application for disqualification under s 6 of that Act after the elapse of two years from the company going into liquidation unless he obtains leave of the court. In *Re Tasbian Ltd* one event of insolvency (the appointment of an administrative receiver) had occurred outside the two year period while another (the making a winding up order) had occurred within it; the question before the court was from what date did the two year period run. Peter Gibson J held that the date ran from the first event of insolvency which would justify an application under s 6. The Secretary of State can still apply for leave, but in many ways it would be preferable if time was to run from the last event of insolvency; this will normally be winding up and it seems inevitable that this procedure will reveal more about the operation of a company's affairs than an administrative receivership and therefore it is reasonable that time should run from this date.

Re McNulty's Interchange Ltd [1989] BCLC 709 once again underscores what has become a dominant theme of decisions in this area and that is that a disqualification order will not be made where all that a director has been guilty of was commercial misjudgment; something more is needed such as gross mismanagement or a want of probity. In particular, Browne-Wilkinson V-C considered it 'untenable' that a director deserved disqualification where he had relied on what appeared to be competent professional advice but failed to appreciate that the advice was not competent. As the courts have consistently emphasised in this area, a director who relies on professional advice will normally not be disqualified. (See also *Re Majestic Recording Studios Ltd* [1989] BCLC 1; *Re Cu Fittings Ltd* [1989] BCLC 556.)

Meetings

Byng v London Life Association Ltd [1989] BCLC 400 explores some of the technicalities of law relating to the conduct of meetings and in particular the powers of the chairman to adjourn a meeting. In that case a meeting of the company was summoned for venue A at which it could not be properly held because of the numbers turning up and the difficulty in having them registered. The chairman summoned a meeting for the same afternoon at venue B and a resolution was carried at this adjourned meeting. A member commenced an action alleging that the whole proceedings were irregular. Firstly, it was alleged that the first meeting was not a meeting properly so called because provision had been made for members to congregate in overflow rooms which were interconnected to the main meeting room by telephonic links and therefore it was anticipated that all attending could not congregate in the same room. Browne-Wilkinson V-C held that there was no requirement that for the holding of a valid meeting those attending had to be physically present in the same room and, provided those attending were able to participate in an exchange of views, this would be a valid meeting. Secondly, although the circumstances surrounding the holding of the meeting at venue A were such that the business for which the meeting was summoned could not be conducted, it did not follow that nothing could be done at all. The meeting was sufficiently constituted for the chairman to be able to adjourn it. Thirdly, the fact that the articles provided that the chairman could adjourn the meeting with the consent of the shareholders did not mean that he could not exercise his inherent powers to adjourn the meeting when it became impossible for the meeting to conduct business. Lastly, the question had to be determined whether the chairman had validly exercised his residual power to adjourn the meeting held at venue A and to reconvene it at venue B. The evaluation of the propriety of the chairman's decision had to be determined by the application of the equivalent of the *Wednesbury* ([1947] 2 All ER 680) principles; namely, was there evidence on the facts which the chairman 'knew or ought to have known' that—

> 'he failed to take into account all the relevant factors, took into account irrelevant factors or reached a conclusion which no reasonable chairman, properly directing himself as to his duties, could have reached . . .' (at 412).

The court held that the chairman's decision to adjourn failed this test since he had failed to take into consideration a factor which he should have done and that was the clear inability of some of those present at venue A to attend the adjourned meeting at venue B; accordingly the meeting at venue B had not been properly convened.

Also of relevance to the question of validly summoned meetings is *Bradman v Trinity Estates plc* [1989] BCLC 757. In that case Hoffmann J held that there was an arguable case that summonses of a meeting sent out to shareholders during a postal strike had not been validly served and accordingly any ensuing meeting would not have been validly constituted.

Winding up

There have been a number of cases dealing with winding up but only a few need to be noted. *Re Calmex Ltd* [1989] BCLC 299 indicates that under the new Insolvency Rules 1986 the court now has jurisdiction to rescind a winding up order (rather than merely grant a stay) and in addition the court can order the registrar to delete the order from the company's register since the registrar cannot register something that is a nullity. *Re Esal (Commodities) Ltd* [1989] BCLC 59 is an interesting recognition of the reality of groups in the context of winding up. The court held that it would be proper for a parent company to release to its subsidiaries documents that it had obtained under s 561 of the Companies Act 1985 (now ss 236 and 237 of the Insolvency Act 1986) to enable the subsidiaries to conduct litigation against the person from whom the information had been obtained.

Auditors

Caparo Industries plc v Dickman [1989] BCLC 154 (O'Connor LJ dissenting in part) is an important case on the liability of auditors in negligence to a company's shareholders and prospective investors. Bingham LJ, who gave the leading judgment, held that auditors owed a duty of care to existing shareholders both as investors in additional shares in the company or as sellers of the company's shares. Thus shareholders who suffered damage by relying on negligent audited accounts would be entitled to recover damages. However, no such duty was owed to prospective investors either because there was not a sufficient degree of proximity or because it would be unfair to impose such liability. Section 310 of the Companies Act 1985 has been amended by s 137 of the 1989 Act so as to enable a company to maintain an insurance policy for officers or auditors with respect to the type of liability referred to in that section; it does not however allow a company and an auditor to agree to any limitation with respect to the auditor's liability to the company.

Legal proceedings by a company

Re Fletcher Hunt (Bristol) Ltd [1989] BCLC 108 reaffirms, what is a salutary warning, that the court has jurisdiction to make a solicitor liable for costs where he has initiated legal proceedings that are unauthorised. This jurisdiction can be invoked even where a solicitor is blameless in the sense that he acted reasonably and on advice. In the context of legal proceedings commenced by a company there can often be a dispute as to whether the proceedings have been properly authorised. This was the issue before the court in *Re Fletcher Hunt (Bristol) Ltd*. On the facts of the *Fletcher Hunt* case, the court found that since all the members knew that the solicitors were acting for the company and had consented to it, there was no basis for the court finding that the proceedings had not been properly authorised.

Breckland Group Holdings Ltd v London and Suffolk Properties Ltd [1989] BCLC 100 raises fundamental questions as to the relationship between the board of directors and shareholders as regards the initiation of litigation. It also throws some light on a relatively unexplored aspect of a director's duties, namely whether a director can bind the exercise of his discretion. The facts in the *Breckland* case were as follows. C Ltd was a 51% shareholder in L Ltd, the remaining 49% of the shares being held by B Ltd. There was a shareholder's agreement under which C Ltd and B Ltd could appoint directors to the board of L Ltd and which also provided that material legal proceedings could not be commenced without the consent of a C Ltd director and of a B Ltd director. C Ltd commenced an action on behalf of L Ltd against six defendants one of whom was A who was the managing director of L Ltd and the principal shareholder in B Ltd. B Ltd sought to restrain C Ltd from continuing the action in the name of L Ltd. There were two lines of defence raised to the action of B Ltd.

First, it was conceded that the action on behalf of L Ltd had not been validly authorised. But a meeting of the board of L Ltd had been summoned at which a resolution was to be put that the action should be adopted and, if it were passed, this would have the effect of validating the proceedings from their commencement (see *Danish Mercantile Co Ltd v Beaumont* [1951] 1 All ER 925). It was further submitted that at the board meeting, A, against whom the proceedings were being brought, would because of this conflict of interest have to vote for their continuance, hence the outcome of the directors' meeting was inevitable. Harman J refused to accept this. It was not possible for a fiduciary to exercise a fiduciary discretion nunc pro tunc; the discretion had to be exercised in the light of all the circumstances existing at the time it was exercised. This is thus clear authority for what has been generally accepted and, that is, that a director as a fiduciary cannot bind his discretion in advance. This of course still leaves open the question of how a valid exercise of power by directors is to be distinguished from an improper fettering of discretion (see *Dawson International plc v Coats Paton plc* [1989] BCLC 233 commented on under 'Take-over bids').

The second line of defence was that since C Ltd held 51% of the shares of L Ltd it would be inevitable that at any shareholders' meeting held to determine whether or not the action had been properly commenced that the action would be approved. This, according to Harman J, raised the following point of law (at 104):

'. . . can a general meeting in circumstances of this sort pass a resolution to adopt [legal proceedings] when by the provisions of . . . the articles of association which govern the company . . . such a matter is within the remit of the board?'

Harman J had little doubt that when matters are confided by the articles to the directors then the shareholders could not intervene. He considered the decision of Neville J in *Marshall's Valve Gear Co Ltd v Manning Wardle & Co Ltd* [1909] 1 Ch 267, which was to the contrary, was in conflict with appellate authority holding otherwise. Accordingly, as the right to commence legal proceedings in the name of the company was vested in the board, the proceedings in the present case had been commenced without authority and the order sought by the plaintiff shareholder to restrain the company from continuing with the litigation should be granted. In granting the order he implicitly recognised that at the minimum a shareholder had a right to compel the company to comply with the provisions in its articles vesting management power in a particular organ if not a broader right to compel the company to comply with its articles as a whole (see Wedderburn (1989) 52 MLR 401).

Minority shareholder oppression

From the volume of reported cases, it is clear that s 459 of the 1985 Act is being invoked with some frequency. What is interesting about the case law so far is that most of the cases are first instance judgments normally involving

proceedings to strike out a petition under s 459 as showing no cause of action
or as otherwise being an abuse of the process of the court. *Re a company (No
006834 of 1988), ex p Kremer* [1989] BCLC 365 is one such case. In this case
Hoffmann J reiterated his view that where there has been a breakdown in the
relationship between the members of a company and it is clear which
member should depart (for example, because of age or lack of business
acumen) then it is not unfairly prejudicial for such a member to have to
transfer his shares to the other members where they are valued pursuant to a
provision in the company's articles of association for determining the fair
value of the shares. (See also *Re Abbey Leisure Ltd* [1989] BCLC 619 where he
held that a shareholder was acting unreasonably in not making use of the
pre-emption provisions in a company's articles and therefore accordingly
refused to grant a remedy either under s 459 or s 122(1)(g) of the Insolvency
Act 1986.) The savings in costs to shareholders of this approach are obvious,
but it is an approach that must be treated with caution. This is for at least four
reasons: (a) it almost provides the majority with a carte blanche to oust the
minority; (b) it could be unfair in that the majority can choose an opportune
time to oust the minority so as to reduce the amount that they have to pay for
the minority's shares; (c) it treats a normal pre-emption provision as applying
to a forced sale whereas more often than not it is designed to deal with agreed
sales; and (d) it fails to give the minority shareholder the means to ensure that
the valuation has been carried out in a manner which adequately protects his
interests. As regards the last point (the issue of valuation), Peter Gibson J in
Re a company (No 005134 of 1986), ex p Harries [1989] BCLC 383 declined to
apply the principle enunciated by Nourse J in *Re Bird Precision Bellows Ltd*
[1984] BCLC 195 that normally the shares of a minority shareholder ordered
to be purchased by the majority should be valued on a pro rata basis and not
discounted because they were a minority. He rightly pointed out that Nourse
J did not consider this to be the invariable rule and, on the particular facts
before him, since the minority shareholder had himself elected to terminate
his relationship with the company, it would not be approrpiate to value the
shares on a pro rata basis.

Conflict of Laws

J G COLLIER, MA, LLB
Barrister, Vice-Master of Trinity Hall, Cambridge

Jurisdiction: service abroad; standard of proof

A plaintiff who seeks leave to serve a writ out of the jurisdiction under RSC Ord 11, r 1 must, on his ex parte application, make it 'sufficiently to appear' that the case is a proper one for service abroad. If the defendant applies for service to be set aside, the question may arise as to what is the standard of proof required of the plaintiff that the action falls within the rule. The Supreme Court Practice (Vol I, para 1/1/6) summarises the authorities, in particular *Tyne Improvement Comrs v Armement Anversois SA, The Brabo* [1949] 1 All ER 294 and *Vitkovice Horni a Hutni Tezirstvo v Korner* [1951] 2 All ER 334, as requiring the plaintiff to show a 'good arguable case'. This is taken to indicate that 'though the court will not require proof of the plaintiff's case to its satisfaction, it will expect something better than a mere prima facie case'.

The matter was considered by the Court of Appeal (Staughton LJ, with whom Sir Nicolas Browne-Wilkinson VC and Woolf LJ agreed) in *Attock Cement Co Ltd v Romanian Bank for Foreign Trade* [1989] 1 All ER 1189. Whether the plaintiff could be given leave depended on whether a contract was governed by English law, which it failed to satisfy the court was the case (see p 52 below). The court asked whether, as the plaintiff argued, it should look only to the plaintiff's case and in effect ignore such evidence as, at this stage, the defendant might adduce. If this were true, the defendant might be compelled to defend the action in England though the plaintiff's assertions should turn out to have been without foundation. Also, unlike a case where the defendant's liability might be open to argument at the trial, so that the issue has to be determined at the leave stage and again at trial, this was a case in which the issue was not likely to be raised at trial, so that an assumption of jurisdiction would in effect determine liability.

Staughton LJ carried out a re-examination of the authorities, and concluded that the standard of proof fell between a prima facie case on the one hand and proof to the full satisfaction of the court on the other. But where between those two extremes did it fall? He answered that the plaintiff's case must not be given sole or even primary consideration, but that the judge should look at all the admissible material before him and reach a provisional or tentative conclusion that the plaintiff is probably right on it before he allows service to stand. This appears to be as good a formulation as can be achieved.

In *E F Hutton & Co (London) Ltd v Mofarrij* [1989] 2 All ER 633, the court held that the action did fall within Ord 11 (see above). Kerr LJ stated that where the test of 'a good arguable' case on the part of the plaintiff is to be applied, the test applies both to issues which will or may and to those which will not or may not, be further investigated at the trial.

Jurisdiction: service abroad in case of injunction

In *Siskina (cargo owners) v Distos Cia Naviera SA, The Siskina* [1977] 3 All ER 803, the House of Lords held that what is now Ord 11, r 1(1)(*b*), which permits of service out of the jurisdiction 'where an injunction is sought ordering the defendant to do or refrain from doing anything within the jurisdiction, whether or not damages are also claimed in respect of a failure to do or the doing of that thing', was not available where the plaintiff had no other cause of action in England and all that he sought was a *Mareva* injunction to restrain the defendant from removing assets from England, in aid of an action abroad.

In consequence of the United Kingdom becoming a party to the Brussels Convention 1968 on Jurisdiction and the Enforcement of Judgments in Civil and Criminal Matters, it became party to art 24 thereof, which provides that application may be made to the courts of a contracting state for such provisional, including protective, measures as are available in those courts even if, under the Convention, the courts of another contracting state have jurisdiction over the substance of the matter. The Civil Jurisdiction and Judgments Act 1982, s 25, provides that the High Court shall have power to grant interim relief where proceedings which are within the scope of the 1968 Convention 'have been or are to be commenced in a Contracting State other than the United Kingdom'. The purposes of s 25 were to enact art 24 of the Convention into English law and to override *The Siskina*.

In *X v Y* [1989] 3 All ER 689, the plaintiff French bank brought an action against the defendant, a Saudi Arabian businessman, in the French courts. In support of those proceedings the bank obtained a *Mareva* injunction in respect of the defendant's English assets and was given leave to serve an originating summons seeking similar relief on the defendant in Saudi Arabia. The defendant argued that the bank's claim did not fall within RSC Ord 11 and, though s 25(1) of the 1982 Act gave the court power to grant interim relief in aid of French proceedings, Ord 11, r 1(1) did not authorise service on a defendant who was not domiciled in a country which was a party to the 1968 Convention. He also argued that the court had no jurisdiction under r 1(1)(*b*) where the injunction sought was not one to which the plaintiff's cause of action entitled it, as where the English court had no jurisdiction over the substantive action.

Mr Anthony Diamond QC, sitting as a deputy judge of the High Court, rejected these contentions. Since s 25 of the 1982 Act was enacted to confer the powers which art 24 of the 1968 Convention entitled it to exercise, the second argument was plainly wrong, because it was effectively based on *The Siskina*. The first argument was also wrong, since neither art 24 nor s 25 was in terms limited to cases where the defendant was domiciled in a contracting state.

Jurisdiction: service abroad in cases of contract

RSC Ord 11, r 1(1)(*d*) permits service out of the jurisdiction when a claim is brought to '. . . rescind, dissolve, annul or otherwise affect a contract' in certain cases, one of which (r 1(1)(*d*)(ii)) is where the contract was made by or through an agent trading or residing in England. In *Finnish Marine Insurance*

Co Ltd v Protective National Insurance Co [1989] 2 All ER 929 the plaintiffs, a Finnish insurance company, issued a writ against the defendant Nebraskan corporation. They sought a declaration that the London branch of a Guernsey firm of underwriters, acting as agents for the plaintiffs (or rather, the predecessors in title to their business) had issued two reinsurance policies to the defendants without authority, so that the plaintiff was not party to any contract with the defendant and that the defendants must account for sums paid to them and repay these. Mr Adrian Hamilton QC, sitting as a deputy judge of the High Court, had to decide whether the claim 'affected' a contract, so that he could allow the plaintiffs to serve the writ out of the jurisdiction under r 1(1)(*d*)(ii) or (*e*), which is concerned with breach of a contract committed within the jurisdiction.

The plaintiffs attempted to argue that it was enough to show that the plaintiffs' contract with the defendants 'affected' their contract with their 'agents', and that the contract in question does not have to be between the plaintiff and defendant. The deputy judge rejected this argument. Then the question arose, whether the plaintiffs' claim could be said to 'affect a contract' with the defendant, the existence of which contract the plaintiffs were denying. There was no authority on this point. It has been held that a claim that a contract has been discharged by frustration 'affects' a contract (*BP Exploration Co (Libya) Ltd v Hunt* [1976] 3 All ER 879) but to claim that a contract has been frustrated involves accepting that it did exist. The deputy judge quite rightly held that a claim that a contract never existed cannot possibly be said to affect such contract. The opposite conclusion would involve a singular self-contradiction.

The claim for an account was rejected since such a claim was not properly disclosed by the writ, though if such a claim did exist it could, in principle, fall within r 1(1)(*d*) and (*e*).

An argument that a claim on one contract between the plaintiff and defendant 'affected' a different contract between them succeeded, however, in *E F Hutton & Co (London) Ltd v Mofarrij* [1989] 2 All ER 633. The English plaintiffs and the Greek defendants had entered into a brokerage contract, which was governed by English law, by which the defendant agreed to provide a bank guarantee for any indebtedness he might incur under that contract. Pending the issue thereof the defendant drew a cheque in Greece on a Greek bank for $US 300,000, payable in Greece, and delivered it to the plaintiffs' representative in Greece. This cheque was governed by Greek law. The plaintiffs obtained leave to serve the defendants under Ord 11, r 1(1)(*d*)(iii) in respect of a claim for damages for breach of the brokerage contract and then were given leave to amend the writ so as to claim damages also in respect of the cheque, which had been dishonoured, and to serve the defendants with the amended writ. The defendants appealed against these orders, arguing that the claim in respect of the cheque did not fall within Ord 11, since it was not 'governed by its terms or implication' by English law.

Obviously, if the claim on the cheque had been the only one made, it would not have fallen within Ord 11. Nevertheless, the Court of Appeal (Kerr LJ and Ewbank J) held that, since payment of the Greek cheque would have immediately reduced the amount due from the defendant under the English brokerage contract, breach of the former contract directly affected the defendant's obligations under the latter. Therefore the claim 'affected' the

English brokerage contract and was within r 1(1)(d). It did so as well, because the breach of the cheque contract was a breach of the brokerage contract and the defendant's promise to honour the cheque was part of his consideration under that contract.

This decision on a novel point is ingenious and sensible. But it should be observed that Kerr LJ accepted that there must be some situations to which it cannot apply. In the instant case the claim on the Greek cheque affected the English contract directly and not consequentially. A claim on one contract does not always 'affect' another simply because the two contracts are between the same parties. The mere fact that a clearly 'foreign' claim might have some consequence for, or repercussion on, an English contract may be said in a sense to affect that contract, but not so as to bring the claim within the rule. One example of this, which was accepted by Kerr LJ, is where the parties conclude a foreign contract for prefabrication, which is outside Ord 11. They also conclude an English construction contract to be performed in England by the use of materials to be prefabricated abroad under the first contract. A breach of the first contract would have consequences for or repercussions on the second. Another example is where the defendant has committed a tort abroad which has had consequences on an English contract between the parties to be performed here.

It may be noted that the argument which succeeded in this case would not have been open to the plaintiffs in a case such as *Attock Cement Co Ltd v Romanian Bank for Foreign Trade* [1989] 1 All ER 1189 (see p 49 above and p 54 below) since in that case, the two contracts involved were not between the same parties. Moreover, it was intended that the second, Romanian, contract contained in the performance bond should be entirely separate from the first, the English construction contract.

Jurisdiction: service abroad in case of tort

Until RSC Ord 11 was amended in 1983, in order for the court to allow service out of the jurisdiction in the case of a claim in tort, the tort had to be committed in England. Following the advice of the Privy Council in *Distillers Co (Biochemicals) v Thompson* [1971] 1 All ER 694 the courts applied a test in cases of a 'transnational tort', wherein some elements of the tort occur in a foreign country and some in England, in order to determine whether or not it was committed here, of 'where was the tort in substance committed?' (See for example *Castree v ER Squibb & Sons Ltd* [1980] 2 All ER 589 and *Multinational Gas and Petrochemical Co v Multinational Gas and Petrochemical Services Ltd* [1983] 2 All ER 563.) The current Ord 11, r 1(1)(f) was altered, in accordance with the interpretation placed upon art 5(3) of the EEC Convention on Jurisdiction and the Recognition of Judgments in Civil and Commercial Matters 1968 by the European Court of Justice in *Bier v Mines de Potasse d'Alsace* [1978] QB 708. It now reads, where 'the claim is founded on a tort and the damage was sustained, or resulted from an act committed, within the jurisdiction'. In *Metall und Rohstoff AG v Donaldson Lufkin & Jenrette Inc* [1988] 3 All ER 116 (see All ER Rev 1988 p 46), Gatehouse J held that, when, in respect of conduct which had taken place in New York whose consequences occurred in England, the plaintiff had established that it had good arguable causes of action in conspiracy and in inducing breach of contract as a matter of

English domestic law alone, service was permissible under r 1(1)(*f*) because the damage was sustained within the jurisdiction.

The Court of Appeal ([1989] 3 All ER 14) reversed Gatehouse J on the conspiracy point, holding that as a matter of English law no such action was available to the plaintiffs. However, it upheld him on two points: (i) that the plaintiffs had a good arguable case as respects the tort of inducing breach of contract and (ii) that this claim fell within r 1(1)(*f*), so that the plaintiffs could have leave to serve out of the jurisdiction in respect of that cause of action. But the court arrived at this conclusion by a very much more convoluted method and by resort to an argument which had not been propounded before Gatehouse J. It determined whether the plaintiffs had an arguable case in tort not by reference exclusively to English domestic law, but by resort also to the choice of law rules of English private international law. The court, whose judgment was that of Slade LJ, proceeded thus. If the wrong was committed in England, all one need ask is whether it gave rise to liability in English law. If it was committed in New York, in order to decide whether the plaintiff had a cause of action in tort, one must apply the double actionability test, which is now agreed to be the upshot of the House of Lords' decision in *Chaplin v Boys* [1969] 2 All ER 1085. That test means that the conduct must be actionable in tort under English law, which in the instant case it was, and it must give rise to civil actionability in damages by the law of the place in which the alleged tort was committed, which it did not, since an action in New York for inducing a breach of contract would be time-barred by the law of New York. In that event the plaintiffs would have no claim in tort and the fact that they had sustained damage in England would not bring the action within Ord 11.

But the day was saved for the plaintiffs since the court, by application of the 'substance of the tort' test, held that it had been committed in England, and service abroad could be permitted.

This is rather odd, and as the proceedings at first instance suggest, somewhat unnecessary. It is odd for two reasons. First the question before the court was one of jurisdiction. The rule in *Chaplin v Boys* is a choice of law rule; it is used to help determine substantive liability. This does not arise unless and until the court decides that it has jurisdiction. Jurisdiction is decided by the lex fori (ie English domestic law) alone. (Art 5(3) of the 1968 Convention, on which, as we have seen, Ord 11, r 1(1)(*f*) is modelled, is only concerned with jurisdiction, as is the whole Convention and not choice of law). If, for example, leave is sought under Ord 11 on the ground that the claim is in contract and the contract was concluded in England, its proper law may well be that of New York. But the court does not investigate at that stage whether the contract is, say, frustrated under New York law. Second, r 1(1)(*f*) is not concerned with where the tort as a whole was committed, but only with where the damage was sustained or where the defendant acted, wherever it might be said that the tort was committed. The requirement that the claim should be in tort is a reference to the claim as the plaintiff frames it, as contrasted with a claim framed, for example, in contract, which would fall under a different head of the rule.

The method by which the Court of Appeal proceeded entails, in effect, that the defendant's liability is being tried in order to decide whether the court has jurisdiction to determine the defendant's liability. From a strictly legal point of view, the method apparently argued before and adopted by Gatehouse J is, it is submitted, preferable in principle. It leads to the same result and does not involve arguing in a circle.

It has to be admitted that the Court of Appeal's approach has something to commend it. Suppose that by applying English law alone the court had held that the plaintiffs had an arguable claim in tort and that they had suffered damage in England and then allowed service in New York. It might later be decided at the trial that the tort was committed in New York and, by application of *Chaplin v Boys*, the defendants were not liable because they were not liable by New York law. Granting leave to serve out of the jurisdiction would, in that scenario, have been purposeless and an expensive waste of time and effort. But this could have been avoided by the court simply exercising its discretion to refuse the plaintiff leave.

Jurisdiction: service abroad, exercise of discretion

In *Metall und Rohstoff AG v Donaldson Lufkin & Jenrette Inc* [1989] 3 All ER 14 the Court of Appeal held that Gatehouse J had properly exercised his discretion to permit service out of the jurisdiction under RSC Ord 11 and had correctly followed the guidelines laid down in *Spiliada Maritime Corp v Cansulex Ltd, The Spiliada* [1986] 3 All ER 843 (see 1986 All ER Rev p 59). Though some of the factors, such as the location and place of business of the defendants, were in favour of trial in New York, others, such as the location of witnesses and experts and work done on the litigation by lawyers, were more or less evenly balanced and the trial of the action in England was in some ways a continuation of an earlier English action. The fact that the plaintiffs had not taken out a protective writ to prevent their action in New York being time-barred was not held against them; since this was not a deliberate omission but at the most due to negligence, this factor was regarded as neutral. The crucial factor in making England the appropriate place for trial was that the alleged tort was substantially committed here.

In *Attock Cement Co Ltd v Romanian Bank for Foreign Trade* [1989] 1 All ER 1189, the action was held not to fall within Ord 11 anyway, but Staughton LJ discussed (at 1200) matters concerning the exercise of discretion if it had. The plaintiffs alleged that there was an oral agreement that any dispute arising out of the performance bond should be tried in England. But, said the court, if there had been such a clause, it would certainly be a possible view that this was a deliberate choice of a neutral forum so that though many of the factors to be considered under *The Spiliada* decision would not point to the English court as the appropriate forum, the choice of that court was a factor to be taken into account. It is submitted that the action would have fallen under Ord 11, r 1(1)(d)(iv) in that the contract contained a term to the effect that the High Court shall have jurisdiction to hear and determine any action in respect of it, and that there is authority, not cited in *Attock Cement*, to the effect that the court does not have to be so careful about allowing service out of the jurisdiction in this type of case as it does in the others set forth in the rule: *Unterweser Reederei GmbH v Zapata Off-Shore Co, The Chapparal* [1968] 2 Lloyd's Rep 158. In such a case has the plaintiff not done enough to show that the case is a proper one for service out of the jurisdiction under Ord 11, r 4(2) by pointing to the defendant's agreement? The defendant should then be required to show reason why service on him should not be allowed.

Jurisdiction: staying of actions

In what seems to be the only case of its kind, Sir Nicolas Browne-Wilkinson V-C held that when a plaintiff starts an action here and abroad against the same defendant, the *Spiliada* guidelines are not really applicable. The plaintiff, by bringing an action here when the foreign court is more appropriate, is verging on being vexatious. He must elect which action to pursue and if he elects to continue the foreign proceedings, as he did in *Australian Commercial Research and Development Ltd v ANZ McCaughan Merchant Bank Ltd* [1989] 3 All ER 65, the English action would be dismissed and not merely stayed. The court, in the event, gave the plaintiff leave to discontinue and stayed a counterclaim put forward by the defendant.

Jurisdiction: submission

If a foreign defendant seeks to have an English action stayed by a summons under s 1 of the Arbitration Act 1975, where he is entitled to a stay as of right, does that amount to a voluntary submission to the jurisdiction of the court? In view of *Williams & Glyn's Bank plc v Astro Dinamico Cia Naviera SA* [1984] 1 All ER 760 and *The Sydney Express* [1988] 2 Lloyd's Rep 257, where it was held that an application for a stay under s 49(3) of the Supreme Court Act 1981 or under an exclusive jurisdiction clause is not a voluntary submission, it would be surprising if it does. But in *Henry v Geopresco International Ltd* [1975] 2 All ER 702, it was held that such an application to a foreign court was a submission to its jurisdiction.

However, Mr Adrian Hamilton QC, sitting as a deputy High Court judge, held in *Finnish Marine Insurance Co Ltd v Protective National Insurance Co* [1989] 2 All ER 929 that the last mentioned decision did not apply to the jurisdiction of the English courts (it has, in any case, been reversed by the Civil Jurisdiction and Judgments Act 1982, s 33) and that an application for a stay is not a submission to the court's jurisdiction to decide the merits, but an invocation of the court's jurisdiction to decide if it has jurisdiction. The defendants were, however, allowed to withdraw the summons to stay which they had issued by mistake and had not pressed.

Jurisdiction: Brussels Convention 1968 and actions in rem

The effect of the Brussels Convention 1968 on Jurisdiction and the Enforcement of Judgments in Civil Commercial Matters on actions in rem has until recently been somewhat unclear. (much light has been shed on the matter recently by T H Hartley in Law Quarterly Review, vol 105 (1989), 640). A case in which one aspect of the matter was considered was *The Deichland* [1989] 2 All ER 1066. The plaintiff issued a writ in rem against a ship in respect of cargo damage. It named as defendants the charterers of the vessel at the relevant time; when the writ was served on the ship in England the charterer's P & I Club gave an undertaking to satisfy any judgment, so the ship was not arrested. The charterers were a Panamanian corporation whose central management and control was in Germany. The defendants argued that the English court had no jurisdiction by virtue of the 1968 Convention since they were domiciled in Germany and by art 2 should be sued there and not here. The judge (Sheen J) held that while the action was solely in rem the charterers were not defendants so that art 2 of the Convention did not apply.

The Court of Appeal allowed the defendant's appeal. The first of three questions which arose was whether the 1968 Convention applied to an action in rem which remains solely in rem; it certainly applies if the action has become an action in personam. The court held that, having regard to its purpose, the Convention was intended to cover all forms of proceedings in civil and commercial matters. The plaintiffs argued, in effect, that in an action in rem there is no personal defendant; to this the court replied that since the charterers would wish to contest liability and the plaintiffs would themselves wish to proceed in personam against them if they entered appearance, in reality the charterers were being 'sued' within art 2. Moreover, should the charterers enter an appearance the action would then continue as an action in personam against them. On this point the decision accords with the general principles of interpretation of the Convention to which the European Court of Justice has adhered; that it should be given a 'community' meaning and not one attuned to the technical vagaries of any particular legal system.

Still, art 2 of the Convention would only apply if the defendant was 'domiciled' in Germany; it would not apply if it were domiciled only in Panama. By art 53 of the Convention, 'a corporation is domiciled where it has its seat'. For the purpose of English proceedings this is determined by English private international law. Section 42(6) of the Civil Jurisdiction and Judgments 1982 Act provides that where the seat of a corporation is not in the United Kingdom, it is in another country if either the corporation (a) was incorporated under the law of that country and has its registered office or some other official address therein or (b) has its central management or control in that country. Under (b) the defendant was clearly domiciled in Germany. It was also, under (a), domiciled in Panama. To the plaintiff's argument that it cannot be domiciled in two countries the clear answer was that under the Convention it can (indeed, under the 1982 Act, a United Kingdom company can have three domiciles). The Convention clearly envisages the possibility that in several situations more than one contracting state's courts may have jurisdiction (though this was not so in *The Deichland* since Panama is not such a state), as is clear from its provisions regarding declining of jurisdiction and staying of proceedings (arts 21, 22).

The third question was whether, in spite of all this, the English court nevertheless had jurisdiction by virtue of art 57 of the Convention, which provides that the Convention is without prejudice to any jurisdiction which the courts of a contracting state possess by virtue of another Convention dealing with a specific matter. The plaintiffs urged that if art 57 was read with the 1952 International Convention for the Unification of Certain Rules relating to the Arrest of Sea-going Ships, the jurisdiction of the English court was preserved. The court held that this was not so; the 1952 Convention only gives jurisdiction if the ship has been arrested. Since *The Deichland* had not been arrested, the Convention did not give the English courts jurisdiction. This seems to be right; but the moral of the story is that if you want the English court to have jurisdiction in such a case, then you had better arrest the ship before accepting any security.

Foreign judgment: fraud

In proceedings brought at common law to enforce a judgment obtained in a foreign court, once it is established that the foreign court had jurisdiction over the case in the eyes of the English court by reason of the defendant's presence or residence in the foreign country at the time the action commenced or by his submission, the defendant has available to him very few defences to enforcement. Provided the judgment was final and conclusive and for a fixed or determinable sum of money (not being for taxes or a penalty), just about the only defences are that its enforcement would be contrary to English public policy, that it was given in breach of natural justice or that it was initiated by fraud on the part either of the foreign court or of the plaintiff.

Fraud on the part of the plaintiff may be 'collateral' fraud, an example of which is fraudulently inducing the court to assume jurisdiction when otherwise it would not have done so (examples of this, both of which concerned foreign divorce decrees, are *Macalpine v Macalpine* [1957] 3 All ER 134 and *Kendall v Kendall* [1977] 3 All ER 471). Or the fraud may vitiate the decision of the foreign court on the merits of the case. By an exception to the general rule that a judgment given by a foreign court of competent jurisdiction cannot be reopened before the English courts, where fraud of this type is alleged the English court may investigate anew the facts which were in issue before the foreign court and which it had investigated: *Abouloff v Oppenheimer* (1882) 10 QBD 295; *Vadala v Lawes* (1890) 25 QBD 310. That is to say, in this type of case, the conclusion of the foreign court as to whether the plaintiff was or was not fraudulent is not conclusive as far as the English court is concerned.

In *Jet Holdings Inc v Patel* [1989] 2 All ER 648, the Court of Appeal held that this is true also where the fraud was 'collateral'. The action was to enforce a judgment of a Californian State court and the plaintiff sought summary judgment under RSC Ord 14. The defendant sought leave to defend on the grounds that the judgment was obtained by fraud; alternatively that the Californian proceedings were opposed to natural justice. The facts, which are somewhat alarming, if the defendant's story was true, were as follows. Patel had worked in California as an accountant for the three plaintiff companies. In 1983 the president of the companies alleged that Patel had stolen large sums of money and dismissed him; Patel denied the allegations. According to him, on three occasions, once in California and twice in England, he had suffered threatened or actual violence at the hands of persons acting on behalf of the president and money was extorted from him; this was denied. As a result of an attempted extortion in England, the president was convicted at the Central Criminal Court and served a sentence of imprisonment. The companies started an action against Patel in California and he submitted to the court's jurisdiction, but he did not attend the trial or comply with other court orders which would have required him to visit California, because, he said, he was in fear of his life. At an early stage he ceased to be represented by lawyers because, he said, he had no money, the plaintiffs having extorted $100,000 from him by violence and threats. The Californian judge had read a declaration by Patel in which he had recited the substance of these matters. The judge proceeded to award damages against Patel.

The Court of Appeal held that, just as the fact that the foreign court's view that it has jurisdiction under its own rules is not conclusive so far as our courts are concerned, ('to put it bluntly, if not vulgarly, the court cannot haul itself up by its own bootstraps'), logically the same reasoning must apply where enforcement is resisted on the ground of fraud. 'The lesson for the plaintiff is that he should sue in the first place where he expects to be able to enforce a judgment'. Assuming, for Ord 14 purposes, the facts to be as they are deposed to by the defendant unless he is plainly lying, Patel had a good arguable defence, though the alleged fraud was collateral and not as to the merits of the case. This seems, with respect, to be correct; no distinction can logically be drawn between the two types of fraud.

The court did not decide the natural justice point, or whether it was a defence that the Californian judgement did not comply with English views of substantial justice. But Staughton LJ thought that, again, the fact that the foreign court thought it was observing natural justice should not be conclusive, if the English court considers that the foreign court was not doing so. He doubted both the correctness of the apparent assertion to the contrary in Dicey and Morris *The Conflict of Laws* (11th edn 1987) 475, and whether the case relied on by that work (*Jacobson v Frachon* (1928) 138 LT 386) is authority for it.

Contract: capacity of a corporation

In *Janred Properties Ltd v Ente Nazionale Italiano per il Turismo* [1989] 2 All ER 444, the Court of Appeal applied what is now rule 174 in Dicey and Morris *The Conflict of Laws* (11th edn 1987) 1134. This states that:

(1) The capacity of a corporation to enter into any legal transaction is governed both by the constitution of the corporation and by the law of the country which governs the transaction in question.

(2) All matters concerning the constitution of a corporation are governed by the law of the place of incorporation.

The question before the court concerned the capacity of an Italian state corporation to enter into an English contract for the sale and purchase of English leasehold property, and the court held that this was a matter governed by the corporation's constitution, as interpreted and given effect by Italian law, and by English law in regard to limitations imposed by general law on the capacity of corporations to do certain acts. It then held that even if, because of lack of capacity, the corporation had entered into no contract, subsequent acts of its president amounted under Italian law to ratification of the contract or the entry into a fresh contract on the same terms. The corporation could either avoid the agreement with the consent of the Italian court or ratify it with the approval of the responsible government minister.

In the circumstances of the case the court held that the corporation was estopped by its actions from denying that it was bound by the agreement.

Contract: determination of the proper law

In several cases, the courts have had to ascertain what was the proper law of the contract; in none of them does the result come as any surprise. Thus, in

E F Hutton & Co (London) Ltd v Mofarrij [1989] 2 All ER 633, the Court of Appeal held that a cheque drawn in Greece or a Greek bank and payable in Greece was governed by Greek law, notwithstanding that the contract whose performance it was meant to guarantee was governed by English law. Further, in *Attock Cement Co Ltd v Romanian Bank for Foreign Trade* [1989] 1 All ER 1189, it was held, in a case in which the plaintiffs had failed to prove an alleged oral agreement that a performance bond given by a Romanian state bank to guarantee the performance by a Romanian state trading corporation of a contract governed by English law, should itself be governed by English law, that the bond was not by implication or by any other test governed by that law. Staughton LJ, giving the only reasoned judgment of the Court of Appeal, observed that, like a banker's documentary credit, a performance bond is a contract between different parties to the contract to whose performance it relates and is intended to be entirely divorced from it. Thus, in *Offshore International SA v Banco Central SA* [1976] 3 All ER 749 and *Power Curber International Ltd v National Bank of Kuwait SAK* [1981] 3 All ER 607 it was held that a banker's credit is normally governed by the law of the place of performance. That place is where payment is to be made under it. In the present case, payment under the performance bond was to be made in Romania, not in England, so the proper law of the bond was Romanian law, not English law.

Little needs to be said in this context about the decision of the House of Lords in *Forsikringsaktieselskapet Vesta v Butcher* [1989] 1 All ER 402, which affirmed the decision of the Court of Appeal: [1988] 2 All ER 43 (see All ER Rev 1988 p 50). At first instance, Hobhouse J had held that certain parts of an English contract of reinsurance in respect of a Norwegian insurance contract were governed by Norwegian law: [1986] 2 All ER 488, (see All ER Rev 1986 p 66). But the House of Lords arrived at the same conclusion as Hobhouse J by the different route taken by the Court of Appeal; that is, that the question at issue was simply whether by the application of the English rules as to the construction of a contract governed by English law certain rules of Norwegian insurance law were incorporated into the contract of reinsurance. The conclusion was that they were.

Libyan Arab Foreign Bank v Bankers Trust Co [1989] 3 All ER 252 is a case decided by Staughton J in 1987. This concerned holding accounts kept by the plaintiff Libyan bank with London and New York branches of the defendant United States bank. These accounts were subject to managed account arrangements stipulating that all transactions were to be passed through the New York branch. In an action brought by the plaintiffs after the defendants had refused to release the funds held with the London branch, the question arose as to what was the proper law of the contract. The judge held that the proper law was English law. This accorded with the normal principle that it can be inferred that the proper law of a bank account is the law of the place where the contract is to be performed, that is, where the account is kept, and not where the bank has its headquarters; see *X AG v A Bank* [1983] 2 All ER 464. He was prepared to hold, unusually, that the contract, that is, the managed account arrangement, was governed partly by New York law and partly by English law.

It may be observed that in a later decision, arising out of very similar arrangements and facts, Hirst J held that the defendant bank had raised by its evidence a triable issue as to whether the general rule applied by Staughton J could be displaced and some other law (that is, New York law) govern the contract (*Libyan Arab Foreign Bank v Manufacturers' Hanover Trust Co* [1988] 2 Lloyd's Rep 484).

Contract: illegality

As has been mentioned, Staughton J held in *Libyan Arab Foreign Bank v Bankers Trust Co* [1989] 3 All ER 252 that the proper law of the contract was English law. In answer to the plaintiff's claim for the release to it of the funds held in their London branch, the defendants argued that by reason of 'freezing' orders imposed by US government decree, it would be illegal under US law for them to release the funds. Staughton J held that since the proper law was English law and not US (or New York) law, this was no excuse and the defendants were liable. That is to say, the contract was not, as a matter of English law, frustrated. With respect, this is perfectly correct and that is all that need have been said on the subject.

However, the judgment seems unnecessarily confused on this point, and discusses, if only to reject, arguments based on illegality by the law of the defendant's place of business or by the law of the country where performance necessarily has to take place. These considerations are only material if what is in issue is what might be called 'initial illegality', as for example where the parties intend at the time of contracting that some act should be done in a foreign country which is illegal by that country's law. In the instant case, none of this arose, since there was nothing nefarious about the parties' agreement when it was made. It was a case of supervening illegality and concerned frustration. This is governed only by the proper law of the contract.

Tort: choice of law rule

Among the perplexing features of the judgment of Slade LJ in *Metall und Rohstoff AG v Donaldson Lufkin & Jenrette Inc* [1989] 3 All ER 14 is his discussion, at pp 30–33, of the choice of law rule for torts which have a 'double locality'. As mentioned earlier (see pp 53–54 above), the court accepted the *Chaplin v Boys* test of double actionability in respect of a tort entirely committed abroad and affirmed that English law alone applies in respect of one wholly committed in England. But this is all of no help, it said, in the case of an alleged tort some of whose elements occur in say, New York and some in England, as in the instant case. Slade LJ then discussed some cases, and stated that 'unrestricted by direct authority' the court's conclusion is that, by applying the 'substance of the tort test' propounded in cases concerned with service out of the jurisdiction under the predecessor of the current RSC Ord 11, r 1(1)(f), and so *by reference exclusively to English law*, the court should consider whether the tort was committed in England. If it so finds, it will disregard *Chaplin v Boys* and apply English law alone. If it finds that the tort was in substance committed abroad, it will apply both English law and the law of the country where it was committed to determine the defendant's liability.

What is extraordinarily puzzling about this is why the court thought it was propounding a novel choice of law rule. To a conflicts lawyer there is nothing surprising about it at all. The trouble appears to be that the court did not realise that the place of commission of a tort, just like the place of contracting, a person's domicile and the situs of property, for example, is a connecting factor. The interpretation of a connecting factor is always a matter exclusively for English law as the lex fori. This is elementary, axiomatic and could not be otherwise.

Nor is the matter free of authority. The court is correct in saying that the 'double locality' cases cited and discussed by it were all concerned with jurisdiction and not choice of law. (This is, as has been pointed out, true of the instant case as well.) But among the copious cases which might have been cited to the court the one case which actually is concerned with choice of law, *Church of Scientology of California v Commissioner of Metropolitan Police* (1976) 120 SJ 690, does not seem to have been mentioned at all, though it is set out and discussed at length by Hodgson J in *Coupland v Arabian Gulf Petroleum Co* [1983] 2 All ER 434. This case was cited, but possibly only the report of the Court of Appeal's judgment; still, it is strange that nobody connected the two cases, since in *Coupland* the Court of Appeal also mentioned the *Church of Scientology* case. In the latter case, the Court of Appeal, without any problems at all, held that when a report was composed in England and sent from England to West Berlin to the local police there for their information and for them to act upon, the alleged tort of libel was substantially committed in Berlin, so that *Chaplin v Boys* applied. The instant case presented simply the converse factual situation to that in the *Church of Scientology* case. The problem which Slade LJ and his brethren seem to have thought they were called upon to solve did not actually exist at all.

Public policy: foreign revenue laws

One point which arose in *Re State of Norway's Applications (Nos 1 and 2)* [1989] 1 All ER 745 was whether an order made in pursuance of letters of request issued by a Norwegian court at the behest of the State of Norway, and supported by the estate of a deceased Norwegian taxpayer, for the examination of witnesses in England fell foul of the rule that the English courts will not enforce a foreign revenue law. The proceedings before the Norwegian court were commenced by the taxpayer's estate to have certain assessments to Norwegian tax set aside and the requested evidence was material to those proceedings.

The rule referred to says that the English court will not enforce a foreign revenue law directly, as where the foreign state itself brings an action to recover taxes due to it: *India (Government) Ministry of Finance (Revenue Division) v Taylor* [1955] 1 All ER 292. Nor will it do so indirectly, where, for example, the liquidator of a company sues to enforce debts due to the company, but it is shown that he will have to pay all the proceeds of his action to a foreign revenue authority: see the decision of the Supreme Court of Ireland in *Peter Buchanan Ltd v McVey* [1955] AC 516n, or where the foreign revenue authority makes a claim for possession of goods to enforce its claim for payment of tax: *Brokaw v Seatrain UK Ltd* [1971] 2 All ER 98.

In *Re Norway's Applications* Lord Goff of Chieveley, with whom the rest of their Lordships agreed, discussed (at 760) the theoretical basis of this rule. He rejected, correctly, it is thought, the view that it is a matter of lack of jurisdiction to enforce such a rule, and inclined to the idea, expressed by Lord Keith of Avonholm in the *Government of India* case and by Lord Denning MR in *A–G of New Zealand v Ortiz* [1982] 3 All ER 432 at 457, that a revenue law is an exercise of a state's sovereignty, which is to be confined within that state's territory. This hardly seems to be much of an explanation, since there is nothing in public international law to preclude one state or its courts from allowing another state to exercise acts of sovereignty in the territory of the former, and, in the case of revenue claims, every consideration of international comity in favour of allowing it to do so. There has never been any satisfactory justification for the rule, which simply assists in the evasion of payment of taxes lawfully levied.

Lord Goff refused to apply this rule in the present case, saying that the letters of request were in no way a direct or indirect enforcement in England of the Norwegian revenue laws, but only a request to the courts of this country to assist in their enforcement in Norway. This is a welcome limitation on an unjustifiable rule.

Consumer Law

C J MILLER, BA, LLM
Barrister, Professor of English Law, University of Birmingham

The All England Law Reports for 1989 contain very little in the way of cases within the broad area of consumer law. However, two such cases were concerned with consumer credit and one further case with the powers of the Director General of Fair Trading in relation to allegedly misleading advertisements. There have been developments also in the area of exemption clauses.

Consumer credit

As, no doubt, readers will be fully aware, recent months have seen a steady and apparently inexorable rise in interest rates. Some fortunate individuals have been unaffected, having had the foresight or good luck to borrow at a fixed lower rate of interest for a fixed period. Many others have struggled simply to meet the interest on the outstanding debt, with little prospect of making inroads into the repayment of capital. In *Lombard Tricity Finance Ltd v Paton* [1989] 1 All ER 918 the Court of Appeal had to consider the position of a finance company which sought unilaterally to increase the interest charged on a running-account credit agreement within s 10 of the Consumer Credit Act 1974.

The matter arose because the defendant had borrowed some £218 on a credit charge account to acquire an Amstrad computer from the retailers, Currys. The interest originally charged was 2.3% per month, giving an Annual Percentage Rate of 31.3%. The agreement contained in the appropriate box (known in the trade as 'the holy ground' and described by Staughton LJ as 'the child's guide'), the statement:

> 'Interest is payable on credit balance. Subject to variation by the creditor from time to time on notification as required by law. In calculating the APR no account has been taken of any variation of it which may occur under this Agreement.'

When the rate was increased to 2.45% and later to 2.95% per month, and the defendant defaulted, it was contended that this was insufficient to comply with the provisions which prescribe the form and content of regulated agreements. In particular, the Consumer Credit (Agreements) Regulations 1983, SI 1983 No 1553, Sch 1, para 19 provide under the heading 'Information' for: 'A statement indicating the circumstances in which any variation [eg of interest rates] . . . may occur'.

His Honour Judge Heald held that para 19 had not been complied with and that the relevant 'statement of circumstances' had to refer to external factors (eg base rates) by which the debtor could judge whether the variation was being properly exercised. No doubt to the intense relief of finance companies and banks, the Court of Appeal disagreed. As Staughton LJ explained (at 922):

'No doubt it would be possible for lenders to comply with the judge's requirements, and state the considerations which will induce them to increase or reduce their interest rate; there is nothing which a draftsman cannot achieve if he has clear instructions and enough ink in his pen. But it could well be a cumbersome procedure. It might also tend to defeat the purpose of "the child guide", by cluttering up that part of the agreement with a mass of detail. The alternative solution, for the lender to apply in every case for an enforcement order in the county court because his agreement did not state the circumstances in which the interest rate could be varied, as defined by the judge, would cause grave disruption in the business of the courts.'

His Lordship added that the words on the face of the contract were 'sufficient to convey, to the average reader of modest intelligence, that Lombard have the right to vary the interest rate at will if they choose to do so, subject only to proper notification.' This seems, with respect, to be right. It may also be noted that as a matter of general contract law it is quite possible (although, no doubt, unusual) for an agreement to provide that an important term is to be left to be settled by one of the parties. What they cannot do with respect to such a term is simply to agree to agree in the future. (See, generally, *May & Butcher Ltd v R* [1934] 2 KB 17).

The second reported case, which came in right at the end of the calender year, was *Forward Trust Ltd v Whymark* ([1989] 3 All ER 915). It raised an issue which must be very commonplace and yet was described by Lord Donaldson MR as having 'furrowed many judicial and other legal brows'. The problem arose because the defendant had failed to comply with a default notice served under s 87 of the Consumer Credit Act 1984, thus leading the plaintiffs to issue a county court summons. The loan of £2,527 had been for a ten-year period which would, in principle, attract interest of £3,790. (This might also cause brows to furrow). The total would be subject to a rebate for any early repayment worked out in accordance with the Consumer Credit (Rebate on Early Settlement) Regulations 1983. In fact, had the defendant complied with the notice he would have received a rebate of some £2,689. Since he did not the problems, in the words of Lord Donaldson, were: (i) 'should the lender issue a summons for the whole amount outstanding or for that amount less whatever rebate would be applicable, assuming that the demands in the summons were met within 14 days, and (ii), if the borrower makes no payment, for what sum should the court give judgment?

As his Lordship noted, neither of these alternatives was, of itself, satisfactory. A judgment for an amount net of the statutory rebate would place the creditor at a considerable disadvantage, given that county court judgments did not bear interest. On the other hand, a judgment for the full amount with the rebate being calculated when the judgment was met might create difficulty when enforced by execution against the debtor's goods. This conjured up images of bailiffs running complicated computations through computers in an attempt to work out the appropriate rebate for early settlement following the seizure and sale of the goods.

The correct solution favoured by the Court of Appeal from a technical point of view was that the judgment should be for the full outstanding amount. Lord Donaldson explained this by saying (at 921):

'The effect of his potential entitlement to a rebate is not to reduce his indebtedness, but to enable him, in some circumstances, to discharge that indebtedness by a payment which may be less than 100p in the pound, depending on when he discharges it.'

He added that the judgment debt could be discharged 'by payment of the amount stated in the judgment *less* any rebate which is applicable in respect of such discharge at that date.'

Finally, in order to safeguard the position of the judgment debtor, the Court of Appeal approved a standard indorsement alerting him that the judgment may be satisfied by deducting any rebate for an early settlement. The relevant amount was to be ascertained by inquiry from the judgment creditor with the matter to be determined by the court in the event of dispute. This would also have the advantage of drawing the point to the attention of bailiffs who would have to take account of the amount of any rebate likely to be applicable.

The overall conclusion seems, with respect, to be the most convenient, although these are certain remaining practical problems noted in Lord Donaldson's judgment (at 921) which need to be resolved.

Misleading advertisements

In *Director General of Fair Trading v Tobyward Ltd* [1989] 2 All ER 266 Hoffmann J had the occasion to remark in the course of an important judgment, 'The only way in which a healthy person can lose weight is by eating less calories than his body consumes.' This stark truth is unwelcome to many of us, more especially in periods during which exercise is minimal and the use of calories low. Some understandably look to slimming aids for which they are prepared to pay not inconsiderable sums of money. (Others prefer exercise bikes which are more effective but not an attractive focal point either of a bedroom or of a lounge). It was one such aid 'Speedslim', the principal ingredient of which is guar gum, which attracted the attention of the Director General of Fair Trading (DGFT) in the present case. So far as I am aware, it was the first such reported case invoking the Control of Misleading Advertisements Regulations 1988, which were themselves based on the EEC Council Directive 84/450/EEC.

Advertisements for 'Speedslim' had been published in the 'Sunday Sport' and six fairly specific claims made for it. For example, it was said to be 'an awesome discovery that will enable you to lose weight easily and, most importantly—permanently' and, in another version, that it carried 'A 100% GUARANTEE OF SUCCESS'. The Council of the Advertising Standards Authority considered that the advertisements failed to satisfy the requirements of the relevant section of the British Code of Advertising Practice and when the respondent declined to withdraw them the matter was referred to the DGFT. He then sought an interlocutory injunction which the court had the power to grant under reg 6 of the 1988 Regulations. The application had the support of the expert evidence of Professor Bender, a distinguished nutritionist, and Hoffmann J was satisfied that the necessary prima facie case that the advertisements were misleading had been established. 'Misleading' for this purpose involved being likely to deceive the persons to whom the advertisement's were addressed and to affect their economic behaviour.

The more difficult question concerned the scope of the injunction. Here it is, of course, fundamental that an injunction should, so far as possible, leave the respondent with no doubt as to what must be done to comply with its terms. However, it cannot be so specific that the same allegedly misleading claims can be made in a slightly different way. This is recognised by reg 6(2), which provides that the injunction may relate not only to a particular advertisement but to any advertisement 'in similar terms or likely to convey a similar impression'. In the result, Hoffmann J accepted the submission of the director that the wording should be made more specific by spelling out the six headings under which an advertisement should not be in similar terms or convey a similar impression. Finally, his Lordship held that the case was not an appropriate one for requiring a cross-undertaking in damages.

Exemption clauses and unfair contract terms

In last year's Annual Review reference was made (at pp 68–69) to the cases of *Smith v Eric S Bush (a firm)* [1987] 3 All ER 179 and *Harris v Wyre Forest District Council* [1988] 1 All ER 691. Both cases were decisions of the Court of Appeal and they had reached differing conclusions on the question whether a surveyor's and valuer's disclaimer of liability was subject to the control of the Unfair Contract Terms Act 1977. The opposing argument was that such a disclaimer operated, rather, to prevent the very existence of a duty of care from arising. The matter has now been resolved on further appeal to the House of Lords ([1989] 2 All ER 514) where it was held that such a disclaimer was subject to the requirement of reasonableness imposed by s 2(2). In neither case was the requirement satisfied. This conclusion seems, with respect, to be more apt to give effect to s 13(1) of the Act which provides, in effect, that the notion of excluding or restricting liability also extends to excluding or restricting the relevant obligation or duty.

Contempt of Court

C J MILLER, BA, LLM
Barrister, Professor of English Law, University of Birmingham

The All England Law Reports for 1989 contain a considerable number of cases on contempt of court, many of which raised issues which were of interest or general importance. They ranged from highly publicised proceedings associated with alleged attempts to influence the House of Lords in the Lonrho affair to the technicalities of the law of civil contempt. Further important cases concerned, for example, with the position of journalists seeking to safeguard their sources of information had not been reported by the end of the calendar year: see *Re Goodwin* (now reported in [1990] 1 All ER 608) (Hoffmann J); on appeal *X Ltd v Morgan Grampian (Publishers) Ltd* (now reported in [1990] 1 All ER 616, CA; (1990) *Times*, 5 April, HL).

Contempt in the House of Lords

Re Lonrho plc [1989] 2 All ER 1100 arose almost as a by-product of the complex and bitter struggle of Lonrho and the Al Fayed brothers for control of House of Fraser plc and thereby of Harrods of Knightsbridge. The Al Fayed brothers had acquired control in 1985, but Lonrho continued its campaign by seeking to establish that the brothers were guilty of fraud. The campaign was successful to the extent that the Secretary of State for the Department of Trade and Industry appointed inspectors to investigate and report on the acquisition. He sent their report to the Serious Fraud Office in July 1988, but decided that it should not be published immediately in case any subsequent criminal proceedings might be prejudiced. He decided also that the take-over should not be referred to the Monopolies and Mergers Commission. Lonrho then began proceedings for judicial review, seeking orders of mandamus requiring publication of the report and a reference to the Commission. The orders were granted by the Divisional Court, but set aside by the Court of Appeal. The matter then went on further appeal to the House of Lords where the hearing was fixed for 10 April 1989. Meanwhile, on 23 March, Lonrho obtained a copy of the report, substantial extracts from which were then published on 30 March in a special edition of the Observer newspaper which was itself owned by one of Lonrho's wholly owned subsidiaries. In addition, copies were mailed individually to influential persons on a list which included four Lords of Appeal in Ordinary. To make matters worse, Lord Keith also received through the post a document called *Birds of a Feather*, which alleged bad faith on the part of the Secretary of State and the peripheral involvement of Mr Denis Thatcher. Altogether, the background was such that chance readers of the law reports might have been forgiven for assuming that they were dipping into a copy of Private Eye.

Although the resultant contempt proceedings raised a number of important questions, not all of them were explored as fully as one might have hoped. This was, in part, because the Appellate Committee involved in the judicial review proceedings stepped down so that Lonrho should not be left with a sense of grievance, 'however misguided'. Consequently, the Committee was of three members only and it confined itself to the specific issues which arose for decision. Perhaps this was wise since, as Lord Bridge observed (at 1110), the House, having acted of its own motion, was 'in the unenviable position of being both a tribunal of first instance and a tribunal of last resort'. The issues were themselves restricted by the fact that the evidence indicated that the mailing to individual judges had been unintentional and the result, for the most part, of problems with a word processor. Indeed, specific instructions had been given to exclude the names of judges from the list. Consequently, one was left with the publication to the community at large of the special edition. This fell to be considered both as a potential statutory contempt of court under the Contempt of Court Act 1981 and as a contempt at common law.

So far as the 1981 Act was concerned, the main issue was whether the test of liability under the strict liability rule was satisfied. Section 2(2) provides:

> 'The strict liability rule applies only to a publication which creates a substantial risk that the course of justice in the proceedings in question will be seriously impeded or prejudiced'.

Not surprisingly, the House of Lords held that the publication did not create a substantial risk of serious prejudice to the proceedings, whether through an effect on the court or on the parties themselves. Lord Bridge commented (at 1117):

> 'When a case has proceeded so far it is unlikely, save in exceptional circumstances, that criticism would deter an appellant from pursuing his appeal or induce a respondent to forego the judgment in his favour or to reach a compromise of the appeal. So far as the appellate tribunal is concerned, it is difficult to visualise circumstances in which any court in the United Kingdom exercising appellate jurisdiction would be in the least likely to be influenced by public discussion of the merits of a decision appealed against or of the parties' conduct in the proceedings.'

The more difficult question arose because Lonrho had pre-empted the result of the judicial review proceedings by giving extensive publicity to the inspectors' report. In effect, they had, by extraneous means, secured the objective which the judicial review proceedings were designed to achieve. The problem was whether this should be categorised as a contempt. The only parallel of sorts was with the 'Spycatcher' proceedings in *A-G v Newspaper Publishing plc* [1987] 3 All ER 276, All ER Rev 1987 at 66 where the Court of Appeal had held that it might be a contempt for a third party, not being bound directly by an injunction, to destroy the subject matter of the confidence which the injunction was seeking to protect. However, there was the important difference that no-one had been enjoined not to publish the report; nor indeed was an application for an injunction pending. The House of Lords declined (and, rightly, it is submitted) to extend the law of contempt to cover such self-help. Lord Bridge explained (at 1119):

> 'The example was put in the course of argument of the plaintiff who complains that his neighbour has built a wall obstructing his right of way and seeks an injunction to have it removed. He succeeds at first instance, loses in the Court of

Appeal and appeals to the House of Lords. While the appeal is still pending he loses patience and knocks the wall down. In this example, if the plaintiff succeeds in the appeal, he will no longer need a mandatory injunction.

If he loses, he will have rendered himself liable in damages and possibly criminally. In either event, however deplorable his conduct, it is difficult to see how the course of justice, in determining the legal rights of the parties is likely to have been impeded or prejudiced in any way.'

Another aspect of the publication was its status as a prejudgment of the issues. This involved discussion of the notorious Sunday Times case (*A-G v Times Newspapers Ltd* [1973] 3 All ER 54) where the House of Lords had held it to be a contempt publicly to prejudge the issues in a pending case. Commentators have agreed that the prejudgment rule should be viewed as not having survived the 1981 Act, so that prejudgments would stand or fall under the general test of s 2(2): see, for example, my discussion in Miller *Contempt of Court* (2nd edn 1989) at 148–150 and Borrie and Lowe's *Law of Contempt* (2nd edn 1983) at 63–64, 149–153 . However, the Act does not formally abolish the rule and the point is not wholly clear. Unfortunately, the House of Lords in the *Lonrho* case did not settle the matter beyond all argument. Thus Lord Bridge referred to the relevant passages from the speeches of Lords Reid, Morris and Cross and said (at 1116):

'How far these passages from the speeches of their Lordships may still be relied upon as accurate expressions of the law is extremely doubtful, certainly in relation to the kind of contempt which is the subject matter of the strict liability rule under ss 1 and 2 of the 1981 Act.

He added:

'The only safe course, we think, is to apply the test imposed by the statutory language according to its ordinary meaning, without any preconception derived from *A-G v Times Newspapers Ltd* as to what kind of publication is likely to impede or prejudice the course of justice.'

Although these are fairly clear pointers, they are not conclusive, more especially since the contrary arguments were not fully addressed. In brief, these are that s 2(2) is concerned only with statutory contempts through seriously prejudicing etc 'the proceedings in question', whereas the rationale of the prejudgment rule was concerned with wider issues. Its concern was to prevent a slide towards trial by the media which would undermine public confidence in the administration of justice *generally* and inhibit other suitors from seeking the protection of the courts.

Finally, Lord Bridge considered the possibility of there being a common law contempt founded on intentional interference with the administration of justice. This raises the vexed question of bare or ineffectual attempts. In other words, can there be a contempt where a person intends to interfere with the administration of justice and yet has absolutely no chance of succeeding? English and Australian decisions show no consensus (see, generally, C J Miller, op cit at 162–165) and the point did not need to be explored in detail in the *Lonrho* case once the House of Lords had accepted that the names of the Lords of Appeal hearing the judicial review proceedings had been left on the mailing list inadvertently. None the less the following statement of Lord

Bridge might be thought to lend support to the view of the present writer that a bare intent may be sufficient. His Lordship said (at 1120):

'. . . if the publication created no such risk [scil of impeding justice], as we concluded in considering the question of statutory contempt, common law contempt within the ambit of the particulars relied on in support of charge 1 could only be established if those responsible for the publication intended it to have consequences affecting the appellate proceedings which it neither achieved nor was ever likely to achieve. In the absence of any material in the evidence before us suggesting such an intention, we could see no prospect that cross-examination could satisfy us beyond reasonable doubt that such an intention was entertained. We accordingly decided that no purpose would be served by requiring witnesses to submit to cross-examination.'

Disturbances outside magistrates' courts

Section 12 of the Contempt of Court Act 1981 provides magistrates' courts with an important new power to deal with any person who, inter alia, 'wilfully interrupts the proceedings of the court or otherwise misbehaves in court' (see s 12(1) (b)). Bodden v Commissioner of Police of the Metropolis [1989] 3 All ER 833 raised a short, but interesting, point of statutory construction involving the scope of this provision. The plaintiff, Mr Kendal Bodden, had been using a loudhailer to address a crowd of demonstrators near to Bow Street Magistrates' Court. His purpose, it seems, related to the trial of two persons which was to be held there that morning. In any event, he disturbed other proceedings being heard by a stipendiary magistrate who ordered him to be brought before the court. As Inspector Hoodless was carrying out the order, the plaintiff struggled and he was later arrested for assault and obstruction. No evidence was offered at the trial of these charges whereupon he sued, claiming damages for wrongful arrest. By this somewhat circuitous route the issue was raised as to whether Mr. Bodden had committed a contempt within s 12(1)(b) of the 1981 Act.

As is apparent from this outline of the facts, the case was unusual in that the act giving rise to the interruption took place outside the confines of the court itself. Nevertheless, the Court of Appeal held that this fell within s 12(1)(b) as it was both unnecessary and ungrammatical to read the concluding words 'in court' as though they appeared also after the words 'proceedings of the court'. It is submitted that this was the right conclusion, although care will need to be taken to ensure that the requirement that the interruption be wilful is not held to be satisfied too readily. Of this, the Court of Appeal indicated that the word encompassed recklessness in the sense of a conscious running of a risk. However, Beldam, L J added (at 838) that with the usual street noises (road drills, jackhammers etc)—

'it may well be that it is only possible to draw the prima facie inference of wilful interruption after the disturbance . . . has been brought to the attention of the contractors.'

The decision will, of course, apply to other statutory provisions which are written in identical terms, for example s 118(1)(b) of the County Courts Act 1984. However, it is perhaps regrettable that the Court of Appeal did not choose to comment on the position in the case of other courts for which there is no equivalent statutory provision. For example, coroners' courts are inferior courts of record (see *R v West Yorkshire Coroner, ex p Smith (No 2)* [1985] 1 All ER 100) and as such have power to commit for contempt but only if the contempt is committed 'in the face of the court'. Different jurisdictions have reached differing conclusions on the question whether this extends to conduct of the type which was in issue in the present case.

Contempt and mental health review tribunals

In *A-G v BBC* [1980] 3 All ER 161 the House of Lords held that a valuation court (although styled a 'court') was not an inferior court the proceedings of which might be protected from outside influence and comment through an application to a Divisional Court of the Queen's Bench Division. The general test there laid down was adopted in s 19 of the Contempt of Court Act 1981 which defines 'court' to include 'any tribunal or body exercising the judicial power of the state'. However, the 1981 Act does not provide a list of such bodies since the Lord Chancellor was unable to cause one to be drawn up.

It was against this background that the position of mental health review tribunals fell to be considered in *A-G v Associated Newspapers Group plc* [1989] 1 All E R 604. The Daily Mail and the Liverpool Echo newspapers had both published highly critical articles concerning the apparent willingness of the medical director of Park Lane Hospital, Liverpool (described as the Broadmoor of the North) to support the release of one Peter Pickering. Pickering had pleaded guilty in 1972 to manslaughter following the rape of a schoolgirl and the relevant articles were published shortly before a mental health review tribunal was to hear his application for release. Both articles were hard-hitting (for example, the Liverpool Echo had the headline 'Storm over sex-killer'), but Pickering had an alarming history of sexual assaults and public safety was involved. Two main issues were raised in the ensuing application to commit for contempt. These were (i) whether such a tribunal was a 'court' for the purposes of the 1981 Act and (if so) (ii) whether there was a substantial risk of serious prejudice to its proceedings.

So far as the first issue was concerned, the Divisional Court (Mann LJ and Henry J) held that, although clearly it had to act judicially in the discharge of its functions, a mental health review tribunal was not a 'court' for present purposes. The reasons given were less than convincing. In essence, these were that the tribunals were inheritors of an executive function, they could not deprive a person of liberty and a refusal to discharge was not final, and that the House of Lords (in the *BBC* case) had required the exercise of caution. Doubts as to the correctness of this decision arise from a related case in which Mr Pickering was seeking to restrain publication of information concerning a later application for discharge. In *Pickering v Liverpool Daily Post and Echo Newspapers plc*, now reported in [1990] 1 All ER 335, the Court of Appeal (Lord Donaldson MR, Glidewell and Farquharson LLJ) was unanimous in holding that such tribunals, which have the power to summon witnesses by subpoena, are 'courts' for the purposes of s 19 of the 1981 Act. This case will be commented on in next year's Annual Review.

On the second issue, the decision of the Divisional Court was altogether more straightforward. There was no suggestion of prejudicing the tribunal itself which was chaired by her Honour Judge Ebsworth—although she had said that the case had been 'severely hampered by ill-informed media comment'. In addition, the court concluded that any effect on the medical director (Dr MacCulloch) who was well used to controversy was remote. Hence the test of liability under s 2(2) was not satisfied.

A final point which was raised only briefly was the qualification to liability in s 5 of the Act for good faith discussion of public affairs or other matters of general public interest. This unsatisfactory provision was considered to be inapplicable since the report had been 'limited to the instant case' and had not discussed the matter more generally.

Wardship proceedings

In recent years there has been a series of cases, many of which have very sad backgrounds, in which the courts have had to grapple with the competing needs of press freedom and the protection of wards of court. The general principles applicable were summarised by Booth J in *Re L (a minor)* [1988] 1 All ER 418, commented on in All ER Rev 1988 at 79, a case arising from the Zeebrugge disaster. Similar issues arose again in *Re C (a minor) (wardship: medical treatment) (No 2)* [1989] 2 All ER 791.

The background was that the Court of Appeal had made an order in associated proceedings (see [1989] 2 All ER 782) authorising the treatment to ease the pain (at the expense perhaps of not prolonging the life) of a brain damaged and terminally ill baby who was suffering from hydrocephalus. The order was accompanied by a further order, binding on the world at large, which was intended to protect the child by ensuring inter alia that her identity was not revealed. The newspapers involved in the present application (the Daily Mail and the Mail on Sunday) did not wish to identify the baby or, it seems, her parents. However, they challenged the scope of the original order as granted by Ward J, which was described by Balcombe LJ (at 798) as putting 'a "ring fence" around her and all connected with her'. In the result, they were only partially successful in reducing the scope of the order in as much as the Court of Appeal removed the restriction on identifying the local authority and local health authority involved.

One obvious distinction between the facts of this case and others was that the condition and life-expectancy of the ward was such that she would never be directly affected by any publicity. This was in marked contrast to the position in, for example, *Re X* [1975] 1 All ER 697 (aberrant sexual behaviour of deceased father) and *X CC v A* [1985] 1 All ER 53 (the Mary Bell case). However, the distinction was not seen as crucial.

The main area of dispute concerned the doctors and other medical carers, both present and past, of the child. The Court of Appeal held that neither category could be identified. Identification of those falling into the former category was seen as being likely to add significantly to their emotional and other stress, thereby affecting the quality of their care for the child. The reasoning might seem strained, but few would argue that the media is so disciplined that it can be trusted to desist from harassment through telephone calls, photographers and the like. The non-identification of past carers could not be justified on the same basis. The court justified it, rather, by reference to their obligation of confidentiality to the child. As Lord Donaldson MR explained (at 795):

'In the absence of a compelling public interest pointing in the other direction, in my judgment the court is entitled and bound to safeguard C's right to confidentiality by reinforcing the former carers' professional obligation and creating an obstacle to third parties' possible attempts to induce them to breach it and to the exploitation of any such breaches. In this context, I should mention that in this particular case the carers are likely to be approached not only by the media, but also by pressure groups who may not display even the consideration and sense of responsibility which one always hopes for in representatives of the media.'

No doubt, views will differ as to whether this is convincing. An alternative justification might point, rather, to the potential long-term effects on future wards generally which might accompany a refusal to grant a non-identification order in the individual case. It is not wholly clear that this is a permissible line of reasoning. However, it seems to have been adopted by Lord Donaldson MR in relation to the parents, who had played virtually no part in C's life. Pointing, it appears, to wider considerations, his Lordship said (at 795):

'Many parents would not willingly make or agree to a child being made a ward of court if they thought that this might lead to their being identified and singled out for special attention by the media.'

However, Balcombe LJ looked, rather, to the instant case and reasoned that, if identified, outside pressure or inducement might cause the parents 'to seek to persuade the professional carers to take a course other than that which, in C's interest, they were proposing to take.' In principle, it seems right that the wider considerations should be taken into consideration.

One's overall reaction to the case must ultimately depend on the relative weight one attaches to the competing interests involved. In this context it must be noted that in the judgment in the associated proceedings the court had read in much of the opinion of the professor who had examined the child. His view was that the aim should be the easing of the suffering of C, rather than the short prolongation of a hopeless life. This opinion could, of course, be reported and commented on. It is by no means clear (especially in view of the obligation of confidentiality) that press interviews, photographs and the like, whether of the professor or of the other medical staff involved, would have added significantly to the sum total of informed public knowledge in this area.

[The later case of Re M (minors) (wardship: freedom of publication) [1990] 1 All ER 205, which dealt with similar issues against a background of alleged sexual abuse, will be commented on in next year's Annual Review.]

Sequestration

In the case of individuals, the power to commit to prison for contempt of court provides an obvious sanction underpinning the remedy of an injunction.

In the nature of things, committal is not available where the alleged contempt is by a corporate body, although its directors can, of course, be committed. Companies and their directors can also be fined. However, as has been apparent from a series of cases arising from labour disputes, for example in the mining and printing industries, it is likely that the most powerful coercive force in aid of an injunction will be the sequestration of corporate assets. That the remedy is a drastic one can be seen from the events associated with the miners' strike of the mid 1980's.

It is strange that it was only when *Rose v Laskington Ltd* [1989] 3 All ER 306 came before the Court of Appeal in 1989 that it was authoritatively decided that a county court had jurisdiction to order sequestration. The issue arose in a dispute concerning the depositing of building materials on land and it was the alleged contemnor which claimed that the proper course was to apply to the county court which had granted the injunction. The plaintiff had applied, rather, to the High Court under RSC Ord 52, r 1. The Court of Appeal agreed that the county court did have jurisdiction even though sequestration was not mentioned in the relevant county court rule (CCR Ord 29, r 1) and yet was so mentioned in the corresponding provision for the High Court (RSC Ord 45, r 5). This conclusion was justified on the ground that the power was derived from the general provision in s 38 of the County Courts Act 1984 enabling a county court to 'grant such relief, redress or remedy . . . as ought to be granted or given in the like case by the High Court and in as full and ample a manner.' Having referred to *Jennison v Baker* [1972] 1 All ER 997, which decided that in granting a 'full and ample' remedy a county court could commit as a punishment for past disobedience even though the plaintiff was no longer seeking to enforce the injunction, Stuart-Smith LJ said (at 311–312):

> 'Similar considerations arise in the case of sequestration. It may be said that sequestration is an essential part of the remedy of the grant of an injunction against a corporation, since otherwise there is no direct sanction on the corporation, only a sanction against its directors or officers. Likewise there is inconvenience and expense involved if the county court cannot grant this relief and application has to be made to the Divisional Court.'

This decision is, of course, very much in line with the current tendency not to encourage applications to the High Court when it is felt that the matter can be dealt with at a lower level. However, some may have doubts whether such a remedy is really appropriate for the county courts, albeit that there is now no theoretical limit to the fine which such courts may impose.

A further case concerning sequestration came before Scott Baker J in *Richardson v Richardson* [1989] 3 All ER 779. Following a divorce, an access order had been made in favour of a father of two children whereupon his ex-wife, who had made unsubstantiated allegations of abuse, effectively thwarted it by removing them to the Republic of Ireland. This placed the father in an unenviable position since he then had to resort to the Irish courts and legal aid was not available for this purpose. Meanwhile he obtained a *Mareva* injunction, restraining the mother from removing her assets from the (English) jurisdiction and obtained leave to issue a writ of sequestration. The principal asset involved was a house, which was in the ex-wife's sole name. Scott Baker J summarised the difficulty which then arose as follows (at 782):

> 'The case draws attention to a problem which is pertinent in this case, namely the distinction between sequestrations to enforce orders for the payment of money or fines and those to enforce other orders of the court, eg injunctive

relief. The old practice was that in the latter the sequestrators simply held the assets until the order was complied with, whereas in the former the sequestrators were permitted to utilise the assets to meet the due payment.'

This distinction between the two purposes of sequestration has been acknowledged, although not necessarily approved, in modern cases (see, eg, *Con-Mech (Engineers) Ltd v Amalgamated Union of Engineering Workers (Engineering Section) (No 3)* [1974] ICR 464 at 467 per Donaldson P). Further doubts were also raised by uncertainty as to whether sequestration empowered the court to order the sale of freehold property (see *Hipkin v Hipkin* [1962] 2 All ER 155 at 157 per Simon P).

In the result Scott Baker J did not find it necessary to deal with this latter point since what was required was that the husband should be put in possession of sufficient funds to enable him to meet the costs of the Irish proceedings. This was achieved by an imaginative order giving leave to the sequestrators to use the seized property to raise £8,000 either by letting it and/or by way of charge. An 'ancient tool of the law' had thereby, in his Lordship's words, been 'adapted for use in modern conditions'.

The nature of civil contempt

The juridical nature of civil contempt of court has long been recognised as something of an oddity. It may attract a committal to prison or a fine, the purpose of which may be either to coerce the contemnor into future compliance or to punish him for past disobedience. In view of their likely outcome, civil contempt proceedings rightly attract many of the safeguards associated usually with a criminal trial. For example, the Court of Appeal has held that proof beyond reasonable doubt is required (see, eg, *Dean v Dean* [1987] 1 FLR 517). In some modern cases the court has even gone so far as to describe civil contempt of court as a common law misdemeanour (see, eg, *Lee v Walker* [1985] 1 All ER 781 at 785 per Cumming-Bruce LJ), although this must surely be wrong.

The precise nature of civil contempt was important to the decision in *Garvin v Domus Publishing Ltd* [1989] 2 All ER 344. Here the plaintiff, who had obtained an Anton Piller order, was applying for leave to use documents which had been seized under it to bring proceedings for contempt for alleged breaches of an earlier Mareva injunction. The defendant relied on the privilege against self-incrimination. By s 14(1) of the Civil Evidence Act 1968 this applied in 'any legal proceedings other than criminal proceedings . . . only as regards criminal offences under the law of any part of the United Kingdom and penalties provided for by such law'. Walton J held that the privilege was inapplicable since civil contempt was not a criminal offence. (Presumably, it was also implicitly decided that the proceedings were not criminal proceedings and as such, outwith the scope of s 14). The conclusion is not surprising and it is supported by the decision of the Court of Appeal in *Savings and Investment Bank Ltd v Gasco Investments (Netherlands) BV (No 2)* [1988] 1 All ER 975, All ER Rev 1988 at 80, holding that the hearsay provisions of the Civil Evidence Act 1968 apply to committal proceedings for a civil contempt.

The closeness of the analogy between criminal proceedings and civil contempt was further examined by the Court of Appeal in *El Capistrano SA v A TO Marketing Ltd* [1989] 2 All ER 572. The background was one of passing off in relation to companies promoting time-sharing properties in Spain and committal proceedings in respect of alleged breaches of undertakings. The problem was that the affidavit in support of the application to commit contained hearsay evidence which Harman J (being unaware of the decision in the *Savings and Investment Bank* case, noted above) considered to be inadmissible. The point had been raised as a preliminary issue by the defendants. His Lordship then dismissed the motion without proceeding to consider the merits of the case and on the understanding that the plaintiff would begin afresh. The alternative of adjourning the proceedings for amendment of the affidavit was seen as being a less convenient course. When the fresh motion to commit was issued the defendants pleaded the defence of autrefois acquit or double jeopardy. The plea was allowed by Morritt J who considered that the defendants had been 'imperilled on the first application'. *Jelson (Estates) Ltd v Harvey* [1984] 1 All ER 12, All ER Rev 1984 at 63 was distinguished on the ground that the defect in that case lay in the motion to commit, rather than in the supporting evidence.

Although this distinction is a tenable one, it did not find favour in the Court of Appeal which was clear that the defendants had never in reality been in any peril of punishment on the first application. The court also indicated that the doctrine was to be applied less strictly than in the criminal law, Kerr LJ saying (at 584):

> 'There is no authority or principle which requires a narrow interpretation of the expression "on the merits", or of the doctrine of double jeopardy, in the law of civil contempt. We are entitled to view such cases on a broad basis of justice, and in my view we should clearly do so.'

Balcombe LJ agreed that a broad approach was appropriate so as to enable courts to attempt to do justice to both parties.

The result seems, in effect, to be that the doctrine is now unlikely to be available unless an application has truly been dismissed on the merits, rather than on procedural grounds. Similarly, of course, the doctrine of autrefois convict will prevent subsequent punishments for breach of a single order (see *Danchevsky v Danchevsky (No 2)* (1977) 121 SJ 796). On the whole, this seems right. Certainly, on the facts of the case it is difficult to believe that the defendants could have felt that there was any real substance in their objections.

Breach of undertakings and of contracts

Finally, reference may be made to *Midland Marts Ltd v Hobday* [1989] 3 All ER 246. The dispute in this case was between the plaintiff livestock auctioneers and the defendants whose business it was to organise Sunday markets. The defendants had given certain undertakings to the court (eg in relation to the taking down of a fence) and the same undertakings also formed part of a contract with the plaintiffs. On a subsequent application to commit Vinelott J said (at 251):

> '. . . I can see no reason in principle why the court, if satisfied that the facts proved at the hearing of a motion to commit constitute both a breach of the

undertaking to the court and a breach of contract and also that there is no tenable ground of defence to an action for damages for breach of contract, should not direct an inquiry into damages or in a sufficiently clear case make a summary award of damages. It would, I think, be unjust and give rise to unnecessary multiplicity of proceedings, that an applicant who has established facts which constitute both a breach of an undertaking to the court and of the respondent's contractual undertakings should be put to the delay and expense of instituting separate proceedings in which the question whether there had been a breach of the undertakings would be res judicata.'

His Lordship proceeded to award £500 damages, this figure having been agreed by the defendants as a reasonable estimate of the plaintiffs financial loss.

Although this course seems to have been a novel one, it was obviously convenient. Presumably, it might also be adopted in simple cases of tort, as when there has been a breach of an injunction restraining a nuisance or an entry on land. The decision does not challenge—indeed it rather supports (see at 250)—the standard, if questionable, assumption associated with *Chapman v Honig* [1963] 2 All ER 513 that contempt of court does not *of itself* give rise to a claim for damages by a person who has been injured thereby. In other words, there must be some other peg on which to hang the claim even if this does not necessarily have to be done in separate proceedings.

Contract

MICHAEL P FURMSTON, TD, BCL, MA, LLM
Bencher of Gray's Inn, Professor of Law, University of Bristol

Formation

In the 1988 Annual Review we considered the judgement of Hirst J in *Kleinwort Benson Ltd v Malaysia Mining Corporation Bhd.* It will be remembered that that case concerned the legal effect of a letter of comfort. The plaintiff bank had agreed to make a loan facility of up to £10 million available to the defendants' wholly owned subsidiary, MMC Metals Limited, which was trading in tin on the London Metal Exchange. The defendants had refused to execute a formal guarantee but had written a letter to the plaintiffs stating, 'It is our policy to ensure that the business of [MMC] is at all times in a position to meet its liabilities to you under the [loan facility agreement]'. When the world tin market collapsed, MMC went into liquidation and the bank sought to recover the amount of outstanding debt from the defendants. The defendants argued that the letter did not impose any legal obligation on them.

The approach of Hirst J was that since the transaction was clearly a commercial one there was an inference that it was intended to create legal relations unless the defendants could show wording which negatived any such inference.

This decision was reversed by the Court of Appeal [1989] 1 All ER 785. The Court of Appeal did not question the general principle that in commercial agreements there is a presumption of intention to create legal relations. In the comfort letter itself there were words such as those of paragraph 2, 'We confirm that we will not reduce our current financial interest in MMC Metals Limited', which were appropriate for entering into a legally binding agreement. But the words used in paragraph 3 were carefully chosen so as not to impose any promisory obligation. They were statements of the defendants' policy. If they had been inaccurate statements of the defendants' policy, they might have given rise to liability in misrepresentation but that did not amount to a promise that the defendants would not change their policy in different circumstances. As Ralph Gibson LJ said, 'It is impossible to make up for the lack of express promise by implying such a promise, and indeed, no such implied promise was pleaded.' This confirms the view which we expressed last year that 'the effects of such documents must depend in the final analysis on [their] precise wording.' It is also important to note that in a situation of this kind where the agreement is being negotiated between equally powerful and experienced parties, who are well aware of the difference between a letter of guarantee and a letter of comfort, the documents should not be approached during the process of construction with any preconceived view that they are designed to reach a particular legal effect. The judgment contains some evidence about the process of negotiation leading up to the giving of the letter of comfort in which an employee of the plaintiffs appears to have indicated that he was willing to accept a letter of comfort rather than a guarantee but that a rather higher rate of interest would probably need to be charged. This makes good commercial sense since the plaintiffs might well think it acceptable to take the risk of the defendants changing their policy if this was reflected in the return on the transaction. After all, lending to sovereign states is itself far from a risk free operation!

Contents of the contract

The joint appeals in *Smith v Eric S Bush (a firm)* and *Harris v Wyre Forest District Council* [1989] 2 All ER 514 have led to a decision of the House of Lords which is one of the most important so far on the operation of the Unfair Contract Terms Act 1977. The decision of the Court of Appeal in *Smith* was discussed in 1987 Annual Review at 310, that of the Court of Appeal in *Harris* in 1988 Annual Review at 86. In *Smith*, the Plaintiff applied to a building society for a mortgage, paid an inspection fee and signed an application form which stated that a copy of the survey report and mortgage valuation would be given to the plaintiff. The form contained a disclaimer that neither the society nor its surveyor warranted that the report would be accurate and stating that the report and valuation was supplied without any acceptance of responsibility. In due course the plaintiff received a copy of the report, was granted a mortgage and went ahead with the purchase of the house. In *Harris*, the plaintiffs applied to the defendant local authority for a mortgage; the defendant had the property valued and the valuation surveyor valued it at the asking price. The local authority made a loan of 90%. In this case the application form for the mortgage stated that the valuation was confidential to the defendant and was intended solely for the information of the defendant so that 'no responsibility whatsoever [was] implied or accepted by the [local authority] for the value or condition of the property by reason of [the] inspection and report'. The form also advised purchasers to have their own survey done.

One answer to the plaintiff's claim on such facts would be that the valuer owed no duty of care to the plaintiff to avoid the economic loss which the plaintiff would suffer as the result of a careless valuation. No doubt this is the answer which most lawyers would have unhesitatingly given 30 years ago. In *Yianni v Edwin Evans & Sons (a firm)* [1981] 3 All ER 592, Park J held that on such facts a valuer did owe a duty of care to a purchaser even where the valuer's report was not shown to the purchaser, since on such facts the purchaser would know that the lender would not have made an advance unless a satisfactory report had been obtained from the valuer and it was much more likely than not that a purchaser of a low value house would rely on the lender's valuation rather than obtaining an independent survey himself. Although the attitude of the House of Lords in recent decisions has been restrictive of liability in tort for economic loss, the House of Lords in this case do not appear to have entertained serious doubts that this was an appropriate case in principle for the imposition of liability. This basic tort question is no doubt discussed elsewhere in this Review.

The principal interest of the case for contract lawyers is the effect given to the attempted disclaimer of liability. This question was treated in a fundamentally different way by the two differently constituted Courts of

Appeal which heard the cases below. In *Smith*, the Court of Appeal assumed that such a disclaimer was subject to s 2 of the Unfair Contract Terms Act 1977 and that therefore the only question was whether the disclaimer was reasonable. The court had little difficulty in finding that as between a valuer who could easily obtain professional negligence insurance and a purchaser at the bottom of the market who could not insure against this risk and was very likely to rely on the valuer being careful, it was not reasonable to exclude the liability of the valuer. Holding down the valuer's professional negligence liability premiums or protecting the pockets of the insurance company would be low priorities in this scheme of things. The Court of Appeal in *Harris* took a different view. They treated the disclaimer as going to whether or not there was initial liability. For this purpose they relied heavily on the reasoning of the House of Lords in *Hedley Byrne & Co Ltd v Heller & Partners Ltd* [1963] 2 All ER 575 where liability for careless statements giving rise to economic loss was said to turn on the voluntary assumption of liability. In *Hedley Byrne* itself the defendants were held not liable by the House of Lords because by labelling their reference 'without responsibility' they had made it clear that they were not accepting liability for it.

As a matter of abstract logic, there is much to be said, if one treats the reasoning in *Hedley Byrne* at face value, for the view taken by the Court of Appeal in *Harris*. It was however robustly rejected by the House of Lords. It was said to give inadequate weight to ss 11(3) and 13(1) of the Act and it is interesting to note that the House of Lords thought it permissible to look at the second report of the Law Commission on *Exemption Clauses* (Law Com no 69) which said 'disclaimers of liability made where information or advice is given, should be subject to control'. The judgments are so unequivocal that it must be a waste of time to enter into a routine transaction like valuing a house and hope to defend oneself by attaching to it a standard form disclaimer. On the other hand, it is difficult to believe that there cannot be circumstances in which a person asked for advice cannot say that he does not really know but his best guess is . . . or that he has not time to do research but the answer off the top of his head is . . . or that if paid a proper fee he will give a proper professional answer but that for gratuitous advice his instinctive feeling is . . . In each of these cases, it must be open to argument on the facts that the advice giver has never assumed responsibility for the advice. It is thought therefore that the reasoning in the present case is not conclusive as to exactly where the line is to be drawn in a case of that kind. A distinction should be drawn between assuming liability and trying to wheedle out of it on the one hand and making it clear from the beginning that one has never assumed liability.

Section 2 of the Unfair Contract Terms Act does not prohibit a party from seeking to disclaim liability for negligence leading to financial loss; it subjects such a clause to the test of reasonableness. The House of Lords had no doubt that it was not reasonable to permit the valuer to exclude liability on facts such as those of the present cases. Of course, it must be the case that what is reasonable depends on a careful consideration of all the relevant circumstances but in a very helpful passage in his speech Lord Griffiths drew attention to a number of matters which should always be considered. These were

(1) 'were the parties of equal bargaining power?'

(2) 'In the case of advice, would it have been reasonably practicable to obtain the advice from an alternative source taking into account considerations of costs and time.' This is a very relevant consideration as to where the line should be drawn in the house market. First-time buyers may well feel that they cannot afford the cost of a full structural survey; the same is not necessarily to be said of those buying an expensive up-market house.

(3) 'How difficult is the task being undertaken for which liability is being excluded.' Granted that the valuer only has to achieve the standard of a reasonably careful valuer which is basically carrying out a careful visual examination and pursuing any suspicious factors revealed by that, this does not appear to impose an excessive burden on valuers.

(4) 'What are the practical consequences of a decision on the question of reasonableness.' This leads naturally on to the sums of money at stake and the ability of one or other of the parties to insure the risks involved. This being so, the potential loss to the purchasers is enormous; the potential cost to the valuer in terms of increased professional liability premiums is in contrast modest. There would of course be other cases in which the potential risks of professional negligence would involve sums so large it would be entirely reasonable and proper to seek to exclude or restrict liability.

A final factor in the present case is that in effect building society lending is organised so that the cost of valuation falls on the borrower. If the borrower had engaged the valuer directly, it would have been very difficult to argue that it was reasonable for the valuer to exclude liability; it is arguably no more permissible to allow the valuer to exclude responsibility because his liability to the purchaser is tortious rather than contractual.

Although *Lombard Tricity Finance Ltd v Paton* [1989] 1 All ER 918 involves primarily a discussion of consumer credit law, it does also raise a point of interest to general contract lawyers. In this case, the defendant borrower entered into a credit agreement with the plaintiff on terms where the rate of interest payable on the balance was said to be 'subject to variation by the creditor from time to time on notification as required by law'. The borrower fell into arrears and when sued sought to argue that the provision as to interest was in conflict with the regulations. We may leave this point elsewhere but the holding of the Court of Appeal that the plaintiff's case succeeded necessarily involves a finding that a contract in which an important term (in this case the rate of interest) can be unilaterally changed by one party is in principle a valid contract. If such a contract was not a valid contract no question of construction of the Consumer Credit Act 1974 and the regulations would have arisen. The Court of Appeal expressly held that a contract providing for unilateral variation by one side is a lawful agreement at common law relying on the dictum of Viscount Dunedin in *May & Butcher Ltd v R* [1934] 2 KB 17: 'with regard to price it is a perfectly good contract to say that the price is to be settled by the buyer'.

The decision of the Court of Appeal in *National Bank of Greece SA v Pinios Shipping Co No 1* [1989] 1 All ER 213 is a useful example of the process of implying, or rather not implying, a term into a contract. In this case, a ship was being built in Japan and the buyer paid 30% of the price on delivery. The remainder of the price was secured by a first preferred mortgage in favour of the builders and by 14 promisory notes signed by Pinios payable at six-monthly intervals. The first six promisory notes were guaranteed by the bank under a letter of guarantee and the bank was secured in its turn by a second preferred mortgage and by a personal guarantee given by a Mr Tsitsilianis. The ship was delivered on 19 February 1977 and the first promisory note fell due on 9 August 1977. It was dishonoured and the bank therefore paid the amount of the promisory note. Under the terms of the letter of guarantee the bank could have declared Pinios in default but instead the bank entered into a three party agreement with Pinios and a company called Glafki. Glafki was appointed sole and exclusive agent to manage the vessel in the best interests of Pinios and the bank and to exercise due diligence to protect and safeguard the interests of Pinios and the bank in various specific respects. It became Glafki's duty to place the insurances and they succeeded to Pinios's obligation to insure for not less than 130% of the total amount secured by the mortgage. The insurance policies originally taken out by Pinios were in dollars and were for an adequate amount. During the running of the agreement, the dollar depreciated against the yen and the renewals by Glafki in February and April of 1988 were for less than 130% of the mortgaged amount. The ship was lost and at the time of loss the insurance proceeds were insufficient to discharge the shipowner's indebtedness under the second mortgage. In an earlier action, the shipowners brought an action against Glafki for under-insurance and breach of the management agreement. The action was successful but Glafki did not satisfy the judgment. The bank then sued the shipowners for repayment of the second mortgage. The shipowners set up a defence that the bank was in breach of a duty of care to see that Glafki did not under-insure the vessel. The Court of Appeal held that there was no implied term to this effect. No term could be implied on the theory that a particular term was appropriate to a contract of this kind since the contract was a one-off contract, carefully negotiated and not falling into any clearly recognised legal category. No term could be implied on the basis of giving business efficacy to the agreement or on the officious bystander tests because it was wholly unclear what the response of the parties would have been if they had been asked whether the bank had implicitly undertaken to supervise Glafki in the performance of their duty to insure.

Similar reasoning as to implication of terms is to be found in a second decision of the Court of Appeal in *The Good Luck* [1989] 3 All ER 628, discussed below pp 85–86.

Privity of contract

In *Norwich City Council v Harvey* [1989] 1 All ER 1180 the Plaintiffs entered into a contract for the extension of a swimming pool complex under JCT 1963 (1977 revision) with a firm of contractors. Under cl 20 of this contract, the risk of loss or damage by fire was placed on the employer and the contract required the employer to maintain adequate insurance against loss or damage by fire. In the event both the existing works and the extension were damaged by fire owing to the negligence of an employee of a sub-contractor engaged by the contractor to do certain roofing work. The plaintiffs brought an action for negligence against the sub-contractors and their employee. The Court of Appeal affirmed the judgment of Garland J that the claim failed. On the face of it this is surprising since one would have expected the sub-contractors and their employees to owe a duty of care to the plaintiffs and therefore to have been liable if they were in breach of that duty. The contrary argument which prevailed in the Court of Appeal was that the terms of the main contract showed that as between employer and main contractor the risk of loss or damage by fire was on the employer, even if the loss or damage was caused by the contractor (*Scottish Special Housing Association v Wimpey Construction UK Ltd* [1986] 2 All ER 957). It was said to follow from this that it was unfair to deprive the sub-contractor of the immunity which the contractual scheme had conferred on the contractor. It is probably an essential part of this argument that the term as to risk of fire was to be found both in the main contract and sub contract. An alternative way of putting the same result is to say that the sub contractors did not owe a duty of care to the employers because they entered on the work in the light of the terms of the sub contract and main contract. In pursuing this line of reasoning, the Court of Appeal reviewed a number of recent cases in which the scope of the duty of care has been considered and in effect narrowed but nearly all of these cases were cases of economic loss. It is notoriously difficult to define exactly when a defendant who causes economic loss should be judged to have been under a duty of care to the plaintiff; it is much less difficult to decide that a plaintiff who causes physical damage owes a duty of care. Indeed, one would normally expect that consequence to flow more or less automatically.

It is not necessarily inappropriate to reach the result reached by the Court of Appeal in this case. If the employer had agreed to insure against the risk of loss or damage by fire and had carried out his contractual obligation to the contractor to do this, it was not the employer but the employer's fire insurer who was the real plaintiff. It makes good economic sense for employer, contractor, sub-contractor and Old Uncle Cobley all to be operating on the same regime covered by a single policy. Multiplication of insurance policies only makes money for insurers. However, there are undoubtedly some technical difficulties in reaching the result. It would have been interesting to read the views of the Court of Appeal on *Scruttons Ltd v Midland Silicones Ltd* [1962] 1 All ER 1 which was cited to the court but not discussed in the judgment.

Economic duress

Atlas Express Ltd v Kafco (Importers and Distributors) Ltd [1989] 1 All ER 641 is a useful application of the principle of economic duress. In this case, the plaintiffs entered into a contract with the defendants who were a small company importing and distributing basketware to deliver cartons of basketware which the defendants had sold to Woolworths. The plaintiffs' depot manager had quoted a price of £1.10 per carton. This was based on his guess that each load would contain at least 400 and possibly as many as 600 cartons. In fact, the first load contained only 200 cartons and the plaintiffs' depot manager therefore told the defendants that the plaintiffs would not carry any more cartons unless the defendants agreed to pay at least £440 per load. The defendants could not easily rearrange the carriage of the cartons and were very anxious to ensure that the cartons were delivered on time to Woolworths, on whom they depended. The defendants accordingly agreed to the new terms but later refused to pay. Tucker J held that the defendants were not liable as their agreement to the change of terms was procured by economic duress. It was clear that in the circumstances the plaintiffs had threatened to break their contract; that the defendants were heavily dependant on the contract of carriage being carried out on time and that the plaintiffs well knew this. This combination of factors produced a clear case of economic duress.

Non disclosure

Banque Finacière de la Cité v Westgate Insurance Co Ltd [1989] 2 All ER 952 was discussed in the 1987 Annual Review at 311 under its earlier name of *Banque Keyser Ullman SA v Skandia Insurance Company Ltd*. It will be remembered that a Mr Ballestero persuaded syndicates of banks to lend his company many millions of Swiss Francs and that these loans were secured, partly, by gemstones (which later turned out to be virtually valueless) and partly by credit insurance policies covering failure by the borrowing companies to repay the loans. These policies were issued by the defendant insurers. The policies contained clauses excluding the insurer's liability in the event of fraud. This meant that the lenders could not recover the money they lent to Mr Ballestero's companies when he disappeared with it because the insurance policies themselves were unenforceable since they did not cover the risk of Mr Ballestero's fraud. However, it also appeared that the policies had been procured by an employee of the insurance broker falsely representing that the full amount of the loan was insured when in fact he only held a cover note valid for 14 days and that the insurers had discovered this deception but had not revealed it to the lenders. It was accepted that if the lenders had known of the dishonestty of the insurance broker's employee, they would not have gone through with the loan transactions.

On these facts it was necessary to decide whether the insurers owed a duty of disclosure to the lenders and, if so, what the remedy was. Steyn J held that the insurer was just as much under a duty of disclosure to the insured as the insured is to the insurer. The Court of Appeal took the same view. Slade LJ, delivering the judgment of court, said (at 989):

> 'there is no doubt that the obligation to disclose material facts is a mutual one imposing reciprocal duties on insurer and insured. . . . The occasions where disclosure by the insurer is required may in practice be rare since the circumstances material to the insurance will ordinarily be known only to the proposed insured. Nevertheless such occasions may arise. . . . It is no less clear that where there is obligation to disclose material facts it is an absolute one which is not negatived by the absence of fraud or negligence. The law requires a party to an insurance contract to state not only all those material circumstances within his knowledge which he believes to be material, but those which are in fact so . . . the merely accidental failure to disclose facts, if material facts, will involve a breach of duty.'

A more difficult problem was the test of materiality to be applied to non disclosure by the insurer. It is well established that, in the case of non disclosure by the insured, the test is whether the facts not disclosed would have influenced the judgment of a prudent insurer. How is this test to be adapted to the reverse position? The Court of Appeal did not think that the insurer was under an obligation to disclose everything which might affect the judgment of the insured; for instance, it did not consider that the insurer was under any duty to disclose that another reputable insurer would cover the risk at a lower premium. The court considered that

> 'the duty falling on the insurer must at least extend to disclosing all facts known to him which are material either to the nature of the risk sought to be covered or the recoverability of a claim under the policy which a prudent insured would take into account in deciding whether or not to place the risk for which he seeks cover with that insurer.'

The court thought that applying this test there had been failure to disclose material facts.

The standard remedy for non disclosure is of course to treat the contract of insurance as voidable. This is a satisfactory remedy from the point of view of the insurer since it means that he does not have to meet the claims. The insured, on the other hand, would not normally want to set aside the policy, at least once the risk had occurred. Setting aside the policy would at most lead to return of the premiums. The only effective remedy in such circumstances from the insured's point of view would be an action for damages. Steyn J held that such an action lay but the Court of Appeal took a different view. Steyn J's judgment was driven by a conviction that if the insured had a right to receive disclosure from the insurer, justice required that there was an effective remedy for breach of this obligation. The Court of Appeal disagreed. Slade LJ said (at 993),

> 'If the banks' right to full disclosure of material facts is founded neither on tort nor on contract nor on the existence of a fiduciary duty nor on statute, we find it difficult to see how as a matter of legal analysis it can be said to found a claim for damages.'

It is important in this respect to note that, as the court observed, the duty of disclosure is an absolute one so that to give a remedy by way of damages for failure to disclose would in effect be to create a new tort of strict liability. The position would have been different if it could have been shown that the insurers were fraudulent or guilty of misrepresentation. On the facts this avenue was not effectively open to the plaintiffs. There was a further alternative, which was that the insurers owed a duty of care to the insured in the circumstances. This was carefully considered and analysed by the Court of Appeal with a full review of many of the recent cases on economic loss. The court came to the conclusion that such a tort remedy did not exist. The judgment contained an exceptionally full and careful analysis of these issues of which what has just passed is a most inadequate summary.

By one of those curious coincidences as a result of which cases on the same subject often come before the courts in pairs, a second case on disclosure came before a somewhat differently constituted Court of Appeal (Ralph Gibson LJ being a member of the court in each case) in *Bank of Nova Scotia v Hellenic Mutual War Risks Association (Bermuda) Ltd, The Good Luck* [1989] 3 All ER 628. In this case a group of Greek shipowners owned a number of ships which were mortgaged to the plaintiff bank as security for a loan. The ships were insured with the defendant P & I Club. The insurers were given notice of the assignment and in a letter to the bank undertook to hold the benefit of the insurance policies which the shipowners had assigned to the bank, to the bank's order, and to inform the bank promptly if it ceased to insure any vessel. Under the insurance arrangements, the bank needed to be assured not only that each of the ships against which it had lent was insured but since the loan arrangement contemplated further advances, that the total amount advanced was adequately covered by insurance. This meant that if one of the ships insured ceased to be insured, the amount that could be prudently lent would be at once reduced to a percentage of the value of the remaining ships. The bank therefore had an obvious commercial interest in knowing as quickly as possible if there was any possibility that any of the ships would not be insured.

Under the insurance arrangements there were prohibited zones in which the ships would not be covered while present and additional risk zones into which entry was permitted but in respect of which an additional premium was payable and entry into which triggered a duty on the part of the shipowner to notify the insurer. The owners of the ships consistently pursued a policy of entering both prohibited and extra premium zones without giving any notice and of chartering ships to Iranian charterers who regularly entered prohibited zones. There was evidence which suggested strongly that the insurers were aware of this practice and had taken no effective steps to dissuade the shipowners from it.

One of the shipowners' ships was a total loss when struck by a missile in the prohibited zone. The owners made a claim after purportedly giving notice of entry into the additional premium zone claiming that they did not know of the existence of the prohibited zone. The insurers' agents told the bank that the shipowners' claim was being investigated in the usual way. This was taken by the bank to mean that in due course it would be paid but the agents and the insurers knew that the claim would very probably not be met because the ship was in a prohibited zone. In due course, the insurers rejected the shipowners' claim and the bank brought an action against the insurers. The Court of Appeal held that the insurers were not in breach of their express undertaking to inform the bank promptly if they ceased to insure the ship since the effect of the ship entering the prohibited zone was not to terminate the contract of insurance but to give the insurers a ground on which they could refuse to meet the claim. The insurers had complied with their express undertaking since they had told the bank when they had eventually decided to reject the claim. They were not required by the express agreement to warn the bank that it was very likely that they would reject the claim and that they believed that they had good reasons for doing so.

The Court of Appeal also rejected an alternative argument that the insurers were under a duty of disclosure to the bank. The Court of Appeal thought there was no scope for applying a duty of disclosure wider than the contractual duty or of developing a remedy in tort so as to outflank the unavailability of a contract remedy.

Illegality

Davitt v Titcumb [1989] 3 All ER 417 is not strictly a contract case but it sheds considerable light on an important part of the law relating to illegal contracts. The defendant and the deceased bought a house for £16,900. The price was raised in large part by a mortgage of £14,950 from a building society. Repayment of the mortgage was provided for in part by an endowment policy on the lives of both the defendant and the deceased which was assigned to the building society. The defendant later murdered the deceased. The building society as assignee of the life insurance policy claimed under the policy and received the proceeds which amounted to £14,950. This sum was used to redeem the mortgage. The house was then sold. The question before the court was whether the defendant was entitled to any share of the net proceeds of the sale of the house. He argued that he was not debarred by the benefit from a crime rule from taking a share in the proceeds of the house since he had always been the owner of a share in the house and it was the benefit under the insurance policy which he would have been barred from claiming if it had been he and not the building society which had been the claimant on the life insurance policy. This argument was rejected. The point of interest for contract lawyers is that Scott J expressed the view that Commercial Union was right to pay the policy money to the building society even though the defendant could not have required it to do so. This was an application of the views expressed obiter in *Beresford v Royal Insurance Co Ltd* [1938] 2 All ER 602 that the benefit from a crime rule did not prevent enforcement of a life insurance policy by an assignee at least so far as is necessary to protect the actual interest of the assignee.

Termination

British and Commonwealth Holdings plc v Quadrex Holdings Inc [1989] 3 All ER 492 is an important and interesting case on the circumstances in which time is, or may become, of the essence of the contract. In July 1987 the plaintiff, a British company, made a bid for another company, Mercantile House Holdings Limited (MH) intending if the bid was successful to sell off the wholesale broking division of MH. The defendant, an American company, made a rival bid for MH; its commercial objective was to acquire the wholesale broking division. By an agreement dated 13 August 1987 the plaintiff and defendant agreed that the defendant would withdraw its bid and if the plaintiff's bid was successful, it would sell MH's wholesale broking division to the defendant for £280m plus the settlement of inter company indebtedness. Clause 3 of this contract provided for implementation 'as soon as reasonably practical' after MH had been acquired by the plaintiff.

The plaintiff's bid was in fact successful and the parties later agreed for completion first on 17 December 1987, then on 6 January 1988 but in both cases the defendant was unable to complete because it had not been able to raise the finance from its bankers. On 25 January 1988 the plaintiffs gave the defendant formal notice to complete by 28 February 1988. The defendants were unable to do so and on 29 February the plaintiff gave notice to the defendant that the failure to complete was being treated as a repudiation of the agreement and on the same day the plaintiff issued a writ claiming damages in excess of £100m and applied for summary judgement under RSC Ord 14. The Court of Appeal drew attention to the fact that 'the phrase "time is of the essence of the contract" is capable of causing confusion since the question in each case is whether time is of the essence of the particular contractual term which has been breached.' Accordingly, it was impossible to say that time was originally of the essence of completion since the agreement did not specify a date of completion or fix a time for completion by reference to a formula which subsequently made the date capable of exact definition. If there had been a contractual date of completion, that date would undoubtedly have been of the essence of the contract since the subject matter of the sale (shares in private companies trading in a very volatile sector) was such as to make time of completion of the essence.

So time of completion was not originally of the essence. Was it made of the essence by the notice? The Court of Appeal said that three requirements were needed if time was to be made of the essence by the service of a notice. These were—

'(1) the giver of the notice (the innnocent party) has to be ready, willing and able to complete, (2) the other party (the guilty party) has to have been guilty of unreasonable delay before a notice to complete can be served and (3) the notice when served must limit a reasonable period within which completion is to take place.'

As to the second requirement, it is important to emphasise that it is not sufficient to show that the guilty party has failed to perform on time; it must be shown that the guilty party has been responsible for undue or improper delay. However the Court of Appeal thought that this limitation was clearly inconvenient in cases where in a real commercial sense time was of the essence and ought not to be extended. The court indeed held that since in the present case time for completion would have been of the essence if there had been a contractually agreed date of completion, it was permissible for the innocent party to serve a notice making time of the essence as soon as the guilty party was clearly in breach of contract. The defendants argued as to the third point that the time given for completion was not reasonable, granted that the plaintiffs knew that the reason the defendants had not completed was their difficulties in satisfying their banks as to the terms of the loan agreement and these difficulties arose, at least in part, because of the non co-operation of directors of the MH subsidiaries which made it difficult to satisfy the accounting requirements as to the position of those subsidiaries which the banks were insisting on. The Court of Appeal said that for the purpose of deciding what time was reasonable for completion, the difficulties of the purchaser in raising the purchase price were normally irrelevant. The position would clearly be different if the purchaser had contracted on the basis that the contract was conditional on raising finance.

The reasoning so far would lead to the conclusion that the plaintiffs were entitled to summary judgement under Order 14. However, the contract between the parties required the parties to 'use all reasonable endeavours to bring about the . . . acquisition of the Wholesale Broking Division on the basis set out in the Agreement' and the Court of Appeal thought that the defendants had an arguable case that the plaintiffs were in breach of their obligations under this clause of the contract. This being so, the Court of Appeal gave the defendants conditional leave to defend subject to their making an interim payment of damages of £5m.

Remedies

Since the rule in *Bain v Fothergill* (1874) LR 7 HL 158, [1874–80] All ER Rep 83 has been abolished by the Law Reform (Miscellaneous Provisions) Act 1989, it is ironic that two cases on the rule have been reported this year. The first of these was *Seven Seas Properties Ltd v Al-Essa* [1989] 1 All ER 164 and the second *Suleman v Shahsavari* [1989] 2 All ER 460. The second case was one which fell outside the rule since the vendors' failure to complete the sale did not turn on their inability to make title. In this case a Mr Martinez had purported to act on behalf of the vendors. It was held that he had actual authority from one of the vendors but neither actual nor apparent authority to act on behalf of the other and therefore there was no contract to sell the property binding on the vendors but that Mr Martinez was liable to the purchasers for breach of warranty of authority. The critical question was whether the plaintiffs could recover the difference between the contract price and the value of the house at the contractually agreed date of completion or at the date of judgement. Andrew Park QC, sitting as a deputy High Court judge, held that the purchasers would certainly have been entitled on the basis of *Wroth v Tyler* [1973] 1 All ER 897 and *Johnson v Agnew* [1979] 1 All ER 883 to judgment against the vendors, if the contract had been binding on the vendors, on the basis of a calculation of the difference between the contract price and the value of the house at the date of judgment. The same basis should apply in the case of an action for breach of warranty of authority.

Two cases involved questions as to interest. The simpler was *Janred Properties Ltd v Ente Nazionale Italiano per il Turismo* [1989] 2 All ER 444 where the Court of Appeal applied the basic rule that in a contract for the sale of land a buyer cannot normally recover interest on the purchase price in the event of failure by the purchaser to complete or to complete on time. In this case, the contract in fact provided for interest between the contractual date of completion and the actual date of completion but that provision did not apply since the contract had never been completed.

A more important case is *National Bank of Greece SA v Pinios Shipping Co No 1* [1989] 1 All ER 213, the facts of which have been set out above. In this case, the Court of Appeal held that once a bank unequivocally demanded immediate payment of outstanding sums and thereby closed the account, the relationship of banker and customer was replaced by one of creditor and debtor so that compound interest ceased to be payable in the absence of an express or implied agreement or a binding custom. This decision has subsequently been reversed by the House of Lords and the question will be discussed more fully next year when the House of Lords' decision has been reported.

Perhaps the most interesting remedies case of the year is *Jobson v Johnson* [1989] 1 All ER 621 which contains an interesting discussion of the relationship between the rules about penalties and the rules about equitable relief against forfeiture. In this case the defendant agreed to buy 62,566 shares in a football club for a total purchase price of £351,688. The price was payable by an initial payment of £40,000 and six instalments of £51,948, payable half-yearly. There was a further provision that if the defendant defaulted on payment of the second or any subsequent instalment, he should transfer the shares back to the vendors for £40,000. That sum was not a genuine pre-estimate of the vendor's loss in the event of the defendant's breach and did not reflect the true value of the shares. The defendant paid £140,000 and then defaulted. The plaintiff was the assignee of the vendors and sought specific performance of the agreement for the retransfer of the shares. The defendant claimed that the retransfer agreement was a penalty; the defendant also counterclaimed for relief against forfeiture if the agreement was enforceable. At the trial, the counterclaim was struck out because the defendant had not complied with an undertaking which he had given to disclose certain documents. There was no appeal against the trial judge's decision to strike out the counterclaim but the absence of the counterclaim made the handling of the main issue more difficult. The trial judge, Harman J, held that the clause requiring the retransfer for £40,000 was a penalty but that the penalty clause was enforceable unless the court decided to exercise its equitable jurisdiction to relieve against forfeiture and that since in the instant case the court could not do that because the application for relief had been struck out, the penalty clause could be enforced. The Court of Appeal thought that the trial judge was certainly correct in thinking that the retransfer provision was penal since the price for the retransfer was not related either to the value of the shares or to the loss which the sellers would have suffered by the transaction going off since the resale price was the same, however many instalments had been paid when the purchaser defaulted.

One might no doubt express the rule about penalties either by saying that an agreement for a penalty is not binding or by saying that an agreement for a penalty is binding but that the court has a wide jurisdiction to give relief against unfair consequences. In most cases it would make little if any practical difference which of these solutions one adopted. The present case is an exception because for quite extraneous reasons the possibility of relief against forfeiture was to be excluded.

The majority view was that although equitable relief was not in the circumstances available, the retransfer clause should not be enforced as it stood since it was penal. What remedies might be given the plaintiff granted the defendant's clear default in the payment of the instalments? One possibility would be retransfer of the shares at a fair value but this would be to make a new contract for the parties. A second possibility would be to award the plaintiff damages for loss of the unpaid instalments (of course the plaintiff could have sued for the unpaid instalments and on the face of it could have recovered a summary judgment under Order 14). It seems fairly clear that the plaintiff was much more anxious to get the shares back than to recover the whole of the purchase price. The commercial reason for this is not clear but it is presumably related to the parties' perception of the value of the shares. No clear picture as to the value of the shares emerges from the judgment and indeed in any case the value of shares in a football club is notoriously fed as much by vanity as by commercial considerations. The majority concluded that the plaintiff should be offered either a sale of the 62,566 shares by the court and payment of all unpaid money out of the proceeds or an inquiry as to the plaintiff's actual loss with a view to giving specific performance if the present value of the shares did not exceed by more than £40,000 the present aggregate of the unpaid instalments and the present amount charged on the shares under a charging order obtained by Chartered Standard Bank. Kerr LJ thought that neither of these alternatives was fair to the plaintiff and that the plaintiff should be offered the opportunity of having specific performance of the contract to retransfer the shares subject to his repaying the defendant the money he had received under the contract, perhaps with interest. Granted that the real dispute is probably about the shares and that these were probably regarded by both parties as far more valuable than any sums of money outstanding, this seems in many ways a more attractive remedy. If the defendant's application for relief had not been struck out, it is very likely that a court, in deciding whether to grant relief, would have decided that it was fair to order retransfer of the shares but on different financial terms from those proposed in the contract.

Two decisions of the Court of Appeal involved the application of the well known line of cases starting with *Lumley v Wagner* (1852) 1 De GM & G 604, [1843–60] All ER Rep 368. In *Warren v Mendy* [1989] 3 All ER 103 the plaintiff entered into a contract with a professional boxer (Nigel Benn) to act as his manager for three years from 27 January 1988. Under the terms of this contract the boxer agreed to be managed exclusively by the plaintiff and not to enter into any other agreement with any other manager without the plaintiff's consent. In fact within a few months Nigel Benn became dissatisfied with the plaintiff and signed a contract engaging the defendant as his agent. The plaintiff brought an action against the defendant claiming damages for inducing Nigel Benn to break his contract with the plaintiff. The plaintiff sought injunctions to restrain the defendant from acting as Nigel Benn's manager.

The plaintiff's claim against the defendant was of course a claim in tort. However, the Court of Appeal took the view that in deciding whether to give the plaintiff interlocutory injunctions against the defendant the court needed to take into account the effect on Nigel Benn's contract with the plaintiff of giving the plaintiff an injunction against the defendant. If it was indeed the case that Nigel Benn had lost confidence in the plaintiff as a manager and that the defendant was the only readily available alternative, to grant the injunctions sought by the plaintiff would, indirectly, apply coercive force to Nigel Benn to perform his personal contract of service with the plaintiff which the court would not normally do directly.

In *Provident Financial Group plc v Hayward* [1989] 3 All ER 298 the defendant was employed by the plaintiffs as financial director of the estate agency business which they operated in the north of England and the Midlands. The defendant's contract of service required him to perform the duties assigned to him; to devote the whole of his time to carrying out his duties under the contract; not to undertake any other business or profession or become an employee or agent of anyone else in any other business or profession during the continuance of his employment. On 1 July 1988 the defendant tendered his resignation and the parties agreed that the period of notice should be six months instead of 12 as in the contract, subject to the defendant undertaking not to disclose any confidential information to anyone including future employers for a period of two years from the date of the notice. The defendant continued to work for the plaintiffs until 5 September when he was sent home on full pay. On 13 October the defendant told the plaintiffs that he intended to start work for a supermarket chain as a financial controller of their estate agency offices which were situated in stores throughout the country. The plaintiffs sought an injunction to restrain the defendant from working for anyone else until his notice expired on 31 December 1988. The Court of Appeal rejected the application for the injunction since the defendant did not have any relevant confidential information which would be of use to the rival company and there was in practice no serious risk of damage to the plaintiffs from the defendant working as a financial controller for this company for the short period which was left of the notice.

A final case, which might more appropriately be in a chapter on restitution, which does not exist in this book, is *Rover International Ltd v Cannon Film Sales Ltd (No 3)* [1989] 3 All ER 423. In this case Thorn EMI made a contract on 5 December 1985 with the plaintiffs which purported to appoint the plaintiffs as Italian distributors of Thorn-EMI's films. The contract was of a fairly standard kind involving supply by Thorn of master copies of films of which Rover were to make prints and release them at Rover's own expense in Italy. Thorn were to receive a royalty on Rover's Italian sales and Rover were to pay monthly advances against the anticipated receipts. Rover was to be specifically incorporated for the purpose of making the payments which were to be in US dollars in order to overcome Italian currency restrictions. Unfortunately, Rover had not in fact been incorporated at the date of the agreement of 5 December 1985.

The first advance was paid on 14 January 1986, matters proceeding normally until about 1 May 1986 when Cannon took over Thorn–EMI and assumed control of the management of the agreement. It quickly became clear that Cannon were anxious to escape from or renegotiate the agreement. In the words of Kerr LJ 'There were many unfounded allegations of breaches by Rover.' By July 1986 Rover had issued a writ claiming a declaration that the agreement remained in force and an injunction to restrain Cannon from breaking it. On 25 July 1986 Cannon discovered that Rover had not been incorporated at the date of the December 1985 agreement. Harman J held that the agreement of 5 December 1985 was void ab initio and that there was no way such as estoppel or ratification by which it could become binding. There was no appeal against this conclusion.

In the present appeal, Rover sought repayment of instalments of advance paid after its incorporation and on a quantum meruit basis the full distribution expenses incurred in relation to the films which were released together with reasonable remuneration for the work done in purported pursuance of the agreement.

The Court of Appeal held that Rover were entitled to recover the five payments of advance made after Rover's incorporation. Kerr LJ held that Rover were entitled to do this both on the grounds that the money was paid in respect of a consideration which had totally failed, since it was paid on the basis that there was a binding contract which did not in fact exist and also on the basis that it was money paid under a mistake of fact. In respect of the latter argument Cannon argued that there had been a change of position but Kerr LJ rejected this on the grounds that there had been no disadvantageous change of position by Cannon since, although they had delivered master prints of the films to Rover, that was a disadvantage to Rover since they had then expended time and effort in making copies and dubbing the film. Dillon LJ put his rejection of the argument on the rather different grounds that where money was paid under a mistake of fact it was recoverable unless the payee could show either estoppel by conduct or payment to a mere agent who has accounted to his principal. Nicholls LJ agreed with both Kerr LJ and Dillon LJ.

At the hearing of the appeal, counsel for Cannon conceded that in principle

Rover must be entitled to some payment on a quantum meruit basis for the work they had done by way of distributing the films. The principal dispute here concerned an argument raised by Cannon that Rover should not be able to recover more on a quantum meruit basis than they would have recovered under the contract if the contract had been valid. This argument was rejected by Kerr LJ on the grounds that Cannon, having chosen to rely on their discovery that the contract was invalid when this invalidity had no commercial significance, could not rely on the limiting provisions in the contract. Furthermore, to do so would be one-sided since there was no corresponding limitation on Cannon's entitlement to gross receipts.

Criminal Law, Criminal Procedure and Sentencing

G J BENNETT, MA
Barrister, Lecturer in Law, University of Leeds

BRIAN HOGAN, LLB
Barrister, Professor of Common Law, University of Leeds

CRIMINAL LAW

General principles

Automatism

'As early as 1313', Professor Nigel Walker tells us (*Crime & Insanity in England* at 166), 'the Council of Vienne was responsible for a resolution to the effect that if a child, a madman or a sleeper killed or injured someone he was not to be held culpable.' Apart from demonstrating Professor Walker's formidable learning, this serves to show that over the centuries it is not the problems that have changed, only the answers.

So far as the criminal liability of children is concerned our law is reasonably satisfactory and tolerably clear. Not so with madmen or sleepers. The law relating to insanity and automatism is far from satisfactory and might even be said to border on the ridiculous.

The premise is that a person who has no conscious control of his or her actions cannot have responsibility for harm done whilst in that state. This has led to the so-called defence of automatism, a defence which the courts have consistently viewed with suspicion. That suspicion is said to be based on the fear that the defence is easy to raise and may be difficult to rebut. That many defences, for example that a killing was accidental or that goods were taken without a dishonest intent, may be easy to raise and difficult to rebut, has not aroused similar suspicion. But automatism was not a genie that Lord Denning was prepared to let out of the bottle; according to him it was to be confined to acts done while unconscious, such as a spasm, a reflex action or a convulsion.

Where a person lacks conscious control of his actions this will most often be because of some malfunctioning of the mind but it is not all malfunctionings of the mind on which a defence of automatism may be predicated. All such malfunctionings, assuming they cause a loss of conscious control, lead to an acquittal, but some—those where the malfunctioning is held to constitute a 'disease of the mind' within the M'Naghten Rules—with the catch that the defendant is found 'not guilty by reason of insanity'.

At one time most of us assumed that 'disease of the mind' referred to some form of mental illness (was the defendant mad?) but in *R v Kemp* [1956] 3 All ER 249 Devlin J ruled that any disease which was capable of affecting the mind could be a disease of the mind. It had been argued that a distinction was to be taken between physical disease and mental disease but, said Devlin J,

> 'The distinction between the two categories is irrelevant for the purposes of the law, which is not concerned with the origin of the disease or the cause of it but simply with the mental condition which has brought about the act . . . the law . . . merely has to consider the state of mind in which the accused is, not how he got there.'

This led, and inexorably led, to the House of Lords ruling in *R v Sullivan* [1983] 2 All ER 673, All ER Rev 1983 at 133, that epilepsy was a disease of the mind. In a speech in which all their Lordships concurred, Lord Diplock said that it was natural to feel reluctance to attach the label of insanity to a sufferer from psychomotor epilepsy but he was clear that only Parliament, and not the courts, could do anything about it.

So Lord Denning's restriction of automatism to such things as spasms, reflex actions and convulsions needs to be qualified to the extent that if the cause of the spasm or convulsion is a disease of the mind it is only the qualified form of acquittal on the grounds of insanity that is available and on all but the most serious of charges the defendant will want to sidestep that by pleading guilty. The instances where automatism would lead to an unqualified acquittal might thus be reduced almost to vanishing point.

Take the case of the defendant who receives a blow to the head and in his concussed state unconsciously assaults another. He would seem to have a disease (which according to the OED includes a condition of the body in which its functions are disturbed or deranged) which takes its effect on the mind and literally falls within the prescription of Devlin J. The concussion may be short lived and readjustment may be prompt but, according to Devlin J in *Kemp*, approved by the Court of Appeal in *R v Quick* [1973] 3 All ER 347, the disease may be 'curable or incurable . . . transitory or permanent.' Logic would seem to dictate that the appropriate verdict is an acquittal on the grounds of insanity. But at this point logic has run up against its greatest adversary, namely that indefinable quality called common sense. The common sense answer that has suggested itself to the courts, and in particular to Lord Diplock in *Sullivan*, is that if the loss of conscious control is attributable to an *external* factor (other than the consumption of intoxicants) then automatism may be available; if it is attributable to *internal* factors then an acquittal is available only on the ground of insanity.

But what is an external factor? A blow on the head causing, say, a footballer to unconsciously attack the referee is assumed to be an external factor though note that it may become an internal factor if it causes him to unconsciously assault his wife months (weeks ?—days ?—hours?) later. Medication may be an external factor so that in *Quick* [1973] 3 All ER 347, CA, for example, it was accepted that if the unconscious episode was owing to the taking of insulin and not an underlying condition of diabetes which the insulin was to treat, the proper verdict would be an acquittal on the ground of automatism and not an acquittal on the ground of insanity.

In *R v Hennessy* [1989] 2 All ER 9, CA, the defendant, during what was alleged to be an unconscious episode, had taken a car and driven it while disqualified. He was a diabetic and claimed that he did not know what he was about because he had failed to take insulin as prescribed which resulted in a hyperglycaemic coma. This, of course, would leave his disease—diabetes—as the cause and leave him only with the insanity acquittal. But it was argued on his behalf that the reason why he had failed to take his insulin was because of stress, anxiety and depression owing to marital and employment problems. An argument that these were external factors was rejected by the trial judge who took the view that the unconscious episode, if there was one, was owing to a disease of the mind within the Rules. The defendant thereupon pleaded guilty and appealed. Affirming the trial judge Lord Lane CJ, on behalf of the court said—

> 'In our judgment, stress, anxiety and depression can no doubt be the result of the operation of external factors, but they are not . . . in themselves separately or together external factors of the kind capable in law of causing or contributing to a state of automatism. They constitute a state of mind which is prone to recur. They lack the feature of novelty or accident, which is the basis of the distinction drawn by Lord Diplock in R v Sullivan . . . It does not . . . come within the scope of the exception "some external factor such as a blow on the head . . . or the administration of an anaesthetic . . .".'

This may sound like robust common sense but what would the sages at Vienne have made of a law which acquits a man for harm done during a hypoglycaemic episode while leaving him with no real choice than to plead guilty if he causes harm during a hyperglycaemic episode? And what of their sleepwalker? If this condition is brought about by internal factors, as most often it will be, he has a choice between pleading guilty or an insanity verdict; but he's entitled to a complete acquittal if it is brought on by eating a surfeit of lampreys.

Necessity and duress

Last year in *R v Conway* [1988] 3 All ER 1025, All ER Rev 1988 at 94, the Court of Appeal took a step towards recognising a general defence of necessity; this year in *R v Martin* [1989] 1 All ER 652 the Court of Appeal took another.

In considering necessity as a defence there is an important distinction between necessity as a defence to murder and necessity as a defence to crimes other than murder. The only clear case where necessity is a defence to murder appears to be where it takes the form of self-defence though it may be that, in addition, a killing to prevent crime or to effect an arrest could be justified if, no doubt in extreme circumstances, the killing was found to be 'such force as is reasonable in the circumstances' within s 3 of the Criminal Law Act 1967. Both defences must be accounted a species of the genus necessity. If the necessity takes the form of what has been traditionally called duress per minas (by threats) or what has now been termed duress of circumstances, it is no defence to a principal or secondary party to murder: *R v Howe* [1987] 1 All ER 771, HL; All ER Rev 1987 at 74. While the actual decision in *Howe* has its critics for introducing a restriction on the defence of necessity, the speeches of Lord Hailsham, expressly, and Lord Mackay LC, implicitly, recognising that no sensible distinction could be drawn between duress by threats and duress of circumstances, has opened the door to a rationalisation and expansion of the law where necessity is raised as a defence to crimes other than murder.

In *Martin* the defendant, charged with driving whilst disqualified, sought to raise necessity as a defence but on the trial judge ruling, in effect, that necessity was no defence to an 'absolute' offence, he changed his plea to guilty. The circumstances on which the defendant sought to rely were that his wife's son (the defendant's stepson) was late for work and accordingly in danger of losing his job, and that this had made his wife so distraught that she threatened to commit suicide unless he drove her son to work. There was medical evidence available indicating that it was likely that his wife would have attempted suicide had he not driven her son to work.

The Court of Appeal, quashing the conviction, held that the trial judge should have left the defence to the jury. The authorities were now clear, said the court, and established the following principles. First, the law does recognise a defence of necessity whether arising from wrongful threats of violence to another or from 'objective dangers' (conveniently called duress of circumstances) threatening the defendant or others. Secondly, the defence is available only if the defendant can be objectively said to be acting reasonably and proportionately to avoid the threat of death or serious injury. Thirdly, it is for the jury to determine whether because of what the defendant reasonably believed he had good cause to fear death or serious injury; and, if so, whether a person of reasonable firmness, sharing the characteristics of the defendant, would have responded as the defendant did.

This comes close to stating the law relating to duress by threats and duress of circumstances as set out in cll 42 and 43 of the Draft Criminal Code Bill (Law Com No 177). It does not recognise a general defence of necessity in the sense that a lesser evil may be justified to prevent a greater evil for it is restricted to the situation where the greater evil takes a form that threatens death or serious injury to the defendant. But judicial attitudes to the defence of necessity, leaving aside its decisive rejection as a defence to murder, appear to be changing and it is difficult to see why it should be restricted to situations posing a threat of serious personal injury. Faced with a choice of evils a man who chooses the lesser to avoid the greater should not be accounted a criminal. Other common law jurisdictions that have recognised such a general defence of necessity have not found it subversive.

Parties to crime

It is clearly established, if anything is ever clearly established, that a person may be convicted of murder as principal only if he or she intended to kill or cause serious bodily harm; that the principal is aware that death is possible or even probable suffices to support a conviction for manslaughter but falls short of what is required for murder.

But what of a secondary party to murder? Must he share the principal's intention to kill or cause serious bodily harm or does it suffice that he contemplates that the principal *might* kill or cause grievous bodily harm? The latter view was taken by the Privy Council in *Chan Wing-sui v R* [1984] 3 All ER 877, All ER Rev 1984 at 94, which, though not binding on English courts, seemed obviously right and might have been taken to have settled the point. Though *Chan Wing-sui* was decided in the 'high probability' days of *Hyam v DPP* [1974] 2 All ER 41, it was there held that a secondary party to murder did not, like the principal, have to foresee death as a high probability; it was enough that the secondary party contemplated (ie foresaw a risk) that his principal would kill or cause serious bodily harm with the relevant mens rea. That the House of Lords subsequently resiled from *Hyam* by requiring intention in the *principal* did not affect the ruling in *Chan Wing-sui* as to the nature of the liability of a *secondary* party.

But in *R v Slack* [1989] 3 All FR 90 the Court of Appeal found it necessary, in effect, to restate the law as it had been laid down in *Chan Wing-sui* because there were conflicting decisions of the Court of Appeal on the point. In *Slack* the principal had killed the victim with a knife provided by the defendant who later claimed that he thought the knife would be used only to threaten. Upholding the defendant's conviction for murder the court held that the trial judge was correct to direct the jury that the defendant could be so convicted if he contemplated that the principal might kill or cause serious bodily harm to the victim as part of their joint enterprise.

Shortly stated, then, the principle is that if, during an enterprise in which P (the principal) and S (the secondary party) are engaged, S contemplates that P may bring about the actus reus of any crime with the relevant mens rea of that crime, S is a secondary party to that crime or crimes. Note, with the relevant mens rea. S is not a secondary party to murder if he realises that P is prepared to take a risk of causing death or serious bodily harm though death in fact occurs since recklessness does not suffice to convict P of committing murder. It would be different if S knew that P was prepared to take a risk of breaking a window and does so; criminal damage may be committed recklessly and S is liable because he knows that P has the relevant mens rea.

Offences against the person

Murder and provocation

In *R v Johnson* [1989] 2 All ER 839 the defendant, charged with murder, raised self-defence and, for obvious reasons, his counsel did not wish to compromise this defence by pleading provocation though he invited the trial judge to leave the issue of provocation to the jury. The judge declined to do so because he took the view that the provocation was self-induced.

No doubt the judge thought that the defendant had only himself to blame. He had started it all one evening in a nightclub by abusing and threatening violence to the deceased and his girlfriend. The deceased reacted first by pouring a glass of beer over him and then by seizing him and pinning him to the wall. It was then that the defendant produced a knife and delivered one mortal blow. The jury rejected the defendant's claim that he acted in self defence and he was convicted of murder.

Substituting a conviction for manslaughter the Court of Appeal held that the issue of provocation should have been left to the jury. The court was referred to *Edwards v R* [1973] I All ER 152 in which the Privy Council had held that while a defendant could not rely on the predictable consequences of his own conduct as provocation, the defence of provocation would be available if the retaliation by the deceased was extreme. The court in *Johnson* evidently thought, and with respect rightly, that the law in *Edwards* was misstated. 'In view of the express wording of s 3 . . .', said the court, 'we find it impossible to accept that the mere fact that a defendant caused a reaction in others, which in turn led him to lose his self-control, should result in the issue of provocation being kept outside a jury's consideration . . . If there is any evidence that it may have done, the issue must be left to the jury. The jury would then have to consider all the circumstances of the incident, including all the relevant behaviour of the defendant, in deciding (a) whether he was in fact provoked and (b) whether the provocation was enough to make a reasonable man do what the defendant did.'

Murder and diminished responsibility

By s 2(1) of the Homicide Act 1957 the defence of diminished responsibility is available to a person charged with murder—

'if he was suffering from such abnormality of mind (whether arising from a condition of arrested or retarded development of mind or any inherent causes or induced by disease or injury) as substantially impaired his mental responsibility'

for the killing. For this purpose alcoholism may constitute a disease provided it has damaged the brain to an extent as to grossly impair the ability to make rational judgments and emotional responses. A killing attributable to alcoholism is one thing but a killing attributable to the taking of alcohol is quite another and a line must be drawn between the two though it may be a fine one in some cases. The taking of alcohol inevitably impairs judgment and the ability to control the emotions because of the effect it has on the brain but the transient effects of alcohol cannot be accounted a 'disease' within s 3.

In *R v Tandy* [1989] 1 All ER 267 the defendant was an alcoholic who normally consumed wine but before strangling her daughter during an episode of which she claimed to have no recollection, she had consumed most of a bottle of vodka. Upholding her conviction for murder the Court of Appeal held that the trial judge had correctly directed the jury on the requirements of the defence under s 3. The trial judge had instructed the jury that if they found that the defendant was suffering from an abnormality of mind in the form of grossly impaired judgment and emotional responses *and* if they found that she was so suffering as a consequence of a condition over which she had no immediate control, the defence was available. It was not enough that the choice whether to drink or not was not an easy one for the defendant to make; only if her condition made it impossible for her to resist her craving for alcohol was the defence available. The Court of Appeal approved the direction and, since there was evidence that the defendant could control her drinking, upheld her conviction for murder.

Manslaughter by unlawful act

In *R v Watson* [1989] 2 All ER 865 the defendant and a confederate broke into the victim's house with intent to steal. They woke up the victim, an 87 year-old man with a serious heart condition, and verbally abused him before leaving without taking anything. The police arrived and so did council workmen to board up the window and about an hour and a half after his encounter with the defendant the victim died as the result of a heart attack. The defendant was convicted of his manslaughter.

For unlawful act manslaughter the unlawful act must be such as all sober and reasonable people would inevitably realise would subject the victim to some harm, albeit not serious harm: *R v Church* [1965] 2 All ER 72, CA. On behalf of the defendant it was boldly argued that the unlawful act was completed at the moment of entry and since at that time the defendant knew nothing of the victim's age and condition, he could not be convicted of unlawful act manslaughter. Hardened readers of this Review will not fall off their seats in surprise when it is disclosed to them that the trial judge and the Court of Appeal found this argument less than compelling. The 'burglarious intrusion' was a continuing one and continued past the stage when the defendant was aware that the victim was old and frail.

A more substantial argument was that the trial judge had incorrectly ruled that it did not matter whether the cause of the victim's death, the heart attack, had been precipitated by either the conduct of the defendant or by the advent of the police and council workmen or both provided the advent of the latter was a natural consequence of the defendant's conduct. Not without hesitation the court quashed the defendant's conviction because the ruling withdrew from the jury's consideration whether it could be said that—

'as a matter of logic the burglary was the cause of the police arriving and of the necessity to board up the window and so for the arrival of the council workmen and so for the heart attack, whichever of the three matters may have been the precipitating event.'

Your reviewers share the court's hesitation. The most natural consequence of a burglary is to send for the police and the second most natural consequence is to restore the security of the premises. This would seem to have been a clear case for upholding the conviction by applying the proviso except, perhaps, for the fact that there was some medical evidence to the effect that the stress created by the defendant's conduct would have subsided within 20 minutes of the defendant's conduct. If so then the stress created by the defendant was no longer an operative cause of the heart attack. The jury should have been invited to consider this possibility; had they done so, and in view of countervailing medical evidence that the effects of the stress to the victim would have continued beyond the arrival of the police and the workmen, they might well have rejected it and concluded that the stress caused by the defendant was an operative cause of the victim's death. But this was a jury issue which should not have been withdrawn from them.

Threats to kill

By s 16 of the Offences against the Person Act 1861, as substituted by the Criminal Law Act 1977 it is an offence for a person without lawful excuse to make a threat to another, intending the other to fear it will be carried out, 'to kill that other or a third person'.

In *R v Tait* [1989] 3 All ER 682 the defendant threatened a woman five months pregnant that were she to inform on him to the police he would kill her baby. This might have been interpreted as a threat to kill the fetus in utero or a threat to kill the child when born but the jury was asked to consider the threat only in the former sense and was asked to consider whether they regarded the child in the womb as a third person. The jury evidently did and convicted the defendant.

Quashing the conviction the Court of Appeal was obviously anxious to make it clear that it was concerned only with the interpretation of s 16 and was making no general statement about the rights of the unborn child. But it was clear to the court that on the proper construction of s 16 a fetus could not be regarded as 'a third person'. It is not murder to kill a fetus at any stage of its development and the court was not disposed to assume that the 1861 Act allowed for any distinction between a non-viable and a viable fetus.

The court went on to consider what the position would be if the defendant's threat had been to kill the baby after birth. Where a child is born alive but dies of injuries inflicted by the defendant before birth, a conviction for murder or manslaughter may be sustained. The court thought, however, that s 16 did not extend to a threat made while the child was in the womb to kill that child after birth. The relevant time for this offence was the time of the threat and at that time it was not a 'third person'; otherwise the commission of the offence would turn upon whether or not the child was subsequently born alive.

Offences against property

Theft, deception and appropriation

There is clearly some overlap between the offences of theft under s 1 and deception under s 15 of the Theft Act 1968. The Criminal Law Revision Committee (CLRC) recognised this (*Eighth Report*, para 90) and expressed the view that it was not desirable to make them mutually exclusive. Indeed the Committee spent a considerable time (para 38) considering whether theft should be made to cover obtaining by what was then false pretences. In the end it decided not to do so partly because of the difficulties of definition and partly because, said the Committee, 'Obtaining by false pretences is ordinarily thought of as different from theft, because in the former the owner consents to part with his ownership . . .'

The extent of the overlap and the distinction (if any) between theft and deception has caused courts exercising criminal jurisdiction not a little trouble. In *Dobson v General Accident Fire and Life Assurance Corp plc* [1989] 3 All ER 927 the issue came before the Civil Division of the Court of Appeal. The plaintiff was insured with the defendants against loss by theft and it was accepted in the proceedings that 'theft' meant theft under the 1968 Act. The plaintiff had advertised a watch and a ring for sale at £5,950 and received a telephone call from someone, conveniently referred to as the rogue, who expressed interest.

The rogue called, expressed agreement to the asking price and, as agreed, made payment by a building society cheque and took delivery of the items. The cheque was dishonoured.

Obtaining goods by presenting a worthless cheque is about as straightforward and as common a case of obtaining by deception as it is possible to come across—but does the rogue also steal the goods? Not on the CLRC's view since 'the owner consents to part with his ownership' but the CLRC's view on the intended effect of ss 1 and 15, though it may be regarded as persuasive, is not decisive. The defendants argued that there could be no theft without an appropriation—this much was accepted—and there was no appropriation as defined by the House of Lords in *R v Morris* [1983] 3 All ER 288. It was there said that an appropriation 'involves not an act expressly or impliedly authorised by the owner but an act by way of adverse interference with or usurpation of' the rights of an owner. Since everything done by the rogue in relation to the goods was expressly authorised by the owner there could be no appropriation.

Had *Morris* been the only case in point it is respectfully submitted that this argument would have been unanswerable but the court was faced with the task (and it is one which has considerably exercised the minds of commentators) of accommodating the equally authoritative decision of the House in *Lawrence v Comr of Police for the Metropolis* [1971] 2 All ER 1253, a decision which was expressly approved in *Morris*. In *Lawrence* the defendant, a taxi driver, swindled his victim, a young Italian student with little knowledge of English, by indicating that the £1 which the student tendered for the fare was not enough and taking a further £6 from the wallet which the student held open. It was held that the defendant was properly convicted of theft. To an argument that the owner had consented Viscount Dilhorne said that s 1 was not to be read as though it contained the words 'without the consent of the owner' which were part of the former definition of larceny and apparently regarded it as crucial that ownership in the money had not passed to the defendant at the time when the appropriation took place; when the defendant placed his hands on the money in the wallet, the money still belonged to the student.

It is abundantly clear that in *Dobson* Parker and Bingham LJJ found it difficult, or impossible, to reconcile the decisions in *Lawrence* and *Morris* but were obliged to make the best of the difficulties. Indeed Parker LJ concluded by acknowledging that he might not be applying *Morris* but somehow he had to accommodate *Lawrence*. Both concluded that the rogue in *Dobson* had stolen the plaintiff's goods. Both decided that this was a case where property was intended to pass not when the contract was made but only upon delivery and at the moment of delivery the goods belonged to the plaintiff; at that stage the defendant dishonestly appropriated the goods with intent permanently to deprive and the elements of theft were accordingly satisfied. Neither was happy about, nor confident in, the conclusion they reached. Presumably Mr Dobson was the only one to leave the courtroom grinning from ear to ear.

A second case during the year which considered the meaning of appropriation was *R v Governor of Pentonville Prison, ex p Osman* [1989] 3 All ER 701, QBD, in which (a possible record) 117 cases were cited in the arguments, not all of them, fortunately, concerned with the law of theft.

The applicant's extradition was sought by Hong Kong on various charges. The applicant was chairman of a deposit-taking company, BMFL, and he was alleged to have conspired with others to have made loans above the authorised amounts to a group of companies, the Carrian group, receiving corrupt payments in return. One method employed by the applicant involved sending telex messages to a bank in the USA authorising it to transfer funds to the Carrian group's bank in the USA. For jurisdictional purposes it was necessary to determine whether the appropriation of the thing in action took place in Hong Kong or in the USA and that in turn depended upon whether the appropriation took place on the sending of the telex instructions or when the bank in the USA acted on those instructions by transferring the thing in action. Following *Morris*, where it was held that an appropriation involves assumption of *any* of the owner's rights, the court held that the appropriation was complete on the sending of the telex instructions. This conclusion was reinforced by *Chan Man-sin v A-G of Hong Kong* [1988] 1 All ER 1, PC, All ER Rev 1988 at 97, where it was held that the presentation of a cheque which the defendant is not authorised to draw is an assumption of a right of an owner and is accordingly an appropriation. The sending of a telex instruction without authority was equally an appropriation. This is so, and the appropriation is complete, whether or not the recipient acts on the cheque or the telex instruction and whether or not any loss is inflicted on the victim.

CRIMINAL PROCEDURE

Costs

Costs in criminal proceedings were the subject of a *Practice Note* [1989] 2 All ER 604. Its detailed provisions covering several disparate fields result in the withdrawal of a number of previous Practice Directions.

Extradition

See the article by I M Yeats below at 157.

Indictment

R v Bellman [1989] 1 All ER 22 raises a significant point of principle even if one that is likely to be encountered comparatively rarely. The defendant had obtained money by deception from individuals, the deception being that the money would be used to purchase drugs in the United States which would then be smuggled into Britain and sold at a vast profit. Although the defendant had gone with accomplices to Florida, supposedly to purchase drugs, none in fact materialised. The story which emerged from the evidence was that the bag of drugs had been stolen from the boot of a car before the parties left the United States. Two interpretations of these events were clearly possible. Either the whole trip had been an elaborate charade to deceive the victims of a fraud or it was an attempt to purchase drugs which had come to grief when they were stolen. The defendant accordingly found himself charged with several counts under s 15 of the Theft Act 1968. As an alternative to the deception charges the prosecution included in the indictment counts of conspiracy to evade the prohibition on the importation of controlled drugs contrary to s 170 of the Customs and Excise Management Act 1979. The Court of Appeal quashed the conviction on the s 15 charges but certified the question:

> 'Is it proper when an indictment contains mutually exclusive counts for both counts to be left to the jury for them to decide which, if either, count has been

proven, or should the prosecution be obliged to elect during the course of the trial upon which count they wish to proceed?'

'Mutually exclusive' in the question meant counts which were factually contradictory so that a conviction on one count necessarily involves an acquittal on the other count.

A unanimous House of Lords decided that it was permissible for such contradictory counts to be left to the jury provided evidence established a prima facie case on both sets of counts. It was then for the jury to make up their minds in the rare cases where this was an appropriate prosecution tactic.

At first sight there seems to be an unattractive logical flaw in this approach. How can the prosecution tell a jury that they should find something proved beyond reasonable doubt but qualify this by saying that, if they are not so persuaded, they are entitled to find on the same evidence that a contradictory account of events is proved instead? Nevertheless, as Professor Smith points out ([1989] Crim LR 302) such a result may not be as unreasonable as it sounds when the outcome of a case depends upon the jury's assessment of whether witnesses are telling the truth. It may simply depend upon which version of the stated facts the jury accepts. It would clearly be more difficult if it were a question of drawing inferences of fact which were diametrically opposed from an identical body of evidence.

In the present case it was crucial that it had been conceded in argument that there was at the close of the prosecution's evidence a prima facie case against the defendant both on the deception and conspiracy charges. Lord Griffiths put a simple but telling example of another type of case where this situation might arise. Suppose the police observe a drug pedlar handing over a packet of white powder to an addict who is seen to pay for it. They arrest the pedlar who claims that the packet only contained chalk powder but that he had told the addict it was heroin. If there is other evidence to support the belief that the packet might have contained drugs there would appear to be a prima facie case that the accused was guilty either of supplying a controlled drug or of obtaining by deception. In this case there was no objection in bringing alternative counts. Lord Griffiths conceded that in a case such as this the prosecution might fail to establish either charge. On the other hand, 'it seems . . . unlikely that, looking at the evidence as a whole, a jury would not feel able to be sure which was the true explanation of the transaction.' One might surmise that even if they were not sure, they would be unlikely to acquit.

This case does not have any impact on the principle exemplified in the old case of R v Richardson (1785) 1 Leach 387 and more recently raised in R v Lane (1985) 82 Cr App R 5 that if the evidence shows that one of two accused must have committed a crime but it is impossible to say which of them committed it, at least where one is entirely innocent, both must be acquitted. Nor does it touch the case where no prima facie case can be established to support either crime. As an illustration of such a dilemma the court referred to Tsang Ping-nam v R [1981] 1 WLR 1462. There a police officer made a statement implicating his colleagues on charges of corruption but gave evidence at their trial exonerating them. His appeal against conviction for attempting to pervert the course of justice was allowed by the Privy Council. The Crown's case had naturally been that either the defendant had committed perjury or had given false information to the investigating officers. Either way he was guilty of attempting to pervert the course of justice. The difficulty with this approach was that there was no evidence of corroboration of the perjury charge nor could it be affirmatively proved that the defendant had given false information to the investigating officer. In other words, the Crown could not establish a prima facie case on either count and, surprising though it might at first seem, it was not proper to leave counts to the jury to establish guilt where not even a prima facie case had been established.

Although Lord Griffiths thought it would be rare to join mutually contradictory counts in an indictment there is clearly an analogy with the long-established practice of charging counts of larceny and receiving as alternatives and to the present practice of charging robbery or theft and handling as alternatives in separate counts. Nothing in the present case casts any doubt on the correctness of that approach.

Rule 9 of the Indictment Rules 1971, which relates to the joinder of charges where, 'those charges are founded on the same facts, or form or are part of a series of offences of the same or a similar character', surfaced in last year's Review in the case of *R v Newland* [1988] 2 All ER 891 ([1988] All ER Rev at 103). The implications of that decision are evident in two decisions of the Court of Appeal in this year's Review.

In *R v Lombardi* [1989] 1 All ER 992 the defendant had been committed for trial by the magistrates on a number of offences under the Forgery and Counterfeiting Act 1981. There then appeared two indictments. The first related to the counterfeiting charges. The second indictment contained charges under the Bankruptcy Act 1914 in respect of which there was ample evidence before the justices but there had been no previous charge or committal. The submission on behalf of the defendant before the trial judge was that the second indictment did not comply with the provisions of the Administration of Justice (Miscellaneous Provisions) Act 1933. The Court of Appeal agreed and quashed the convictions under the second indictment. Rule 9 of the Indictment Rules meant that the bankruptcy charges could not simply be added to the indictment containing the counterfeiting charges and the decision in *Newland* emphasised that, even if this had been done, it is not possible to sever an indictment which is not itself valid. Section 2(2) of the 1933 Act and the proviso to that section was restrictive in its tenor and did not give the prosecution the power to prefer a fresh indictment. What this case suggests, as counsel for the defendant urged, is that the only way the prosecution could have legitimately proceeded on the fresh charges would have been to obtain a voluntary bill or else to charge the defendant and apply to have him committed for trial by the justices on those fresh charges.

A more striking example of an indictment which offended r 9 of the Indictment Rules would be harder to find than *R v Follett* [1989] 1 All ER 995. The solution adopted by the court was to allow the prosecution to prefer three further bills of indictment so that each indictment complied with r 9. All proceedings on the original indictment were stayed but it was neither quashed nor were any of the counts in the original indictment amended out of that indictment. The defendant was convicted on one of the three new indictments and appealed on the ground that the prosecution had no power to prefer a fresh series of indictments in order to cure an original indictment which was defective. Reliance was placed on the case of *R v Newland*. The Court of Appeal upheld the convictions and distinguished *Newland*.

That case is certainly authority for the proposition that an invalid indictment cannot be saved by severing the disparate sets of counts and trying each separately. It might be made good by deleting one set of counts and conducting the trial on the basis of what remained. Neither course was adopted in the present case. *Newland* states obiter, and the court confirmed the correctness of this dictum, that once one set of counts have been 'deleted' those counts cannot be the subject of a fresh indictment without the assistance of a voluntary bill. Crucially, in this case, the original indictment had only been stayed, not quashed, since the charges against the defendant were founded on facts or evidence upon which the magistrates had committed him for trial; s 2(2) of the 1933 Act was satisfied. Next, a *Practice Note* [1976] 2 All ER 326 issued by Lord Widgery made clear that there was nothing to prevent two indictments against the same person for the same offence being in existence at the same time, although of course the prosecution would ultimately have to elect on which one to proceed. The result was therefore that the course adopted by the trial court was one perfectly lawful way to deal with the difficulty. Had the original indictment been quashed before preferring a fresh indictment then it is clear that the only way of proceeding would have been by way of a voluntary bill. All of this indicates that, whilst the matter is somewhat complex, a scrupulous adherence to the correct technical steps can salvage an indictment which would otherwise fall foul of r 9. No doubt the simplest solution to the problem, as the court indicated in both *Newland* and the present case, is to have proper regard to the Indictment Rules in the first place.

As a footnote to the above, *Newland* was applied and *Follett* considered in the later case of *R v O'Reilly* [1989] Crim LR 652. What appears to have gone wrong in this case was that the court fell foul of the principle that an indictment which is defective because of a mis-joinder cannot be saved by severing the disparate counts and trying them separately.

Jury

1 Excusal from jury service

Whether adherence to a particular religious belief was capable of amounting to 'good reason' for being excused from jury service under s 9(2) of the Juries Act 1974 fell to be considered in *R v Crown Court at Guildford, ex p Siderfin* [1989] 3 All ER 7. Quite apart, however, from the particular grounds involved the court took the opportunity to give firm general guidance on how such claims should be approached.

The applicant for judicial review was a member of the Plymouth Brethren movement who believed that jury service was contrary to its cardinal tenets. When she was summoned for jury service she wrote to the appropriate officer at the court explaining her objections. On being refused excusal she appealed to the Crown Court, as she was entitled to do, for a hearing before the judge. Her request for an adjournment so that she could be legally represented was refused on the grounds that a request to be excused from jury service was not an appropriate case for legal representation. After a hearing the judge ruled against her application although he did intimate that the trial judge and counsel would be notified of her objections. The Divisional Court quashed the judge's decision and returned the matter to the Crown Court at Guildford for the appeal to be reheard before another judge.

In the view of the court the judge's handling of the situation had been less that satisfactory on several fronts. Whilst Watkins LJ was not persuaded that an applicant had a right to legal representation before the judge he nevertheless considered that there was a discretion to allow such representation. Accordingly the judge had misdirected himself in law on that issue. An application for an adjournment for legal representation where a conscientious objection to jury service is to be advanced should be approached 'most carefully and sympathetically'. The decision to inform the trial judge of what happened was, 'not . . . at all helpful' and it was best to leave it to the juror herself to reveal it at a later stage in her attempt to avoid service. What also weighed with the Divisional Court was that the judge seemed not to have appreciated that the juror's affidavit suggested she would perform her duties in isolation from the other jurors. In other words she would not participate in the usual discussion between jurors which is an integral part of the jury system. That point had been emphasised in the case of *R v Watson* [1988] 1 All ER 897 ([1988] All ER Rev at 104, which cites the relevant passage).

Two broader themes run throughout Watkin LJ's judgment. First, each case must be decided initially by the appropriate officer on its own merits. Membership of a particular faith or movement should not lead to automatic exemption followed by a referral to a judge. The judge's only proper involvement was at the appellate stage after the officer has reached an independent decision. Second, in deciding what amounts to a 'good reason' under s 9(2) of the Act regard must be had to the *Practice Note* [1988] 3 All ER 177 which states that whilst there is a general presumption that those not excused jury service as of right should be required to serve, applications for excusal 'should be dealt with sensitively and sympathetically'. Adherence to a religious belief by itself cannot be regarded as giving an unchallengeable right to excusal from service. It might, however, be a 'good reason' under the Act if such adherence meant that the juror would be unlikely to perform his duties as a juror in a proper way. Excusal is a personal matter and each application must be determined on its own facts.

2 Multi-racial jury

The central legal issue in *R v Ford* [1989] 3 All ER 445 may be simply stated but not so easily disposed of. Does a judge have the power to accede to an application that a black defendant be tried by a multi-racial jury? It is surprising that it has taken so long for the issue to reach an authoritative determination by an appellate court. Some judges in the past, as in *R v Frazer* [1987] Crim LR 418, had seemed to accept the principle that there should be black representation on a jury and were prepared to take some steps to bring this about. It now seems that this liberal trend must come to an end. Lord Lane's emphatic conclusion was that,

> 'however well intentioned the judge's motive might be, the judge has no power to influence the composition of the jury, and that it is wrong for him to attempt to do so.'

This was said to follow from s 5 of the Juries Act 1974 which makes the random selection of jurors a matter for the Lord Chancellor, not the judge. This principle applied not only to the empanelling of a particular jury but also where complaint is made that the panel is not truly random in that a particular minority group is under-represented by comparison with the area from which it is drawn. Only if the summoning officer has shown bias or impropriety would it be possible to challenge for cause. The court does not add that, as a practical matter, that would be very difficult to establish.

This particular difficulty has been considered more than once by the US Supreme Court. An original analytical tool which sheds light on this problem is revealed in Michael Finkelstein's article 'The Application of Statistical Decision Theory to the Jury Discrimination Cases' (1966) 80 Harvard LR 338. This claimed that in the well-known case of *Swain v Alabama* 13 L Ed 2d 759 (1965) the disproportionate under-representation of blacks could have resulted by chance only in one out of a 100 million trillion venires chosen from the population of Talladega County. It seems that this type of analysis must have commended itself to the court in *Whitus v Georgia* 17 L Ed 2d 599 (1967) where it was described as 'interesting' that, in finding a prima facie case of discrimination, the statistical probability under Finkelstein's analysis of the venire containing the number of blacks it did was 0.000006.

Those who experience racial discrimination outside the courts may well fear that such discrimination could be carried into the jury room. In addition, as Alan Dashwood stated in an article not adverted to by the court 'Juries In A Multi-Racial Society' [1972] Crim LR 85, 'The role of the jury in the process of adjudication presupposes a certain instinctual rapport with the accused which cannot be taken for granted in an increasingly heterogeneous society.' Moreover in the past English law seems to have taken a more generous view of the need to supply a jury of what could more readily be felt to be one's peers. In the case of an alien, trial was at one time available per medietatem linguae where half the jury was composed of members of the foreign community. At least until the passing of s 18 of the Juries Act 1949 there were also other less exotic 'special juries' which could be convened to hear cases where their peculiar qualifications might be thought to be particularly apt. At one time an attempt might have been made to produce a multi-racial jury by means of the peremptory challenge, but this option has disappeared with the passing of s 118 of the Criminal Justice Act 1988. Even this would not be so significant were it not for the fact that an English lawyer, unlike his opposite number in the United States, is severely limited on what he may ask a potential juror on the voir dire. An example of this in a racial context is the case of *R v Broderick* [1970] Crim LR 155. One does not necessarily need to embrace the total American experience, in which it can take days or weeks to empanel a jury, to allow that some relaxation in the English rules could sometimes be justified.

Any speculation as to how an English jury comes to its decision is inevitably based more on hunch that empirical testing, and s 8 of the Contempt of Court Act 1981 may help to ensure that this is long likely to be the case. Nevertheless, it might be granted that a jury with all of its preconceived notions does a better job than any individual might do in trying to assess fairly and impartially the evidence before it. As Lawton J observed in *R v Kray* (1969) 53 Cr App R 412 at 415, '. . . the drama, if I may use that term, of a trial almost always has the effect of excluding from recollection that which went before.' Even so, a prime requirement of justice is not only that it should be done but also that it should be seen to be done. This decision by the Court of Appeal will do nothing to alleviate feelings which may be shared by a significant number in the black community, and in other minority groups, that trial by jury is not the bastion of liberty which its proponents often claim.

Legal Aid

A *Practice Note* [1989] 2 All ER 479 concerns the provision of a two counsel order in the Crown Court.

Magistrates

1 Adjournment

There are many reasons for adjourning a case but they must rarely be as original as that found in *R v Walsall Justices, ex p W (a minor)* [1989] 3 All ER 460. The defendant was a juvenile charged with an assault contrary to s 20 of the Offences against The Person Act 1861. He had allegedly shot and wounded a 12-year-old boy. On the day fixed for the trial the prosecution found themselves in a difficulty. If the magistrates were to find, as they might, that the victim was too young to take the oath then s 38(1) of the Children and Young Persons Act 1933 required the child's evidence to be corroborated. No such evidence was available and if the trial were to take place that day the prosecution would offer no evidence so that the defendant would be acquitted. The prosecution then pointed out that the very next day s 34(1) of the Criminal Justice Act 1988 would come into force and abolish the 1933 Act's requirement of corroboration. Their difficulties would be over. The magistrates obligingly acceded to the prosecution's request for an adjournment. Was this a proper basis for an adjournment? The Divisional Court thought not, quashed the magistrates' decision and issued prohibition to prevent them from proceeding with the adjourned trial.

Saville J, giving the judgment of the court, commented that he found the opposing arguments finely balanced. At the end of the day what weighed with the court was that it was not for the magistrates to choose whether or not to apply the law in force depending upon their view of whether it would do proper justice. Having said that, the court seems to have left open the possibility that there may be cases where such an adjournment would be defensible. The present case was concerned with what the court regarded as a 'fundamental and mandatory rule of law'. It is faintly hinted that were it merely a question of 'procedural changes' different considerations might apply and there would then be nothing objectionable in a court adjourning matters to await such changes. Further litigation on this point might therefore be expected.

2 Bias

A point which is likely to be of some significance to licensing committees of magistrates was considered in *R v Bath Licensing Justices, ex p Cooper* [1989] 2 All ER 897. Although not concerned with criminal procedure it does touch upon issues of bias of a kind that might surface in any hearing before magistrates.

The applicants for judicial review had previously applied unsuccessfully to the local licensing justices on two occasions for a licence to sell spirits. After the second application they appealed to the Crown Court against the magistrates' refusal to extend their licence. On this occasion a member of the bench was one of the licensing justices who had dismissed the first application where the arguments were for all practical purposes the same. The Crown Court also dismissed the applicants' appeals and the applicants accordingly applied for judicial review. The grounds were that it was contrary to natural justice for the same licensing justice to have sat on both the first application and the appeal against the second application. In those circumstances justice could not be seen to be done.

The Divisional Court thought the case was near the borderline but granted the application. In effect, the court adopted the formulation, derived from *R v Liverpool City Justices, ex p Topping* [1983] 1 All ER 490 ([1983] All ER Rev at 160): would a reasonable and fair-minded person sitting in court and knowing all the relevant facts have a reasonable suspicion that a fair trial was not possible? There was no suggestion that there had been any bias or impropriety, only that there might be the appearance of it. Although suitably hedged with warnings that it was only a rough rule of thumb, Woolf LJ indicated that had the interval between the first application to the justices and the appeal to the Crown Court been 12 months or more the problem might not have arisen. By then the member of a licensing committee would have heard so many other applications that the facts of such an earlier hearing would no longer be materially present to his mind and would not give the impression that a fair hearing could not be obtained.

3 Civil liability

Although it does not relate directly to criminal procedure, the decision in *R v Manchester City Magistrates' Court, ex p Davies* [1989] 1 All ER 90 was noted in last year's Review ([1988] All ER Rev at 106). Since then the Lord Chancellor has announced his intention to bring forward legislation to give magistrates the same immunity from civil action as judges now enjoy. The same immunity will be applied to stipendiary magistrates and to justices' clerks when exercising the powers of a single justice.

4 Information

Rubin v DPP [1989] 2 All ER 241 is a case that deserves to be noted although its essential features can be briefly summarised. The defendant was charged with exceeding the speed limit, the information being preferred by the Thames Valley Police rather than a named person such as the chief constable. The defendant unsuccessfully contended that this invalidated the information. Watkins LJ took the view that even if the identity of the informant had been masked by the title used for him,

'Where . . . the erroneous title is given in an information, as here, to a person who has a right to prosecute and no one is misled as to the status of that person, such an error does not have the effect of rendering an information invalid. The paramount considerations are the authority to prosecute and the right to know the prosecutor. As to the former, there can in the present case be no doubt. As to the latter, it was clear that a police officer was prosecuting. All that was lacking was his easily ascertainable name.'

Part of the problem in this case seems to have been the use of computers for laying informations and the court took the opportunity to urge that modern technology should not be allowed to cause departure from what should be customary police practice, namely to lay informations by a named person.

Private prosecution

A cautionary tale for private prosecutors is told in *R v Ealing Magistrates' Court, ex p Dixon* [1989] 2 All ER 1050. Search warrants had been obtained by the police under s 21A(1) of the Copyright Act 1956 and were executed with effect at the defendants' premises. As a result they were charged at the police station with copyright offences, the charges being read out and the charge sheet signed by the custody officer. The charge sheet was also signed by the applicant for judicial review as the 'person charging'. The significance of this was that the applicant represented the Federation Against Copyright Theft Ltd (FACT) and the defendants were told that they were being charged on behalf of the Federation and that the police intended that the prosecution would be conducted by the Federation. A solicitor for the Federation was present to prosecute when the defendants were brought before the magistrates but the case against them was dismissed. Since the charges had been brought by the police and no information had been laid by or on behalf of the Federation the proper procedure for bringing a private prosecution had not been followed and the Federation's solicitor had therefore no standing as a prosecutor. The Divisional Court dismissed the application for judicial review of the magistrates' decision.

What in effect went wrong was that the police had complied with the provisions of ss 37 and 38 of the Police and Criminal Evidence Act 1984 in such a way as to inadvertently start a public prosecution. The charging of the defendants instituted proceedings under s 15(2) of the Prosecution of Offences Act 1985 with the result that under s 3(2) of the Act it became the duty of the Director of Public Prosecutions to take over conduct of the proceedings. Although the Director is empowered to appoint someone else to take over the conduct of the proceedings under s 5 of the Act this had not happened here. The police had no power to entrust anyone other than the Crown Prosecution Service with the conduct of the proceedings and the magistrates were accordingly correct to conclude that the solicitor for FACT was not entitled to conduct the committal proceedings.

Of course none of the above prevents the applicant in this situation from commencing a further prosecution. Woolf LJ even made the rather bold suggestion that if an oral application had been made to the justices for an information to be laid on behalf of the applicant, committal proceedings could have taken place after discontinuance of the existing proceedings. If correct, this seems a surprisingly simple expedient to avoid the difficulties in which the applicant found himself. A simpler solution would be of course to avoid such problems in the first place. In this regard counsel for the Director referred to an instruction issued to the Metropolitan Police which makes it clear that shoplifting cases, which frequently involve private prosecutions, would now be dealt with by the Crown Prosecution Service where the police decide to prosecute and if they decide not to prosecute the interested party should be referred to the magistrates' court to apply for process. A similar instruction would now be urgently considered in relation to copyright offences.

Trial

Compared to the United States, where the Sixth Amendment gives constitutional force to the right to effective assitance of counsel, English law seems to contain relatively few cases where the competence of counsel has received exhaustive consideration at the highest level. There is nothing to compare with the standards laid down by the US Supreme Court in *Strickland v Washington* 80 L Ed 2d 674 (1984) and *United States v Cronic* 80 L Ed 2d 657 (1984) after a detailed analysis of the problem. The test ultimately adopted in *Strickland* combines two components. First, the defendant must show that counsel's performance was deficient. Second, it must be shown that such performance prejudiced the defence. Nevertheless the court considered that some cases could be disposed of on the basis of lack of prejudice without inquiring into the first limb of the test. It also stressed that all the circumstances of the case had to be considered and it was not possible to apply rules in a mechanical fashion. The same defence tactic might, after all, prove brilliant in one case and a disaster in another. *Strickland* suggested, in effect, that there is a strong presumption that the challenged conduct by counsel might have been sound trial strategy and the defendant needs to make a colourable showing of innocence. The case of *R v Ensor* [1989] 2 All ER 586 points in rather the same direction in so far as it suggests that it is a plea where the defendant has a considerable burden to discharge to have any prospects of success.

Part of the appeal in *Ensor* which proved successful (see at 593), was based upon the judge's corroboration warning. The ground of appeal relying upon counsel's conduct of the trial was, however, rejected. The basis for this claim arose from the fact that the defendant faced two charges of rape based upon different incidents with different victims. It seems that the defendant made known his wish that the counts should be severed and it seems likely that such an application might have been granted. The Court of Appeal was also willing to assume for the sake of argument that if the indictment had been severed the defendant's chances of acquittal would have been improved. Nevertheless, the defendant's counsel, after apparently considering the matter carefully, declined to make any such application. He had come to the conclusion that the delay in complaint being made in the first charge of rape might well dispose a jury to acquit on that count. Since the evidence on the second count was, if anything, weaker they might well go on to acquit or both charges.

Lord Lane, giving the judgment of the court, cited with approval the words of Taylor J in *R v Gautam* (1987) *Times*, 4 March, when he said:

'. . . it should be clearly understood that if defending counsel in the course of his conduct of the case makes a decision, or takes a course which later appears to have been mistaken or unwise, that generally speaking has never been regarded as a proper ground for an appeal.'

This statement, it was held, should only be subject to the qualification made by O'Connor LJ in *R v Swain* [1988] Crim LR 109 (Note) that, if the court had any lurking doubt that the appellant might have suffered some injustice as a result of flagrantly incompetent advocacy by his advocate, then it would quash the conviction. In fairness to defence counsel it should be stated that there is more than a suggestion that the defendant may have tacitly accepted his counsel's advice to abandon the application for severance. Nevertheless, in any event, the appeal based upon counsel's conduct of the trial failed to reach the level of flagrant incompetence which it emerges is the correct test to apply. One might be justified in concluding that this is a standard which is both vague and intended to be highly restrictive.

SENTENCING

Attorney General's Reference (No 1 of 1989) [1989] 3 All ER 571 is noteworthy not least because it is the first reference made under s 36 of the Criminal Justice Act 1988. This provision gives the Court of Appeal power to increase a sentence thought to be too lenient, and the power was exercised on this occasion so as to double the length of the trial judge's sentence of three years imprisonment. Its more general significance is that it lays down helpful and comparatively detailed guidelines for dealing with cases on incest.

Where the girl is over 16 the sentence should range from a nominal penalty to three years imprisonment. Influencing factors would be the existence of force, degree of harm and corruption to the girl and the desirability of minimising family disruption. Where the girl is 13 to 16 the sentence range should be three to five years, or two to four on a guilty plea. Under 13 the sentence should be about six years if the girl was not far short of 13. Aggravating features, whatever the girl's age, included physical or psychological damage, the fact that incest occurred frequently over a long period, threats or violence, perverted behaviour, the fact that the girl was made pregnant and similar offences against other daughters. Mitigating features included a guilty plea, genuine affection for the victim, previous sexual experience on the part of the girl, deliberate attempts at seduction by the girl, and in rare cases the fact that a shorter term of imprisonment would benefit the victim and family.

This case is to be welcomed as another example of the 'guideline' cases although it does not necessarily follow that every reference under s 36 of the 1988 Act will be such a judgment. In effect, it might be said that this case does for the crime of incest what the earlier case of *R v Billam* [1986] 1 All ER 985 ([1986] All ER Rev at 123) did for sentencing in the case of rape.

Employment Law

IAN SMITH, MA, LLB
Barrister, Senior Lecturer in Law, University of East Anglia

The Transfer of Undertakings (Protection of Employment) Regulations 1981

Perhaps the most important decision reported this year in the area of employment law is that of the House of Lords in *Litster v Forth Dry Dock and Engineering Co Ltd* [1989] 1 All ER 1134, settling a fundamental point of interpretation of these difficult regulations. They were enacted to give effect to an EEC Directive and have proved troublesome ever since, partly because when enacted they were not integrated into existing employment law, but simply superimposed upon it. One major change was that by virtue of reg 5 (see *Harvey on Industrial Relations and Employment Law* VII [369] ff for the text of the regulations and commentary) where there is a relevant transfer of an undertaking, the contracts of employment of those employed by the transferor employer are *automatically* transferred to the transferee employer (whether either side wants that or not); this could be of particular importance to the employees where the old employer is insolvent, though it must be added that there have been cases where it has been the employees who were trying to show that the regulations did not apply, in order to be able to cash in their existing redundancy rights against the old employer and start afresh with the new employer. As always in this area, things are rarely straightforward.

For reg 5 to apply, however, the employees in question must have been employed 'immediately before' the transfer. Earlier case law (especially *Alphafield Ltd v Barratt* [1984] 3 All ER 795, EAT) held that this phrase meant that there could be a gap between a dismissal of the workforce and the actual transfer, and reg 5 would still apply. The attraction of this approach was that it prevented the employers from evading the regulation by the simple device of dismissing the workforce *before* the transfer—the transferee, for example, might want the plant but not the workforce (wanting to use some of his existing workers there) and so might oblige the transferor to dismiss the workforce a few days before the transfer (leaving them to pursue any rights, eg for redundancy payments, against the transferor, who might not be able to satisfy them). Under *Alphafield*, provided that the gap was of an acceptable length (whatever that might have been), that would not work. However, when the matter came before the Court of Appeal in *Secretary of State for Employment v Spence* [1986] 3 All ER 616 (see All ER Rev 1986, p 128) this approach was disapproved and 'immediately before' reconstrued to mean 'at the time of' the transfer, so that any gap would be fatal—the contract of employment must subsist at the very moment of transfer. In *Alphafield* a gap of two days had been permitted, but in *Spence* a gap of three hours (on the same day—dismissed at 11 am, undertaking transferred at 2 pm) was held to mean that reg 5 could not apply, and so the contracts were not transferred.

Although that was in fact what the employees wanted in that topsy-turvy case, the overall effect was to weaken employee protection and to permit the employer tactic of dismissal-in-advance-of-transfer.

The point arose again in *Litster*, where the facts once again showed the problem. The transferor was insolvent; the receivers agreed to sell the assets of the company to the transferor who did not want the workforce (wishing to use other workers instead who were prepared to accept lower wages). At 3.30 pm the receivers dismissed the workforce with immediate effect and at 4.30 pm on the same day the transfer was effected. The dismissed employees sought to claim unfair dismissal against the new owners (the old ones being insolvent). According to *Spence* this should not have been possible, but the House of Lords held that it was. The reasoning is slightly complicated. *Spence* is *not* overruled and *Alphafield* is still wrong, on the meaning of 'immediately before', so that a gap is still not permissible under reg 5 itself. *However* shortly before the appeal in *Litster*, the ECJ had decided *P Bork International A/S (in liq) v Foreningen af Arbejdsledere i Danmark* Case 101/87 [1989] IRLR 41 in which it was held (under the equivalent provisions of the original directive) that an approach akin to that in *Spence* was too narrow—the directive also contains a provision (found in the UK regulations in reg 8) rendering a dismissal ineffective if it is because of the transfer (unless it comes under the special defence of being for 'an economic, technical or organisational reason'). This provision should be wide enough to prevent easy evasion of the automatic transfer of contracts by the simple device of a prior dismissal. Lord Oliver, giving the principal speech in the House of Lords in *Litster* held that the domestic regulations must now be interpreted to put that policy into effect (citing *Pickstone v Freemans plc* [1988] 2 All ER 803, HL, see All ER Rev 1988 p 114, as authority for a more flexible and purposive approach to interpretation when construing legislation designed to give effect to EEC obligations).

This is achieved by reading reg 5 *in the light of reg 8*—if a dismissal is unfair under reg 8 (as it frequently will be in these cases), then for the purposes of reg 5 the employee is *deemed* still to be in the transferor's employment at the time of the transfer, so that reg 5 bites and legal liabilities to the employee are automatically transferred to the transferee employer. The potential problem that reg 8 (unlike the relevant Directive article) only states expressly that the dismissal is unfair (not that it is 'ineffective') is avoided by the above-mentioned purposive interpretation and by the implication into reg 5(3), after the words 'immediately before the transfer', of the words 'or would have been so employed if he had not been unfairly dismissed in the circumstances described in regulation 8(1)'. Thus, although *Spence* was right in its reasoning, that reasoning did not go far enough, and the potential gap of 'prior dismissal' has been effectively closed by this interesting decision of the House of Lords.

Duties of confidence, restraint of trade and injunctions

The reports this year contain four cases concerning the ever-important common law area of restraint of trade or, in the absence of an express restraint clause in the contract, the general implied duty of confidentiality on the part of an employee. Three cases concern important points on the enforcement of such duties, two of them showing circumstances where an injunction might *not* be granted and the third showing concern by the court at attempts by employers to extend other forms of relief into this area. The fourth case is an important decision on the topical subject of 'garden leave' clauses, meant to 'neutralise' an executive after he or she leaves employment simply so that their expertise and abilities cannot be used by a competitor.

In *Warren v Mendy* [1989] 3 All ER 103, CA the plaintiff was a boxing manager who contracted with B, a boxer, to have exclusive rights of management over him. Within a short period of time, B became disillusioned and asked the defendant to act as his agent. The plaintiff sought interlocutory injunctions against the defendant (a) restraining him from inducing a breach of contract between the plaintiff and B and (b) restraining him from acting as B's manager. Although the plaintiff may have had a good cause of action, the question arose whether the injunctions were a proper remedy. The trial judge considered whether on the facts the effect of the injunctions would be to compel B to carry out his contract with the plaintiff, and held that it would. On that ground, the judge refused the injunctions, and the Court of Appeal held that he was correct to do so. They reaffirmed the rule that a court should normally refuse injunctive relief if the effect would be to compel performance of a contract for personal services. That was particularly the case here, since the relationship between a boxer and his manager is an especially close one with a high degree of mutual and fiduciary trust (know what I mean, 'Arry?).

The point at issue in *Re a company's application* [1989] 2 All ER 248, ChD was rather different—on ordinary principles there *was* a good case for an injunction, *but* the question arose as to whether at least some disclosure was warranted in the public interest. The defendant had been employed by the plaintiff company, a provider of financial services, but had been dismissed. During horse trading over dismissal compensation, the defendant alleged against the company irregularities that would be of interest to FIMBRA (the Financial Intermediaries, Managers and Brokers Regulatory Association) and the Inland Revenue. The plaintiffs sought to prevent any such disclosure by him, obtaining an *Anton Piller* order (see below) and an ex parte interlocutory injunction restraining any disclosure of confidential documents. However, at the subsequent inter partes hearing Scott J varied the terms of the injunction—the defendant was under a general duty of confidentiality and so an injunction was appropriate *but* it would *not* apply to disclosure to FIMBRA or the Inland Revenue—such disclosure could be in the public interest, even in a case where it was being alleged by the employer that the disclosure was being threatened maliciously and/or in order to achieve a better settlement of other claims. In his judgment, Scott J only refers for authority to the Spycatcher case (*A-G v Guardian Newspapers Ltd (No 2)* [1988] 3 All ER 545, see All ER Rev 1988, p 55), but the approach in this case may be seen as consistent with that in other employment-related cases, especially *Initial Services Ltd v Putterill* [1967] 3 All ER 145, CA (see Smith and Wood *Industrial Law* (4th edn 1989) at p 70).

The facts of *Lock International plc v Beswick* [1989] 3 All ER 373, Ch D show a classic action based on breach of the duty of fidelity, but its interest lies in the plaintiff's application for an *Anton Piller* order to obtain evidence of the breach. The first eight defendants were ex-employees of the plaintiff company (which manufactures metal detectors); they had left to set up a new company (the ninth defendant), manufacturing metal detectors in competition with the plaintiff company. The latter claimed that they were misusing trade secrets and confidential information. They applied for and were granted an ex parte *Anton Piller* order, allowing them to search the other company's premises and the houses of three of the ex-employees, as a result of which large quantities of papers, drawings, computer records and prototypes were removed and inspected by the plaintiff's employees. On an application to the court, Hoffmann J however discharged the order, stating that it was unnecessary and should never have been made; moreover, following the views of Scott J in *Columbia Picture Industries Inc v Robinson* [1986] 3 All ER 338, Ch D that *Anton Piller* orders have been granted in the past too readily, he said that such applications in actions for breach of the duty of fidelity should be approached with 'a certain initial scepticism'. This is because some employers view the very fact of new competition from an ex-employee as evidence of dishonesty (whereas that is far from the case in law), and may seek to use an oppressive *Anton Piller* order as a way of nipping such competition in the bud.

As stated above, the decision in *Provident Financial Group plc v Hayward* [1989] 3 All ER 298, CA concerns what is known in the current jargon as a 'garden leave' clause in a contract of employment, and its legal enforceability. Such a clause may provide that during a period of notice of dismissal (or, indeed, during a period of suspension of duties) the employee shall not work for any competitor etc, but shall instead continue to receive his wages from the employer. In the case of a key executive, the notice period could be lengthy, and so such a clause allows the employer to 'neutralise' him and require him to spend the time in question tending his garden. Clearly, if the employee is in possession of confidential information and is intending to join a major trade rival straight away, the courts may restrain such a move, either by restraining the divulgence of such information or, more generally, by preventing him entering the new employment during his contractual notice period (provided the employer continues to pay him during that period); the latter can be seen from the decision of the Court of Appeal in *Evening Standard Co Ltd v Henderson* [1987] IRLR 64 where a senior production manager on a newspaper was restrained from working for a rival during the currency of his year's notice, on the basis that the employer was prepared to continue payment throughout the period—this was not a case where the enforcement of a negative, anti-competition clause would mean that the employee must continue working for the employer or starve. The interest in the case was, however, that eventually it was decided that the employee was not in possession of confidential information as such, and so the question arose whether mere use of the employee's expertise could be restrained during the notice period. On the facts it was held that it could, but Lawton LJ said that the whole matter needed reconsideration. This has now happened in *Hayward*. The employee, a financial director, gave six months notice to leave his employers. After two months, the employers said that they did not want him to work the rest of the notice and paid him for it, on the basis that he would not work for anyone else during the period (the contract itself containing a clause against competition during employment). The employee then proposed to start employment with another estate agent after a month and the employers sought an injunction to stop him. It was refused by the judge at first instance, and that refusal was upheld by the Court of Appeal. It is made clear in the principal judgment of Dillon LJ that the granting of relief in such a case remains in the discretion of the court—it is not enough simply to point to a wide, anti-competition clause in the contract and claim that it has been broken. In order to decide whether to give injunctive relief, the court will need to examine whether the new employment proposed by the employee would indeed materially and adversely affect the old employer's business. If not, the court will not prevent the new employment. If, however, there would be such an effect, then the court may well grant an injunction (on whatever terms it considers appropriate) either on the basis of an anti-competition ('garden leave') clause in the contract, or under the court's general powers to restrain breaches of the duty of good faith by an employee (especially where the employee could genuinely be said to be in possession of misusable confidential information). In this case, however, there was no evidence of the possession of such information to any significant degree, nor was there the prospect of serious damage to the employer in the ten weeks left to run of the notice period, and so the judge was correct to refuse the interlocutory injunction. This does not, of course, mean that there would be no action for damages against an employee who pockets the money and then takes employment in breach of a clause in his contract, but in practice it is the injunction that is the desired remedy, and this case gives important guidance on the principles to be applied to that remedy.

Equal pay—man in the same employment

The decision of the House of Lords in *Leverton v Clwyd County Council* [1989] 1 All ER 78 settled an important point on comparability under the Equal Pay Act 1970, and reversed what could have been a very unfortunate majority decision of the Court of Appeal. The claim was one for 'equal value', but this point of interpretation applies to any form of equality claim where the applicant and the male comparator work at different establishments. In that case, s 1(6) of the Act provides:

> '. . . [M]en shall be treated as in the same employment with a woman, if they are men employed by her employer . . . at the same establishment or at establishments in Great Britain which include that one and at which common terms and conditions of employment are observed either generally or for employees of the relevant class.'

The applicant, a woman, was employed by the council as a nursery nurse, earning £5,058 pa for a 32-hour week and working only during school terms. She claimed 'equal value' with male council employees in other establishments on other work who earned £6,081 to £6,532 pa, but who worked longer hours and had less holidays; in fact, in *hourly rate* terms, there was no substantial difference between her pay and theirs. Both she and the male comparators in the other establishments were employed under the same collective agreement for local authority administrative, professional, technical and clerical staff. The majority of the Court of Appeal held that she and they were *not* employed in the same employment, within s 1(6), because their terms and conditions (especially relating to hours and holidays) were significantly different; in effect, however, this was not just a serious threat to the scheme of the Act but also a self-fulfilling prophesy, for it was just those differences (leading, arguably, to a difference in pay) that the applicant was complaining about. The House of Lords, approving May LJ's dissenting judgment, held that where the terms and conditions for the various types and grades of employees at different establishments were governed by the same collective agreement, there were common terms and conditions within s 1(6), and so the relevant comparisons could be made.

However, this case has a sting in the tail, and an instructive one. The above ruling meant that an equality claim could be brought, but in this case it failed because the House of Lords accepts that the employers had made out the defence under s 1(3) of 'genuine material factor' other than sex, genuinely accounting for the difference in annual salaries, that factor being the substantial differences in hours and holidays producing at the end of the day an effectively similar hourly rate. This application of the s 1(3) defence follows the leading case of *Rainey v Greater Glasgow Health Board* [1987] 1 All ER 65, HL (see All ER Rev 1987 p 104), and can also be seen in the speech of Lord Goff in *Hayward v Cammell Laird Shipbuilders Ltd* [1988] 2 All ER 257, HL (see All ER Rev 1988 p 114); it gives considerable ammunition to an employer resisting an equal pay claim (particularly on the basis of equal value) because he says that there are no economically sound grounds for it.

Discrimination—application and meaning

Of the three sex and race discrimination cases reported this year, two are not concerned with employment, but rather with the provision of services. However, it will be recalled that both discrimination statutes start off with common provisions on definition and application, and so these cases are also of interest in the employment field.

With regard to the application of the race legislation, it was held in *Commission for Racial Equality v Dutton* [1989] 1 All ER 306, CA that gipsies were capable of being a separate 'racial group' under s 3(1) of the Race Relations Act 1976, on the basis of their remaining an identifiable group with common 'ethnic origins', the word 'ethnic' not being used in the statute 'in a strictly biological or racial sense' (per Nicholls LJ at 314): *Mandla v Dowell Lee* [1983] 1 All ER 1062, HL applied. Thus, where a publican put up a notice saying; 'Sorry, no travellers', that was capable of being indirect racial discrimination (since it affected gipsies in particular), unless it could be shown to be justified under s 1(1)(*b*); the case was remitted to the county court to determine that question of justification of the facts. In a more specialised context, it was held in *Sheikh v Chief Constable of Greater Manchester Police* [1989] 2 All ER 684, CA that a special constable comes within the protection of the Race Relations Act 1976, s 4 (discrimination in employment), *not* because he satisfies the normal definition of an 'employee', but because s 16 deems to be in employment a person 'holding the office of constable'. After an examination of the Police Act 1964 and related legislation, the Court of Appeal (reversing the EAT) held that that phrase *does* cover a special constable.

Turning to the definition of discrimination, most of the modern case law on sex discrimination tends to concern the somewhat protean head of indirect discrimination (with its possibility of justification). However, cases occasionally still arise on the meaning of straightforward (?) direct discrimination. *James v Eastleigh Borough Council* [1989] 2 All ER 914, CA is one such case. It arose from facts that could be considered petty, but raises a basic point. The plaintiff (a man) objected to having to pay 75p to use a swimming pool when his wife of the same age (61) could enter free. This was because of council policy, which was to admit free those 'who have reached the state pension age' of 65 for a man and 60 for a woman. At 61, he was in fact retired, but of course was not over 65. With the aid of the EOC, he complained to the county court of direct discrimination. This is, of course, not an employment discrimination case, but the definition of discrimination is common to all areas.

It appears to be settled that there is no need under s 1(1)(a) of the Sex Discrimination Act 1975 (or s 1(1)(a) of the Race Relations Act 1976) to prove an intention to discriminate, still less a motive to do so: *Equal Opportunities Commission v Birmingham City Council* [1989] 1 All ER 769, HL. However, in the instant case the Court of Appeal held that the plaintiff had *not* been discriminated against on the grounds of sex, not because of any involved arguments relating to retirement ages and EEC law, but rather on the fundamental ground that there was actually no discrimination at all under s 1(1)(a). Browne-Wilkinson V-C explained it thus—there is only discrimination 'on the ground of' sex where, subjectively, the defendant has treated the plaintiff less favourably because of his or her sex; the court or tribunal, therefore, has to look at the reason why the defendant treated the plaintiff less favourably, not merely at whether there is a causative link between the defendant's behaviour and the detriment to the plaintiff. On the facts of the case, the council's reason for giving free swimming to persons over pensionable age was to aid the needy, not to give preference to one sex over the other. The Vice-Chancellor explained that this approach does not contravene the views of the House of Lords in the *Equal Opportunities Commission* case and does not mean that an intention to discriminate now becomes necessary:

> 'In my judgement there is a clear distinction between the ground or reason for which a person acts and his intention in so acting' (at p 919).

However, at least one leading commentator has taken a radically different view, arguing that such an approach does bring in questions of motive and could have 'potentially disastrous ramifications for discrimination law'. It is possible that this case may go on further appeal.

Industrial disputes—tortious liability

As pointed out in the final paragraph of last year's chapter (All ER Rev 1988 p 121), the fact that the government keeps altering the trade disputes legislation to increase the categories of case where the statutory immunities in the Trade Union and Labour Relations Act 1976, s 13 do *not* apply (most recently in the Employment Bill 1990, before Parliament at the time of writing) has meant some renewed interest in the basic definitions of the specific torts that may be committed by a union when taking industrial action; this is because if a union is deprived of the immunity, its only hope of avoiding an injunction is to show that no tort has been committed in the first place. Guidance on this has come this year in three reported cases (the first two in commercial contexts, but applicable in principle to trade dispute cases).

First, the problem of whether there is a defence of justification to the tort of conspiracy by unlawful means appears to have been resolved in the affirmative by the Court of Appeal in *Metall und Rohstoff AG v Donaldson Lufkin & Jenrette Inc* [1989] 3 All ER 14—they reversed Gatehouse J's decision and held (approving the judgment of Hirst J in *Allied Arab Bank Ltd v Hajjar (No 2)* [1988] 3 All ER 103) that the speech of Lord Diplock in *Lonrho Ltd v Shell Petroleum Co Ltd* [1981] 2 All ER 456, HL *was* to be read as making a change to the pre-existing 'anomalous' tort of conspiracy, so that in *all* of its forms the plaintiff had to show that the sole or predominant purpose of the defendant's agreement was to injure him or his interests; putting this the other way around, it meant that it is open to the defendants to plead justification (usually the prosecution of their own independent interests), where it is alleged that unlawful means have been used. Secondly, however, in *Lonrho plc v Fayed* [1989] 2 All ER 65, the Court of Appeal held that a similar rule does not apply to the entirely separate tort of wrongful interference with trade or business. As Woolf LJ pointed out, this tort is still of uncertain ambit, but its existence is now beyond doubt. While it is necessary for the plaintiff to show that the wrongful act in question was directed against him or was intended to harm him, it was held that he does *not* have to go further and show that the defendant's predominant purpose was to injure him, rather than to further his own interests; to hold otherwise would be to confuse this tort with that of conspiracy, whereas in *Lonrho Ltd v Shell Petroleum Co Ltd* (above), Lord Diplock had treated them as entirely separate. Although the leading judgment was by Dillon LJ, the following passage from Woolf LJ at p 73 is of use:

> 'So far as conspiracy is concerned, there is good reason for requiring that predominant intent should be an ingredient of the tort. Great difficulty would, in my view, arise if a requirement of predominant intent to injure were to be introduced into [unlawful interference]. This tort is not based on any agreement, but interference, and frequently it will be fully appreciated by a defendant that a course of conduct that he is embarking on will have a particular consequence to a plaintiff, and the defendant will have decided to pursue that course of conduct knowing what the consequence will be. Albeit that he may have no desire to bring about that consequence in order to achieve what he regards as his ultimate ends, from the point of view of the plaintiff, whatever the motive of the defendant, the damage which he suffers will be the same. If a defendant has deliberately embarked on a course of conduct, the probable consequence of which on the plaintiff he appreciated, I do not see why the plaintiff should not be compensated'.

Thirdly, in a newsworthy decision at the time (set against the backdrop of the impending abolition of the dock labour scheme by the Dock Work Act 1989), the House of Lords discharged an injunction based on the even more uncertain tort of inducement to breach of statutory duty, in *Associated British Ports v Transport and General Workers Union* [1989] 3 All ER 822. However, their decision was based on a narrow (but vital) point. The employers were seeking an interlocutory injunction on the grounds that it was arguable that the strike call would constitute either interference with business by the unlawful means of inducing breach of statutory duty by the dockworkers or a separate tort of inducement to breach of statutory duty. This all hinged on a construction of the Dock Labour Scheme, clause 8(5)(b) (that dockers should 'work for such periods as are reasonable'), that it constituted a definite statutory duty, the inducement of a breach of which could have the above tortious results (which lay outside the protection of the Trade Union and Labour Relations Act 1974, s 13(1)). Lord Goff, giving the principal speech, said that clause 8 could not be so construed—it merely regulated the hours that a dockworker was contractually obliged to work; breach of it, therefore, only amounted to breach of contract by the dockers and so the union would only be guilty of inducement to breach of contract which *is* covered by the Trade Union and Labour Relations Act 1974, s 13. There was, therefore, no arguable basis for the injunction, which was discharged. In the light of this finding, Lord Goff stated that it was not necessary for the House of Lords to examine the ambit of the torts invoked by the employers which, therefore, remain, as they have always been, a grey area awaiting clarification at the highest level. It is true that there are interesting observations on these points in the decision of the Court of Appeal (reported at [1989] 3 All ER 796) *but*, while any guidance in this area is welcome, it must be remembered that it has recently been held that (on general grounds of stare decisis) if the House of Lords decide an appeal on grounds different from those relied upon by the Court of Appeal and (as here) express no views as to the soundness or otherwise of the Court of Appeal's reasoning, then that decision of the Court of Appeal has little or no precedent value: *R v Secretary of State for the Home Department, ex p Al-Mehdawi* [1989] 1 All ER 777, CA.

Industrial disputes—picketing 'at or near the place of work'

When the picketing immunity in the Trade Union and Labour Relations Act 1974, s 15 was amended by the Employment Act 1980, inter alia so that picketing is only lawful if 'at or near his own place of work', it was a deliberate attempt to narrow the immunity and circumscribe picketing more closely. The case law since then has shown the effectiveness of this, with some fairly narrow and literal decisions (for example banning picketing altogether outside an employer's new place of work when the old, dismissed workforce had not worked there at all, a factor of some importance in the News International dispute with the newspaper's move to Wapping, see *News Group Newspapers Ltd v SOGAT' 82* [1986] IRLR 337, QBD and, on slightly different facts, *Union Traffic Ltd v Transport and General Workers' Union* [1989] IRLR 127, CA). However, the decision of the Court of Appeal in *Rayware Ltd v Transport and General Workers' Union* [1989] 3 All ER 583 shows a rather more purposive and, arguably, realistic approach to the problems faced by pickets under s 15.

The employers leased a site on a trading estate, 0.7 miles from the road entrance to the estate. During the course of a trade dispute, the union set up a picket line at the estate entrance. In order for it to be lawful, the picketing had to be 'at or near' the place of work. The judge at first instance, granting an injunction, applied a geographical test, holding that to be 'at or near' the picketing had to be within sight or sound of the employer's premises. However, the Court of Appeal (allowing the union's appeal) held that this was too restrictive a view; the phrase 'at or near' was not a term of art, but rather had to be construed in a realistic sense. Counsel for the union had pointed out that the rest of the trading estate was private property and so the entrance was the closest point at which a picket could be organised without trespassing. Both May LJ and Nourse LJ state that s 15 was not to be construed in a way that would make it impractible to picket lawfully at all in a case such as this. On the facts, this picketing was 'at or near' the place of work, and so within the protection of the section.

Health and safety at work—meaning of 'process'

In the All ER Rev 1987 at p 108 there was considered the case of *R v AI Industrial Products plc* [1987] 2 All ER 368 in which the Court of Appeal held that a single operation (in that case, the demolition of a kiln) could not in itself constitute a 'process'. That case concerned the Asbestos Regulations 1969, but the point was made there that the decision would apply equally under the Factories Act 1961, where the word appears in the definition of a factory, and which gave the vires for many such regulations. This point has arisen now before the House of Lords in *Nurse v Morganite Crucible Ltd* [1989] 1 All ER 113, in which *R v AI Products plc* has been overruled. The facts again concerned asbestos, this time escaping when the defendant company's employees were demolishing certain brickdriers, parts of which contained the asbestos. The company were prosecuted under the Factories Act 1961, s 155 for breach of the Asbestos Regulations, but argued that this one-off demolition job was not a 'process' for the purposes of the legislation. The Divisional Court reluctantly agreed, being bound by the previous Court of Appeal decision, but the House of Lords allowed the prosecutor's appeal—the word 'process' should be construed broadly to cover any operation or activity of more than minimal duration, which involves some degree of continuity or repetition of a series of acts. Here, the demolition had taken about nine days and so it *was* a process involving materials containing asbestos, so that the relevant regulations were applicable.

Health and safety at work—duties to another's employees

Sections 2 and 3 of the Health and Safety at Work Act 1974 lay down broad general duties on employers and the self-employed to secure reasonable safety for their employees, and persons other than their employees but nevertheless affected by their undertakings. Section 4 then goes on to impose rather more specific duties on 'persons concerned with premises to persons other than their employees'. This is particularly relevant where an employer/occupier brings in an outside contractor and/or his employees to work on the premises—the contractor will be liable in the ordinary way to secure the health and safety of his own employees, but the occupier may also be liable in certain circumstances for any breaches of health and safety to that contractor's employees—by virtue of s 4(2) the occupier must:

> '. . . take such measures as it is reasonable for a person in his position to take to ensure, so far as is reasonably practicable, that the premises, all means of access thereto or egress therefrom . . . and any plant or substance in the premises or, as the case may be, provided for use there, is or are safe and without risks to health.'

Clearly there is potentially a difficult balance to strike here—certain duties must be placed on the occupier, but at the same time the very reason for engaging the contractor may have been to use the latter's resources, skills etc and to rely on that delegation. In *Mailer v Austin Rover Group plc* [1989] 2 All ER 1087, HL the company had engaged a contractor to clean a spray painting booth which contained highly flammable material; a flash fire occurred in the sump under the booth, leading to the death of one of the contractor's employees. The contractor was prosecuted and convicted of failing to provide a safe system of work for his employees. The question in the case was whether the company was also liable under s 4. Lord Jauncey held that under that section the prosecution had to prove (1) that premises made available for use by others were unsafe and constituted a risk to health, (2) that the defendant had a degree of control over those premises and (3) that, having regard to the degree of control and his knowledge of the likely use, it would have been reasonable for the defendant to have taken measures to secure safety or lack of risk to health; once these have been shown, the onus shifts to the defendant to show that it was not reasonably practicable to take those measures (which will involve the usual balancing operation, setting off the risk to safety or health against the practicability, including cost, of taking those measures). On the facts of the case, there had been unanticipated misuse of the premises by the contractor's employees ('. . . a number of events took place which should not have taken place if [the contractors] or their servants had acted as they should have done in accordance with the contract or their instructions', per Lord Jauncey at 1099) and so it was not reasonable for the company to have taken measures to prevent such misuse; the inspector's appeal against the Divisional Court's decision that the company were not in breach of s 4 was dismissed.

European Community Law

CHRISTOPHER GREENWOOD, MA, LLB
Barrister, Fellow of Magdalene College, Cambridge

Relationship of Community law and English law: supremacy

In last year's Review, it was suggested (at p 122) that the English courts had yet to provide a clear answer to the question how they would deal with a conflict between a directly effective rule of European Community law and a subsequent Act of Parliament. Two decisions of the House of Lords during 1989—*Litster v Forth Dry Dock and Engineering Co Ltd* [1989] 1 All ER 1134 and *Factortame Ltd v Secretary of State for Transport* [1989] 2 All ER 692—show the courts edging towards a resolution of this problem.

The Court of Justice of the European Communities has repeatedly held that national courts are under a duty to accord priority to directly effective Community law (ie those provisions of Community law which confer rights or impose obligations directly upon individuals) over inconsistent national laws. According to the Court of Justice, Community law is supreme whether the national legislation was enacted before or after the Community law in question and irrespective of the status of the national legislation within the national legal system (see, in particular, Case 106/77 *Simmenthal (No 2)* [1978] ECR 629 and Case 11/70 *Internationale Handelsgesellschaft* [1970] ECR 1125). The Court of Justice has also held that it is the duty of the national courts to ensure that rights derived from Community law are effectively protected.

When the United Kingdom joined the European Communities, Parliament sought to accommodate the Community law principle of direct effect by enacting s 2(1) of the European Communities Act 1972:

> 'All such rights, powers, liabilities, obligations and restrictions from time to time created or arising by or under the Treaties, and all such remedies and procedures from time to time provided for by or under the Treaties, as in accordance with the Treaties are without further enactment to be given legal effect or used in the United Kingdom [ie all directly effective provisions of Community law] shall be recognized and available in law, and be enforced, followed and allowed accordingly . . .'

The supremacy of Community law over national legislation was dealt with in more circumspect fashion (perhaps because of the controversy surrounding this subject at a time when the British Government was having difficulty getting a majority in the House of Commons for United Kingdom membership of the Communities). Section 2(4) provides that:

> '. . . any enactment passed or to be passed, other than one contained in this Part of this Act, shall be construed and have effect subject to the foregoing provisions of this section.'

Since the 'foregoing provisions of this section' include s 2(1), s 2(4) appears to provide that all Acts of Parliament are to be construed and take effect subject to the directly effective provisions of Community law which the English courts are required to enforce under s 2(1).

The problem with this approach is that it is apparently incompatible with the more extreme version of the doctrine of Parliamentary sovereignty, according to which the one limitation upon the powers of Parliament is that it can in no way bind its successors. The Court of Appeal in *Ellen Street Estates Ltd v Minister of Health* [1934] 1 KB 590 stated (albeit obiter) that this principle even precluded the entrenchment of legislation against implied or inadvertent repeal; a court must, it said, give effect to the intention of Parliament as expressed in the latest piece of legislation before it, irrespective of any provisions in earlier legislation. If this dictum does indeed represent the law, then s 2(4) of the European Communities Act 1972 has no greater force than any other statutory provision and cannot bind an English court to give priority to a provision of Community law over the clear words of an Act of Parliament passed subsequent to the entry into force of the Community provision.

In most cases the problem will not arise, because the words used in the Act of Parliament will not be so totally free of ambiguity that a court cannot interpret them in such a way as to reconcile the British statute with the prior provisions of Community law. That was the approach recommended by Lord Diplock in *Garland v British Rail Engineering Ltd* [1982] 2 All ER 402 and followed by the House of Lords in *Pickstone v Freemans plc* [1988] 2 All ER 803 (noted in All ER Review 1988, p 127). The English courts have always been somewhat coy, however, about what they would do if an Act of Parliament was so worded that it could not be reconciled with prior directly effective Community law by a process of interpretation, although Lord Denning MR in *Macarthys Ltd v Smith* [1979] 3 All ER 325 suggested (obiter) that in such circumstances the English courts would give priority to the Community law, unless Parliament had made clear that in passing the legislation it intended to override any inconsistent provisions of Community law. Even if the English courts were to adopt the approach urged by Lord Denning, great uncertainty remained regarding the remedies which they might grant in such a case.

Factorame Ltd v Secretary of State for Transport

In *Factortame v Secretary of State for Transport* [1989] 2 All ER 692, however, everyone seemed to take the answer to the underlying question of supremacy for granted. The case concerned the system of national quotas under the common fisheries policy. That system, embodied in EC Council Regulation 170/83, aims to prevent overfishing of Community waters by setting total allowable catches which are then divided into national quotas allocated to each member state. When the system was introduced, fishing vessels registered in Spain, which was not then a member of the Communities, were substantially excluded. Factortame and the other applicant companies in the present case were companies incorporated in the United Kingdom but largely owned by Spanish nationals, which operated some 95 fishing vessels, all of which flew the British flag and were registered in the United Kingdom under the Merchant Shipping Act 1894. As such, they were entitled to share in the United Kingdom national quota. Many of the applicant companies' vessels had originally been registered in Spain. Part II of the Merchant

Shipping Act 1988 introduced new criteria for registration of fishing vessels in the United Kingdom, under which only vessels owned by British citizens domiciled and resident in the United Kingdom or by companies 75% of whose shareholders and directors were British citizens domiciled and resident in the United Kingdom might be registered as British fishing vessels. None of the applicants' vessels met these criteria.

The applicants sought judicial review, claiming that the application to them of the new criteria violated their directly effective rights under Community law, in particular the right to establish themselves in business anywhere in the Community (EEC Treaty, arts 52 and 58), to participate in the capital of the applicant companies (EEC Treaty, art 221) and to freedom from discrimination on grounds of nationality (EEC Treaty, art 7). The Government countered that the provisions of the 1988 Act were not incompatible with these fundamental provisions of Community law but were intended only to ensure that fishing vessels flying the British flag had a genuine link with the United Kingdom, as required by international law. The Community fisheries policy was based upon a system of national quotas and Community law left each state free to determine for itself who qualified as its nationals.

The Divisional Court ([1989] 2 CMLR 353) requested a preliminary ruling from the Court of Justice, under the EEC Treaty, art 177, on the extent of the rights claimed by the applicants and, in effect, the compatibility of the 1988 Act with those rights. It was conceded by the Attorney General that if the Court of Justice gave a ruling favourable to the applicants, then the English courts would have to give the applicants' Community law rights priority over any provisions of the 1988 Act which might be inconsistent with them. The backlog of cases before the Court of Justice meant, however, that it was likely to be two years before a ruling was given. In the meantime, the applicants argued, they faced ruin if their ships could not be used as British fishing vessels. If the Court of Justice gave a ruling favourable to the applicants at the end of that time, the decision of the Court of Appeal in *Bourgoin SA v Ministry of Agriculture Fisheries and Food* [1985] 3 All ER 585 (noted in All ER Review 1985, p 152) meant that the applicants would be unable to obtain damages for their losses during the two years when the case had been pending. The applicants therefore asked the Divisional Court for interim relief in the form of an order 'disapplying' the 1988 Act insofar as it affected the applicants.

The Divisional Court held that it had jurisdiction to grant the interim relief requested and made an order that:

'(1) Pending final judgment or further order herein the operation of Part II of the Merchant Shipping Act 1988 and the Merchant Shipping (Registration of Fishing Vessels) Regulations 1988 be disapplied and the Secretary of State be restrained from enforcing the same in respect of any of the Applicants and any vessel now owned (in whole or in part) managed operated or chartered by any of them so as to enable registration of any such vessel under the Merchant Shipping Act 1894 and/or the Sea Fishing Boats (Scotland) Act 1886 to continue in being . . .'

The grant of an interim injunction restraining the Crown from applying an Act of Parliament was, of course, an unprecedented step which provoked a small outcry in the House of Commons. It was not, however, a step which attracted either the Court of Appeal ([1989] 2 CMLR 353) or the House of Lords ([1989] 2 All ER 692). The Court of Appeal allowed an appeal by the Secretary of State on the ground that under the United Kingdom constitution an English court had no jurisdiction to grant an interim order disapplying a statute—Bingham LJ described the Divisional Court's order as a 'constitutional enormity'.

On appeal to the House of Lords, the judgment of the Court of Appeal was affirmed, though on somewhat different grounds. Lord Bridge (with whom the rest of the House agreed) held that until a ruling was given by the Court of Justice there was a presumption that the 1988 Act was valid. He accepted that the court would not lend its assistance to the enforcement of the relevant provision of the Act (eg if a prosecution was brought under the Act it would be stayed pending the ruling of the Court of Justice) but denied that the court could go further and take positive steps to prevent the Secretary of State from bringing into operation provisions which did not require the assistance of the court for their operation. Lord Bridge also held (overruling the Court of Appeal's decision in *R v Licensing Authority, ex p Smith Kline & French Laboratories Ltd (No 2)* [1989] 2 All ER 113) that the courts had no power to grant an interim injunction against the Crown in judicial review proceedings.

In many ways, the most striking feature of this case is the one which received least attention in the judgments: the point, conceded by the Crown and accepted by all three courts, that directly effective Community law must prevail over inconsistent subsequent legislation. Lord Bridge's speech in the House of Lords contains the most authoritative statement of the supremacy of Community law yet made by an English court:

> 'By virtue of s 2(4) of the [European Communities Act 1972] Pt II of the 1988 Act is to be construed and take effect subject to directly enforceable Community rights and those rights are, by s 2(1) of the 1972 Act, to be "recognized and available in law, and . . . enforced, allowed and followed accordingly . . ." This has precisely the same effect as if a section were incorporated in Pt II of the 1988 Act which in terms enacted that the provisions with respect to registration of British fishing vessels were to be without prejudice to the directly enforceable Community rights of nationals of any Member State of the EEC. Thus it is common ground that, in so far as the applicants succeed before the European Court in obtaining a ruling in support of the Community rights which they claim, those rights will prevail over the restrictions imposed on registration of British fishing vessles by Pt II of the 1988 Act and the Divisional Court will, in the final determination of the application for judicial review, be obliged to make appropriate declarations to give effect to those rights;' (at pp 700–701).

The recognition by the English courts that directly effective Community law prevails over subsequent national legislation deserves a warm welcome, coming as it does at a time when the West German courts are abandoning their constitutional reservations about the supremacy of Community law (see *Wunsche Handelsgesellschaft* [1987] 3 CMLR 225). Nevertheless, the treatment of this question in *Factortame* is far from satisfactory.

In the first place, it is a matter for regret that the House of Lords did not discuss the constitutional issues raised by the supremacy of Community law. The effect of the Crown's concession was that a major constitutional law controversy seems to have ended not with a bang but a whimper. It is impossible to see how the effect accorded to s 2(4) of the European Communities Act 1972 can be reconciled with the comments of the Court of Appeal in *Ellen Street Estates*. However, is the correct inference that *Ellen Street Estates* should no longer be regarded as persuasive in relation to any legislation or only that it is not applicable to legislation which conflicts with Community law? Does *Factortame* represent a rejection of the extreme view of Parliamentary sovereignty or is it simply an accommodation of that doctrine with the principles of Community law? The European Communities Act 1972 is a statute of such immense constitutional significance that it should probably be regarded as sui generis and the effects of *Factortame* should be limited accordingly. Nevertheless, Lord Bridge's comments, and those made in the lower courts, suggest that the *Ellen Street Estates* decision may now be easier to challenge.

Secondly, Lord Bridge's approach to the supremacy of Community law is based solely upon the effect of s 2(4) of the European Communities Act. According to the passage from his speech quoted above, directly effective Community rights prevail over a subsequent Act of Parliament because the effect of s 2(4) is to write into each Act of Parliament passed after the 1972 Act an implied provision that that Act shall take effect subject to directly effective Community law. There is a marked difference between this approach and the basis on which the Court of Justice has placed the supremacy of Community law:

> 'By creating a Community of unlimited duration, having its own institutions, its own personality, its own legal capacity and capacity of representation on the international plane and, more particularly, real powers stemming from a limitation of sovereignty or a transfer of powers from the States to the Community, the Member States have limited their sovereign rights, albeit within limited fields, and have thus created a body of law which binds both their nationals and themselves.' (*Costa v ENEL* [1964] ECR 585 at 593.)

The difference of approach is of more than theoretical importance. Like Lord Denning in *Macarthys Ltd v Smith*, Lord Bridge seems to have left open the possibility that Parliament might deliberately legislate contrary to Community law and that if it chose to do so and made its intentions clear, the English courts would give effect to the legislation notwithstanding anything in Community law. By contrast, the Court of Justice's theory that Community law is based upon a transfer of sovereign powers would preclude a national parliament overriding Community rights in this way. That is not to say that Lord Bridge's approach is not to be preferred—it is certainly a better reflection of political realities in the United Kingdom today than is that of the Court of Justice—but the matter deserves more consideration than it has so far received.

The decision of the House of Lords on the main point in *Factortame*—the grant of interim relief—has had a mixed reception (contrast the criticisms expressed by Gravells in 'Disapplying an Act of Parliament pending a Preliminary Ruling: Constitutional Enormity or Community Law Right' (1989) PL 568 with the more favourable reaction of Lewis 'Statutes and The EEC: Interim Relief and the Crown' (1989) 48 CLJ 347). The result is certainly no surprise, although it is disappointing that the House of Lords should have rejected the whole notion that the courts may grant interim injunctions against the Crown. As Lord Bridge put it:

> 'If the applicants fail to establish the rights they claim before the European Court, the effect of the interim relief granted [by the Divisional Court] would be to have conferred on them rights directly contrary to Parliament's sovereign will . . .' (p 703).

Yet this aspect of the decision is open to criticism on the ground that it does not adequately protect such Community law rights as the applicants may have. To be fair, Lord Bridge recognised that possibility; he considered, however, that *as a matter of English law* the courts had no jurisdiction to grant interim relief for the protection of those rights. He accepted, however, that Community law might empower or require the courts to grant interim relief and referred this question to the Court of Justice in addition to the questions already referred by the Divisional Court.

In the meantime, the applicants' immediate problems have been solved by a decision of the Court of Justice requiring the United Kingdom to:

> '. . . suspend the application of the nationality requirements laid down in section 14(1)(a) and (c) of the Merchant Shipping Act 1988, read in conjunction with paragraphs (2) and (7) of that section, as regards the nationals of other member States and in respect of fishing vessels which, until 31 March 1989, were pursuing a fishing activity under the British flag and under a British fishing licence.' (*EC Commission v United Kingdom* Case 246/89R [1989] 3 CMLR 601 at 610).

These measures were granted by the court in the exercise of its own power to grant interim relief under the EEC Treaty, art 186, in a separate set of proceedings concerning the 1988 Act brought by the Commission againt the United Kingdom.

Litster v Forth Dry Dock and Engineering Co Ltd

Litster v Forth Dry Dock and Engineering Co Ltd [1989] 1 All ER 1134 raised a somewhat different question about the relationship of Community law and English law. The case concerned the interpretation of EC Council Directive 77/187, the object of which was to protect the rights of employees in the event of a change of employer, and the Transfer of Undertakings (Protection of Employment) Regulations 1981 which were made in order to give effect to the directive. Article 5(1) of the Regulations (which follows art 3 of the Directive) provides that where an undertaking is transferred from its old owner ('the transferor') to a new owner ('the transferee'), the contracts of employment of those employed by the transferor '. . . shall have effect after the transfer as if originally made between the person so employed and the transferee'. The effect is also to transfer the employment protection rights associated with the contract, including the right not to be unfairly dismissed. Under art 5(3) of the Regulations, the employees whose rights are transferred in this way are those 'employed immediately before the transfer' in the undertaking which is transferred.

In *Litster* the transferor was in receivership and its receivers agreed to sell the business to the transferee, which intended to replace the existing employees with workers who had been unemployed for a while and who, 'chastened by unemployment' were willing to work for lower wages. In what seems to have been an attempt to circumvent art 5(1) by taking advantage of the wording of art 5(3), the transferee insisted that the receivers dismiss the entire work force one hour before the transfer took effect. The transferee then argued that the work force were not 'employed immediately before the transfer' and so fell outside the protection of the Regulations. This very literal interpretation of art 5(3), which succeeded before the Court of Session, would, as Lord Keith said (at p 1136), have driven 'a coach and four' through art 5 of the Regulations. It would also have meant that the Regulations had failed adequately to implement the Directive, since the Court of Justice held in *P Bork International A/S (in liq) v Foreningen af Arbejdsledere i Danmark* Case 101/87 [1989] IRLR 41 that where employees were dismissed by a transferor, for reasons connected with the transfer, before the transfer took effect, they were to be treated as still employed by the undertaking at the time of the transfer.

The House of Lords had no hesitation in overruling the Court of Session and giving the Regulations a more liberal interpretation. Lord Oliver accepted that if he had had to apply the normal canons of construction applicable to a purely domestic statute, he would have had difficulty reading the words of the Regulations in such a way as to achieve the same result as the Court of Justice had attributed to the Directive. He stated, however, that:

> '*Pickstone v Freemans plc* [1988] 2 All ER 803, [1989] AC 66 has established that the greater flexibility available to the court in applying a purposive construction to legislation designed to give effect to the United Kingdom's treaty obligations to the Community enables the court, where necessary, to supply by implication words appropriate to comply with those obligations:' (p 1153).

Since the Regulations had been adopted specifically to implement the Directive, it was the duty of the court to construe them in such a way as to give effect to the Directive as it had been interpreted in the subsequent decisions of the Court of Justice (see especially Lord Keith at p 1136).

Following the decision in *Marshall v Southampton and South West Hampshire Area Health Authority (Teaching)* [1986] 2 All ER 584 (All ER Review 1986, p 136), the Directive did not have direct effect in these proceedings, so that unlike *Factortame* the case did not turn on s 2(1) and (4) of the European Communities Act 1972. Had the Regulations not been adopted specifically to give effect to the Directive, therefore, the decision in *Duke v GEC Reliance Ltd* [1988] 1 All ER 626 (All ER Review 1988, p 123) shows that the United Kingdom courts would not have been willing to do violence to the wording of the Regulations in order to ensure that they achieved the same result as the Directive. What distinguished *Litster* and *Pickstone* from *Duke* was that in the former cases the United Kingdom legislation had been adopted in order to give effect to the relevant Community law instruments. Where *Litster* goes beyond *Pickstone* is in making clear that the duty of the United Kingdom court is to construe an implementing measure (whether it takes the form of primary or secondary legislation) not merely in the light of the terms of the Directive it is designed to implement but so as to give effect to the interpretation placed upon that Directive by subsequent decisions of the Court of Justice.

Free movement of goods; intellectual property

Pharmaceutical Society case

Ever since the decision of the Court of Justice in the famous *Cassis de Dijon* case (*Rewe-Zentral AG v Bundesmonopolverwaltung fur Branntwein* Case 120/78 [1979] ECR 649), national laws which may have an effect upon trade between member states have come under close scrutiny even if they are not specifically concerned with imports. The decision of the Court of Justice in joined Cases 266 and 267/87 *R v Royal Pharmaceutical Society of GB, ex p Association of Pharmaceutical Importers* [1989] 2 All ER 758 breaks no new ground but gives an indication of the limitations of the 'Cassis' principle.

Since the price of most pharmaceutical products varies considerably from one member state to another, there is a substantial market in 'parallel imports', with large quantities of drugs being imported from a country where their price is low into those states where it is high. A series of decisions of the Court of Justice in the 1970's established that once a company which owned the patent or trade mark rights in a product had marketed that product in one member state, Community law did not permit it to use its intellectual property rights to prevent the goods which it had thus put into circulation from being imported into another member state even if the imports undercut its prices there. British pharmacists are reimbursed for drugs which they supply on National Health Service (NHS) prescriptions (approximately 95% of all drugs supplied on prescription in Britain) according to a scale based on the normal price of the drugs in Britain, irrespective of where the drugs are in fact obtained. There is thus a financial incentive for the pharmacist to use parallel imports obtained from a member state where prices are lower. If the drug prescribed is sold under the same name in Britain and the other member state, no problem arises. However, the same drug is frequently marketed by the same company or group of companies using different names in different member states. In addition, the same drug may be available under both a proprietary name and a non-proprietary 'generic' name.

At the relevant time the NHS generally permitted doctors to prescribe drugs using the British proprietary names if they wished and many did so. A practice of 'substitution' therefore developed, whereby some pharmacists given a prescription for a particular drug described by its British brand name would substitute a quantity of the same drug obtained from a parallel importer and bearing a different brand name. The Royal Pharmaceutical Society (the Society), a professional body with responsibility for ethics and discipline amongst pharmacists, adopted a Code of Ethics and notes for guidance which stipulated that a pharmacist was required to supply the product named in a prescription and which prohibited the substitution, except in an emergency, of any other product, even if its therapeutic effects were identical to those of the product named in the prescription. The Association of Pharmaceutical Importers (API), which was the main source of parallel imports of drugs into Britain, maintained that the Code and guidance notes and the relevant provisions of the statutory instrument issued by the Secretary of State concerning the duties of pharmacists in supplying drugs prescribed under the NHS amounted to a quantitative restriction on imports, contrary to the EEC Treaty, art 30, and sought judicial review. The Court of Appeal referred the matter for a preliminary ruling by the Court of

Justice under the EEC Treaty, art 177. Before the Court of Justice, the API, which was supported in part by the EC Commission, contended that the prohibition of 'substitution' effectively operated to bar parallel imports from the main part of the British drugs market in all cases where a drug was marketed under different names in different states.

An interesting preliminary question was whether the Code and guidance notes could amount to measures falling within the EEC Treaty, art 30. Noting that the Society was incorporated by royal charter, had been given certain powers by legislation and was responsible for exercising authority over a profession, the court held that measures adopted by the Society could fall within art 30. This decision makes good sense. Britain is unusual in entrusting the regulation of many professions to autonomous bodies created by the profession in question: in most other member states the functions of the society would be performed by a state agency of some kind. In those circumstances, it is manifestly right to treat the rules adopted by the society as though they had been imposed by the state itself.

Both Advocate General Darmon and the court, however, held that the prohibition of 'substitution' did not contravene art 30, although they reached that conclusion by different routes. Advocate General Darmon (who did not conceal his view that the arguments of the Commission and the API amounted to an invitation to the court to cast common sense to the winds) thought that the requirement that the pharmacist supply exactly what was named in the prescription did not fall within art 30 at all. He advised that a rule of this kind was not to be regarded as a trading rule within the principle in Case 8/74 *Procureur du Roi v Dassonville* [1974] ECR 837 and thus did not constitute an obstacle to trade. On this view the API failed at the threshold of art 30; there was therefore no need to consider whether the measures in question could be justified either under the mandatory requirements identified in *Cassis* or under art 36.

The court was not prepared to go that far. Without finally committing itself, it left open the possibility that the measures might constitute an obstacle to trade within art 30:

'. . . the court cannot exclude the possibility that, in the particular circumstances of the case, the said rule is capable of hindering intra-community trade. For that reason, and without there being any need to decide whether a rule prohibiting a pharmacist from substituting another product with the same therapeutic effect for the medicinal product prescribed by the doctor treating the patient generally constitutes a measure having equivalent effect within the meaning of art 30 of the EEC Treaty, it is necessary to consider whether such a rule may be justified under art 36 . . .' (p 780).

The court's refusal to follow the line suggested by the Advocate General on this point may simply reflect a cautious approach but it may be an indication that the court is now less willing than it had been a few years earlier to restrict the scope of the *Cassis* rule by excluding whole categories of national measures from the scope of art 30 ab initio by classifying them as measures which do not constitute obstacles to trade. It is interesting to note that in the Sunday Trading cases the court seems to have taken a similar view. This new approach may be constrasted with the court's earlier attitude in cases such as Case 75/81 *Blesgen v Belgium* [1982] ECR 1211 and, of particular relevance because it also concerned payment for drugs supplied on prescription, Case 238/82 *Duphar BV v Netherlands* [1984] ECR 523.

The court nevertheless quite rightly held that if the measures adopted by the society fell within art 30, they were justified under art 36 as measures taken to protect public health. The relationship between doctor and pharmacist and the degree to which it was necessary to prevent a pharmacist from substituting a therapeutically equivalent drug for that prescribed by the doctor were matters for the national public health service in the absence of Community regulation. In particular the court emphasised the possible psychological reasons for which it might be appropriate to prescribe a particular brand name drug. The court rejected, however, the suggestion that the measures prohibiting substitution might also be justified in order to protect intellectual property rights, since the reason why the same drug was sold under different names in different member states might be as part of a strategy on the part of the trademark owner to partition the market along national lines.

Thetford v Fiamma

The intellectual property exception under EEC Treaty art 36 was, however, at the heart of Case 35/87 *Thetford Corp v Fiamma SpA* [1989] 2 All ER 801. Thetford Corp were the owners of the United Kingdom patent relating to portable toilets. Fiamma SpA manufactured portable toilets in Italy, where no patent in the product existed, and imported them into the United Kingdom. Thetford sought an injunction to restrain this breach of its British patent. Since Thetford had not in any way consented to Fiamma's manufacture of the toilets in Italy, there was no question of Thetford having exhausted its rights. On the face of it, therefore, the grant of an injunction would not have violated art 30, since it would have been within the exception for industrial and commercial property rights in art 36.

Fiamma argued, however, that the protection of Thetford's patent did not fall within art 36 since, even if it was valid in Britain, it would not have been valid in any other Community state (with the possible exception of Ireland) because there was nothing novel about the 'invention' which Thetford had registered, for a number of specifications had been filed in respect of similar portable toilets many years before the grant of the patent to Thetford. Thetford's patent was valid in the United Kingdom only because the Patents Act 1949 contained a notion of 'relative novelty' or re-invention under which the fact that other specifications had been filed in respect of an invention more than fifty years before the current specification was filed did not mean that the current specification was to be treated as having been anticipated and thus disqualified from the grant of a patent. The earlier specifications for portable toilets apparently fell within the scope of this provision. Fiamma maintained that this peculiarity of the 1949 Act meant that there was no genuine specific subject matter of the Thetford patent and that the normal rules of Community law regarding intellectual property should not therefore be applied. Alternatively, Fiamma argued that even if it was legitimate to enforce the patent, Community law precluded the grant of an injunction, so that the only relief which might be granted was an order for the payment of a reasonable royalty. The Court of Appeal referred these questions to the Court of Justice under art 177.

Fiamma's arguments received short shrift from the Commission, the Advocate General and the Court of Justice. All rejected the notion that art 36 did not justify the enforcement of a patent which was valid only because of a rule of national law not found in the laws of most other member states. The court followed its earlier decision in Case 144/81 *Keurkoop BV v Nancy Kean Gifts BV* [1982] ECR 2853 that until such time as there was a Community law standard for the grant of intellectual property rights, it was for national law to determine the conditions under which protection was granted. The fact that United Kingdom law was almost unique in granting protection to rediscovered inventions was irrelevant. Nor did the court accept the suggestion that Community law limited relief to an order for the payment of royalties. The court had recognised such a limitation in case 434/85 *Allen & Hanburys Ltd v Generics (UK) Ltd* [1988] 2 All ER 454 (All ER Rev 1988, p 130) because the basis on which an injunction would have been granted would have discriminated between goods produced in the United Kingdom and goods imported from another member state. In the present case, however, Thetford would have been able to obtain an injunction whether Fiamma imported the goods or manufactured them in Britain.

The decision shows that while the court has developed Community law in such a way that it imposes substantial limitations upon the exercise of intellectual property rights conferred by national law, those rights nevertheless remain part of the national law of the state concerned. A member state is free, therefore, to make the grant of those rights subject to conditions which differ from those applicable in the rest of the Community.

Freedom of establishment: companies

The EEC Treaty, art 52 guarantees to nationals of the member states the freedom to establish themselves in business anywhere in the Community. Art 52 provides that:

> 'Freedom of establishment shall include the right . . . to set up and manage undertakings, in particular companies or firms, within the meaning of the second paragraph of article 58, under the conditions laid down for its own nationals by the law of the country where such establishment is effected, subject to the provisions of the Chapter relating to capital.'

Although this part of Community law is directed principally to ensuring that the authorities of the host state allowed a national of another member state to establish himself there, it also imposes obligations upon the state of origin to permit one of its nationals to establish himself in another member state. So far as natural persons are concerned, these principles are now quite clear and are reflected in a large body of case law, as well as legislation such as Council Directive 73/148 (which makes clear that a member state must allow one of its nationals to depart in order to establish himself in business elsewhere in the Community.

The rights of companies and other legal persons have not, hitherto, received as much attention. The special problems which may arise in their case were highlighted by Case 81/87 *R v HM Treasury, ex p Daily Mail and General Trust plc* [1989] 1 All ER 328. In English law a distinction is drawn between the state of incorporation of a company and the residence of that company, so that a company may be incorporated in England, yet have its central management and control and, therefore, its residence elsewhere. The distinction can be important because the company's liability to United Kingdom taxes is generally dependent on the company being resident in the United Kingdom. For that reason, s 428(1) of the Income and Corporation Taxes Act 1970 makes it unlawful for a company resident in the United Kingdom to cease to be so resident unless the Treasury gives its consent. The applicant, a holding company, was incorporated and resident in England. It sought Treasury consent to transfer its central management to the Netherlands and to become resident there. It was common ground that the company wished to make this move so that it could avoid becoming liable to United Kingdom capital gains and corporation taxes on a series of capital transactions which it envisaged. When the Treasury raised objections, the company sought judicial review, arguing that it had a right under Community law to establish itself in another member state and that the United Kingdom could not make the exercise of that right dependent upon Treasury consent.

The company relied upon art 58, which provides that:

> 'Companies or firms formed in accordance with the law of a Member State and having their registered office, central administration or principal place of business within the Community shall, for the purposes of this Chapter, be treated in the same way as natural persons who are nationals of Member States.'

The company argued that this provision gave it the same entitlement under Directive 73/148 as a natural person. The High Court referred a series of questions for a preliminary ruling by the Court of Justice under art 177.

The company's argument was undoubtedly logical and apparently in accord with the text of the EEC Treaty as well as a long line of decisions from the Court of Justice that a member state was not entitled to subject the exercise of a fundamental Community law right to conditions such as obtaining the consent of national authorities. A complicating factor, however, was that the United Kingdom was unusual amongst Community countries in allowing a company to move its management to another state and yet retain its legal personality as a United Kingdom company. Many other member states regarded the transfer of a company's central management as equivalent to the winding up of the company and, of course, insisted that a full tax settlement be a feature of such a winding up. It seems to be generally accepted that such a requirement is not contrary to Community law.

The Commission nevertheless considered that where a member state permitted a company to change its residence without having to be wound up, that company had the same rights as a natural person and the member state could not make the transfer of residence dependent upon consent from the national fiscal authorities even if the principal purpose of the move was to reduce liability to tax. Advocate General Darmon thought that:

> 'It would be paradoxical if a member state not requiring winding up were to find itself placed by Community law in a less favourable fiscal position precisely because its legislation on companies is more consistent with Community objectives in regard to establishment.' (p 345).

Advocate General Darmon accepted the Commission's position that the transfer to another member state of the central management of a company could constitute a form of exercise of the right of freedom of establishment and that, since this was a fundamental Community law right, a member state could not make the transfer dependent upon prior authorisation. However, he added two important qualifications. First, he considered that there would be no exercise of the Community law right where a company proposed to make a transfer which was not 'genuine', in the sense that it involved no real integration of the company into the economic life of the host state but was merely a token change of residence to avoid the application of national law. Secondly, he advised that a member state was entitled to insist that a company which exercised its right to transfer its central management should settle its tax position with regard to any assets affected by the transfer. His opinion was thus, in effect, a rejection of the applicant company's arguments on the facts of the present case.

The court also rejected the company's submissions but on more fundamental grounds. Notwithstanding the provisions of art 58, the court held that:

> '. . . unlike natural persons, companies are creatures of the law and, in the present state of Community law, creatures of national law. They exist only by virtue of the varying national legislation which determines their incorporation and functioning.' (pp 348–349).

The court thus concluded that Directive 73/148 was inapplicable to legal persons and that the rules on freedom of establishment did not deal with the question of whether a company might transfer its residence from one member state to another while retaining the status of a company incorporated under the laws of the first member state. Until the Community adopted further legislation on companies or the member states concluded conventions (for which provision is made by art 220 although none have so far been concluded) on the retention of legal personality by companies transferring their registered offices from one state to another, it was for each member state to decide whether to allow companies incorporated under its laws to transfer their residence to another member state and under what conditions.

Court of Justice: interim measures

1989 was not a good year for the net book agreement, the agreement between the major United Kingdom publishers which effectively fixes the price of most books published in the United Kingdom and sold in the United Kingdom and Ireland. In Britain the agreement has been challenged by at least one major chain of book stores. In Brussels the Commission ruled that the agreement violated art 85 by restricting competition within part of the common market.

The net book agreement was concluded in 1957 and has twice been the subject of a decision in the Restrictive Practices Court which, in each case, accepted the argument of the Publishers Association that the agreement's benefits in ensuring the supply of a wide range of books outweighed any adverse effects it might have. When the United Kingdom joined the Community in 1973 the agreement, and the network of rules and documents which supported it, were notified to the Commission and thus enjoyed provisional validity. In December 1988, however, the Commission decided (Decision EEC 89/44) that the agreement was contrary to EEC Treaty art 85(1) (a point which was not seriously contested by the Publishers Association) and that it should not be given exemption under art 85(3). The decision required the Publishers Association to take immediate steps to put an end to its infringement of art 85(1). The decision also had the effect of terminating the provisional validity which the agreement had enjoyed since 1973, rendering the agreement void from the date of the decision.

The Publishers Association brought an action in the Court of Justice under EEC Treaty art 173, contesting the validity of the decision. They also sought interim measures suspending the decision until the court gave judgment on the merits (Case 56/89R *Publishers Association v EC Commission* [1989] 2 All ER 1059). In this respect the Association has been partially successful. The President of the court held that the two decisions of the Restrictive Practices Court in the 1960s evaluating the advantages of the agreement demonstrated that the Association had a prima facie case. He also held that if the Association was to comply with the decision, it would have to dismantle most of the system based upon the agreement and that this might cause serious and irreparable damage (the criterion for the grant of interim relief) to the members of the Association. Balancing these considerations against the interest of the Commission in bringing an immediate end to any violation of art 85(1), the President decided to order the suspension of those parts of the decision which refused exemption and ordered immediate compliance. He did not, however, suspend the part of the decision which ruled that the agreement violated art 85(1), since the Association had failed to show a prima facie case that this part of the decision was unfounded. If the court eventually finds against the Association, the fact that this part of the Commission's decision was not suspended may have important consequences, since the provisional validity of the agreement will have ceased from the date of the Commission's decision rather than the date of the court's ruling on the merits.

Whatever one's views of the merits of this case or the desirability of dismantling the net book agreement, the decision on interim measures must be regarded as correct. The failure to grant interim relief would have had very serious effects, whereas the Commission's interest in bringing an immediate end to any violation cannot be regarded as particularly strong, given (as the President pointed out) that the Commission had taken 16 years to deal with the agreement. A particularly welcome feature of the court's decision is the fact that due deference was shown to the earlier decisions of the Restrictive Practices Court on the beneficial effects of the agreement. It may well be reasonable for the Commission to take a different view from the Restrictive Practices Court but it would be most damaging to the relationship between national and Community competition laws for the court not to have taken into account the views of the national court in deciding whether or not to grant interim relief.

Cases not reviewed

Space does not permit discussion of the following cases which also involved points of Community law: *Customs and Excise Commissioners v Bell Concord Educational Trust* [1989] 2 All ER 217 (value added tax Directive), Case 416/85 *EC Commission v United Kingdom* [1989] 1 All ER 364 (value added tax exemptions—noted in last year's Review at p 133), *Kelly v Shulman* [1989] 1 All ER 106 (rest periods for drivers of commercial vehicles) and *Smith Kline & French Laboratories v Licensing Authority* [1989] 1 All ER 578 (medicines Directive).

Evidence

A A S ZUCKERMAN
Fellow of University College, Oxford

Hearsay

The hearsay rule has been under retreat for many years. As a common law principle it has long since ceased to acknowledge the need to adapt to contemporary needs. But the world does not stand still simply because the hearsay rule refuses to acknowledge progress even in the computer age. One of the great revolutions of our generation has been brought about by computer use. Today a great deal of information is processed and stored by computers. Computer printouts containing factual statements fall foul, however, of the hearsay prohibition. But, as Steyn J has observed in *R v Minors* [1989] 2 All ER 208 at 210, if 'computer output cannot relatively readily be used as evidence in criminal cases, much crime . . . will in practice be immune from prosecution.' Practical needs of this kind have been met in one of two ways: by judicial evasion or by statutory exception. The two appeals before Steyn J involved the latter.

In both appeals the issue concerned the admissibility of computer records. In one case the record in question described the accused's state of account with a building society and in the other the printout contained a list of season tickets which had been stolen from London Regional Transport. Section 69 of the Police and Criminal Evidence Act 1984 makes computer records admissible subject to certain conditions which amount, in effect, to proof that the computer in question was properly used and that it properly functioned. Further, Pt II of Sch 3 provides that a certificate concerning these matters may be admitted as proof of the required conditions. This is fairly straightforward. The problem was whether on proof of the conditions in s 69, the printout becomes ipso facto admissible or, alternatively, whether it has to be further proved that the situation falls under one of the recognised exceptions to the hearsay rule.

Section 68 of the 1984 Act, for example, renders admissible in certain circumstances documents which have been compiled by a person acting under a duty. These circumstances include the unavailability of the supplier of the information, due to various reasons enumerated in the section, and the fact that the supplier of the information cannot reasonably be expected to remember it by the date of the trial. Section 68 has now been replaced by s 24 of the Criminal Justice Act 1988 which follows the same pattern in a more relaxed form. Steyn J decided that s 69 does not constitute a 'self-contained code governing the admissibility of computer records' but must be read subject to s 68. Thus before s 69 can render admissible a computer record, the situation must be brought under one of the exceptions in s 68. Thus it must be proved by oral evidence that the supplier of the information is either unavailable for one of the reasons mentioned there or cannot reasonably be expected to have any recollection of the matter in question. This ruling will hold equally good in respect of s 24 of the 1988 Act.

There is irresistible logic in this decision. If it were otherwise, all hearsay will become admissible provided it has been entered into a computer in accordance with the requirements of s 69. For instance, it would be admissible for the prosecution to adduce evidence of what witnesses told the police provided that the police entered the witnesses' statements into a word processor. Although as a matter of interpretation the result in this case is sound, the process of arriving at it illustrates the price paid for the statutory reform of the hearsay rule.

The construction of new exceptions which are designed to keep up with technical developments often involves ambiguity and fine technical distinctions. In the instant appeals 'it became obvious that in each case prosecuting counsel, defence counsel and the judge fundamentally misunderstood the meaning of these statutory provisions . . .' [1989] 2 All ER at 210. As a result Steyn J found that the computer printouts were wrongly admitted in both cases under appeal. In one case the conviction was upheld by the application of the proviso but in the other it had to be quashed. This is hardly satisfactory. It is important that criminal cases should be decided on their factual merits rather than on abstruse points of interpretation.

It is not as if now that we have the Steyn J interpretation, no further ambiguities of construction remain. Some further ambiguities have already surfaced in *R v Governor of Pentonville Prison, ex p Osman* [1989] 3 All ER 701. Lloyd LJ had to pronounce on the vexed question of what is a record for the purpose of s 68 of the 1984 Act. Faced with decisions which, on the one hand hold a bill of lading to be a record and, on the other hand, deny the same status to a file of correspondence or to a report by a Companies Act 1948 inspector, he embraced the definition in *H v Schering Chemicals Ltd* [1983] 1 All ER 849 at 852, which defines documents as those written statements which:

> 'a historian would regard as original or primary sources, that is documents which either give effect to a transaction itself or which contain a contemporaneous register of information supplied by those with direct knowledge of the facts.'

This definition will be workable only if it is not taken literally. The reference to the criterion of historians is unsatisfactory. A historian is not concerned with whether a document may be categorised as primary but with its probative value. Furthermore, it is not clear what is meant by the requirement of contemporaneity. Section 68 neither requires contemporaneity with the event in question nor with the original reporting by the witness who possesses first hand knowledge.

It was accepted before Lloyd LJ that company minutes, cheques and bank statements were records. He further held that tickets, confirmation slips and telexes used in the course of banking activities were also records. However, according to Steyn J in *Minors* [1989] 2 All ER at 212, some of these documents may not amount to hearsay at all. Steyn J thought that bank statements produced by computers were 'real evidence' and were therefore unaffected by the hearsay prohibition. The distinction between hearsay and real evidence, which is often used as a means of evading the hearsay prohibition, opens up a considerable field for conceptual disputes. It might even be argued that documents which carry out banking transactions are not hearsay because they are 'operative acts'; another convenient label for avoiding hearsay complications. Moreover, in one of the appeals in *Minors* it may well have been possible to evade the hearsay prohibition by a further route. Instead of adducing the computer lists of stolen tickets, under ss 68 and 69 of the 1984 Act, the prosecution may have been able to call a witness to testify that the tickets in question did not appear in the list of lawfully sold tickets and thus invoke the doctrine of negative inference. According to this doctrine, inferences drawn from the non-existence of an entry do not infringe the hearsay prohibition.

A number of other points of construction were clarified by Lloyd LJ in the *Osman* case. He held that the conditions set out in s 68(2) of the Police and Criminal Evidence Act 1984 were alternative and not cumulative, and he explained the relation between s 68 of the 1984 Act and s 11 of the Fugitive Offenders Act 1967.

It is undesirable that in criminal trials so much legal ingenuity and energy should be devoted to technical points which have little, if any, bearing on whether the accused committed the crime charged. However, it would be misleading to suggest that the statutory exceptions considered above turn only on legal niceties. Section 69 does draw attention to important factors of reliability and s 72(2) of the 1984 Act preserves the discretion of the court to exclude documents notwithstanding their admissibility; a discretion reiterated in s 25 of the 1988 Act.

This kind of discretion has its roots in the common law discretion to ensure a fair trial, which has been considered by the Privy Council in *Scott v R* [1989] 2 All ER 305, where it was illustrated how the discretion should be exercised. 'It is the quality of the evidence', Lord Griffiths observed (p 313), 'that is the crucial factor that should determine the exercise of the discretion.' Thus the trial judge must first consider whether a proffered statement falls into a recognised exception. He must then assess whether its probative quality justifies its admission in evidence. Lastly, when the statement has been admitted, the trial judge has to ask the jury to consider carefully the fact that the court has been deprived of the benefits of cross-examination. With such meticulous care being given to quality and to jury direction it is not easy to continue to justify a blanket hearsay exclusion subject to narrowly defined exceptions.

There is no reason why admissibility should not depend on quality from first to last. If quality became the sole consideration some of the factors that are relevant to present day exceptions would retain some importance. For example, the availability of the original maker of a statement to give oral testimony in court will obviously be important. Adducing the hearsay statement of an available eye witness will cast grave doubt on the motives for submitting inferior evidence and would normally lead to exclusion. However, unlike the present hearsay exceptions, a test of quality would not attempt to capture the reasons for the acceptability of hearsay within tight legal definitions. In a complicated or doubtful case a trial within a trial would have to be held in order to determine admissibility (as it must now be held in situations such as *Minors* [1989] 2 All ER at 214) but it will then be devoted on to considerations of merit.

Best evidence rule

One of the more esoteric points to emerge this year concerns the best evidence rule to which Lloyd LJ would have been more than happy to say goodbye: *R v Governor of Pentonville Prison, ex p Osman* [1989] 3 All ER 701 at 728. Although now largely defunct, the principle has still a flicker of life in it: a party who possesses an original document in court, or could have it in court without difficulty, may not adduce a copy instead. It is difficult to believe that the situation would be altered in this respect even if the best evidence rule were to disappear altogether.

Cross-examination of a co-accused

R v Rowson [1985] 2 All ER 539 decided that if a co-accused gives evidence which incriminates the accused, the latter is entitled to cross-examine the former on a previous inconsistent statement which contains a self-incriminating admission by the co-accused. This is so even where such self-incriminating statement is inadmissible as evidence for the prosecution. The reason is straightforward: an accused must have an uninhibited right to challenge the evidence against him and establish his innocence. This has now been reiterated in the Privy Council in *Lui Mei-lin v R* [1989] 1 All ER 359. However, the refinements accompanying this reiteration do little credit to the administration of justice.

Lord Roskill said that when a co-accused has been cross-examined on an inadmissible confession the judge must instruct the jury not to

> 'use the statement in any way as evidence . . . of the prosecution's case and that its only relevance is to test the credibility of the evidence which the maker of the statement has given against his co-accused.' (362-3)

It is difficult to see how a jury, or anyone else for that matter, can discriminate between these different evidential uses. Suppose that the co-accused is cross-examined on an otherwise inadmissible confession in which the co-accused declared that he did the beating while the accused was waiting outside. At the trial the co-accused testifies that it was he who waited outside while the accused did the beating. As a result of the cross-examination, the jury are persuaded that the co-accused's testimony is false and that his out of court statement is true. Is it reasonable to expect rational persons to say to themselves that this conclusion holds good only for the accused, but not for the co-accused?

Of course, it is possible for jurors to come to the view that they are not sure which is the correct version and give the benefit of the doubt to both the accused and the co-accused. But short of this situation, a conclusion that the out of court statement of the co-accused was after all right must be good for all purposes. In *R v Sharp* [1988] 1 All ER 65 at 75, Lord Havers said

> 'that a jury will make little of a direction that attempts to draw a distinction between evidence which is evidence of facts and evidence in the same statement which whilst not being evidence of facts is nevertheless evidentiary material of which they may make use in evaluating evidence which is evidence of the facts.'

The same may be said, mutatis mutandis, of the present attempt to draw a distinction between the co-accused's credibility and the truth of his statements.

To the above dictum on the divisibility of the co-accused's credit Lord Roskill added two riders. First, that the judge should inform the jury why the inconsistent statement had previously been excluded and stress that it cannot be relied on by the prosecution. Further, the jury should be told about the circumstances surrounding the inadmissible confession and that they may well have affected its credibility. These precautions are sensible, but they can hardly alter the fact that once the jurors have decided to believe the out of court statement of the co-accused, their belief will inexorably affect the fate of the co-accused as well as that of the accused. This inescapable outcome remains unaffected by Lord Roskill's second rider (at 363) that

> 'the cross-examiner is bound by the answers which he receives and that it is not legitimate to reopen all the circumstances in which the excluded statement was taken.'

Suppose that on being shown the inadmissible confession mentioned above, the co-accused says that it was obtained from him by police torture. Surely, the accused is allowed to challenge this claim and press the co-accused in an attempt to make him retract his claim of torture. Indeed, in appropriate circumstances justice will demand that the accused be allowed to disprove by means of independent evidence the co-accused's claim of torture.

Clearly, cross-examination of a co-accused on an inadmissible confession places the co-accused in a very difficult situation. A possible solution to this problem is to sever the trials of the two accused. Lord Roskill is right to suggest that, at the conclusion of the voir dire, the accused should indicate whether he proposes to cross-examine the co-accused on the inadmissible confession so that severance may be considered at that stage. But, as his Lordship observed, severance would be rare. The reason for this is not difficult to fathom. If the trials are severed, the co-accused would be unlikely to testify against the accused and the court would be deprived of an opportunity to test the relative merits of the accused and co-accused's claims against each other (see Zuckerman, *The Principles of Criminal Evidence* (1989) 283). The prosecution was therefore correct to argue in *Lui Mei-lin* that

> 'the trial judge might have to carry out . . . a balancing exercise, balancing the interests of the maker of the statement against the interests of the co-accused on whose behalf it was sought to cross-examine, before deciding whether or not to permit the proposed cross-examination' ([1989] 1 All ER at 363).

Unfortunately, this suggestion has been rejected, but the trial judge may still have an opportunity to strike a just balance. Lord Roskill stressed the importance of the relevance of the inconsistent statement. Thus, trial judges have to be satisfied that the cross-examination is likely to elicit sufficiently useful information about the co-accused's credibility before allowing examination on an inadmissible confession. In this regard there is some scope for balancing the benefit to the accused against the harm to the co-accused.

Confessions and the observance of the Code of Practice

In recent years the courts have demonstrated increasing support for the rights of suspects in custody and for the enforcement of the Code of Practice for the Detention, Treatment and Questioning of Persons by Police Officers.

Prominent amongst decisions to this effect is *R v Samuel* [1988] 2 All ER 135, where it has been held that a denial of a right to consult a solicitor would often result in the exclusion of a confession. This year the Court of Appeal has decided that serious breaches of the provisions of the Code of Practice that are concerned with the recording of interviews can also have similar consequences.

In *R v Keenan* [1989] 3 All ER 598, the accused was arrested after a car chase on suspicion of taking the car without authority. Subsequently his car was searched in his absence and the police claimed to have found a home-made spear in it. The accused was charged with various driving offences and with possession of an offensive weapon. At his committal the prosecution tendered statements from two policemen who claimed to have found the spear in the car. After the committal statements from two further policemen were served. In these the officers claimed that on arrival at the police station, the accused was interviewed by them and admitted possession of the spear. However, the statements of these officers were dated some six weeks after the accused's arrest. Objection was taken to the admissibility of the accused's confession contained in these statements on the grounds that it had been taken in breach of paras 11.3(*b*)(ii), 11.6 and 12.12 of the Code. These provisions require that an interview with a suspect be recorded during the course of the interview, that where a record is not completed during the interview the reason must be recorded, and that a copy of the record should be shown to the suspect who should be asked to sign it as correct or indicate any inaccuracies.

Most breaches of the Code are not, as it were, actionable per se; they do not automatically result in the exclusion of evidence obtained in breach of the Code. Section 67(1) of the Police and Criminal Evidence Act 1984 empowers the court to take into account the provisions of the Code. Section 78(1) empowers the court to exclude evidence

> 'if it appears . . . that, having regard to all the circumstances, including the circumstances in which the evidence was obtained, the admission of the evidence would have such an adverse effect on the fairness of the proceedings that the court ought not to admit it.'

The trial judge in *Keenan* refused to exclude the confession under s 78 because, it was assumed, he did not know at the voir dire stage that the accused would deny making the confession and because he thought that any unfairness would be dissipated if the accused testified about his own version of the interview. This mode of reasoning throws into relief one of the main problems involved in dealing with breaches of the Code under the s 78 discretion. An argument for discretionary exclusion has to be made when the prosecution proposes to adduce the evidence. But at that point in the trial the judge does not necessarily know what course the trial is going to take and he may therefore find it difficult to assess the impact that the evidence, to which objection has been taken, will have on the fairness of the proceedings as a whole. Hodgson J has now provided a solution to this conundrum.

He has done so by invoking the rationale of the 1984 Act (PACE) and of the Code of practice. The provisions of PACE and the Code, he observed, embody guarantees for the proper treatment of suspects in custody and for the reliable recording of their statements during interrogation. Breaches of these provisions may rob the suspect of his protection, as would the denial of access to a solicitor, or may rob the court of reliable means of determining whether the statements attributed to the suspect were in fact made, as happened in the present case. As Lord Lane CJ observed in *R v Delaney* (1989) 88 Cr App R 338 at 341–342, where similar omissions by the police were considered, by 'failing to make a contemporaneous note . . . as soon as practicable, the officers deprived the court of what was, in all likelihood, the most cogent evidence of what did indeed happen during these interviews and what did induce the appellant to confess.' If a failure to comply with the recording provisions undermines the court's ability to determine the truth, it follows that the effectiveness of the fact finding process is dulled and the fairness of the trial is adversely affected.

Exclusion in such situations, Hodgson J explained, is not ordered because the court wishes to punish the police for its breaches of the Code. He insisted that only breaches that were 'significant and substantial' should result in exclusion. This significance is measured in terms of its effect on the criminal process as a whole (see [1989] 3 All ER at 609). The novelty of this approach lies in the notion of procedural fairness as an independent value of justice. The exclusionary discretion does not rest principally on considerations of probative value and even less on a desire to discipline the police. Rather, it tries to maintain adequate standards in the investigatory process because it is intimately connected with the trial procedure; so much so that procedural defects at the investigation can undermine the effectiveness and fairness of the trial itself.

His Lordship analysed the unfair consequences of the breaches in the case of *Keenan*. If the accused intended not to testify, then the admission of the confession would effectively rob him of his right to remain silent because in practice he would have had to go into the witness box and deny the confession . If the accused intended to argue, as in the event he did, that his statement had been concocted, then its admission placed him at a disadvantage because it forced him to attack the character of the police officers and thus expose himself to cross-examination on his own character. If his contention were that his answers had been inaccurately recorded, then he would be placed at a disadvantage in that he had been given no contemporaneous opportunity to correct the inaccuracies.

This decision goes a long way towards giving content to the notion of unfairness and will doubtless enhance, along with other similar decisions, the fairness of the criminal process.

Special procedure material

The Police and Criminal Evidence Act 1984 instituted a new procedure whereby a constable could obtain access to what is defined in s 14 as 'special procedure material'. This is, essentially, material acquired or created in the course of any business or profession (not being material subject to legal privilege or 'excluded' material) and held subject to a duty of confidentiality. A typical instance is provided by a bank account, in respect of which the bank owes a duty of confidence to its client. An order to allow the police access to such material may be made by a circuit judge upon an application by the police and upon proof of certain conditions. There are three parties involved: the police seeking the order, the party in possession of the material, and the party entitled to control over the information and who is the object of the police investigation (in our example the account holder); the latter will henceforth be referred to as 'the person entitled to confidence'.

Schedule 1 sets out the conditions for obtaining an order for the disclosure of special procedure material (henceforth 'the material') and the procedure to be followed. An application for such order must be made to a circuit judge inter partes (paras 4, 7). An order under para 4 directs the person in possession of the material to let a constable have access to it or take it away. It is clear therefore that notice of the application, as required by para 8, must be served on such person. But what are the procedural rights of the person entitled to confidence; the account holder in our example? Is he entitled to notice and may he resist the application at the hearing? Has he any right to demand resistance of the application from the person in possession, the bank? These questions were considered in *Barclays Bank plc v Taylor* [1989] 3 All ER 563, and *R v Crown Court at Manchester, ex p Taylor* [1988] 2 All ER 769, decided last year.

The cumulative effect of these decisions is as follows. The account holder has no locus standi in these proceedings and no notice need be given to him by the police. The bank is not required by law, nor by implication from contract, to notify the account holder of the fact that an application has been made or to contest such application and probe the supporting evidence. The police may ask the bank not to divulge to the account holder the fact that an application has been made. The bank, on its part, is not obliged in law to abide by such request but a judicial hope has been expressed that banks would co-operate with the police.

Lastly, although the notice served by the police on the bank has to identify the material subject to the application, this and other relevant information may be given orally.

Our starting point has to be that by devising a special procedure for obtaining access to confidential information Parliament intended to create special safeguards for such information. This is reflected by the provisions of Sch 1 which require the police to establish certain facts as a condition to obtaining an order. These include, the commission of a serious offence; that the material is likely to be of substantial value in the investigation and of relevance at a trial; that other methods of obtaining the material are not available. Finally, it is incumbent on the circuit judge to give due consideration both to the interest in assisting the investigation and to the protection of privacy (para 2(c)). However, the interpretation given to the new procedure in recent decisions has emptied the safeguards contained in the procedure of much of their practical content.

If the person entitled to privacy, the account holder, is not given notice of the application and is afforded no opportunity to participate at the hearing, this person will not be able to challenge the application or probe the grounds upon which it relies. The bank, on its part, has neither an interest to resist the application nor the information necessary for doing so. The procedural safeguards of notice, it has been decided, are merely intended to protect the interests of the person in possession of the material, against whom the order is sought. Yet it is clear that the party who requires the procedural protection is not the disinterested person who happens to be in possession of the material but the person whose confidential information is entrusted to another and whose affairs are investigated. This fact has not been overlooked but it has been held that the interests of the person entitled to confidence are left to the protection of the circuit judge who, according to Glidewell LJ, 'must exercise his powers and his discretion fairly and properly' ([1988] 2 All ER at 722; see also [1989] 3 All ER at 569, 570).

Usually the protection of a litigant's interests is not left to the judge alone. In an adversarial system the interests of a person affected by a judicial decision are protected by a procedural right to be heard before a decision is made. The right to be heard is therefore an important constitutional as well as procedural right. It is only in cases of pressing urgency that our law makes exceptions. The search warrant procedure constitutes one such exception. We must therefore ask whether the procedure described in Sch 1 forms another exception.

A study of Sch 1 reveals that the legislature intended to make only a limited exception to the right to be heard. Schedule 1 sets out not one procedure but two for the purpose of obtaining confidential material. The one is an inter partes application under para 4. The other procedural route is, however, via an ex parte application for a search warrant to be made under para 12. One of the conditions for obtaining an ex parte warrant is, according to para 14(d), 'that service of a notice of an application under paragraph 4 above may seriously prejudice the investigation.' Otherwise, the police have to establish the same facts that are required under an inter partes application. It follows that the legislature saw justification for secrecy only where the police could establish a risk that by alerting the person in possession or anyone else concerned, the investigation would be impeded. The decisions under consideration have given the police virtually all the advantages of an ex parte application without demanding any proof that there is a real danger of this kind.

As we have seen, under the present interpretation of the para 4 procedure the person entitled has no right to be notified either by the police or by the person in possession of the material and has no right to be heard before the circuit judge. It follows that such person is in no better procedural position than under the normal search warrant procedure. If it were the case that the legislature regarded the exercise of discretion by the circuit judge as offering satisfactory protection for confidential material, the legislature would hardly have made a distinction between inter partes orders and ex parte warrants. (For further discussion see my article 'The Weakness of the PACE Special Procedure for Protecting Confidential Material' [1990] Cr LR, July issue).

Legal professional privilege

Over the last few years attention has been drawn on the pages of this Review to a judicial indulgence towards claims for legal professional privilege. This trend has now been sharply arrested.

In *Dubai Bank Ltd v Galadari* [1989] 3 All ER 769 the defendants had a dispute at some point with one of their employees. A copy of the employee's affidavit was sent to the defendants who, in turn, submitted either that very copy, or a photocopy of it, to their solicitors for advice. The dispute with the employee was subsequently settled. Later the plaintiffs brought an unrelated action against the defendants and sought inspection of the affidavit. The defendants claimed legal privilege in respect of the copy of the affidavit in the hands of their solicitor. The defendants relied on *R v Board of Inland Revenue, ex p Goldberg* [1988] 3 All ER 248, where Watkins LJ held that a photocopy made for the purpose of obtaining legal advice is privileged even where the original itself is not privileged. On the facts of the *Dubai Bank* case it was not clear whether the copy in the hands of the defendants' solicitors was the very copy that the defendants had received, in which case there would be no privilege, or a copy of the copy made by them for submission to their solicitors, in which case it would be privileged. Dillon LJ found it 'incredible that the line of privilege should depend on such a fine distinction' (at 772).

For reasons similar to those outlined in last year's commentary Dillon LJ has now found the authorities relied on by Watkins LJ in *Ex p Goldberg* insufficient to support the conclusion reached (see [1988] All ER Rev 135–136). The Court of Appeal has now decided that where an original document in the hands of the client is not privileged, a copy thereof made for the purpose of obtaining legal advice could not be privileged either ([1989] 3 All ER at 775). In arriving at this conclusion the Court of Appeal has both reversed a rule that threatened to bring legal professional privilege into disrepute and, at the same time, has removed temptation for underhand practices.

There is however one aspect which seems to have been left in disarray. In *Ex p Goldberg* Watkins LJ relied on *Watson v Cammell Laird & Co (Shipbuilders and Engineers) Ltd* [1959] 2 All ER 757, where the plaintiff sued the defendant in respect of an accident. The plaintiff's solicitors obtained copies of hospital records concerned with the plaintiff's treatment. The Court of Appeal held that these copies were privileged notwithstanding that the originals could be obtained by the defendants from the hospital by means of a subpoena duces tecum. In *Dubai Bank* ([1989] 3 All ER at 774) Dillon LJ seems to have endorsed Lord Evershed MR's view that although 'copies, the mere replacement of something which the defendant himself would have to produce, must be produced' ([1959] 2 All ER 757 at 758). Dillon LJ distinguished the *Watson* case on the grounds that there the document in question was never in the plaintiff's possession whereas in *Dubai Bank* the document was at one point in the defendants hands in an unprivileged state.

Of itself the fact that the originals were never in the hands of the party claiming privilege could not be of any great importance. But if this fact is put together with the doctrine that the advice given by a lawyer to his client is not disclosable, it could support the conclusion arrived at by Lord Evershed MR. The reasoning being that by revealing the lawyer's copies, the lawyer's advice or strategy would emerge. In *Watson v Cammell Laird* Lord Evershed MR went so far as to suggest that copies made by a lawyer were the fruits of the lawyer's expertise; 'in so far as skill is involved it was part of his [the solicitor's] professional skill in assisting his client to go to the hospital to get it [the copy]' [1959] 2 All ER at 759. In the *Dubai Bank* case Farquharson LJ observed that the decision in *Ex p Goldberg* might be supportable on the grounds that 'the solicitor had prepared the documents for counsel by a process of selection and sifting and himself copying them' and that the copy in question was one of these documents ([1989] 3 All ER at 776).

The result would appear to be that if, in preparation for litigation or for the purpose of legal advice, the lawyer makes copies of documents not otherwise privileged, the copies may still be privileged. The scope of this rule is wholly unclear. According to the dictum in *Watson v Cammell Laird* that 'the mere replacement of something which the defendant himself would have to produce, must be produced' ([1959] 2 All ER at 758), if the original of the document was at one point in the hands of the client, the copy in the hands of his lawyer will not be privileged. But according to Farquharson LJ in the *Dubai Bank* case, such copy may well be privileged if 'the solicitor had prepared the documents for counsel by a process of selection and sifting and himself cop[ied] them' ([1989] 3 All ER at 776).

Whichever form the rule takes, it is hardly acceptable that a copy of an unprivileged document should be privileged merely because it was made by a lawyer. Such a result is clearly not required by the need to promote candour between client and lawyer. Nor does the risk that the opponent would be able to figure out the lawyer's advice, by learning what copies are in the hands of the proponent's lawyer, offer substantial support to such a rule. This is because the mere existence of copies must be disclosed in the list of documents served on the opponent after the close of pleadings; RSC Ord 24, r 1. On learning of their existence, the opponent would usually be able to obtain copies from other sources. Moreover, in many cases the disclosure of the contents of pre-existing documents could not possibly reveal the legal advice given. The only authority cited for Lord Evershed MR's dictum in *Watson v Cammell Laird* was *The Palermo* (1883) 9 PD 6. However, as I argued in last year's Review, *The Palermo* was really a case of public interest immunity and could not support Lord Evershed MR's conclusion. The sooner any remnant of the rule which offers privilege to a copy of an unprivileged document is put to rest the better.

A further case that has restored a measure of good sense to legal professional privilege is *Webster v James Chapman & Co (a firm)* [1989] 3 All ER 939. In an action for personal injuries against his employers the plaintiff commissioned, through his solicitors, a report form consulting engineers. The report dealt with the method of unloading lorries at the defendants' premises and was partly unfavourable to the plaintiff's claim. Through a clerical error the plaintiff's solicitors sent the report to the defendants' solicitors. When they discovered their mistake, the plaintiffs' solicitors sought an order for the return of the report and for restraining its use in the proceedings. Scott J found himself faced with the apparently irreconcilable decisions of *Calcraft v Guest* [1898] 1 QB 759, and *Lord Ashburton v Pape* [1913] 2 Ch 469, and with two more recent decisions of the Court of Appeal which did little to remove the conflict.

Calcraft v Guest decided that once a document subject to legal privilege has fallen into the hands of a third party, the privilege no longer attaches to it and it may be adduced in evidence. *Ashburton v Pape* decided that a client whose privileged documents fell into the hands of a stranger may obtain an injunction for the return of the documents and restrain the stranger from their use in any legal proceedings. In *Goddard v Nationwide Building Society* [1986] 3 All ER 264 the Court of Appeal held that both decisions were right. Nourse LJ explained:

> 'The crucial point is that the party who desires the protection must seek it before the other party has adduced the confidential communication in evidence or otherwise relied on it at trial' ([1986] 3 All ER at 271).

In the commentary on this case three years ago it was suggested that the main flaw in the Court of Appeal's reasoning lay in a failure to recognise that our famous pair of cases was concerned with two entirely different matters ([1986] All ER Rev 160). A distinction needs to be drawn between privilege and confidence. Legal professional privilege confers immunity from the compulsory process of obtaining evidence; it prevents the courts from issuing subpoenas for obtaining such evidence or from ordering witnesses to answer questions designed to elicit privileged information. All that *Calcraft v Guest* decided was that when a privileged document is no longer in the hands of those entitled to claim immunity from the process of obtaining production or answers, there is nothing to prevent its use in evidence. But of course if a person has a right to confidence in a document, such person can protect his right by injunction, and this is what lay behind *Ashburton v Pape*. In *Webster v James Chapman & Co (a firm)* [1989] 3 All ER 939 Scott J has reached a similar conclusion. More importantly, Scott J found that although a court had jurisdiction to restrain breach of confidence by injunction, there was no automatic right to such an order. Indeed, it is a matter of first principle that injunctions are not granted as a matter of right but only in the exercise of discretion on the merits. In the *Goddard* case, Scott J explained, the Court of Appeal could not have held that the courts are duty bound to grant automatic injunctions to those who wished to restrain breach of confidence ([1989] 3 All ER at 944–945).

Scott J outlined the way in which this discretion should be exercised. He referred to the principles outlined in *Guinness Peat Properties Ltd v Fitzroy Robinson Partnership (a firm)* [1987] 2 All ER 716. There Slade LJ held that once a privileged document has been inadvertently disclosed in discovery proceedings, it is generally too late to claim injunctive relief. He indicated that the courts would normally give such relief if disclosure was obtained by fraud or trick of if the person who received the privileged document immediately realised the mistake by which the document came into his possession. To this Scott J added two important riders. First, that

> 'if the document had come into the possession of the other side not through trick or fraud but due to a mistake or carelessness on the part of the party entitled to the document or by his advisers, the balance will be very different from the balance in a fraud case' ([1989] 3 All ER at 946–947).

Second, and more significant still, he considered that if an injunction to prevent the use of information in litigation could inhibit the party, who possesses the information, in the conduct of the litigation, an injunction should not be normally issued; especially where the document was divulged through carelessness (at 947).

It is illuminating to study the way in which Scott J exercised his discretion. The plaintiff sought not only to suppress the consultants' report but also to adduce a second report prepared by the same consultants. This second report, apparently, took into account the plaintiff's comments on the unfavourable conclusions in the first report and those conclusions were not repeated in the later report. Scott J refused to oblige the plaintiff in suppressing the first report and remarked that

> 'the conduct of the defendant's case would be seriously embarrassed if the defendant and its legal advisers were not able to make use of their knowledge of the contents of the original report, knowledge that has come into their possession through no fault of theirs' ([1989] 3 All ER at 947).

If counsel cross-examining the consultants had been forbidden to use the information gleaned from the first report, counsel would have found it impossible to probe the consultants' conclusions without feeling that some of the questions came to mind because of the about-turn of the second report. Once we have learnt something, we cannot erase the knowledge from our mind (although we may unselfconsciously forget what we knew).

The exercise of the discretion in deciding whether to restrain the use of confidential material involves, as will have become clear, the striking of a balance between the interests of the plaintiff who seeks to suppress confidential information and the interests of the defendant who seeks to use it in evidence. Into this balance Scott J has thrown, as we have seen, the effect that knowledge has on the conduct of one's case and has thereby greatly reduced the scope of orders to prevent the use of information that had once been immune from production. However, the very existence of a discretion, albeit limited, to restrain the use in evidence of confidential material must be subject to serious doubt.

The general principle is that, if called upon to do so, one must produce in court all relevant evidence. Subpoenas ad testificandum and subpoenas duces tecum are the compulsory instruments by which the courts secure the evidence necessary to determine the truth about the facts in issue. It is no answer to a subpoena to say that one is bound in contract or in honour not to tell what the court wants to know. Legal professional privilege entitles lawyers and their clients to keep their communications to themselves. They are immune from compulsory process. This immunity may extend to third parties, such as consultants who are recruited to help with the preparation of a case for trial. However, once the material has got out, it should not be kept out of court on account of its confidential nature any more than would any other confidential material.

In this respect the decision in *R v Governor of Pentonville Prison, ex p Osman* [1989] 3 All ER 701 makes good sense. In extradition proceedings initiated in England by the Government of Hong Kong against Osman, it was alleged that Osman had accepted corrupt payments which were transmitted to him through his solicitors in Malaysia. The solicitors were ordered to testify abroad, where objection to their testimony was taken on the grounds of legal professional privilege. The objection was overruled and the solicitors gave evidence accordingly. In the extradition proceedings before a magistrate in England objection was taken afresh to the admissibility of the solicitors' statements on grounds of privilege. Lloyd LJ referred to *R v Tompkins* (1977) 67 Cr App R 181 at 184, and invoked the distinction discussed earlier between immunity form production, on the one hand, and inadmissibility, on the other. Lloyd LJ concluded that once privileged material has come out, it cannot be excluded ([1989] 3 All ER at 730). Thus Lloyd LJ was prepared to countenance admissibility even though the material may have come out through a judicial mistake.

This ruling is laudable. It would make a mockery of justice for a court to turn its back on incriminating evidence merely because the solicitors should not have been ordered to divulge the information in the first place. Such a prospect, of keeping the court in ignorance of material evidence known to both parties, did not however deter the Court of Appeal in *Guinness Peat Properties Ltd v Fitzroy Robinson Partnership (a firm)* [1987] 2 All ER 716; [1987]

All ER Rev 123; in *Goddard v Nationwide Building Society* [1986] 3 All ER 264; [1986] All ER Rev 160; or in *British Coal Corp v Dennis Rye Ltd (No 2)* [1988] 3 All ER 816; [1988] All ER Rev 140. True, in the *Osman* case it was also held that the privilege was lost because the client had used his legal advisers for the purpose of furthering crime. But it would appear that Lloyd LJ was prepared to admit the solicitor's evidence quite independently of this factor.

The *Osman* case establishes another significant point. Where it is alleged that legal privilege is overridden by the consideration that the client acted in furtherance of crime, the court is entitled to inspect the material before ruling on the point even if there is not extraneous evidence to support the claim of furtherance of crime: [1989] 3 All ER at 730.

In what seems to have been a sustained campaign this year against abuse of privilege, the courts have also turned their attention to bankruptcy situations. A person was declared bankrupt and the question arose whether that person could assert legal privilege against his trustee in bankruptcy in relation to pre-bankruptcy proprietary dispositions. Peter Gibson J held that at common law a

> 'trustee is no ordinary third party. In him are automatically vested all the assets of the bankrupt divisible among his creditors . . . A successor in title to property succeeds to and is entitled to assert the privilege of a predecessor in title and so stands in the predecessor's shoes to that extent . . .'

Re Konigsberg (a bankrupt), ex parte the trustee v Konigsberg [1989] 3 All ER 289 at 297. This conclusion is now reinforced by s 311 of the Insolvency Act 1986.

Two further points were clarified in the last mentioned case. It has been held that where a solicitor is employed by two clients in a conveyancing transaction, the communications concerning the transaction between either of them and the solicitor are disclosable in favour of the other. Further, once a client has revealed in court part of the communication between himself and his solicitor regarding a transaction in issue, the client has thereby waived his privilege with respect to all communications connected with the same transaction.

Public interest immunity and the protection of innocence

The criminal procedure has to accommodate two goals which are at times at odds with each other. On the one hand, it has to afford accused persons an adequate opportunity to establish their innocence. On the other hand, it has to promote the detection of crime. One source of conflict between these two aims was considered in *R v Johnson* [1989] 1 All ER 121. To a charge of supplying controlled drugs the accused's defence was, inter alia, that he was buying rather than selling at the relevant time. The evidence against him consisted of the testimony of police officers who secretly observed the accused from premises belonging to private residents, who agreed to provide the police with observation posts. The prosecution was granted permission to withhold any information which could lead to the identification of these premises. As a result, counsel for the accused was not allowed to cross-examine the officers about the location of their observation posts and of the nature of any obstructions to their view.

The prosecution relied on public interest immunity as justifying the withholding of information about the observation posts. It is well established that the police may suppress the identity of informants in the interests of combating crime. It is therefore understandable that suppression should also be allowed in order to maintain the secrecy of observation posts; see *R v Rankine* [1986] 2 All ER 566. It is, after all, as important to secure the co-operation of the public in providing suitable observation posts as it is to encourage the public to come forward with information. The case under consideration is important from another point of view. It outlines the evidence to be supplied and the procedure to be followed when a claim for public interest immunity is made in such circumstances. It also provides some indication of how the balance between the interests of the accused and those of the prosecution must be struck.

A number of requirements have to be met in order to satisfy the trial judge that there is a real need to prevent identification of premises. It has been decided that an officer of a rank of sergeant, or above, ought to be in charge of surreptitious observation of this kind. Such officer must consult the occupiers of the proposed posts in advance and establish their attitude to possible disclosure in legal proceedings. Further, after observations have taken place, a chief inspector must again consult the occupiers and ascertain their attitude to disclosure. A claim for immunity would be entertained only if the owners of the premises in question object to being identified. Having satisfied himself on this score at a hearing conducted in the absence of the jury, the judge must then consider whether the suppression of the location of the observation posts could result in injustice to the accused.

In this regard the judge must be convinced that the jury would be able to make a proper assessment of the reliability of the constables' testimony even in the absence of cross-examination about the precise location from which they observed the crime. This is the most tricky part of the procedure adopted in this case. All that the jury heard was the policemen's testimony that they had observed the accused from some posts which were within one hundred yards and from other posts within one hundred and fifty yards from the place where the accused stood. However, without further information it is difficult to see how the trier of fact could assess the accuracy of the observations; especially when the issue is not so much the identity of the accused but whether he was the purchaser or the seller of the drugs. The precaution was taken of informing the jury of the reasons for the curtailment of the cross-examination. They were told of the necessity of protecting the citizens who co-operated with the police. This, however, offers meagre safeguard to the accused. First, knowing that there was justification for curtailing the cross-examination does not help in the assessment of the accuracy of the observation. Second, the information that residents face threats from a criminal community to which the accused may well have belonged could create prejudice and incline the jury to take the police evidence on trust. It is hard to escape the feeling that for the sake of crime detection and prevention the court has weakened the protection of the innocent and has set a dangerous precedent.

Public interest immunity

In *Conway v Rimmer* [1968] 1 All ER 874 the House of Lords took a momentous and progressive step. It discarded the notion of Crown privilege which had been used by ministers to claim immunity from production in evidence of all sorts of material regardless of importance or of possible impact on the functioning of government. In its stead it introduced a special procedure for making and judging claims for immunity. This procedure is known as the balancing exercise which requires the judge to place on the one side of the scales the harm to the public interest that may result from the production of the evidence in question, and on the other side the harm that may ensue from withholding evidence to the administration of justice and to the interests of the litigant seeking production. This procedure requires ministers to explain the public interest and enjoins the courts to judge on a case by case basis whether acceptance of a claim of immunity would unduly sacrifice the interests of the administration of justice and the prospects of the particular litigant to make out his case. Underlying the philosophy of *Conway v Rimmer* is the assumption that withholding relevant evidence from the court requires strict justification. It follows that it is for the party seeking to withhold relevant evidence to justify his request and not for the party seeking production. We have however come a long way from 1968 and although the notion of Crown privilege has not been fully revived, the law has reverted to a position that is now close to this discard doctrine.

Evans v Chief Constable of Surrey Constabulary (A-G intervening) [1989] 2 All ER 594 illustrates a number of the obstacles that litter the way of litigants seeking disclosure from public bodies. The plaintiff was arrested on suspicion of murder. Before he was charged, another person admitted the commission of the murder and was convicted. The plaintiff sued the police for wrongful arrest and false imprisonment and asked to see the report sent by the police to the DPP following his arrest. Although the police seemed prepared to let him have it, the Attorney General intervened claiming public interest immunity.

Wood J explained that even before the balancing test is used, the plaintiff must make out a case for production in discovery. In ordinary circumstances all that is needed is relevance: *Cie Financière et Commerciale du Pacifique v Peruvian Guano Co* (1882) 11 QBD 55, 63. Not so when a claim for public interest immunity has been made. Here, according to *Burmah Oil Co Ltd v Bank of England and A-G* [1979] 3 All ER 700, 726, the litigant seeking disclosure has to show a 'reasonable probability of finding support' in the document sought. There would be few cases where a party who has no access to a document could surmount this obstacle for the simple reason that he who has no access to a document and is ignorant of its contents can prove nothing about the document. It follows that once a claim for immunity has been made, the judge need not even engage in the balancing process, except in the wholly exceptionl situation where the litigant knows what is in the document. If this is right, the balancing process is virtually redundant. As we have seen, a person cannot prove the usefulness of a document of the contents of which he is ignorant. Where, by distinction, the party seeking disclosure is familiar with the document, it would be hard to make a case against disclosure because any damage to the public interest will have already taken place and no further purpose can be achieved by keeping the court ignorant of evidence known to both parties.

In the present case Wood J reached the predictable conclusion that the plaintiff had not established that the report to the DPP would advance his case; indeed, how could he? This was sufficient to dispose of the case but having heard argument on public interest immunity, Wood J felt inclined to carry out the balancing exercise. This consisted simply of accepting the Attorney General's explanation that immunity was necessary in order to maintain freedom of communication between police officers and the DPP. The argument from candour was criticised by the House of Lords in *Conway v Rimmer*. Indeed, the very existence of the balancing exercise entails that disclosure could in appropriate circumstances be ordered and public servants cannot therefore expect invariable secrecy. Wood J gave no consideration to the other side of the scales and did not weigh the interest of the plaintiff because, presumably, the right of the latter to see the document had already been defeated in the pre-balancing obstacle.

It has to be said in fairness to Wood J that he has not created this state of affairs, there was ample authority to support him. He merely reflects a general judicial opinion when he says that—

> 'if a public interest immunity claim is raised, and it is usually only raised on sound or solid ground, it is necessary for those who seek to overcome it to demonstrate the existence of a counteracting interest calling for disclosure . . .'; [1989] 2 All ER at 598.

A study of the history of Crown privilege reveals that the assumption that immunity is usually claimed on solid grounds is incorrect. The sad truth is that current judicial opinion no longer accords with the exalted aims of *Conway v Rimmer*.

Extradition

I M YEATS, BCL, MA
Barrister, Senior Lecturer in Law, Queen Mary and Westfield College, University of London

A state has sought the return of a fugitive criminal from the United Kingdom. To what extent should it have to establish that the conduct alleged against the fugitive would also have been contrary to the law of the United Kingdom? The Fugitive Offenders Act 1881 (enacted at a time when the political and legal character of all the relevant states was very similar) imposed no requirement of double criminality, but expressly provided that it 'shall apply to an offence notwithstanding that by the law of the part of Her Majesty's dominions in or on his way to which the fugitive is or is suspected of being it is not an offence': s 9. By s 26 of the Extradition Act 1870, however, an extradition crime was defined as 'a crime which, if committed in England or within English jurisdiction, would be one of the crimes described in the first schedule to this Act.'

A meeting of Commonwealth law ministers was held in 1966 to review the scheme for the surrender of fugitive criminals within the Commonwealth in the light of developments since 1881. Paragraph 10 of the *Scheme relating to the Rendition of Fugitive Offenders within the Commonwealth* (Cmnd 3008) (1966) specifically provided for a double-criminality rule:

> 'The return of a fugitive offender will either be precluded by law or be subject to refusal by the competent executive authority if the facts on which the request for his return is grounded do not constitute an offence under the law of the country or territory in which he is found.'

Section 3(1) of the Fugitive Offenders Act 1967 gave effect to that rule in the United Kingdom by providing that—

> '. . . an offence of which a person is accused or has been convicted in a designated Commonwealth country or United Kingdom dependency is a relevant offence if— . . . (c) . . . the act or omission constituting the offence, or the equivalent act of omission, would constitute an offence against the law of the United Kingdom if it took place within the United Kingdom . . .'

The House of Lords has had to determine the meaning of that provision in *Government of Canada v Aronson* [1989] 2 All ER 1025. Part of the problem is caused by the ambiguity of the expression 'offence'. To the question, 'Of what offence is John White accused?', both, 'Murder' and, 'The murder of Anne Black in Ottawa in May' would be acceptable answers. But the act or omission constituting murder does not mean the same as the act or omission constituting the murder of Anne Black. What degree of correspondence between the laws of the requesting state and of the United Kingdom has to be established?

Three principles would seem to be clear. First, a person should not be returned to another Commonwealth country if what he is alleged to have done would not have been criminal if done in the United Kingdom. This is ensured partly by s 3(1)(c) and partly by s 7(5) which requires the court of committal also to be satisfied 'that the evidence would be sufficient to warrant his trial for that offence if it had been committed within the jurisdiction of the court'. Secondly, the scheme is designed to ensure that persons who have committed criminal offences should be sent for trial in some country which has jurisdiction over them, and this purpose should not be defeated by relying on technical differences in the definitions of criminal offences between the laws of various Commonwealth countries. Thirdly, it must be possible to give effect to s 4(3) which requires that there should be satisfactory arrangements with the requesting state to ensure that the fugitive criminal will not be tried after his return except for—

> '(a) The offence in respect of which his return under this Act is requested; (b) any lesser offence proved by the facts proved before the court of committal; or (c) any other offence being a relevant offence in respect of which the Secretary of State may consent to his being so dealt with . . .'

A fugitive is surrendered to the requesting state because the magistrate is satisfied that there is sufficient evidence in respect of all the elements of an English crime. If he were then to be convicted in the requesting state without any proof of one of those elements (because it is not an ingredient of the crime under that law), would he still have been convicted of the offence in respect of which his return had been requested? If he would, how is the purpose of s 4(3) to be achieved?

Aronson was sought by the Canadian authorities who alleged that he had committed 77 offences of dishonesty in Canada. In respect of 69 of these there was an argument that they were not relevant offences under s 3(1)(c) of the Fugitive Offenders Act 1967. In each case the Canadian crime (as defined in the Criminal Code of Canada) did not require proof of an element which was essential to the nearest corresponding English crime. For example 32 offences arose under s 338(1) of the Criminal Code which provides:

> 'Everyone who, by deceit, falsehood or other fraudulent means, whether or not it is a false pretence within the meaning of this Act, defrauds the public . . . is guilty of an indictable offence.'

There is no need to perpetrate deception or to intend to deprive the victim permanently of the goods or money obtained. A person could be convicted under that section who could not be convicted of any corresponding offence under English law. On the other hand many of those convicted under it could in fact also have satisfied the additional requirements demanded by English law. The evidence against Aronson apparently did demonstrate that the conduct on which he was actually alleged to have engaged fell within the scope of the English offence. A majority of the House of Lords held that in these circumstances Aronson could not be surrendered to stand trial in Canada on these charges or on other charges to which similar objection could be taken.

The problem first arose in *R v Governor of Brixton Prison, ex p Gardner* [1968] 1 All ER 636. Warrants were issued in New Zealand for the arrest of Gardner, alleging that he had obtained sums of money with intent to defraud by means of false pretences, the particulars being that he had falsely represented that a company would supply distributors with cosmetics. In each case the false representation related to the future, which was not then criminal under English law The Divisional Court granted his application for habeas corpus on the basis that the offences with which he was charged were not relevant offences under s 3(1)(c) of the Fugitive Offenders Act 1967. The reasoning was similar to that now adopted by a majority of the House of Lords, although it appears that in any event the actual conduct alleged against Gardner did not fall within the scope of the English criminal law.

The statute is ambiguous, but the alternative constructions are not easy to set out even in descriptive language. Lord Griffiths (who, with Lord Jauncey of Tullichettle, dissented) expressed the choice in these terms:

> 'Do these words refer to the conduct of the accused so that s 3(1)(c) is satisfied if what he did would constitute a crime if committed in this country? Or do the words refer to the ingredients of the Canadian offence, so that s 3(1)(c) is only satisfied if the definition of the offence in the Canadian Criminal Code contains all the ingredients in the definition of a corresponding English offence?' ([1989] 2 All ER at 1030).

If that is the correct way of expressing the alternatives, it is not surprising that Lord Griffiths preferred the first. The second would indeed make the scheme of rendition unworkable, for it would never be possible to secure the return of an offender for an offence which was defined in significantly wider terms in the law of the requesting state than in that of the United Kingdom. Two awkward consequences might however follow and Lord Griffiths's answer to them was not wholly convincing. The first is the requirement of s 4(3), referred to above. Lord Griffiths took the view that the offence for which the fugitive was surrendered was the offence as particularised in the magistrate's warrant of committal and this warrant should contain clear particulars of each relevant offence. It would then apparently follow that the authorities in the requesting state would be alert to the need to prove some element which was disclosed in those particulars but was not an ingredient of the offence under their own law. The second difficulty is that s 3(1) applies not only to the situation where a fugitive is wanted in order to stand trial but also to the situation where a convicted criminal has escaped from custody, where the surrendering state would have no information other than the fact of the conviction for an allegedly relevant offence, and could not be expected to examine in detail the evidence presented at the trial. Requests for the surrender of a convicted criminal are of course rarer and Lord Griffiths was of the opinion (at 1032) that it would normally be possible to determine whether the crime for which the accused was convicted was founded on facts that constituted an English crime. Where there was some doubt that this was so, surrender would be refused.

It is not clear that the majority saw the choice of statutory constructions in the same terms. Lord Bridge of Harwich (at 1027) posed it in this way.

> 'Does it [s 3(1)(c)] mean that the ingredients of the Commonwealth offence, as disclosed by the particulars of the offence in the charge, would, if proved, establish guilt of a corresponding United Kingdom offence (the narrow construction)? Or does it mean that the totality of the evidence relied on to prove the Commonwealth offence would, if accepted, prove guilt of a corresponding United Kingdom offence (the wide construction)?'

Lord Bridge's second question appears to be Lord Griffiths's first? But Lord Bridge's first (which he adopted) does not seem to be the same as Lord Griffiths's second? Lord Bridge refers not just to the Commonwealth crime as defined in the Code but to the ingredients of the crime as disclosed by the particulars of the offence in the charge. This is clear also in the speech of Lord Lowry, who gave the fullest speech for the majority. He referred (at 1036) to 'the criminal conduct specifically alleged against him in the Commonwealth country's warrant' and not to 'the criminal conduct covered in the Commonwealth country's code'. Again, after citing with apparent approval the judgment of Edmund Davies LJ in ex p Gardner [1968] 1 All ER 636 at 642, his Lordship continued (at 1045–1046),

> 'Ex p Gardner does not appear to say that a magistrate would never be justified in committing a fugitive under s 7(5)(a) to face trial on a New Zealand charge of false pretences just because a person could be convicted under New Zealand law by reason of a false pretence as to the future, whereas it would in 1968 have required proof of a false pretence as to the present in order to justify conviction in England. It concentrates attention on what is charged in the warrant. I conceive that, if the particulars of the offence given in or annexed to the warrant had alleged a false pretence as to the present, the magistrate could then properly have committed the fugitive to await his return to New Zealand, since the charge specified in the warrant and the particulars given therein or annexed thereto constitute the offence in respect of which the fugitive's return is requested.'

The primary responsibility therefore rests on the requesting state so to frame the charges as expressed in the warrant sent to the United Kingdom as to reveal (if the facts justify it) conduct which would be criminal under the law of the United Kingdom. In some cases that might not be intelligible in terms of the local law, but in many it would. There seems to be no reason why the charges in ex p Gardner could not have made clear (if such were the facts) that the representations which he was alleged to have made related to the present. If expressed in this way, the problems with the approach of Lord Griffiths largely disappear. There is no problem with s 4(3) because the offence for which the fugitive was surrendered would be the offence as set out in the warrant from the requesting state. There would still be some problem with the case of the fugitive convicted criminal, since the charges in that case would not have been framed with a view to future extradition proceedings, but in many cases it would be reasonably clear that the offence of which he was convicted was a relevant offence under s 3(1)(c).

Section 3(1)(c) figured also in the judgment of the Divisional Court in R v Governor of Pentonville Prison, ex p Osman [1989] 3 All ER 701. It was held that, where the offences were alleged to have taken place partly within the territory of the requesting state and partly in third countries, the question to ask was whether there would have been a crime against the law of England (which would have been indictable in England) if those acts which took place in the requesting state had taken place within the jurisdiction of the English courts. After an analysis of complex provisions of the English criminal law, the court concluded that this requirement was satisfied and that Osman could be surrendered to Hong Kong to face various charges of conspiracy, theft and false accounting allegedly committed while he was chairman of the board of Bumiputra Malaysia Finance Ltd, a wholly owned subsidiary of a major

Malaysian bank, the Bumiputra Bank. The authority to proceed against Osman had been dated 13 May 1986 (following an earlier authority dated 24 January) and he had been committed to custody awaiting return pursuant to an order made on 1 June 1987 by the Chief Metropolitan Magistrate. Since the failure of the application for habeas corpus in the reported proceedings (judgment in which was given on 30 March 1988) he has made two further unsuccessful applications and was still in custody at the end of 1989, his continued detention having become the subject of parliamentary questions.

In *Aronson* Lord Lowry emphasised (at 1048–1049) that the requirements for surrender within the Commonwealth were different from those under the Extradition Act 1870 for surrender to foreign countries. A decision under the latter Act was not necessarily relevant to proceedings under the 1967 Act and in particular reliance on *Government of Denmark v Nielsen* [1984] 2 All ER 81, [1984] AC 606 had been misplaced. In *Osman* (which was decided before, but reported after, *Aronson*) *Nielsen* was referred to (at 724–725) and the Divisional Court suggested that the practice in Commonwealth cases should be brought into line with that in extradition cases and the foreign warrant should not be annexed to the authority to proceed. In the light of *Aronson* this may no longer be appropriate.

The Divisional Court in *Osman* also considered the respective roles of the magistrate and the Divisional Court and in particular the language which should be used to describe those roles. The task of the magistrate is formulated as being to consider the evidence to see whether that evidence is such that on it a reasonable jury properly directed could convict (720–721). The task of the Divisional Court has been phrased in different ways in earlier cases. The present Divisional Court took the view that these did not represent different meanings, but that the most appropriate approach was to define the task in *Wednesbury* terms, whether there was evidence on which a reasonable magistrate, properly directing himself in law, could commit (722–723).

An unusual point on the Fugitive Offenders Act 1967 was raised in *R v Brixton Prison Governor, ex p Kahan* [1989] 2 All ER 368, after the government of the Republic of Fiji applied under that Act for the return of a fugitive criminal after it had become a republic and, according to a statement by Commonwealth leaders, its membership of the Commonwealth had lapsed. No steps had however been taken to amend the Order in Council under which Fiji had been named as a designated Commonwealth country for the purposes of the Act. The Act throughout referred to 'the designated Commonwealth country' without there being any qualification that the country had in fact to be recognised as such. Accordingly, the Divisional Court held that it was still competent to order the surrender to Fiji under that statute.

The Divisional Court had to consider a narrow point of extradition law in *R v Chief Metropolitan Stipendiary Magistrate, ex p Secretary of State for the Home Department* [1989] 1 All ER 151 and in doing so refused to follow its own previous decision in *R v Governor of Pentonville Prison, ex p Khubchandani* (1980) 71 Cr App R 241. The magistrate had refused to order the return to Norway in respect of some of the specified charges of a fugitive who had been convicted of extradition crimes involving false accounting, forgery and theft because he held that these were in different ways concerned with tax evasion and that to order surrender would be to enforce the revenue laws of a foreign state. The Divisional Court disagreed with the conclusion that the magistrate had been bound by authority to reach. Even if there were a general common law rule deriving from international law that prevented the enforcement through extradition proceedings of the revenue laws of a foreign state, there was no trace of its surviving in the provisions of the Extradition Act 1870. That Act had incorporated specifically two other common law restrictions on the right to secure extradition, viz the exception for political offences and the requirement that the fugitive could be tried only for those offences for which he had been extradited. There was no room for the inference that another common law exception had survived intact. Provided the offence was an extradition crime, surrender was still possible even if it had been committed in the context of the revenue laws.

The Privy Council was concerned in *United States Government v Bowe* [1989] 3 All ER 315 with extradition from the Bahamas to the United States. However, the Extradition Act 1870 and the extradition treaty between the United Kingdom and the United States (brought into force by the United States of America (Extradition) Order in Council 1935, SR & O 1935/574) were held to continue to regulate extradition from the Bahamas. The principal point in issue was whether the offences with which Bowe was charged of conspiracy to import and distribute cocaine were extraditable offences under the treaty as well as extradition crimes under the Extradition Act. Article 3(24) of the treaty included in the list of extraditable offences 'Crimes or offences or attempted crimes or offences in connection with the traffic in dangerous drugs'. The argument for the fugitive was that, since art 3(24) did not refer to a conspiracy whereas other provisions in art 3 did (eg 3(1) 'murder or attempt or conspiracy to murder') there was an implication that conspiracy in connection with drug offences was not an extraditable offence. The Privy Council had no difficulty in rejecting this argument. Conspiracy is a crime and therefore prima facie a reference to crimes in connection with the traffic in dangerous drugs would include a conspiracy; an express reference to conspiracy was necessary only where the treaty referred to a specific crime such as murder and not to crimes in general terms. The Privy Council was critical of the form which the proceedings had taken in that the magistrate had broken off the committal proceedings in order that application should be made to the Supreme Court for orders of certiorari and prohibition and suggested that the entire case should be presented to the magistrate, including all the evidence, before a prerogative remedy was sought. In that way the order of the Privy Council would achieve finality.

Family Law

S M CRETNEY, MA, DCL, FBA
Solicitor, Professor of Law, University of Bristol

Justice or efficiency?

Courts exercise the judicial power of the state (Contempt of Court Act 1981, s 19); and it is axiomatic that those concerned must be accorded the basic rights conveniently summarised in the phrase 'due process of law'. But there is, particularly in family cases, a tension between the apparent legalism to which that process may give rise, and the desire to maximise efficiency by defining the issues which require adjudication in an attempt to save time at the hearing and to focus the parties' minds in advance on those issues in the hope that a consensus may be reached and a hostile court hearing avoided.

This tension is well illustrated by the case of *Dimino v Dimino* [1989] 2 All ER 280, CA. In a father's custody application the court ordered that a court welfare officer make a report; and that report was—in accordance with a routine procedure at the court in question—referred to a judge. The parties were subsequently notified that the judge had read the report and proposed that an order be made in specified terms. The notice asked the parties to notify the court whether they agreed with the proposal, or whether a hearing would be required.

The Court of Appeal emphatically condemned this practice (although perhaps surprisingly did not upset the order which, after a full hearing, the judge had made). The notice procedure—although intended, as a lawyer might well understand, simply to save the time and costs of litigation—was likely to convey to the mind of the recipient that the judge had predetermined the case. It is of the highest importance that a judge should avoid any suggestion that he has reached a view on the appropriate relief, before he has considered the evidence; and parties should not be given any ground for thinking that the judge had arrived at even a preliminary view as to the order which will ultimately be made. The practice should therefore be discontinued.

Nature of care proceedings

The word 'adversarial' has unpleasant overtones; but in relation to judicial proceedings it merely indicates a system under which the judge acts as an umpire, determining the issues which the parties choose to raise rather than conducting an inquiry on behalf of society at large: *Jones v National Coal Board* [1957] 2 All ER 155 at 159, per Lord Denning MR. The adversarial system characterises English criminal and civil procedure; but much of English family law is influenced by the inquisitorial model of procedure in which the court has certain duties of inquiry, irrespective of the parties wishes: see *Re E (SA) (a minor) (wardship)* [1984] 1 All ER 289, per Lord Scarman; and note the duty to inquire which is statutorily imposed on the divorce court by the

Matrimonial Causes Act 1973, s 1(3) (duty to inquire into facts in divorce proceedings) and s 41 (duty to inquire into arrangements proposed for children).

Many of the most difficult and far reaching decisions about children are taken by magistrates' courts in the exercise of the jurisdiction conferred by the Children and Young Persons Act 1969. That Act bears all too many traces of its origins as a measure intended to be appropriate as a framework for dealing with both the deprived and the 'depraved' or delinquent. In particular, the structure of the legislation (and of the procedural rules governing its administration: Magistrates' Courts (Children and Young Persons) Rules 1988, SI No 913) frequently suggests an adversarial structure in which the applicant must establish the case before the court can consider material relevant to the child's welfare: see eg Magistrates' Courts (Children and Young Persons) Rules 1988, SI No 913, r 25(3). Yet statute (see Children and Young Persons Act 1969, s 32B(3)) and rules now provide for the appointment in most care proceedings of a guardian ad litem charged to safeguard the child's interests; and some recent judicial decisions emphasise that care proceedings are to be regarded as 'essentially non-adversary, non-party proceedings': *Humberside CC v DPR (an infant)* [1977] 3 All ER 964 at 967, per Lord Widgery CJ.

The conflict between these two approaches came to a head in *R v Birmingham Juvenile Court, ex p G and others (minors)* [1989] 3 All ER 336. After proceedings had been started, the local authority decided that there was no longer any need for a care order; but the guardian ad litem appointed by the court was (in the light of her own inquiries) of a contrary opinion. She considered that voluntary supervision would not adequately safeguard the children's interests. At the hearing counsel for the authority sought leave to withdraw the application; but the justices (in the exercise of their discretion: *R v Wandsworth West Juvenile Court, ex p S* [1984] FLR 713) rejected this application. Counsel then stated that he proposed to offer no evidence. The justices refused the guardian's application to adduce evidence, and, applying the principle that the proceedings were adversarial, dismissed the case. The Court of Appeal agreed with Stephen Brown P in the Divisional Court ([1988] 3 All ER 726, [1988] All ER Rev 159) that they had been wrong to do so.

The Court of Appeal emphasised the court's duty to 'have regard' to the child's welfare (Children and Young Persons Act 1933, s 44); and also its duty to hear evidence—in this case the guardian's report—available as a result of orders made by the court earlier in the proceedings. In a case where the welfare of children is involved, to prevent the admission of evidence prepared by order of the court itself and bearing directly on those very issues would (said Purchas LJ at 345) be 'not only an affront to common sense but a denial of justice.' The case reveals a conflict not only between the adversarial and inquisitorial models of procedure; but also (as Dillon LJ pointed out) between the principle that child care decisions have been entrusted to local authorities (see *W v Hertfordshire CC* [1985] 2 All ER 301) and the principle that a juvenile court is a court of law which has to exercise a judicial discretion and therefore has to hear any evidence tendered to it. In the present case, the inquisitorial role of the court has been significantly emphasised; and the balance of decision-taking power shifted marginally away from the local authority to the courts.

The guardian and her duties

The crucial importance of the guardian ad litem is also emphasised by the decision of Ewbank J (sitting as an additional judge of the Queen's Bench Division) in *R v North Yorkshire County Council, ex p M* [1989] 1 All ER 143. The parents of a child in care, faced with the local authority's decision that adoption—if possible by a family which would accept continued access by the parents—would be appropriate for their child, applied for the discharge of the care order. The court appointed a guardian ad litem under the provisions of s 32A of the Children and Young Persons Act 1969. Six weeks before the date fixed for the final hearing of the parents' application the local authority decided to place the child for adoption, the adoption panel having previously recommended that access be phased out with a view to termination.

The parents applied for judicial review of the local authority's decision on the basis that the decision would seriously prejudice the pending proceedings in the juvenile court and was for that reason unreasonable and improperly made. Ewbank J rejected this argument; and held that the local authority's decision to act in accordance with the child's best interests could not be faulted on these grounds. But the decision was flawed for a different reason. This was that the guardian ad litem has a duty to regard the need to safeguard and promote the child's welfare as paramount, and to investigate all circumstances relevant to the proceedings: see now Magistrate's Courts (Children and Young Persons) Rules 1988, SI No 913, r 31(6)(a) and (b). That imposed a corresponding reciprocal duty on the local authority to disclose to the guardian ad litem any major proposed change in the circumstances of the child, and indeed to listen to her views about any such proposal. The authority's failure to do so vitiated their decision, which the court accordingly quashed.

The parents' victory in the initial application for judicial review (*R v North Yorkshire County Council, ex p M* [1989] 1 All ER 143) may appear to have been a pyrrhic one: the guardian's request that she be allowed to attend the subsequent meeting of the adoption panel was refused and an application to quash that refusal was rejected (*R v North Yorkshire County Council, ex p M (No 2)* [1989] 2 FLR 79). Moreover, the parents were effectively debarred from themselves warding the child by the fact that care proceedings were on foot: *A v Liverpool City Council* [1981] 2 All ER 385; and the local authority took no action to ward the child notwithstanding the recommendation by the judge who had initially granted leave to proceed to judicial review that they should consider doing so: *R v North Yorkshire County Council, ex p M* [1989] 1 All ER 143 at 144. Finally, the court rejected the parent's suggestion that it should itself ward the children since—although there could be exceptional circumstances in which the court, on a successful application for judicial review, could and should exercise the inherent jurisdiction and ward a child of its own motion—the present was not such an exceptional case: *R v North Yorkshire County Council, ex p M (No 3)* [1989] 2 FLR 82. But in fact the parents' persistence may have paid off in the end, since it appears that, faced with a further appeal by the parents and the guardian, the local authority itself warded the child: see [1990] Fam Law 91.

Access to wardship?

The two cases discussed above suggest that the guardian ad litem's duty to safeguard the child's interests before the court (Children and Young Persons Act 1969, s 32B(3)) places her in a very special position in care proceedings. But in *Re T and others (minors) (wardship: jurisdiction)* [1989] 1 All ER 297 the Court of Appeal declined to accord to the guardian any additional status or authority outside those proceedings. Care proceedings relating to children of a family were pending in two different juvenile courts. The two courts appointed the same guardian to act for all the children; and the guardian was concerned by difficulties which she apprehended she would face in dealing with two different proceedings in two different courts, the more so since there was a conflict of interest between the children. She accordingly issued an originating summons in wardship in an attempt to ensure that one court would be able to exercise jurisdiction over the whole family. The local authorities applied unsuccessfully to Booth J (see [1988] 3 WLR 713) to discharge the wardship; but they succeeded on appeal to the Court of Appeal.

The Court of Appeal held, first, that the applicant had no standing as a guardian ad litem to initiate wardship proceedings; and secondly that, even if she had, the principle of *A v Liverpool City Council* [1981] 2 All ER 385, prevented the court from exercising the wardship jurisdiction.

The decision seems surprising for two reasons. First, it is a cardinal principle of the wardship jurisdiction that any person with a sufficient interest may invoke it: see eg *Re D (a minor) (wardship: sterilisation)* [1976] 1 All ER 326 (application by concerned social worker)—and indeed it was accepted that the guardian could, as a private individual, properly have warded the children. Secondly, the House of Lords in *A v Liverpool City Council* [1981] 2 All ER 385 (particularly per Lord Wilberforce at 372) accepted that the court's inherent power remained available to fill gaps; and Booth J had concluded that neither juvenile court had the necessary statutory powers to safeguard and protect the welfare of the children precisely because she thought their interests should not be considered in isolation one from another. However, the Court of Appeal brushed this argument aside: neither local authority felt any difficulty in dealing with the cases under the statutory jurisdiction; and the court did not itself consider the fact that the application of the statutory code would inevitably result in the juvenile court considering individual children rather than the family as a whole to be a sufficient ground to justify removing the proceedings to the High Court.

In the light of these cases, it is difficult to resist the feeling that there are two inconsistent attitudes to the use of wardship in care situations: on the one hand, there is the highly restrictive approach adopted by the House of Lords and other appellate courts; and on the other, there is the more flexible attitude of some Family Division judges: see notably per Latey J, *R v Newham London Borough Council, ex p McL* [1988] 1 FLR 416. Be that as it may, the restrictive approach appears to have won the day, since provisions of the Children Act 1989 go a long way towards making it impossible for wardship to be invoked in local authority care cases. However, the Act does introduce a much more flexible system for transferring cases between courts; and it may well be that the new flexibility will enable some of the problems encountered in the administration of the law at the moment to be overcome.

The Children Act also seems to be based on the assumption that the High Court has an inherent jurisdiction over children which is unconnected with and exercisable without reference to wardship; and that this inherent jurisdiction will be available—for example, if injunctive relief is needed in respect of a child in care, or if there is a particularly difficult issue (such as irreversible medical treatment) to be resolved: see Lord Mackay of Clashfern, Joseph Jackson Memorial Lecture (1989) 139 NLJ 505 at 507. However, there seems to be a good deal of uncertainty as to the scope of such an inherent jurisdiction as can between from the decision of the Court of Appeal in *Re C and another (minors) (wardship: adoption)* [1989] 1 All ER 395.

In that case, the court in reliance on *Re McGrath (infants)* [1893] 1 Ch 143 had purported to appoint a guardian for a ward of court in the exercise of its inherent jurisdiction (thereby enabling the guardians to overcome the statutory prohibition on removal of children from this country for the purpose of adoption: Adoption Act 1976, s 56(1)). The Court of Appeal thought it doubtful whether any such inherent power existed; but held that in any case it had been wrong to make such an appointment: in wardship, ultimate responsibility for the child must remain with the court, and to appoint a guardian would inevitably be a derogation from the wardship court's powers over the child.

There seems to be little to suggest that the relationship between the statutory and other jurisdictions will cease to be troublesome; and this has certainly proved to be the case in relation to the Child Abduction Act 1985 (which gives effect to the Hague Convention on the Civil Aspects of International Child Abduction.) For example, in *Re J (minor: abduction: ward of court)* [1989] 3 All ER 590 the mother of a ward took her abroad without the consent of the court. The father—who had access rights—sought to invoke the procedures of the Convention; but these were dependent on proof that there had been an infringement of 'rights of custody' relating to the child and attributed to a 'person, institution or other body'. Swinton Thomas J held that there had been such an infringement in respect of the court's rights: the custody of a ward remained in the court, and the court came within the definition of a person institution or body for the purpose of the Convention. (See also *C v C (minor: abduction: rights of custody abroad)* [1989] 2 All ER 465.)

Wardship not to be used to question administrative decisions

The reluctance to allow wardship to be invoked in care cases is based on the general principle of constitutional law that where Parliament has by statute entrusted to a public authority an administrative power subject to safeguards which, however, contain no provision that the High Court is to be required to review the merits of decisions taken pursuant to the power, the High Court has no right to intervene: *W v Hertfordshire CC* [1985] 2 All ER 301 at 304, per Lord Scarman. Thus, long before it had become fashionable to invoke wardship in an attempt to question local authority decisions in care cases it was accepted that wardship could not be invoked to challenge immigration decisions: *Re A (an infant)* [1968] 2 All ER 145. It is therefore at first sight surprising that in *Re F (a minor)* [1989] 1 All ER 1155 the Court of appeal allowed an appeal from the decision of Hollings J striking out an originating summons issued so as to impede the Secretary of State from exercising his discretion to remove a 7 year old Nigerian child from the country.

The Court of Appeal accepted that wardship should not be used to hamper the immigration authorities in removing minors from the jurisdiction (see *Re A (an infant), Hanif v Secretary of State for Home Affairs* [1968] 2 All ER 145 at 153, per Russell LJ); but there could (so the court held) be exceptional cases in which the exercise of the jurisdiction was necessary to protect the child's welfare in circumstances in which immigration decisions would not thereby be put in issue. On the facts, the present case was exceptional in so far as those caring for the child in this country were entitled to have their position regularised by order of the court; and the Secretary of State's discretion was not affected since he had already undertaken not to remove the child pending the outcome of adoption proceedings. The case is logically consistent with decisions refusing to allow 'exceptional circumstances' to be invoked to question local authority decisions, yet may still be thought to evidence a different attitude.

The court as a parent

An immigration decision clearly cannot be allowed to be upset (or even questioned) on the basis that the welfare of an individual child must be the paramount consideration; and the same is even more axiomatic in relation to the criminal law—notwithstanding the statutory directive that the court should 'have regard' to the child offender's welfare: Children and Young Persons Act 1933, s 44. But the system of formally cautioning juvenile offenders who admit their guilt—now used in more than a third of all cases of detected and admitted offences by juveniles—involves an element of parental choice: the juvenile's parents or guardians must consent to the caution being issued: Home Office Circular 14/1985, para 4(c); and in *Re A (a minor) (wardship: criminal proceedings)* [1989] 3 All ER 610 Cazalet J had to decide what should happen when the juvenile in question was a ward of court. He held that the administration of a caution—which would be recorded, might influence future prosecution decisions, and could be cited on any future finding of guilt—was an important step in the ward's life, and that accordingly the court in its role as the child's parent should take the decision on the basis of whether or not it should be in the ward's interests so to do.

Important though a decision on accepting a caution may be, it pales into insignificance compared with a decision on the medical care of the severely disabled (*In re B (A minor) (Wardship: Medical Treatment)* [1981] 1 WLR 1421—the Court of Appeal overrode the decision of parents and of the judge at first instance and directed surgery to preserve the life of the severely disabled child). In relation to children, the availability of wardship at least allows the court to apply the comprehensible and defensible test that it will adopt whichever course will best promote the child's welfare? (cf *F v West Berkshire Health Authority (Mental Health Act Commission intervening)* [1989] 2 All ER 545 for an illustration of the conceptual difficulties that can arise in dealing with the incapable in the absence of any prerogative powers). The principle is of course easier to state than to apply, as is dramatically illustrated by the facts of *Re C (a minor) (wardship: medical treatment)* [1989] 2 All ER 782, CA. A new born baby had severe brain damage and had become terminally ill before birth. The Court of Appeal declined to accept that the child be given the treatment which would have been appropriate to a non-handicapped child; and accepted that treatment should be given in accordance with medical advice with the aim of relieving the baby's suffering rather than seeking to achieve a short prolongation of her life.

Not surprisingly, such cases arouse considerable public interest or curiosity; and an injunction was granted to prevent the publication of information about the ward, her parents, or those who had cared for her. The justification for granting an injunction in such wide terms was the need to protect the ward's welfare. She would never know what was being published about her; but publicity could indirectly affect the quality of care given to her. Moreover—and possibly of most interest from the family law viewpoint—Lord Donaldson regarded it as axiomatic that parents owe their child a duty of confidentiality save in so far as the child's welfare requires disclosure: *Re C (a minor) (wardship: medical treatment) (No 2)* [1989] 2 All ER 791 at 795, CA. In contrast, in *Van Oppen v Clerk to the Bedford Charity Trustees* [1989] 1 All ER 273 (Boreham J), [1989] 3 All ER 389, CA, it seems to have been accepted that a parent has no duty to insure a child against the risk of accidental injury: see at 290, 312,

Judicial review as a remedy?

The concept of a court taking a child into its care (which is how Lord Cross of Chelsea—in line with a long line of authority: see eg *R v Gyngall* [1893] 2 QB 233 at 239, per Lord Esher MR—described the essence of wardship: (1967) 83 LQR 200 at 207) is no doubt inconsistent with modern ideas of the proper role of an efficient system of judicial administration; and the modern trend is to seek to confine the courts' involvement to the taking of broad decisions, and to minimise its supervisory role. In particular, judicial review of particular local authority decisions is preferred to the detailed supervision once provided by wardship.

The most striking example of the utility of judicial review in the year under discussion is the decision of Waite J in *R v Norfolk County Council, ex p M* [1989] 2 All ER 359—which involved a recommendation by a case conference, rather than a decision directly relating to the care provided to a child by the local authority.

Fairness to suspected abusers

Local authorities have extensive statutory duties to investigate reports that children are at risk, and to take appropriate action; and child abuse registers (or child protection registers)—registers of the names of all children who are known to have been abused or who are considered to be at risk—are kept by all authorities as one of the methods employed to discharge those duties, specifically by ensuring that there will be a list available of all children who are the subject of an inter-agency protection and that those plans are regularly reviewed: *Working Together*, DHSS (1988) para 5.32. But although such registers are confidential, they effectively constitute blacklists; and as such have dangerous potential as instruments of injustice or oppression: per Waite J, *R v Norfolk County Council, ex p M* [1989] 2 All ER 359 at 366.

The decision to place a child's name on such a register will normally be taken at an inter-agency case conference; and it is of course axiomatic that the procedure should be fair. But what does that mean? The courts are concerned that a procedure intended to protect the welfare of children should not be stultified by excessive legalism, even if the result may be that the interests of an adult have to take second place to the need to protect the child: *R v Harrow London Borough Council, ex p D* [1990] 2 FLR 79 (parent not entitled to attend conference at which recommendation made that child's name be placed on register). But in *R v Norfolk County Council, ex p M* [1989] 2 All ER 359 the case conference was held to have acted unfairly and unreasonably in effectively branding a man of good character as an abuser on the basis of an unsubstantiated complaint by a disturbed 13 year old girl after a brief and one-sided investigation during which he had no opportunity to meet the allegations made against him. Waite J emphasised that the concept of fairness was a flexible one; that social workers ought to be allowed a sensible latitude in deciding how the requirements of fairness should be met; and that if genuine attempts had been made to reconcile the duties of child protection and the duty of fairness to the alleged abuser it was unlikely that the court should interfere. But on the facts of the case the applicant was entitled to have the decision quashed.

Money after divorce

There have been surprisingly few cases reported in 1989 about the exercise of the courts' powers to make financial orders in divorce. In *J v J (C intervening)* [1989] 1 All ER 1121 the court had refused to order an increase in children's maintenance since the children were entitled contingently on attaining the age of 18 to their mother's estate, on the basis that the exercise of the trustees' powers under s 31 of the Trustee Act 1925 to make payments for the children's maintenance rendered it unnecessary to increase the burden on the father. But the Court of Appeal held that the judge had been wrong to assume that the whole income should become available to the children. The trustees have a discretion; and the court will not bring improper pressure to bear upon them to exercise that discretion in a way which they should not otherwise have thought appropriate: *Howard v Howard* [1945] 1 All ER 91. But in assessing the worth of the children's interest the court was (per O'Connor LJ at 1125) entitled to assume that they would act reasonably in all the circumstances of the case. Rich fathers should not expect to get much relief; but poor fathers should not have the last drop of money extracted from them.

A deterrent to forum-shopping

In *Holmes v Holmes* [1989] 3 All ER 786, husband and wife had lived for a substantial part of their marriage in New York; and the New York court had granted a divorce, and made financial orders. The wife returned to England and took up residence in a cottage which, under the New York court's order would be sold with the proceeds going to the parties equally. The wife was unable to raise funds to buy out the husband; and there was evidence that the child of the marriage was distressed by the prospect of a move. Nonetheless, the New York court confirmed its order.

Part III of the Matrimonial and Family Proceedings Act 1984 allows a former spouse to seek financial relief in this country notwithstanding the fact that the marriage has been terminated by a foreign divorce, even if the foreign court has exercised its own powers to order financial relief. However, perhaps in an attempt to minimise the potential for abuse and blackmailing applications, it is provided that an applicant must apply ex parte for leave to make the application, and must on that application satisfy the court that there is a substantial ground for making the application. In the present case the wife's application was rejected, and her appeal was dismissed. The object of the legislation was (per Purchas LJ) to remit hardship arising from the absence of appropriate relief in a foreign court (see eg *Quazi v Quazi* [1979] 3 All ER 897); it was not to vest in the English court a power to review or correct orders made by a foreign court in a procedure not dissimilar to that provided by English law. In particular, an appellate court should be very slow indeed to interfere with the decision of the judge to whom the application for leave had been originally made.

Land Law and Trusts

P J CLARKE, BCL, MA
Barrister, Fellow of Jesus College, Oxford

Tenancy or licence?

Since, at least, Parliament's intervention to protect tenants from the perceived iniquities of landlords, landlords (having, in many cases, access to better—or at least more expensive—legal advice) have attempted to find methods within the law which will ensure that the legislation does not interfere with arrangements they may make with those who wish, for a consideration, to occupy their property and which will give them advantages the Rent Acts forbid. In the decade before 1985, there was a very considerable number of cases, mainly in the Court of Appeal, attempting to resolve the tensions inherent in this area of law. The House of Lords' first foray into the area, *Street v Mountford* [1985] 2 All ER 289, All ER Rev 1985 190–196, may, not unkindly, be regarded as a simplistic attempt to solve the problem: if the occupier had had a right to occupy premises for a term at a rent (and even this last was not strictly necessary: *Ashburn Anstalt v Arnold* [1988] 2 All ER 147, All ER Rev 1988 176–177, 185–186) there was, save in exceptional circumstances (which were not exhaustively listed), a tenancy. *Street v Mountford* spawned its own brood of litigation (see the citations in 1986 All ER Rev 154–155), and the House of Lords returned to the charge in the conjoined appeal in *AG Securities v Vaughan* and *Antoniades v Villiers* [1988] 3 All ER 1058, All ER Rev 1988 172–177, 186–191 which attempted to deal with the problem (which had not arisen in *Street v Mountford* itself) of 'sharing' agreements. It is clear from these cases that the general thrust of *Street v Mountford* is to be followed; in particular, the court seemed willing to be astute to detect 'shams' (or as the House of Lords now seem to prefer—for no particular stated reason—'pretences') either affecting the agreement as a whole, or particular clauses within it. (Sir Denys Buckley did not adopt this 'astute' approach in *Stribling v Wickham* [1989] 2 EGLR 36 at 40, preferring to be 'even-handed'). Further, to Lord Templeman at least, the function of the courts was to uphold the policy of the Rents Act and not to allow this to be easily circumvented.

1989 has seen three further reports in the All Englands on this subject, all in the Court of Appeal. Of these, the conjoined appeals in *Aslan v Murphy (Nos 1 and 2)* and *Duke v Wynne* [1989] 3 All ER 130 are the most important: notwithstanding that this was an appeal from a county court there was a full—and strong—Court of Appeal in which Lord Donaldson MR gave the unanimous judgement 'in order to reduce the scope for argument whether we all mean the same thing, which in fact we do.' ([1989] 3 All ER at 132j). Both appeals concerned issues similar to those in *Street v Mountford* itself; again, there was no 'sharing'. The court laid down some general principles; (i) the status of a tenant is different from a lodger (the court tends throughout its judgment to eschew the word 'licence'); (ii) owners of property can make accommodation available on either basis (the court makes no reference to any presumption as to the operation of the Rent Acts), and it is not a crime, nor contrary to public policy, to licence occupiers to occupy on the basis other than a tenancy: [1989] 3 All ER at 133b, 135c; (iii) which basis is adopted depends on the difficult question of ascertaining the parties' true intention; (iv) the labels the parties have attached are not conclusive; indeed, they do not give 'any guidance at all' [1989] 3 All ER at 133d; (v) the exclusivity or non-exclusivity of the occupation is the 'touchstone' [1989] 3 All ER at 133e which distinguishes a licence from a tenancy, though making that distinction will depend on a number of factors; (vi) the agreement between the parties may not, in whole or part, reflect the true bargain between them; (vii) if an occupier would otherwise be protected—

> 'by the Rent Acts, he does not lose that protection by agreeing that he will surrender it either immediately or in the future and whether directly and in terms or indirectly . . .' ([1989] 3 All ER at 133j).

This last point is the only direct reference to the Rent Acts, but there is a possible ambiguity in the phrase 'would otherwise be protected'. The court presumably means that an occupier who has signed an agreement or is in possession under an agreement which would otherwise be protected cannot lose that protection—ie he *is* protected by the Rent Acts. An alternative construction is that anyone who *would have been* within the protection of the Rent Acts when he signed the agreement or entered into possession *if* the agreement had not been entered into in that particular form, would still be protected. This latter view, however, seems incompatible with (ii) above. Presumably a genuine sharing agreement, intended as such from the beginning, will still be permitted: this is different from 'agreeing to substitute a shared for an exclusive right of occupation should the owner so require'— which the court states in terms is not permissible: [1989] 3 All ER at 133j. There is no indication that the court should lean in favour of construing an agreement so as to further the policy of the Rent Acts; this was also the approach of Sir Denys Buckley in *Stribling v Wickham* [1989] 2 EGLR 35 at 40.

In *Aslan v Murphy* the defendant, who occupied one room 4ft 3in by 12ft 6in, was required, under the terms of his agreement to share his accommodation (if required) with the licensor or his invitees or licences, and was not allowed to occupy it between 10.30 am and noon each day. The Court of Appeal held that both provisions were wholly unrealistic and clearly pretences (cf *Crancour Ltd v Da Silvaesa* (1986) 52 P & CR 204). A second justification for a licence was that the owner had expressly reserved the right (which he had exercised) to retain the keys to the room. The Court of Appeal, properly and summarily, rejected this argument—what mattered was not the retention of the keys as such but the reason for the retention: the genuine provision of genuine services, for example, (no such services being provided in *Aslan v Murphy*) would assist in making the inference that the occupier was a lodger, whereas the need to enter for purposes of emergency, repair, meter-reading and so on would not justify any inference that the owner was behaving otherwise than a normal landlord concerned for his property and to fulfil his obligations as lessor.

Duke v Wynne involved totally different facts. The defendants were granted an express non-occupation licence of a three-bedroomed house, the plaintiff owner to have the right to insist on others sharing the house with them and their children. Such sharing would have been possible: the Wynne family could have slept in two bedrooms, the third being available for another occupier. The court found that there was a tenancy; the position would have been different if there had been evidence that the plaintiff was seeking two separate sets of people, but absent such intention, it was 'inherently more likely' ([1989] 3 All ER at 138b) that the occupiers would be tenants.

There is no doubt that the Court of Appeal's restatement of the law—for that is what it is—will be of great assistance to hard-pressed circuit judges and recorders. But it is doubtful if it will lighten the load of legal advisers: everything is still very much a question of fact. Certainly Mrs Duke's advisers, with the benefit of hindsight, could have organised matters so as to protect her position: if she had consistently sought a co-lodger, the defendants would not have been tenants and thus protected by the Rent Acts. At a time—and in an area—of housing shortage, the defendants would presumably have accepted the owner's terms. The facts do not make it clear why a shorthold tenancy was not agreed by the parties.

Mikeover Ltd v Brady [1989] 3 All ER 618 was decided by the Court of Appeal before *Aslan v Murphy*, but being reported later, was not considered in it. Here a couple occupied the plaintiff's flat (which had been advertised as a flat for people to share) on the basis of two identical licence agreements, each occupier being liable to pay a sum of £86.66 per month for a period of six months to the plaintiff. (The form of agreement was substantially the same as in *Aldrington Garages Ltd v Fielder* (1978) 3 P & CR 461, criticised in *Street v Mountford*, save that in the earlier case a licensee could give a week's notice, thus leaving the owner with the risk of being out of pocket for the remainder of the term). The two occupiers were thus obliged to share with each other for the full period of six months; there was no right in the landlord to share the property with them (cf *Antoniades v Villier* [1988] 3 All ER 1058). However, the matter did not end there: for there to be a tenancy by the couple the tenancy had to be joint—ie the unities of possession, title, time and interest had to be present. 'Interest' included 'the bundle of rights and obligations representing the interest'—and the interest had to be the same in extent, nature and duration. As each occupier was separately liable to the payment of a sum of money each month (and it mattered not that the sums were identical) there was no such unity: this followed from *Antoniades v Villiers*. There was no sham; and there was no joint tenancy: the dictum of Lord Templeman in *Antoniades v Villiers* [1988] 3 All ER at 1066 that—

> 'A tenancy remains a tenancy even though the landlord may choose to require each of two joint tenants to agree expressly to pay one-half of the rent'

was not followed, the more orthodox statements of Lord Oliver and Lord Jauncey (at 1073 and 1075) being preferred. Support was also gained from a statement of Parker LJ, giving the judgment of the Court of Appeal in *Stribling v Wickham* [1989] 2 EGLR 35 to the effect that where a co-occupier is liable only for a specific sum being less than the total rent, that is wholly inconsistent with a joint tenancy. *Stribling v Wickham* itself (noted JEM (1989) Conv 192) is a not dissimilar case, and shows that in 'sharing' cases the courts are much more likely to find licences or 'lodgments'. (Parker LJ made the point in that case that if earlier agreements between the owner and the occupiers were entered into separately—ie at separate times—it did not matter that replacement agreements were entered into simultaneously. This seems in accord both with common sense and with *AG Securities v Vaughan*). But, once again, what of the defendants in *Duke v Wynne*? Assume that Mrs Duke advertised her house as suitable for a couple to share—and that she agreed that Mr Wynne must pay a certain sum per month and Mrs Wynne an identical amount. The fact that the couple were married makes the situation look different: but as the Court of Appeal in *Mikeover Ltd v Brady* were not apparently concerned at all with the relationship between the occupiers, why should it matter? A married couple can share a flat—so can two (entirely platonic) friends. It may be that the courts would have been astute to find a sham if there was an intention to live in connubial bliss, but why should this be so? Slade LJ in *Mikeover Ltd* states 'the monetary obligations of each licensee were genuinely intended to be entirely independent from those of the other': [1989] 3 All ER at 628a. Such obligations can exist as well within as without marriage: indeed, could a feminist—strident or otherwise—ask for anything more? Applying the tests suggested by the Court of Appeal in *Aslan v Murphy*, *Duke v Wynne*, the pointers are, on the view of the facts taken by the Court of Appeal in *Mikeover Ltd v Brady*, all in favour of a licence, with the possible exception of (v): the exclusivity or non exclusivity of the occupation is the 'touchstone'. At first sight, the couple were entitled to exclude all others, including the owners, but, given that they were not joint tenants they could not be tenants at all, and each was not entitled to exclude the other, and therefore neither had exclusive possession. This reasoning, however, smacks of circularity: *if* there is a joint tenancy, there is exclusive possession; if there is exclusive possession, there cannot be a licence. If the court concentrates on the formal requirements in a situation where there is sharing, it is likely to find that there is no joint tenancy and thus no exclusive possession; if, however, the court looks at what it perceives as the reality of the position and finds there is exclusive possession, there may well be a tendency (providing the unities of time, title and possession are present) to find that there is a tenancy. One point that was not considered in *Mikeover Ltd v Brady*, as it had not been considered in *AG Securities v Vaughan*, is why there was not a tenancy in common. Of course there cannot be a tenancy in common at law, but the Law of Property Act 1925, s 34(2) provides that an attempt to create one results in a legal joint tenancy held by the joint tenants (or, if more than four, the first four of them) on trust for the purported joint tenants, but as tenants in common. If, as in *Mikeover Ltd v Brady* all the occupiers had signed agreements at the same time, for the same duration, does not a tenancy in common more neatly fit the true nature of the arrangement? Where there is a shifting population of occupiers, as in *AG Securities v Vaughan*, a tenancy in common will be much less likely; but *Mikeover Ltd v Brady* appears and, it is submitted, is fundamentally different.

The third case is *Ogwr BC v Dykes* [1989] 2 All ER 880 (JEM (1989) Conv 92) , a case decided before the decisions of the House of Lords in *Antoniades v Villiers* and *AG Securities v Vaughan*, and before that of the Court of Appeal in *Aslan v Murphy*, *Duke v Wynne*. This case involved an arrangement made by the plaintiffs in fulfilment of their obligation under the Housing Act 1985 to provide accommodation to an intentionally homeless person. Such arrangements could be by way of tenancy: *Eastleigh BC v Walsh* [1985] 2 All ER 112, All ER Rev 1985, 190, 216, but *Ogwr BC v Dykes* states that a licence can also be created in such circumstances. This possibility had first been floated by Sir John Donaldson MR in *South Holland DC v Keyte* (1985) 84 LGR 347 at 352, and was accepted by the Court of Appeal. The main judgment, that of Purchas LJ, relied on the judgment of Fox LJ in *AG Securities v Vaughan* [1988] 2 All ER 173, (later reversed); the judge seems expressly to find a licence exclusively to occupy: however, he then states that, 'By its very nature a licence, if it is proved to exist in appropriate conditions, negates the concept of exclusive possession' ([1989] 2 All ER at 886e). This latter statement—but not the former—accords with the judgment of the Court of Appeal in *Aslan v Murphy, Duke v Wynne*; unfortunately, the *Ogwr* case was not cited to the court, and so the point remains unclear. Purchas and Ralph Gibson LJJ relied, however, on the legal relationship of duty between the defendant and the council under the Housing (Homeless Persons) Act 1977: and this, it is submitted, may be a safer ground: the tensions in the private owner/occupier relationship are not present in the same way where a local authority is carrying out its duties towards the intentionally homeless. Even so, however, the decision in *Eastleigh BC v Walsh* shows that there can be a tenancy in such situations, so the 'duty' of the local authority cannot by itself provide an answer. (In *Family Housing Assoication v Jones* [1990] 1 All ER 385, the Court of Appeal states that *Owgr BC v Dykes* is irreconcilable with *AG Securities v Vaughan*: see Balcombe LJ at 393e, Slade LJ at 396h, Farquharson LJ at 397a).

Adverse possession

Buckinghamshire CC v Moran [1989] 2 All ER 225 (Gerald McCormack (1989) Conv 211) restores order to a small corner of the law of adverse possession. The plaintiffs had acquired in 1955 a plot of land with a view to using it for a road at some unspecified future time. The plot adjoined both a highway (which the plaintiffs fenced off from the land with access by a gate) and the garden of the defendant's predecessor in title, X, who thus controlled the only other access to it: there was no fence between X's land and the plot, and both X and the defendent (who purchased the land in 1971) had padlocked the gate from the plot with their own padlock, without apparent objection from the plaintiffs. The defendant had also planted grass seed and bulbs. The plaintiffs' main argument was that the use to which the defendant had put the land was not inconsistent with the purposes for which they (the plaintiffs) intended to use the land. The Court of Appeal agreed that for a claimant to show that he had acquired title by adverse possession (i) the true owner must either have discontinued possession or have been dispossessed; (ii) the claimant must have been in possession (iii) that was adverse to the true owner, (iv) for 12 years next before action brought. The issue arose in connection with the third point. In the 1970s, a line of cases, based on dicta of Bramwell LJ in *Leigh v Jack* (1879) 5 Ex D 264 at 273, tended to show that in one context only, a licence would be implied from the true owner in favour of the squatter without any factual basis for such implication, namely where what the possessor was doing on the land was not such as substantially to interfere with any plans the true owner may have for future use of undeveloped land: see *Wallis's Cayton Bay Holiday Camp Ltd v Shell-Mex and BP Ltd* [1974] 3 All ER 575, *Gray v Wykeham-Martin* [1977] CA Transcript 10A, and *Treloar v Nute* [1977] 1 All ER 230. These decisions were criticised both by Slade J (himself a member of the Court of Appeal in *Moran*) in *Powell v McFarlane* (1977) 38 P & CR 452, and by the Law Reform Committee in their Twenty-First Report (Cmnd 6923) paras 3.47–3.52, as they give little weight to the ordinary meanings of the words 'possessors' or 'depossessors'. Parliament abrogated the doctrine in the Limitation Act 1980, Sch 1, para 8(4):

> 'For the purpose of determining whether a person occupying any land is in adverse possession of the land it shall not be assumed by implication of law that his occupation is by permission of the person entitled to the land merely by virtue of the fact that his occupation is not inconsistent with the latter's present or future enjoyment of the land. This provision shall not be taken as prejudicing a finding to the effect that a person's occupation of any land is by implied permission of the person entitled to the land in any case where such a finding is justified on the actual facts of the case.'

Wallis and the other cases cited above were thus cast into the legal lumber room. However, what para 8(4) left unclear was whether the statement of Bramwell LJ in *Leigh v Jack* (1879) 5 Ex D 264 at 273 was still law.

In the context of the need for inconsistent acts by the would-be adverse possessor, Bramwell LJ's judgment stated—

> 'that is not the case . . . where the intention of the plaintiff and her predecessors in title was not either to build upon or to cultivate the land, but to devote it at some future time to public purposes.'

The Court of Appeal in *Moran* noted that the other members of the Court of Appeal in *Leigh v Jack* (Cockburn CJ and Cotton LJ) did not adopt Bramwell LJ's formulation, preferring to rely on the fact that the squatter's actions prevented him from having sufficient intention to take possession. Slade LJ in *Moran* ([1989] 2 All ER at 234f) regarded Bramwell LJ's proposition as too wide: everything depended on the nature of the land, the nature of the acts of dispossession and the nature of the would-be adverse possessor's intention (see the dissenting judgment of Stamp LJ in *Wallis's* case: [1974] 3 All ER 575 at 585). Nourse LJ, indeed, went so far as to say that the intention of the true owner was, with one exception, irrelevant in practice. (This exception was that where the true owner's intention was known to the squatter, the latter's intention might thereby be affected, which would be a matter of fact in each case.)

On the facts, the plaintiffs had acquired, by the relevant date, control of the land: the land was enclosed (cf *Seddon v Smith* (1877) 36 LT 168 at 169 per Cockburn CJ and *George Wimpey & Co Ltd v Sohn* [1966] 1 All ER 232 at 240); he had planted it with bulbs and with grass seed; and he had locked the gate to the highway with his own padlock and key. The Court of Appeal, however, were faced with one problem: the plaintiff had perhaps admitted that he would have to give up the plot if the defendants required it for the road-widening scheme for which they had originally purchased it. The defendant clearly, however, had an intention *for the time being* (Slade LJ's italics: [1989] 2 All ER at 238b) to possess the land, and that was sufficient, given the other circumstances.

Moran thus emphasises that possession by a squatter must be adverse, and that this will in every case depend on the circumstances. What are seen as artificial rules to protect the holder of the paper—or registered—title are not to be upheld: Parliament showed the way in 1980, and the Court of Appeal has followed enthusiastically. As registered title becomes the norm, it may be queried whether adverse possession should be so willingly confirmed: the concept of limitation of actions is that a would-be plaintiff loses a right to sue which he has been dilatory in enforcing, rather than property which (on legal advice, in most cases) he believed he owned. The justification is presumably that a landowner who does not assert his rights will lose them, and that the courts will only aid the vigilant. Large corporations, local authorities and absentee owners may thus find themselves at a disadvantage, whereas the owner-occupier is much more likely to be protected.

Part of the oddity appears because of the use of the law of limitation rather than of prescription, a distinction between the civilian and the common land systems elegantly explained by Nourse LJ in *Moran* at [1989] 2 All ER 238–239. However it cannot surely be right to suggest as Nourse LJ does that, for there to be prescription, the possession must be 'as of right', save in the sense that it must not be by permission: if possession was rightful in the first place, there would be no need for prescription. A possessor may believe he has a right (which is often the situation in adverse possession cases) and thus acquire a title; just as, under the Prescription Act 1832, a dominant owner, who at the beginning of the prescription period has no easement, may prescribe an easement against a servient owner, so long as the acquisition is peaceable, open, and without permission: nec vi, nec clam, nec precario. After all, the Romans had recognised this point nearly 2000 years ago with their sophisticated development of their Actio Publiciana: this clearly distinguished the position of someone who had rights informally created from someone who was merely a bona fide possessor.

Restrictive covenants

The passing of the benefit of restrictive covenants made after 1925 is commonly regarded as having been revolutionised by the interpretation of the Law of Property Act 1925 (LPA), s 78 in *Federated Homes Ltd v Mill Lodge Properties Ltd* [1980] 1 All ER 371. In *J Sainsbury plc v Enfield London Borough Council* [1989] 2 All ER 817 (JEM (1989) Conv 358–359), Morritt J had to consider the effect of the predecessor of s 78, ie the Conveyancing and Law of Property Act 1881, s 58. On the facts, it was agreed that the land retained by the original covenantee was capable of benefitting from the covenants, and was sufficiently identified for the covenants to be annexed to it. After 1925, such a covenant would clearly fall within s 78.

Before considering the statute, however, the judge considered, if on the authorities, ignoring the statute, the benefit of the covenant attached to the land. The first point was whether the intention that the covenant should run with the land could be inferred from the circumstances alone rather than from the terms of the relevant conveyance. The judge referred to the one authority which seemed clearly to offer support for such a view: *Marten v Flight Refuelling Ltd* [1961] 2 All ER 696, (though cf PV Baker 84 LQR 24, and EC Ryder 36 Conv (NS) 20). He did not, however, analyse that much-contested decision, preferring to consider other authorities such as *Renals v Cowlishaw* (1878) 9 Ch D 125 which contemplated that the relevant intention should be detected either within the conveyance or outside it. However, Morritt J adopted the restrictive approach manifested (so far as annexation as distinct from assignment was concerned) in cases such as *Miles v Easter* [1933] All ER Rep 355 and *Newton Abbot Co-op Society Ltd* v *Williamson & Treadgold Ltd* [1952] 1 All ER 279, in that he was obliged 'to construe the conveyance . . . in the light of the relevant circumstances' ([1989] 2 All ER at 823d). This was the conventional view of the law before *Federated Homes*, and manifests the reluctance on the part of the judiciary to extend the enforceability of restrictive covenants which was also shown by Judge Baker QC in *Roake v Chadha* [1983] 3 All ER 503, All ER Rev 1983 232–233. The point was not taken that the onus of proof is on a person seeking to argue that a covenant is not capable of benefitting the land to satisfy the court of that view: *Wrotham Park Estate Co v Parkside Homes Ltd* [1974] 2 All ER 321, per Brightman J; nor, apparently, was the argument raised that the defendants had notice of the covenant, and that therefore they should be liable at the suit of the plaintiff, unless there was a compelling reason to the contrary.

Having found, ignoring the effect of statute, that the benefit of the covenant was not attached to the land, the judge then considered the Conveyancing and Law of Property Act 1881, s 58. The narrowness of s 58, compared with the width of LPA, s 78 had already been noted by Brightman LJ in *Federated Homes* [1980] 1 All ER 371 at 379: s 78, moreover, was clearly stated (s 78(2)) to affect only covenants made after the 1925 legislation came into effect, but the effect of the 1881 Act, s 58 on covenants already in existence was expressly preserved. Morritt J therefore held, entirely correctly, that s 58 had no effect. Two points, however, were conceded before the judge though reserved if the case went to appeal: (i) whether the Conveyancing and Law of Property Act 1881, s 6 (later LPA, s 62) would operate to pass the benefit, (cf *Roake v Chadha* [1983] 3 All ER 503 at 508–509, 1983 All ER Rev 233 per Judge Baker QC where s 6/s 62 was held not to apply), (ii) that the covenant was annexed to each and every part of the land and not only to the whole of it (cf *Re Ballard's Conveyance* [1937] 2 All ER 691).

The rule in *Bain v Fothergill*

The rule in *Bain v Fothergill* [1874–80] All ER Rep 83 provides that if a purchaser is unable to complete his purchase of land because of the vendor's inability to make title, all he is able to recover is wasted conveyancing expenses and costs. The rule, properly known as the rule in *Flureau v Thornhill* [1775–1802] All ER Rep 91, has been heavily criticised both judicially (*Sharneyford Supplies Ltd v Edge* [1987] 1 All ER 588, All ER Rev 1987 p 317) and by the Law Commission (Law Com Report No 166) and has been repealed with effect from 27 September 1989 by the Law of Property (Miscellaneous Provisions) Act 1989, s 3. However, in *Seven Seas Properties Ltd v Al-Essa* [1989] 1 All ER 164 Hoffmann J applied the rule to a sub-sale where completion had been delayed because the sub-vendor (the original purchaser) had been unable to obtain title from his vendor.

Land registration

Belcourt v Belcourt [1989] 2 All ER 35 (Morritt J) provides a useful guide to the interpretation of the Land Registration Rules, rr 298–302. These rules are headed 'Hearings before the Registrar', but r 301 provides, inter alia, that a notice of intention to appeal from an order or decision of the chief land registrar or the court shall be entered on the register. In *Belcourt*, a judge had ordered removal of a caution entered on the register by the plaintiff (who claimed an interest in the beneficial proceeds of sale of the property) from the Land Registry: the plaintiff had appealed and notice of it had been served on the registrar. The defendant agreed that r 301 did not apply to appeals from the High Court under its general original jurisdiction. Morritt J rejected the argument: r 301 was of general application, and was designed to clarify that dealings for valuable consideration previously registered would not be affected by the entry of a notice concerning an appeal; other dealings would be affected. Given that approach, there was no justification for limiting the rule's scope. Notwithstanding the—now apparently misleading—heading to this part of the rules—this seems correct. The main problem, however, is that notice of appeal may be entered on dubious grounds, and thus effectively prevent the successful respondent from dealing with the property. If a highly profitable sale were thereby lost, there is no obvious remedy available to the respondent, though the unsuccessful appellant would be liable to costs. On the other hand, the meritorious appellant is much better able to protect his position. The answer to the problem may be (as the judge had suggested) to provide for attachment of the proceeds of sale.

Commons

Re Merthyr Mawr Common [1989] 3 All ER 451 clarifies one part on the procedure to confirm the provisional registration of land as common land under the Commons Registration Act 1965. Where a right of common has been extinguished between the date of provisional registration and the date of the hearing before a commons commissioner the position at the latter, rather than the former, date is the relevant one: Mervyn Davies J followed dicta of Reginald Goff J in *Central Electricity Generating Board v Clwyd CC* [1976] 1 All ER 251 at 256 and Nourse J in *Re Burton Heath* (12 May 1983 unreported); he also confirmed the view expressed by Slade LJ in *Re West Anstey Common* [1985] 1 All ER 618 at 625 (All ER Rev 1985 p 203) that the onus of proving rights provisionally registered was on the claimant of those rights.

Land: miscellaneous

A-G (ex rel Yorkshire Derwent Trust Ltd) v Brotherton [1989] 2 All ER 423 (Angela Sydenham (1989) Conv 448) holds that a right of navigation is not a right of way under the Highways Act 1980, s 31; the definition of land in s 31(3) as including 'land covered with water' deals with fords and causeways: it was difficult to see how, for example, a notice could be placed by an owner of a private right of navigation so as to make it clear that a public right is not thereby created. *Reed v Madon* [1989] 2 All ER 431 explains the nature of an exclusive right of burial in a reserved plot in Brookwood

Necropolis, the company's private Act incorporating the Cemeteries Clauses Act 1847 and the Lands Clauses Consolidation Act 1845: Morritt J held that such a right was to be equated with a right of property, and, therefore, protected the owner of the plot against any infringer, even though there was no body buried, and even though the infringement (in part) only affected the surface of the plot. As briefly noted last year, the Court of Appeal in *Inglewood Investment Co Ltd v Forestry Commission* [1989] 1 All ER 1 upheld the decision of Harman J [1988] 1 All ER 783, All ER Rev 1988 p 184, that 'game' in an indenture of 1921 meant 'feathered game' and not 'terrestrial game': deer were therefore excluded from the ambit of the relevant clause. *Suleman v Shahsavari* [1989] 2 All ER 460, a case on the measure of damages for the sale of land, is dealt with at p 89 above.

Charity: religion

Re Hetherington (decd) [1989] 2 All ER 129 (John Hopkins (1989) CLJ 373, DM Parry (1989) Conv 453, considers the question of whether a gift for the saying of masses is charitable. The testatrix left £2,000 'to the Roman Catholic Church Bishop of Westminster for the repose of the souls of [named persons, including herself]'; the residue 'is to be given to the Roman Catholic Church St Edwards Golders Green for masses for my soul'.

It has long been established that gifts for the furtherance of religion are prima facie charitable, even if the religion or sect in question might be regarded as on the fringes of orthodoxy: see *Thornton v Howe* (1862) 31 Beav 14 (the writings of Joanna Southcote) and *Re Watson (decd)* [1973] 3 All ER 678 (the writings of HG Hobbs, on undenominational christianity). However, even this rule has its limits: there must be sufficient element of public benefit: *Gilmour v Coats* [1949] 1 All ER 848. In this case a gift to an order of totally cloistered nuns was held not charitable as the only benefits alleged were edification to the world by example and the effect of intercessory prayer, which were not regarded as sufficient or susceptible of proof. The question of private masses thus appears to fall midway between these two principles. The House of Lords in *Bourne v Keane* [1918–19] All ER Rep 167 held that a gift for the saying of masses was not illegal under the Dissolution of Colleges Act 1547 (as some 19th century decisions had held) and held the gift was valid, leaving open the question whether such gifts were charitable or were examples 'where Homer had nodded' of non-charitable purpose trusts without an obvious human beneficiary. Luxmoore J in *Re Caus* [1933] All ER Rep 818 regarded a gift for the saying of masses for the repose of souls as charitable, but the correction of this decision was expressly left open by four members of the House of Lords in *Gilmour v Coats*.

Sir Nicolas Browne-Wilkinson V-C was able to avoid the need to make a final decision on the issue of whether private masses were charitable. The testatrix had not stated whether the masses were to be said privately or in public, though it was clear that such masses were for (as she would have seen it) the souls of herself and those named in the will. In *Re Hetherington* there was uncontradicted evidence that such masses would be said publicly, even though there was no requirement of canon law to that effect. The judge, however, did indicate his view that the performance in private of a religious ritual act was not charitable as being for the public benefit: [1989] 2 All ER at

134g. (This is consistent with the approach adopted by the court in, admittedly, the slightly different context of whether a building was a place of worship for the purposes of the General Rate Act 1967, s 39(2) in *Broxtowe BC v Birch* [1983] 1 All ER 641). This, however, was not an end of the matter. Although, as a matter of practice the masses would be said in public, there would be a possibility—totally compatible with the terms of the gift—that the masses should be celebrated privately. The Vice-Chancellor overcame this by holding that the gift should be construed as capable of being carried out only by modes that were exclusively charitable: following *Re White* [1891–4] All ER Rep 242 at 244–5 and *Re Banfield (decd)* [1968] 2 All ER 276. This is clearly an example of the approach in construing a gift so as to give charity the benefit of the doubt: see eg *IRC v McMullen* [1980] 1 All ER 884 at 890c per Lord Hailsham. However, the issue is not that simple: there is a well established (if unfortunate) line of cases that holds that gifts for 'charitable or benevolent' purposes are not exclusively charitable and must thus fail: *Chichester Diocesan Fund & Board of Finance Inc v Simpson* [1944] 2 All ER 60, [1944] AC 341. Why should a more benevolent approach be adopted in some contexts than in others? It may be that, 40 years after the period when the House of Lords, under the influence of Viscount Simonds, adopted a restrictive approach to the law of charity, a more flexible attitude is now being manifested (cf *IRC v McMullen* and *Re Koeppler's Will Trusts* [1985] 2 All ER 869; All ER Rev 1985 at 270, 321, 322. However, this leads to other problems: does *Re Hetherington* imply that a four-year covenant by a Roman Catholic to his parish priest to say masses for his family's souls will attract tax relief? If this is so—and it seems logically correct—the law is moving towards a very broad concept of public benefit, at least in the context of religion. It is well established that a gift by a taxpayer to have his children educated privately is not charitable, neither, one assumes, is a gift by the same taxpayer to a private hospital in consideration of his family being provided with free medical treatment charitable. Obviously these examples are reconcilable because of the different concepts of public benefit adopted under the different heads of charity: it is the attitude of the courts, however, that is uncertain.

The second ground adopted by the Vice-Chancellor is, however, a safer one, at least from the point of precedent: ie that there was sufficient public benefit in the endowment of the priesthood. This had been adopted by Luxmoore J in *Re Caus*, and had not been impugned by the House of Lords in *Gilmour v Coats*. The resources of the Roman Catholic Church thus freed could be used for purposes other than the augmentation of the stipend of the priest in question. This approach is partially consistent with other examples elsewhere in the law of charities: thus, a gift to a private hospital (at least where it is linked in some way with a public one: *Le Cras v Perpetual Trustee Co Ltd* [1967] 3 All ER 915, [1969] 1 AC 514) is charitable as it allows other resources to be devoted to the public good in the area of the provision of medical services; a gift for the provision of scholarships at a school or college—even, anomalously, for a preference to be given to 'founders' kin', *Spencer v All Souls College* (1762) Wilm 163, *A-G v Sidney Sussex College* (1869) LR 4 Ch App 722—allows that institution's resources to be deployed elsewhere. At a time when the role of state intervention for public welfare is a matter of political controversy and public debate, the possibility of an expansion of the frontiers of charity to fill a vacuum left by the withdrawal or lessening of public funding is not without interest.

Charity commissioners: tort

The ambit of the tort of negligence has this year, as in previous years, been a subject of debate in appellate courts: see pp 329–341 below. Even the law of charity has not been exempt: apart from the decision (on substantive law) of *Van Oppen v Clerk to the Bedford Charity Trustees* [1989] 1 All ER 273, affd [1989] 3 All ER 389, p 331 below, there is *Mills v Winchester Diocesan Board of Finance* [1989] 2 All ER 317. An application was made under the Charities Act 1960, s 28 that advice given by the charity commissioners on application by charity trustees under the Charities Act 1960, s 24 was erroneous. This action was struck out as disclosing no course of action; the plaintiffs then brought an action against the commissioners for negligence causing damage, which was struck out for a similar reason. Knox J held, as matters of procedure, first that the charity commissioners were not proper parties to questions of construction or to questions of whether trusts had failed, and secondly, that they should not be joined for the purpose of recovering costs. He also decided the main issue in favour of the commissioners: the provision of an appeal under s 28 of the Act, and the duplication of costs if actions in negligence were allowed, militated against the extension of tortious liability. He prayed in aid Cardozo CJ's statement in *Ultramares Corp v Touche* (1931) 255 NY 170, and noted the absence of any judicial support for such extension in the history of the charity commissioners. The decision thus protects the charity commissioners; cases such as *A-G v Cocke* [1988] 2 All ER 391 (All ER Rev 1988 at 183–184) show that if misfeasance is alleged, a recipient—or potential recipient—of charity is not left without remedy.

Landlord and Tenant

PHILIP H PETTIT, MA
Barrister, Professor of Equity, University of Buckingham

The lease/licence distinction

Aslan v Murphy (Nos 1 and 2, and *Duke v Wynne* were three appeals, reported together at [1989] 3 All ER 130, on the troublesome lease/licence distinction which has so often come before the courts in recent years, though on this occasion the court chose throughout the judgment to speak in terms of tenant or lodger—a point to which we shall return. As the Master of the Rolls explained, the reasons for holding that in each case the defendant was a tenant were given 'in a single judgment to which we have all contributed in order to reduce the scope for argument whether we all mean the same thing, which in fact we do'. A procedure not without merit.

One can, perhaps, summarize the propositions of law with which the judgment began as follows:
 (i) There is an essential difference between a tenant and a lodger. Owners of accommodation may make it available on either basis. Which basis applies in any particular case depends on what was the true bargain between the parties.
 (ii) The labels which the parties agree to attach to themselves or to their agreements are never conclusive and in this particular field 'they give no guidance at all'.
 (iii) 'The occupier has in the end to be a tenant or a lodger.' The touchstone is whether occupation is exclusive or non-exclusive. It is necessary to consider the rights and duties of both the owner and other occupiers.
 (iv) Without castigating the whole agreement as a sham, it may on the face of it contain provisions which are not in fact any part of the true bargain. Having stripped away pretences the question is whether the true bargain as revealed indicates that the occupier is a tenant or a lodger.
 (v) If an occupier would otherwise be protected by the Rent Acts, he does not lose that protection by agreeing that he will surrender it either immediately or in the future and whether directly in terms or indirectly.

Two brief comments may be made on the above propositions. First, in relation to (ii), it is submitted that, though it may well be so in a particular case, it is somewhat extreme to deny that the label can never be of any assistance. Secondly the statement in (iii) that an occupier must be either a tenant or a lodger disregards the special cases referred to in *Street v Mountford* [1985] 2 All ER 289. It is to be observed that when Lord Templeman drew the tenant/lodger distinction in *AG Securities v Vaughan* [1988] 3 All ER 1058 he was careful to make the proviso 'save in the exceptional circumstances mentioned in *Street v Mountford*'. It is submitted that while a lodger is necessarily a licensee, not a tenant, a licensee is not necessarily a lodger. Assuming this is so, it is further submitted that the principles stated by the court apply to any case of a licence, whether or not the licensee can properly be called a lodger.

Having stated the law, the court proceeded to apply it to the facts of each case. In *Aslan v Murphy (No 1)* the provisions of the agreement in relation to a room 4ft 3ins by 12ft 6ins that it should be used in common with the 'licensor' and such other 'licensees' as the licensor should permit to use the room, and that the 'licensee' should only be permitted to use the room between midnight and 10.30 am and between noon and midnight were wholly unrealistic and clearly pretences. The holding of a key by the 'licensor' was of no great significance: it was not needed to provide the services referred to in the agreement for in fact virtually no services were provided. The occupier had exclusive possession at a rent for a term and was accordingly a tenant. It may be noted that the Court of Appeal has recently reasserted that the retention of a key by itself cannot be decisive—*Family Housing Association v Jones* (1989) 139 NLJ 1709.

In *Duke v Wynne* the landlord had previously lived in the house in question as the matrimonial home. Having left the house she refurbished it, but wished to wait a couple of years before deciding whether to sell. The agreement purported to be a bare licence outside the Rent Act 1977 and to give the occupier a non-exclusive right of occupation reserving to the owner the right to place other occupiers in the premises at any time. Here, unlike *Aslan v Murphy*, sharing with another occupant would have been physically possible, though there was no evidence that the owner intended to introduce another occupant and she did not in fact do so. The question, it was said, was whether

(i) the true bargain was that the occupier was entitled to exclusive possession unless and until the owner required him to share. If so *Antoniades v Villiers* [1988] 3 All ER 1058 is authority for saying that the occupier was a tenant whose status could not at some future date be unilaterally converted into that of lodger by the owner putting in some other occupier with whom he would have to share, or

(ii) the true bargain was that the occupier's entitlement was only to a share in the right to occupy, when he could never achieve the status of a tenant. It would not affect the result if for the time being there was no other occupant so that it would be impractical and unreasonable to seek to prevent de facto occupation of the whole premises.

On the facts a tenancy was clearly established.

Aslan v Murphy (No 2) was a second possession action between the same landlord and the same tenant as in *Aslan v Murphy (No 1)*. Though the landlord had got his possession order in the first action, a stay of execution had been granted pending the appeal. In the meantime the local authority served a closing order on the plaintiff in respect of the premises, the effect of which was to take away the statutory security of tenure under the Rent Act. The court held that the county court judge had been wrong to grant an order for possession in the second action, for the landlord had taken no steps to determine the tenancy which (as it had been decided in *No 1*) the tenant held. The closing order did not constitute a ground for possession: it merely removed the Rent Act protection the tenant would otherwise have. There was, of course, nothing to prevent the landlord now serving notice to quit, on the expiry of which there would be no answer to a claim to possession.

Mikeover Ltd v Brady [1989] 3 All ER 618, though reported after *Aslan v Murphy (Nos 1 and 2)*, was in fact decided about a month earlier by a differently constituted Court of Appeal, and raised somewhat different issues. The facts were that the defendant and a Miss Guile agreed to take a flat advertised by the plaintiffs as a flat for two people to share, the layout being such that it was clearly only suitable for occupation by persons who were personally acceptable to one another. The defendant and Miss Guile signed at substantially the same time separate but identical agreements put before them by the plaintiffs in which each was called a 'Licensee'. Each agreement purported in clause 1 to grant the 'Licensee' 'the right to use in common with others who have been granted the like right' the flat and furniture therein. In the agreement the 'Licensee' agreed, inter alia,

> '2(1) To pay the sum of £86.66 per month for the right to share in the use of the said rooms . . .
> 2(4) Not to impede the use of the said rooms . . . nor . . . to impede the use of any services supplied to the said rooms . . . by such other persons not exceeding one in number to whom the Owner shall grant [a] licence'

and to pay a deposit of £40.00.

Each 'licensee' was given a key to the flat, and the defendant and Miss Guile were allowed to continue in occupation on a monthly basis when the original six month term expired. After about 18 months Miss Guile physically moved out and subsequently wrote to the plaintiffs terminating the contract and returning her key. The plaintiffs returned to her the deposit she had paid when she entered into the agreement. At about the same time the defendant offered to pay monthly sums of £173.32 (representing twice £86.66), but the plaintiffs refused to accept them, holding him responsible for his share only. Subsequently the defendant fell into arrears with his payments. The plaintiffs purported to determine his 'licence' and brought a possession action. It was common ground that the plaintiffs must succeed if the defendant was indeed a licensee, but that the defendant would be entitled to Rent Act protection if he was a tenant.

The court considered that its first task was to construe the terms of the agreement. It observed that his agreement gave the defendant a right to use the flat in common with others 'who *have been* granted the like right' (court's emphasis) and that it was not qualified by any obligation to share such use with any others who might be granted such right *in the future* (court's emphasis). The court was not persuaded that there was to be implied a power in the plaintiffs to introduce a new occupant in the flat should Miss Guile leave: the agreement by clause 1 gave the defendant the right to exclusive occupation of the flat in common only with Miss Guile during its currency, and by clause 2(4) imposed on him a corresponding obligation not to impede the use of the flat by Miss Guile during the currency of the term. However an absolutely strict and literal interpretation of the emphasised phrases (*have been* and *in the future*) was implicitly not insisted upon as the two agreements were substantially contemporaneous. It was, it was said, 'quite plain that one must construe the provisions of the defendants's agreement having full regard to the fact that Miss Guile had just executed or was about to execute an agreement in identical form (and vice versa)'.

The court adopted the well-known definition of a sham given by Diplock LJ in *Snook v London and West Riding Investments Ltd* [1967] 1 All ER 518 at 528 and distinguished *Antoniades v Villiers* [1988] 3 All ER 1058, where the facts were not wholly dissimilar. However in that case it was held that the true nature of the arrangement was to create a joint tenancy and the purported retention by the alleged licensor of the right to share the occupation of the small flat or to introduce an indefinite number of third parties to do so was clearly a pretence intended to deprive them of the protection of the Rent Acts. In the instant case, as we have seen, the agreements did not, on their true construction, reserve to the plaintiffs the right to impose a co-occupant on the defendant or Miss Guile during the term of either agreement. They did, however, confer on the defendant and Miss Guile together a right of joint exclusive occupation of the property. Did this create a tenancy? *Street v Mountford* [1985] 2 All ER 289 was referred to as authority for the proposition that, save in exceptional circumstances, the enjoyment by one person of exclusive occupation of premises for a term in consideration of periodical payments creates a tenancy, and *Antoniades v Villiers* as illustrating that the enjoyment by more than one person of joint exclusive occupation of premises for the same term in consideration of periodical payments is capable of creating a joint tenancy.

The court then went back to the basic principle, recently affirmed by the House of Lords in *AG Securities v Vaughan* [1988] 3 All ER 1058, that for the creation of a joint tenancy the four unities must be present. In the instant case the unities of possession, time and title were admitted to be present, but could it be said that there was unity of interest, which imports the existence of joint rights and joint obligations? The county court judge had found that the agreements were not shams, in which, the court said, he was amply justified. Though at first sight the employment of two forms of agreement, rather than one, had an air of artificiality about it, on the particular facts of the case no sham device or artificial transaction was involved. The agreements imposed on each party individual and separate obligations to pay a deposit of £40 and monthly payments of £86.66, but no joint monetary obligation. There was no joint obligation and therefore no complete unity of interest from which it followed inevitably that there was no joint tenancy. Since neither the defendant nor Miss Guile had power to exclude the other from occupation of any part of the premises, their respective several rights during the period of their joint occupation could never have been greater than those of licensees. It was not contended, the court thought rightly, that the defendant's status became that of tenant after Miss Guile's departure. The plaintiffs were accordingly entitled to succeed in their possession action.

Lastly, there is *Ogwr Borough Council v Dykes* [1989] 2 All ER 880, CA. It is, however, at the outset essential to realise that this case was decided before— actually the day before—the House of Lords handed down its decision reversing *AG Securities v Vaughan* and *Antoniades v Villiers*. In *Family Housing Association v Jones* (1989) 139 NLJ 1710 Balcombe LJ, with whose judgment Slade and Farquharson LJJ agreed, observed that *Ogwr Borough Council v Dykes* is irreconcilable with the House of Lords decision in *Antoniades v Villiers*. This latter decision, which supports the argument of counsel for the defendant in *Ogwr Borough Council v Dykes*, deprives that case of much of its authority. In it the lease/licence distinction came up in the context of the duty of a council under s 65(3) of the Housing Act 1985, in the case of a person with a priority need who has become intentionally homeless, to 'secure that accommodation is made available for his occupation for such period as they consider will give him a reasonable opportunity of securing accommodation for his occupation.' In pursuance of their statutory duty the council granted the defendant what it claimed to be a licence for 13 weeks from 10 March 1986. The council allowed the defendant to continue in occupation after the expiry of that period, but purported to determine the alleged licence by a letter dated 19 February 1987 demanding vacant possession not later than 4 March 1987. It is significant that the specified date of termination was less than 12 months after the commencement of the alleged licence: by para 4 of Sch 1 to the 1985 Act a tenancy granted in pursuance of s 65(3) is not a secure tenancy before the expiry of 12 months from the specified date, ie the date when the tenant received notification under s 64(1) or 68(3). Although by s 79(3) a licence is considered for the purposes of Pt IV of the Act as a tenancy, it was vital to the defendant's case to establish that she had had a tenancy, and not a licence. The reason for that was that if, as the council claimed, the defendant only had a licence it was duly determined by the letter of 19 February 1987 before it had run for 12 months. If however it was a tenancy the letter, which gave less than the four weeks notice required by s 5 of the Protection from Eviction Act 1977, would not have been effective to determine it and the council would be unable to bring the case within para 4 of Sch 1. It may be noted that the council did not in fact start proceedings for a possession order until August 1987, but it was held that this act of leniency on the part of the council did not prejudice its position. There was no evidence of receipt of rent during this extended period.

The case therefore turned on whether, applying the principles laid down by the House of Lords in *Street v Mountford* [1985] 2 All ER 289, [1985] AC 809, the letter of 10 March 1986, which in terms purported to grant a licence, was in fact to be construed as creating a tenancy. Under the homeless persons legislation, now to be found in the Housing Act 1985, the first duty of a local authority is to decide whether or not a claimant is entitled to relief at their hands. If it decides that he is, any relief granted falls within the area of private law and is governed by the ordinary rules: it may involve the grant of a tenancy or a licence or the taking of other appropriate steps. What had to be decided on the facts of the instant case was the legal effect of the action taken by the council.

The substance of the argument on behalf of the defendant was that the three criteria set out in *Street v Mountford*, namely, a fixed term, exclusive occupation and a fixed rent were present and that she must therefore have obtained a tenancy and not a licence. Purchas LJ, who gave the leading judgment, referred to the judgment of Fox LJ in *AG Securities v Vaughan* [1988] 2 All ER 173 at 178 setting out the principles to be derived from *Street v Mountford*. Although the decision was reversed by the House of Lords [1988] 3 All ER 1058, no adverse comment was made on these observations. Purchas LJ adopted the first two criteria declared by Fox LJ, namely:

> '(1) Exclusive possession is of the first importance in deciding whether an occupier is a tenant . . . (2) Exclusive possession is not decisive because there are circumstances in which an occupier who has exclusive possession is not a tenant. Thus, he may be an owner in fee simple, a trespasser, a mortgagee in possession, an object of charity or a service occupier.'

The two paragraphs in the judgment of Purchas LJ following this citation raise some difficulties. The broad sweep of his argument seems to be that there are circumstances in which a person may enjoy exclusive possession yet not be a tenant, but rather a licensee. And on the facts, in the light of the provisions of the Housing Act 1985, the defendant had indeed been a licensee without any right to remain after her licence had been duly determined. The brief judgment of Ralph Gibson LJ agreeing with the judgment of Purchas LJ confirms this, for he states clearly that under the homeless persons legislation the council had the capacity to grant a licence only 'notwithstanding the fact that exclusive possession of the dwelling house was thereby given for a term' at a rent.

Going back to the judgment of Purchas LJ, he seems clearly to have taken the view that exceptionally there might be exclusive possession without a tenancy (at 886d and e). Immediately following this there are two sentences which are difficult to reconcile with each other and with what has gone before. The first of these two sentences seems to follow naturally from his preceding observations. 'Of course', he said, 'no one has written the possibility of a licence existing out of the law of England in this context.' This appears to accept that a person who has exclusive possession but who is not a tenant may in some circumstances at least be a licensee. However he immediately goes on to say, 'By its very nature a licence, if it is proved to exist in appropriate conditions, negates the concept of exclusive possession'. This is so difficult to reconcile with the preceding statements and with the broad sweep of the judgment that one wonders whether this is what Purchas LJ in fact said, or intended to say.

As already pointed out this decision can no longer be relied on.

Common law and general statutory provisions

Barrett v Lounova (1982) Ltd [1989] 1 All ER 351, decided in the Court of Appeal, concerned a Rent Act tenancy which began as long ago as 1941, the present tenant being the second successor of the original tenant. The outside of the premises were in a bad state of repair and dilapidated, and the issue was whether the landlord was under an obligation to repair it.

The tenancy agreement appears to have been made by deed (though nothing turned on this), because Kerr LJ referred to it as containing a covenant that the tenant would keep the inside in good repair and giving the landlord access for any reasonable purpose. But there was no express obligation on anyone to keep the outside in repair. Should any obligation to repair be implied? It is clear from the books that in general there is no implied undertaking that the landlord will do any repairs whatever. (See, e g, in addition to *Woodfall on Landlord and Tenant* (28th edn) cited by Kerr LJ, Cheshire and Burn's *Modern Law of Real Property* (14th edn 1988) at 373 and Megarry and Wade's *Law of Real Property* (5th edn 1984) at 696, 697). To this general rule there are certain well-known exceptions, namely (i) furnished houses, (ii) premises in multiple occupation—*Liverpool City Council v Irwin* [1976] 2 All ER 39, (iii) houses let at a low rent—ss 8–10 of the Landlord and Tenant Act 1985, (iv) houses let for a short term—ss 11–16 of the Landlord and Tenant Act 1985, and (v) there may be a duty of care in tort—see the Defective Premises Act 1972. In addition it is clear that a tenancy agreement, like any other agreement, must be read as a whole and in construing the agreement it may be proper to imply an obligation on the landlord to do repairs. The issue before the court was whether such an implication should be made in the case before it.

In his judgment Kerr LJ referred to the observations of Slade LJ in *Duke of Westminster v Guild* [1984] 3 All ER 144, who had said that in some instances it would be proper for the court to imply an obligation against the landlord, on whom an obligation is not in terms imposed by the relevant lease, to match a correlative obligation thereby expressly imposed on the other party. Applying that to the facts of the case before him Kerr LJ said that there was an express covenant by the tenant, clearly intended to be enforceable throughout the tenancy, to keep the inside and fixtures in good repair, order and condition. Sooner or later it would become impossible to comply with this covenant unless the outside had been kept in repair. It was therefore necessary, as a matter of business efficacy to make the agreement workable, that an obligation to keep the outside in repair must be imposed on someone.

To the question who that someone should be there were three possible answers. First, the obligation could be put on the tenant. This was rejected as being unbusinesslike and unrealistic. Moreover, it would be wrong, as a matter of construction, where there was an express tenant's covenant relative to the inside, to imply a covenant relating to the outside as well. Secondly, there could be the implication of a joint obligation on both parties to keep the outside in good repair. This too was rejected, as being obviously unworkable. The first two possibilities having been rejected, the court was left only with the third solution, an implied obligation on the landlord. This was the only solution which made business sense. The landlord's appeal against the county court decision that a repairing obligation was to be implied was accordingly dismissed. The tenant was entitled to agreed damages of £1,250, and a mandatory injunction to compel the landlord to carry out the work in an agreed schedule of dilapidations, estimated to cost about £10,000. On the face of it this imposed a heavy burden on the landlord, for the current rent was only £15 per week, but the indications were that the landlord had spent nothing on the property for many years. Kerr LJ finally referred briefly to the alternative claim that the landlord was in breach of the duty of care owed to the tenant under s 4(1) of the Defective Premises Act 1972. If the appeal on the main issue had been allowed, the court would have remitted the matter back to the county court to deal with the alternative claim under the Act. There was no reason of principle or jurisdiction why an injunction should not be granted to enforce the statutory obligations in appropriate circumstances.

In *Coronation Street Industrial Properties Ltd v Ingall Industries plc* [1989] 1 All ER 979 the House of Lords had to decide whether the principles it had laid down in the previous year in *P & A Swift Investments (a firm) v Combined English Stores Group plc* [1988] 2 All ER 885 and discussed in All ER Rev 1988 at 192 applied to the facts before it. It will be recalled that in the last mentioned case the question was whether the assignee of the reversion could sue the surety on his covenant to guarantee performance of the tenant's obligation to pay the rent. There had been no express assignment of the benefit of the surety's covenant to the assignee of the reversion, and the assignee could therefore only succeed if he could establish that the covenant touched and concerned the land and accordingly ran with it. It was held that it did. In the instant case the assignee was likewise suing the surety who had not only guaranteed the performance of the tenant's covenants, but had also covenanted with the original landlord that in the event of the tenant going into liquidation and the lease being disclaimed, which event happened, it would accept from the landlord a lease of the demised premises for the unexpired residue of the term. It was argued on behalf of the surety that the second covenant conferred an option on the landlords to create a new lease and that with the single anomalous exception of an option to the tenant to renew his lease options in leases did not touch and concern the land. Lord Templeman did not consider that the cases relied on by counsel for the surety were concerned with the position where a new lease is substituted for an old lease which through no fault of the landlord ceases to be effective. In giving its consent to the disclaiming of the lease by the liquidator of the tenant the court must have believed that the landlords would not be prejudicially affected thereby. Lord Templeman cited his own colourful metaphor in the *Swift Investments* case:

> 'A surety for a tenant is a quasi tenant who volunteers to be a substitute or twelfth man for the tenant's team and is subject to the same rules and regulations as the player he replaces'

and continued: 'As a result of the disclaimer the tenant retires mortally wounded and the surety is the substitute.' He concluded that the covenant by the surety to accept a new lease did touch and concern the land and was accordingly enforceable against him by the assignee of the reversion. In reaching this conclusion their Lordships agreed that the working test propounded by Lord Oliver in the *Swift Investments* case as to whether, in a given case, a covenant touches and concerns the land was satisfied.

The Court of Appeal, in *Rhodes v Allied Dunbar Pension Services Ltd* [1989] 1 All ER 1161, reversed the decision of the judge below, reported in [1988] 1 All ER 524, and discussed in All ER Rev 1988 at 194, on the basis of an argument not put to the court at first instance. The essential facts, it may be recalled, were that trustee landlords, the appellants, had granted leases of freehold property they owned to Offshore Ventilation Ltd (the company) which had granted underleases of parts of the demised property. On 3 March 1986 the company entered into a debenture in favour of its bankers to secure all money from time to time owing. The debenture granted the bank a first legal charge over the company's interest in the demised property and in the usual way a fixed charge over all the book debts and other debts of the company, present and future, and a floating charge on all the undertakings and property of the company. On 31 July 1986 the bank under its powers in the debenture appointed the respondents to be joint receivers and managers of the company. Rent was due to the appellants from the company, which itself had not been paid rents due from the undertenants. The appellants, who were aware of the appointment of the receivers, served notices on the undertenants under s 6 of the Law of Distress Amendment Act 1908 requiring the undertenants to pay future instalments of rent direct to them. The response of the receivers was, two or three days later, to levy distress in respect of the rent due from the undertenants, and they applied to the court for directions regarding the moneys in their hands which they had obtained through the distress.

Prima facie the effect of the notices was to assign to the appellants as superior landlords the right to receive the undertenants' rents: in the words of the section they operated 'to transfer to the superior landlord the right to recover, receive and give a discharge for' all future payments of rent by the undertenants until the arrears of rent due to the superior landlords had been paid. On this basis the receivers were not entitled to recover the rents and the distress they had levied was unlawful. The moneys they had received under the distress should be paid to the appellants. At first instance, however, the judge accepted the argument that the s 6 notices were not effectual against the bank. It was a case of successive assignments of a chose in action, viz the right to be paid the undertenants' rents. Though the s 6 notices brought about a statutory assignment of the chose in action, it was held that there was a prior assignment. On the appointment of the receivers the right to future payments of rent was assigned in equity to the bank and under the rule in *Dearle v Hall* [1824–34] All ER Rep 28 the appellants, who knew of the appointment of the receivers, and, hence, of the prior assignment to the bank could not acquire priority by serving s 6 notices. At first instance it had been common ground that the crystallisation of the floating charge by the appointment of a receiver had the effect of assigning to the bank in equity the right to future payment of the undertenants' rent. This 'starting point', as it was called by Nicholls LJ, was challenged in the Court of Appeal by counsel for the appellants (who had not represented them in the court below), and the analysis put forward by him was accepted by the court.

The proper analysis of the debenture, in so far as it created a charge by way of legal mortgage, was that it gave the bank the protection, powers and remedies referred to in s 87 of the Law of Property Act 1925. The bank as mortgagee could, and did, allow the company as mortgagor to remain in possession, and in those circumstances the mortgagor remained entitled to receive and retain the income of the mortgaged property, including the rents under the underleases, without any liability to account at law or in equity. Nor was the position altered by the appointment of the receivers for, as is usual, they were by the terms of the debenture itself deemed to be the agents of the company. Though the receivers were entitled to payment of the undertenants' rents, their entitlement was as agents of the company. Further it was held that the first legal charge over the land then owned by the company was intended to state, and was effective to state, what was to be the nature of the bank's charge over such land. There was no scope for the operation of the subsequent fixed charge or floating charge in relation thereto.

Having accepted this analysis of the debenture the position was tolerably clear. As Nicholls LJ, with whose judgment the other members of the court agreed, said: 'The spectre of successive assignments of the same chose in action vanishes.' The company, as the undertenants' immediate landlord was clearly entitled to their payments of rent before the debenture was executed. The position was unaffected by the execution of the debenture, the bank not having exercised its right to take possession, and, as explained above, the appointment of the receivers made no difference. There was no question of competing assignments and the s 6 notices operated in the ordinary way to assign to the appellants as superior landlords the right to receive the undertenants' rents.

In conclusion Nicholls LJ observed that the result was neither surprising nor unfair. Section 6 would clearly have been available to the appellants if the company had never executed the debenture but had failed to pay the rent. Again an assignee of a lease, or a person such as a mortgagee who takes a subterm carved out of the headlease, acquires an estate which from its inception is subject to the rights conferred on superior tenants and undertenants by the Act. Thus if the bank had gone into possession of the property under the debenture and had not paid rent to the appellants as head landlords, s 6 would have been available to the appellants. It would have been surprising if s 6 would not have been available where the bank had not gone into possession but had appointed a receiver.

Phillips v Mobil Oil Ltd [1989] 3 All ER 97 raised a question of construction of the Land Charges Act 1972. The plaintiff was the assignee of the reversion of a 25 year lease to the defendants which expired on 25 March 1986. The lease contained an option to renew for a further term of 25 years, and Mobil exercised this option in February 1985. The plaintiff (whose company was an undertenant of the defendants) refused to renew on the ground that the option had not been registered in the land charges register and was therefore void against him for want of registration. The simple question of law was whether a renewal option contained in a lease falls within the Land Charges Act in 1972 as a land charge class C (iv) (the Land Charges Act 1925, in force at the time of the relevant sale was for present purposes in terms not materially different). This is defined as:

'Any contract by an estate owner or by a person entitled at the date of the contract to have a legal estate conveyed to him to convey or create a legal estate, including a contract conferring either expressly or by statutory implication a valid option of purchase, a right of pre-emption or any other like right (in this Act referred to as "an estate contract").'

Before 1926 it was settled law that the burden of an option in favour of a tenant to buy the reversion did not touch and concern the land and so did not run with the reversion, but it was otherwise in the case of an option to renew the lease. It was argued in *Taylor Fashions Ltd v Liverpool Victoria Trustees Co Ltd* [1981] 1 All ER 897 that the land charges provisions were designed to replace the equitable doctrine of notice, and that an option to renew might fall within the Act and be void as a land charge. However, it was contended, this would not touch contractual obligations which by statute and independently of any equitable doctrine of notice, bind a purchaser as an integral part of the land purchased: the obligation resting on a reversioner under an option to renew is a contractual obligation which has run with the land and bound the reversioner regardless of any question of notice. Oliver J thought there was logic in the argument which, he said, accorded 'with the view of the original authors of Wolstenholme and Cherry, with what Harman J thought was the policy of the legislation in *Hollington Brothers Ltd v Rhodes* [1951] 2 All ER 578n and with the practice of the legal profession up to 1960'. The reference to 1960 is an indirect reference to *Beesly v Hallwood Estates Ltd* [1960] 2 All ER 314 (affd on other grounds [1961] 1 All ER 90) where Buckley J decided that a covenant to renew was registrable as an estate contract and, if not registered, would be void as against a purchaser of a legal estate for money or money's worth. As a direct authority which had been adopted as correct, though apparently without argument, by the Court of Appeal in *Greene v Church*

Commissioners for England [1974] 3 All ER 609 and *Kitney v MEPC Ltd* [1978] 1 All ER 595, Oliver J felt bound to follow *Beesly v Hallwood Estates Ltd*, observing that it was a considered judgment on a difficult point of statutory interpretation which had been followed and acted on by conveyancers for some 18 years—now, as the Court of Appeal pointed out, nearly 30.

Nichols LJ, with whose judgment the other members of the court agreed, took a robust approach. In his view a renewal covenant in a lease fell within the definition of an estate contract—and prima facie this is clearly so—and there was nothing in the context or legislative antecedents to alter this. He could see no inconsistency between (a) Parliament enacting s 142 of the Law of Property Act and leaving untouched the established principle that a renewal covenant in a lease runs with the reversion and (b) Parliament intending that in future, unless registered, a renewal covenant in a lease should be void as regards purchasers of a legal estate for money or money's worth. On the question of construction Nicholls LJ was probably right, and he was certainly right to show the same reluctance as Oliver J in the earlier case to overrule a decision acted on by conveyancers in innumerable transactions for nearly 30 years. He cited, inter alia, the recent observations of Lord Bridge in *Otter v Norman* [1988] 2 All ER 897, 901 that in this sort of case a settled construction should not be upset even if a different construction could reasonably be placed upon the relevant provision. In conclusion Nicholls LJ said that he derived some comfort from noting that since *Beesly's* case Parliament had revisited the Land Charges Act 1925 more than once without taking any steps to reverse it.

Practitioners can now rely on *Beesly's* case with even greater confidence, or, to look at it another way, should take even greater care when acting for a tenant to ensure that the option is duly registered so as to protect both the client—and also themselves from the risk of an action for negligence. Indeed it is a matter of concern to the original landlord also, for if the option is not registered and is void as against a purchaser, the original landlord may be contractually liable in damages—*Stuart v Joy* [1904] 1 KB 368; *Wright v Dean* [1948] 2 All ER 415; *Hollington Bros Ltd v Rhodes* [1951] 2 All ER 578n.

Finally it is submitted that consideration should be given to an amendment of the law. One possibility would be, by analogy with the definition of a restrictive covenant (land charge class D (ii)) in s 2(5) of the 1972 Act), to exclude from the definition of an estate contract an option to renew (and other like rights) contained in a lease. At the same time consideration might be given to the anomalous distinction between an option to renew the lease and an option to purchase the reversion.

Hammersmith and Fulham London BC v Top Shop Centres Ltd [1989] 2 All ER 655 is the latest case in the long running saga concerning Parway Estates. The earlier cases are discussed in All ER Rev 1984 at pp 196–198 and All ER Rev 1985 at pp 210, 211. An admirable and concise summary of the complicated history of the case occupies the first five pages or so of the instant report. The essence, for present purposes, is that Parway (which had since been wound up) had been granted a building lease by the charity trustees in 1961. Underleases had been granted to the plaintiff council among others. Parway's lease was forfeited on 19 July 1982, and a vesting order was made in favour of mortgagees in 1984 in respect of the residue of the term granted to Parway, less one day. As a consequence of subsequent dealings the freehold became vested in the defendants and the lease was surrendered. The question before the court was whether the council's underleases were good against the defendants.

It was not disputed that as a result of the forfeiture of Parway's lease, all interests derived therefrom, including the council's underleases, ceased to exist. However neither the trustees nor the mortgagees nor the receivers appointed by them took any formal steps to apprise the underlesees of the situation, and the managing agents at all material times demanded and received rents on the footing that the underleases still subsisited. In these circumstances the defendants argued that the council held a yearly tenancy terminable on six months notice on the terms of the underleases so far as applicable to a tenancy from year to year.

The council put its case in three ways:
  (i) that the vesting order under s 146(4) in favour of the mortgagees had the effect of automatically reinstating the council's erstwhile underleases as underleases to which that lease was subject. If this was so, it is well settled that the surrender of the lease would not extinguish the underleases but leave the freehold subject to them.
 (ii) that the conduct of the trustees and the mortgagees gave rise to an estoppel binding on the defendants which precluded them from denying that the council's underleases were still subsisting.
(iii) that it was not too late for the council to apply for relief under s 146(4) of the Law of Property Act 1925.

As to contention (i), Warner J said that the only authority on the point was the dictum of Scott J in one of the earlier Parway cases, *Official Custodian for Charities v Mackey* [1984] 3 All ER 689, 701 where he said that the vesting order could not reinstate the various leases. In following and applying this dictum Warner J nevertheless saw the attraction of applying the same rule as that which applies where relief is granted to a lessee under s 146(2) where it is settled that the effect is automatically to reinstate all derivative interests. He observed, however, that the grant of relief under sub-s (2) restores the original lease as if there had been no forfeiture while the grant of relief under sub-s (4) creates a new lease as from the date of the court's order, and he distinguished *Chelsea Estates Investment Trust Co Ltd v Marche* [1955] 1 All ER 195 where it had been held that the mortgagee of a lease which had been forfeited held under a new lease vested in him under s 146(4) subject to the equity of redemption of the mortgagor. In the instant case there was no similar equity: the rights of the former underlessees depended entirely upon common law and statute. Further, Warner J thought a decisive consideration was the fact that s 146(4) confers a wide discretion on the court. Save that it cannot vest in the applicant under that sub-section a lease beginning before the date of its order or ending later than the original lease would have done the discretion of the court is unfettered. The court could, for instance, order a new lease at a different rent from that reserved by the original underlease; for a term ending sooner than the term granted thereby; with different covenants: or for a lesser part of the property demised by the forfeited lease than was comprised in the original lease. This is inconsistent with the proposition that all interests derived from the original underlease should automatically be reinstated. As to contention (iii), s 146(4) begins in words identical to the corresponding part of s 146(2), 'where a lessor is proceeding to enforce a right of re-entry or forfeiture . . .' The question is when the lessor's 'proceeding' to enforce his right of re-entry is at an end. The starting point is that underlessees are, vis-à-vis the freeholder, trespassers once the headlease has been forfeited. The freeholder, however, has not fully enforced his right of re-entry until he has effectively asserted that right, for instance by compelling the underlessees to take new leases or give up possession. The mere receipt from them of the rents payable under the erstwhile leases is not sufficient. On the facts the council had not lost its right to apply for relief under s 146(4).

The view of the court on contention (ii), however, made it unnecessary for the council to rely on sub-s (4). In considering whether a case of proprietary estoppel was made out Warner J followed the prevailing (though not universal—see *Coombes v Smith* [1986] 1 WLR 808) trend which, while not ignoring the classical five probanda set out by Fry J in *Willmott v Barber* (1880) 15 Ch D 96 and adopted by Scarman LJ in *Crabb v Arun DC* [1975] 3 All ER 865, treats them more as indicators than prerequisites. He cited the judgment of Oliver J in *Taylor Fashions Ltd v Liverpool Victoria Trustees Co Ltd* [1981] 1 All ER 897 to the effect that what is required is a broad approach

> 'which is directed to ascertaining whether, in particular individual circumstances, it would be unconscionable for a party to be permitted to deny that which, knowingly or unknowingly, he has allowed or encouraged another to assume to his detriment . . .'

Counsel for the defendants argued that the receipt of rent by their predecessors in title did no more than enable the council to claim a yearly tenancy. It was held that, on the facts, there was more than a mere receipt of rent, and that the defendants' predecessors in title had knowingly allowed or knowingly encouraged the council to assume that it still held its underleases, giving rise to an estoppel which bound the defendants as their successors in title. For the council to succeed on the basis of proprietary estoppel it had to be shown that it had acted to its detriment as a result of its belief in the continued existence of its underleases. The court accepted that a detriment had been shown, most significantly by its failure to negotiate with the mortgagees for the grant of new leases or to apply for relief under s 146(4). Did this detriment flow from a reliance on the belief induced by the defendants' predecessors in title? There was no direct evidence to this effect, but no evidence to the contrary either. In these circumstances the judge followed recent authority that reliance may be presumed—see *Greasley v Cooke* [1980] 3 All ER 710 and *Re Basham (decd)* [1987] 1 All ER 405. The defendants were accordingly estopped from denying that the council still held under the under-leases.

Particular statutory provisions

The most important point decided in *Pittalis v Grant* [1989] 2 All ER 622 was a procedural one, namely that the rule in *Smith v Baker and Sons* [1891] AC 325, [1891–4] All ER Rep 69 ought no longer to be applied. This was the rule that said that there was no right of appeal from a county court on a question of law, even on a pure question of law, which was not raised and submitted to the county court judge at the trial. Since that is not a landlord and tenant point it will not be further discussed here, and we will concentrate on the substantive question which arose under the Rent Act 1977. This was a pure question of the construction of s 137(3) which in some circumstances protects a sub-tenant when a head tenancy comes to an end, even though that head tenancy is not itself a statutorily protected tenancy. This sub-section is a statutory exception, first introduced by s 41 of the Housing Repairs and Rent Act 1954, to the principle established in *Cow v Casey* [1949] 1 All ER 197 that [s 137(2)] only applies where the head tenancy which has determined was one to which the Act applied. In the opinion of Lord Greene MR in that case any other decision would have enabled an unprotected head tenant to saddle his landlord with protected tenants when his head tenancy expired.

Section 137(3) applies where two conditions are fulfilled, namely, where a dwelling-house—

> '(a) forms part of premises which have been let as a whole on a superior tenancy but do not constitute a dwelling-house let on a statutorily protected tenancy; and
> (b) is itself subject to a protected or statutory tenancy . . .'

The sub-section was primarily intended to deal with the situation where the sub-tenant could not obtain protection because the premises comprised in the head tenancy were of too high a rateable value, but it is not in terms directed to that situation. In *Maunsell v Olins* [1975] 1 All ER 16 the premises let on the superior tenancy comprised not a dwelling-house but an agricultural holding. It was held by the House of Lords that the word 'premises' in s 137(3)(a) was to be construed as being limited to premises which for the purposes of the Act are treated as dwelling-houses. Accordingly the case did not fall within the Act and the sub-tenant was unprotected notwithstanding that as between the head tenant and the sub-tenant there was a tenancy protected by the Acts. That decision has been statutorily reversed by the addition of a final paragraph to s 137(3) which provides that 'premises' includes an agricultural holding, but the principle stated by the House of Lords remains and was held to apply in the instant case where the head lease was one to which Part II of the Landlord and Tenant Act 1954 applied and accordingly was not a regulated tenancy.

In the instant case Nourse LJ, giving the judgment of the Court of Appeal, said that even if this view was wrong, there was a second reason why the tenant could not succeed. Where conditions (a) and (b) are satisfied, the sub-section provides that, from the coming to an end of the superior tenancy, the Act should apply in relation to the dwelling-house comprised in the sub-tenancy:

> 'as if, in lieu of the superior tenancy, there had been separate tenancies of the dwelling-house and of the remainder of the premises, for the like purposes as under the superior tenancy . . .'

It had been argued that 'purposes' should be construed distributively, so that you look at the purposes for which each part of the property was used at the material date, and it was admitted that the property comprised in the subtenancy was used for residential purposes. The court held, however, that this was not the proper approach. The purposes under the superior tenancy were those under the head lease, which were partly business and partly residential, and it was for those *dual* purposes that the notional separate tenancies of each part of the property would be deemed to be granted. Such dual purposes would not give rise to a tenancy within the Act.

In *Lester v Ridd* [1989] 1 All ER 1111 the Court of Appeal was faced with a question under the Leasehold Reform Act 1967 which was easy to ask but which the court found difficult to answer, though ultimately all the members of the court were agreed on their decision. The relevant facts were that a 99 year lease had been granted from 25 December 1901 under which the demised premises for very many years up to at least 1963 were used for agriculture by way of trade or business. In that year the farming partnership between the two persons who were then the tenants was dissolved. Glebe House together with two acres of surrounding land (the Glebe House property) was assigned to one partner for the unexpired residue of the term, and the remainder of the demised property, some 18 acres of land, was likewise assigned to the other partner. These 18 acres have continued to be used as agricultural land at all material times. The Glebe House property was assigned to the appellants in 1982, who from the date of purchase used it as a residence, and it was subsequent to this that the respondent landlord learnt of the 1963 partition. The appellants were now seeking to acquire the freehold of the Glebe House property under the 1967 Act, and all the relevant conditions but one were clearly satisfied. The question arose in relation to the qualification contained in s 1(3) of the Act, which excludes a house from the operation of the Act at any time when '(*b*) it is comprised in an agricultural holding within the meaning of the Agricultural Holdings Act 1948'. Though the Agricultural Holdings Act 1986, a consolidating Act which repealed the 1948 Act, was only enacted after the proceedings had been commenced the court accepted the agreement of counsel that it would be convenient to look at the provisions of the 1986 Act since in relation to what is 'comprised in an agricultural holding' its provisions concisely set out the effect of the corresponding provisions of the 1948 Act as interpreted by the courts.

By s 1(1) of the 1986 Act 'agricultural holding' means the aggregate of the land comprised in a contract of tenancy which is a contract for an agricultural tenancy, which in turn, by s 1(2), means a contract where

> 'the whole of the land comprised in the contract, subject to such exceptions only as do not substantially affect the character of the tenancy, is let for use as agricultural land.'

It was common ground that before the partition in 1963 the Glebe House property was comprised in one 'agricultural holding' consisting of the aggregate of the land comprised in the 'contract for an agricultural tenancy' embodied in the original 99 year lease. The main question was whether the effect of the partition was to create two separate tenancies of two separate holdings, each of which had to be looked at on its own. If so, the Glebe House property would no longer be comprised in an agricultural holding and would not be excluded from enfranchisement under s 1(3)(*b*). If not, the land in the original lease had still to be looked at as a whole, and, looked at as a whole, the whole of the land, with an exception (the Glebe House property) which did not substantially affect the character of the tenancy, was still let for use as agricultural land.

As Slade LJ explained, if the landlord had concurred in the partition this might well have given rise to the emergence of two new 'contracts of tenancy', by way of novation, to each of which the landlord was a party. However the landlord did not consent and was not to be prejudiced by the partition. It would be unjust to thrust upon him by a transaction to which he was not a party a separate tenancy of the Glebe House property which carried with it the potential right to enfranchisement under the Leasehold Reform Act 1967. Moreover the notion that two separate tenancies were created by the partition was said to be wholly inconsistent with the recognised position in law that the whole of the rent under the original lease could, despite the partition and separate assignments, be recovered by distress levied on any part of the land originally comprised in the lease. Accordingly the Glebe House property was still comprised in an agricultural holding within the meaning of the Act and s 1(3)(b) operated to deprive the appellants of any right of enfranchisement which they might otherwise have enjoyed.

Medical Law

ANDREW GRUBB, MA
Barrister, Senior Lecturer in Law, King's College, University of London

In 1989 three important medical law cases were reported. These concerned the scope of lawful authority to treat an incompetent patient without consent (*F v West Berkshire HA* [1989] 2 All ER 545); a doctor's duty to treat a seriously ill (or handicapped) newborn child (*Re C (a minor) (wardship: medical treatment)* [1989] 2 All ER 782) and the obligation of confidence (*W v Egdell* [1989] 1 All ER 1089). In these cases we see the courts shaping the common law to deal with difficult legal and moral questions arising from medical practice.

Consent and the incompetent

In the previous two issues of this Review there was an extended analysis of cases concerned with the legality of sterilising mentally handicapped minors (*Re B (a minor) (wardship: sterilisation)* [1987] 2 All ER 206) and adult women (*T v T* [1988] 1 All ER 613). In *F v West Berkshire HA* [1989] 2 All ER 545 the House of Lords has finally determined many of the legal issues concerned with sterilisation and adult women.

F was aged 36. Due to disease suffered as a baby she was permanently mentally disabled. She had the verbal capacity of a 2 year-old child and the mental capacity of one aged 4 or 5. She was a voluntary inpatient at a mental hospital where she had formed a sexual relationship with another patient. Her doctors feared that she would become pregnant and that because of her mental disability she would not be able to cope with, nor understand, pregnancy, labour or delivery and she would not subsequently be able to care for the child. The only method of contraception which was both effective and feasible because of her condition was considered to be surgical sterilisation. However, F could not consent to the operation because of her mental disability. Her mother sought a declaration from the court that the sterilisation of F would not amount to an unlawful act by reason only of the absence of F's consent. Both the trial judge, Scott Baker J, and the Court of Appeal granted the declaration. The Official Solicitor, acting on behalf of F, appealed to the House of Lords.

In granting a declaration, the House of Lords addressed two principal substantive issues. First, who, if anyone, can give a valid consent to medical treatment on behalf of an incompetent patient (proxy consent). In particular, the House considered whether the court can (or, indeed, must in the case of a sterilisation) authorise the treatment. Secondly, the House defined the circumstances in which an incompetent patient can be treated without consent if no one can consent on her behalf (necessity and public policy).

1. Proxy consent

(a) by an individual

It seems to have been assumed in *F* that at common law no one has the power to consent to medical treatment upon another adult. It was never suggested that F's parents had any such authority. It has often been assumed in the medical profession that spouses or next of kin have such a power. One judge even made a passing remark which assumed the existence of this power *(Wilson v Pringle* [1986] 2 All ER 440 at 447 per Croom-Johnson LJ). Perhaps this particular myth, without legal foundation, has now been put to rest once and for all.

Instead, F's mother argued that a number of statutory provisions vested decision-making power in another. The House rejected this argument confirming the earlier views of Wood J in *T v T* (see All ER Rev 1988 200 at 206–211). The House held that the guardianship provisions of the Mental Health Act 1983 do not permit an appointed guardian of a mentally disordered patient to consent to medical treatment.

(b) by the court

Further, the House rejected the arguments that the court, either in exercising its powers qua Court of Protection under the Mental Health Act or under its inherent parens patriae power, might consent on behalf of an incompetent patient. In deciding that the court *could* not consent, the House of Lords rejected the argument that legally the court *must* authorise the procedure.

As to the former source of power, Lord Brandon (with whom the others agreed) held that the Court of Protection's powers under ss 95 and 96 of the Mental Health Act were restricted to 'the property and affairs of persons under disability'. Seen in the context of the 1983 Act, this statutory phrase did not extend to medical treatment but was limited to 'business matters, legal transactions and other dealings of a similar kind.' This confirms the generally accepted view before *F* (see *In re W (EEM)* [1971] Ch 123 and *T v T*).

As to the parens patriae power, Lord Brandon accepted that the court had once possessed such a power over 'lunatics and idiots' but that the combined effect of the coming into force of the Mental Health Act 1959 and the revocation in 1960 of the warrant from the Crown delegating to the power to the judges meant that the power no longer existed. However, Lord Brandon's explanation is not entirely clear. Has the parens patriae power been abrogated or, more accurately, been placed in abeyance by the legislation (a constitutional argument) or is it that the power is just not currently vested in the judges because of the revocation of the delegation in 1960 (a procedural argument)? The distinction is important because it might be thought desirable in the future that the courts should have the parens patriae power in view of the procedural and substantive difficulties of the current law which *F* highlights.

The better argument is the procedural one (see Grubb and Pearl, 'Sterilisation and the Courts' (1987) CLJ 439 at 461–462). Lord Brandon's language is ambiguous referring to the effect of the revocation of the warrant (relevant to the procedural argument) and the impact of the legislation (relevant to the constitutional argument). But, it is not repeated by Lord Goff or Lord Griffiths who speak in terms more consistent with revocation than abrogation (at 562 and 561 respectively). Consequently, the Crown may still possess the power though it is not currently delegated to the judges.

2. *Necessity and public policy*

What, then, was the basis for the court's declaration? First, the House accepted that, as a general rule, consent is required for medical treatment to be lawful because without it any treatment would amount to a trespass to the person. The argument, based upon the Court of Appeal's decision in *Wilson v Pringle* [1986] 2 All ER 440, which would place all medical touchings outside the scope of the law of trespass because they are not 'hostile' was rejected. Secondly, the judges rejected, or chose not to rely upon, two arguments which might justify treating an incompetent patient.

It is sometimes argued that an incompetent patient's consent to medical treatment can be implied. This argument is tenable in the case of the temporarily unconscious upon whom it is proposed to perform a medical procedure which is clearly beneficial because of its life or limb saving qualities, for example, an emergency patient who has been involved in a car accident. However, in the case of a permanently incompetent patient upon whom it is proposed to perform a procedure which is not so clearly therapeutic, for example, a sterilisation on a mentally handicapped woman, the argument that she impliedly consents takes on the air of the unreal. For this reason, in *T v T* Wood J rejected the implied consent argument. In *F* Lord Brandon did not mention implied consent and Lord Goff, who did, arguably rejected it preferring to rely upon the principle of necessity.

Further, Lord Goff rejected the view that consent was not necessary because medical procedures came within the recognised exception of physical contact 'generally acceptable in the ordinary conduct of everyday life' *(Collins v Wilcock* [1984] 3 All ER 374 at 378 per Goff LJ). Lord Goff restricted this exception to physical contacts which are ordinary events in everyday life, for instance, jostling in a public place. It could not be said that '[m]edical treatment, even treatment for minor ailments . . . [falls] within that category of events.'

Instead, the House of Lords relied upon the common law principle of necessity to justify treatment of an incompetent patient without consent. The principle of necessity as a legal justification for treating unconscious patients in situations of emergency has been anticipated by legal commentators (eg Skegg 'A Justification for Medical Procedures Performed Without Consent' (1974) 90 LQR 512).

Lord Goff analysed the principle of necessity as follows. First, there must be a necessity to act when it is not practicable to communicate with the person who is unable to consent and secondly, the action taken must be such as a reasonable person would in all the circumstances take, acting in the best interests of the incompetent person.

This principle was not restricted to cases of emergency, indeed the circumstances of *F* could not properly be described as an emergency. It could apply where there was no emergency but the individual was temporarily or permanently incapable of consenting to medical treatment. Lord Goff recognised that there were limitations on the scope of the principle. First, it would not justify officious intervention. Secondly, it could not operate where the doctor proposed to act contrary to the known wishes of the patient. Therefore, a doctor could not lawfully give, for example, a blood transfusion to a known Jehovah's Witness who was unconscious (see *Malette v Shulman* (1988) 63 OR (2d) 243). Thirdly, Lord Goff noted that in the case of the temporarily incompetent patient a doctor could only carry out such procedures which are 'reasonably required, in the best interests of the patient' before the patient regains his competence. Consider for example the temporarily unconscious patient; a doctor should only do that which is reasonably necessary before the patient regains consciousness (see, for example, *Marshall v Curry* [1933] 3 DLR 260 and *Murray v McMurchy* [1949] 2 DLR 442). Fourthly, Lord Goff accepted that in the case of the permanently incompetent patient a doctor might be justified in performing a wider range of procedures than in the case of the emergency or temporarily incompetent patient. For example, not only surgical procedures or other substantial medical treatment could be performed but also routine medical procedures and other 'humdrum matters' which are in the patient's best interests and which could not otherwise be performed.

The importance of *F* lies not primarily in the recognition of the existence of the common law justification for treating the incompetent but in the extended scope given to it by the House of Lords and, in particular, its application to cases of surgical sterilisation.

How does a doctor determine whether a particular medical procedure may lawfully be performed without consent? As we have seen, the House of Lords held that the scope of the principle of necessity was to act *reasonably in the best interests of the patient*. The House applied the *Bolam* test (*Bolam v Friern Hospital Management Committee* [1957] 2 All ER 118) developed in the tort of negligence which defines the scope of a doctor's duty of care in terms of the 'reasonable doctor'. A doctor will satisfy this standard if his action is in accordance with *a* body of accepted medical opinion. Consequently, disagreement within the medical profession will not affect the legality of the intervention which has not been consented to. Lord Brandon and Lord Goff pointed out that not to adopt *Bolam* might put the doctor who has decided treatment is in the patient's best interests in an invidious position. If he does not treat, he could be in breach of his duty of care and so liable in an action in negligence and yet, if he does treat, he might be at risk of being sued for trespass to the person because he had not obtained the patient's consent if a more stringent test is adopted under the principle of necessity. To avoid this situation a doctor's duty (as defined by the *Bolam* test) must also determine the extent of the principle of necessity.

On reflection, does this, admittedly problematic, situation arise? In the case of a competent patient, a doctor's duty is limited by the need for his patient's consent. A doctor cannot act in what he perceives to be his patient's best interests *unless* his patient also consents to the medical intervention. The need for consent, and in this situation, the scope of the principle of necessity, limit the doctor's duty. In the case of an incompetent patient, therefore, it is question begging to say that it is the doctor's duty to intervene because it is in a patient's best interests and so the intervention must be lawful notwithstanding the lack of consent. It is not illogical, therefore, for the scope of the principle of necessity to be narrower than what would be the doctor's duty in the tort of negligence. Indeed, in the factually similar case of *T v T*, Wood J held that the scope of lawful intervention was defined by what 'good medical practice demands' which the judge explained required that 'there are really no two way views of what course is for the best' (discussed All ER Rev

1988 200 at 206–211). In the Court of Appeal in *F* the judges applied more restrictive tests than *Bolam*. Lord Donaldson MR required that the doctor follow a practice *rightly* accepted by the medical profession. Neill and Butler Sloss LJJ required that the doctor act in accordance with the 'general body of medical opinion'.

In view of the personal liberty interests which are protected by the tort of trespass to the person perhaps a more restrictive approach, like that of Wood J or the Court of Appeal in *F*, could have been justified. Nevertheless, the House of Lords' rejection of these and its use of the 'reasonable doctor' standard along with *Bolam* might be acceptable if the court retained a role in defining (and determining) what a 'reasonable doctor' would do in a particular situation. This should be especially vital when dealing with cases of surgical sterilisation of the mentally handicapped. The *Bolam* test, however, hands over to the medical profession the determination of the scope of the duty of care in the tort of negligence *(Sidaway v Bethlem Royal Hospital Governors* [1985] AC 871 at 881 per Lord Scarman). Does it have the same effect when applied to determine the scope of the common law justification of necessity?

There are a number of indications in the opinions of Lord Brandon and Lord Goff that it may not. We have already seen how Lord Goff attempted to circumscribe the conduct of the 'reasonable doctor' in certain situations. Other indications exist. First, both judges appeared to define, as a matter of law, the factors which must be considered by a doctor in assessing a patient's best interests and which must be the basis for the 'competent body of medical opinion' under *Bolam*. Lord Brandon stated that a procedure would only be in a patient's best interests if it is carried out in order to save life or to ensure improvement or prevent deterioration in physical or mental health. Similarly, Lord Goff spoke of a doctor acting to preserve life or health, although he may have diluted this a little by also including action to preserve an individual's well-being.

The judges seemed to be marking out the proper scope of medical opinion as a matter of law. This is significant and is not the normal application of *Bolam*. In the case of most medical procedures performed on an incompetent this limitation will not be vital. However, in the case of surgical sterilisation it would restrict a doctor's mind, in determining his patient's best interests, to medical factors and exclude such social factors as the interests of others who may have the care of the incompetent or of any children that might be otherwise born. In truth, of course, doctors often 'dress up' social factors in terms of health factors such as the patient's mental health. The experience of the availability of abortions on grounds of risk to the mental health of the pregnant woman illustrates this. Sterilisation decisions may often involve the very same fudging. Indeed, might this not explain the actual decision in *F*?

The second limitation on allowing the *Bolam* test to govern uncontrolled is the insistence by all the judges that in applying the *Bolam* test in sterilisation cases such as *F*, an application to the court for a declaration is desirable in order to obtain an 'independent, objective and authoritative view' of the legality of the sterilisation procedure (per Lord Goff). The judges put sterilisation procedures in a special category although it was recognised that other procedures might exist. Perhaps, for example, the judges had in mind abortion or inter vivos organ donations (on which see now the Human

Organ Transplant Act 1989, s 2). Lord Brandon identified six features that put sterilisation in this special category. First, the operation is irreversible; second, it will deprive the woman of the fundamental human right to reproduce; third, this involves moral and emotional considerations; fourth, there is a risk that a mistake will be made in determining the woman's best interests; fifth, there is a risk that the operation may be carried out for improper reasons or motives; and sixth, court involvement will protect doctors from adverse claims or criticisms.

The desirability of court involvement is clear. Lord Griffiths would have gone further and required that the court be asked to authorise a sterilisation. However, his view is untenable once the judges determined that the court lacked any parens patriae power. Indeed, even if that power existed the court's approval could not be required until the court was seized of the matter. That would certainly seem to be the law in relation to the analogous wardship jurisdiction of the court over minors. Only if the minor is already a ward, or a specific application to ward is made to deal with the sterilisation operation, would the court's consent be necessary (see Grubb and Pearl at 452–456). Nevertheless the House of Lords gave a clear indication that it hoped all cases would be brought before the court using the declaratory procedure which was approved in F. No doubt, following the earlier decision of the House of Lords in Re B (a minor) (wardship: sterilisation) [1987] 2 All ER 206, this will also be desirable in the case of minor girls.

Assuming these cases are brought before the courts, what sort of limitation is this on medical decision-making when all the judges (contra Lord Griffiths) accept that a sterilisation will be lawful if it is in a patient's best interests even without the court's involvement? Lord Goff gave the impression that the court will make its own determination of where the patient's best interests lie when a case comes before it—forming an 'independent, objective and authoritative view'. Perhaps the analogy would be with a court exercising wardship jurisdiction over a minor in similar circumstances. But this cannot be correct because in cases such as F the court is limited to determining the legality of the doctor's action under the Bolam test. Providing the doctor has relied upon the proper criteria defined by the judges, namely health factors, and a body of competent medical opinion would agree with his assessment of these factors, the proposed sterilisation will be lawful. If the court seeks to exercise any greater review power then it must reject the application of the Bolam test. If the court seeks independent expert evidence upon the issue of the patient's best interests and the evidence reaches a contrary conclusion to that of the doctor, the court cannot, in applying Bolam, prefer this evidence to that of the doctor who has the care of the patient if his views are supported elsewhere in the medical profession (Maynard v West Midlands Regional Health Authority [1985] 1 All ER 635). It is curious, therefore, that Lord Goff both approved Bolam and, at the same time, stated that 'where expert opinions are expressed, those opinions are listened to with great respect; but, in the end, the validity of the opinion has to be weighed and judged by the court'. Does this not flatly contradict the effect of Bolam? It is interesting that Lord Brandon did not appear to envision such a role for the court in applying the Bolam test. The other Law Lords agreed with them both!

F has given some clarity to the law of treating the incompetent patient. It has, however, introduced a potentially wide ranging justification for treating such individuals. In cases of sterilisation, the substantive and procedural safeguards offered by the court may prove illusory. The Official Solicitor has subsequently published guidance containing detailed requirements before he will support an application to the court for sterilisation ((1989) NLJ 1380). While these create significant hurdles before a sterilisation could be performed, as the court recently pointed out (*In re C, Times*, 13 February 1990) they are not binding on the court which must always act in the individual's best interests.

In *F* the merits of the case were not considered in the House of Lords because the sterilisation was conceded as being in F's best interests. There may be some validity in this if one views the adverse consequences for F without the operation as being that much greater than undergoing the operation because of the inevitable deprivation of liberty she would otherwise have to undergo in order to prevent pregnancy. If these are the reasons for many sterilisations, then perhaps these reasons should be expressly stated. They would then be subject to much closer scrutiny; they are after all social and not medical and these cases leave the impression that doctors (and courts) are making medical decisions. At present there is a distinct possibility that social reasons are fudged into medical reasons and the courts accordingly give their blessings. Such an approach arguably raises issues beyond the province of judicial decision and more the province of Parliament.

Treating handicapped neonate

It can be a tragedy for a couple when a handicapped child is born. The effect on their lives could be devastating. Many couples would chose an abortion if the child's condition could be detected prior to birth. The law has for some time permitted the performance of an abortion on the ground of the unborn child's physical or mental handicap (Abortion Act 1967, s 1(1)(*b*)) and more recent developments in the law of medical negligence have provided compensation if a doctor carelessly fails to advise the mother of the option of abortion. Techniques such as amniocentesis and chorionic villus sampling now permit doctors to detect many handicaps while the baby is in utero. A failure to detect a handicap such as spina bifida or Down's Syndrome has lead to negligence actions when the handicapped child is born if the mother can prove that, if she had been fully informed, she would have sought an abortion (for a recent example, see, *Rance v Mid-Down Health Authority* (1990) NLJR 325).

What, however, is the doctor's duty to the child once it is born? Two cases have previously arisen in England; *In re B (a minor)* [1981] 1 WLR 1421 (Down's Syndrome baby with duodenal atresia) and *R v Arthur*, (1981) *Times*, 6 November (Down's Syndrome baby). To what extent should the wishes of the parents determine the treatment the child should receive? In what circumstances will the law allow a doctor to treat a newborn so that death will follow? Some of these issues were considered by the Court of Appeal in *Re C (a minor) (wardship: medical treatment)* [1989] 2 All ER 782.

C was born prematurely with hydrocephalus. In addition to the blockage of cerebral fluid associated with this condition, her brain structure was poorly formed. Shortly after her birth, a shunt was inserted to relieve the pressure on her brain caused by the build up of fluid. However, the damage to C's brain and the handicap it caused was irreversible. As C was for other reasons a ward of court, the local authority sought the direction of the court as to the appropriate treatment for C. The Official Solicitor, acting on behalf of C, obtained the expert opinion of a consultant pediatrician. His view was that C was physically and mentally severely disabled. She suffered from spasticity in all her limbs, was blind, probably deaf, incapable of properly absorbing foods given to her and cried as if in pain. C had little or no interaction with the world. The expert's view was that it was inconceivable that C would acquire any developmental skills or abilities. He described her ultimate prognosis as 'hopeless'.

In addition the expert also stated that C should not be treated for any intervening infection nor given artificial hydration and nutrition should these become necessary. Only if the nurses who had the care of C thought that C was in pain and suffering should such procedures be undertaken. To do otherwise would prolong 'a life which has no future and which appears to be unhappy for her'.

The trial judge, Ward J, held that C's handicap was 'severe and irreparable' and her intellectual functioning was 'negligible'. When coupled with her physical handicap this combination meant that her 'quality of . . . life will be demonstrably awful and intolerable'. Consequently, he directed that C be 'treat[ed] . . . in such a way that she may end her life and die peacefully with the greatest dignity and the least of pain, suffering and distress'.

The Court of Appeal reached the same conclusion though the reasoning was somewhat different. As we have seen, Ward J applied a 'quality of life' test, balancing the benefits of treatment against its burdens in the light of C's physical and mental condition. The Court of Appeal adopted the opinion of the expert as the definition of the legal duty of C's carers. It is to be expected that the court should look to expert evidence on the diagnosis and prognosis of a patient but it is, at first blush, surprising that the court considered expert opinion on the proper treatment determinative of a doctor's duty. However, we have already seen how in F the House of Lords adopted the Bolam test. Perhaps this is further notice from the court of the importance of expert evidence in all cases where a doctor's legal duty is under examination. Even so, it seems inappropriate, as we saw in relation to F, for the court to become blinkered by medical evidence. It could be that the expert's opinion in Re C simply coincided with the judges' independently reached views of the scope of the doctor's duty but it is far from clear that the court was adopting this independent role.

By approving the expert's report and adopting its suggested treatment regime, the court simply dealt with the case before it. Nevertheless, the case does provide some guidance for the future as to a doctor's duty in treating handicapped neonates. A number of points need to be made.

1. C was 'dying'

Lord Donaldson emphasized that C was dying. He said that 'one fundamental and inescapable fact [is that] Baby C is dying and nothing that the court can do, nothing that the doctors can do and nothing known to medical science can alter that fact.' Later he added that the only question was 'how soon this would happen.' On the face of it, therefore, *Re C* was a case concerned with a terminally ill and handicapped baby. While it is true that Baby C was dying that would, to an extent, be true of every human being. We are all born and are thereafter dying. What the Master of the Rolls meant, of course, was that medicine could not sustain her life. Arguably, this might not have been the case. Probably the court's view was based on the expert's opinion that C's prognosis was 'hopeless'. But surely this could mean no more than C's physical and mental handicaps were irreversible not that her death was imminent or inevitable anymore than anyone's death is inevitable. It looks likely that C's quality of life would have been minimal but that with medical intervention opportunistic diseases such as pneumonia could have been treated and, if called for, artificial hydration and nutrition could have sustained what little quality of life she had. Perhaps her condition might reduce her life expectancy but not shorten it to the extent of suggesting death was an imminent possibility.

Why should the court want to categorise C as a 'dying' child? The answer is two-fold. The court did not want to be seen to be authorising the killing of the child. Nor did it want it to be thought that the medical team was killing the child. The court criticized Ward J for initially ordering the doctors to 'treat the minor to die'. Instead, the Court of Appeal approved the withholding of life-saving treatment and artificial hydration and nutrition (subject to the provision of symptomatic relief if the nurses thought proper). Surely any difference is merely a matter of form? In substance the court authorised the doctors to do precisely what the court stated it was not authorising, namely to 'treat . . . C in a way designed to bring about her death.' Withholding life-sustaining treatment is bringing about a patient's death albeit by allowing an underlying cause or medical condition to take its course.

Further, the categorisation seemed important because of the court's perception that non-intervention by the medical team would be more justifiable if death was imminent. Consequently, the court distinguished the two earlier cases of *In re B (A minor) (wardship: medical treatment)* [1981] 1 WLR 1421 and *Re SD* [1983] 3 WWR 618. In *Re B* the Court of Appeal authorised the performance of a surgical procedure upon a Down's Syndrome baby. The operation would have been normal in a baby without B's handicap and the court held that it was in B's best interests to operate when the baby had a life expectancy of 20 to 30 years albeit with the physical and mental handicaps of Down's Syndrome. Similarly, in *Re SD* a Canadian court exercising wardship jurisdiction authorised the insertion of a shunt in the head of a severely mentally handicapped aged 6. The court took the view that the child's 'best interests' lay in life (albeit handicapped) and not death; particularly since not performing the procedure might lead to pain and suffering by the child rather than death.

The difference between the cases, particularly *Re C* and *Re B*, lies not exclusively in the fact that C was dying in any event (assuming this to be the case) while B was not, but rather in the effect this has in determining the baby's 'best interests'. In both cases the courts accepted that the child's 'best interests' were the determining factor. However, the way in which this is utilised in these handicapped neonate cases is really to require the court to assess the quality of life of the baby. The length of a baby's life may be significant in assessing that baby's quality of life. A quality of life assessment requires the court to weigh the benefits of interventions against the burdens they may impose upon the baby. The benefits may well be less if the baby has a minimal life expectancy. Consequently, the burdens of intervening with aggressive treatment for opportunistic diseases are more likely to outweigh the benefits for a baby in C's situation than in B's. The courts in *Re C* and *Re B* are, it is suggested, making just this kind of assessment. The expert's opinion in *Re C* is clearly couched in terms of quality of life. For example he states that to aggressively intervene 'would be prolonging a life which has no future and which appears to be unhappy for her.' Perhaps the quality of life approach is emphasised by the expert's view that aggressive intervention would be appropriate if the nurses thought this would relieve pain. In other words, interventions intended to sustain life would not be appropriate because of the prolongation of suffering for a doomed child but would be if the purpose was otherwise. The Court of Appeal accepted the expert's view as reflecting the legal duty of C's doctors.

In *Re B* although the court authorised intervention, Templeman LJ recognised that 'if the life of [the] child is demonstrably going to be awful' because its life was 'so bound to be full of pain and suffering' then the court might not authorise intervention. This too is an acceptance that a baby's quality of life is important. Even though Templeman LJ's remarks were doubted by Stephenson and Ackner LJ in *McKay v Essex Area Health Authority* [1982] 2 All ER 771 at 781 and 787, certainly Balcombe LJ considered C's situation to fall within Templeman LJ's words.

The Court of Appeal in *Re C* has accepted that a handicapped child's quality of life may be such that medical intervention to overcome opportunistic infections or to sustain life through artificial hydration and nutrition is not legally required. It is the first time that a court in England has reached such a decision on the facts. It should not, however, be seen as permitting the withholding or withdrawing of treatment other than in clear cases where the doctors reasonably conclude that the considerable burdens of treatment and sustained life outweigh the benefits to the baby of intervention. *Re C* is not a carte blanche to treat selectively handicapped neonates.

2. Parental role

A curious comment of Lord Donaldson MR in *Re C* concerns the role of the parents in making decisions concerning the treatment their baby should receive. When, as in *Re C*, the baby is a ward of court then it is well recognised that the court must determine where the baby's 'best interests' lie. What, however, is the situation when no court is involved? Clearly, the baby's parents have decision-making power. Lord Donaldson stated that in such a case any decision concerning C's medical treatment would 'have been solely a matter' for them. This could be interpreted as meaning that the parents can make any determination they wish in the child's 'best interests'. In other words, the parents have an unlimited discretion in determining the fate of their child. In *Re B* Dunn LJ made a comment which would support this interpretation. In that case the parents were opposed to the surgical intervention but they were overruled by the court and yet Dunn LJ stated that the decision of the parents was accepted by everyone as 'an entirely responsible one.' Considered and honest the decision might be but responsible it cannot be when the court applying the same 'best interests' test as the parents reaches a diametrically opposed decision on the fate of the child. The better view is that the law vests prima facie decision-making power in the parents to act in their child's 'best interests'. While presumptively their decision will be taken to be in the child's 'best interests' unless challenged in court, it is the court which imposes legal limits and prescribes the range of decisions that a prudent parent applying the 'best interests' test may reach (see Kennedy and Grubb *Medical Law: Text and Materials* (1989) ch 12). Lord Donaldson's comment should be interpreted in the light of this.

Confidentiality

Until recently there was almost no case law in England concerned with a doctor's duty or obligation of confidentiality owed to his patient. In last year's Review (All ER Rev 1988 200 at 214–216) we saw the case of *X v Y* [1988] 2 All ER 648 concerned with the confidentiality of information relating to an AIDS patient. In *W v Egdell* [1989] 1 All ER 1089 the scope of a doctor's obligation of confidence and the existence of any exception to that duty was again before the court. W was detained in a secure hospital after he shot and killed four people and was convicted of manslaughter on the grounds of diminished responsibility. He was considered a potential danger to the public. Ten years later he made an application to a mental health review tribunal to be discharged or transferred to a regional secure unit. In pursuance of his application, W sought a report on his condition and was examined by Dr Egdell an independent psychiatrist. The report was not favourable and W's solicitors withdrew W's application to the tribunal. The report was not disclosed to the tribunal or the hospital where W was held. When Dr Egdell discovered this he sent a copy of the report to the hospital and a copy was forwarded to the Home Secretary and in turn he sent a copy to the tribunal. W sought an injunction against each of these parties seeking to restrain them from disclosing or using the report. His principle claim was that Dr Egdell was in breach of his duty of confidentiality in sending the report to the hospital and hence to the Home Secretary and the tribunal.

Scott J refused the relief sought. As regards Dr Egdell's disclosure to the hospital, Scott J held this was not a breach of confidence for two reasons. First, he adopted para 81(b) of the General Medical Council's *Advice on Standards of Professional Conduct and of Medical Ethics* contained in the so-called 'Blue Book'. Following this, he held that disclosure was justified on the basis that the information was being 'shared with other registered medical practitioners who participate in and assume responsibility for clinical management of the patient . . .' As Scott J stated 'Dr Egdell was expressing opinions which were relevant to the nature of the treatment and care to be accorded to W at the hospital.'

Secondly, the judge decided that there was no breach of confidence on a broader ground. The judge held that Dr Egdell owed a duty to the public at large because of the circumstances of W's dangerousness. Consequently, he did not owe a duty of confidentiality to W. The judge said:

'In my view, a doctor called on, as Dr Egdell was, to examine a patient such as W owes a duty not only to his patient but also a duty to the public. His duty to the public would require him, in my opinion, to place before the proper authorities the result of his examination if, in his opinion, the public interest so required. This would be so, in my opinion, whether or not the patient instructed him to do so.'

Consequently disclosure to all the parties was justified because of Dr Egdell's concern that W was still a danger to the public if released.

The first approach of Scott J, looking as it does to a discretion to disclose, is the more attractive. Surely, Dr Egdell did owe a duty of confidentiality to W but an exception based upon the public interest in disclosure justified his action? Otherwise, it might be difficult to restrain publication, for example, to a newspaper if there is no obligation of confidence. It is better to recognise that there is a duty but that the law confers a discretion to disclose. That would allow a court to restrain publication to a newspaper because that would not be justified in the public interest. Scott J's judgment is heavily influenced by the context of a psychiatric patient who is detained in hospital after a criminal conviction. There is no indication in his judgment that he would necessarily conclude that generally a psychiatrist owed a duty to the public when he discovers that he has a dangerous patient.

Another way of interpreting Scott J's judgment is a twist upon his second approach. The judge recognised that Dr Egdell owed a duty of confidentiality to W but that the public interest justified disclosure because of W's danger to the public if he were released (see para 81(g) of GMC's Blue Book). This interpretation (adopted by the Court of Appeal subsequently, W v E (1989) Times, 20 November) leads to the possibility that a doctor who knows that his patient is a real danger to another may (but not must) act to try and prevent harm. It might justify, for example, a psychiatrist disclosing to a victim the desire of his patient to kill or harm that other. It might justify a doctor in warning the sexual partner of a patient who is HIV positive if the patient refuses to take precautions to avoid transmission to that sexual partner (see All ER Rev 1988 200 at 216). What this approach does not do is create a legally enforceable duty to the potential victim or sexual partner which could lead to a tort action if the doctor does not warn them (as in Tarasoff v Regents of the University of California (1976) 551 P 2d 334).

Serious professional misconduct

Beyond these three important cases one other case reported in 1989 calls for brief comment. In Lanford v General Medical Council [1989] 2 All ER 921 the Privy Council held that the criminal rules of evidence relating to similar fact evidence applied in proceedings before the professional conduct committee. The appellant was charged with serious professional misconduct in that he used obscene and indecent language and behaved improperly towards two different female patients. The Privy Council held, applying the rule in criminal cases, that similar fact evidence was admissible if its similarities were striking. On the facts, the Privy Council held that the account of each of the patients was capable of corroborating the other even though the similarity lay only in what the appellant said to each woman and not in what he actually did to them.

Practice and Procedure

ADRIAN A S ZUCKERMAN, LLM, MA
Fellow of University College, Oxford

Mareva injunctions

The effect of world wide Mareva injunctions

It will be recollected that the Mareva jurisdiction had its origin in attempts to prevent foreign residents from removing their assets out of the jurisdiction in order to frustrate English judgments against them. That innovation has proved so successful that attention has now turned to measures to extend the reach of English judgments to foreigners whose assets as well as their persons are abroad. In *Babanaft International Co SA v Bassatne* [1989] 1 All ER 433 the plaintiffs obtained judgment for some $15m against the defendants who lived and conducted their business abroad and whose life style was described as peripatetic. When the defendants failed to pay, the plaintiffs obtained an order for the examination of the defendants under RSC Ord 48 to determine their assets. The defendants were ordered to file an affidavit disclosing their assets wherever situated and, in the meantime, to refrain from dealing with their assets outside the jurisdiction.

An injunction against a foreign defendant directing him to refrain from doing something abroad clearly raises difficulties. How is the court to enforce such order? What is the court to do when foreign banks holding the defendant's money disregard the order and allow the defendant to dispose of the money? Over the defendant himself an English court has at least jurisdiction otherwise there would be no action against him. But over foreign third parties who deal with the defendant's assets abroad there is not even jurisdiction. The Court of Appeal recognised that an unqualified Mareva injunction over foreign assets could not be issued. It drew a distinction between personal jurisdiction over a defendant and jurisdiction over his foreign assets. By virtue of their jurisdiction over defendants, English courts are empowered to order only defendants themselves to refrain from disposing of their assets, wherever situated.

In so holding the Court of Appeal explained away *Ashtiani v Kashi* [1986] 2 All ER 970 where it was suggested that the Mareva jurisdiction was confined to assets within the jurisdiction. Since English courts do not have extra-territorial jurisdiction, a Mareva injunction, it has been held, should be qualified so as to make it clear that it did not seek to control the activities of third parties abroad. Thus, a foreign bank notified of such injunction will be under no duty to freeze the defendants' accounts.

The fact that there is jurisdiction over a foreign defendant does not of itself mean that he can be made to comply with the court's order. Here, however, the 1968 Brussels Convention on Jurisdiction and the Enforcement of Judgments in Civil and Commercial Matters which has been incorporated into English law by the Civil Jurisdiction and Judgments Act 1982 comes to the aid of English courts. Article 24 of the 1968 Convention provides—

'Applications may be made to the courts of a Contracting State for such provisional, including protective, measures as may be available under the law of that State, even if, under this Convention, the courts of another Contracting State have jurisdiction as to the substance of the matter.'

This provision authorises the courts of a contracting state to give provisional remedies in aid of proceedings pending in another state. Thus, for example, a French court could freeze the assets of a person who is a defendant in an English action so as to prevent the defendant from defeating an English judgment. In the *Babanaft* case Kerr LJ would have preferred not to qualify the effect of the injunction to the defendant personally so as to explicitly exclude third parties from its ambit. He would have rather granted a Mareva injunction in general terms but adding the qualification that it would affect third parties abroad only 'to the extent that it is enforced by the courts of the states in which any of the defendants' assets are located'; [1989] 1 All ER at 447. Armed with an injunction in these terms, he felt, the plaintiffs could then take the matter to the courts in the countries where the defendants' assets were located and seek help in accordance with art 24 of the 1968 Convention.

Republic of Haiti v Duvalier [1989] 1 All ER 456 which, as we shall shortly see, was also concerned with an extra-territorial injunction added a gloss on the issue of the effect of Mareva injunctions on third parties out of the jurisdiction. The Court of Appeal in this case felt that individual third parties, as distinguished from companies, who hold the defendant's assets abroad but who are resident in England should not be excluded from the operation of the injunction. Thus if an English resident happens to have control over the defendant's assets in France, he should be guilty of contempt if he helps the defendant to dispose of the French assets (a similar position was adopted by the Court of Appeal in *Derby & Co Ltd v Weldon (No 1)* [1989] 1 All ER 469). Companies were excluded from enforcing Mareva orders at their foreign branches in order to avoid placing English companies with branches abroad in an invidious position. However, in the later case of *Derby & Co Ltd v Weldon (No 2)* [1989] 1 All ER 1002 objections were raised to this distinction. Lord Donaldson MR pointed out that it was unjustified to distinguish between companies and partnerships for example. Further, he observed that by excluding English companies from the order they are denied an excuse they may wish to use to prevent the defendant from removing his assets. The Master of the Rolls preferred an injunction which would exclude persons resident abroad, except and to the extent that the foreign courts gave effect to the injunction, but would include

'persons who are subject to the jurisdiction of this court and (i) have been given written notice of this order at their residence or place of business within the jurisdiction, and (ii) are able to prevent acts or omissions outside the jurisdiction of this court which assist in the breach of the terms of this order'; [1989] 1 All ER at 1013.

'Persons' in this context include companies. This new formula was used in *Securities and Investments Board v Pantell SA* [1989] 2 All ER 673, 678, where an injunction freezing an account at Barclays Bank in Guernsey was said to restrain the bank from disposing of the assets in the Guernsey accounts because the bank was resident in England.

It is not, however, altogether clear what is meant by the words 'are able to prevent acts or omissions' in Lord Donaldson MR's dictum. Suppose that the defendant has a deposit in a Belgian bank in Brussels. The plaintiff has obtained a worldwide Mareva injunction and has served it on a branch of the Belgian bank in London. Is the bank obliged to freeze the defendant's account in Brussels? If this were so, the court would indeed be purporting to regulate the conduct of the Belgian bank in Brussels.

In the *Babanaft* case it was envisaged that the English plaintiffs would seek Mareva type relief in other European countries in aid of English actions. In *Republic of Haiti v Duvalier* [1989] 1 All ER 456 foreign plaintiffs sought Mareva relief in England. The Republic of Haiti brought proceedings in France against the Duvalier family for the recovery of $120m which were allegedly embezzled by them while in power. The Republic obtained an order in England to restrain the defendants from dealing with the proceeds of the money so embezzled wherever they might be and an order freezing the defendants' assets in England and ordering the defendants' solicitors to disclose the whereabouts of the defendants assets and restraining the solicitors from disclosing the order to their clients.

Before the Civil Jurisdiction and Judgments Act 1982, an English court could not grant Mareva relief in aid of a claim that proceeded abroad and over the substance of which English courts had no jurisdiction: *The Siskina* [1977] 3 All ER 803. But section 25(1) of the 1982 Act provides:

'The High Court . . . shall have power to grant interim relief where—(a) proceedings have been or are to be commenced in a Contracting State other than the United Kingdom . . .'

According to RSC Ord 11, r 1(2)(a) service of a writ out of the jurisdiction is permissible without leave for 'a claim which by virtue of the Civil Jurisdiction and Judgments Act 1982 the Court has power to hear'. However, this is subject to the condition in r 1(2)(a)(i) that 'no proceedings between the parties concerning the same cause of action are pending in the courts of any other part of the United Kingdom or of any other Convention territory'. It was argued that the same action was pending in France and no service could therefore take place. Staughton LJ rejected this argument—

'Either a claim for interim relief does not involve or concern any cause of action, or it is based on a new and distinct cause of action created by s 25. Whichever be right, the condition in Ord 11, r 1(2)(a)(i) is satisfied because any cause of action with which the English proceedings are concerned or involved is not the same as that with which the French action is concerned or involved:' [1989] 1 All ER at 462.

An interesting objection to service abroad was also raised in *X v Y* [1989] 3 All ER 689 in this regard. The plaintiffs brought proceedings in France against a defendant who was resident in Saudi Arabia, and sought an injunction in England to freeze the defendant's account here pending the French action. The defendant contended that although the Civil Jurisdiction and Judgments Act 1982, s 25(1) gave English courts power to grant interim relief in aid of foreign proceedings, notice of the proceedings had to be served abroad in accordance with Ord 11, r 1(1). However, he contended, since r 1(1) makes no provision for this situation, notice could not be served and the power under s 25(1) of the 1982 Act is unexercisable. This argument was rejected by A E Diamond QC, sitting in the Queens Bench Division, who held that it was plainly the purpose of the 1982 legislation to give effect to the 1968 Convention and in particular to art 24 of the Convention.

In *Republic of Haiti v Duvalier* [1989] 1 All ER 456 Staughton LJ took the opportunity to outline the approach that the courts would take with regard to foreign assets. Like Kerr LJ in the *Babanaft* case, he drew a distinction between a pre-judgment and a post-judgment injunction. The latter, he observed, would be granted more readily because the plaintiff's right has already been established. Amongst pre-trial applications for injunctions he distinguished between a proprietary tracing claim, whereby the plaintiff seeks to recover his property or the proceeds thereof, and a claim to damages. He thought that a plaintiff pursuing the former type of claim 'will more readily be afforded interim remedies in order to preserve the asset which he is seeking to recover, than one who merely seeks a judgment for debt or damages'; [1989] 1 All ER at 464.

The Republic of Haiti brought the proceedings in England mainly for the purpose of discovering where the defendants' assets were located. Staughton LJ expressed the view, obiter, that in such a situation the duration of the injunction restraining the disposal of assets abroad should be limited to the time needed to enable the plaintiff to seek a remedy in the country where the assets are located.

This brings us to a vexed and difficult question. The general rule is that a party who has obtained information from the opponent in discovery may not use the information for any purpose outside the proceedings in which it was obtained, except by the leave of the court. Where the Mareva device is used in cases such as the present, the plaintiff's main object is to locate the defendant's assets so that they may be frozen where they are found. Having served the Mareva order and having obtained the desired information, does the plaintiff need to apply for permission to go after the assets which were disclosed in the information? Although this question did not arise directly in *Babanaft*, Kerr LJ thought that as a general rule it was unnecessary to require an undertaking from the plaintiff not to use the information without leave of the court. By contrast, Nicholls LJ was of the view that the courts should exercise control over the use of information disclosed compulsorily about assets situated overseas: [1989] 1 All ER at 455. In the *Republic of Haiti* case Staughton LJ tended to the former view stressing the fact that it would be difficult to police compliance with plaintiffs undertaking not to use the information, other than by seeking bank guarantees which, he thought, would not be appropriate: [1989] 1 All ER at 467.

This point received further attention in *Derby & Co Ltd v Weldon (No 1)* [1989] 1 All ER 469. It was felt that if plaintiffs had an unfettered freedom to use the information obtained from defendants concerning the whereabouts of assets abroad, plaintiffs would be in a position to harass defendants. Harassment could take the form of engaging defendants in a multiplicity of proceedings abroad with the aim of either exhausting the defendants' resources or disrupting their business. To prevent oppressive practices the Court of Appeal decided that world wide Mareva injunctions should usually be granted on the plaintiff's undertaking not to use information obtained from the defendant without leave of the court. Thus the courts retain supervision over the use of the information.

The factors justifying world wide injunctions

The cases that we have been discussing illustrate the breadth of the Mareva jurisdiction. A Mareva injunction may be granted in order to restrain the disposal of assets abroad; it may be granted both after judgment and before judgment; disclosure orders may be made in respect of foreign assets both after and before judgment; orders may be made both where the main action proceeds in England and where it takes place elsewhere. Although it is repeatedly stressed that worldwide Mareva orders will only very rarely be made, it is difficult to identify any special factors that are required to be established in an application for a world wide order, as distinguished from a local order. In the *Babanaft* case the order was made after the plaintiff had obtained judgment. In the *Republic of Haiti* case the order was made before judgment, but there the plaintiffs alleged fraud and maintained a proprietary claim to the assets sought. In *Derby & Co Ltd (No 1)* the application was made before judgment and there was not more than 'a seriously arguable case' that the plaintiffs had an interest under a constructive trust and there was no clear evidence of fraud. The common feature in these cases has been a serious risk that the defendant would put his assets beyond the reach of the court. Having acknowledged that a world wide injunction is a 'draconian order' Nicholls LJ added—

> 'The risk of prejudice to which, in the absence of such an order, the plaintiff will be subject is that of the dissipation or secretion of assets *abroad*. This risk must, on the facts, be appropriately grave before it will be just and convenient for such a draconian order to be made.' [1989] 1 All ER at 478.

One would have, however, thought that the risk must also be grave before a local order will be made. Indeed, the need for special factors was rejected in the sequel to *Derby & Co Ltd (No 1)*. In *Derby & Co Ltd v Weldon (No 2)* [1989] 1 All ER 1002 Lord Donaldson MR explained that there was no list of special conditions for obtaining a world wide Mareva injunction. The only guiding principle is that 'no court should permit a defendant to take action designed to frustrate subsequent orders of the court'; [1989] 1 All ER at 1009.

On the principle that equity does not act in vain the courts do not issue injunctions that they cannot enforce. But it would appear that in the Mareva situations the courts hardly ever lack the means of enforcement. The Court of Appeal has held that English courts possess an ultimate sanction at their disposal: 'in the event of disobedience, the court could bar the defendants' right to defend'; [1989] 1 All ER at 1010. It means that there is a sanction in all cases where the substantive claim is pending in an English court. In *Derby & Co Ltd v Weldon (No 2)* [1989] 1 All ER 1002 the Court of Appeal was prepared to contemplate an order against a Panamanian company, even though Panama was not a party to the Convention concerning the enforcement of judgments and even though it was not even proved that this company had any assets.

Receivers in Mareva situations

Ever since the inception of the Mareva jurisdiction attention has been focused on injunctions to prevent dissipation of assets. The present source of this jurisdiction is s 37 of the Supreme Court Act 1981, but this section empowers the court not only to grant injunctions but also to appoint a receiver. This last device was employed in *Derby & Co Ltd v Weldon (No 2)* [1989] 1 All ER 1002 where the plaintiffs had very substantial claims against two individual defendants. These defendants were the managers of a company that the plaintiffs bought and which the defendants continued to manage. The company bought by the plaintiffs had been owned by a Panamanian company and by a Luxemburg company, both of which were under the control of the two individual defendants. The plaintiffs claimed that they suffered some £35m losses through the malpractice of the individual defendants and their companies. In addition to world wide Mareva injunctions, the plaintiffs sought the appointment of receivers for the Luxemburg and the Panamanian companies notwithstanding that the companies were resident out of the jurisdiction and had no assets within the jurisdiction.

Browne-Wilkinson V-C who heard the application observed that—

> 'the court should not appoint receivers over non-residents in relation to assets which are not within the jurisdiction of this court, unless satisfied that the local court either of residence or of the situation of the assets will act in aid of the English court in enforcing it'; [1989] 1 All ER at 1013.

Consequently he made the order appointing a receiver for the Luxemburg company subject to the proviso that it would be enforceable only to the extent that the Luxemburg court gives effect to it. Lord Donaldson MR expressed reservation about this approach. He observed that one ought to distinguish between two separate aspects of the 1968 Brussels Convention on Jurisdiction and the Enforcement of Judgments in Civil and Commercial Matters: first, the enforcement of the judgments of country A by the courts of country B: arts 25 and 45; and, second, obtaining protective orders in country B in support of proceedings pending in country A: art 24. According to Lord Donaldson MR the present situation came under arts 25 and 45. Consequently, the order vesting the assets of the Luxemburg company in the receiver should not have been made subject to the condition that it be recognised by the Luxemburg courts. He explained that although the company in question was a Luxemburg company,

> 'it is a party to the action and can properly be ordered to deal with its assets in accordance with the orders of this court, regardless of whether the order is recognised and enforced in Luxemburg. The only effect of non-recognition would be to remove one of the potential sanctions for disobedience'; [1989] 1 All ER at 1014.

The Master of the Rolls took matters further. He thought that it was appropriate to appoint a receiver in respect of the assets of the Panamanian company even though Panama was not a party to the European Judgments Convention or to an agreement to enforce English judgments. He said—

> 'What really matters is the extent to which the receiver could effectively carry out his task, whatever that might be. In the instant case it would be to preserve any assets of Milco [the Panamanian company]. He would be assisted by the sanction that, absent co-operation, Milco would not be allowed to defend the action. He would also be able to make use of the European Judgments

Convention if, as seems not unlikely, any assets of Milco were situated in countries which were parties to that convention'; [1989] 1 All ER at 1014.

If the Master of the Rolls is correct, then the appointment of receivers is a more powerful remedy than the Mareva injunction. When the latter is granted in respect of assets abroad it has to be made subject to the *Babanaft* proviso that it would not affect the rights of third parties abroad except to the extent that the courts of the foreign jurisdiction supported it. The appointment of a receiver vests the assets of the company or person affected by the appointment in the receiver. This vesting of rights can, and normally would, affect the position of third parties. For example, the receiver can go and claim assets of the Luxemburg company from whoever is in possession wherever that may be. Having devoted so much care to avoiding infringement of foreign jurisdictions by Mareva injunctions this attitude to receivers seems to throw all caution to the winds.

Debt owed by a third party to the defendant

An interesting problem was considered in *Bank Mellat v Kazmi* [1989] 1 All ER 925. The defendant was subject to a Mareva injunction freezing his bank account and ordering him to refrain from disposing of his assets. The plaintiffs were the victim of a fraud committed by the defendant, who had been their employee and had been convicted for the fraud. The plaintiffs got to know that the Department of Social Services (DSS) owed the defendant a substantial sum of money in respect of supplementary benefits. The question was whether and how the plaintiffs could prevent that money from coming into the hands of the defendant who was likely to dissipate it.

Nourse LJ's starting point was that—

'mere notice of the existence of a Mareva injunction cannot render it a contempt of court for a third party to make over an asset to the defendant direct'; [1989] 1 All ER at 928.

However, where the third party has notice of a probability that the asset will be disposed of in breach of the injunction, the third party could well be guilty of contempt. In such a situation the proper course is to order the third party to pay the money into court or, if there is already a frozen account with a bank to order the money to be paid into that account: at 929. It might be tempting in such circumstances, for a defendant to forgive the debt owed to him but this ploy seems to have been blocked by the observation that a waiver of a debt would constitute disposal of an asset and would amount to breach of the Mareva injunction.

There was a further complication in this case. Under the Crown Proceedings Act 1947, ss 25(4), 27(1), and the Supplementary Benefits Act 1976, s 16(1), no attachment order can be made against the Crown and any charge or assignment of a supplementary benefit is void. It has been decided that these provisions do not prevent an order of the kind discussed above because a Mareva injunction does not amount to an attachment; it does not deprive the defendant of his rights in the assets but merely acts in personam and prevents him from disposing of it. Further, even if the order had amounted to an attachment it would not be prevented by the legislation because it did not order the government to make payment, which it was ready to do, but simply gave it directions how to discharge its obligation to the defendant. These reasons are not altogether convincing. The legislation is intended to prevent social security benefits from becoming subject to execution process, yet this is precisely the result that the court has now sanctioned. An alternative route to the same result was outlined by Nourse LJ who said that if the money were paid to the defendant, he would immediately come under an obligation not to dispose of it. The court would then be bound to come to the aid of the subsisting Mareva injunction and order the defendant to pay the money into the frozen account. The present order, Nourse LJ explained, is merely a short cut for achieving that result. If the legislator intended to place supplementary benefits beyond execution, it would not be right to restrain a person entitled to supplementary benefit from disposing of the money because this would be an indirect method of achieving the prohibited result.

Another short cut procedure to prevent a person from disposing of monies received, or to be received, from a certain source emerges from *Seven Seas Properties Ltd v Al-Essa* [1989] 1 All ER 164. The plaintiffs obtained an order of specific performance for the conveyance to them of land that they had agreed to purchase from the defendants. The plaintiffs also had a claim in damages against the defendants in respect of the same transaction. Hoffmann J held that it was possible to add a Mareva remedy to an order for specific performance and order that part of the proceeds be paid into the joint names of plaintiffs and defendants pending the damages action. Retention in joint names, Hoffmann J observed, gave the plaintiffs better protection against other creditors than a Mareva freezing order. But this point was not argued.

Non-disclosure of material facts

Attention was drawn last year to judicial concern about the failure of applicants for Mareva injunctions to disclose material facts (All ER Rev 1988 218) and to different approaches adopted in this regard. This year the Court of Appeal has displayed a stiffer resolve in dealing with this problem and a number of important points have been made in *Behbehani v Salem* [1989] 2 All ER 143.

First, it has been spelt out what is meant by improper, or at any rate non-innocent, non-disclosure. This is a deliberate failure to disclose facts that are known to be material. Woolf LJ was not happy to extend the definition to facts that ought to have been known to be material; [1989] 2 All ER at 148–149. However, lest it be thought that plaintiffs or their legal advisers would be wise to seek comfort in ignorance, the Court of Appeal stressed that it was the duty of plaintiffs' solicitors to discover the material facts; see 152, 157. Furthermore, Nourse LJ thought that where there is evidence that the plaintiff's solicitors were aware of the existence of certain facts, the onus is on them to prove that they thought that the facts were immaterial; [1989] 2 All ER at 156. If there is a duty on the plaintiff's solicitors to ascertain the facts, and if there is a presumption that the solicitors are alive to the materiality of facts known to them, would it not be simpler and more economical to hold that non-disclosure of material is culpable when solicitors fail to disclose facts which they ought to have known?

The sanction for non-disclosure is a discharge of the injunction, but the courts preserve a discretion to regrant the injunction, if justice so requires. Concern was expressed last year that if the needs of the plaintiff prevail in considering a regrant of the injunction, the sanction for non-disclosure would be weakened. This year the concern was shared by Woolf LJ who said that if

> 'the right approach is one which requires the court to measure the materiality of the non-disclosure . . ., then it cannot be right just to sweep that aside on the basis of the strength of the plaintiffs' case against the defendants'; [1989] 2 All ER at 155.

Further, the defendant need not show that the judge who originally made the injunction would have reached a different conclusion, had the full facts been disclosed. Where the non-disclosure has been sufficiently serious, an injunction would be discharged notwithstanding that full disclosure may not have altered the result and notwithstanding that the plaintiff's case is a strong one (cf *Ali & Fahd Shobokshi Group Ltd v Moneim* [1989] 2 All ER 404). The injunction was discharged, albeit on the defendant giving certain limited undertakings, on the grounds of serious non-disclosure.

Mareva injunctions for the benefit of the public

A Mareva injunction has been granted at the request of a statutory body, the Securities and Investment Board (SIB), against a person who has carried out illegal investment business in this country. The Financial Services Act 1986 gives the SIB various powers, including the right to obtain an order to secure monies derived from the illegal business. Sir Nicolas Browne-Wilkinson V-C has held that SIB was entitled to seek an injunction to protect the money of investors. In so holding the Vice-Chancellor distinguished *Chief Constable of Leicestershire v M* [1988] 3 All ER 1015 where it was held that the police could not obtain an injunction to ensure that money is available for the payment of a fine. The Vice Chancellor explained that unlike the SIB the police does not have a statutory power to take action and that the police was not attempting to protect a traceable interest of investors.

Self-incrimination in Mareva proceedings

In *Arab Monetary Fund v Hashim* [1989] 3 All ER 466 the defendant, who was ordered to disclose the whereabouts of his assets, objected to disclosure on the grounds that such disclosure would show that he had breached Iraqi law prohibiting Iraqi citizens from holding assets abroad and would expose him to the death penalty in Iraq. Morritt J held that under the Civil Evidence Act 1968, s 14(1), the privilege applied only where the evidence sought incriminated the witness under the law of the United Kingdom. At the same time, since the Mareva jurisdiction was discretionary, the fact of incrimination under a foreign law may be taken into account in the exercise of discretion. In the event it was not felt necessary to accede to the defendant's request to be released from the obligation of disclosure.

Section 14(1) has also been considered in *Garvin v Domus Publishing Ltd* [1989] 2 All ER 344. The plaintiff obtained a Mareva injunction. Later suspecting breaches of the injunction, the plaintiff obtained an Anton Piller order and claimed to have discovered a document which tended to prove breach of the injunction. She then applied to court for permission to use the document in the committal of the defendant for contempt. Section 14(1) confers a privilege to refuse to testify or produce a document tending to expose the person affected 'to proceedings for an offence'. Walton J decided that contempt was not a criminal offence and that, consequently, there is no privilege to withhold evidence showing contempt of court. The defendant then relied on the risk that the use of that document might lay him open to a charge of forgery. This argument was rejected on the grounds that the document belonged to the company of which the defendant was an employee and one could not claim privilege in someone else's document.

Secrecy of information disclosed in Mareva proceedings

Morritt J ordered that certain facts disclosed by the defendants be disclosed to the plaintiffs' solicitors on the undertaking that the latter did not disclose the facts to their clients, the plaintiffs. This information consisted of the identity of persons in Iraq who might suffer as a result of their identity becoming known to the plaintiffs. Such procedure has been disapproved of in *WEA Records Ltd v Visions Channel 4 Ltd* [1983] 2 All ER 589, but the judge felt that the circumstances were such as to justify this course of action.

Anton Piller orders

In 1986 Scott J delivered a powerful warning against the abuse of the Anton Piller procedure: *Columbia Picture Industries Inc v Robinson* [1986] 3 All ER 338, All ER Rev 1986 225. Judging from the decision in *Lock International plc v Beswick* [1989] 3 All ER 373 little note was taken of this warning for Hoffmann J reports a common experience of 'evident surprise' on the part of counsel when he has refused applications for Anton Piller orders. Such reactions have lead him to conclude that Scott J had been right to say that—

> 'the practice of the court has allowed the balance to swing much too far in favour of plaintiffs and that Anton Piller orders have been too readily granted with insufficient safeguards for respondents.'

The plaintiffs in this last case, a large manufacturing company, were displeased when a number of their employees left them to set up a business of their own and to produce a product in competition with that of the plaintiffs. They obtained an ex parte interlocutory injunction to restrain the employees and their new company, the defendants, from using the plaintiffs' trade secrets, and an Anton Piller order. In the execution of this order the plaintiffs seized from the defendant's place of work and from their private homes virtually all their drawings, commercial information and computer records, and also private papers. The defendants applied for and obtained a discharge of both orders.

In relation to the interlocutory injunction Hoffmann J explained that a person is entitled to set up in competition with a former employer and to use in his business skill and knowledge gained in his former service. What a person is not entitled to do is to use his employer's trade secrets. He found that the plaintiffs' application for the orders did not sufficiently identify the secrets alleged to have been misused by the defendants. Moreover, at the inter partes hearing the plaintiffs claimed that the defendants had misused trade secrets but when all the parties were heard at the inter partes stage this claim turned out to be hollow.

Hoffmann J explained why he also found that the plaintiffs had no good reason to obtain an Anton Piller order for—

> '. . . there must be *proportionality* between the perceived threat to the plaintiff's rights and the remedy granted. The fact that there is overwhelming evidence that the defendant has behaved wrongfully in his commercial relationship does not necessarily justify an Anton Piller order . . . Not everyone who is misusing confidential information will destroy documents in the face of a court order requiring him to preserve them.' [1989] 3 All ER at 384.

In many cases, he added, it will be sufficient to order that the plaintiff's documents be delivered to their solicitors or, where the documents belong to the defendant, that the latter preserve them or allow the plaintiff's solicitors to take copies. As for orders allowing searches of the defendant's premises Hoffmann J said—

> 'The making of an intrusive order ex parte even against a guilty defendant is contrary to normal principles of justice and can only be done when there is a paramount need to prevent a denial of justice to the plaintiff.'

The idea of paramount need to prevent injustice has been present ever since the birth of the Anton Piller jurisdiction but it has proved very difficult to give it substance in practice. The reason is simple: our adversarial procedure works well only where there is adversity between opponents who are able to meet each other's claims on an equal footing. At the ex parte stage there is no equality. In the absence of one's adversary it is all to easy to make one's case look strong. The Anton Piller procedure has therefore made it all too tempting for employers to 'launch a pre-emptive strike to crush the unhatched competition in the egg by causing severe strains on the financial and management resources of the defendants or even a withdrawal of their financial support'; [1989] 3 All ER at 383. This inequality explains why the plaintiffs and their solicitors were able to obtain Anton Piller orders against persons whose honesty could not be doubted, who had fixed addresses and lead normal family lives, who made no secret of their commercial activities, and who were supported by highly respected financial institutions. It was enough to hear the defendants' side of the story to persuade the judge that the orders should never have been made.

The plaintiffs were also found guilty of non-disclosure of material facts in that they gave a misleading picture of their own financial standing. Their financial position was relevant in considering the value of their cross-undertaking. This was of great importance because the interlocutory injunction, accompanied as it was by an Anton Piller order, could deal a severe blow to the defendants' business. It was therefore important to establish whether the plaintiffs were in a position to compensate the defendants, if it turned out that the plaintiffs' action had been unjustified.

The readers of this Review will be aware that it is not for the first time that judges have spoken strongly against plaintiffs who take unjustified advantage of the Anton Piller procedure. But few practical measures have been taken against such plaintiffs; see All ER Rev 1986 at 226. In the present case, however, Hoffmann J discharged the injunction and ordered an inquiry as to damages. There were a number of reasons, he explained, for awarding damages right away rather than leaving the matter to be dealt with at the trial: the question of whether the order should have been made did not involve an investigation of conflicting evidence, the issues relevant to this question would not require further investigation at the trial and, perhaps most significantly, in view of the plaintiffs' questionable finances it was unfair to expose the defendants to the risk of going without compensation. The plaintiffs were also ordered to return all material seized from the defendants and all copies made thereof.

If this stern attitude to unwarranted Anton Piller proceedings is taken up by the courts, there is a chance that plaintiffs will in future be deterred from indulging too freely in the kind of stratagems employed in this case. But more could be done at the ex parte stage to make plaintiffs think long and hard before asking for Anton Piller orders. For example, plaintiffs might be asked, especially in commercial cases, to give an adequate security as a condition to being granted an order.

Interim injunction against the Crown

The House of Lords has held that the court had no jurisdiction to grant an interim injunction against the Crown in judicial review proceedings: *Factortame Ltd v Secretary of State for Transport* [1989] 2 All ER 692; for discussion of this decision see the article on administrative law.

Stay of action not absolute

In an action brought by the plaintiffs against the defendants a settlement was reached and a consent order was made that 'all further proceedings in this action be stayed'. Shortly afterwards an intervener, who had a substantial interest in the result of the litigation, sought to be joined as a defendant in accordance with RSC Ord 15, r 6(2). Joinder may be ordered, according to the opening words of the rule, 'at any stage of the proceedings'. The issue in *ROFA Sport Management AG v DHL International (UK) Ltd* [1989] 2 All ER 743, was whether there was a stage in the proceedings still subsisting once the above consent order had been made.

It was not in dispute that had the action been dismissed by consent or discontinued under Ord 21, r 3, the action would have been at an end and there would have been no action to which a new defendant could be joined. Neill LJ observed that earlier practice gave rise to a distinction between absolute stay and conditional stay. The former being equivalent to a discontinuance or a dismissal while the latter amounted to a suspension which could be lifted so as to allow for the action to continue. Speaking for the Court of Appeal Neill LJ thought, however, that there was no room for such distinction in modern practice. He explained—

> 'In my judgment, for the sake of clarity and certainty the word "stay" in an order should not be treated as a possible equivalent of a dismissal or a discontinuance. There may well, of course, be cases, however, where the

person who wishes to have the stay removed will face great difficulties. An action which has been stayed by consent following a compromise provides an obvious example. But, as it seems to me, the action following a stay remains technically in being. The action cannot proceed or resume its active life without an order of the court, but I do not consider that it can properly be regarded as dead in the same way as an action which has been dismissed or discontinued by order.' ([1989] 2 All ER at 749).

The decision to allow joinder of the intervener as a defendant did not put an end to the matter for the question immediately arose as to what was to become of the settlement between the plaintiffs and the defendants which, as will be recollected, resulted in the stay order. The Court of Appeal held that the settlement would be protected and that the 'action will proceed but effectively only between Sport-Billy [the intervener] and the plaintiffs'. This, however, puts considerable strain on the notion that the original action is still in existence. The action brought by plaintiffs against the defendants has been resolved and their settlement cannot be undone. How can it be said that the original action is still alive and that it proceeds against the intervener? Is it not more realistic to say that this is an altogether new action?

Amendment of writ after judgment

The plaintiff bought air tickets from Sterling Travel. The tickets were returned but a refund was not forthcoming. The plaintiff sued Sterling Travel and obtained judgment by default only to discover that 'Sterling Travel' was the trade name of the defendant company. The defendant then applied to have the judgment set aside as having been obtained in an incorrect name. An order was made to set the judgment aside and permit the defendant to defend on condition that he pay into court the full sum claimed. The plaintiff was given permission to amend the writ so as to name the defendant company instead of Sterling Travel. The defendants appealed on the grounds that the mistake rendered the judgment a nullity and it should have been set aside as of right and free of any conditions. Further, the defendant argued that there was no power in the court to allow amendment of writ after final judgment; not even after the judgment has been set aside. Finally, it was argued that the failure of serving the writ at the company's registered office, as required by s 725 of the Companies Act 1985, rendered the service void and could not be cured.

The Court of Appeal rejected these arguments in *Singh v Atombrook Ltd* [1989] 1 All ER 385. It held that the court has wide powers under RSC Ord 2, r 1(2) and Ord 20, r 5, to amend the writ. Further, it was held that even if the provision in s 725(1) of the Companies Act 1985, and the related provisions in Ord 20, r 1(2) and (7) and Ord 65, r 3(2) were mandatory, non-compliance did not render the proceedings a nullity and the irregularity could be cured within Ord 2, r 1(1).

These rulings bear out the wisdom of the policy of Ord 2, r 1 which aims to abolish the distinction between forms of non-compliance with the rules which render proceedings a nullity and forms that render proceedings merely irregular and, therefore, remediable. To have accepted the defendants' argument that the proceedings were a nullity and that the plaintiff had to start afresh, when the former contributed to the plaintiff's mistakes, would have cast a serious blemish on the law.

Representative proceedings

In *Irish Shipping Ltd v Commercial Union Assurance Co plc* [1989] 3 All ER 853, the plaintiff shipowners found themselves saddled with liabilities incurred by their charterers who were in liquidation. The charterers were insured against those liabilities with some 77 insurers. The policies were identical, except in relation to the amount of risk undertaken by different insurers. The policies included a leading underwriter clause by which a resolution of a dispute by the leading underwriter was binding on all underwriters in proportion to their respective share. The plaintiffs brought a representative action under Ord 15, r 12 against the largest insurer and the leading underwriter suing them as representatives of all the insurers. The insurers argued that a representative action was not allowed in the circumstance of this case because the insurers did not have 'the same interest' in the proceedings, as required by Ord 15, r 12(1). It was argued on behalf of the insurers that since each insurer was severally liable for his own proportion of the risk they did not have one interest but each had a different interest.

The Court of Appeal rejected this argument holding that what mattered was not whether the defendants were jointly or severally liable but, rather, whether there was an identical issue and an identical interest to contest that issue. Here all the insurance contracts were the same and all the insurers had an identical interest in resisting the claim on the grounds that the benefit of the charterers' insurance had not passed to the shipowner under the Third Parties (Rights against Insurers) Act 1930.

There was a possibility that the foreign insurers amongst the group of 77 might have a defence on account of the fact that the situs of their obligation was abroad and was therefore not caught by the 1930 Act. But this, it was held, went to show that the foreign insurers had an additional defence and not that they did not have the same interest in the action as the representatives against whom the action was brought. It was emphasised that the rule gave the court discretion to discontinue a representative action where there was a risk that judgment may be enforced against a party who had no opportunity to be heard. There was, however, no such risk in this case. Lastly, those interested in the history of Ord 15, r 12 will find the judgment of Purchas LJ most informative.

Service out of the jurisdiction

When a plaintiff applies for leave to serve abroad under Ord 11, r 1, all he has to show is that if the facts to which he deposes are true, the case is brought within the rules. But what burden does he bear at the later inter partes stage when the defendant applies to set aside the service? This question was considered in *Attock Cement Co Ltd v Romanian Bank for Foreign Trade* [1989] 1 All ER 1189. It called for the consideration of two separate problems. The first concerned the standard of proof; the degree of persuasion that has to be reached with regard to the factors which justify service abroad. The other problem was concerned with the range of evidential material to be looked at in arriving at a factual decision.

The first problem was fairly straightforward. The plaintiff applying for leave to serve abroad has to establish a good arguable case that facts exist which bring the action within RSC Ord 11, r 1. This means that, before allowing the service to stand, the judge has to reach the conclusion that the plaintiff is probably right on the disputed facts. But on what material was the judge required to form his view? It has often been said that the judge must not conduct a trial of fact on the basis of affidavits. This broad assumption has led the plaintiff to argue that the judge has to arrive at the conclusion exclusively on the basis of the plaintiff's affidavits and ignore any contradiction of his assertions that may be contained in the defendant's affidavits. This can hardly be right; a conclusion that the plaintiff has a good arguable case may well look untenable if the totality of the facts in both parties' affidavits is taken into account. Yet if the judge has to consider the conflicting affidavits, how can he avoid trying the issue on the basis of these affidavits?

This conundrum has only one logical solution. The task of the judge is to reach a conclusion about the strength of the plaintiff's case, not about its actual truth. The strength of the plaintiff's case is, inevitably, relative to the strength of the defendant's. It follows that a conclusion regarding the former is tied to the view taken of the latter. This was Staughton LJ's conclusion. He explained that the task of the judge is to assess all the material before him in reaching his conclusion. However, to avoid at that stage a full blown trial of the issue, the judge has to bear in mind that he is only required to reach a provisional and tentative conclusion for the purpose of determining the propriety of the service; [1989] 1 All ER at 1196–1197.

There are, however, situations where the issue contested for the purpose of service abroad under Ord 11, r 1 will not, if leave is granted, arise again at the trial. Some dicta suggest that in such situations the plaintiff bears a heavier burden, but the Court of Appeal found it unnecessary to decide this point. A more definite view was expressed on this aspect by Kerr LJ in *E F Hutton & Co (London) Ltd v Mofarrij* [1989] 2 All ER 633, 639–640, where he said that the test of a good arguable case applies both where the issue will be considered at the trial and where it will not. This seems, however, to have been contradicted by Slade LJ in *Metall und Rohstoff AG v Donaldson Lufkin & Jenrette Inc* [1989] 3 All ER 14, 23, where he said that—

> 'the plaintiff must show a strong probability that the claim falls within the letter and the spirit of . . . Ord 11, r 1(1) . . . This requirement is treated strictly, since if leave is given (and, if challenged, upheld) it will never thereafter be investigated . . .'

It would therefore appear that the matter cannot be taken as settled. But perhaps not too much should be made of this diversity of views since the difference between a good arguable case, which means in this context a good chance of success, and a strong probability may not be very significant. It is also to be borne in mind, and this point was emphasised in the last mentioned case, that as well as showing a strong case that his claim comes within Ord 11, r 1, the plaintiff must also show a good chance of succeeding on the merits.

E F Hutton & Co (London) Ltd v Mofarrij [1989] 2 All ER 633 settles another point. The plaintiff obtained permission to serve on the defendant abroad a claim founded on a contract which was governed by English law. Under the terms of the contract the defendant, who operated his business in Greece, gave the plaintiff a cheque as security for performing his obligations under the contract. The cheque was drawn in Greece on a Greek bank and was payable in Greece. When the cheque had been dishonoured, the plaintiff applied for leave to serve on the defendant abroad an amendment of the writ so as to add to the existing claim a claim on the cheque. The defendant objected on the grounds that the cheque represented a separate contract which was governed by Greek law and over which jurisdiction rested with the Greek courts.

The plaintiff relied on Ord 11, r 1(1)(d)(iii) which allows service abroad where 'the claim is brought to enforce . . . or otherwise affect a contract . . . which . . . is . . . governed by English law'. Kerr LJ held that the cheque was so directly and intricately connected with the contract that its enforcement amounted to an enforcement of the contract. The plaintiff had a right to present the cheque only where the defendant failed to meet his indebtedness under the contract. Once the cheque has been honoured, the defendant's liability under the contract was pro tanto discharged. The contract included therefore an undertaking by the defendant that the cheque, being a security for his obligations under the contract, would be honoured when presented in accordance with the terms of the contract. Kerr LJ was, however, careful to stress that where the connection between a cheque and a contract was not so immediate, service abroad will not be allowed simply because the cheque contract will in some way affect the performance of the English contract.

Underlying Kerr LJ's judgment was the assumption that the words 'affect a contract' in Ord 11, r 1(d)(iii) meant 'have a bearing on a contract'. But a reading of the rule does not bear out this interpretation. The rule does not envisage two contracts: one English and another foreign. The rule is not concerned with the effect that a foreign contract has on an English contract. On the contrary, the rule contemplates only one contract and a claim to affect, ie to give effect to, this contract which is governed by English law. If this is the correct reading, there is no need to worry about the possibility that too loose a connection between the foreign contract and the English contract will open the flood gates nor about the degree of connection between the two contracts. The only question that falls to be considered is whether there is a claim to affect a contract governed by English law.

This interpretation was adopted by Adrian Hamilton QC in *Finnish Marine Insurance Co Ltd v Protective National Insurance Co* [1989] 2 All ER 929. Referring to Ord 11, r 1(d), he said—

> '. . . all the earlier grounds ("enforce, rescind, dissolve, annul") can only relate to a contract between plaintiff and defendant. There is nothing to indicate that a different type of contract becomes available when the claim is to "affect" a contract. In each case the word "contract" means a contract between plaintiff and defendant;' (at 933).

There are several proceedings that although not amounting to enforcement, rescission, dissolution or annulment are nevertheless claims to affect the contract. One of these would be a claim for declaratory judgment in connection with the contract. However, it has been held in the last mentioned case that where a party seeks a declaration that a contract has never existed, the action cannot be brought within the rule because it is not an action to affect a contract. In this case, after the writ was served, the defendant applied for stay of proceedings under s 1(1) of the Arbitration Act 1975, as well as to set aside the service. The plaintiff claimed that an application to stay the proceedings pending arbitration amounted to a voluntary submission to jurisdiction on behalf of the defendant. This argument was rejected. An application to stay proceedings in these circumstances cannot possibly be construed as an acceptance of the jurisdiction of the court to deal with the merits of the claim. On the contrary, it amounts to a waiver of the court's jurisdiction in favour of arbitration.

An important point concerning legal arguments in pleadings intended for service abroad emerges from *Metall und Rohstoff AG v Donaldson Lufkin & Jenrette Inc* [1989] 3 All ER 14. The general rule is that it is sufficient for the pleader to state the material facts; he need not state the legal result. If he does state the legal result, he is not limited by what he has stated. This principle, it has been held, does not apply in pleadings intended to be served out of the jurisdiction. Slade LJ explained (at 24) that—

> 'if the draftsman of a pleading . . . can be reasonably understood as presenting a particular head of claim on one specific legal basis only, the plaintiff cannot thereafter, for the purpose of justifying his application under Ord 11, r 1 . . . be permitted to contend that that head of claim can also be justified on another legal basis . . .'

The reason for taking a different line in cases of service abroad is that the court must be fully appraised of the nature of the claim at the ex parte case and so must the defendant when he receives service abroad.

Service within the jurisdiction

An interesting issue concerning the ambit of RSC Ord 10, r 1(2) was considered in *Barclays Bank of Swaziland Ltd v Hahn* [1989] 2 All ER 398. The plaintiffs sought to sue the defendant whom they found rather elusive for the purpose of service. The defendant was a national of South Africa but lived in different places in Europe. He had a home in England where he spent several months every year. The plaintiffs' agents found out that the defendant was due to return to his English flat and placed a writ in his letter box as is authorised by Ord 10, r 1(2)(b). At that very moment the defendant was not in England but on board of an aircraft bound for London. He landed a few hours after the writ was left at his address. He heard about this before returning home and, soon after, boarded a plane and left the jurisdiction. The defendant contended that the writ had not been duly served on him since at the time at which it was left at his address he was not within the jurisdiction. Rule 1(2) provides—

> 'A writ for service on a defendant within the jurisdiction may, instead of being served personally on him, be served (a) by sending a copy of the writ by ordinary first-class post to the defendant at his usual or last known address, or (b) if there is a letter box for that address, by inserting through the letter box a copy of the writ . . .'

Rule 1(3) of Ord 10 contains a number of provisions relevant to the present issue—

> 'Where a writ is served in accordance with paragraph (2)—(a) the date of service shall, unless the contrary is shown, be deemed to be the seventh day . . . after the date on which the copy was sent to or, as the case may be, inserted through

the letter box for the address in question; (b) an affidavit proving due service of the writ must contain a statement to the effect that—(i) in the opinion of the deponent . . . the copy of the writ, if sent to, or, as the case may be, inserted through the letter box for, the address in question, will have come to the knowledge of the defendant within 7 days thereafter . . .'

The Court of Appeal and the House of Lords took different views regarding the interpretation of the rules. Speaking in the Court of Appeal Fox LJ explained that—

'the words "A writ for service on a defendant within the jurisdiction" are descriptive of the writ and its service and not of the defendant . . . they are directed at the distinction between a writ for service within the jurisdiction and one for service out of the jurisdiction'; [1989] 1 All ER 193, 195.

On this view, if the writ is of the kind that is used for service within the jurisdiction and is left at the defendant's address in accordance with the above provisions, it matters not the defendant happened to be abroad at the moment at which the writ was placed in his letter box or was posted to him. The House of Lords disapproved of this construction which, according to Lord Brightman—

'would mean that a writ could validly be served under Ord 10 on a defendant who had once had an address in England but had permanently left this country and settled elsewhere by inserting the copy writ through the letter box of his last address, provided that the plaintiff was able within seven days to communicate to the defendant the existence of the copy writ; for in such circumstances the plaintiff could properly depose that the copy writ would have come to the knowledge of the defendant within seven days after it was left in the letter box of his last known address'; [1989] 2 All ER at 402.

The Court of Appeal was not unaware of this possibility of abuse. Fox LJ drew attention to r 2(3)(b) and observed that this provision is designed to—

'protect the person who has ceased to have any real connection with the address at which the service is made. The opinion that is required to be sworn to on behalf of the plaintiff, involving, as it does, the likelihood that the writ will come to the knowledge of the defendant within seven days, assumes a substantial degree of contact with this country on the part of the defendant served'; [1989] 1 All ER at 196.

Fox LJ's view is strengthened in this regard by the wording of the rule which requires the plaintiff's affidavit to state not that the writ has, as a matter of fact, reached the defendant's knowledge but rather that it 'will have come to the knowledge of the defendant within 7 days thereafter'. Thus the plaintiff has to swear that at the time of the placing of the writ in the defendant's letter box, the defendant's circumstances and connection with his address were such that the writ was likely to reach him.

In the event the House of Lords agreed with the result reached by the Court of Appeal that there has been proper service on the defendant, but arrived et this conclusion by a circuitous route. Lord Brightman focused on r 1(3)(a) which says that where 'a writ is served in accordance with paragraph (2)—(a) the date of the service shall, unless the contrary is shown, be deemed to be the seventh day . . . after the date on which the copy was . . . inserted through the letter box . . .' According to his Lordship the words 'unless the contrary is shown' could only refer to the defendant's reception of the writ. He concluded that—

> 'a plaintiff or a defendant may displace the deemed date of service by proving that the defendant acquired knowledge of the writ at some other date'; [1989] 2 All ER at 402.

In this case, the defendant found out about the writ soon after landing and therefore he was properly served within the rules.

There are a number of difficulties about this interpretation. First, it fits ill with the wording of paragraph (3) which begins with the words 'Where a writ is served in accordance with paragraph (2)'. Thus the 'contrary' may be shown only about a writ that has already been served in accordance with the last mentioned paragraph. If we go back to this paragraph which deals with a 'writ for service on a defendant within the jurisdiction', and we give it Lord Brightman's interpretation as requiring that the defendant be within the jurisdiction, it follows that, in a case such as the present, where the defendant was out of the jurisdiction at the time of the insertion of the writ into his letter box, paragraph (3) has no application at all; there is no opportunity for proving the contrary of anything.

There is a more serious objection to the House of Lords' decision. It introduces an unnecessary complication into the service process by requiring the server of the writ, as Croom-Johnson LJ observed, 'to ensure that the proposed defendant was personally present inside the jurisdiction of the court at the moment when the writ was . . . put in a postal box'; [1989] 1 All ER at 197. This rather defeats the purpose of substitute service under Ord 10, the point of which is to relieve the plaintiff of having to prove facts about the defendant's precise whereabouts and his actual knowledge of the writ where the defendant has a place of abode in this country. The House of Lords' decision makes substitute service more hazardous and probably more costly and its consequences will in all probability demand consideration from the Rules Committee.

Discovery

Discovery in judicial review

The applicant in *R v Inland Revenue Commissioners, ex p Taylor* [1989] 1 All ER 906 challenged in judicial review proceedings a notice, served on him by an inspector of the Inland Revenue under the Taxes Management Act 1970, s 20(2), and requiring disclosure of documents relevant to his tax assessment. In his affidavit the inspector relied on a report produced by an employee of the Inland Revenue who looked into the applicant's affairs. The applicant sought disclosure of this report arguing that the report formed part of the inspector's decision-making process and could throw light on whether the inspector acted in bad faith, as the applicant alleged.

RSC Ord 53, r 8(1) applies Ord 24 to proceedings for judicial review. Ord 24 deals with discovery and inspection of documents and r 13(1) provides that no order for the production of documents shall be made 'unless the Court is of opinion that the order is necessary either for disposing fairly of the cause or matter of for saving costs.' Normally the fact that a document is relevant would suffice to establish this condition. But the position seems to be different in proceedings for judicial review because the Court of Appeal now reached the conclusion that it is upon the applicant 'to show that it is necessary for the fair disposal of the case' to order disclosure; [1989] 1 All ER at 916. Requiring an applicant to show that the sought-after document helps, or is likely to help, his case is to impose on him an impossible burden because it is not the applicant but his opponent who is in possession of the document. How can the applicant show that a document in his opponent's possession is likely to give a real boost to his case? It is, however, likely that the Court of Appeal did not mean to lay down a hard and fast rule in this respect. Indeed, O'Connor LJ explained that it might be necessary to reconsider the question of discovery at a later stage in the proceedings when the applicant's line of attack on the inspector's decision has developed further. It is therefore possible that all the court has decided is that where an applicant has no evidence of impropriety in the decision–making process, he would not be helped to fish around for documents so as to find whether there are any grounds for complaint.

Discovery of material used in previous arbitration

The rule in *Riddick v Thames Board Mills Ltd* [1977] 3 All ER 677 was relied upon in *Shearson Lehman Hutton Inc v Maclaine Watson & Co Ltd* [1989] 1 All ER 1056. According to this rule documents revealed in discovery in one action may not be used in other proceedings. In the present case the plaintiffs sought from the defendants discovery of documents which related to arbitration proceedings which had taken place between the defendants and third parties. Webster J held that the rule in *Riddick* obtained only where documents were disclosed under a compulsory procedure of discovery or as a result of an Anton Piller order. Here the documents had been voluntarily produced in private arbitration, Webster J explained, and were therefore disclosable.

The reasoning that lead to this conclusion is far from straightforward. The *Riddick* rationale is that immunity from disclosure is required to remove inhibition form making full disclosure. It was said in this case that this rationale does not apply to arbitration because parties to arbitration are unlikely to be inhibited. In view of the law's policy to encourage arbitration this reasoning is doubtful for it makes discovery in arbitration more hazardous than in court proceedings. The source of the trouble lies in the *Riddick* rule itself which has been criticised on the pages of this review; see All ER Rev 1987 193. All that can therefore be said in defence of Webster J's decision is that it has restricted the scope of the *Riddick* rule.

Discovery before writ

Under s 33(2) of the Supreme Court Act 1981 and RSC Ord 24, r 7A a person who is likely to bring proceedings for personal injuries may obtain discovery of documents from a person who is likely to be a party to such proceedings. In *Harris v Newcastle Health Authority* [1989] 2 All ER 273 a person (the 'likely plaintiff') who intended to bring proceedings against a health authority applied for disclosure but was met with the objection that the limitation period had long since elapsed and that no disclosure should be ordered since there was little chance of overcoming this obstacle.

In the Court of Appeal Kerr LJ distinguished between jurisdiction and discretion in the matter of ordering disclosure. All that had to be established for jurisdiction was that the applicant was 'likely to be a party to . . . proceedings'. Where a limitation defence was certain to succeed, the matter went to jurisdiction, since the court would conclude that no responsible counsel would advise proceedings and there would therefore be no reasonable likelihood of proceedings. A probability, as distinguished from a certainty, of success of a limitation defence went to the discretion that the court had in ordering disclosure under s 33. Where an action is bound to fail it would not be necessary or desirable in the interests of justice to order discovery.

However, under s 33 of the Limitation Act 1980 the court has discretion in personal injury cases to forgive the lapse of the limitation period. This possibility must be taken into account before concluding that an action is clearly bound to be defeated by a plea of limitation. Since an application for discovery is made before any pleadings have taken place, it is obviously difficult, if not impossible, for the court hearing the application for discovery to assess the likely outcome of a limitation plea, let alone to conclude that it is certain to succeed. It is therefore undesirable, the Court of Appeal has held, to go into the question of limitation at this stage unless the circumstances are exceptional. Hence, discretion would not normally be exercised against discovery on the grounds that the action is bound to be defeated by limitation.

Discovery orders against the police

For over a century now it has been settled that discovery is not limited to documents which would be admissible in evidence but extends to material that may lead to a train of inquiry which may help a party advance his case or damage that of the adversary: *The Supreme Court Practice 1988*, vol 1, para 24/2/5. The rule has evolved in this way because the truth is most likely to emerge where both parties have full excess to material that is directly or indirectly connected with the issues. This policy has already been undermined by the doctrine of public interest immunity (see article on evidence). The Court of Appeal has now dealt it a further blow in *Thorpe v Chief Constable of the Greater Manchester Police* [1989] 2 All ER 827.

The plaintiff had been charged with obstructing the highway in connection with a demonstration. Quashing his conviction by the magistrates, the Crown Court expressed a view that the arresting constables had given false evidence. The plaintiff brought an action against the police in respect of assault, unlawful arrest and malicious prosecution. The issue before the Court of Appeal was whether the plaintiff could insist on production of the disciplinary convictions of the constables for offences similar to those which they allegedly committed against the plaintiff. The constables' misbehaviour on previous occasions was capable of being relevant in two ways: it could undermine their denials of misbehaviour in the plaintiff's case and it could establish a propensity for such misbehaviour. It has been decided that neither of these grounds of relevance justified production: it would be oppressive to make a party disclose material relevant to his credit and discovery of similar fact evidence should not be ordered, except where it is relevant to rebut a defence of accident or where it is necessary to prove system.

The Court of Appeal thus inserted into the law of civil discovery two rules drawn from the law of criminal evidence where, notwithstanding their popularity, they have caused a good deal of trouble. The distinction between relevance to credit and relevance to issue is largely unhelpful and the case under consideration will illustrate this. Suppose that the court were left with a choice between the testimony of the constables, on the one hand, and that of the plaintiff, on the other. Where the only evidence is that of conflicting testimony, the issue must needs be resolved by testing the credibility of the opponents. The better the court is able to determine credibility, the greater is the likelihood of a correct decision. A piece of evidence that shows that the constables are lying, such as the fact that they have been disciplined for repeated false accusations against peaceful protestors, would remove their credibility and would ipso facto affect outcome. It follows that the distinction between relevance to credibility and relevance to issue has little to do with the ascertainment of truth which is the object of discovery in civil cases.

The similar fact rule was invoked by the Court of Appeal because of a possibility that the action would be tried with a jury. In jury trials care must be taken to avoid undue prejudice and the similar fact rule governs the reception of such evidence at the trial. But here the plaintiff was not seeking to adduce the evidence, he was only asking to see it. The similar fact rule has no relevance to the question of discovery. The Court of Appeal held that discovery of similar fact evidence will be ordered only where it is relevant to rebut a defence of accident or to prove system. In doing so the court seems to have invoked the pre Boardman rule. However, according to Boardman v DPP [1974] 3 All ER 887, similar fact evidence is admissible not because it can be categorised as rebutting a defence or as proving a system but only where its probative contribution outweighs its prejudicial effect. This balance can be performed only in the light of how the case has evolved at the trial and what evidence has beed adduced, none of which can be known at the discovery stage.

One cannot help feeling that the criminal evidence rules have provided an excuse for blocking access to police information just as the doctrine of public interest immunity did in the case of *Evans v Chief Constable of Surrey Constabulary* [1989] 2 All ER 594, discussed in the article on evidence. The trouble is, however, that while the impact of public interest immunity may be contained the newly declared doctrines are not so limited.

Summary judgment

The parties to an insurance contract were in dispute about the meaning of a clause in their agreement. Although the contract provided for arbitration, the plaintiff applied to the court for summary judgment under RSC Ord 14 contending that the defendant had no real defence on the point of construction. An arbitration agreement is no obstacle to such course because arbitrators are bound by the law and if the law is clear on a point of construction, there is no real dispute to be referred to arbitration. What may not, however, be altogether certain is when may an issue of law be considered so clear as to be fit for summary resolution. This was the point that was considered by the Court of Appeal in *Home and Overseas Insurance Co Ltd v Mentor Insurance Co (UK) Ltd (in liq)* [1989] 3 All ER 74. It has been held that a court will conclude that there is no defence only where it is immediately obvious that the point of law raised by the defendant is misconceived, or where it can be shown to be so by short argument. However, in dealing with Ord 14 applications the court must not embark on a consideration of legal issues that require lengthy argument or to allow application for summary judgment to become a spurious device for securing immediate trial of the action.

To deter plaintiffs from taking such course where they had agreed to arbitration Parker LJ observed that—

'when a plaintiff seeks immediate judgment in other than a clear case and resists the submission of the dispute to the tribunal on which he has agreed, one is bound to wonder whether the course which he has taken is prompted by the knowledge that the chosen tribunal with its more intimate knowledge of the trade may reach a conclusion adverse to him . . .'; [1989] 3 All ER at 78.

Interim payment

Two years ago the Court of Appeal decided that where a plaintiff makes two alternative claims, one for damages and another for the price of goods supplied, and it is clear that he is bound to succeed on one or the other, interim payment may be awarded under Ord 29: *Shearson Lehman Bros Inc v Maclaine Watson & Co Ltd* [1987] 2 All ER 181. This year the Court of Appeal faced a situation where it was clear that a plaintiff was bound to recover from one of two defendants but it was not clear from which of them: *Ricci Burns Ltd v Toole* [1989] 3 All ER 478. It has been held that before a defendant can be ordered to make interim payment, the plaintiff must prove a likelihood of success against that particular defendant; it is not enough to show that the plaintiff is bound to succeed against one or the other of the defendants. Although the court regretted this outcome since it involved hardship for the plaintiff, it considered it necessary for the protection of defendants to insist on individualised proof.

The connection between unconditional leave to defend and interim payment is not altogether clear. A defendant who has obtained unconditional leave to defend must have had an arguable case and may therefore win at the end of the day. If so, what justification is there for making him hand over to the plaintiff an interim payment when on winning the case he may find that the plaintiff has spent the money and is not in a position to repay it? This problem was met head on in *British and Commonwealth Holdings plc v Quadrex Holdings Inc* [1989] 3 All ER 492.

Order 29, r 11(1) authorises the court to make an order for interim payment if 'the Court is satisfied . . . (c) that, if the action proceeds to trial, the plaintiff would obtain judgment . . .' Speaking in the Court of Appeal Browne-Wilkinson V-C said that he found it—

'an impossible concept that the same court can be simultaneously "satisfied" that the plaintiff *will* succeed at trial and at the same time consider that the defendant has an arguable defence sufficient to warrant unconditional leave to defend'; [1989] 3 All ER at 511.

He concluded therefore that it is impossible to make an order for interim payment where unconditional leave to defend has been given. Where no leave to defend has been given summary judgment against the defendant will be entered and there is no scope for interim orders. It follows that interim payment may be ordered only where there is room for conditional leave to defend. That is—

> 'in cases where on the evidence then before it, the court entertains sufficient doubt as to the genuineness of the defence to give only conditional leave to defend, it is possible for the court to be satisfied that the plaintiff will succeed at trial'; [1989] 3 All ER at 511.

Interim payment becomes therefore a species of a condition to defend. An ordinary condition to defend usually entails payment into court whereas interim payment is made outright to the plaintiff. But even where there is only conditional leave to defend, there must still be some possibility that the defence would prove successful. Interim payment is justified here because the defendant's defence is shadowy and his prospects of success very small. Even so, before the defendant is subjected to a risk that he may not recover the interim payment, the court, according to Browne-Wilkinson V-C, must give due consideration to the defendant's ability to make an interim payment and the disruptive effect that it may have upon his business.

Striking out for want of prosecution

Where there has been inordinate and inexcusable delay on the part of the plaintiff his action may be dismissed, if the delay created a risk that it would not be possible to have a fair trial or has caused prejudice to the defendant. Further, an action will not be struck out within the limitation period because the plaintiff will be free to renew it. Lastly, the time that has elapsed up to the issue of the writ within the limitation period cannot constitute inordinate delay and cannot be taken into account in determining the risk to fair trial or the prejudice to the defendant. These rules received the endorsement of the House of Lords in *Birkett v James* [1977] 2 All ER 801 but have recently been criticised in lower instances as too lenient. In *Department of Transport v Chris Smaller (Transport) Ltd* [1989] 1 All ER 897 the House of Lords was called upon to tighten up the law so that firmer action may be taken against deleterious plaintiffs. This the House of Lords has declined to do.

Experience has shown that the main stumbling block to dismissal is the need to prove risk to fair trial or prejudice. But Lord Griffiths found no reason for doing away with the above requirements—

> 'What would be the purpose of striking out in such circumstances? If there can be a fair trial and the defendant has suffered no prejudice, it clearly cannot be to do justice between the parties before the court; as between the plaintiff and defendant such an order is manifestly an injustice to the plaintiff. The only possible purpose of such an order would be as a disciplinary measure which by punishing the plaintiff will have a beneficent effect on the administration of justice by deterring others from similar delays;' [1989] 1 All ER at 903

While not altering the existing law the House of Lords has clarified two points. First, that prejudice entitling the defendant to seek to strike out the action is not confined to prejudice affecting the conduct of the trial but extends to prejudice to the defendant's interests generally, such as the running of his business. It warned however against giving too easy a recognition to anxiety as a form of prejudice. Second, where a long delay before the issue of the writ caused the defendant prejudice, he only needs to show little more then minimal extra prejudice arising from post-writ delay to justify striking out.

Lord Griffiths did not delude himself into thinking that the present law provides an effective solution to the serious problem of delay. He preferred, however, to leave a radical solution to the reform of civil procedure recommended by the Report of the Review Body on Civil Justice. If these proposals, which include a strict timetable for actions, do not materialise, the House of Lords may yet have to reconsider its decision.

Disclosure of witness statements

As the practice of exchanging witness statements before trial in accordance with RSC Ord 38, r 2A gains momentum, the courts have been called upon to rule on the uses that may be made of exchanged statements. In *Fairfield-Mabey Ltd v Shell UK Ltd* [1989] 1 All ER 576, Judge Bowsher QC laid down a number of guidelines. He proceeded from the assumption that a proponent who serves a statement on his opponent has a right of confidence in the statement and that the opponent is duty bound to respect this confidence until the proponent has called the witness to testify and the latter has verified the statement on oath, or the proponent has waived the privilege. This assumption is, however, not entirely correct. A party who discloses to the opponent a document does so subject to the undertaking that the opponent will not use the document for any extraneous purpose (see *Home Office v Harman* [1982] 1 All ER 532). Under this rule the opponent may use the document in connection with the proceedings in which it has been disclosed. Suppose, for example, that the proponent, who served a witness statement, calls the witness to testify but the latter gives an account which is at odds with his earlier statement. Surely, the opponent is entitled to cross-examine the witness on his earlier inconsistent statement.

Judge Bowsher QC thought that, before a witness statement has been put in evidence by the proponent, the opponent should not be able to use the statement for cross-examining other witnesses, because the party who served the statement may choose not to rely on it. While it is right to discourage the insinuation of witness statements by the back door, the solution adopted here is not altogether satisfactory. Litigants should not be allowed to play cat and mouse with each other. They should be required to state at the earliest opportunity, and no later than the beginning of the trial, whether they intend to put their witness statements in evidence. This practice will obviate the situation where, for instance, a plaintiff is inhibited from examining the defendant on statements served by the latter because the defendant has not yet declared his intention to use these statements in evidence. Such a plaintiff would either be deprived of the opportunity of obtaining the defendant's reaction to his own witness statements or, alternatively, the plaintiff would have to ask for the defendant to be recalled at a later stage. None of these courses is desirable.

Lastly, it was held that a party who has served a witness statement may choose to cross-examine the opponent's witnesses on this statement thereby waiving the confidence in the statement. But according to Judge Bowsher QC—

'When this course is adopted, the judge should direct himself that the unsworn statement being put to the witness is not evidence and that the only evidence will be the answers of the witness in relation to it.' [1989] 1 All ER at 577.

This dictum introduces into civil litigation the distinction between relevance to credibility and relevance to issue which causes so much confusion in criminal trials. There is precious little justification for the distinction in criminal cases but there is even less so in civil litigation. Hearsay evidence is, to all intents and purposes, admissible in civil cases. Out of court statements are therefore admissible in principle. If a party chooses to introduce his own witness statement when cross-examining a witness for the opponent, he should be taken to have thereby introduced the statement in evidence. It would be absurd to allow this party to claim that the statement upon which he himself relies is only to be taken as a test of the reliability of the witness whom he was cross-examining but should not be regarded as evidence of facts stated therein. Of course, a party introducing a witness statement is not thereby bound to accept it as true in all respects and in all circumstances. But if a party disputes facts stated in a document used by him, he should state so and give reasons.

Clearly, the uses that may be made of witnesses' statements deserve closer consideration. The starting point should be that such statements may be put in evidence by both parties. Suppose that the plaintiff has served the statement of witness X on the defendant. If it is held that the latter is not entitled to put this statement in evidence, he is still free to call X to testify on his behalf. But why should the defendant be put to the expense and the trouble of serving a subpoena on X, if he is willing to content himself with the statement prepared by the plaintiff?

Sequestration by the county court

The power of the county court to issue injunctions is derived from s 38 of the County Courts Act 1984. But CCR Ord 29, r 1, unlike its counterpart RSC Ord 45, r 5, does not mention the possibility of sequestration. Sequestration is the only practical sanction against a company that disobeys an injunction. It has been decided in *Rose v Laskington Ltd* [1989] 3 All ER 306 that the county court does have the power of sequestration and that the aggrieved party need not and must not seek this remedy in the High Court.

Costs

Costs when payment into court has taken place

It has been assumed that to be effective to save the defendant's costs after payment into court, the payment must be made no later that 21 days before the beginning of the trial. This assumption was based on RSC Ord 22, r 3(1) which gives the plaintiff 21 days 'before the trial or hearing of the action begins' to accept the money in satisfaction of his cause of action. However, there is nothing in Ord 22 to suggest that later payment is ineffective. On the contrary, Ord 22, r 3(2) provides that where money is paid into court after the trial has begun, the plaintiff has two days in which to accept the payment. It has been held by the Court of Appeal in *King v Weston-Howell* [1989] 2 All ER 375 that where payment has been made less than 21 days before the trial, the plaintiff has the remainder of the pre-trial period within which to accept. Having regard to r 3(2) the plaintiff must have at least two days for making up his mind.

Under Ord 62, r 9(1)(b) the court 'in exercising its discretion as to costs shall take into account . . . any payment of money into court and the amount of such payment . . .'. It has been held that if payment is made after 21 days before the trial this must still be taken into account in determining the costs. The general rule in this respect is that if at the end of the trial the plaintiff recovers no more than the amount that the defendant has paid into court, the plaintiff will be entitled to costs only up to the date on which payment into court was made. Thereafter, the defendant is to be considered as the winning party and entitled to costs. Further, where delay on the part of the plaintiff has prevented the defendant from making payment into court which he would have done, the judge has discretion to regard the cut-off date for costs such earlier date as he considers just in the circumstances.

Costs against person maintaining action

The Criminal Law Act 1967, s 14, abolished liability in tort for maintenance and champerty. This does not mean, according to Macpherson J in *Singh v Observer Ltd* [1989] 2 All ER 751 that persons who maintain the litigation of others cannot be ordered to pay costs. In *The Vimeria* [1986] 2 All ER 409 it was held that the discretion conferred by s 51(1) of the Supreme Court Act 1981 to award costs was not confined to orders of costs against the parties to the proceedings. This enabled Macpherson J to conclude that costs may be ordered against a person who has kept an action going 'without the maintainer having any interest whatsoever in the litigation'; [1989] 2 All ER at 756. Moreover, the solicitor of the party whose action has been maintained by an outsider may be made to disclose the identity of the maintainer so that the court may investigate his interest in the litigation and the extent of the assistance provided. It will come as a surprise to those contributing to the costs of worthy litigants to find out that they could be found liable for the costs of the opponents as well.

Appeal from the county court on a point of law not raised below

The general rule governing the raising of a fresh point of law on appeal is as follows. Generally a point of law may not be raised for the first time on appeal, but the appellate court has a discretion to allow such point to be raised if, first, the opponent has had sufficient opportunity to meet the point, second, the opponent has not acted to his detriment by relying on the omission to raise the point earlier and, third, the opponent can be adequately protected in costs. However, as a result of the decision in *Smith v Baker & Sons* [1891] AC 325 a different rule governed appeals from the county court to the Court of Appeal according to which an appeal could not deal with a point of law not raised in the county court.

In *Pittalis v Grant* [1989] 2 All ER 622 the Court of Appeal reviewed the history of this special rule and reached the conclusion that the reasons that lead to its creation have long since disappeared and that it should be abandoned. Henceforth appeals from the county court will be governed by the same general rule that governs appeals from the High Court.

Public International Law

CHRISTOPHER GREENWOOD, MA, LLB
Barrister, Fellow of Magdalene College, Cambridge

The International Tin Council litigation

The litigation concerning the collapse of the International Tin Council (ITC), which dominates the chapter on Public International Law in 1989 as it did in 1987 and 1988 is now, at last, drawing to a close. In *Maclaine Watson & Co Ltd v Department of Trade and Industry* [1989] 3 All ER 523 the House of Lords dismissed appeals by creditors of the ITC from two judgments of the Court of Appeal (noted in last year's Review at pp 241–247). Although the decisions of the House of Lords by no means disposed of all the litigation in the English courts (let alone that in courts elsewhere), the rejection of the appeals paved the way for a settlement of all outstanding claims which seems to have put a stop to the litigation.

Background

In October 1985 the ITC, an international organisation established to ensure an orderly market in tin, announced that it was unable to pay debts estimated at between £700 million and £900 million, most of which was owed to commodity brokers who had bought and sold tin with the ITC and banks who had lent money to the ITC. The members of the ITC were the United Kingdom, 22 other States and the EEC. At the relevant time the ITC operated under the terms of the Sixth International Tin Agreement 1982 (ITA6). According to the terms of a Headquarters Agreement concluded between the ITC and the United Kingdom in 1972 (the Headquarters Agreement) the headquarters of the ITC were established in London. The Headquarters Agreement was given effect in English law by the International Tin Council (Immunities and Privileges) Order 1972 (the 1972 Order), a statutory instrument made under the International Organisations Act 1968. The principal provisions of these texts are considered at All ER Rev 1987 pp 210–11.

Outline of the Litigation

The main cases reported to date in the All England Law Reports and Butterworths Company Law Cases are as follows:

1 *Standard Chartered Bank v International Tin Council* [1986] 3 All ER 257 (All ER Rev 1987 p 212). In this case Bingham J held that the ITC had waived its immunity by virtue of a clause in its loan agreement with Standard Chartered and gave judgment against the ITC. The case was subsequently settled out of court. In most cases, however, it was not possible for the creditors to secure payment from the ITC itself, because of the organisation's

lack of funds. The other cases therefore involved a variety of attempts to obtain payment from the members of the ITC.

2 *The 'direct actions'.* In these actions a number of banks and brokers proceeded directly against the members of the ITC, arguing that they were liable on the contracts concluded by the ITC. The actions were struck out by Millett J in *Maclaine Watson & Co Ltd v Department of Trade and Industry* [1987] BCLC 707 and Staughton J in *JH Rayner (Mincing Lane) Ltd v Department of Trade and Industry* [1987] BCLC 667 (All ER Rev 1987 p 216). The Court of Appeal dismissed appeals from both judgments *sub nom Maclaine Watson & Co Ltd v Department of Trade and Industry* [1988] 3 All ER 257 (All ER Rev 1988 p 241). An appeal to the House of Lords was dismissed in the 1989 judgment (below).

3 *The 'receivership action'.* In *Maclaine Watson & Co Ltd v International Tin Council* a broker who had obtained an arbitration award against the ITC and then converted it into a judgment sought the appointment of a receiver by way of equitable execution over the assets of the ITC which, the broker alleged, included a right on the part of the ITC to be indemnified by or to obtain contributions from the members. This action was struck out by Millett J [1987] 3 All ER 787 (All ER Rev 1987 p 216) and an appeal was dismissed by the Court of Appeal, [1988] 3 All ER 257 at 364 (All ER Rev 1988 p 245). An appeal to the House of Lords was also dismissed in the 1989 judgment (below).

4 *The 'winding up action'.* In *Re International Tin Council* an attempt was made to have the ITC wound up under Pt XXI of the Companies Act 1985. This action was struck out by Millett J [1987] 1 All ER 890 (All ER Rev 1987 p 214). The Court of Appeal dismissed an appeal, [1988] 3 All ER 257 at 359 (All ER Rev 1988 p 244). There was no appeal to the House of Lords.

5 *The 'discovery of assets action'.* In *Maclaine Watson & Co Ltd v ITC (No 2)* Millett J ordered that an officer of the ITC disclose details of the ITC's assets with a view to execution being levied against them [1987] 3 All ER 886 (All ER Rev 1987 p 213). The ITC's appeal was dismissed by the Court of Appeal, [1988] 3 All ER 257 at 376 (All ER Rev 1988 p 245). The ITC did not appeal to the House of Lords.

6 *Shearson Lehman Bros Inc v Maclaine Watson & Co Ltd (International Tin Council intervening) (No 2)* [1988] 1 All ER 116. The ITC intervened unsuccessfully in an attempt to prevent the use of documents emanating from the ITC in litigation between two brokers concerning the 1985 collapse. The decision of the House of Lords is noted at All ER Rev 1987 p 217. Further decisions in this case have not involved points of public international law.

Other decisions, including some from courts outside the United Kingdom, are reported in volumes 77, 80 and 81 of the International Law Reports. A number of decisions which have not yet been reported will also appear in that series in due course.

The House of Lords' judgment: the direct actions

The direct actions turned on whether the ITC possessed a legal personality separate from its members and, if it did, on the nature of that personality. Article 16 of ITA6 provided that the ITC was to have legal personality, including 'the capacity to contract, to acquire and dispose of movable and immovable property and to institute legal proceedings.' This provision was repeated in art 3 of the Headquarters Agreement. Neither provision was incorporated into English law but the 1972 Order provided, in art 5, that the ITC should have 'the legal capacities of a body corporate'. Did these provisions have the effect that the ITC possessed a legal personality similar to that possessed by a limited company in English law, so that its members would not be liable for its debts. The creditors argued that they did not and advanced four alternative arguments to show that the ITC's members were liable for the debts of the ITC:

> *Submission A:* under English law the ITC was not a legal entity distinct from its members but only a collective trading name under which the members did business;
>
> *Submission B(1):* if the ITC did possess separate legal personality, as a matter of English law that personality was not such as to exclude the liability of its members:
>
> *Submission B(2):* as an international organisation, the ITC derived its legal personality from international law under which the members of an international organisation remained liable for its debts, at least in the absence of an express provision to the contrary in the treaty constituting the organisation.
>
> *Submission C:* the constitution of the ITC was such that it had contracted as agent for its members.

The House of Lords was unanimous in rejecting all four arguments. Lord Templeman had little patience with any of them but Lord Oliver clearly thought that submission B(2) deserved rather more consideration than the other arguments. The rest of the House joined in these opinions.

Submission A foundered on the interpretation of the 1972 Order. While this did not expressly incorporate the ITC, both Lord Templeman and Lord Oliver considered that it conferred a legal personality of some kind. Lord Oliver added that if the 1972 Order had been ambiguous, reference to ITA6 and the Headquarters Agreement (which would have been necessary since the 1972 Order was plainly designed to implement the Headquarters Agreement and the forerunner of ITA6) would have removed that ambiguity since both treaties made clear that the ITC was to have legal personality. Submission B(1) was couched entirely in terms of English law and also failed on the interpretation of the Order. Lord Oliver conceded that Parliament could, if it wished, have conferred upon the ITC a personality similar to that of a 'mixed entity' such as a Scottish partnership but found nothing in the Order to suggest that it had done so. On the contrary, all the indications were that the intention had been to treat the ITC as though it were a body corporate.

The essence of submission B(2) was that the ITC, as an international organisation derived its personality from international law, so that the English courts had to look to international law to determine the nature of that personality, in the same way as they would look to French law to ascertain the nature of the legal personality of a French company. To succeed in this submission the creditors had to show:

(a) that art 5 of the 1972 Order did not confer legal personality upon the ITC but merely recognised and gave effect to a legal personality which already existed under international law;

(b) that the English courts could apply the rules of international law which defined the attributes of that personality and, in particular, the rules which determined whether the members of the ITC were liable for its debts; and

(c) that there was a rule of international law which provided that the members of an international organisation were liable for the debts of that organisation, at least in the absence of provision to the contrary in the organisation's constitution.

In the Court of Appeal Nourse LJ, who dissented, had accepted these three propositions and Kerr LJ had been attracted by the first and third. The House of Lords, however, rejected the first proposition and thus the entire argument. An international organisation, Lord Oliver held, was not in the same position as a company incorporated under foreign law. When a company was incorporated in France, French law made that company a legal person distinct from its shareholders and it could assert that personality in England by, for example, becoming party to contracts there. When the ITC was created as an international organisation, the legal personality which it thus acquired existed only on the plane of international law—it had no personality which it could assert on the level of English law until art 5 of the 1972 Order bestowed such personality upon it. The ITC thus had an existence in English law separate and distinct from its existence in international law. As Lord Oliver put it:

> 'Let it be assumed, for the moment, that the international entity known as the ITC is, by the treaty, one for the engagements of which the member states become liable in international law, that entity is not the entity which entered into the contract relevant to these appeals. Those contracts were effected by the separate persona ficta which was created by the 1972 Order.' (p 552).

In effect, the correct analogy was not with a French company doing business directly in England but with a French company which does business in England through the medium of an English subsidiary.

Having rejected the first proposition on which submission B(2) was based, it was not strictly necessary for the House of Lords to consider the other two propositions. However, Lords Templeman and Oliver went on to state that even if the personality of the ITC had been derived from international law, any principle of international law which might exist imposing upon the members of an international organisation liability for that organisation's debts was non-justiciable in the English courts. Lord Templeman held that:

> '. . . if there existed a rule of international law which implied in a treaty or imposed on sovereign states which enter into a treaty an obligation (in default of a clear disclaimer in the treaty) to discharge the debts of an international organisation established by that treaty, the rule of international law could only be enforced under international law. Treaty rights and obligations conferred or imposed by agreement or by international law cannot be enforced by the courts of the United Kingdom.' (p 529)

In fact neither Lord Templeman nor Lord Oliver was persuaded that international law contained any such rule.

The agency argument (submission C) also received short shrift. In the Court of Appeal, Kerr and Nourse LJJ had been willing to look at the terms of ITA6 to ascertain whether they supported the creditors' theory of 'constitutional agency' (ie that the constitution of the ITC was such that it necessarily contracted as agent for the members) but found nothing in ITA6 to sustain the creditors' argument. In the House of Lords, Lord Oliver agreed that the submission had to be rejected for the reasons given by the Court of Appeal but also stated that even to look at ITA6 in the way that Kerr and Nourse LJJ had done was contrary to the principle of non-justiciability.

The House of Lords' judgment: the receivership action

The appeal in the receivership action also failed on the non-justiciability ground. Like the Court of Appeal, Lords Templeman and Oliver held that any rights which the ITC might have against its members were derived from ITA6 and therefore were non-justiciable in an English court, because of the principle that a treaty cannot create rights enforceable in the English courts. A majority of the Court of Appeal, however, had rejected an alternative argument advanced by the member states that the receivership action should also be rejected on the basis of the decision in *Buttes Gas and Oil Co v Hammer (No 2)* [1981] 3 All ER 616. In the House of Lords, Lord Oliver questioned whether this argument should have been rejected but held that it was unnecessary to decide the point. The limitations which the majority of the Court of Appeal imposed (quite correctly, it is respectfully submitted) on the *Buttes* doctrine should still be taken as representing the law.

The effects of the House of Lords's decision

The decision of the House of Lords is likely to have far-reaching implications for United Kingdom foreign relations law (to borrow an American phrase). In this writer's view, very few of those effects are beneficial. There is, perhaps, room for more than one view about whether the creditors were badly treated (especially in the light of the settlement discussed below). Moreover, it is far from clear whether international law does indeed impose liability upon the members of an international organisation for the debts of that organisation. Yet instead of basing their rejection of submission B(2) on a decision about the liability of members of an international organisation in international law, the House of Lords relied upon a doctrinaire dualist view, in which international law and English law inhabit totally different planes. This approach is particularly evident in two parts of the decision.

First, their Lordships' approach to the question of the source of the ITC's legal personality is based upon the assumption that the personality which the ITC derived from international law was one which could exist only on the ethereal plane of international relations. To enter into the commodities market in London, the ITC had first to acquire a fresh personality which might be used in the more down to earth world of English law, a personality which was supplied by the 1972 Order. In much the same way, the gods of classical legend could descend from Mount Olympus and reveal themselves to men only by assuming the forms of earthly creatures (although they were always prone to revert to divine status at a moment's notice). This approach is highly artificial. Did anybody who worked for, dealt with or lent money to the ITC in London imagine that he was dealing not with an international organisation but a creature of English law, something rather like a subsidiary of the organisation created by ITA6? Moreover, this artificial approach is not even as simple as it may appear. The problems to which it can give rise were highlighted by the decision of Hoffmann J in *Arab Monetary Fund v Hashim (No 3)* [1990] 1 All ER 685. The Arab Monetary Fund (AMF) is an international organisation of which the United Kingdom is not a member and in respect of which no order has been made under the International Organisations Act 1968. When it sued its former director-general and various other parties in the High Court, the defendants argued that the AMF was not a legal person in the eyes of English law and thus had no standing to sue. The obvious riposte to this argument is that the AMF is a person under international law and, as such, can sue and be sued in the English courts just as a company incorporated under foreign law can sue and be sued. Hoffmann J, however, considered that the decision in the Tin appeals precluded this sensible approach.

Instead, he felt constrained to hold that as the treaty establishing the AMF had been incorporated into the law of Abu Dhabi (where the AMF had its headquarters), he could treat the AMF as an entity established under the law of Abu Dhabi. This decision is entirely in keeping with the decision of the House of Lords in *Maclaine Watson* but the result is absurd: a body which is plainly a creation of international law has to be treated as though it were a creation of Abu Dhabi law, which it plainly is not. Worse, the AMF treaty may well have been incorporated into the domestic law of more than one member state. Is there, therefore, a separate AMF in each such state? Which one is the party to a given transaction? Can one AMF sue another in the English courts? Small wonder that Hoffmann J (who was delighted not to have to answer those questions on the facts of the case before him) described these as questions of 'Trinitarian subtlety'.

Secondly, the approach of the House of Lords led it to extend the scope of non-justiciability without, it appears, any clear rationale for doing so. There is, in truth, more than one principle of non-justiciability. The first is that, with minor exceptions that are not relevant here, the Crown, which is the body responsible for concluding treaties on behalf of the United Kingdom, cannot change English law by the exercise of its prerogative power to conclude treaties. Thus, a treaty cannot create rights or obligations in English law; any changes in English law necessitated by United Kingdom participation in a treaty must be effected by legislation which (if Parliament chooses) may take the form of the incorporation of the whole treaty into English law. This principle is nothing to do with the nature of international law; it is a well established principle of the British Constitution. It is the reason why the receivership appeal failed, since any rights which the ITC might have had against its members had to have been created by ITA6.

This constitutional principle of non-justiciability did not, however, require the rejection of submission B(2) in the direct actions. If, as maintained by the creditors, there is a rule of international law that the members of an international organisation are liable for the organisation's debts unless they exclude that liability, that rule is derived not from any one treaty creating an international organisation but from the customary international law concerning the effects of such treaties. Moreover, that rule does not purport to change English law, any more than the French legislation on corporations purports to change English law merely because a French company does business in England. All that the international law rules do is to provide the framework for the creation of an international person and to define the nature and effects of its personality.

Some English decisions suggest that there is a second, quite different, principle of non-justiciability based upon the inherent unsuitability of national courts adjudicating upon certain matters of international relations. As Lord Oliver put it:

> 'It is axiomatic that municipal courts have not and cannot have the competence to adjudicate on or to enforce the rights arising out of transactions entered into by independent sovereign states between themselves on the plane of international law.' (p 544).

This statement, together with a number of other comments in the opinions of Lords Oliver and Templeman, cannot be explained on the basis of any constitutional doctrine about treaties not changing English law, since they are expressed in terms which embrace rights not created by treaty. Yet the reason for such a wide principle of non-justiciability and the explanation of why adjudication by English courts of rights arising out of events on the international plane is inappropriate are not clearly articulated in *Maclaine Watson*. That is a pity. If there are areas of international law into which it is not proper for English courts to venture, we should be told why that is so. In particular, even if it is wrong for an English court to adjudicate upon certain activities of States and intentional organisations, do the same considerations apply to the activities of an organisation which functioned almost entirely by trading on a national commodities market?

The settlement

According to press reports, in December 1989 the ITC and its creditors agreed upon a settlement of all the claims arising out of the collapse of the ITC. Under the terms of the settlement, the creditors were to receive £182.5 million. Since the full extent of the ITC's liabilities was never established in the proceedings and it is unclear how far the creditors were able to mitigate their losses by the sale of tin held as security, it is impossible to say what percentage of the ITC's liabilities will be paid. Nevertheless, the conclusion of the settlement is a considerable achievement. It is understood that, as part of this settlement, the remaining actions against the ITC and its members have now been discontinued.

Treaties and statutory interpretation

In addition to the decision in *Maclaine Watson* (above) and the case of *Factortame Ltd v Secretary of State for Transport* [1989] 2 All ER 692 (discussed in the chapter on European Community Law), two other decisions reported in 1989 raise interesting points regarding the way in which English courts will refer to treaties as an aid to the interpretation of legislation.

Re State of Norway's Applications

It is well established that where a statute is passed to give effect to a treaty, the

English courts should have regard to the treaty in interpreting the statute. In *Re State of Norway's Applications (Nos 1 and 2)* [1989] 1 All ER 745 the House of Lords had to consider the implications of this principle in relation to other methods of statutory interpretation. Following the death of a wealthy Norwegian citizen, a Norwegian county tax committee raised a retrospective tax assessment against his estate on the ground that he had allegedly failed to disclose part of his assets. The estate challenged this decision in a Norwegian court and that court issued letters of request to the High Court in England requesting the High Court to secure the attendance of two witnesses to be examined before an examiner in London. One of the questions which arose was whether the High Court had jurisdiction to order the examination of the witnesses under s 1 of the Evidence (Proceedings in Other Jurisdictions) Act 1975.

The witnesses argued that s 1 applied only to civil proceedings, which were defined in s 9 as proceedings in 'a civil or commercial matter', and the Norwegian proceedings were not civil proceedings in this sense. The 1975 Act, they contended, had been passed in order to give effect to the Convention relating to the Taking of Evidence Abroad in Civil or Commercial Matters 1970, and had to be interpreted in the light of that Convention. The witnesses maintained that, under that Convention, the term 'civil or commercial matter' had an internationally accepted meaning. It should be taken as referring not to the nature of the procedure (ie proceedings in a criminal or civil court) but to the substance of the issues before the foreign court, construed in the light of the distinction in civil law countries (which made up the majority of the parties to the 1970 Convention) between civil and public law proceedings and that, since fiscal matters were classified as public law proceedings under this approach, the Norwegian court's request had to be interpreted as falling outside the scope of s 1 of the Act, even though the Norwegian court itself had classified the proceedings as civil. It was also suggested that, since the 1975 Act had been passed to give effect to the Convention, it would be wrong to look to previous legislation dealing with requests from foreign courts as an aid to interpretation of the 1975 Act. This approach succeeded in the Court of Appeal in *Re State of Norway's Application (No 2)* [1989] 1 All ER 701 but was rejected in the House of Lords.

Lord Goff, with whom the rest of the House agreed, held that although the implementation of the 1970 Convention had been a principal purpose of the 1975 Act, it had not been the only reason for its enactment. The Act had also been passed with a view to bringing together in one statute the various enactments relating to judicial assistance. In these circumstances, he held that reference to the earlier legislation was entirely appropriate. Under that legislation, the powers of the English courts had not been restricted to civil or commercial matters in the narrow sense, excluding public law proceedings, and Lord Goff refused to hold that the 1975 Act, the wording of which varied only slightly from that of the earlier statutes, had been intended to restrict the jurisdiction of the English courts in such a way, especially since the 1975 Act also applied to requests from common law countries not party to the 1970 Convention. One might add that, in any event, the broader interpretation of the phrase 'civil or commercial matter' did not mean that English law conflicted with the Convention but only that it went beyond what was required by the Convention.

The House of Lords also held that, even if it had been constrained to interpret the 1975 Act by reference to a substantive approach to the meaning of 'civil or commercial matter', a comparative law analysis showed that there was no intentionally accepted definition of those terms. The House concluded that a request was to be treated as having been made in relation to a 'civil or commercial matter' if it was made in the context of proceedings classified as civil or commercial under both English law and the law of the requesting State. Under English law, the term referred to any proceedings other than criminal proceedings.

R v Secretary of State for Transport, ex p Pegasus Holidays

In *R v Secretary of State for Transport, ex p Pegasus Holidays (London) Ltd* [1989] 2 All ER 481 Schiemann J had to consider a decision by the Secretary of State for Transport to suspend a permit granted under the Air Navigation Order 1985 to Tarom, a Romanian airline. The permit allowed Tarom to operate charter flights using Romanian pilots and required that Tarom ensure that its crews met the licensing requirements of the Romanian Civil Aviation Authority. Five of the pilots concerned took an examination set by the United Kingdom Civil Aviation Authority (CAA), although they were not required to do so, and failed it. The CAA then expressed concern to the Secretary of State about the ability of Tarom's pilots and the Secretary of State decided to suspend Tarom's permit pending an inquiry into the Romanian licensing requirements and the ability of T's pilots to comply with them.

Pegasus Holidays, a London tour operator which used flights operated by Tarom, sought judicial review of this decision on the ground, inter alia, that it contravened the Chicago Convention on International Civil Aviation 1944. Schiemann J held that the Secretary of State was required to comply with the Chicago Convention in exercising his powers, either because the Air Navigation Order itself had to be in accordance with the Convention or because the court was required to interpret the Order in such a way as to conform to the Convention if possible. He reached this result, however, not because of any general principle about the relationship between treaties and English law but principally because of the wording of s 60(2) of the Civil Aviation Act 1982, which provided that:

> 'An Air Navigation Order may contain such provision as appears to Her Majesty in Council to be requisite or expedient – (*a*) for carrying out the Chicago Convention, any Annex thereto relating to international standards and recommended practices . . . (*b*) generally for regulating air navigation.'

Schiemann J rejected an argument that the effect of this section was to incorporate the Convention into English law but held that, properly construed, s 60(2) showed that Parliament had not given the Secretary of State power to make an Order containing provisions which conflicted with the Convention. An Order might go further than was required by the Convention but could not run counter to it. The logical conclusion is that had the 1985 Order run counter to the Convention it would have been ultra vires. As an alternative he held that the 1985 Order had to be interpreted, where possible, in such a way as to comply with the Convention. Schiemann J held, however, that, on the facts, the Secretary of State had not acted contrary to the provisions of the Convention.

Jurisdiction: United Kingdom statutes

The decision of the House of Lords in *Holmes v Bangladesh Biman Corp* [1989] 1 All ER 852 is an application of the principle that United Kingdom statutes are presumed not to have extra-territorial effect. The plaintiff was the widow and executor of a British citizen killed when one of the defendant's aircraft crashed on an internal flight within Bangladesh. Liability was admitted and only the amount of damages was in issue. Under Bangladesh law, the maximum which the plaintiff could recover was £913, whereas if an order made under the Carriage by Air Act 1961 applied, the plaintiff could recover £83,763. The 1961 Act was passed to give effect to the Hague Convention 1955, and Schedule 1 to the Act effectively incorporated the Convention into English law. It was common ground that the Hague Convention (and its precursor, the Warsaw Convention) did not apply on the facts of this case. The plaintiff relied upon the terms of a 1967 Order in Council made under s 10(1) of the 1961 Act, which gave power to apply the provisions of the Act (and hence of the Hague Convention) to 'carriage by air, not being carriage by air to which the Convention applies'.

Despite the broad terms of s 10(2), the House of Lords unanimously held that it had to be read subject to the presumption against extra-territorial legislation and thus conferred a power to extend the application of the Act only to flights within British territory or between British territory and the territory of a foreign State. As Lord Griffiths put it:

> 'The basis of the rules that statutes do not have extra-territorial effect is the presumption that our own Parliament will not seek to intervene in matters that are legitimately the concern of another country. Countries respect one another's sovereignty and the right of each country to legislate for matters within their own boundaries.' (p 864)

The limitation of damages resulting from the crash of an internal Bangladesh flight was pre-eminently a matter within the legislative sovereignty of Bangladesh and, harsh as the decision is, it is undoubtedly correct.

Jurisdiction: effect of foreign public laws

Two cases raised questions about the effect within the United Kingdom of foreign public legislation.

In *Libyan Arab Foreign Bank v Bankers Trust Co* [1989] 3 All ER 252 (a case discussed in more detail in the chapter on Conflict of Laws), Staughton J had to consider the effect of United States executive orders imposing economic sanctions against Libya. The Libyan Arab Foreign Bank had a demand (or current) account with the Bankers Trust Co in New York and a call (or deposit) account with the London branch of the same bank. Both accounts were denominated in dollars. Under a managed account arrangement, a peg balance of US $500,000 had to be kept in the New York account. Each day Bankers Trust was entitled to transfer funds from the London account if the New York account fell below that balance and was required to transfer any surplus in the New York account to the London account. At 4.10 pm New York Time on 8 January 1986, a United States executive order froze all Libyan assets (including those of the plaintiff) in the United States or held by the overseas branches of United States banks. The plaintiff sued Bankers Trust claiming, inter alia, some US $131 million held in the London account at the time of the executive order and some US $161 million held in the New York account but which, the plaintiff argued, Bankers Trust should have transferred to the London account at 2.00 pm on 8 January, before the executive order was signed.

Staughton J found in favour of the Libyan Bank on both claims. He held that the London account was governed by English law not the law of New York (or any other part of the United States) and that the Libyan Bank was thus entitled to demand payment of all sums held in the account and the sum which, he held, Bankers Trusts should have transferred to the account. He accepted that the English courts would not require a party to a contract governed by English law to do something which would be unlawful by the law of the place of performance but held that the place of performance in this case was London. The fact that Bankers Trust might have to draw on dollar reserves in New York, an act which would have violated United States law, was irrelevant. Bankers Trust was not being required to perform in New York but would merely be equipping itself in New York for performance in London.

The position of Bankers Trust was an unenviable one. The executive order prohibited it from paying even the funds held in the London account. On the other hand, English law required it to pay over those funds. Bankers Trust did not seek to argue (though it wished to reserve the point for argument in the event the case went to the House of Lords) that the English courts should give extra-territorial effect to the executive order. Yet it is the attempt by the United States to apply economic sanctions on an extra-territorial basis which is at the root of the case. In a series of disputes stretching back many years successive United States administrations have sought to require United States companies with overseas branches not to honour obligations incurred under the laws of other States. In doing so they have forced a conflict between the principle that a State has jurisdiction over its own citizens and the principle of territorial jurisdiction. In the circumstances, they cannot expect the courts of other States to co-operate in the enforcement of such measures taken on a unilateral basis by the United States.

The rule that English courts will not enforce a foreign public law was discussed in *Re State of Norway's Applications (Nos 1 and 2)* (the facts of which are considered above). After reviewing the decision in *Government of India, Ministry of Finance (Revenue Division) v Taylor* [1955] 1 All ER 292, the House of Lords held that the rule did not go to the jurisdiction of the English courts (as stated in *Dicey and Morris on the Conflict of Laws*) but merely gave the court a discretion to decline to exercise its jurisdiction. Lord Goff, with whom the rest of the House agreed, also inclined to the view that the rule is rooted in considerations of public international law to the effect that one state had no right to assert sovereign power in the territory of another state. However, the House of Lords held that the rule did not prevent an English court assisting a foreign state to assert its sovereign powers within its own territory by collecting evidence for use in the foreign state. By seeking the assistance of the English courts in obtaining evidence which would be used in revenue proceedings in Norway, Norway was not attempting to enforce its public laws extra-territorially.

Coup d'état: Fiji

Following the coup d'état in Fiji in 1986, Fiji became a republic and ceased to be a member of the Commonwealth. In *R v Brixton Prison Governor, ex p Kahan* [1989] 2 All ER 368, the applicant tried to resist a request by Fiji for his extradition under the Fugitive Offenders Act 1967 by arguing that the Act was no longer applicable to Fiji now that Fiji had ceased to be a Commonwealth country. According to s 1 of the Act, the Act applied to requests from any Commonwealth country designated by Order in Council made under s 2 of the Act. Fiji had been designated by an Order made in 1970 which had not been repealed. The Divisional Court treated the matter as a simple question of construction and held that the fact that Fiji's membership of the Commonwealth had lapsed did not remove it from the list of designated countries or render the 1967 Act inapplicable to it.

The decision, it is submitted, makes good sense. If there is a problem, it is that the case highlights the fact that extradition arrangements concluded at a time when a state was a democracy will remain in place after that state has undergone major internal upheavals. The solution to that problem, however, cannot be crafted by the courts.

Coup d'état: Haiti

Following the overthrow of his government, the former President of Haiti fled the country. In 1986 the new government began proceedings in the French courts to recover some £120 million which it accused the former president of having embezzled. The Republic of Haiti later commenced proceedings in the English courts and obtained a Mareva injunction restraining the defendants (various members of the Duvalier family and their associates and a bank) from dealing with assets, wherever they might be located, which represented the proceeds subject to the French action, freezing the assets of the defendants within the jurisdiction and ordering the defendants' solicitors to disclose certain information about the whereabouts of those assets. The Court of Appeal held that the English courts had jurisdiction to grant an injunction regarding assets held outside the United Kingdom in view of the defendants' admitted intention of moving their assets out of reach of the courts and the skill they had already shown in doing so. The case (*Republic of Haiti v Duvalier* [1989] 1 All ER 456), thought Staughton LJ, was one which 'demands international co-operation between all nations' (p 467).

This case, like the Marcos litigation in the United States (reported in volume 81 of the International Law Reports) illustrates the difficulties facing states seeking to recover funds allegedly misappropriated by a former dictator. The decision of the Court of Appeal seems to be based upon the assumption that a foreign state with which the United Kingdom has diplomatic relations should be assisted in ensuring that the funds involved are not removed from the reach of the courts which will eventually try the action. The Court of Appeal also proceeded on the basis that a foreign state should, in general, be presumed to be acting in good faith. Thus, in considering an argument that an undertaking by the Republic of Haiti not to use information obtained by virtue of the injunction was insufficient unless the court had sufficient control over the Republic to ensure compliance, Staughton LJ said:

> 'It is difficult to see how, as a matter of law, the court *could* ensure that it had that degree of control over the Republic of Haiti, short of requiring a bank guarantee in a very large sum which could be called on in the event that the undertaking was broken. But I doubt if the court should make such a demand on a foreign sovereign state, or assume that it would be at all likely to break an undertaking given to the court.' (p 467)

If the undertaking was broken, he thought, the courts of the European states which might have to try the main action could be expected to take that breach into account in the exercise of any discretionary power which might be relevant.

Judicial review of the prerogative in foreign affairs

Ever since the decsion of the House of Lords in *Council of Civil Service Unions v Minister for the Civil Service* [1984] 3 All ER 935 (All ER Rev 1984, pp 1–5 and 251), the courts have asserted a right to review the exercise of some prerogative powers. In *R v Secretary of State for Foreign and Commonwealth Affairs, ex p Everett* [1989] 1 All ER 655 the Court of Appeal held that it had the power to review the decision of the Foreign and Commonwealth Office to refuse to issue a new passport to a British citizen resident abroad who was wanted for questioning by police in England. The decision is a welcome assertion of the power of the courts to review the grant or refusal of travel documents. The Secretary of State had argued that because 'the grant of a passport involves a request in the name of the Queen to a foreign power to afford the holder free passage and protection' and extends 'the protection and assistance of the Crown to the holder whilst he is abroad' (p 660) the power to issue passports had to be regarded as an aspect of the prerogative to conduct foreign policy—an area of prerogative powers generally conceded to be unreviewable. The argument was rejected by the Court of Appeal and Taylor LJ drew a clear distinction between matters of high policy in the conduct of foreign affairs and routine matters such as the issue of a passport which, as Taylor LJ noted, was no more likely to have foreign policy repercussions than decisions made under the Immigration Act which are, of course, subject to judicial review. The case is a timely reminder that not all prerogative powers which may have a bearing on foreign relations are necessarily immune from judicial review, although the courts (as both this case and *Maclaine Watson* make clear) will not review the exercise of the treaty making power or other powers which genuinely involve questions of high policy.

Shipping Law

R P GRIME, BA, BCL
Professor of Law, University of Southampton

In a commercial sense, the end of the eighties saw the revival of the shipping industry. Perhaps inevitably, however, the law reports in the penultimate year of the decade are full of the sad consequences of harder times: insolvency, default and even fraud.

Mortgagee's managers and ships

One example of the problems of lenders whose loans are secured on ships was provided by the latest stage in the long-running Maira litigation, *National Bank of Greece SA v Pinios Shipping Co No 1 and another, The Maira* [1989] 1 All ER 213. The 'Maira' was a 10,000 ton dry-cargo ship belonging to Pinios. In 1978, when little more than a year old, she blew up off Australia and became a total loss. The insurance did not cover the bank's claim. Several actions ensued. The instant litigation concerned the question whether *the bank* owed any duty to the shipowner with regard to the careful management of a ship.

The price of the 'Maira' had been secured by a first mortgage and 14 promissory notes in favour of the builder. The bank was guarantor of the promissory notes. Its guarantee was secured by a second mortgage. The first two promissory notes were dishonoured. At that point, the bank no doubt considered, as do many lenders on the security of commercial property in a falling market, that a better road to financial salvation lay in the continued exploitation of the ship than in foreclosure. It decided to put in a manager. This was done under a 'Tripartite Agreement' involving the bank, Pinios and Glafki Shipping as managers.

Glafki was a regular commercial ship–management company. As such, it was to play a fairly vigorous part, rather different from the sometimes quite passive role undertaken by ordinary mortgagee's managers. It was to have total control of the 'Maira', subject only to the bank's directions under the terms of the second mortgage. For all practical commercial purposes, it was to be owner. Pinios was very much the junior partner in these arrangements: indeed, it was strongly urged that the tripartite agreement had been forced on the shipowners.

It was a term of both first and second mortgages that the owners keep the 'Maira' insured to 130% of the amount secured. This Pinios had done on delivery, effecting cover valued at US$10 million: but the creditor was a Japanese yard, the debt was in yen and in 1978/9 the US dollar was depreciating rapidly against the yen. By the time the insurance came up for renewal, Glafki was in place and making all the management decisions: it renewed the insurance at the same level (in dollars) as had pertained in the expired year. Ten days later the 'Maira' exploded and there proved to be insufficient insurance moneys to pay the bank what its guarantee had cost.

When its guarantee had been activated, the bank had debited Pinios. It now demanded immediate settlement of that debt. Pinios sued Glafki for breach of the tripartite agreement, under which Glafki was obliged to maintain all insurances in accordance with the mortgages (ie to 130% of the value of the secured advances) and won in the Court of Appeal and the House of Lords: *Glafki Shipping Co SA v Pinios Shipping Co No 1, The Maira (No 2)* [1984] 1 Lloyd's Rep 660 (Hobhouse J); [1985] 1 Lloyd's Rep 300 (CA); [1986] 2 Lloyd's Rep 12 (HL). (The first litigation concerning the 'Maira' had been *Glafki Shipping Co SA v Pinios Shipping Co No 1, The Maira* [1982] 1 Lloyd's Rep 257 (CA on appeal from Parker J) in which the court held that the arbitrator did not have the power to impose a condition that Glafki, whom he suspected of using delaying tactics on Pinios' claim, put up substantial security before he would state a special case. History would seem to demonstrate that *someone's* delaying tactics were successful.)

Glafki proved to be a broken reed. So Pinios turned and sued the bank, alleging that it owed a duty to see that Glafki carried out its insurance obligations properly. At first instance, Leggatt J held 'on orthodox lines' that no such duty arose either in tort or under the tripartite agreement. The Court of Appeal agreed. Lloyd LJ gave the leading judgment, paying due respects to his 'educated reflex to facts' (see per Lord Goff in *Smith v Littlewoods Organisation Ltd (Chief Constable, Fife Constabulary, third party)* [1987] 1 All ER 710 at 736) which led him to favour the bank. It is, of course, a matter of refinement of taste, but Lord Goff's phrase in other contexts is regularly rendered as a 'gut reaction', or in transatlantic academia a 'judicial hunch'. However expressed, it cannot be a bad way to start the hunt for an implied term.

Lloyd LJ found no great difficulty in discovering that the terms of the tripartite agreement contained no obligation of the sort contended for. Pinios' interests were simply not catered for: power lay with Glafki, which was appointed to act for the bank. The bank did not undertake to look after the interests of Pinios: neither expressly nor impliedly. MacKinnon LJ's friendly creation, the officious bystander, was trundled out from his semi-retirement in the text-books and given a rare airing in the courts. Indeed, to press the metaphor further, he was invited to sit by the judge on the bench. Instead of having his naive intervention testily suppressed by the parties' common 'oh, of course', Lloyd LJ came close to putting into his mouth a much more apposite, even judicial remark:

> 'The argument was put concisely and forcefully by counsel for the defendants at the outset of his submissions as follows: "There was nobody to look after Pinios's interests, once the management agreement had been entered into. The bank owed a duty of care to those that it had deprived of the opportunity of protecting themselves." But in the course of developing his submission, counsel shied away from the "officious bystander" test. In this he was wise. For, so far from it being obvious that the bank would have agreed to the suggested implied term, it seems to me quite obvious that it would not. Why should it?'

Lloyd LJ may have added to the Moorcock literature. Certainly a 'why should it' test for terms implied in fact, introducing as it may concepts of economic interest and commercial practice, might move us back from the chimera of tacit agreement towards some more practical notion of reasonable implication.

So much for terms implied in fact. What of terms implied in law? Lloyd LJ considered the leading authorities, *Liverpool City Council v Irwin* [1976] 2 All ER 39 and *Lister v Romford Ice and Cold Storage Co Ltd* [1957] 1 All ER 125, and investigated the question whether the contract between Pinios and the bank was one of a class of 'contracts of a defined type', like sale of goods or employment, upon which standard legal duties might be imposed through the mechanism of a term implied by law. The answer was negative. Although an ordinary banking contract could easily be such, the tripartite agreement was 'a carefully drawn "one-off" contract between three parties, made for a particular purpose in special circumstances, and apparently making full provision for that purpose'. In any event, preferring Lord Wilberforce to Lord Cross in *Liverpool City Council v Irwin* Lloyd LJ required *necessity* for the implication of a term in law. There was none such here.

But would the law impose a duty of care on any other grounds? It was alleged that the bank had meddled in Glafki's decision-making on the renewal of the insurance, but that allegation failed on the facts. What of tort? Pinios had argued 'strenuously' on the basis of the 'much discussed and increasingly precarious dictum' of Lord Wilberforce in *Anns v Merton London Borough Council* [1977] 2 All ER 492 at 498. Perhaps surprisingly, Lloyd LJ's answer was taken from the speech of Lord Scarman in *Tai Hing Cotton Mill Ltd v Liu Chong Hing Bank Ltd* [1985] 2 All ER 947 (PC) at 957, to the effect that in a case where a plaintiff might arguably sue in contract or in tort, if he fails in contract he must necessarily fail in tort.

From a broad-based point of view of shipping law, *The Maira* may be seen as yet another case raising difficult issues about ship-managers, whose use is now everyday. Many of the assumptions of shipping law are tested by that common usage. Who is 'carrier'? What is the relevance of the manager's inaction in limitation proceedings? How does the manager fit the scheme of in rem proceedings? And this, the short but significant point, how is the duty to insure distributed?

On a further point, whether the bank could continue to treat Pinios as a regular banking customer for the purpose of charging compound interest for the period after the bank had demanded the sum due to it, the Court of Appeal found in favour of Pinios: the bank successfully appealed to the House of Lords. That appeal is reported at [1990] 1 All ER 78.

The ill luck of the 'Good Luck'

In *Bank of Nova Scotia v Hellenic Mutual War Risks Association (Bermuda) Ltd, The Good Luck* [1989] 3 All ER 628 the Court of Appeal was again dealing with an indirect consequence of bad times in shipping and again it ended by examining the same knotty conceptual questions on the borders of contract and tort as it had in *The Maira*. But the road travelled was very different.

The insurance of war risks in the marine market might have been designed to demonstrate basic principles of insurance law. War, of its nature, is a volatile business. Furthermore, apart from the unlucky chance of running down a derelict mine, the risks of war damage to an innocent merchantmen have, in a geographical sense, a kind of 'all-or-nothing' quality: a ship is either where the missiles fly or it is not. All this being so, it has long been apparent that the practice of insuring hulls for long (say 12 month) periods will not do for war risks. The chosen solution has a certain elegance.

War risks insurance is offered, at extremely low rates, for standard periods, essentially on condition that the insured vessel does not enter any area in which it is likely to suffer the effects of war. These areas are termed additional premium areas (APAs). They are made the subject of a negative undertaking by the insured, in the language of marine insurance, a warranty, strictly, a trading warranty. A 'warranty' in insurance law, much to the confusion of general common lawyers, is a 'condition which must be exactly complied with'. In *marine* insurance it is also traditionally considered to be a condition precedent to liability. Hence, in virtue of s 33(3) of the Marine Insurance Act 1906 'subject to any express provision in the policy, the insurer is discharged from liability as from the date of the breach of warranty', while remaining liable for claims arising before the date of the breach. If this provision be taken at its face value, rather than the insurer being granted the option to reject the claim or to affirm the cover, he is *automatically* 'discharged', subject to waiver (s 34(3)) and subject to 'any express provision in the policy'.

In war risk policies, such automatic effect is tempered by the 'express provision' of a 'held covered' clause. The effect of such a clause is to maintain the cover (to use a traditional formulation) 'provided notice be given to the underwriters immediately upon receipt of advices and any amended terms of cover and any additional premium required by them agreed'. Notice given in war risks cover leads to a very high premium for a very short stay (say 14 days), just enough to get in and out. In more modern policies, the language may be somewhat streamlined: they commonly contain a war risk trading warranties clause simply declaring that should the vessel enter an APA an additional premium is payable and that prompt notice of intention to enter should be given.

The temptations this system places before an impecunious shipowner are great. The real costs only accrue when he gives notice, which may be fine so long as he can pass those costs on to the charterer. But that depends on the terms of the charterparty, the attitude of the charterer and the market. It may not be possible. Furthermore, war risk policies rarely place the shipowner under any *obligation* to give notice and pay the additional premium: many allow for the option of uninsured entry, with suspension of cover—although in such a case the insurer is likely to wish to reserve his position on whether the cover be continued after the suspension and, if so, on what terms.

So why not take a chance? If the shipowner's luck holds, he gets in and out undamaged and slightly wealthier. If it does not, an apologetic late notice can always be given shortly after the event: a notice closely followed by a claim. And what then is the legal position? Clearly a breach of contract has been committed in the lateness of the notice. And the insured is therefore liable in damages. But he is still, on the face of it, insured: particularly so under the terms of a modern war risk trading warranties clause. And what is the correct measure of damages? What have the underwriters lost? The shipowner will be more than willing to pay the additional premium.

One escape-route from this underwriters' dilemma was provided by Hirst J in *Black King Shipping Corp and Wayang (Panama) SA v Massie, The Litsion Pride* [1985] 1 Lloyd's Rep 437. A shipowner who tried his luck in this way found himself by the same token providing evidence of lack of good faith, thus enabling the insurer to repudiate liability under s 17 of the Marine Insurance Act 1906, which declares contracts of marine insurance to be contracts uberrimae fidei. The decision was a little unexpected and caused some doubts, since it appeared to impose upon the assured some 'post-contractual' duty of disclosure, somewhat contrary to the spirit of ss 18, 19 and 21 of the Marine Insurance Act 1906 (the non-disclosure sections): a point which weighed heavily with the Supreme Court of New South Wales, which refused to follow *Litsion Pride* in *New South Wales Medical Defence Union v Transport Industries Insurance Co* (1985) 4 NSWLR 107.

The Good Luck gave the Court of Appeal the opportunity to examine the ramifications of this dilemma further. The ineptly-named vessel was owned by the ironically-titled Good Faith Shipping Co SA. She was regularly chartered to Iranian interests for voyages into the Arabian Gulf (an APA) during the Iran/Iraq conflict. Such charterers might be expected to be unwilling to meet the additional premiums. Rule 20 of the rules of the defendant war risk club, in the usual way, allowed for entry into an APA either *on* risk on payment of the additional premium, or *off* risk, with cover temporarily suspended. In either case, prompt notice had to be given to the club. Perhaps to deal specifically with *The Litsion Pride* problem, the rule also strengthened the underwriter's hand by expressly conferring on the club the specific power to reject claims if prompt notice had *not* been given.

Entry without notice ('trying one's luck') was not permitted by the rules. It brought into operation rule 25. This applied the regime of s 33(3) of the Marine Insurance Act 1906, as traditionally understood, generally to the situation where the shipowner/member failed to obey such 'orders, prohibitions, directions or recommendations' as the directors of the club were entitled to give. It was accepted that the designation of an area as an APA operated as such a 'prohibition'. Thus, on undeclared entry, in virtue of s 33(3), a vessel would automatically go off risk.

As in *The Maira* there was a bank. The whole Good Faith fleet was mortgaged to the plaintiff. The security lay in the vessels or, in the event of loss, the insurance proceeds. Appropriate assignments and loss payable clauses in the policies were therefore necessary. Further, to protect its interest the bank specifically required of the shipowner that if entry to a war zone was contemplated proper notice be given not only to the insurers but also to the bank, and that the additional premium be paid. Thus, as a condition of the mortgage, uninsured entry was forbidden.

None the less, Good Faith ships traded in the Gulf without declarations. The club managers noted this and a meeting was held with Good Faith, but to no practical avail. Eventually, as might perhaps have been predicted, the 'Good Luck' while at Bandar Khomeyni was hit by a missile and lost. The suspicions of the club managers were immediately aroused and eventually the claim was rejected. While all this was happening, Good Faith was re-scheduling its debts. The bank had agreed to make advances of two thirds of the book-value of the fleet: taking account of the rolling over of existing debt, that left some $2,679,120 to be drawn down as working capital by Good Faith. The 'Good Luck', or its insurance proceeds, accounted in that calculation for $4.8 million gross. Its removal would have so reduced the level of 'permitted advances' as to leave it more than $500,000 short of what was required to roll over existing debt: nothing at all should have been drawn down in cash.

The issue before the court was whether the bank had a claim against the club. Presumably, the falling shipping market in 1982 had rendered the arithmetical balance of security after the deduction of the 'Good Luck' (of around $21.4 million) of theoretical value only. At first instance, Hobhouse J ([1988] 1 Lloyd's Rep 514) found as a fact that, had the bank known of the doubts surrounding the 'Good Luck', that vessel would not have appeared in the security and held that the club was under a duty towards the bank. That duty, he further held, derived from the express terms of the letter of undertaking given by the club to the bank. The purpose of this document is primarily to declare that the policy (in the case of a mutual insurance association, the certificate of entry) is held to the order of the bank. The club undertakes to insert and operate a loss payable clause whereby all or part of the proceeds of any claim would be paid directly to the bank as secured lender. However, the letter also contained an express undertaking to advise the bank if the club ceased to insure or if any of the ships ceased to be entered in the club. Hobhouse J held that the fact that the 'Good Luck' had, to the knowledge of the club (or its managers) been up the Arabian Gulf without declarations, and thus had become 'automatically' uninsured in virtue of the operation of rule 25 and s 33(3), was a matter which should have been communicated to the bank under that paragraph.

He further held the club to be in breach of an implied obligation to inform the bank when the latter was about to be defrauded, but did not impose upon the club a general 'duty to speak' deriving from an obligation of uberrima fides. There was, he said, also a duty of care, of which the club was in breach. The club appealed. The bank cross-appealed against the finding by the judge that their relationship with the insurer was not one of the utmost good faith.

The judgment of the Court of Appeal was delivered by May LJ. It was radical. The first belief challenged was the traditional analysis of a warranty. In non-marine insurance, the effect of a breach of warranty is exactly the same as the effect of a breach of condition in the general law of contract: the insurer, the innocent party, may repudiate or affirm at his option. The contract is, as some say, voidable not void. Thus the automatic discharge of the underwriter from liability as from the date of the breach, without prejudice to liability incurred beforehand, if it is to exist, must be a peculiar rule of *marine* insurance. The language of the 1906 Act certainly supports that peculiarity but closer investigation discloses a more complicated picture. First, as May LJ pointed out, the position before the Act was far from clear: the first draft of s 33(3) used the traditional 'voidability' approach. Second, and perhaps in explanation of the confusion, the automatic effect must be qualified by the possibility of waiver by the insurer, which must of necessity occur after the breach. It is more than a debating point that a void obligation cannot be resuscitated.

The true difficulty arises from the economical use of language among marine insurers: the same form of words is used for provisions designed to delimit the risk (eg 'warranted free from capture and seizure') which can easily be seen to operate as conditions precedent to the underwriter's liability, and *promissory* warranties, that a state of affairs will continue to exist (eg trading warranties, that the vessel will not enter, etc), which are much less easy so to understand. The point was accurately identified by Donaldson J, as he then was, in *de Maurier (Jewels) Ltd v Bastion Insurance Co Ltd* [1967] 2

Lloyd's Rep 550 and he concluded that, even in marine insurance, 'breach of a warranty of a promissory character . . . rendered the contract voidable'. May LJ, therefore, held that s 33(3) was to be understood as 'enacting the same rule as that which applies . . . to breach of express promissory warranties in the field of non-marine insurance'. Thus the breach by Good Faith of rule 25 did not render their ships 'uninsured' for the purpose of the club's letter of undertaking. The club was in breach of no expressly undertaken obligation.

The significance of this re-examination of the legal significance of a warranty in marine insurance cannot be underestimated. The analysis is convincing, the conclusion rational. The legacy is not simply that the lawyers will now need to distinguish between warranties that are and warranties that are not conditions precedent to liability, which may not prove too difficult, but that insurers will now need to be aware of the risks of delay or inaction when faced by a breach of warranty. No longer may they rely upon the protection given by the 'automatic' discharge of s 33(3).

Hobhouse J had gone beyond the terms of the letter of undertaking. He had further found the club to be in breach of other duties owed to the bank. It had been urged upon him that the relationship created by the letter of undertaking was one of the utmost good faith. This he had rejected, but he had concluded that the club might have *some* 'duty to speak', almost incidentally giving strong support to the proposition of Hirst J in *Litsion Pride* that duties (deriving from utmost good faith) might persist after the moment when the contract was concluded. In his careful analysis, he relied heavily on the advice of the Privy Council in *Tai Hing Cotton Mill Ltd v Liu Chong Hing Bank Ltd* [1985] 2 All ER 947, a case whose declaration of policy towards the overlap between contract and tort was so seriously considered by Lloyd LJ in *The Maira*. He also made much use of the judgment of Steyn J in *Banque Keyser Ullman SA v Skandia (UK) Insurance Co Ltd* [1987] 2 All ER 923, a case very similar to the present save that the security lay in gemstones not ships and that the insurance used as collateral security was 'credit insurance', direct insurance of the borrower's ability to repay, rather than insurance of the primary security. Hobhouse J, like Steyn J, had taken very great care to distinguish between a duty which might give rise to damages and one which might give rise merely to other 'remedies', such as an estoppel or rescission. Clearly, while 'rescission', or resisting a claim, is the usual remedy sought by an insurer for non-disclosure, damages were the only sensible remedy here. However, like Steyn J, he had discovered an ordinary common law duty of care. There was ample evidence of failure by the club to take reasonable care to avoid reasonably foreseeable risks of loss by the bank. Like Steyn J, he found breach and awarded damages.

The Court of Appeal had two advantages over Hobhouse J: since his decision, Steyn J in the *Banque Keyser Ullman* case had been reversed on appeal (sub nom *Banque Financière de la Cité SA v Westgate Insurance Co Ltd* [1989] 2 All ER 952) and Lloyd LJ had discussed the matter still further in *The Maira*. May LJ approached the problem from a slightly different angle. First, if there was a relationship of uberrima fides between the club and the bank, that relationship could not bear an action for damages. In this conclusion he applied a dictum of Slade LJ in the *Banque Keyser Ullman* litigation in the Court of Appeal and expressly disapproved a contrary dictum of Hirst J in

Litsion Pride. He expressly approved (surely obiter?) the main proposition of *Litsion Pride*, however. Where there was utmost good faith, the duty to speak could exist in both pre- and in post-contractual forms. But, so derived, it was not a term of the contract, despite what had been said in the Court of Appeal and the House of Lords in the hallowed case of *Blackburn Low and Co v Vigors* (1887) 12 App Cas 531 (HL), rvsg (1886) 17 QBD 553 (CA).

Nor could it be a tort, and for four reasons: like duress and undue influence, non-disclosure derived from the equitable jurisdiction to relieve from imposition, which did not carry with it damages; *CTI v Oceanus* [1984] 1 Lloyd's Rep 476, in which a Court of Appeal consisting of Stephenson, Kerr and Parker LJJ had rather surprisingly held a non-disclosure operative despite the fact that it had no discernible effect upon the insurer because it *would* have affected a *prudent* insurer, demonstrated that consequential loss (or no) was irrelevant; the right to damages was not in the contemplation of the draughtsman of the Marine Insurance Act 1906; the obligation to disclose was absolute and any tort would be a tort of strict liability.

So the principle of *uberrima fides* is neither contract nor tort, gives no claim for damages and arises by operation of law. Without deciding exhaustively, or in general terms, where it might arise, May LJ was satisfied that it did not arise in the relationship between club and bank. It could not be applied to the letter of undertaking because, as Hobhouse J had held, that was a 'straightforward commercial contract' not in need of such equitable addition. Nor could the good faith which clearly applied in the insurance contract be utilised for the benefit of the bank through the 'assignment' of the club membership (if it were so) contained in the letter of undertaking.

Nor was there any room for the implication of any duty to speak outside the doctrine of utmost good faith into the contract between the club and the bank on other, common law, grounds. The letter of undertaking was complete in itself and the possibility of default, even fraud, by the Good Faith group was clearly in the contemplation of both the club and the bank. The club did not expressly undertake the obligation to 'shop' the shipowner: to imply such an obligation would have unjustifiably extended the obligation that was expressly undertaken. No implied term meant that, utilising the approach of the *Tai Hing* case, there should be no tort either.

Two points might be made. First, while it is always welcome to have principles stated in terms as wide as possible, there is one very important commercial fact about club insurance which might have been thought to have a special bearing on the issue. Protection and indemnity associations, the Clubs, operate on mutual principles. These are more than historical curiosities. Despite the Clubs now being universally incorporated, for obvious tax reasons, they are still to a remarkable extent run by their members, the assureds. To have imposed upon the managers the duty to make full disclosure to a member's bank would not have made much sense in the real world.

The second point is this. The overlap, or gap, between contract and tort has been one of the more intractable theoretical legal questions of the eighties. The problems are great: there are difficulties in the extent of duty, the nature of the obligation, the measure of damages. In 1989, we have seen the Court of Appeal in both *The Maira* and *The Good Luck* exhaustively examining questions of the use of tort duties in contexts more usually considered contractual. In both, careful and complex journeys have reached precise and specific negative conclusions. More simple-minded commentators had thought that a shorter and easier path had been provided by Lord Brandon in *Leigh & Sillavan Ltd v Aliakmon Shipping Co Ltd, The Aliakmon* [1986] 2 All ER 145.

What is TOVALOP?

There is a hoary old story regularly trundled out after law students' dinners, in which Serjeant Sullivan (or possibly F E Smith) responds to the tetchy judicial intervention: 'Surely Serjeant Sullivan (or possibly Mr Smith) your client has heard of the maxim *res ipsa loquitur* (or possibly *volenti non fit injuria*)?' with: 'In the part of Ireland (or possibly Wales) from which my client comes it is almost the sole topic of conversation.' It is tempting to think that there might have been the chance of performing the story for real, changing the subject-matter to TOVALOP and the actors to the crofters of the Shetlands in *Esso Petroleum Co Ltd v Hall Russell and Co Ltd (Shetland Islands Council, third party), The Esso Bernicia* [1989] 1 All ER 37.

The advantages of suing shipbuilders after accidents, particularly those which create great liabilities, have been well known since the Amoco Cadiz litigation. In December 1978 the Esso Bernicia struck a number of mooring dolphins at Sullom Voe and spilt a large quantity of bunker oil. The resulting bills picked up by Esso amounted to £4,695,376.42. Esso sued Hall Russell, the builders of the tug Stanechakker, which had caught fire because a failed joint had deposited hydraulic fluid onto a hot exhaust pipe while assisting the Esso Bernicia to berth, leading her to cast off the towline and so precipitating the collision between the tanker and the dolphins. It also sued the manufacturers of the towing winch aboard the Stanechakker whence the trouble had emanated, and the operator and the owner of the tug. Hall Russell joined four other parties, including the Shetland Islands Council, the employer of the pilot aboard the Esso Bernicia at the time of the collision. By the time the case got to the House of Lords, there were but three parties left: Esso, Hall Russell and the Shetlands Islands Council.

The case came to the Lords before proof, as had another famous Scottish proceeding, on the questions of law only. Of these, there were essentially three. First, could the manufacturers of the tug be liable for the consequences of the collision between the tanker and the jetty; second, how much could Esso recover; third, was the council liable for any negligence of the pilot. Only the first was at all easy. Lord Jauncey, who delivered the only comprehensive speech, had no doubts that the allegation of negligence was worth examination. The Stanechakker had been built for the specific purpose of berthing tankers at Sullom Voe. It could hardly be argued that its failure could not foreseeably cause damage and oil pollution there.

The second issue was much more complicated. Of the sums claimed by Esso only some £170,000 related to damage to the vessel and loss of the bunker oil: the total included over half a million paid to the crofters and over four million to the terminal operators. Both crofters and terminal operator had claims under TOVALOP (Tanker Owners Voluntary Agreement Concerning Liability for Oil Pollution) for pollution and, in the case of the terminal operator, clean-up costs and the costs of arbitration, but the terminal operators had also had a separate claim for damage to the jetty. The legal regime of most UK harbours is governed by the Harbours, Docks and Piers Clauses Act 1847, s 74, or an equivalent, which makes the owners of vessels causing damage to harbour installations strictly liable.

Esso's first argument was that, having paid the crofters and the terminal operator under TOVALOP, it was subrogated to their rights against whoever was legally liable for the collision. Subrogation is a principle most commonly met with in insurance: an insurer who has settled a claim is subrogated to the rights of the assured pertaining to the matter of the claim. But the underlying principle is wider.

> 'I know of no foundation for the right of underwriters, except the well-known principle of law that where one person has agreed to indemnify another he will, on making good the indemnity, be entitled to succeed to all the ways and means by which the person indemnified might have protected himself or reimbursed himself for the loss,'

said Lord Cairns in *Simpson & Co v Thomson* (1877) 3 App Cas 279 at 284. If Esso, when paying the crofters and the terminal operator under TOVALOP was an indemnifier, then they would be subrogated.

But how? In the ordinary insurance situation, the insurer settles and conducts proceedings against the third party in the name of the assured. The power to do this without the active cooperation of the assured is maintained by an express subrogation clause in the policy and by the so-called 'equity' wherewith the courts will intervene to require the assured to permit an action to go ahead in his name. In practice, the procedure is short-circuited by the insurer bringing an action against the assured and the third party in which he seeks an order that the assured authorise him to proceed against the third party. The insurer still as a matter of law does not proceed in his own name but in the name of the person indemnified. But here there was no thought of the crofters or the terminal operator suing Hall Russell. The action had begun with Esso as pursuers and the others were now time-barred.

Esso argued that an exception to the general rule might be found where they, the subrogated claimants, had themselves suffered physical damage (as they had) as a result of the same negligence. In support of this, Esso in effect argued for a necessary exception to the rule in *Cattle v Stockton Waterworks Co* (1875) LR 10 QB 453. That case is usually considered to support the substantive proposition that A cannot sue for economic loss suffered by him because of damage to B's property. But the language of 1875 cast the proposition in terms beguilingly similar to those used in subrogation: 'can Cattle sue in his own name for the loss which he has in fact sustained in consequence of the damage which the defendants have done to the property of Knight . . .' said Blackburn J. Lord Jauncey would have none if it. *Cattle* was not about subrogation: see *Candlewood Navigation Corp Ltd v Mitsui OSK Lines Ltd, The Mineral Transporter* [1985] 2 All ER 935 and *The Aliakmon* [1986] 2 All ER 145.

Could Esso make the same claim substantively? They had an action against Hall Russell, could their payments under TOVALOP appear as a head of damage? There is no difficulty in principle. According to the arbitrary irrationality which passes for logical distinction in the law of tort, financial loss suffered in consequence of physical damage is recoverable, provided that the physical damage is to the claimant's own person or to property which he owns. All other financial loss is economic loss and irrecoverable. So the question was whether the payments under TOVALOP were a consequence of the damage to the Esso Berenicia. The answer was negative. Had the payments been made under the Civil Liability Convention, the answer would have been different: there the shipowner would have been legally liable to make good the damage and costs in virtue of the Merchant Shipping (Oil Pollution) Act 1971. Indeed, the making good of the damage to the dolphins and the jetty was recoverable as a head of damage in Esso's claim, since Esso was strictly liable for that under the Harbours, Docks and Piers Clauses Act 1847 and the Zetland County Council Act 1974. TOVALOP was a 'gratuitous contract of indemnity'.

To what extent is TOVALOP a 'gratuitous' contract? It is rather more than an ad hoc voluntary agreement between tanker-owners. TOVALOP is administered by the International Tanker Owners' Pollution Federation Ltd, 'the Federation'. Application to join TOVALOP is made to, and accepted by, the Federation and, although by the terms of TOVALOP the Federation undertakes no liabilities, members must inform the Federation and the Federation may (and does) play a role in dealing with the consequences of spills. In practice, claims, though routed through the members, are met from liability insurance. The Federation must be satisfied of a member's insured capacity to pay and to that end has set up the International Tanker Indemnity Association Ltd, a specialised mutual insurance club. In short, TOVALOP may be slightly more than a member's club. It may even be that the contract of membership is made with the Federation. If a member failed to meet a proper claim, could the Federation enforce the membership rules? Could it do so at the behest of an unpaid claimant? These questions have not been posed, let alone answered. But it is not impossible that a participating member of TOVALOP might be legally required to meet the obligations laid upon it by the agreement.

None the less, it is quite clear that in a legal system which does not recognise a jus quaesitum tertio the crofters could not have sued Esso on TOVALOP. This was crucial for Lord Jauncey. For Lord Goff, who also addressed the question, the matter might be put more broadly. 'The damage to the ship did no more than trigger off the event which led to the pollution in respect of which Esso became bound under the terms of TOVALOP to make the payments . . .' The payments were not losses consequent upon the physical damage. They were a separate head of damage, irrecoverable under *Simpson & Co v Thomson* or *Mineral Transporter*. With respect, this seems to be a narrow and perhaps unrealistic approach to the question of the causal connection. Everyone, certainly every reasonable tug-builder, knows of TOVALOP and that tanker-operators are all members. Since 1969, the shipping world has operated on the basis that if a tanker spills oil, its operator pays at least some of the consequential costs. Why should such costs not be as recoverable as the businessman's car-hire after a traffic accident has laid his vehicle up for a week?

Lord Goff, as might be expected, examined the possibility of restitution, but only to reject it. Since payments under TOVALOP did not decrease the rights the crofters or the terminal operator might have to sue Hall Russell, the latter could not be said to have been enriched. So Esso had no claim in restitution.

The final point in the case takes us to the extremely difficult waters sailed by the 'Towerfield': the decision of the House of Lords in *Workington Harbour and Dock Board v Towerfield (owners)* [1950] 2 All ER 414. In that case a ship went aground damaging both itself and the harbour partly because of the negligence of the harbour authority and partly through the negligence of a compulsory Trinity House pilot. The case arose before the coming into force of the Law Reform (Contributory Negligence) Act 1945. The House held that s 15 of the Pilotage Act 1913 which rendered a shipowner 'answerable' for loss or damage caused by faulty navigation while the vessel was under compulsory pilotage meant that the owners were not only responsible for the damage to the harbour but were unable to claim for the damage to their own vessel. The case was difficult because the clear purpose of s 15 was to abolish the defence of compulsory pilotage: the thrust of the section is in its final words: 'the owner or master . . . shall be answerable . . . in the same manner as he would if pilotage were not compulsory.' A long line of authority has established that a shipowner is liable for the negligent navigation of a ship when in receipt of the services of a voluntary pilot, but has not clearly established the legal basis of that liability. The purpose of s 15 is clear. By giving the meaning they did to 'answerable' the House had avoided the difficult unanswered question. Is he a servant pro hac vice? An independent professional adviser?

The pilot of the Esso Bernicia was employed by the Shetland Islands Council, the pilotage authority under the Sullom Voe, Shetland Pilotage Order 1976, SI 1976/1541. Hall Russell averred that he was their servant and that they were vicariously liable for his negligence. The contention failed. First, because a pilot was an independent professional who in fact operated as principal not agent of the pilotage authority when aboard the ship. That must be an accurate conclusion. Pilots do so act. They advise the navigators from their special knowledge. Furthermore, the Pilotage Act, as interpreted, makes the use of pilotage services responsible. There is no room for ordinary employer's vicarious liability. So the rule in *The Towerfield* is to be maintained. Which some might think harsh on shipowners.

In rem, arrest and charterers

The need to come to terms with different concepts of arrest and in rem proceedings has been brought to the forefront by the passage of the Civil Jurisdiction and Judgements Act 1982. In the Review for 1988, we noted *The Nordglimt* [1988] 2 All ER 531, a case which concerned inter alia the question whether art 57 of the Jurisdiction Convention (enacted by the 1982 Act) preserves any jurisdiction based on arrest, despite the express prohibition thereof in art 3, through its recognition of other conventions which 'govern jurisdiction'. The Arrest Convention 1952 is not of itself a jurisdiction convention. It regulates the arrest of ships, a procedure which in many countries has no jurisdictional relevance. It does, however, somewhat indirectly, envisage the possibility of jurisdiction based upon arrest conferred by domestic law. The Arrest Convention was enacted in jurisdictional terms in the UK. Hobhouse J held that jurisdiction 'recognised or granted by the 1952 convention' was so preserved. In *The Linda* [1988] 1 Lloyd's Rep 175 and *The Deichland* [1988] 2 Lloyd's Rep 454, Sheen J, fortified by the decision in *The Nordglimt* asserted a jurisdiction in rem which was not caught by the exclusive 'domicile of the defendant' principle of the Jurisdiction Convention. *The Deichland* has now gone to appeal ([1989] 2 All ER 1066).

The case concerned rusty steel coils. The cargo owners issued a writ in rem while the ship was demise-chartered. The writ was served, service being acknowledged by the demise-charterers, but the vessel was never arrested, since the P & I club issued a letter of guarantee, in the usual way. Between issue and service of the writ, the demise charterparty had ended: the charterers acknowledged service only to contest jurisdiction. The ground was the Jurisdiction Convention. They were domiciled in the Federal Republic of Germany. Sheen J held that the proceedings were in rem, not against the defendants, until the defendants entered an appearance (acknowledgement of service to protest jurisdiction was clearly insufficient), after which the case could proceed in personam on the basis of a submission to the jurisdiction, an allowed exception to the 'domicile principle' of the Jurisdiction Convention (art 18). 'The special purpose of an action in rem,' said the judge, 'is to induce the owner of the res to submit to the jurisdiction of the court.' A rousing statement of the procedural theory, indeed. And not one which sits easily with the sharp distinction he drew between the action in rem which was not to be considered to be in breach of art 2 of the Convention requiring 'persons' to be sued in the countries of their domicile.

The Court of Appeal (Neill, Stuart-Smith LJJ and Sir Denys Buckley) allowed the appeal. A demise charterer of a ship served with a writ in rem was being 'sued' in the courts in which the writ was issued. Neill LJ said, at p 1074:

> 'I have come to the conclusion that the right approach when one is considering the effect of an international convention is to take account of the purpose or purposes of the convention. Plainly the 1968 convention was intended, inter alia, to regulate the circumstances in which a person domiciled in one contracting state might be brought before the courts of another contracting state "in civil or commercial matters". Accordingly, it seems to me that all forms of proceedings in civil and commercial matters were intended to be covered except in so far as some special provisions such as art 57 might otherwise prescribe.'

And art 57 did not so prescribe: for what was preserved was jurisdiction granted by other conventions. The 1952 Arrest Convention granted jurisdiction only in respect of 'arrest'. The difference between arrest and other proceedings falling short thereof (release on bail, club letters, etc) was not unknown to those who drafted the convention. Indeed it was recognised in arts 3 and 6. If the English court had jurisdiction over the 'Deichland', it had it in virtue of ss 20 and 21 of the Supreme Court Act 1981, not in virtue of any implementation of the Arrest Convention.

An even firmer assertion of the procedural principle. And a decision which must be seen as true to the purpose of the Jurisdiction Convention. The lesson to EEC shipowners is clear: always be sure to get a club letter quickly. Only actual arrest is allowed to make a breach in the domicile principle, so *The Nordglimt* stays, as does *The Linda*.

Misdelivery and theft

A short point arose for decision by Hirst J in *Cia Portorafti Commerciale SA v Ultramar Panama Inc and others, The Captain Gregos* [1989] 2 All ER 54. If the carrier steals the cargo, can he take the benefit of the one-year limitation period in the Hauge–Visby Rules, art III, rule 6?

The answer was negative. The rule speaks of 'all liability whatsoever in respect of the goods'. This formulation replaced the Hague Rules provision: 'all liability in respect of loss or damage'. The shipowners invited Hirst J to rely on the powerful dicta of Lords Wilberforce and Scarman in *Gatoil International Inc v Arkwright–Boston Manufacturers Mutual Insurance Co* [1985] 1 All ER 129 (noted all ER Rev 1985 at 238), the interpretation might be 'reinforced' by reference to the travaux préparatoires. The cargo-receivers, on the other hand, pressed the argument, supported by equally strong dicta of Kerr LJ in *D/S A/S Idaho v Peninsular and Oriental Steam Navigation Co, The Strathnewton* [1983] 1 Lloyd's Rep 219, that the rules had to be read as a 'package', which would confine the operation of art III to the 'Risks' as set out in art II. This would exclude *all* misdelivery, since art II envisages a carriage of the goods concluding with a discharge under the contract.

Hirst J adopted a 'broad and purposive' approach, adopted the 'package' analysis and concluded that 'as a matter of construction that misdelivery, whether dishonest, honestly intentional or merely mistaken, is entirely outside the scope of the rule.' If, however, he was wrong, recognising the 'cautious criteria' laid down by Lord Wilberforce, he found nothing in the Stockholm Conference to 'support a view that there was a legislative intention that the time limit should apply in such cases, of which the present case is alleged to be an instance': that is *deliberate* misdelivery by the carrier.

The case has gone to appeal. A Court of Appeal consisting of Bingham, Stocker and Slade LJJ unanimously reversed Hirst J on 14 December 1989. The decision has not yet been reported: the appeal was adjourned for further consideration of the points in the case raised by the reversal. Clearly, there is much more to be said on the matter.

A pound ain't worth what it used to be . . .

The Rosa S [1989] 1 All ER 489 concerned a very valuable shipment. A complete aluminium casting and rolling plant was consigned from Livorno to Mombasa in 222 cases. The carriage was subject to the Hague Rules, unamended, unadorned. One case was damaged: the loss was put at £K107,758.53. Article IV, rule 5 limits liability to '£100 per package'. The question for Hobhouse J was: how much is £100?

The French text (the only authentic test of the Hague Rules) made it clear that pounds sterling were envisaged, rather than Kenyan pounds. The argument for the cargo-receivers, however, was that those pounds should be understood as 'sterling gold value': in other words, gold sovereigns. Although they are no longer used in the shops, gold and silver coinage still exists as recipients of the Queen's maundy money, and a few dealers, will testify. They are defined by the Coinage Acts, currently, the Coinage Act 1971, which declares, in Sch 1, the official gold content of the sovereign as 798,805 milligrams of gold of millesimal fineness of 916.66. The calculation gives a per package limit of £K6,491.25. Not much as compared to £K107,758.53, but better than nothing. And Hobhouse J held in favour of cargo.

Maritime lawyers are well used to gold-standard currency: this was the standard method adopted to avoid the excesses of currency fluctuations before the use of the standard drawing right of the International Monetary Fund. The unit commonly used was the gold, or Poincaré, franc. But when used, it tends to be specifically referred to in the substantive part of the relevant convention (eg the 1957 Limitation Convention) and precisely defined by it. In 1924, however, the draft Hague Rules referred simply to £stg100. In the final version, however, there appeared art IX, which begins: 'The monetary unit mentioned in this Convention are to be taken to be gold value.' A statement more obviously meaningful at a time when the pound sterling *did* have a gold value in ordinary commerce.

When the Hague Rules were enacted, various solutions were offered. The US Carriage of Goods by Sea Act 1936 replaced £100 with $500 and had no truck with gold value. The UK Carriage of Goods by Sea Act 1924 compulsorily incorporated the draft Hague Rules into relevant bills of lading, but with the addition of the first sentence of art IX: a decision which led to disagreement. One view was that the 'English' Hague Rules intended £stg100 in contracts governed by English law and £100 gold value in contracts governed by foreign laws. But in *The Rosa S* there could be no such problem, for it was the Hague Rules 'raw', unsullied by legislation, that this contract incorporated. Put crudely, therefore, the question was whether the reference to £100 referred to money of payment or to money of account. Only if it were the former could an argument be raised in favour of 'real' pounds. It was not and the cargo-receivers were entitled to a little bit more.

In *Brown Boveri (Australia) Pty Ltd v Baltic Shipping Co, the Nadezhda Krupskaya* [1989] 1 Lloyd's Rep 518, the Court of Appeal of the Supreme Court of New South Wales, approved and followed the decision of Hobhouse J in an exactly similar case, as part of a 'stream of overseas authority'. It cannot be denied that the decision fits well with international expectations.

Salvage in the Thames: again

The Powstaniec Wielkopolski [1989] 1 All ER 198 is a kind of footnote to *The Goring* [1988] 1 All ER 641 (All ER Rev 1988 at 268, 1987 at 226). Three tugs rendered salvage services to the defendant ship in the Gravesend Reach of the River Thames, which is part of the Port of London. The owners resisted payment on the grounds, inter alia, that s 742 of the Merchant Shipping Act 1894, the general definition section, so defined 'tidal water' as to exclude 'harbour'. If *The Goring* had decided that true salvage services could be rendered only in tidal waters, did that not therefore exclude from salvage services rendered in harbours?

The point had been identified but not settled by Lord Brandon in *The Goring*. The predecessor of s 742, s 476 of the Merchant Shipping Act 1854, included in salvage services rendered 'upon the High Seas or within the Body of a County', a phrase which had presented its own problems for the court in *The Goring* but which at least made no special disposition for harbours.

Further, between 1854 and 1894 services rendered in tidal harbours were treated as salvage: *The Tees, The Pentucket* (1862) Lush 505 and *The Zeta* (1875) LR 4 A&E 460 both concerned events in the Thames. Did the definition section of the 1894 Act change the law? If it had, the change had not been noticed. Five cases had been found in the reports dated after 1894 in which services rendered in Gravesend Reach had been duly rewarded as salvage.

No, it did not, held Sheen J. First, because the 1894 Act was a consolidation statute. Second because that construction would be contrary to public interest. The public interest his Lordship found in two places. On the one hand the clear policy that voluntary salvage should be encouraged. On the other, the provisions of para 3 of Sch 5 to the Merchant Shipping Act 1988 which assumed that tidal harbours were covered for salvage by making special provision for non-tidal parts directly connected thereto.

Having identified the desired end, Sheen J proceeded towards it. As a matter of construction, it was not necessary to incorporate the detailed definition contained in the 'harbour' heading in s 742 (which actually includes 'estuaries and navigable rivers') in order to provide a working meaning of the word 'harbour' as incidentally included in a succeeding heading in the same section, that of 'tidal water'. What then *does* 'harbour' mean in the context of 'tidal water'? Sheen J did not make that clear, save to say that a ship in the Gravesend Reach was clearly not in harbour. No doubt it would be in harbour if tied up to wharf. But when the services were rendered to the 'Powstaniec Wielkopolski' she was moored fore and aft, awaiting a berth, apparently taking on bunkers from a bunkering barge. Clearly, some further difficult lines have yet to be drawn.

Norwegian fish in the House of Lords

In the All England Law Reports Review for 1988 we commented on the case of *Forsikringsaktieselskapet Vesta v Butcher and others* [1988] 2 All ER 43 (All ER Rev 1988 at 266) in the Court of Appeal. That court had decided that British reinsurers were obliged to reimburse Norwegian insurers on a reinsurance contract in London form governed by English law despite there being a clear breach of a warranty which would have afforded a complete defence in English law and practice. The reason was that such a breach did *not* afford a defence in Norwegian law and the insurers' exposure that was reinsured arose from a Norwegian policy. All documents had been drafted in similar, English, form by the brokers whose idea the scheme was. The insurers had paid and were now asserting a 'to follow settlements' clause in the reinsurance contract: such a clause obliges reinsurers to follow settlements reached by insurers. The reinsurers asserted a 'claims management' clause, also in the reinsurance policy, which granted to the reinsurers 'sole control' of the negotiations. The Court of Appeal had cut *that* Gordian knot by interpreting the 'claims' over which the management clause granted control to the reinsurers as 'claims in accordance with Norwegian law', thus avoiding Hobhouse J's flirtation with the 'hybrid' conflicts of law solution of having the reinsurance contract *partly* governed by Norwegian law (see [1986] 2 All ER 488).

This point was appealed to the House of Lords and is reported as

Forsikringsaktieselskapet Vesta v Butcher and others (No 1) [1989] 1 All ER 402. Lord Lowry, who delivered the main speech, effectively affirmed and reinforced the approach adopted in the Court of Appeal. A reinsurance contract, as he clearly and exhaustively demonstrated, is a contract of indemnity: it indemnifies the insurer for his liability on the insurance he has written. In this context it does not matter that the two policies may not be perceived as interactive or 'back-to-back'. Even in the English reinsurance contract, the 'failure to comply' with the 24-hour watch warranty could only mean 'relevant' or 'causative' failure to comply. Which meant relevant in the context of the Norwegian insurance policy.

A short clear answer to a complicated point, with no appeal to any legal principles more abstruse than those governing the interpretation of contract terms. The speech of Lord Lowry is however notable not for its brevity but for its careful analysis, clear common-sense and understanding of the commercial realities. Such is also the tenor of the shorter concurring speeches of Lords Templeman and Griffiths. In the view of their Lordships, the problem lies not so much in the balancing of irreconcilable interests but in making practical sense of confused and confusing language. Lord Griffiths was particularly explicit. It is not merely the practice of incorporating contradictory clauses such as the 'claims management' and the 'to follow settlements' clauses into the one document, but the basic method of writing reinsurance on the same terms as insurance. As Lord Griffiths pointed out, 'The two contracts are dealing with entirely different subject matter.' Lord Bridge virtually confined his intervention in the case to the following comments:

> 'I wish also to record my concurrence in the views expressed by my noble and learned friend Lord Griffiths regarding the relationship normally to be found between contracts of insurance and contracts of reinsurance. I entirely agree with him as to the desirability of the Lloyd's standard form of reinsurance being redrafted in grammatical, intelligible and unambiguous language. The only people who can expect to profit from the obscurities of the present Form J1 are the lawyers.'

The first Lloyd's policy was reputedly settled about 1779. That was described by Buller J, in an oft-quoted phrase, as 'an absurd and incoherent instrument' (*Brough v Whitmore* 4 TR 206). That case was reported in 1791. Between 1982 and 1984 the Lloyd's policies were comprehensively re-drafted. Plus ça change.

The more interesting part of the Court of Appeal decision was its readiness to uphold the claim of the Norwegian insurers, Vesta, against the brokers, Bain Dawes, who in a commercial sense were the creators of the whole scheme. It will be remembered that the court, following *General Accident Fire and Life Assurance Corpn v Tanter, the Zephyr* [1985] 2 Lloyd's Rep 529 (CA), was not only prepared to impose a duty of care in the fixing of the reinsurance (despite it having been arranged long before the insurance itself), but was also prepared to apply the Law Reform (Contributory Negligence) Act 1925 and make adjustments to take account of the insurers' own carelessness, despite the obligations having arisen ex contractu. This development has attracted judicial attention in several cases, amongst them the *Banque Keyser Ullman* litigation and *The Good Luck*. It seems a pity that this aspect will not apparently reach the House of Lords.

Set-off and freight in the House of Lords

In *Colonial Bank v European Grain and Shipping Ltd, The Dominique* [1988] 3 All ER 233, reviewed All ER Rev 1988 at 257, Mustill LJ, giving the judgment of the Court of Appeal, allowed a charterer in a freight prepaid voyage charterparty to deduct from the freight owed a claim against the shipowner based on the repudiation of the charterparty. In so doing, he departed from the ancient rule that the right to freight is absolute, which had been affirmed by the House of Lords in *Aries Tanker Corp v Total Transport Ltd, The Aries* [1977] 1 All ER 398, surviving even the introduction of the equitable doctrine of set-off by the unification of law and equity. *The Aries* he distinguished on the grounds that the right to freight had never been held to survive the termination of the charter through the shipowner's repudiation.

The decision has now been reversed by the House of Lords. The appeal is reported *sub nom Bank of Boston Connecticut v European Grain and Shipping Ltd, The Dominique* [1989] 1 All ER 545. Lord Brandon gave the judgment of the court. It was admitted that the absolute right to freight survived non-repudiatory breach: Lord Brandon simply did not accept the distinction adopted in the Court of Appeal. There was no set-off whatever the nature of the breach. He offered three reasons, two practical, one theoretical.

First, a breach may be non-repudiatory and cause more damage to the charterer than a repudiation. That must be the case so long as repudiation is defined in any way which is not determined by the consequences of the breach. Second, the value of the set-off depends upon the financial worth of the carrier: nothing is lost if he is solvent and available. Freight can be paid and he can be sued. There may be much in this, but if the argument was made otherwise than by Lord Brandon, one might have suspected a degree of disingenuousness. The solvent available carrier may sometimes seem almost mythical.

The third point turns upon the nature and consequences of frustration, to which repudiatory breach is conceptually similar. Lord Brandon pointed out that the common law rule of frustration was that losses and gains lay where they fell except upon total failure of consideration for payments due before frustration: *Fibrosa Spolka Akcyjna v Fairbairn Lawson Combe Barbour Ltd* [1942] 2 All ER 122. This simple pattern had been replaced by the 'elaborate code' of the Law Reform (Frustrated Contracts) Act 1943. But the 1943 Act expressly excluded from its operation voyage charterparties. The only reason for that would be the need to preserve the 'indefeasibility of an accrued right to advance freight'. It should similarly be preserved in circumstances of repudiation.

In the Court of Appeal, Mustill LJ had appealed to the principle of fair dealing in commercial matters, relying in part on the dicta of Lord Denning in *Federal Commerce and Navigation Ltd v Molena Alpha Inc, The Nanfri* [1978] 3 All ER 1066. It was pointed out that Lord Denning in *Henriksens Rederi A/S v T H Z Rolimpex, The Brede* [1973] 3 All ER 589, a case directly in point, had made an equally fervent appeal to the principle of security of commercial transactions. Lord Brandon seems to agree with Lord Denning's earlier thoughts.

Solicitors

BRIAN HARVEY, MA, LLM
Solicitor, Professor of Property Law, University of Birmingham

A review of 1989 reveals rather less activity concerning the work, status and professional position of solicitors in the courts than in the debating chambers of the legislature. This years' cases have nevertheless thrown a certain amount of light on a few important areas of everyday activity.

Access to prisoners

Can a Chief Constable give instructions to his force whose effect is to encourage his senior officers to deny access to persons held in police custody by named solicitors' clerks? This was the issue posed in *R v Chief Constable of the Avon and Somerset Constabulary, ex p Robinson* [1989] 2 All ER 15.

As Mann LJ explained in the Court of Appeal, which was adjudicating on an application for judicial review, the applicant was a solicitor from a firm specialising in legal aid defences in criminal cases concerning the black community in Bristol. As the judge mordantly remarked—this is not a remunerative field of activity. Evidence was given that in order to be economic it was necessary to employ persons who had no professional qualifications to attend at the interviews of suspects. In fact the five clerks named in the proceedings were employed by companies controlled by the applicant ie service companies—formed for fiscal reasons and operating without objection from the Revenue or the Law Society. The clerks were regarded as being, in effect, employed by the applicant.

The answer lay in the correct interpretation of the *Code of Practice for the Detention, Treatment and Questioning of Persons by Police Officers* issued under s 66 of the Police and Criminal Evidence Act 1984. That Act, by s 58, entitles a person arrested and held in custody in a police station or other premises 'to consult a solicitor privately at any time'. This entitlement is expanded by the provisions of the Code which enables a solicitor to send a clerk or legal executive to provide advice on his behalf 'unless an officer of the rank of inspector or above considers that such a visit will hinder the investigation of crime and directs otherwise'.

A preliminary question was—who is 'a clerk or legal executive?' The meaning of 'legal executive' was thought to be obvious, but the meaning of a 'clerk' was not so self-evident. The learned judge suggested 'that the person must be a "clerk" genuinely so-called and not someone recruited, so to speak, off the streets masquerading as a clerk.' If that is the case the police are entitled to exclude him from the station. However, if a person is ostensibly capable of giving advice the Court of Appeal was of the opinion that the police could not refuse admission on the basis that the quality of the advice would be poor. Nevertheless the Court of Appeal expressed itself as being anxious about quality. Whereas under the Duty Solicitors Scheme the solicitor's representative in these circumstances must have had at least three years experience of criminal defence work, no such provisions apply where a solicitor is privately chosen. The Court of Appeal asked the Law Society to 'consider urgently' whether the Duty Solicitors Scheme requirement should not be made general.

The problem in this case was that the clerks nominated by the Chief Constable in his advice to his senior officers were 'well known to officers of the Bristol division', and in one specific case the clerk had a conviction for conspiracy to defraud. The Chief Constable therefore adopted a device of issuing instructions to his force naming the clerks in question and, without issuing a 'blanket ban', stating: 'It is my opinion that there will be very few occasions on which it would be appropriate to allow this man access to persons in custody.'

The Court of Appeal concluded that the Chief Constable had paid scrupulous regard to the 1984 Act and to the Code. His instructions recognised that the decision was one for the individual police officer who must decide whether such a visit might hinder the investigation of a crime. The Chief Constable's instructions were therefore not contrary to para 6.9 of the Code. The Court of Appeal, in dismissing the application, nevertheless drew attention to paragraph 6.10 of the Code under which in the circumstances the Inspector must notify the solicitor of the refusal of access and give that solicitor an opportunity of making alternative arrangements:

> 'However, inspectors do not inform the solicitor why his clerk was refused an attendance. This seems to us to be a wise practice because of the risks of an action for defamation. A result of the present proceedings has been that the chief constable has undertaken to inform a solicitor why a particular clerk has been refused presence at an interview' (at 21).

This case reveals a state of affairs of which our much vaunted system of criminal justice can hardly be proud. The solicitors doing important work in inner city areas are entitled to be paid properly for their activities. Equally, persons in custody are entitled to advice of proper quality. It is much to be hoped that the Law Society is able to accept the Court of Appeal's invitation to improve the working of this area of activity.

Costs in criminal cases

Attention is drawn to a Practice Note appearing at [1989] 2 All ER 604. Amongst other things Part VIII deals with 'awards of costs against solicitors'. Rule 8 amplifies the procedure to be followed where the court in the exercise of its inherent jurisdiction over officers of the court orders a solicitor personally to pay costs thrown away by reason of some improper act or omission on his part or that of his staff. Reasonable notice must be given to the solicitor of the matter alleged against him before such an order is made, and that solicitor must be given a reasonable opportunity of being heard in reply. Significantly the Practice Note goes on to state:

> 'There is no power to award costs to be paid personally by counsel but where counsel acts under legal aid the court may make observations to the determining authority.'

There have been reported cases in the last few years where the fault as a result of which costs have been thrown away has been entirely, or almost entirely, that of counsel. It is surely high time that this discriminatory distinction was properly reviewed, if necessary by the legislature.

Costs in civil cases

In *King v Weston-Howell* [1989] 2 All ER 375 the Court of Appeal had to consider a technical point as to the costs consequential on failure to pay a sum into court. In this case, involving medical negligence, the defendant had admitted liability. Twelve days before the trial on the issue of quantum was due to begin the plaintiff's solicitors provided particulars of the damages claimed. The defendant would have in fact paid £290,000 into court but considered on existing authority that it was now too late to do so and the trial on quantum proceeded. Judgment was later given for the plaintiff for £276,651. The trial judge held, amongst other things, that, the plaintiff's solicitors should personally pay part of the defendant's costs. This was because it was alleged that the solicitor's conduct, principally in palpable delay in providing particulars of the damages claimed, had had the effect of unduly prolonging the trial and depriving the defendant of the opportunity to make an effective payment into court.

To cut a complex story short, it was held that there was nothing in RSC Ord 22, r 1(1) which provided that a payment into court made less than 21 days before the trial was ineffective. Such a payment would be effective and the defendant had not been deprived of his protection in costs. It followed, therefore, that the plaintiff's solicitors could not be made personally liable on the basis adopted by the trial judge. Previous authority, particulary *Bowen v Mills & Knight Ltd* [1973] 1 Lloyd's Rep 580 was overruled.

Actions for negligence against solicitors

The limitation on the solicitor's immunity from negligence in litigation is, as *Cordery on Solicitors* (8th edn 1988) trenchantly states; 'a solicitor acting as an advocate is immune from an action for negligence in and about the conduct of his client's case in court' (at 142). This statement is founded on the House of Lords' decision in *Saif Ali v Sydney Mitchell & Co (a firm)* [1978] 3 All ER 1033, [1980] AC 158 and *Rondel v Worsley* [1967] 3 All ER 993, [1969] 1 AC 191. The question arising in *Somasundaram v M Julius Melchior & Co (a firm)* [1989] 1 All ER 129 was whether this immunity extends to solicitors advising a convicted person on the plea to a charge, particularly where the plea was decided upon on the advice of counsel.

The facts, in brief, were that the plaintiff had been charged with the unlawful and malicious wounding of his wife whom he had stabbed during an argument. His initial instructions to his solicitors were that he intended to plead not guilty, relying on the defence of accident or self-defence. The plaintiff subsequently changed his story in such a way that it was clear that a not guilty plea was not sustainable. At a conference with counsel the appellant stuck to his revised story and counsel consequently advised him that he had no defence. The appellant then decided that he would plead guilty, which in the event he did and he was sentenced to a term of imprisonment, reduced on appeal to 18 months.

In the view of May LJ it was possible that the appellant changed his story in the hope of achieving some reconciliation with his wife. At the time there were serious matrimonial difficulties and the respondents were acting as his solicitors in the matrimonial proceedings between him and his wife. The appellant then alleged that because of this background his solicitors had 'over persuaded' him to change his story and plead guilty. The appellant alleged negligence. A master had ordered that the appellant's action be struck out on the ground that it disclosed no reasonable cause of action and was frivolous and vexatious and an abuse of process. This decision was upheld by the judge. The appellant then appealed to the Court of Appeal.

The Court of Appeal made it clear that the appellant had no reasonable chance of establishing negligence and that consequently this claim could be struck out as being frivolous and vexatious. However, a more fundamental question was (a) whether the civil action was an abuse of the process of the court (in that the appellant was seeking to attack in civil proceedings the final decision of a criminal court of competent jurisdiction), and (b) whether the respondents were immune from suit in respect of the allegations of negligence and there could therefore be no case to answer in any event.

With regard to the legitimacy of challenging a final decision of the criminal court through a civil appeal, in this case the Court of Appeal held that it was an abuse of the process of the court for the appellant to bring this action. It necessarily involved an attack on the conviction and sentence imposed by the Crown Court and upheld in the Court of Appeal, Criminal Division, subject to a reduction in the sentence. The Court relied on the decision of the House of Lords in *Hunter v Chief Constable of West Midlands* [1981] 3 All ER 727, [1982] AC 529, and Lord Morris's speech in *Rondel v Worsley* [1967] 3 All ER 93, [1969] 1 AC 191, where the public policy reasons for this principle were fully expanded.

The remaining ground on which it was submitted that the action for negligence against the solicitor should be struck out was based on the principle of immunity from suit, as set out above. On this most important point, the Court of Appeal accepted that it was well established that advice as to a plea is something which is so intimately connected with the conduct of the litigation that it can fairly be said to be a preliminary decision affecting the way that the cause is to be conducted when it comes to a hearing, and therefore within the immunity. It was submitted here that such immunity must extend to a solicitor. The Court of Appeal stated that in previous cases the solicitor's immunity was limited to the occasions when acting as advocate (eg in the magistrates' or county courts or, occasionally, in Crown Courts where solicitors have rights of audience). Could it be, here, that there was therefore a difference between the immunity of counsel and of a solicitor when advising on plea in a criminal case at which counsel appeared as advocate? It is clear that the Court of Appeal here, and courts in previous cases, were reluctant to extend this immunity further than was deemed to be necessary in the interests of justice in public policy. Accordingly, although it was not necessary to the decision here, the Court of Appeal stated that this immunity does *not* apply to solicitors when a barrister has also been engaged to advise. It follows, therefore, that a solicitor is theoretically exposed to a negligence action in these circumstances. However, it does not therefore follow that the solicitor has *in fact* been negligent since, as the Court of Appeal here pointed out, to get the solicitor before the court at all would probably involve a civil court adjudicating on a final criminal decision (which it cannot do). Even if the civil court were able to proceed, if the advice as to plea was later confirmed by counsel, any action against the solicitor would almost certainly fail either because the solicitor would submit that he had been advised by counsel and was not therefore negligent, or on the matter of causation since counsel's intervention broke any link between the solicitor's advice and the eventual plea. For all these reasons the aggrieved prisoner's appeal was dismissed.

Legal professional privilege

Problems concerning the extent of the right of a solicitor to refuse to produce documents on the ground of privilege occur almost annually in the All England Law Reports. 1989 brings its own clutch of cases on this point.

In the first one, *R v Governor of Pentonville Prison, ex p Osman* [1989] 3 All ER 701, the Queen's Bench Divisional Court had before it a complex appeal concerning Mr Osman, who had applied for habeas corpus. The events centred on the affairs of a Malaysian bank operating in Hong Kong as a deposit-taking company. This case, incidentally, usefully indicates how the extremely sophisticated loan-syndication frauds were alleged to have operated, but the point of immediate relevance here was an incidental one. The magistrate had ruled that certain documents were admissible under s 11 of the Fugitive Offenders Act 1967 and s 68 of the Police and Criminal Evidence Act 1984 although there was a claim for privilege in respect of some of these documents.

The point arose in this way. The magistrate had found that there was evidence of an agreement in Hong Kong for the applicant to accept corrupt payments. It was alleged that these payments could be traced into the hands of two Malaysian solicitors, both of whom acted for Osman. To help establish these facts, the prosecution sought the evidence of the two solicitors. When that evidence was being taken, there was an objection that all communications between Osman and his solicitors were privileged. That objection was overruled when taken, so the evidence was on the file. The point was then re-argued before the magistrate. Counsel for the respondents argued that the argument was ill-founded because (1) many of the documents produced by the solicitors were not privileged on any view (eg simple accounting documents not connected with the purpose of Osman obtaining advice), (2) privilege could not be claimed for any communication between Osman and his solicitors if the purpose of the communication was the furtherance of crime (*R v Cox and Railton* (1884) 14 QBD 153), and (3) even if the communication would have been privileged under English law or practice, the evidence was now available and it was therefore too late to argue privilege. The documents were now to hand. Privilege had in previous proceedings been unsuccessfully argued abroad, and there was nothing now to prevent them being used.

With regard to the important point as to whether a communication between a solicitor and his client is not privileged because its purpose was for the furtherance of crime, it was held here that the court was entitled to look at the document in question without requiring the party who objects the claims of privilege to prove by evidence au dehors the document that it came into existence for the purpose of furthering crime. And the Divisional Court here confirmed the principle that provided the evidence has not been obtained with impropriety and is then available to the court, a claim for privilege protects the client against the production of the documents; it does not affec their admissability in evidence once produced (see *Calcraft v Guest* [1898] QB 759, [1895–9] All ER Rep 346.

Privilege

Re Konigsberg (a bankrupt), ex p the trustee v Konigsberg [1989] 3 All ER 289

These proceedings arose out of events leading up to the bankruptcy of Mr K. Mr and Mrs K jointly owned the matrimonial home. At a time when Mr K was in financial difficulties and a writ had been issued against him by the Commissioners of Customs and Excise, Mr and Mrs K conveyed the property into Mrs K's sole name, the transfer being expressed to be 'in consideration of natural love and affection'. Mrs K then re-borrowed sufficient money to discharge the existing mortgage and various other debts including solicitors' costs. Shortly afterwards a receiving order was made against Mr K and he was adjudicated bankrupt in January 1986. In July 1986 the trustee in bankruptcy asked for a declaration that the transfer was a voluntary settlement and void against the trustee under s 42 of the Bankruptcy Act 1914. The wife swore an affidavit claiming that she was not aware at the time of the transfer that the bankrupt was in serious financial difficulties, and claimed that the transfer was for valuable consideration. She denied that she understood the significance of the words 'in consideration of natural love and affection'. The solicitor acting for the parties swore an affidavit filed on behalf of the trustee directly contradicting the wife's assertion that the transfer was for valuable consideration. The wife's response to this was to seek an order that the solicitor's affidavit and its exhibits be excluded from the hearing of the trustee's motion since it related to communications between the solicitor and both clients or the solicitor in his joint capacity and the wife alone. Her counsel conceded, however, that this could not be taken too far, since counsel could not expect to succeed in an application to exclude all the solicitor's evidence if his own client had put in evidence already what she claimed to have told her solicitor. It would be unfair to allow only Mrs K's version for the matter to be received in evidence when her solicitor contradicted it. Accordingly, the claim for privilege extended only to communications between the solicitor and the bankrupt and Mrs K jointly and between the solicitor and Mrs K alone. It did not apply to evidence in the solicitor's affidavit rebutting evidence given by Mrs K at the hearing of the trustee's motion as to such communications.

Distilling the essence of this rather complex case, the first question was whether, where two parties employ the same solicitor, communications between them and their solicitor, in his joint capacity, should be disclosed in favour of the other. *Phipson on Evidence* (13th edn 1982) clearly states that in these circumstances there is no legal privilege relating to these communications. The only exception is where communications are made to the solicitor in his *exclusive*, rather than joint, capacity. This proposition was not really challenged by Mrs K's counsel. The crucial question was whether the trustee in bankruptcy could be said to stand in the shoes of Mr K for the purpose of the rule, or whether the trustee is to be treated as a third party. If the trustee was simply a third party then it was a sustainable proposition that one joint client, Mrs K, could insist on the maintenance of privilege (to the extent that she had not waived it) even if the other joint client was prepared to waive it: see *Rochefoucauld v Boustead* (1896) 65 LJ Ch 794.

Dubai Bank Ltd v Galadari and others [1989] 3 All ER 769

This case concerned the problem of whether an affidavit prepared for one set of proceedings can be ordered to be produced, for the purposes of evidence, in unrelated proceedings.

Here Mr M was a former employee of a company controlled by the defendants who had dismissed him. He had a claim against the company, not in issue in the present proceedings, for wrongful dismissal. He swore an affidavit in November 1985, disclosed in the present action, but never having been filed. This affidavit which had been disclosed in the present action referred to an earlier affidavit. The original of the earlier affidavit was not in the possession of any of the parties, but the solicitors of the first two defendants did have in their possession a copy of it. The first two defendants objected to the disclosure of that copy on the ground that it was protected by 'legal professional privilege' because a copy was sent to the solicitors so that they could advise the first and second defendants in respect of the claims which Mr M was then making for unfair dismissal, a claim unrelated to the present proceedings.

Dillon LJ, in an appeal against the judge at first instance who had rejected the claimed privilege, found it necessary to examine the basis of the privilege asserted. It lies, of course, in the principle that a client should be able to confide fully in his solicitor on the basis that communications so made should be kept secret unless revealed with his consent. Otherwise it would not be possible properly to conduct litigation.

The judge neatly avoided the issue on the facts by finding that (a) the claimed privilege would only apply to a document made by the defendants themselves for the purpose of obtaining legal advice, (b) that the onus of establishing privilege is on the party refusing to disclose the relevant document and (c) an alternative reason for the existence of the photocopy of the affidavit passed by the defendants to their solicitors was that it was for the purpose of service in the contemplated proceedings. On the latter basis privilege could not be asserted on the facts, since the document was clearly intended for the public domain. There was a further reason in law why the document could not be privileged.

In law, privilege would not have attached to the original affidavit since it had not been brought into existence for the purpose of obtaining legal advice for assembling evidence for trial. The fact that a photocopy of the affidavit had been made for the purpose of obtaining legal advice did not thereby confer privilege on the photocopy. In reaching this conclusion a number of previous authorities were considered and some doubt was thrown on the decision of the Divisional Court in *R v Board of Inland Revenue, ex p Goldberg* [1988] 3 All ER 248, [1989] QB 267. But the underlying difficulty in the case for the second defendant, alleging privilege, was (as Farquharson LJ pointed out at 776) that he had to submit that the copy of the document which he had made for the purpose of obtaining legal advice is the subject of privilege when the original document clearly was not. It followed that in so far as *ex p Goldberg* decided that copy documents relating to a lay client's tax affairs supplied to a Queen's Counsel became privileged when supplied to counsel by the taxpayer, although the original documents could not in themselves attract privilege, *ex p Goldberg* was disapproved.

None of this affects the general principle, however, that documents and copies of documents brought into existence by *solicitors* for the purpose of litigation are privileged. Equally, documents prepared by the client for the purpose of litigation for the obtaining of legal advice remain privileged on the same basis. The *Dubai Bank* case makes it clear that photocopying a non-privileged document for use in other circumstances does not confer a magical new status upon it!

Sport and the Law

EDWARD GRAYSON, MA
Barrister, South Eastern Circuit

Introduction

Sport and the Law made its debut in these pages, to coin the standard sporting phrase, for the All ER Annual Review 1987 during 1988: the year when Butterworths published my book *Sport and the Law*. As I explained on that occasion, it

> 'listed 200 reported cases which are merely the tip of a more discoverable iceberg from the last 100 years. Their ripples extend beyond any single boundary. During 1987 four separate judicial areas swam into the sporting world.'

During 1989 not only did five judicial examples surface; the year also witnessed British sport's most disastrous experience with 95 fatalities at Sheffield Wednesday's Hillsborough Stadium at the FA Cup semi-final between Liverpool and Nottingham Forest. That led concurrently to the first of two Reports of a Judicial Inquiry into the tragedy conducted by Lord Justice Taylor and the acceleration of the Football Spectators Act 1989, both of which were published within the twelve month span of 1989.

Furthermore, the year began and ended with generous references and citations from *Sport and the Law* by two of my learned friends. In Public Law for 1989 at 95 Michael J Beloff QC published a paper he had read to the Bar Conference at the end of 1988 in which he concluded, at 110:

> '. . . it is often the case that, once the courts have shown the willingness to intervene, the standards of the bodies at risk of their intervention tends to improve. The threat of litigation averts its actuality.
> There is therefore no reason why the field of sport cannot define law's new or at any rate next, frontier; and if Britain can no longer head the world in sport itself, perhaps it can do so in sporting litigation.'

David Pannick concluded an address to the Central Council of Physical Recreation's 18th National Conference of Sport and Recreation in December 1989 with a suggestion that

> '. . . it might be that the way forward for sports law was the creation of an expert sports tribunal to hear appeals from the decisions of sports bodies. The advantages of such a scheme would be to ensure the development of expert and consistent principles in this complex area and the probability that courts would be even less likely to interfere with the decisions which were reached.'

The flaw inherent in that last reasoning is that no sports tribunal, however expert, would ever be advised responsibly to usurp the function of the courts in the areas where they were called upon to intervene during 1989 for civil compensation for violent foul play; criminal custodial sentencing for similar illegality; taxation disputation with the Inland Revenue; and the rights or wrongs of unfair or unreasonable disciplinary process (irrespective of the overriding principle against ouster of the courts' jurisdiction: *Scott v Avery* (1856) 5 HL Cas 811, 10 ER 1121; *Enderby Town Football Club Ltd v The Football Association Ltd* [1971] 1 All ER 215 at 219c). Those examples together with Lord Justice Taylor's Interim Report (Cm 765), the Football Spectators Act, and a re-enacted section within the Finance Act 1989 relating to expenditure on stands at sports grounds, all point towards a continuing inevitability linking the law with sport for its own self-protection and the protection of all associated with it.

Civil compensation for violent foul play

Three developments during 1989 all suggest that the manner in which the Court of Appeal in *Condon v Basi* [1985] 2 All ER 453 upheld a Warwick County Court judicial award of £4,900 for a broken leg, suffered in a violent foul soccer tackle, based upon a claim in negligence, and an unappealable award of £5,400 for a similar injury incident pleaded as trespass to the person twenty years ago, in *Lewis v Brookshaw* which I noted in the New Law Journal (1970) vol 120 at 413), have yet to filter through to players of all levels.

The Daily Mirror for 7 February 1989 alone recorded that a claim by Tottenham Hotspur's former England international, Danny Thomas, against Queen's Park Rangers and one of its former players, Jim Maguire, for ligament injuries suffered in a foul tackle, resulting in a loss of career as a professional footballer, was settled for a sum of £130,000.

No other known reference to this appeared in the national press; and its lack of jurisprudential novelty, but interest from the quantum standpoint in respect of loss of a professional career, is consistent with the comment of another learned friend, Oliver Wise. He drew my attention to a further county court award with which he had been concerned professionally during 1989. At Basingstoke County Court a kick to an opponent during the course of play, which was adjudicated to have been deliberate on the spur of the moment, resulted in two nights in hospital and an award of £400 general damages for a claim of trespass to the person. He commented to me that it may not contribute to jurisprudence. Yet it does illustrate a sanction which sporting governing bodies cannot impose (*Vermont v Green*).

Further during 1989, a chance meeting with Judge John A Baker, DL, at Kingston-upon-Thames County Court during a lull in court business resulted in a casual inquiry whether a judgment which he had delivered in the Epsom County Court a few years earlier for a soccer playing injury would be of interest and assistance for the *Sport and the Law* archives. The response was positive and with the generous assistance of the county court staff it is possible to acknowledge that 1989 was the year in which it became possible to record that at Epsom County Court in 1983 His Honour Judge John A Baker DL awarded £400 general damages, £5.80 special damages and costs for a head butt (pleaded as a civil assault in trespass to the person) during a soccer match which resulted in a broken nose and black eyes to a 38 years old player in a local league match (*Hewish v Smailes*).

Finally, bearing in mind that the London Court of Appeal in *Condon v Basi* (supra) adopted the judgments of two Australian sources, Barwick CJ and Kitto J in *Rootes v Shelton* [1986] ALR 33, a negligence claim for injuries suffered from a water-skiing accident, it is appropriate to record a judgment of Finlay J in the Australian Supreme Court during 1989 in which he awarded damages of $A 121, 490 in a claim for civil assault and negligence brought by one jockey against another. A broken thigh and back was suffered by the injured plaintiff in a fall caused by the defendant's horse under his rider's guidance crossing in front of two other runners as reported in the Racing Post for 19 and 26 May 1989: *Fraser v Johnston*.

The categories of sporting negligence are never closed; and anyone who considers that the world of sport is capable of doing justice to victims and protecting its domain against violent offenders should recall how the Football Association was constrained to deal with the Arsenal defender, Paul Davis, who broke the jaw of a Southampton opponent, Glenn Cockerill, in full view of millions of tv spectators shortly before 1989. He was fined £3,000 and banned from playing in nine matches. The FA was unable, of course, to order compensation to the victim.

Criminal liability for violent foul play

1989 marked another notch in the ratchet of penal consequences for breaches of Rugby Law 26 or Soccer Law 12 which prohibit violent foul play. The principles for prosecuting in such circumstances are of more than a century's antiquity but were reaffirmed by the Court of Appeal, Criminal Division, as relatively recently as 1975 in *R v Venna* [1975] 3 All ER 788 (793 f-g) explaining, '*R v Bradshaw* (1878) 14 Cox CC 83 [the first traceable prosecution for a soccer-playing injury] can be read as supporting the view that unlawful physical force applied recklessly constitutes a criminal assault'.

A century later the first ever prosecution for a rugby-playing offence was recorded in *R v Billinghurst* [1978] Crim LR 553. A fractured jaw in two places from an off-the-ball punch in a club rugby match in South Wales was indicted as inflicting grievous bodily harm, contrary to s 20 of the Offences against the Person Act 1861; the conviction after a not guilty plea resulted in a 9-months suspended sentence. During the next ten years the sentencing pattern zig-zagged from 6 months custody reduced on appeal for a fractured jaw, nose and cheekbone to 2 months custody (*R v Gingell* [1980] Crim LR 661); via one month custody on a guilty plea to common assault for causing concussion in an off-the-ball rugby union match, reduced on appeal to one month suspended for a year (*R v Bishop* (1986) *Times*, 12 October), to 6 months custody for an ear bite after a tackle in a policy Rugby Union match on a conviction for inflicting grievous bodily harm with intent, contrary to s 18 of the Offences against the Person Act 1861, which was confirmed on appeal: *R v Johnson* (1986) 8 Cr App R (S) 343.

In 1988, however, after an opponent in an amateur rugby match suffered a broken cheekbone when kicked on the ground during the course of play, an 18 months custodial sentence was imposed at Bristol Crown Court (*R v Lloyd* (1988) *Times*, 15 September). In the same year at St Albans Crown Court this level of custody was imposed on a soccer player who caused concussion by kicking an opponent on the ground, and after a jury had failed to agree on a s 18 Offences against the Person Act 1861 indictment, he pleaded guilty to causing grievous bodily harm without the element of intent under s 20. He was nevertheless sentenced to 18 months custody (*R v Chapman*).

On appeal, during 1989 that St Albans Crown Court 18 months sentence was affirmed without the authorities considering a necessity to report this development. The significance, however, of that decision, together with the fragmented and personal manner in which the civil compensation awards levels have come to my attention, is that this particular area of adjudication is essentially a legal lottery.

In the case of *R v Johnson* (supra: the police officer who was convicted of biting an opponent's ear) counsel conducting the appeal prayed in aid the variation of one month's custody on a guilty plea of common assault to a suspended sentence of one month for a year, in the case of *R v Bishop* (supra: a former Welsh international rugby player). Lord Lane CJ commented as recorded in *Sport and the Law* 19, 20 that Bishop may 'consider himself lucky to be treated so leniently'. Correspondingly, in November 1989 the Criminal Appeal Office Index Supplement to the 43rd edition of *Archbold* noted a decision attributable to Tudor Evans J that 6 months was too harsh and 2 months was substituted for kicking an opposing player and causing a wound which required 13 stitches, although he was also fined £100 by West Wales Football League and banned for two years from playing any type of football (*R v Shervill*, 6 June 1989 No 2635-W-89, transcript p 13).

Insurance and school sport

Any doubts about the law being required to fill the gaps which sport cannot fill in the circumstances cited above should be dispelled by a report published in the 16 April 1989 issue of the Sunday Mirror by its medical correspondent, Alan Burns. He cited the findings of the Institute for the Study of Children in Sport. There, according to its director, Dr Martin Lee, a study carried out at Bedford College of Higher Education on 160 children disclosed that, 'More than 33 per cent of ten-year-olds are prepared to commit a foul to gain an advantage'.

This figure was comparable to that disclosed a decade earlier by two Guys Hospital doctors as recorded in the British Medical Journal for December 1978 and in *Sport and the Law*. J E Davies, Research Registrar, now the honorary physician to the Welsh Rugby Union and medical officer to the British Lions, and T Gibson, Consultant Physician, disclosed in an article entitled 'Injuries in Rugby Union football':

> 'in a prospective study of 185 players attached to 10 British clubs . . . foul play might have caused as many as 47(31%) of all reported injuries. Complete eradication of deliberately dangerous play would considerably reduce the high incidence of injuries in this sport.'

Against that background it was hardly surprising that the responsibility efficient Medical Officers Schools Association (MOSA) should have recommended less than a year later in July 1979 insurance for all rugby playing schools. For administrative reasons in respect of which no one at Bedford School could be adversely criticised these MOSA proposals were not implemented until July 1981. During the intervening November 1980 a then 16 years-old schoolboy, Simon Van Oppen, was seriously injured during an inter-house school match.

In due course High Court proceedings were begun alleging negligence under the two heads pleaded of (1) inadequate rugby coaching or instructions and (2) absence of personal accident insurance. In an action which lasted 26 days, and occupied 100 pages of a typescripted reserved judgment, Boreham J dismissed the claim, but said of the insurance limb, 'It is accepted that this case breaks new ground; it cannot be brought precisely within the categories so far identified and recognised by authority. This, therefore, is a novel claim'.

An appeal concentrated only on the insurance claim, and the judgment based on the common law negligence plea was affirmed. Balcombe, Croom-Johnson and O'Connor LJJ explained schools were obliged to take reasonable care for the health and safety of pupils, but owed no legal duty to insure against accidents. They also said that the appeal amounted to a claim there was a general legal duty on schools to have regard to the economic welfare of pupils, but there was no such duty. Furthermore, even if there was, it would be unfair and unreasonable to impose it on the school. It also rejected an alternative claim that the school had assumed a special responsibility on the insurance question.

What does not appear to have been pleaded before Boreham J or the Court of Appeal is the fiduciary duty in equity of trustees to have disclosed the crucial medical information contained in the MOSA report to parents. Boreham J's judgment contained a vital passage that the plaintiff's father, a solicitor, had said that had he been 'appraised of the dangers of rugby and of the need for insurance he would have sought insurance cover; in other words, he would have heeded the advice. There is no reason to doubt his evidence'.

The school was sued technically through the formal status of the Clerk to the Bedford Charity Trustees (*Van Oppen v Clerk to the Bedford Charity Trustees* [1989] 1 All ER 273, 274); and the case must be read as limited to only its special facts related to common law negligence. A potential claim for breach of trust by non-disclosure of crucial information for the advantage of an infant beneficiary to whom school trustees stand in loco parentis will now have to wait for another day and another claim. At first instance the case was considered in the New Law Journal vol 138 for Friday 29 July 1988 at 532–533.

A more clear-cut decision was reported briefly in The Daily Telegraph 13 April 1989. Leonard J upheld a claim that a 14 year-old schoolboy who had suffered a broken skull from an inadequately supervised playground 'kicking game' based on martial arts films had established liability against his school (*Townsend v Croydon London Borough Education Authority*). This decision was consistent with the extended seam of cases confirming liability for inadequate supervision and collected in Chapter 6, in respect of the parent–pupil relationship in *Sport and the Law* at 119–122.

Taxation

Compensation of a different kind from that obtained by Tottenham Hotspur's Danny Thomas for personal injuries was claimed by England's international goalkeeper, Peter Shilton, upon his transfer form Nottingham Forest to Southampton in 1982. The selling club paid him a £75,000 slice of the transfer fee it received from Southampton. He was assessed under s 181 of the ICTA 1970 (now s 19 of the ICTA 1988 'in respect of any office or employment on emoluments therefrom', and the commissioners decided that the receipt by Shilton of the payment from Nottingham Forest was an emolument 'flowing from' the services rendered or to be rendered to Southampton, and thereby liable to tax.

Morritt J on appeal held that because Nottingham Forest had no continuing interest in Shilton's services with Southampton after the transfer, and of payment by Nottingham Forest to Shilton, that the sum paid was not an ordinary emolument and chargeable under s 181: *Shilton v Wilmshurst (Inspector of Taxes)* [1988] STC 868 (and see also Annual Review 1988 at 300). On appeal during 1989 the Court of Appeal affirmed the judge, holding that a payment was not assessable under s 181/s 19 if it was attributable to the *creation* of a contract of employment, irrespective of the services to be rendered under it. Nottingham Forest's only interest was to ensure that Shilton would sign for Southampton contractually to release the transfer fee for his future services only with Southampton ([1990] STC 55).

Disciplinary process

A less successul appeal was also decided in December 1989, on this occasion by a Divisional Court which rejected an attempt to bring the Jockey Club within the jurisdiction of judicial review. The claim concerned a local steward whose conduct or actions as the Doncaster disciplinary meeting chairman was unacceptable to the Jockey Club, which concluded that he should not act as chairmen.

A dispute centred on whether the Jockey Club's disciplinary committee had or had not acted unfairly towards the applicant, but the main issue concerned the extent to which a domestic sporting governing body could be subjected to judicial review.

The Jockey Club operated in more than one dimension. Under the grant of a Royal Charter its powers and actions had a public flavour and potential impact alongside its functions of a domestic nature which also created contractual rights and relationships. Neill LJ, as recorded in the Times newspaper report for 3 January 1990 in respect of the judgment dated 20 December 1989, felt that if the matter had been free from authority 'he would have been disposed to conclude that some decisions at least of the Jockey Club were capable of being reviewed by the process of judicial review'; *R v Disciplinary Committee of the Jockey Club, ex p Massingberd-Mundy* (1990) *Times*, 3 January.

That authority is *Law v National Greyhound Racing Club Ltd* [1983] 3 All ER 300 where the Court of Appeal held that the power of the stewards of the National Greyhound Racing Club to suspend a trainer's licence was derived wholly from a contract between him and the club. Since the Divisional Court judgments of 20 December 1980, the Jockey Club was again unsuccessfully brought to court in a vain attempt to invoke the judicial review machinery. On this occasion, however, Stuart-Smith LJ was reported as saying that Roch J in the *Massingberd-Mundy* decision also had said

'that, in the absence of authority, he would have concluded that the Jockey Club was amenable to judicial review and suggested that in cases where the authority

of the club's stewards was not derived wholly from contract, judicial review
might be available.'

R v Jockey Club, ex p RAM Racecourse Ltd (1990) *Times*, 6 April. On this latter
occasion, Simon Brown J however foreshadowed,

> 'This was a dynamic area of law, well able to embrace new situations as justice
> required . . . just occasionally, as when exercising the quasi-licensing power
> here under challenge, his Lordship would regard the Jockey Club as subject to
> review.'

By the time these pages appear, or at least before the next Annual Review,
it is conceivable that this 'dynamic area of the law' will have exploded the
immunity of sporting domestic governing bodies from the 'time-warp' of
contract which under the constraints of *Law v NGRC Ltd* ties the court's
jurisdiction to contract in this field.

Parliament

No authority at government level was sufficiently affected or minded to act
with sufficient energy upon any one of the eight government reports between
the Wembley Stadium overcrowding at its first-ever FA Cup Final in 1923
(Cmnd 2088: 1924) and Lord Justice Taylor's Interim Report of the inquiry
into the Hillsborough Stadium Disaster on 15 April 1989 (Cm 765) to
prevent the greatest disaster in British sporting history. The Ibrox fatalities in
1971 were followed by the Wheatley Report in 1972 (Cmnd 4952) which
resulted in a Highway Code styled Green Guide published in 1973 without
legal effect and the Safety of Sports Ground Act 1975. The Bradford City fire
inferno produced in 1985 Mr Justice Popplewell's Interim (Cmnd 9585) and
Final (Cmnd 9710) Reports, which in turn created the Fire Safety and Safety
of Places of Sport Act 1987 with 40 sections and five Schedules. It did not
come into force until 1 January 1988 by a Commencement Order (SI 1987 No
1762) with also an amended Green Guide Code. Yet neither statute prevented
Hillsborough.

While Lord Justice Taylor's Interim Inquiry and Report were being
prepared for recommendations to be made relating to crowd safety and
control for the forthcoming soccer season 1989–1990, Parliament was
struggling with the controversial contents of the Football Spectators Act
which received the Royal Assent on 16 November 1989. Its main objects
were to provide—

(1) a statutory framework for a national membership scheme for spectators
    at designated football matches in England and Wales,
(2) the licensing of grounds, and
(3) courts' powers to impose restrictions on persons convicted of certain
    offences for the purpose of preventing violence or disorder at or in
    connection with designated football matches played outside England and
    Wales.

The Act was due to come into force on a day to be appointed. This was
announced during the second half of the soccer season 1989–1990, at the time
of writing on the eve of the first anniversary of the Hillsborough disaster, and
before the coroner's inquest had formally begun during April 1990. It had not

been implemented during 1989. The recommendations of Lord Justice Taylor's Final Report published in January 1990 (Cm 962) did not support the concept of a membership scheme for practical reasons; and anyone familiar with the company club shareholding structure of professional football in the United Kingdom knew that this particular concept did not fit within any corporate or unincorporated membership criteria, such as that associated with Corinthian Casuals, Harlequins or MCC, known to Anglo-Saxon law.

This bizarre and unreal creation was consistent with no attention having been given to drawing Lord Justice Taylor's Interim Inquiry to the taxation advantages for capital allowances to be given as on machinery and plant, with a disposal value to be taken as nil, under s 119 of the Finance Act 1989, for expenditure on stands at sports grounds to satisfy safety requirements under the Fire Provision and Safety of Places of Sport Act 1987 (which re-enacted the comparable earlier provisions relating to the Safety of Sports Grounds Act 1975). The costs inherent in his 43 recommendations at the Interim Report stage would always be crucial to their capacity for implementation.

Such fragmented and uncoordinated elements which float around sporting government areas are completely consistent with the lacunae seen nearly 30 years ago when Lord Hailsham of St Marylebone recognised, as I have explained on the first two pages of *Sport and the Law*,

> 'the absence of any "coherent body of doctrine, perhaps even a philosophy or government encouragement"'

and also,

> '"a need, not for a Ministry, but for a focal point under a Minister".'

That Minister, of which Lord Hailsham of St Marylebone was the first when doubling up with his Cabinet post of Minister for Science and Technology, has never since been granted Cabinet Status, and, apart from the Rt Hon Denis Howell MP (with the rank of Minister of State), has never been above the constitutional status of an Under-Secretary in the Department of the Environment. Yet Lord Justice Taylor's and all earlier government reports into sporting crowd problems have always been commissioned for delivery to the Home Office, while problems of overseas offenders inevitably involve the Foreign and Commonwealth Office. The Junior Ministers and their Department with responsibility for Sport have no direct connection with sporting crowd safety and control. Therein lies a natural recipe for disaster, of which Ibrox (1971), Bradford (1985) and Hillsborough (1989) are direct testimony. Only when Lord Hailsham's awareness of the absence of any 'coherent body of doctrine, perhaps even a philosophy or government encouragement' is recognised by the bureaucrats in Whitehall or the vote-catching politicians at Westminster will this crucial constitutional gap in sporting legal affairs be capable of being filled.

Conclusion

If anyone ever doubted the manner in which the law today can rescue sport from its own built-in limitations the developments during 1989 provide the self-evident answers. Without adherence to the rules of play on the field and the rule of law off it anarchy would prevail for sport as well as society. That is why, in addition to the practical examples explained here for sport's efficient functioning, sport and the law are here to stay, together, forever.

Statute Law

FRANCIS BENNION, MA (OXON)
Barrister, Research Associate of the University of Oxford Centre for Socio-Legal Studies, former UK Parliamentary Counsel

Introductory note

For the convenience of readers this article, like its predecessors in the All ER Annual Review series, conforms to the Code set out in the author's book *Statutory Interpretation* (1984, Suppl 1989). A reference to the relevant section of the Code is given after each heading in the notes below.

Ignorantia juris neminem excusat (Code s 9)

In *Greenwich London Borough Council v Powell* [1989] 1 All ER 65 the House of Lords took judicial notice of the fact that an enactment which it was called on to construe originated as a government Bill, and relied on that in arriving at the legal meaning of the enactment (see the note on p 299 below related to Code s 316).

The subject: mandatory and directory requirements (Code s 10)

Where a statutory power or discretion is conferred on a court or other body, but the enactment is silent on whether it can be exercised conditionally, that question can be decided only by considering the purpose of the enactment. The court, when pronouncing on the exercise of statutory powers, is disposed to allow maximum flexibility. Principle tends to give way to convenience, mainly because of the difficulty of foreseeing future circumstances.

In *R v Crown Court at Southwark, ex p Customs and Excise Commissioners* [1989] 3 All ER 673 the Divisional Court was required to decide whether conditions could be imposed on the making of an order under the Drug Trafficking Offences Act 1986, s 27(2) (which empowers a Crown Court to order production of, or access to, certain material for the purpose of an investigation into drug trafficking). The Act being silent on the point, the Divisional Court held that the Crown Court, if it decided to make an order, must make it in the unconditional terms laid down by s 27(2). It would however be open to the Crown Court, in an exceptional case (which did not exist here), to decline to make the order unless specified undertakings were given by the party seeking it. The giving of these would be equivalent to the imposing of conditions when making the order.

Enforcement agencies: courts and other adjudicating authorities (Code s 19)

No jurisdiction by consent

Parties to litigation cannot by their mutual agreement confer upon a court or other adjudicating authority any jurisdiction which, under the Acts establishing or regulating it, it does not possess: *R v Secretary of State for Social Services, ex p Child Poverty Action Group* [1989] 1 All ER 1047.

Stare decisis

A court must not decline a jurisdiction which it is satisfied Parliament intended to confer on it, even though to exercise the jurisdiction means treating an otherwise binding decision as having been arrived at per incuriam.

In *Rickards v Rickards* [1989] 3 All ER 193 the Court of Appeal declined to follow its own previous decision in *Podbery v Peak* [1981] Ch 344. This decided that the House of Lords decision in *Lane v Esdaile* [1891] AC 210 that there is no right of appeal against a grant or refusal of leave to appeal applied to a refusal to extend the time for appeal. In *Rickards* Balcombe LJ said (at 201):

> 'We are justified in refusing to follow *Podbury v Peake* because to do so would require us to decline a jurisdiction which I am satisfied Parliament has conferred on us.'

He said (ibid) that the true ratio of *Lane v Esdaile*

> 'is that where there is a provision that an appeal shall lie only with the leave of a particular court or courts neither the grant nor the refusal of leave is itself appealable, otherwise the introduction of the "filter" requiring leave would be pointless.'

Transactions between states

Municipal courts do not have the competence to adjudicate on or enforce the rights arising out of transactions entered into by independent sovereign states between themselves on the plane of international law *(Maclaine Watson & Co Ltd v International Tin Council* [1989] 3 All ER 523, per Lord Oliver at 544; see also *Secretary of State in Council of India v Kamachee Boye Sahaba* (1859) 13 Moo PCC 22 at 75 (15 ER 9 at 28–29) and *Cook v Sprigg* [1899] AC 572 at 578).

Court orders valid until quashed

In *Barclays Bank plc v Taylor* [1989] 3 All ER 563 at 565 Lord Donaldson MR said 'a court order which is valid on its face is fully effective and demands compliance unless and until it is set aside by due process of law.'

Enforcement agencies: judicial review (Code s 24)

Terminology

In *R v Inland Revenue Commissioners, ex p Taylor (No 2)* [1989] 3 All ER 353 at 357–358 Glidewell LJ delivered an important dictum concerning the terminology used in judicial review—

> '[The argument] is that, in the circumstances of this case, the use by the Board [of Inland Revenue] of s 20(2) [of the Taxes Management Act 1970] . . . was unreasonable in the *Wednesbury* sense (see *Associated Provincial Picture Houses Ltd v Wednesbury Corp* [1947] 2 All ER 680, [1948] 1 KB 223). That phraseology, though we still adhere to it out of usage if not affection, is one that properly has been replaced by the use of the word "irrational" derived from the well-known

speech of Lord Diplock in *Council of Civil Service Unions v Minister for the Civil Service* [1984] 3 All ER 935, [1985] AC 374. It will be remembered that Lord Diplock made it clear that in order for a court to find that a particular decision or action on the part of a body whose traverse was irrational, it had to be—"a decision which is so outrageous in its defiance of logic or of accepted moral standards that no sensible person who had applied his mind to the question to be decided could have arrived at it." (See [1984] 3 All ER 935 at 951, [1985] AC 374 at 410.)'

In *Al-Mehdawi v Secretary of State for the Home Department* [1989] 3 All ER 843 at 846 Lord Bridge confirmed that in relation to the three heads of illegality, irrationality and procedural impropriety laid down by Lord Diplock in *Council of Civil Service Unions v Minister for the Civil Service* [1985] AC 374 at 410 as the grounds for judicial review it is 'the third head which embraces breaches of natural justice.'

Enforcement agencies: dynamic processing of legislation by (Code s 26)

Where a sub-rule laid down by judicial decision has through the passing of subsequent legislation become inappropriate, it ceases to apply. It may then be disregarded even by a court inferior to that which laid down the sub-rule.

In *Pittalis v Grant* [1989] 2 All ER 622 the Court of Appeal reviewed the decision of the House of Lords in *Smith v Baker & Sons* [1891] AC 325 laying down that under the enactments providing for an appeal from a county court to the Court of Appeal a point of law could not be taken in the Court of Appeal if it had not been raised in the court below. *Held* In view of the change made by the Supreme Court Act 1981 removing the restriction whereby an appeal from a county court lay only on a point of law, the rule in *Smith v Baker & Sons* was no longer applicable and should be treated as obsolete. Nourse LJ said (at 632)—

> 'We are conscious that it may seem a strong thing for this court to hold thus of a rule established by the House of Lords, albeit one enfeebled by exceptions, the statutory support which gave it life at last turned off. But, where it can see that the decision of the higher court has become obsolete, the lower court, if it is not to deny justice to the parties in the suit, is bound to say so and to act accordingly.'

Delegated legislation: doctrine of ultra vires (Code s 58)

Presumption of validity

It was stated by Lord Bridge in *Factortame Ltd v Secretary of State for Transport* [1989] 2 All ER 692 at 709, following *F Hoffmann-La Roche & Co AG v Secretary of State for Trade and Industry* [1975] AC 295, that it is a principle of English law 'that delegated legislation must be presumed to be valid unless and until declared invalid'.

Severance

Where a person is prosecuted for infringement of a byelaw it is not a defence to show that a provision of the byelaw is ultra vires if the accused would still have been guilty of the offence even had that provision not been included in the byelaw.

The case of *DPP v Hutchinson* [1989] 1 All ER 1060 concerned byelaws made with respect to common land under the Military Lands Act 1892, s 14(1) (which states that no byelaw made under it shall authorise interference with rights of common). The applicant, who was convicted of an offence under the byelaws, possessed no right of common in respect of the land. The byelaws thus interfered with no rights of common of hers, even though they may have interfered with rights of common possessed by other persons. *Held* The conviction was lawful. Schiemann J said (at 1070) that in upholding the conviction the court was performing an exercise which was essentially the alteration of a decision made by another authority (namely the authority which made the byelaws in question). It should do this only when sure that the altered decision represented that which that authority would have enacted had he appreciated the limitation on his powers. Here it was clear that if this limitation had been appreciated the byelaws would still have been made, but would have been restricted to non-commoners. In that case the applicant would have been justly convicted.

Presumption against extra-territoriality

In *Holmes v Bangladesh Biman Corp* [1989] 1 All ER 852 the House of Lords held that a power to make delegated legislation may by implication be treated as narrowed by the application of the presumption against extra-territoriality (see the note on p 296 below related to Code s 223).

The enactment: challenges to validity of (Code s 75)

European Community law

The European Communities Act 1972, s 2(1) was stated by Lord Bridge in *Factortame Ltd v Secretary of State for Transport* [1989] 2 All ER 692 at 701 to have precisely the same effect in relation to any subsequent Act as if a section were incorporated in the later Act which in terms enacted that the provisions of the later Act were to be without prejudice to the directly enforceable Community rights of nationals of any member state of the EEC. Earlier (at 697) Lord Bridge suggested that the phrase 'directly enforceable Community rights' was a convenient expression to use to denote 'those rights in Community law which have direct effect in the national law of member states of the EEC'. He defined 'Community law' as embracing 'the EEC Treaty, subordinate legislation of institutions of the European Economic Community (the EEC) and the jurisprudence developed by the Court of Justice of the European Communities'.

In *Factortame* the House of Lords held that a court had no power to make an order postponing the coming into force of a British statute pending the determination of a reference to the European Court to determine its validity. Lord Bridge said (at 702–703) that—

> 'the presumption that an Act of Parliament is compatible with Community law unless and until declared to be incompatible must be at least as strong as the presumption that delegated legislation is valid unless and until declared invalid.'

Filling in the detail: implications (when legitimate) (Code s 109)

Incidental statutory powers

In *Bodden v Commissioner of Police of the Metropolis* [1989] 3 All ER 833 the question arose whether a magistrate was empowered by the Contempt of Court Act 1981, s 12(2) to order a person who was committing a possible contempt of court *outside* the court (in this case by using in the street a loud-hailer which interrupted court proceedings) to be brought before him immediately, when all that the enactment says is that the court may order the offender to be detained until the rising of the court. The Court of Appeal held that the power was implied. Beldam LJ said (at 837)—

> 'In giving the magistrates' court jurisdiction to deal with the different kinds of contempt referred to in s 12(1)(a) and (b), Parliament obviously intended to confer all incidental powers necessary to enable the court to exercise the jurisdiction in a judicial manner.'

The common law rule that a statutory power by implication carries with it all incidental powers necessary for its operation is very important. It is for example the basis for the well-known rule that, except where the contrary intention appears, the exercise of a statutory power cannot in itself amount to a nuisance (see Code pp 738–739). (As to this case see also the note on p 299 below related to Code s 284).

Filling in the detail: implications affecting related law (Code s 110)

Where courts reject statutory analogy

The case of *Singh v Observer Ltd* [1989] 2 All ER 751 provides a further example of the tendency of the courts not to follow the lead set by Parliament in abolishing a criminal offence or tort (for earlier examples see Code pp 248–249). Notwithstanding that the Criminal Law Act 1967, ss 13 and 14 abolished criminal and civil liability for the maintenance of actions Macpherson J held that this remained contrary to public policy, so that it was open to the court to order a maintainer to disclose his identity and pay the costs of the maintained action.

On the other hand in *Kirkham v Chief Constable of the Greater Manchester Police* [1989] 3 All ER 882 Tudor Evans J followed the lead of the Suicide Act 1961, s 1 (by which suicide ceased to be a criminal offence) in rejecting the argument that because of its unlawful nature damages could not be recovered where police had negligently allowed a prisoner known to be suicidal to be kept without proper safeguards, so that he did in fact commit suicide (affirmed by the Court of Appeal: *The Independent* 16 January 1990). However *R v City of London Coroner, ex p Barber* [1975] Crim LR 515; Code p 248, which went the other way, was not cited to the court. (As to this case see also the note on p 294 below related to Code s 126).

Commonsense construction rule (Code s 122)

Meaning of 'forthwith'

Where an enactment requires that a thing is to be done 'forthwith' this does not mean it is to be done before the conditions necessary for doing it are satisfied. The Social Security Act 1975, s 98 requires a claim for benefit to be 'submitted forthwith to an adjudication officer'. In *R v Secretary of State for Social Services, ex p Child Poverty Action Group* [1989] 1 All ER 1047 the Court of Appeal held that this did not require a claim to be submitted for determination at a point in time when it was incapable of being determined because relevant facts had not yet been ascertained.

Statutory definitions (Code s 125)

Potency of the defined term

It is pointed out at Code p 276 that the natural meaning of a defined term may have a potency sufficient to override the literal meaning of the statutory definition. An extraordinary example of judicial ignoring of this important principle arose in *R v Brixton Prison Governor, ex p Kahan* [1989] 2 All ER 368, where the defined term was 'designated Commonwealth country'. The definition of this contained in the Fugitive Offenders Act 1967, s 2(1) states that it is a country designated by an Order in Council made under s 2(1) (which empowers designation of any country for the time being mentioned in the British Nationality Act 1981, Sch 3 'or any other country within the Commonwealth'). Fiji was so designated by the Fugitive Offenders (Designated Commonwealth Countries) (No 3) Order 1970, art 2. Despite the fact that Fiji left the Commonwealth on 15 October 1986 this Order had not been amended.

The applicant for habeas corpus, Mr Kahan, was the subject of an authority to proceed against him under the 1967 Act issued by the Home Secretary on 26 September 1988. This authority would have been invalid if on that date Fiji was not a 'designated Commonwealth country' within the legal meaning of that expression. Since on that date it was not a Commonwealth country at all, the argument could scarcely be stronger for saying that the literal meaning of the definition was overridden. When it is considered that the 1967 Act is penal to a very strong degree, the argument becomes overwhelming. Nevertheless the Divisional Court applied the literal meaning and dismissed Mr Kahan's application.

The term 'person'

It is submitted that it is clear law, as well as common sense, that unless the contrary intention appears the term 'person' in an enactment does not include a foetus in utero.

This question again came before the Court of Appeal in *R v Tait* [1989] 3 All ER 682. The court considered it afresh, even though it might be thought to have been concluded by the earlier Court of Appeal decision in *Re F (in utero)* [1988] 2 All ER 193. In that case the court held that since a foetus has no existence independent of its mother it does not become a person unless and until born, and so cannot be made a ward of court.

The enactment in question in *Tait* was the Offences against the Person Act 1861, s 16, as substituted by the Criminal Law Act 1977, s 65 and Sch 12. This says (emphasis added):

'A person who without lawful excuse makes to another a threat, intending that that other would fear it would be carried out, to kill that other *or a third person* shall be guilty of an offence.'

The question was whether a threat made to a pregnant woman to kill her foetus contravened this provision.

Although strangely the Court of Appeal did not deal with the point in this straightforward way, it clearly begins and ends with the question whether a pregnant woman's foetus falls within the legal meaning of the phrase 'a third person' (the first and second persons respectively being the one making the threat and the one to whom it is made).

The foetus cannot be 'a third person' unless it is a person, so the question is simply whether a foetus is in law a person. The court declined to treat *Re F (in utero)* as a relevant authority on the ground that it related to civil or family law, though it is submitted that this is not a sound reason for disregarding it. It confirms what has been a general principle of our law, that a foetus is not a person in its own right since it is part of the person of its mother.

After much difficulty, which it is submitted did not truly arise, the court reached the obvious conclusion (at 688): 'We feel constrained to say that the fetus in utero was not, in the ordinary sense, "another person", distinct from its mother.' The court did not specify in what extraordinary sense it might be held to be 'another person' in a different context. It seems that a clear contrary intention would need to be spelt out in the enactment for such a construction to be correct.

Principles derived from legal policy: nature of legal policy (Code s 126)

In ascertaining and applying legal policy for the purposes of statutory interpretation the court will have regard to the underlying principles of all systems of law comprised in the common law, using that term in the widest sense. In *Kirkham v Chief Constable of the Greater Manchester Police* [1989] 3 All ER 882 at 892–893 Tudor Evans J, in considering whether legal policy required damages for negligence to be disallowed where it consisted in allowing a suicidal person an opportunity (which he took) actually to commit suicide, had regard to the fact that suicide is an ecclesiastical offence. He cited the dictum of Lord Denning M R in *Hyde v Tameside Area Health Authority* [1981] CA Transcript 130 that suicide is contrary to the ecclesiastical law 'which was, and still is, part of the general law of England'. Lord Denning had cited the following dictum of Lord Blackburn in *Mackonochie v Lord Penzance* (1881) 6 App Cas 424 at 446:

'The ecclesiastical law of England is not a foreign law. It is a part of the general law of England—of the common law—in that wider sense which embraces all the ancient and approved customs of England which form law, including not only that law administered in the Courts of Queen's Bench, Common Pleas, and Exchequer,to which the term Common Law is sometimes in a narrower sense confined, but also that law administered in Chancery and commonly called Equity, and also that law administered in the Courts Ecclesiastical, that last law consisting of such canons and constitutions ecclesiastical as have been allowed by general consent and custom within the realm—and form, as is laid down in *Caudre's Case* 5 Rep 1, the King's ecclesiastical law.'

(As to *Kirkham v Chief Constable of the Greater Manchester Police* [1989] 3 All ER 882 see also the note on p 292 above related to Code s 110.)

Presumption that updating construction to be applied (Code s 146)

In *Smith v Braintree District Council* [1989] 3 All ER 897 the House of Lords, in determining that the power conferred by the Insolvency Act 1986, s 285(1) to stay any legal process brought 'against the property or person of the debtor' extended to proceedings for commitment under the General Rate Act 1967, s 102, declined to follow *Re Smith, Hands v Andrews* [1893] 2 Ch 1 and *Re Edgcome, ex p Edgcome* [1902] 2 KB 403. Those cases were decided, under a similar provision in the Bankruptcy Act 1669, on the ground that proceedings for recovery of rates were 'coercive', following a dictum of Lord Hatherley in 1871. In rejecting these authorities Lord Jauncey of Tullichettle said (at 907):

> '. . . not only has the legislative approach to individual bankruptcy altered since the mid-nineteenth century, but social views as to what conduct involves delinquency, as to punishment and as to the desirability of imprisonment have drastically changed. It is, for example, most unlikely that anyone today analysing the six exceptions in s 4 of the 1869 Act would conclude,as did Lord Hatherley LC in 1871, that they all involved an element of delinquency.'

(Compare *Rayware Ltd v Transport and General Workers' Union* [1989] 3 All ER 583, discussed in the note on pp 296–297 below related to Code s 231.)

Weighing the interpretative factors (Code s 158)

In *A-G's Reference (No 1 of 1988)* [1989] 2 All ER 1 the House of Lords considered the legal meaning of the word 'obtained' in the Company Securities (Insider Dealing) Act 1985, s 1(3). This restricts the use by an individual of 'information which he knowingly obtained (directly or indirectly) from [an insider]'. The question was whether this covers only information acquired by purpose and effort or also covers the case where the individual merely receives the information without doing anything active. Finding for the wider meaning, the House rejected the argument that since the statute was penal the narrower meaning must be preferred. Giving the principal judgment, Lord Lowry (at 8) said that 'having carefully weighed the points on either side' he was satisfied that the wider meaning was correct. This confirms the argument of Code s 158 that all relevant interpretative factors are to be weighed in the balance.

Commencement of an enactment (Code ss 164–169)

Judicial postponement of commencement date

In *Factortame Ltd v Secretary of State for Transport* [1989] 2 All ER 692 the House of Lords held that a court has no power to make an order postponing the coming into force of a statute pending the determination of a reference to the European Court to determine its effectiveness. (As to this case see also the note on p 290 above related to Code s 58).

Judicial alteration of commencement date

A court has no power effectively to alter the commencement date appointed for an enactment by adjourning until after that date a matter which has come before it earlier.

In *R v Walsall Justices, ex p W (a minor)* [1989] 3 All ER 460 the prosecution indicated on the date fixed for the trial before magistrates of a person accused of wounding a boy of twelve that it would offer no evidence unless the magistrates adjourned the trial until after the commencement of the Criminal Justice Act 1988, s 34(1). This enactment abolished the rule requiring the unsworn evidence of a child to be corroborated. In the present case no corroborating evidence was available. The magistrates adjourned the trial accordingly. *Held* They had no power to do so. Although the power of adjournment conferred by the Magistrates' Courts Act 1980, s 10(1)is in terms unconditional, by implication it does not empower a court to circumvent the date fixed by the legislature for the coming into effect of a change in the law. To do so contravenes the rule laid down in *R v Boteler* (1864) 4 B & S 959, 122 ER 718 that a court is not entitled to refuse to apply the current law on the ground that in their opinion it is lacking in justice.

Extra-territorial application of Act (Code s 223)

The Carriage by Air Act 1961, s 10(1) says that an Order in Council may apply Sch 1 to the Act, which sets out the 1955 Hague Convention, 'to carriage by air, not being carriage by air to which the Convention applies, of such descriptions as may be specified in the Order'. In *Holmes v Bangladesh Biman Corp* [1989] 1 All ER 852 the House of Lords held that this literally-unrestricted wording must be treated as impliedly cut down by the presumption against extra-territoriality. It therefore did not authorise the making of an Order in respect of non-Convention carriage by air where none of the following were within British territory: (1) the place of departure, (2) any agreed stopping place en route, or (3) the place of destination. The House rejected the argument that s 10(1) could be given an unrestricted construction because, under the doctrine of forum non conveniens, the carrier would be likely to obtain in the appropriate foreign court a stay of any proceedings inappropriately commenced in a British court.

The case illustrates that just because an enactment is to some extent extra-territorial (perhaps because, as here, its purpose is to implement an international convention), that does not mean the presumption against extra-territoriality ceases to apply to it in other respects. As Lord Griffiths said (at 864):

> 'If as a result of international co-operation a number of countries agree to adopt the same law, the domestic legislation that gives effect to this international agreement in this country is not extra-territorial within the meaning of the rule. In such circumstances our domestic legislation is not an interference with the sovereignty of the other countries but the recognition of their wish that we should alter our own law to accord with the common will.'

Pre-enacting history: the earlier law (Code s 231)

In using earlier legislative treatment of a particular mischief as a guide to interpretation, the court must keep in mind changes of approach. In *Rayware Ltd v Transport and General Workers' Union* [1989] 3 All ER 583 the Court of Appeal was required to construe the Trade Union and Labour Relations Act 1974, s 15(1), which authorises an employee to take part in picketing provided it is 'at or near his own place of work'. The nearest point at which it was possible to picket the place of work without trespassing was just over half a mile away. Holding that in the circumstances this satisfied the test of nearness, May LJ (at 587) said of the history of earlier versions of s 15: 'The approach of different generations to what may appear to be the same or a similar problem sometimes alters radically.' (Compare *Smith v Braintree District Council* [1989] 3 All ER 897, discussed in the note on p 295 above related to Code s 146.)

Rayware illustrates the judicial treatment of a term which has been previously processed by the courts. Both May LJ (at 587) and Nourse LJ (at 589) adopted the dictum of Byles LJ in *Tyne River Keelmen v Davison* (1864) 16 CBNS 612 at 622; 143 ER 1267 at 1271 that 'the word "near" is not a restraining, but an expanding, word, to be extended so far as to give effect to the intention of the legislature'.

Enacting history: as an indication of Parliament's intention (Code s 240)

Government policy

For the court's reference to government policy as an indication of legislative intention see the note on pp 299–300 below related to Code s 316.

Enacting history: special restriction on parliamentary materials (Code s 241)

Speeches by Ministers

In *Maclaine Watson & Co Ltd v International Tin Council* [1989] 3 All ER 523 at 531 Lord Griffiths, after saying that we do not, as yet, have resort to the parliamentary history of an enactment as an aid to statutory interpretation, quoted from the speech of a Government minister on the second reading of the Bill that became the Diplomatic Privileges (Extension) Act 1944. His purpose was to show that the power conferred by the 1944 Act (later reproduced in the International Organisations Act 1968, s 1(2)) to confer the legal capacities of a body corporate on an international organisation by Order in Council was not intended to deprive persons dealing with such an organisation of relief in case of default, but that such relief was intended to be given by state action rather than a legally-enforceable remedy.

This illustrates the reluctance of judges to be bound by the self-imposed restriction on reference to parliamentary materials when they feel this has a distorting effect on their construction of an enactment. The truth is that, despite the restriction, the court is master of its procedure and will be influenced by parliamentary materials where this is necessary in order to do justice.

Enacting history: international treaties (Code s 242)

Uniform construction

Where a treaty is referred to in the construction of an enactment, the court should ensure that its interpretation of it is not out of line with that of other countries which are parties to the treaty. Accordingly the use in a treaty of a term which has a particular meaning in the municipal law of the court does not require that it be given that meaning if to do so would be out of step with the general treatment of the term in countries which are parties to the treaty.

C v C [1989] 2 All ER 465 concerned the legal meaning of the term 'custody' in the Child Abduction and Custody Act 1985, which implements provisions of the 1980 Convention on the Civil Aspects of International Child Abduction. Lord Donaldson MR said (at 472):

> 'The whole purpose of such a code is to produce a situation in which the courts of all contracting states may be expected to interpret and apply it in similar ways, save in so far as the national legislatures have decreed otherwise. Subject then to . . . [such exceptions] . . . the definitions contained in the convention should be applied and the words of the convention, including the definitions, construed in the ordinary meaning of the words used and in disregard of any special meaning which might attach to them in the context of legislation not having this international character.'

Post-enacting history: judicial decisions on Act (Code s 256)

Tacit legislation

Where it is alleged that a previous judicial decision on the legal meaning of an enactment was erroneous, the court will be influenced by the fact that, although Parliament has had an opportunity to rectify the alleged error, it has not chosen to do so. This may indicate tacit approval of the decision in question.

In *Phillips v Mobil Oil Co Ltd* [1989] 3 All ER 97 it was argued that the decision of Buckley J in *Beesly v Hallwood Estates Ltd* [1960] 2 All ER 314, [1960] 1 WLR 549 that a renewal covenant in a lease falls within the definition of 'estate contract' in the Land Charges Act 1925, s 10, and is therefore registrable as a Class C(iv) land charge, was erroneous. The Court of Appeal rejected the argument partly on the ground that on two occasions since the ruling in that case Parliament had made amendments to the 1925 Act without taking the opportunity to reverse it.

Unamendable descriptive components of Act: format (Code s 283)

Division of Act into Parts

In *R v Inland Revenue Commissioners, ex p Taylor (No 2)* [1989] 3 All ER 353 the Divisional Court rejected the contention that when an appeal is pending the power to require production of documents conferred by the Taxes Management Act 1970, s 20 (which is in Pt III of the Act) is replaced by the somewhat different power conferred by s 51 (which is in Pt V). Glidewell LJ (at 357) gave valuable guidance on the significance of an Act being divided into Parts. After pointing out that Pt III of the 1970 Act is concerned with tax returns and information, Pt IV with assessments and claims, and Pt V with appeals, he went on—

> 'The fact that the 1970 Act proceeds in a logical order, first of all dealing with returns and then with assessment and claims and then with appeals, does not mean that, so to speak, each section is in watertight compartments or that procedures provided in one part of the Act necessarily supersede or rule out the use of procedures provided in other parts of the Act. If that were the case, there would have to be some words in the statute that made it clear.'

Unamendable descriptive component of Act: punctuation (Code s 284)

Use of commas

An example of where the presence or absence of commas can make a difference to the meaning of an enactment arose in *Bodden v Commissioner of Police of the Metropolis* [1989] 3 All ER 833. The enactment in question was the Contempt of Court Act 1981, s 12(1)(*b*), which gives a magistrate jurisdiction to deal with any person who 'wilfully interrupts the proceedings of the court or otherwise misbehaves *in court*' (emphasis added). The draftsman had taken this wording from provisions deriving from the County Courts Act 1846, s 113, which said that if 'any Person . . . shall wilfully interrupt the Proceedings of the Court, or otherwise misbehave in Court, it shall be lawful [to take him into custody]'. *Bodden* concerned a person who had interrupted court proceedings by using, in the street outside the court house, a loud-hailer for the purpose of addressing a demonstration protesting about another case which was being heard inside. In rejecting the argument that the words 'in court' governed the first limb of the enactment as well as the second, the Court of Appeal had regard to this legislative history, though it appears they would have come to the same conclusion anyway. (As to this case see also the note on p 292 above related to Code s 109).

Purposive-and-strained construction (Code s 315)

Potency of defined term

An important category of cases where a purposive-and-strained construction is required is that where the potency of a defined term overrides the literal meaning of the definition. For an example see the note on p 293 above related to Code s 125.

Purposive construction: statements of purpose (Code s 316)

Purpose based on govenment policy

In interpreting an enactment the court may refer to a line of government policy which Parliament clearly had in mind when framing the enactment. In *Greenwich London Borough Council v Powell* [1989] 1 All ER 65 the House of Lords construed the definition of 'protected site' in the Mobile Homes Act 1983, s 5(1) by reference to government policy regarding the provision by local authorities of caravan sites for gipsies. The definition says that the term 'does not include any land occupied by a local authority as a caravan site providing accommodation for gipsies'. Lord Bridge, who delivered the only judgment, relied on government advice to local authorities contained in a Department of Environment circular as an indication that the definition referred to sites for gipsies who were nomadic for part of the year only as well as those who were continuously nomadic. He said (at 70):

> 'The Bill which became the 1983 Act was a government Bill and it would be quite unrealistic not to recognise that the distinction between the two classes of site made in [the definition of "protected site"] must have been made with full knowledge of the policy which had been followed since 1970 . . . [and which] . . . is, in my opinion, fully cognisable as a powerful pointer to the intention of the legislature . . .'

Purposive construction: Community law (Code s 320)

In *Litster v Forth Dry Dock and Engineering Co Ltd* [1989] 1 All ER 1134 the House of Lords, following its decision in *Pickstone v Freemans plc* [1988] 2 All ER 803, [1989] AC 66, held, as Lord Templeman put it (at 1139), that where necessary to implement their purpose—

> 'the courts of the United Kingdom are under a duty to follow the practice of the European Court by giving a purposive [that is purposive-and-strained] construction to directives and to regulations issued for the purpose of complying with directives.'

The applicants, employees of Forth Dry Dock, were dismissed one hour before Forth Dry Dock's transfer to Forth Estuary Engineering took effect. *Held* They must be treated for the purposes of the Transfer of Undertakings (Protection of Employment) Regulations 1981, reg 5 as having been employed by Forth Dry Dock 'immediately before' the transfer. Otherwise there would not be compliance with the spirit of EC Council Directive 77/187, art 3, the clear object of which is to protect the rights of employees in the event of a change of employer.

Avoiding a futile or pointless result (Code s 324)

For an example see *Lane v Esdaile* [1891] AC 210, as explained in the note on p 289 above related to *Rickards v Rickards* [1989] 3 AlL ER 193.

Implied application of ancillary rules: constitutional law rules (Code s 334)

Parens patriae doctrine

For reasons that are not clear or convincing, under current constitutional doctrine as laid down by the courts the Crown cannot act directly as *parens patriae*. Therefore in a particular case the Crown cannot act in this capacity where no functionary is for the time being appointed by the Crown to act in such matters on its behalf.

On the commencement of the Mental Health Act 1959, which contained provisions corresponding to those previously exercised under the *parens patriae* doctrine, the warrant dated 10 April 1956 by which the jurisdiction of the Crown in lunacy had been assigned to the Lord Chancellor and judges of the Chancery Division, was revoked by a further warrant. The consequence was, as it was put by Lord Brandon in *F v West Berkshire Health Authority* [1989] 2 All ER 545 at 552, that 'so much of the parens patriae jurisdiction as related to persons of unsound mind no longer exists'. (Although Lord Brandon gave as an additional reason the provisions of the 1959 Act itself, now embodied in the Mental Health Act 1983, this was clearly erroneous. The 1959 Act made no reference to the royal prerogative, and did not affect it.)

Hearing both sides: audi alteram partem (Code s 346)

The decision of the Court of Appeal in *R v Diggines, ex p Rahmani* [1985] 1 All ER 1073, [1985] QB 1109; All ER Rev 1985, p 266; Code Supplement p 82, which at [1986] 1 All ER 921, [1986] AC 475 was affirmed by the House of Lords on grounds not relevant to the audi alteram partem rule, was reversed by the House of Lords so far as it related to that rule in *Al-Mehdawi v Secretary of State for the Home Department* [1989] 3 All ER 843. The House held that an appellant under the Immigration Act 1971, s 15(1) who had been deprived of the opportunity to be heard on the appeal through the negligence of his solicitors in sending notice to him at the wrong address was not entitled to judicial review on the ground of breach of natural justice. There can be no such breach where the process of justice has not itself proved defective. In this connection a litigant must be identified with his legal adviser. If the adviser proves deficient the litigant's remedy (if any) can only be against the adviser, since the state's administration of justice is not at fault.

Lord Bridge confirmed (at 846) that, in relation to the three heads of illegality, irrationality and procedural impropriety laid down by Lord Diplock in *Council of Civil Service Unions v Minister for the Civil Service* [1985] AC 374 at 410 as the grounds for judicial review, it is 'the third head which embraces breaches of natural justice'.

Ordinary meaning of words (Code s 363)

Word with no ordinary meaning

Where a word used in an enactment has no settled meaning, its legal meaning as so used must be determined from the context. In *Inglewood Investment Co Ltd v Forestry Commission* [1989] 1 All ER 1 it was held by the Court of Appeal that the word 'game' in relation to hunting, shooting and other sporting rights 'is without comprehensive basic definition' (per Dillon LJ at 4).

Implication where statutory description only partly met (Code s 396)

Exercise of power partly ultra vires

In *Robbins v Secretary of State for the Environment* [1989] 1 All ER 878 the House of Lords considered a case where a repairs notice served under the Town and Country Planning Act 1971, s 115 required the carrying out of work some of which was within the power conferred by the section and some of which was not. *Held* The notice was not invalidated by the inclusion of invalid items of work, since the appeals machinery provided by the Act was enough to prevent hardship to the building owner. Lord Ackner said (at 890):

> 'so long as there is not inextricably mingled in the repairs notice works which have not the character of work of preservation, such works can properly be excised from the repairs notice, leaving the notice valid as respects [the remainder].'

Succession

C H SHERRIN, LLM, PHD
Barrister, Reader in Law, University of Bristol

Wills

The most interesting of the cases on wills reported this year is the Court of Appeal's decision in *Re Berger (deceased)* [1989] 1 All ER 591, affirming Warner J's decision at first instance. The case was concerned with the testaments of Mr Gerson Berger who was an orthodox Jew, domiciled in England, and who had executed a series of parallel documents. One category comprised a series of English wills in due form and clearly intended to be subject to the jurisdiction of the English Court of Probate. But in addition there were a number of holograph documents written in Hebrew and known as zavah, which contained a mixture of religious exhortations and dispositions of his movable property. It appeared that the zavah were intended to be binding in Jewish law and to be enforced in the rabbinical court but it was not clear what their relationship was to the English wills, or whether they were also intended to be enforceable in the English courts.

The order of execution of the last few crucial documents was as follows. A will and a zavah both executed on 18 December 1972. A will executed on 15 July 1975. A zavah executed on 11 February 1976. On Sunday 6 August 1977 he executed, with the formalities required by the Wills Act 1837, a zavah. At that time he was in possession of his last will, but didn't execute it until Tuesday 9 August 1977 when he signed it with one witness. By reason of the single witness this will clearly failed for want of due formality. Probate was sought and granted of the August zavah, with the August will incorporated in it. This conclusion of Warner J's was affirmed by the Court of Appeal.

The basic dilemma posed by the case was that the testator almost certainly did not intend that the zavah should operate in tandem with the English wills in the sense of being read in conjunction with the latest will as dispositions to which the English courts would give effect. Thus could such a document, probably not intended to be a probated will, be granted probate notwithstanding?

There was a surprising absence of expert evidence available to the court as to the nature and effect of the zavah, which as a matter of fact and law could surely have been supplied. But the real problem centered on the proof or discovery of the testator's intentions regarding the two series of documents. In technical term whether Mr Berger had sufficient animus testandi regarding the zavah. Mustill LJ, after reviewing a series of basic propositions governing the proof of wills, dealt with the problem as follows:

> 'Thus, if one is to seek out the intention of Mr Berger, the right question is this: what did he intend to be the status of the zavah as a document to be admitted to probate, on the unforeseen contingency that the English will was ineffectual? To this question there is no rational answer, for in reality Mr Berger had no intention at all, since the possibility that the English will might fail obviously

never crossed his mind: and if it had done, he would have looked into the matter, and the course of events would have been different. But, whatever intention should be imputed to him, I see no reason to suppose that he intended a document designed to be enforced by the rabbinical tribunal , and written in the appropriate terms, to be enforced by a court to which its terminology and social underpinnings were entirely alien, and still less that he would have wished a linguistic and intellectual hybrid between a valid zavah and an invalid English will to be enforced by an English court, and this is what the plaintiffs' argument entails.'

It was thought that if Mr Berger had included an express statement denying probate of the zavah, that would exclude the will from proof. But the will disclosed no such statement; no evidence was really forthcoming on the testator's intention in the circumstances that had happened.

The Lord Justice concluded that the zavah were intended to operate in the shadow of the English wills. Thus the rights created by the English wills were alone to be those recognised by the mechanism of English law, but the persons who were beneficiaries of those rights were to hold them subject to a further group of rights and duties as to the manner in which they were to be enjoyed; the enforcement of which was the business of the rabbinical tribunal. Further, the zavah were designed to impose on persons who had received property during the deceased's lifetime, obligations with respect to the disposition of those assets, again to be enforceable by the rabbinical tribunal (at 598).

Since the evidence of intention was largely conjectural the judge was forced back onto two undoubted propositions of fact. First, that the testator made a document containing directions for the disposal of his property, the language of which was dispositive. Secondly, that it was executed in a form sufficient to render it enforceable by the English courts. On this basis the judge was prepared to admit the zavah to probate with the existing, though subsequently invalidly executed, English will incorporated into it. However, it can be said that this fails to give sufficient prominence to the central issue of the case, namely whether Mr Berger had animus testandi with reference to the zavah. Mustill LJ had earlier stated the axiomatic proposition that 'An instrument cannot be a "provable will" unless the maker had an "animus testandi".' Unfortunately he had also stated with equal force the much more questionable proposition that, 'If the document has the necessary dispositive effect and is duly executed, the necessary animus will be presumed.' In his concluding paragraph the Lord Justice makes no reference to animus other than the observation that 'Mr Berger would have been startled to learn that the zavah was to be administered by the English court, rather than the tribunal to whose religious and cultural norms it so plainly appealed.' A comment which surely tends to negate animus rather than support it.

Sir Denys Buckley agreed that the zavah should be admitted to probate; his judgment is more satisfactory since it centres analytically on the question of animus testandi. He stated the law as follows:

'English law does not require a document which is intended to have testamentary effect to assume any particular form or to be couched in language technically appropriate to its testamentary character. It is, says Jarman [on Wills (8th edn, 1951)] p 32, sufficient that the instrument, however irregular in form or artificial in expression, discloses the intention of the maker respecting the posthumous destination of his property. It may be made in any language. If it is made in a foreign language, the court must be furnished with an authenticated translation made by a qualified translator. It is that translation, not the text in the foreign language, which is admitted to probate. It is from the document so admitted to probate together with any other relevant testamentary instruments that an English court will ascertain the testator's testamentary intentions and determine their effect and validity.'

Then, referring to the following passage in the will,

'Each of my sons . . . should know that what I have written in this will is binding on you and additional to what was written in the English language will, and should any clarification be needed, the present will (in the Holy Tongue) [Hebrew] is the definitive one.'

He concludes:

'This seems to me to be irreconcilable with any suggestion that that zavah was not intended to have any testamentary force. On the contrary, the deceased's signature on it was attested by two witnesses which, according to the evidence, would render its provisions judicially enforceable in a rabbinical court.'

A conclusion which is certainly possible on the facts even if one hesitates to agree with it.

Sir Denys Buckley's judgment also contains useful comment on the different jurisdiction of the Chancery judge, trying a probate action, from the jurisdiction of a judge of that Division trying an administration action. This was prompted by the knowledge, perhaps, that the decision in the case on the probate issue would cause constructional and administrative problems for those charged with giving effect to the Berger 'will', for the zavah and the will did not lie happily together: (at 602). Secondly, the law governing the distribution of movable property of a testator domiciled in England is restated, with particular reference to the problems that arise where the will is written in a foreign language with reference to a foreign system of law (at 603). Finally, the law relating to incorporation of documents by reference is restated and applied (at 604, 605).

Intestacy

One of the murkier and more obscure backwaters of the law of succession is the provision in s 1(1) of the Legitimacy Act 1976. The section was the subject of the recent decision in *Re Spence (deceased), Spence v Dennis* [1989] 2 All ER 679.

Consider this scenario. A marries B and gives birth to a child C. A leaves B and goes to live with D and has a child E, and subsequently two more children F & G. Then A who has never been divorced from B, goes through a ceremony of marriage with D, which D, without knowledge of B, believes to be a valid marriage. Many years later, E dies intestate and C claims entitlement to his estate claiming to be the lawful half sister of E. This is contested by G who claims to be the lawful brother of the full blood to E; if that is so then his claim, based on full blood relationship, will oust that of C, based on half blood relationship. Remember also that at the time of E's death, in 1985, a person could not claim any inheritance from the estate of his illegitimate brother (see the 1969 Family Law Reform Act, although the position would now be different under the 1987 Family law Reform Act) and it will be appreciated that the success of both C and G's claims depends on showing that G, and F and E, were legitimated by the subsequent ceremony of marriage entered into by their parents. If that was the case then clearly G's claim will succeed.

The usual rule would be that a child of a void marriage would be illegitimate, in so far as that status now has any relevance in view of the provisions of the Family Law Reform Act 1987. However, a common reason for a marriage being void is that it is bigamous and such marriages often involve an innocent party, as where one party knows that a previous marriage is still subsisting and that his or her second 'marriage' is void for that reason, but the other party has no knowledge of that and thinks he or she is contracting a valid marriage. In such circumstances the section under consideration states:

> '(1) The child of a void marriage, whenever born, shall, subject to subsection (2) below and Schedule 1 to this Act, be treated as the legitimate child of his parents if at the time of the act of intercourse resulting in the birth (or at the time of the celebration of the marriage if later) both or either of the parties reasonably believed that the marriage was valid.
>
> (2) This section only applies where the father of the child was domiciled in England and Wales at the time of the birth or, if he died before the birth, was so domiciled immediately before his death.'

Why the belief of the parents should have any effect on the illegitimacy of the child defies logical explanation but presumably the provision has some pragmatic justification. It is also interesting to note that the section does not operate to actually legitimate the child but simply states that he or she is to 'be treated as the legitimate child of his parents' (see s 10 which contains a definition of 'legitimated person'). There are differences in the status and legal rights of these two categories, but these need not concern us here (see Morritt J at 682).

The precise point that arose in Re Spence was whether the section applied to legitimise a child who was born before his parents entered into a void marriage. The usual case is, of course, that the child is born after the celebration of the void marriage.

It can certainly be argued that s 1(1) of the 1976 Act should apply whenever the child is born in view of the clear reference in the section to 'whenever born'. Further the reference to 'if at the time of the act of intercourse resulting in the birth (or at the time of the celebration of the marriage if later)' can be said to recognise that the birth may precede the marriage. These arguments did not persuade the court. It was pointed out that the phrase above merely recognises that the conception may precede the marriage not that the birth may. In rejecting the argument that the section applied to the facts of the case the court was influenced by two factors.

Firstly, the requisite birth is not of any child but is of a 'child of a void marriage'. Secondly, a child born to parents who subsequently contract a void marriage is born illegitimate and if the section were to apply, this would involve a change of status during his life, which it was thought the Act did not recognise or intend. Accordingly, the claims of both the half sister, and the brother of the whole blood, failed, since at the time of the death in 1985 the law did not recognise any intestate entitlement between brothers or sisters based on illegitimate relationships. There being no other relatives the property passed to the Crown as bona vacantia.

As a tailpiece it can be noted that s 1(1) of the Legitimacy Act 1976 which is still the applicable legislation has been amended by s 28 of the Family Law Reform Act 1987. These specific amendments do not affect the precise point decided in *Re Spence*, but it will be appreciated that the change in the entitlement of illegitimate persons or intestacy effected by the more general provisions of that Act would.

Charities

The holograph will in *Re Hetherington (deceased), Gibbs v McDonnell* [1989] 2 All ER 129 reopened the debate on public benefit raised by a gift for the saying of masses. The testator bequeathed £2,000 to the Roman Catholic Bishop of Westminster for 'masses for the repose of the souls of my husband and my parents and my sisters and also myself when I die.' The residue was given to a named church for 'masses for my soul'. The question simply was whether these were valid charitable gifts. It has been settled since *Bourne v Keane* [1919] 1 AC 815 that a gift for the saying of masses is a valid gift. The House of Lords' decision in that case centred on the finding that such a gift was not void as being for a superstitious use by reason of being rendered illegal by the Dissolution of Colleges Act 1547. What was not clear was whether this validity rested on a finding that such a gift was a valid charitable trust or whether gifts for the saying of masses fell within the anomalous category of non-charitable purpose trusts that had been recognised over the years. Students of trusts usually encounter the case in the latter context under the heading non-charitable purpose trust. But in *Re Caus* [1934] Ch 162 Luxmoore J held that trusts for private or public masses were charitable, a decision which prior to *Re Hetherington* often elicited a critical comment. It is perhaps necessary to recognise that trusts for the saying of masses can be public in the sense of being performed in the public, or private, performed in closed services to which the public is not admitted and either can be for the repose of the souls of everyone generally or for the repose of souls of specified individuals.

The decision which is usually regarded as casting doubts on *Re Caus* is *Gilmour v Coats* [1949] 1 All ER 848, a case too well known to need further rehearsal here. So the Vice-Chancellor, Sir Nicolas Browne-Wilkinson, in *Re Hetherington* was faced with the decision whether to follow *Re Caus* and uphold the trust as charitable, or follow *Gilmour v Coats* and hold it invalid for charitable purposes as lacking public benefit. Somewhat surprisingly he adopted the former. He summarised his conclusions in four propositions: (1) A trust for the advancement of education, the relief of poverty or the advancement of religion is prima facie charitable and assumed to be for the public benefit. (2) The celebration of a religious rite in public does confer a sufficient public benefit because of the edifying and improving effect of such celebration on the members of the public who attend. (3) The celebration of a religious rite in private does not contain the necessary element of public benefit since any benefit by prayer or example is incapable of proof in the legal sense, and any element of edification is limited to a private, not public, class of those present at the celebration: (4) Where there is a gift for a religious purpose which could be carried out in a way which is beneficial to the public (ie by public masses) but could also be carried out in a way which would not have sufficient element of public benefit (ie by private masses), the gift is to be construed as a gift to be carried out only by the methods that are charitable, all non-charitable methods being excluded.

The judge thought that the necessary public benefit could be found in the fact that the masses were to be celebrated in public and that the money would in effect go in satisfaction of the stipends that the church would otherwise have to pay its priests. The first justification misses the point; it is not sufficient that an activity be performed in public with free access for the public to attend; the issue is whether the activity itself confers or contains sufficient element of public benefit. The second is frankly too tenuous to be persuasive. While one sympathises with any desire to liberalise the definition of charities in English law, for too long the tax benefits, jealously guarded by the Inland Revenue Commissioners, have imposed a straight jacket on sensible expansion; it is doubtful if this trust should have received such favourable attention. *Gilmour v Coats* is an established case bearing the authority of a strong House of Lords and, it is submitted, tends to negate any finding of public benefit in trusts for the saying of masses. This has certainly been the view in other jurisdictions when *Gilmour v Coats* has been considered. In *Re Alsagoff Trusts*, a decision from Singapore (1956) 22 MLJ 244, for example, it was held that the performance of religious rites in public was not charitable following the House of Lords' decision.

Taxation

JOHN TILEY, MA, BCL
Reader in the Law of Taxation, University of Cambridge
Fellow of Queen's College, Cambridge

1989 was a year of marking time in tax case law. A number of important issues came before the courts but progress was slight.

Avoidance schemes and the new approach

There have been three cases of interest in the light of the fluctuating fortunes of *Furniss v Dawson* [1984] 1 All ER 530 and the new approach. They may be of concern rather than interest to the authorities since the Crown lost in all three.

In *Ensign Tankers (Leasing) Ltd v Stokes (Inspector of Taxes)* [1989] STC 705 the commissioners found that a limited partnership was not trading and therefore the taxpayer could not use its losses. This finding was reversed by Millett J (see p 768). The commissioners also found that the transactions were preordained as a series of transactions and that the creation of the limited partnership served no commercial purpose. Millett J found the first unexceptionable but the second to be untenable.

The story begins with the taxpayer company, Ensign. Ensign became interested in films when it discovered from the Revenue's Statement of Practice SP9/79 that as from 1 June 1979, first-year allowances would be available in respect of capital expenditure on their production. It became a partner in two limited partnerships (Victory and Outland) set up to finance the production and exploitation of two films called 'Escape to Victory' and 'Outland'. The Victory partners, including Ensign, contributed a total of 25% of the cost of 'Escape to Victory' (the Outland partners contributed 25.5% to 'Outland') and borrowed the remainder by way of loans repayable exclusively out of the receipts of the films (ie non-recourse loans). The partnerships thus acquired the entire interest in each venture. All the transactions relating to the Victory partnership took place on 14 July 1980 and those relating to Outland on 5 November 1980. The Victory and Outland partnerships appointed sole and exclusive agents to distribute and exploit the films on their behalf.

Under the Revenue's Statement of Practice SP9/79 master prints of films were to be treated as plant for the purposes of FA 1971, s 41(1) if ownership carried the right to distribute and exploit the films. Ensign claimed first-year allowance on its percentage of the capital expenditure incurred on the films under s 41(1) of the Act.

Among the many arguments advanced by the Revenue to counter this scheme was one that the Ramsay principle applied (*WT Ramsay Ltd v IRC* [1981] STC 174, *Furniss (Inspector of Taxes) v Dawson* [1984] STC 153), the transactions having been entered into purely with a fiscal motive.

In rejecting this argument Millett J held that there was commercial purpose here and so the principle could not apply. He said (770–771):

> 'It was commercially essential for there to be some structure to regulate the relationship of the parties, preferably one with limited liability. The chosen structure was that of a limited partnership, which not only served a commercial purpose but became the taxable entity (for the Crown seeks to tax the film receipts . . . while denying the deduction of the expenditure which made the receipts possible). . . .
>
> The question is whether some step in a preordained transaction is so closely connected with the rest that it is to be treated not as having an independent effect but as merely an element in a different and larger whole. If so, then a question of statutory construction arises, for it is still necessary to apply the terms of the taxing Act to the composite whole. . . .
>
> I am unable to comprehend how the creation of the two limited partnerships can be treated as a step in some other and larger transaction without any independent effect of its own.'

The Crown also argued that the transactions in the present case should be disregarded as being not merely paper transactions without any commercial effect, or single transactions artificially broken up into separate stages. This submission too was rejected. It could not stand as an independent point since it was logically impossible at one and the same time to find that the partnerships were trading and that the transaction into which they entered had no commercial purpose. While agreeing with this conclusion one must however note the shift from 'no commercial effect' in the formulation of the point to 'no commercial purpose' in the answer; Lord Brightman in *Furniss v Dawson* of course talks about the absence of commercial effect as distinct from purpose.

The question of the meaning of a composite transaction was also considered in *Shepherd (Inspector of Taxes) v Lyntress Ltd; News International plc v Shepherd (Inspector of Taxes)* [1989] STC 617, Vinelott J. Again the Revenue lost. Under the *Craven v White* [1988] 3 All ER 495 approach the question whether an A–B transfer which is followed by a B–C transfer is to be treated as an A–C transfer depends upon there being not an existing *decision* at the time of the A–B transfer that there will be a B–C transfer but an *arrangement* that there will be one. Moreover the mere fact that the two are close in time is not enough to make them linked.

Grendon Trust plce owned M Ltd which by 1978 had suffered heavy losses and was worth very little. Grendon acquired a number of shell companies in which it held not less than 75% of the shares. Lyntress Ltd was one of them. Grendon then transferred its shares in M Ltd to them. Those shares were exchanged for shares in M Holdings (MH) which was not a 75% subsidiary of Grendon. At that stage the transfer of the shares to Lyntress had no fiscal consequences. However if Lyntress ceased to be a 75% subsidiary of Grendon or sold the MH shares outside the group, the loss on those shares would be realised.

In 1979 Grendon decided to utilise the loss by selling Lyntress to a company with chargeable gains which could be set off against Lyntress's losses on the MH shares; News International plc (News) became interested. There were two problems—one was a preemption provisions in the articles of association of MH; the other was CGTA 1979, s 62(3) which provides that if a disposal to a connected person gives rise to a loss the loss can be used only against gains accruing from disposal between the same persons; thus it was necessary for Grendon to cease to be in control of Lyntress before the sale of the MH shares.

The transaction was to be divided into three stages. The first stage was to be the sale to News of sufficient shares (35%) to ensure that Lyntress ceased to be a member of the Grendon group. That would realise an allowable loss which was not within s 62(3) and Lyntress could then carry out the second step, ie sell its MH shares to another Grendon subsidiary without giving rise to any further loss which would have fallen within s 62(3) or come within the provisions of MH's articles of association. Finally the third step; the sale of the balance of Lyntress's shares to News.

On 26 November 1979 News acquired 35% of Lyntress from Grendon. On 28 November News acquired the remaining 65%. Between those two dates Lyntress sold its shares in MH to another subsidiary of Grendon, Manilsa Ltd. News also acquired another company, Salcombe Securities Ltd (Salcombe) which had accrued capital losses. News intended to utilise those losses by setting them off against any gains arising on the disposal of its shareholdings in LWT, News Corporation and Broken Hill, which had considerably appreciated in value. In 1980 News sold substantial blocks of those shares, below market value to Lyntress and Salcombe, and within a few days the companies sold the shares in the market at a profit. Similar transactions were carried out in 1981.

Vinelott J first dealt with the sale to News on 26 November of 35% of Lyntress's shares which resulted in Lyntress leaving the Grendon group and there was on that date a deemed disposal of the MH shares which gave rise to an allowable loss. He held that that loss remained an allowable loss after News had acquired all the shares of Lyntress and the gains accruing to Lyntress after it had become a member of the News Group could therefore be set against it (s 62(3) not applying).

As the commissioners had pointed out, at this point, ie the acquisition of the Lyntress shares by News,

> 'there had been no occasion to utilise the loss on the [M] shares which crystallised at the moment when Lyntress left the Grendon group for the purposes of [TA 1970] s 278(3) . . . The composite transaction which is pointed to stops short of a significant event, so that the Revenue's subsequent submissions have nothing on which to bite.'

Vinelott J said at 650:

> 'In my judgment they were clearly right to reject those submissions. The case presented by the Crown was nothing less than a frontal assault on the ability of a group to hive down losses into a subsidiary and to sell the subsidiary to another group willing to purchase it so that it can set its own gains against the losses. It is surprising that losses can be bought and sold in this way, but if the law is to be changed it must be by the legislature.'

The other matter concerned the sale by News of the shares with accrued gains to Lyntress followed by the sale of those shares by Lyntress on the London and Australian Stock Exchanges. The commissioners had concluded that these had to be treated as disposals by News rather than by Lyntress. Vinelott J held that on the facts it was impossible to conclude that the transfer of the shares in LWT, News Corporation and Broken Hill by News to Lyntress and the subsequent sales of those shares by Lyntress were in each case part of a single composite transaction within the Ramsay principle. It was not enough to say that the shares were transferred to Lyntress with the intention that they should be sold, so that the gains could be set off against the losses in those companies. There was no ground for inferring from the brevity of the period between the transfer of the shares by News to Lyntress and the sale of those shares by Lyntress on the market that arrangements had been made for the sale before the transfer. Accordingly the gains on the shares of LWT, News Corporation and Broken Hill sold to Lyntress by News and sold in the open market by Lyntress were gains realised by Lyntress and not by News. The appeal by News would therefore be allowed.

Vinelott J observed that the brevity of the period may be an important event or even a decisive one in determining whether the two steps were part of a single composite transaction. But there is an important factual difference between a sale of, for instance, shares in an unlisted company and a sale of shares in a listed company. Negotiations for the sale of shares in an unlisted company are often and indeed normally are protracted. For a sale of shares listed on the Stock Exchange all that is normally required is a telephone call to a stockbroker.

Lastly one should note the decision of the Court of Appeal in the VAT prepayment case of *Customs and Excise Comrs v Faith Construction Ltd* [1989] STC 539, [1989] 2 All ER 938. All three judges rejected the argument based on *Furniss v Dawson* on the basis that the true legal construction of the facts showed that the payment was not received for the supplies as and when the loan was repaid; that concluded the point.

Schedule E

(a) *Bray (Inspector of Taxes) v Best* [1989] STC 159, [1989] 1 All ER 969 is the decision of the House of Lords on a case which has been commented on in earlier years. One might have wished for a more ringing endorsement of the principle that for income to be taxable the source must exist in the year of assessment however nonsensical that principle may be. In any event the decision has been reversed by the Finance Act 1989, ss 36–42.

(b) General principle. *Shilton v Wilmshurst (Inspector of Taxes)* [1990] STC 55, Court of Appeal; golden handshake or emolument—payment by third party—general test of emolument.

(c) Benefits in kind. There are two cases on benefits in kind. In *Stones v Hall (Inspector of Taxes)* [1989] STC 138 an assessment was made on the taxpayers in respect of rent-free accommodation and other benefits in kind; under the legislation these charges should be reduced to the extent that the costs were made good by them. The taxpayers sought reductions on account of (i) the value rendered by them to the company under their contracts of service and (ii) including certain interest-free loans made by them to the company. Warner J held that in the absence of evidence to link the interest-free loans to the benefits no allowance could be made for them. He also held that as a matter of principle the value of these services rendered to the company under the contracts of service could not be taken into account at all.

While it was true that the taxpayer did indeed render services to the farm in managing it and its investments. However—

> 'To my mind it is implicit in that legislation that the provision of services in exchange for the provision of benefits in kind cannot be either the payment of rent or a making good of the cost to the company of providing the benefits in kind. That is because the whole purpose of Sch E is to tax remuneration for services and the purpose of the present sections is to assimilate remuneration in the form of benefits in kind to remuneration in the form of emoluments directly taxable under the charging section of Sch E [TA 1988, s 19].' (148h)

Of course if the company had paid for his services its profits would have been reduced and therefore its tax would have been reduced and so, in a sense, the Revenue were getting at a slice of profits twice; once in the hands of the company and now in the hands of the employee; but that was immaterial, the only issue was the taxable income of the taxpayer and not what adjustment might be made to the income of the company.

Gurney (Inspector of Taxes) v Richards [1989] STC 682 is a short case in which Millett J had to consider the tax liability of a deputy chief fire officer for whom a vehicle equipped with telephone and flashing light was provided by his employer. The vehicle was used by him at all times while he was on duty, including journeys between home and office. Millett J held that it was used exclusively for business purposes but that it was not a car and so escaped a charge under TA 1988, s 157. The case was remitted to the commissioners to see whether any other head of charge might apply.

Johnson v Holleran (Inspector of Taxes) [1989] STC 1 is concerned with the question 'what is a pension?' The taxpayer suffered a period of ill-health and was on sick-leave from his company for one year from 12 March 1982 to 12 March 1983. In February 1983, he was informed that following the reorganisation of the company, he would be declared redundant with effect from 31 March 1983 and that since he had been on sick leave from 12 March 1982, he would receive, in addition to the redundancy payments, a monthly disability benefit from the company's staff pension scheme. The taxpayer argued that these monthly payments should be treated not as pension but as benefits in accordance with the terms of his notice of redundancy, so being in consideration of the termination of his employment (and so exempt from charge to tax by virtue of s 188(1)(a)). The argument failed but the planning lessons are clear. The taxpayer received sums of money from the trustees of the pension fund after the cesser of his employment in recognition of his previous employment and because of his disability and in those circumstances the commissioners were entitled to find that the payments were a pension. The fact that the payments were made on account of disability rather than for past services was immaterial.

Schedule D, Case I

Kirkham v Williams (Inspector of Taxes) [1989] STC 333 is an interesting case on the scope of the Schedule. Its importance lies in the statement of Vinelott J that there was no overriding principle that if it was a purpose of the taxpayer to acquire something as a capital asset of his business that was sufficient to show that the steps which he took in order to acquire it could not be an adventure in the nature of trade.

The taxpayer carried on business as a general dealer, demolition contractor and hirer of plant. In 1978 he purchased a 10 acre site including a mill. The General Commissioners found that the site was acquired principally to provide office accommodation and storage space for his demolition and plant hire business. He also intended to carry on limited farming activities on the land. In 1977, before he acquired the site, he applied for planning permission to erect an agricultural worker's dwelling. That application and a subsequent one in 1978 were refused. Planning permission was granted in 1980 for the erection of a dwelling house, which the taxpayer built himself. He sold the whole site and house in October 1982 and moved to a farm. The commissioners found that the taxpayer did not terminate his business as a general dealer and demolition contractor when he moved to his new premises.

The taxpayer claimed that the site was part of the fixed capital of his business and that the gain realised on the sale of the land, being a gain on the sale of a capital asset, was capable of being rolled over and set against the purchase price of his new premises. The commissioners found that the taxpayer did not intend to use the whole of the land for office and storage space nor to live there. They confirmed the assessment holding that the purchase, development and resale of the land was an adventure in the nature of trade and the gain realised was assessable under Sch D, Case I as a trading profit.

Vinelott J held that there was ample foundation for the conclusion that the taxpayer in order to get a site for his demolition and plant hire business embarked on a transaction which had all the characteristics of trading and the commissioners' finding was not inconsistent with that conclusion. He also rejected an argument based on apportionment, holding that the site had been acquired as a whole and the taxpayer had not established that he had bought part of the land for his demolition and plant hire business and part for development and resale as a separate trading transaction.

Richfield International Land and Investment Co Ltd v Inland Revenue Commissioner [1989] STC 820 is a short and entirely predictable Privy Council decision on appeal from Hong Kong. The taxpayer, a company engaged in business of long-term property investment which had purchased seven properties in Hong Kong, had been content to be taxed on profits from sale of two of the properties as on sale of trading stock and had invited taxation on that basis in relation to profits arising from sale of a third property. It now wanted capital gains treatment on a fourth property—and failed.

Eckel v Board of Inland Revenue [1989] STC 305 is an equally straightforward Privy Council case as far as scope is concerned but is of some interest on the issue of timing. In September 1969 W, a married woman living with her husband, agreed to buy six parcels of land. A year later she agreed to resell them to a company (E Ltd) of which she and her husband were the sole directors, at a higher price; the price was to be paid (a) as to $10,000 as soon as E Ltd accepted her title (on which date E Ltd would be let into possession); (b) as to the balance (plus interest thereon, from that date of payment, at the current bank rate for overdrafts), on or before 26 September 1972. During 1971 W acquired title. She was not paid the balance of the price in September 1972, but during the fiscal years 1973 and 1974 she respectively conveyed two parcels of the contract land to the order of the company. The Tax Appeal

Board held that W had acquired the land with a trading intention but that she was not trading in 1973 and 1974; this was rejected by the Privy Council. The correct analysis was that she did not become assessable until 1973 and 1974. She could not be held to have earned the profit until she had done all that was needed to earn it, ie by executing a conveyance of the property.

The question whether a fiscally motivated transaction can be a trading transaction has arisen in connection with two attempts to establish trading losses. The taxpayer lost in the first case but succeeded in the second. In *Overseas Containers (Finance) Ltd v Stoker (Inspector of Taxes)* [1989] STC 364 the Court of Appeal held in favour of the Revenue and rejected a scheme designed to get relief for foreign exchange losses by passing them through a finance subsidiary.

The taxpayer company was a wholly owned subsidiary of the parent shipping company (OCL) which was engaged in the container trade; it was formed so that gains and losses incurred on foreign loans would enter into the parent company's computation of liability to tax through group relief. The court held that when one looked at all the circumstances and not merely at the taxpayer company's in isolation, it was clear that the loan transactions had no commercial element in them. The interest differential obtained by the taxpayer company merely represented a transfer of income from the group to the taxpayer company. Accordingly there was no ground on which it could be held that the short and medium-term loan transactions were trading transactions. Another way of putting it would have been to say, according to one commentator, 'that the company had been formed in an attempt to circumvent the potential tax disadvantage but that this failed and a genuine loss did not therefore secure deduction;' Atkinson in *Tolley's Tax Planning* 1989–90 p 370. Against this one may make the point that if finance companies were allowed to operate in the way desired by the taxpayer it might enable taxpayers to use such vehicles where the risk was one way and different vehicles where the risk was the other way.

In *Ensign Tankers (Leasing) Ltd v Stokes (Inspector of Taxes)* [1989] STC 705 the question was whether two partnerships could be said to be trading; the taxpayer was one of the partners. The partnerships produced films with a view to their distribution and exploitation for profit but the partnerships' finances were obtained from investors, whose primary purpose was to gain a fiscal advantage. Millett J held that the partnerships were trading. He dealt with the relevance of fiscal motives thus—

> 'Fiscal considerations naturally affect the taxpayer's evaluations of the financial risks and rewards of any proposed venture, and are often the decisive factor in persuading him to enter into it. First year allowances, enterprise zones, government grants and the like operate as financial inducements to businessmen to engage in commercial activities which would be financially unattractive or unacceptably speculative without them. Such motivations, even if paramount, do not alter the character of the activities in question. But while a fiscal motive, even an overriding fiscal motive, is irrelevant in itself, it becomes highly relevant if it affects, not just the shape or structure of the transaction, but its commerciality so that . . . "the shape and character of the transaction *is no longer that of a trading transaction*". . . . nothing less will do.' (763, 764).

This passage is highly abstract and is hard to analyse—how does one assess the commerciality of the transaction?—but is important as an expression of the view that the fiscal motive must be very powerful before the court will intervene. He dealt with the earlier Court of Appeal case thus (at 763):

> 'the alleged commercial profit consisted of a payment from one wholly-owned subsidiary to another in the same group; such a payment disappears on consolidation and serves no commercial purpose of any kind.'

Donald Fisher (Ealing) Ltd v Spencer (Inspector of Taxes) [1989] STC 256 is the Court of Appeal decision on the taxation of compensation payments by an agent following his negligent failure to serve a counter-notice in a rent review; the court agreed with Walton J that the payments to compensate the company for the exess rents it had to pay were not for any diminution in value of a capital asset or for loss of profits and so taxable as trading receipts.

Beauchamp (Inspector of Taxes) v F W Woolworth plc [1989] STC 510 is a major decision. The case concerned exchange losses on the repayment of loan capital which took the form of Swiss franc loans for fixed five-year terms. The House of Lords reversed the decision of the Court of Appeal and reinstated that of Hoffmann J who had reversed the commissioners. Giving the only reasoned speech Lord Templeman said that a loan was a revenue transaction only if it was temporary and fluctuating in nature and was incurred in meeting the ordinary running expenses of the business. This loan was therefore on capital account so that the exchange loss went unrelieved. He thought that a five-year loan was quite distinct from a five-year petrol tie which had been classified as revenue expenditure in *Regent Oil Co Ltd v Strick* [1966] AC 295, [1965] 3 All ER 174 (on which see Whiteman (1966) BTR 115). The petrol tie was an integral and essential method of trading in petroleum products, and the petrol tie had become 'an ordinary incident of marketing.' (518b). He might have added that in *Regent Oil* itself the five-year lease was held to be capital. Lord Templeman went on to reject the opinion in the Court of Appeal that this was a question of fact; rather it was a matter of law. Unfortunately there is not the slightest indication here of any guidance as to how one tells fact from law. The case is also interesting because no trace of any argument based on TA 1988, s 74(f) appears in Lord Templeman's speech; presumably the Revenue accept the opinion of the Court of Appeal that that section does not apply.

The case leaves some unease. It is all very well for Lord Templeman to refer to the possibility of amending legislation, but the problem has been known for a long time and various efforts to get round it (see *Overseas Containers (Finance) Ltd v Stoker* supra) have failed. Meanwhile the business community are left with unrelieved losses.

Rolfe (Inspector of Taxes) v Wimpey Waste Management Ltd [1989] STC 455 is another Court of Appeal decision upholding a first instance decision. However this one is to be reversed by legislation (Finance Bill 1990, clause 69; presumably because of its green character). The taxpayer carried on a waste disposal business and subsequent restoration of sites suitable for tipping waste. Once the tipping space was exhausted the company would sell the sites. The court held that the assets acquired by the taxpayer company were not airspace but land on which the taxpayer company carried on its business and, taking into account all the factors, in particular the average length of time for which the sites had been used, it was clear that what the taxpayer company had acquired was a capital asset. One should add that the sites were usually disused gravel pits or quarries and that the taxpayer acquired either the freehold or a long or short lease of the property; this would seem to be one way of distinguishing *Golden Horse Shoe (New) Ltd v Thurgood* [1934] 1 KB 548, 18 TC 280 where the acquisition of tailings by a refining company was held to be the acquisition of trade stock.

MacKinlay (Inspector of Taxes) v Arthur Young McClelland Moores & Co [1989] STC 898 is the House of Lords decision on partnership expenses and personal expenses. The Court of Appeal decision was commented upon adversely last year, 1988 All ER Rev at 303–305. The House of Lords has reversed that decision. The removal expenses of a partner met by the firm, being at least partly personal in nature, were not deductible in computing partnership profits. The speech of Lord Oliver is a model of sound technical sense.

R v Inspector of Taxes, ex p Brumfield [1989] STC 151, QBD Peter Gibson J is a short case on the interpretation of a Statement of Practice. SP4/85, para 3 concerns the deduction of interest on loans used to buy land occupied for partnerships purposes. This case holds that it is available only where the loan is taken out by the individual partner (as distinct from the partnership).

Baylis (Inspector of Taxes) v Roberts [1989] STC 693 is yet another case on the meaning of the word 'may'. TA 1988, s 63 provides the basis of assessment for closing years and provides that if the actual profits of the last two full years are greater than those produced by the normal preceding year basis of assessment the inspector may make an assessment in that higher sum. Knox J held that 'may' here means shall and that the inspector has no discretion about it. *R v HM Inspector of Taxes, ex p Lansing Bagnall Ltd* [1986] STC 453, (see 1986 All ER Rev) was distinguished.

Schedules C and D, Case III

Here there are a number of smallish points. *Esso Petroleum Co Ltd v Ministry of Defence* [1989] STC 805 raised the question whether interest on damages awarded against a government department fell within Schedule C as a public revenue dividend or Schedule D Case III. Harman J held in favour of Schedule D and so was not subject to deduction of tax at source.

Peracha v Miley (Inspector of Taxes) [1989] STC 76 is another case on whether interest has been received for the purposes of TA 1988, s 59. Sums held in a deposit account were held as a guarantee for a loan; interest had accumulated in the frozen account over several years; the taxpayer was liable to repay the loan personally but had no access to the account. Vinelott J held that he had received the interest because it had enured to his benefit within the meaning of that phrase as interpreted in *Dunmore v McGowan (Inspector of Taxes)* [1978] STC 217, [1978] 2 All ER 85. *Macpherson v Bond (Inspector of Taxes)* [1985] STC 678 was distinguishable because in that case the loan had not been guaranteed by the taxpayer.

Essex County Council v Ellam (Inspector of Taxes) [1989] STC 317 is the Court of Appeal decision in the case on pure income profit (discussed 1988 All ER Rev p 317). The first instance decision was upheld—rightly in the writer's opinion.

Capital allowances

There are two important cases. The first is *Wimpy International Ltd v Warland (Inspector of Taxes)* [1989] STC 273, the Court of Appeal decision on the distinction between plant and setting, to use familiar but imprecise terminology. The case holds that something which had become part of the premises, instead of merely embellishing them, cannot be plant, except in the rare case when the premises themselves were plant (such as *IRC v Barclay Curle & Co Ltd* [1969] 1 All ER 732, 45 TC 221 where a dry dock was held to be plant and *Cooke (Inspector of Taxes) v Beach Station Caravans Ltd* [1974] 3 All ER 159, [1974] STC 402 where a swimming pool and a paddling pool were held to be plant. The fact that something which is part of the premises has a function (eg in creating atmophere) is not enough save in these exceptional cases.

The case is of interest for two other reasons. The first is the comment of Lloyd LJ that the task of the appellant taxpayer was not to argue that the judge had erred in law in his reasons for not reversing the commissioners but that the commissioners had erred in the first place (285j). The other is the statement also by Lloyd LJ, about the attention to be paid to the reasons of the commissioners. At 286 he said:

> 'There is no universal formula which can solve every problem. Nor, unfortunately, is this a field where one can fall back on that useful resort—so often the last resort—that plant, though difficult to define, is, like an elephant, easy enough to recognise when one sees it. For . . . no ordinary man, whether literate or semi-literate, would think of a horse or a swimming pool as plant.
>
> So what is to be done? The answer is, I think, that in these cases the courts should be especially reluctant to upset the decisions of commissioners, unless it can be shown not only that they have erred in law but also that their error is palpable. It is not enough to show that they may have applied the wrong test, as seems to be suggested by counsel for the taxpayer companies at one stage, or that they have not stated the test in the most precise language, or that they have omitted to refer to some factor which they ought to have taken into account. Where the judges have themselves failed to find a universal test, the commissioners are not to have their language examined too closely or dissected line by line.'

The second important case is *Ensign Tankers (Leasing) Ltd v Stokes (Inspector of Taxes)* [1989] STC 705 again. The Crown argued that the taxpayer was not entitled to capital allowances in respect of the master copy of a film on the ground that the film did not belong to the partnership. This was because the partnerships, immediately after acquiring the films, had parted with the right to distribute and exploit them in perpetuity. This was rejected by Millett J first on the ground that, even accepting this analysis, there had been some scintilla temporis in which the film had belonged to the partnership. However he went on to reject the analysis itself; by entering into the various distributorship agreements, the partnerships did not part with the right to exploit the films, but instead exploited them.

Millett J then dealt with the Revenue argument that the taxpayer had not incurred that part of the expenditure which was funded by a non-recourse loan. This too was rejected. 'To incur' means 'to render oneself liable to' and expenditure is incurred by a taxpayer if he has legally committed himself to it.

For the purposes of s 41 of the Finance Act 1971, expenditure is treated as incurred when the sum in question became payable. A borrower who obtains a non-recourse loan incurs no personal liability to repay the lender but that is irrelevant; in the case of borrowed money s 41 is concerned with the taxpayer's liability to expend it on the acquisition of plant, not on his liability to repay the lender: see p 769.

Corporation tax

Again there are two interesting cases. *Dunstan (Inspector of Taxes) v Young Austen and Young Ltd* [1989] STC 69 is the Court of Appeal decision on the meaning of the term reorganisation and whether the situations in CGTA 1979, s 77(2) are exhaustive. The court held that the situations are not exhaustive, allowed the appeal and restored the decision of the commissioner. In reversing the decision of Warner J the court stated that an increase of share capital could be a reorganisation notwithstanding that it did not come within the precise wording of s 77(2)(a)(i), provided that the new shares were acquired by existing shareholders because they were existing shareholders, and in proportion to their existing beneficial holdings.

Gallic Leasing Ltd v Coburn (Inspector of Taxes) [1989] STC 354 is a case on what is needed to make a valid claim for group relief. Vinelott J held that all that was required was for the claimant company to make it clear to the inspector that a claim was being made; there was no requirement for the claimant company at the time of making the claim to identify the surrendering companies or the amount of losses to be surrendered by each of them; the taxpayer's appeal was allowed.

Inheritance tax

Montague Trust Co (Jersey) Ltd v Inland Revenue Commissioners [1989] STC 477, Ch D, concerns the issue of whether there was excluded settled property. Under the Inheritance Tax Act 1984, s 48(4) where securities issued by the Treasury subject to a condition that they are to be free of tax while in the beneficial ownership of persons neither domiciled nor ordinarily resident in the United Kingdom are comprised in a settlement they will be excluded property if (a) a person neither domiciled nor ordinarily resident in the UK is entitled to a qualifying interest in possession in them or (b) no qualifying interest in possession subsists in them but it is shown that all known persons for whose benefit the settled property or income from it has been or might be applied, or who are or might become beneficially entitled to an interest in possession in it, are persons neither domiciled nor ordinarily resident in the UK.

By a settlement made in 1970, Mrs K settled shares on discretionary trusts for the benefit of her daughter, Mrs W, and her four children, and other members of her own and her husband's family. The trustees were authorised, in the exercise of a power of appointment, to transfer the trust fund, subject to the settlement, to another body of trustees and to delegate the exercise of the power of appointment. The class of beneficiaries under the 1970 settlement included persons domiciled and ordinarily resident within the United Kingdom.

In 1974 Mrs Wallis and her family emigrated to Israel where they became domiciled. The plaintiffs, resident in Jersey, were appointed trustees of the 1970 settlement in 1976 and they reinvested the trust fund in a single holding of 6½% Treasury Loan 1976 which were exempt securities so long as the securities remained in the beneficial ownership of persons neither domiciled nor ordinarily resident in the United Kingdom.

On 11 May 1976, a settlement was made between Mrs W as settlor, the plaintiffs as trustees and her minor children and their issue as beneficiaries, all of whom were domiciled outside the United Kingdom. The powers of appointment were similar to those in the 1970 settlement.

By a deed dated 11 May 1976 (the first 1976 appointment) the plaintiffs transferred the 1970 settlement trust fund, subject to the trusts of the 1970 settlement, to themselves as trustees of the 1976 settlement, to be held on trusts for the exclusive benefit of Mrs W's four children and their issue. Vinelott J held that it could not be inferred from the terms of the first 1976 appointment that the trustees, as trustees of the 1970 settlement, intended to create absolute interests in favour of the four children and so the trust fund was not excluded property.

On the following day, 12 May 1976 (the second 1976 appointment), the trustees executed a deed of appointment whereby each child became entitled to an interest in possession of one quarter of the trust fund. That share could be divested on death under the age of 30 years in favour of the deceased's issue. Vinelott J held that while this appointment removed the possibility of persons resident in the United Kingdom benefiting, what is now s 48(4) had to be applied to the situation which existed immediately before that appointment. On that footing the trusts created by the appointment had to be disregarded. It followed therefore that there was a capital distribution when the second appointment creating interests in possession in the trust fund was made and capital transfer tax was therefore payable.

Lake v Lake [1989] STC 865 is a remarkable case on the use of the equitable remedy of rectification to take advantage of the rule allowing variations of testamentary dispositions to be treated as if made by the deceased (Inheritance Tax Act 1984, s 142—Capital Gains Tax Act 1979, s 49).

A deed to vary distribution was made. Unfortunately, in the course of finalising the draft deed prepared by counsel to that end, a clerical error in the office of the solicitors concerned led to the specification of the property to be given in quarter shares to the children and the grandchildren becoming prefaced by the words 'I give free of tax'. A further deed varying the first one was ineffective by reason of the decision in *Russell v IRC* [1988] STC 195 (see 1988 All ER Rev p 313) and so the widow now sought an order for the rectification of the first deed by substituting for the words 'free of tax' in that deed, the words 'such gifts to bear their own tax'.

Mervyn Davies J held that on the evidence he was completely satisfied that the common intention of the parties, when executing the first deed, had been that the assets specifically bequeathed in four equal shares to the children and the grandchildren should bear their own tax. The fact that all the parties desired the order sought was no bar to it being made! The parties were able to save some £145,000 in tax.

Trusts and settlements

Butler (Inspector of Taxes) v Wildin [1989] STC 22 is a case on TA 1988, s 663. The taxpayers (two brothers) had given shares in a newly incorporated company to themselves and their four infant children and the question was whether the dividends should be treated as his income by reason of that provision.

The infants' shares were paid for out of money provided by their grandparents and the price agreed was par value of £1 per share. Subsequently, two more children were born, first P, who received 12 shares from his father and seven shares from his uncle and later, L who received five shares from her father and 11 shares from the five existing infant shareholders. Both P and L also paid £1 for each share out of their own resources. At that stage none of the shares remained in the possession of the taxpayers.

The company commenced trading by acquiring a disused railway yard from British Rail for development in 1981. It was financed by a bank loan guaranteed by the taxpayers. No profits were made until the accounting year ending 31 October 1985. Dividends were declared in March 1985 which were paid to each infant shareholder.

When the matter came before a Special Commissioner the Revenue contended that the taxpayers, by incorporating the company and allotting shares to the children which they could have allotted to themselves, by adopting the whole risk of the venture for the benefit of the children, by giving their personal guarantees to the bank and acting as directors without any remuneration, entered into an arrangement which had elements of bounty and had provided funds directly or indirectly for the purpose of the arrangement. Accordingly they were settlors and since the dividends to the children in question were derived from the arrangement, they fell to be treated as the income of the taxpayers by virtue of s 437 of the 1970 Act. In the case of L's shares transferred from her father, the Revenue conceded before the commissioner that she had paid market value for them. The Special Commissioner allowed the taxpayers' appeals holding that s 437 did not apply. The Revenue appealed. Vinelott J in allowing the Revenue's appeal said that the taxpayers were the architects of a reciprocal arrangement to which both had contributed by the provision of skills or services, to ensure that the company, and so indirectly the children took the benefit of the development at no cost or risk to themselves. The dividends were paid to the four older children 'by virtue or in consequence of any settlement' within s 663. That arrangement contained an element of 'bounty' since the children contributed nothing except trifling sums, they were exposed to no risk, which was borne by the taxpayers, who lent money to the company and guaranteed bank loans and they gave their services as directors free of charge.

Secondly Vinelott J held that, in the absence of any findings by the Special Commissioner, he could not infer that the original arrangement was that the taxpayers would pass on their shares to the afterborn children. The shares received by P from his uncle could be disregarded because there was no evidence of any reciprocity; however the 12 shares transfered by the child's father clearly fell within s 663. The burden lay on the taxpayer to show that full value had been given for the shares by the son.

A further parcel of shares were transferred to L out of the holdings of the other infant shareholders. This transfer was not part of any reciprocal arrangement between the taxpayers. The Revenue had conceded that the transfer of shares to L by her father was for full market value with L paying out of her own resources. This concession attracted a certain amount of judicial incredulity but apparently rested on the fact that the Share Valuation Office had accepted par value as full value for the purposes of stamp duty. As Vinelott J put it, the Revenue said they

> 'would face criticism and a possible application for judicial review if they were to claim in another context that the transfers were not for full value. I express no opinion on that point. What is remarkable is that, as I have pointed out, the letter from the stamp office charged voluntary disposition duty.'

In the light of the concession the learned judge felt he had to conclude that there was no settlement of these shares and so none of the income from L's shares should be aggregated with that of the taxpayer. One is left sharing the judge's comments on the concession and his view that this is an entirely correct application of s 663.

Dawson v Inland Revenue Commissioners [1989] STC 473 is the House of Lords decision on the problem of trustees and their residence. It adds nothing to what had gone on in the lower courts and has been reversed by legislation; see FA 1989, ss 110 (trustees) and 111 (personal representatives).

Jenkins (Inspector of Taxes) v Brown [1989] STC 557, Ch D is a decision on the meaning of settled property for CGT. The case follows and greatly resembles, *Booth v Ellard (Inspector of Taxes)* [1980] STC 555.

In 1971 WB and his five children, the taxpayers, executed a deed setting up a family trust into which they conveyed farms to which they were individually absolutely entitled. Pooling the farms was intended to retain them within the family. The terms of the deed of settlement provided that each taxpayer had an undivided unequal percentage share in the trust fund in proportion to the value of the property which he had transferred into the trust. It was accepted that the taxpayers were abolutely entitled to the settled property as against the trustees within the meaning of s 46(1) of the Capital Gains Tax Act 1979.

After the death of WB, three of the children wished to alter the pooling arrangement and revert to owning the land which they had transferred into the trust. All the parties agreed and a deed of rearrangement was executed in 1980 under which certain parcels of land were taken out of the trust holding and distributed to the three children. The remainder of the trust property was held by the trustees under the terms of the 1971 settlement. The value of the distributed parcels of land corresponded with the value of the percentage interests in the corpus of the settled property previously owned by the three children.

The question was whether the deed of rearrangement had resulted in a disposal of assets. Knox J, dismissing the Crown's appeal, held that the beneficial interests of the settlors in the mass of the trust reflected precisely their respective beneficial proprietary interests prior to the creation of the trust and that those interests remained unaffected by the deed of rearrangement.

It was agreed that the undivided shares in the land were assets and that the undivided shares in the land were not interest in settled property—because of

CGTA 1979, s 46(1); he also accepted that those interests fell to be treated as vested in the beneficiaries themselves rather than the trustees. However he argued that the 1980 deed involved each of the ten taxpayers giving up their undivided shares in favour of one or more of the other taxpayers. Knox J relied heavily on a passage from the judgment of Buckley LJ in *Booth v Ellard* where he said,

> 'The effect of the trust was to subject all the trust shares to powers and discretions conferred on the trustees for what was conceived to be the collective benefit of the settlors, but, subject to those powers and discretions which the settlors collectively could override, the measure of the beneficial interests of the settlors remained unaffected by the trust. There was no transfer of any beneficial interest from any one of them to any other.' [1980] STC 555 at 560.

That analysis, said Knox J, was based on a comparison of their respective entitlements before and after. There was no disposal for CGT purposes because there was no alteration in those respective entitlements; the fact that there had been a change on a proper legal analysis in the subject matter of any given participant was irrelevant: see p 594a.

Capital gains

Owen v Elliott (Inspector of Taxes) [1989] STC 44 involved an ingenious but unsuccessful argument by the taxpayer. The taxpayer owned and lived in premises which consisted of a main building and an annexe. He and his wife carried on the business of a private hotel or boarding-house in those premises by receiving guests for reward. During the summer season, when visitors normally stayed for one or two weeks the taxpayer and his family lived in the annexe. In the winter, there were few guests who stayed for several months and the taxpayer and his family occupied the whole building in common with them. Thus during the taxpayer's ownership of the hotel the whole of it was from time to time used as his main residence. It was sold, and the taxpayer agreed with the inspector that one-third of the gain from the disposal should be exempt from capital gains tax under ss 101 and 102.

The taxpayer's ingenious argument was his claim that he was entitled to further relief under FA 1980, s 80(1) on the ground that the talking in of guests for reward as carried on by him amounted to letting of the premises wholly or partly as residential accommodation. The taxpayer's appeal was rejected by Millett J who said that the phrase 'let by him as residential accommodation' referred not to the quality of occupation by the occupier but to the quality of letting by the home-owner and was satisfied only if the kind of letting in which he was engaged was the provision of accommodation for people who would use the premises as their home. The learned judge went on to explain that the relief would normally be available to the home owner who provides lodging for university students or accommodation for hospital nurses, or who takes in lodgers from time to time but not to someone who is simply carrying on an hotel or boarding house business. The question was one of fact.

Pennine Raceway Ltd v Kirklees Metropolitan Council (No 2) [1989] STC 122 is an indirect case on the tax treatment of a right to compensation. A company had planning permission to conduct drag racing under licence but that permission was revoked by the local authority. The company was entitled to compensation but there was some uncertainty as to tax to be levied on compensation. Following *Zim Properties Ltd v Procter* [1985] STC 90 the Court of Appeal held that the licence was an asset for CGT purposes and that the capital sum was derived from that asset. Alternatively the sums would be taxable as compensation as income for loss of profit. Since the sums would be taxable in either event, the damages should be paid. This decision although convincing in the case itself enabled the court to avoid having to decide which was the appropriate basis for taxation and so avoid some knotty problems arising under the decision of the House of Lords in *British Transport Commission v Gourley* [1956] AC 185, [1955] 3 All ER 796.

Finally there are two cases involving assets held since before April 1965. The first is *Morgan (Inspector of Taxes) v Gibson* [1989] STC 568 and concerns the determination of the current use value of the land. The issue was whether the gain should be determined on a straight line basis under CGTA 1979, Sch 5, para 11 or by reference to the market value of the land on 6 April 1965 as directed by Sch 5, para 9. This turned on whether the consideration for the disposal of the asset exceeded its current use value. The case involved 10 acres of market garden land adjacent to Heathrow Airport; numerous applications for planning permission were refused and there was no change of use of the land between 1948 and 1984 when it was sold for £160,000. The Revenue view was that the consideration obtained on the disposal of the land exceeded the current use value of the land.

Scott J upheld the Revenue view; the legislation defined that value on the assumption that no material development was permissible or would become permissible. On that footing no element of hope value or development value could be included in the current use value. There was an element of development value on the facts.

The other case, *Richart (Inspector of Taxes) v J Lyons & Co Ltd* [1989] STC 665, concerns roll-over relief. That relief is excluded in whole or in part to the extent that the asset has not been used for the purposes of the trade throughout the period of ownership. The Court of Appeal held that periods of ownership before 1965 should be included in this calculation, a decision which favoured the taxpayer as his periods of non-trade use were after 1965.

Double taxation relief

The first case, *George Wimpey International Ltd v Rolfe (Inspector of Taxes)* [1989] STC 609, upholds the orthodox (and restrictive) view of the scope of this relief.

The taxpayer company (W) carried on a worldwide construction business. In 1984 it made a trading loss computed for income tax purposes in accordance with Schedule D Case I in the sums of £2,479,061. That loss took into account profits of £3,858,268 earned in Gabon, Hong Kong and Jordan on which the company had paid £1,153,376 by way of income tax under the law of those territories. In the same year the company had other non-trading income and chargeable gains amounting to over £4m. W thus had total profits on which the company was chargeable to corporation tax under TA 1988, s 9(3). Could W use the foreign tax as a unilateral credit under TA 1988, s 790? Under s 790(4) 'credit for tax paid under the law of the territory

outside the [UK] and computed by reference to income arising in that
territory [is] allowed against any [UK] . . . corporation tax computed by
reference to that income'. The foreign income had been taken into account in
computing the total profits. Did it follow that the UK corporation tax was
'computed by reference to' that foreign income?

Hoffmann J resorted to the scheme of the legislation and said that it led to
the need to identify exactly the fund charged to overseas tax with a fund
chargeable also to United Kingdom tax.

> 'The reference in s [790(4)] to United Kingdom tax being "computed by
> reference to" the income on which the foreign tax had been computed was
> introduced . . . in consequence of the decision in *Duckering (Inspector of Taxes)
> v Gollan* 42 TC 333, and was intended to ensure that the identity was not
> between funds which might notionally be regarded as the taxable income in the
> foreign territory and the United Kingdom but between the actual funds by
> reference to which the computation of tax was made. This identification of the
> income subject to United Kingdom corporation tax can, in my judgment, only
> be made in accordance with income tax principles. On this basis it seems to me
> that the income in respect of which the taxpayer company became liable to
> corporation tax was its non-trading income notwithstanding that the
> computation of that income was made subject to deduction for losses which
> took into account the company's trading in the three territories. The taxpayer
> company was not chargeable to any tax in respect of the income which had been
> subject to foreign tax. No credit can therefore be allowed.' (p 616).

R v Inland Revenue Commissioners, ex p Camacq Corporation [1989] STC 785 is
of general interest because of the argument advanced by the Crown that
foreign sovereigns were liable to income tax on income accruing within the
United Kingdom and that sovereign immunity from income tax meant no
more than the immunity of the sovereign from being sued therefore in the
United Kingdom courts. From a taxation viewpoint the case is of interest as
an example of judicial review to seek a review of the Revenue decision to
revoke a permission to pay a dividend gross. On the facts both Kennedy J and
the Court of Appeal held that it was proper for the Revenue to revoke the
permission.

There are also two obsolete cases. *Padmore v Inland Revenue Commissioners*
[1989] STC 493 is the Court of Appeal decision rejecting the Revenue
arguments in relation to the UK-Jersey convention. The reasons are the same
as those of Peter Gibson J that the partnerships referred to in the convention
must include mixed partnerships; this partnership was resident in Jersey
because it was managed and controlled there and its profits were therefore
exempt. This decision has been comprehensively reversed by what is now
TA 1988, s 112(4)(5). The same fate has overtaken *Collard (Inspector of Taxes)
v Mining and Industrial Holdings Ltd* [1989] STC 384 on the interaction of the
foreign tax credit and ACT; see FA 1986, s 49 now TA 1988, s 797. The
House of Lords dismissed the Revenue appeal. Lord Oliver said that the
structure and language of the legislation pointed strongly to the conclusion
that, in making the necessary corporation tax computations, the deduction of
double taxation relief was intended to precede the set-off of advance
corporation tax.

Administrative matters

First there is the decision of Nolan J in *Woolwich Equitable Building Society v Inland Revenue Commissioners* [1989] STC 111. The issue was whether a taxpayer has a right to recover a payment made to the Revenue by way of tax if the demand is later shown to be without lawful authority. Orthodox restitutionary thinking would say that such a payment was made under a mistake of law and therefore irrecoverable. However Nolan J held that where a taxpayer paid money in response to a tax demand by the Revenue without lawful authority, that money was recoverable if there was an agreement for repayment in the event that the money paid turned out not in fact to be payable. In the absence of statutory provision, such an agreement would be implied whenever money was paid to the Revenue pending the outcome of a dispute which would determine whether or not the Revenue was entitled to the money, but there was no right to interest unless also agreed. He rejected the taxpayer's alternative argument that it had been paid under duress; the possible damage to Woolwich's reputation and interest liabilities arising from a refusal to pay did not amount to duress on the part of the Revenue. He also held that in the circumstances, by virtue of what is now TA 1988, Sch 16, para 10(4) the Revenue must be assumed to have accepted Woolwich's payments on terms that they would be repaid if the judicial review proceedings went against them.

The status of Revenue advice as possible grounds for judicial review if that advice is withdrawn was considered in *R v Inland Revenue Commissioners, ex p MFK Underwriting Agencies Ltd* [1989] STC 873 where the Court of Appeal said that the Revenue would be bound if it agreed to, or represented that it would, forego tax which might arguably be payable on a proper construction of the relevant legislation, and the taxpayer relied on such agreement or representation. However the Revenue would only be bound in the case of an informal approach if the taxpayer gave full details of the specific transaction on which he sought the Revenue's ruling, indicated the ruling sought and made it plain that a fully considered ruling was sought, and indicated the use he intended to make of any ruling given, and the ruling or statement made was clear, unambiguous and devoid of qualification. The advice did not fall within this category in this case. A similar approach was taken in *R v Inland Revenue Commissioners, ex p Camacq Corporation* [1989] STC 785.

In *Burford v Durkin (Inspector of Taxes)* [1989] STC 845 the question was whether an assessment signed by one inspector on instructions from another is made by the former or the latter. For most situations this will be covered by TMA 1970, s 113(1B) but that section did not apply in this case. Surprisingly Mervyn Davies J held that the assessment was made by the person who gave the instructions and was therefore valid; which leaves one wondering whether s 113(1B) was needed. He went out of his way to distinguish *Honig v Sarsfield* [1986] STC 246 which had held that the 30 day period for appeal did not begin to run until it was actually signed.

One should record a victory for the taxpayer on a case under TMA, s 20. In *R v Inland Revenue Commissioners, ex p TC Coombs & Co* [1989] STC 520, TMA 1970, s 20(3), (4), (7) the inspector's belief was held to be unreasonable so that the notice under that section was invalid. To preserve a balance one should also note *R v Collector of Taxes, ex p Robert Goodall (Builders) Ltd*

[1989] STC 206 in which Schiemann J held that a particular collector of taxes did not have a closed mind.

There have been the usual crop of cases on appeals to commissioners. In two the taxpayer was able to show that the commissioners had behaved incorrectly in refusing an application for an adjournment of a hearing, so opening the way to judicial review. In *R v Ward (Inspector of Taxes), R v Special Commissioner, ex p Stipplechoice Ltd (No 3)* [1989] STC 93 the matter concerned a revision by the inspector of the terminal date of accounting period under appeal using his powers under TA 1988, s 12(8). Notice of the revision was not received by the taxpayer prior to the hearing and in consequence the taxpayer was not represented at the hearing of appeal. The determination of the appeal was quashed by Nolan J. In *R v Sevenoaks General Commissioners and Inland Revenue Commissioners, ex p Thorne* [1989] STC 560 the taxpayer was unable to attend the hearing owing to ill health; the commissioners' refusal of the request for an adjournment on the taxpayer's behalf was held unreasonable; *Dick v Piller* [1943] KB 497 applied. This case is also interesting because of a comment by Morritt J on the meaning of TMA 1970, s 118(2). Morritt J said that if the taxpayer had genuinely and reasonably believed and relied on what his bank had told him, it was arguable that this could constitute a reasonable excuse within TMA 1970, s 118(2).

It is necessary to distinguish from these cases the decision of Vinelott J in *Fletcher v Harvey (Inspector of Taxes)* [1989] STC 826, Ch D. Here the taxpayers' accountant's car broke down so the appeal was heard without him and a finding of wilful default against the taxpayers was made. He asked the commissioners to reopen the appeals in view of the large amounts of the assessments. He produced a statement of profits which the inspector had already seen. The commissioners decided that the determinations for the years 1976–77 to 1982–83 should stand in view of the fact that the taxpayers had failed to produce any evidence to displace the Revenue's case but that the determinations for the years 1983–84 to 1985–86 should be reopened and a final adjournment be granted until the commissioners' meeting on 22 January 1987. Vinelott J held that there had been nothing controversial in the inspector's evidence before the commissioners and nothing had been put before the comissioners that had not previously been put before the taxpayers. The taxpayers were not deprived of an opportunity of putting evidence to rebut the inspector's evidence or to adduce any other evidence. Therefore it could not be said that the commissioners had acted unreasonably or unfairly and in a way capable of causing injustice when they declined to adjourn the hearing. The appeal was therefore dismissed.

Lord Advocate v McKenna [1989] STC 485 is a lesson on the dangers of failing to appeal alternative assessments. Assessments had been made on the taxpayer under Sch D Case I, TA 1988, s 776 and to capital gains tax. The taxpayer appealed only against the Sch D assessment. The court held that the other assessments had become final, and there was no defence to the Revenue's action for payment due under the s 776 assessment.

There are three cases on matters which should occasion little surprise. *Gibson v General Commissioners for Stroud and Morgan (Inspector of Taxes)* [1989] STC 421, Ch D considered whether an appeal is determined when the commissioners determine the method of assessment or when the figures are subsequently agreed between the inspector and the taxpayer or when the commissioners hold the hearing for the formal confirmation of the figures. As the matter concerned the running of the thirty-day period under TMA 1970, s 56(2) it is no surprise that the last of these dates was held to be correct. *Montague v Hampstead General Commissioners and Inland Revenue Commissioners* [1989] STC 818 holds that an appeal determined by commissioners without the presence of the taxpayer is valid and cannot be set aside simply on that ground. *R v Inspector of Taxes, ex p Brumfield* [1989] STC 151 holds that a delay of 26 months in asking for judicial review is inexcusable.

Many interesting issues arose in *Shepherd (Inspector of Taxes) v Lyntress Ltd* [1989] STC 617; one of them was what issues can be raised on appeal? After the decision in one part of the appeal the question arose whether on the facts found by the commissioners the court had jurisdiction to hear the Crown's claim that the gain would be treated as the gain of another party to the litigation. Although the only issue in the other party's appeal was whether a particular loss accrued to that taxpayer in one situation, the court held that it had a discretion to allow any point of law that could be raised properly on the facts found by the commissioners unless the point raised was unfair to one of the parties.

There are numerous cases saying that the particular issue is one of fact not of law or that the burden of proof against an assessment is on the taxpayer. Examples are *Barnes-Sherrocks v McIntosh (Inspector of Taxes)* [1989] STC 674, *Billows v Robinson (Inspector of Taxes)* [1990] STC 161 and *Phillimore v Heaton (Inspector of Taxes)* [1989] STC 374.

Interpretation and miscellaneous points

Finally there are one or two small points. The task of interpreting the tax statutes is one of extreme difficulty; by reason of the complexity of the subject matter and the arid nature of the exercises as carried out by Chancery judges. However it is welcome to see references to the scheme of the Act as a whole in *George Wimpey International Ltd v Rolfe* and to the structure and language of the legislation in *Collard v Mining and Industrial Holdings Ltd* [1989] STC 384; we also find references to the objects and intentions of capital gains tax in *Owen v Elliott* [1989] STC 44. These questions are however ultimately ones of impression; *Dunstan v Young Austen and Young Ltd* [1989] STC 69 at 74j.

Smith v Fox (Inspector of Taxes) [1989] STC 378 is a charming tailpiece. The taxpayer sought to deduct certain expenses of travel. He was unable to produce any evidence of the nature of the contracts to put before the commissioners because a substantial part of his work concerned contracts between his company and the Ministry of Defence and was therefore covered by the Official Secrets Act 1911. In this case Vinelott J declined to upset an assessment and counselled the taxpayer on the desirability of professional representation in future.

Tort

B A HEPPLE, MA, LLB
Barrister, Professor of English Law, University College, University of London

Negligence

Economic loss

The continuing uncertainty about the limits of liability for economic loss was reflected in a number of lengthy reported judgments. Among the issues inconclusively canvassed were whether 'pure' economic loss can ever be recovered without an assumption of responsibility, whether such an assumption can arise from silence and whether a plaintiff who has an option to sue in contract or tort can succeed in tort where the contractual claim fails. Most of these issues arose in the context of cases where false information or advice was alleged to have caused economic loss (below). But these and related questions were also raised in several other cases.

The basic rule of tort law, that a person claiming for loss resulting from damage to property must have had a proprietary or possessory interest in the property damaged at the relevant time, was confirmed by the House of Lords in *Esso Petroleum Co Ltd v Hall Russell & Co Ltd (Shetland Islands Council, third party), The Esso Bernicia* [1989] 1 All ER 37. It was also made clear that the mere fact that a plaintiff who has suffered economic loss has also sustained damage to his own property is not sufficient to entitle him to claim for the economic loss unless it is consequent upon, and not merely additional to, the damage to his property. The *Esso Bernicia* had collided with the jetty at Sullom Voe terminal in the Shetlands and bunker oil escaped polluting the foreshore. This had happened when a coupling blew out of a hydraulic pipe above the starboard engine of the *Stanechakker*, one of three tugs helping to berth the *Bernicia*. A fire started and the towing line was cast off causing the *Bernicia* to go out of control. This action was raised by Esso, the shipowners, against Hall Russell, the designers and builders of the *Stanechakker*, averring negligence. The claims were for (1) £170,000-odd for the value of bunker oil lost, cost of repair to the *Bernicia* etc; (2) £527,000 for sums paid by Esso to local crofters in respect of damage to sheep due to pollution of the foreshore; and (3) £3.7 million paid by Esso to BP, the terminal operators, to clear up the foreshore. These two last-mentioned sums had been paid in terms of an agreement, called TOVALOP, under which tanker operators have agreed inter se to assume liability to victims for pollution damage caused by oil escaping or discharged from their tankers.

The first issue with which the House of Lords had to deal, in relation to the claim in negligence, was that of remoteness. Like the Lord Ordinary and the First Division, their Lordships had no difficulty in rejecting the argument that the damage to the *Bernicia* and the resultant spillage were not reasonable and probable consequences of the alleged negligence. There was, therefore, no further defence on the pleadings (proof had not yet taken place) to the claim in respect of physical damage to the tanker and consequential financial loss (eg loss of use, loss of bunker oil etc). The problem was the payments to the crofters and BP under TOVALOP. This was economic loss, and the House said that this was irrecoverable because it was not consequent upon the physical damage to the tanker, but a result of the damage to the sheep and terminal which Esso had agreed under TOVALOP to indemnify. Thus far, the decision is an impeccable application of first principles established ever since *Simpson & Co v Thomson* (1877) 3 App Cas 279.

However, the House made a further finding which is difficult to reconcile with these principles. This was that Esso were prima facie entitled to claim from Hall Russell the sum which they were liable under statute to pay the owner of the jetty for colliding with it. This, like the irrecoverable economic loss, was not consequent upon damage to the tanker, but consequent upon damage to the jetty. On delictual principles it should have been excluded, but it was not. The first difference in the eyes of their Lordships appears to be that this payment was involuntary (under statute) while the other heads were the result of TOVALOP, a 'voluntary' agreement. This seems to imply that the claim by Esso was, in English terms, one for 'restitution' of payments made by them to the jetty owners under statute, not a claim in tort. Even accepting the somewhat dubious description of the payments to the crofters and BP as 'voluntary' (TOVALOP was a 'binding' agreement between tanker owners entered into some time previously), the second reason given by their Lordships for differentiating between the statutory and TOVALOP payments is curious. This was that the payments had not enriched Hall Russell, because they did not discharge Hall Russell's liability to the crofters and BP. But if the claims were, as argued, in tort (delict) it is difficult to see why the payments already made to them would not have been deductible had the crofters and BP proceeded against Hall Russell. Lord Jauncey's equation of the TOVALOP payments with 'gratuities from a disaster fund' (at 54) seems to ignore the commercial realities which led Esso to enter into a 'binding' agreement under which BP had been paid pursuant to an arbitral award.

Esso also argued that the doctrine of subrogation entitled them to recover in their own name sums paid out by them in terms of TOVALOP. This was rejected on the grounds that if an indemnifier is subrogated to the rights of someone whom he has indemnified he can only pursue those rights in the name of that person and not in his own name. Esso could have taken an assignation (assignment in England) of the crofters' and BP's claims against Hall Russell, or, if this had been refused, Esso might (as in insurance cases) have brought a single action against the payees and Hall Russell claiming (1) an order that the payees should authorise Esso to proceed against Hall Russell, and (2) relief against Hall Russell, so authorised. Esso failed because they did not follow these forms of action, which are designed to protect the debtor from two actions from a single obligation. The fiction upon which this rests is that the victim of a tort who has been paid by his insurer (or, as here, a third party) has not been compensated at all.

The Court of Appeal was concerned with the duty to insure, or to advise insurance, in respect of injuries to another person, in two cases. In *Reid v Rush & Tompkins Group plc* [1989] 3 All ER 228, it was held that there was no duty of care in tort owed by an employer who posted an employee overseas to provide the employee with personal accident insurance against special risks arising out of the posting or to advise the employee to obtain such cover. The court was also unwilling to imply a term to that effect into the contract of employment. The result was that Frederick Reid was left uncompensated for severe injuries suffered while driving a Land Rover for his employers in Ethiopia, the accident being the sole fault of an unidentified lorry driver. In *Van Oppen v Clerk to the Bedford Charity Trustees* [1989] 3 All ER 389, affirming a decision of Boreham J [1989] 1 All ER 273, the Court of Appeal held that a school was under no duty of care in tort to take out personal accident insurance for pupils playing rugby or to advise parents to do so. The result was that Simon Van Oppen was left uncompensated for severe spinal injuries sustained during an inter-house rugby football match. Boreham J had held that the school had not been negligent in its rugby coaching and the injuries were the result of an accident rather than negligence on anyone's part. There was no appeal against this aspect of his decision, but only as regards the insurance claim.

The first of these decisions is a remarkable illustration of judicial reluctance either to see tort actions as a means of avoiding uncompensated injury, or to invent compulsory insurance where Parliament has feared to tread. Compulsory insurance against liability to employees has been required ever since 1972, by the Employers' Liability (Compulsory Insurance) Act 1969, but save in exceptional cases, this applies only to injuries in the course of employment in Great Britain. The underlying policy of the Act is that the employer is the best cost avoider of industrial accidents because he is in a better position than the employee to estimate the risks, to prevent accidents, and to absorb or pass on the costs to employees and customers. Those arguments apply with even greater force to work in a foreign country where the employee is unlikely to know the special risks involved. Broad policy arguments of this kind, were brushed aside by the court. Ralph Gibson LJ (at 235–236) simply noted that going uncompensated is an 'ordinary risk', given the large number of cases where there is no protection from a statutory scheme. The policy arguments were even less persuasive in *Van Oppen*, because a duty to insure would impose a higher duty on the school than on a parent who, even if advised to insure against the risk of accidental injuries to the child, is under no obligation to do so.

In *Reid*, it was submitted that there were two distinct sources of duty. The first was that owed by the defendants as employers to protect the 'economic welfare' of the employee while acting in the course of his employment. The court was unwilling to accept that the mere status of employer and employee could justify this novel extension of the duty of care which until now has been held to apply only to the the physical well-being of the employee. The second submission was that the defendants by employing the plaintiff to work for them in Ethiopia impliedly undertook a duty of care to advise the plaintiff of any special risks, and that he relied on this undertaking. The defendants argued that only if there was an assumption of responsibility and corresponding reliance thereon under the principles of *Hedley Byrne & Co Ltd v Heller & Partners Ltd* [1963] 2 All ER 575 could the plaintiff recover his alleged economic loss. Ralph Gibson LJ, after examining recent authorities (including the *Keyser Ullman* case, below) concluded that this was not necessarily so (at 239), a point on which the other members of the court reserved their opinion. This issue was not necessary to the decision, because all members of the court were agreed that (a) on the facts alleged it was impossible to imply a term into the plaintiff's contract of service which would entitle him to recover damages for the loss sustained, and (b) that it was not open to the court to impose a duty of care in tort which was not contained in any express or implied term of the contract. So this decision is clear authority for the proposition that the law of tort cannot be used to extend the parties' own (express or implied) bargain. In Ralph Gibson LJ's words (at 242):

> 'where there is a contract between the parties, and any "voluntary assumption of responsibility" occurred, if at all, at the time of making and by reasons of the contract, it seems unreal to me to try to separate a duty of care arising from the relationship created by the contract from one "voluntarily assumed" but not specifically assumed by a term of the contract itself.'

In *Van Oppen*, the court was unwilling to find any assumption of responsibility in relation to insurance, or reliance upon it, in the particular circumstances of the case. The court also held that there was no general duty to have regard to the economic welfare of pupils arising from the relationship of school and pupil. This is fully in accord with the decision in *Reid*, on which heavy reliance was placed.

An attempt to establish a duty in tort where the plaintiff had failed in contract was also unsuccessful in *National Bank of Greece SA v Pinios Shipping Co No 1, The Maira* [1989] 1 All ER 213, CA. It was alleged that there was a duty of care on a bank, which had entered into a tripartite management agreement with owners of a vessel mortgaged to the bank and a management agent, to see that the management agent did not under-insure the vessel. This duty was said to arise either as a term implied by law in the contract or in tort. Having held that there was no contractual duty of care applying to all contracts of a generalised type into which the management agreement could be fitted or a duty arising from the particular facts of the case, the Court of Appeal held without hesitation that in a case such as this 'if . . . the plaintiff fails in contract he must necessarily fail in tort' (at 223 per Lloyd LJ; see too, Nicholls LJ at 232). Lloyd LJ pointed out that the position would be different if the contract and tort lay in different fields:

> '. . . if, to take a simple example, I give my employee a lift home and injure him by my careless driving, then obviously he will not be prevented from recovering from me in tort because of the existence between us of a contract of employment' (at 223–224).

The approach taken in *The Maira* to filling contractual gaps was approved and followed by another division of the Court of Appeal in *Bank of Nova Scotia v Hellenic Mutual War Risks Association (Bermuda) Ltd, The Good Luck* [1989] 3 All ER 628 at 669–672, considered in the Chapter on Commercial Law, above.

In *Minories Finance Ltd v Arthur Young (a firm) (Bank of England, third party); Johnson Matthey plc v Arthur Young (a firm) (Bank of England, third party)* [1989] 2 All ER 105, Saville J applied the criterion of 'common sense and reason' when deciding that the Bank of England was not under a legal obligation to an individual commercial bank to exercise reasonable care and skill in carrying out its supervisory functions. The responsibility for conducting their commercial dealings prudently and carefully must rest on the banks themselves. In the same case it was argued that the bank owed no duty of care to a depositor in the commercial bank and reliance was placed on *Yuen Kun-yeu v A-G of Hong Kong* [1987] 2 All ER 705, All ER Rev 1987 at 285. Saville J pointed out that the latter case concerned a different supervisory banking authority and could not be considered as conclusive so far as the Bank of England was concerned. However, there was an 'insuperable barrier' against liability on the part of the bank, namely that the depositor in the present case was a parent company of the commercial bank and deposits by such companies were outside the Bank of England's supervisory powers and responsibilities under the Banking Act 1979.

False information and advice

In *Smith v Eric S Bush (a firm)* [1989] 2 All ER 514, the House of Lords affirmed the decision of the Court of Appeal, [1987] 3 All ER 179, All ER Rev 1987 at 310, but in the simultaneously heard appeal in *Harris v Wyre Forest DC* [1989] 2 All ER 514, the House reversed the decision of the Court of Appeal, [1988] 1 All ER 691, All ER Rev 1988 at 68, 86, 327. In both cases the question was whether a surveyor instructed by a mortgagee to value a house owed the prospective purchaser a duty in tort to carry out the valuation with reasonable skill and care and whether a disclaimer of liability for negligence by the surveyor was effective. Approving *Yianni v Edwin & Sons (a firm)* [1981] 3 All ER 592, the House of Lords held that there was a duty of care owed by the valuer to both the mortgagee and the purchaser by agreeing to carry out a valuation for mortgage purposes knowing that the valuation fee has been paid by the purchaser and that the valuation will probably be relied upon by the purchaser in order to decide whether or not to enter into a contract to buy the house. It made no difference whether the valuer was employed by the mortgagee or acted on his own account or was employed by a firm of independent valuers. Nor did the statutory duty of the building society or local authority to value the house prevent the valuer coming under a contractual or tortious duty of care to the purchaser. However, the liability was limited to the purchaser of the house and did not extend to subsequent purchasers.

From a theoretical point of view, the difficulty is to fit this type of case into the *Hedley Byrne* concept of 'voluntary assumption of responsibility'. As Lord Jauncey pointed out (at 541) a contract existed between the building society and the surveyors in *Smith v Bush*, and there was no room for a contract between the purchasers and the surveyor. This tripartite situation is different from the kind of direct relationship equivalent to contract which gave rise to liability in *Hedley Byrne*. Both Lord Griffiths (at 534, 536) and Lord Jauncey (at 541) based the duty on a 'deemed' rather than an actual assumption of responsibility by the surveyors to the purchasers in the light of the close degree of proximity between them. It was emphasised that the mere fact that the valuer knows that the valuation will be shown to the purchaser is not enough; knowledge, actual or implied, of the purchaser's 'likely' (at 541) or even 'highly probable' (at 536) reliance must be brought home to the surveyor. While such an implication can readily be made in relation to a potential mortgagor at the lower end of the housing market, it is far less likely in the case of an expensive residential or commercial property where the purchaser may be expected to rely on his own survey. The House of Lords also considered the effect of the disclaimer clauses under s 2 (2) of the Unfair Contract Terms Act 1977. This aspect is discussed in the chapter on Contract, above.

The standard of care expected of a surveyor in such situations was considered by Ian Kennedy J in *Roberts v J Hampson & Co (a firm)* [1989] 2 All ER 504, after hearing expert evidence, in a passage (at 510) expressly approved by Lord Templeman in *Harris v Wyre Forest DC* (at 525):

> 'If a surveyor misses a defect because its signs are hidden, that is a risk that his client must accept. But, if there is a specific ground for suspicion and the trail of suspicion leads behind furniture or under carpets, the surveyor must take reasonable steps to follow the trail until he has all the information which it is reasonable for him to have before making his valuation.'

In *Caparo Industries plc v Dickman* [1989] 1 All ER 798, the Court of Appeal held by a majority (Bingham and Taylor LJJ, O'Connor LJ dissenting) that the statutory auditor of a public company owed a duty of care to individual shareholders to carry out his audit using reasonable care and skill and that this duty was owed in respect of the purchase by a shareholder of further shares in the company. However, such a duty was not owed to non-shareholding potential investors or take-over bidders. The House of Lords has subsequently overturned the first part of this decision holding that the duty is owed neither to individual shareholders nor to potential investors ([1990] 1 All ER 568). Discussion of this important case must, therefore, be postponed to the the 1990 issue of this Review. *Caparo* in the Court of Appeal was said by Millett J in *Al Saudi Banque v Clark Pixley (a firm)* [1989] 3 All ER 361 at 371, to mark 'the furthest limit to which the duty of care for negligent misstatement has so far been taken in England' but its reasoning did not lead him to conclude that the auditors of a company owed a duty of care to a bank which lent money to the company. He held that there was no duty of care, regardless whether the bank was an existing creditor of the company making further advances or was only a potential creditor. It is worth noting that neither Bingham LJ nor Taylor LJ in *Caparo* regarded 'voluntary assumption of responsibility' as the 'single, simple litmus test of proximity' in cases of false information or advice. They preferred a more wide-ranging inquiry based on the now familiar elements of foreseeability, proximity and whether it is 'just and reasonable' to impose a duty.

The reserved judgments of the Court of Appeal in *Caparo* were handed down the day after the reserved judgments in *Banque Financière de la Cité SA v Westgate Insurance Co Ltd* [1989] 2 All ER 952, CA, so that the judgments in the one were made in ignorance of the judgments in the other. The latter is generally known as the *Keyser Ullman* case, that being the operative part of the former name of Banque Financière. An appeal was allowed from the decision of Steyn J, [1987] 2 All ER 923, All ER Rev 1987 at 20, 290. The plaintiff banks had made loans to B who had perpetrated a massive fraud on them by pledging as security gemstones which turned out to be worthless. The hapless banks were also the victims of dishonest conduct by L, the manager of the firm which had arranged insurance policies (containing fraud exclusion clauses) to protect the lending banks in the event of borrowing companies being unable to repay the loans. His misconduct, unconnected with that of B, consisted in representing to the banks that they had full cover when that was not the case. D, an employee of the insurers, had become aware of L's dishonesty but had failed to disclose it to the banks. The banks claimed that if L's dishonesty had been disclosed to them, they would have lent no further sums to B and so would not have incurred any further losses. Steyn J had allowed the banks to claim damages from the insurers. The Court of Appeal had to consider 11 specific issues on an appeal by one of the insurance companies ('Hodge') by whom D was employed. Two of these are relevant for purposes of this chapter. The first was whether the economic loss suffered by the banks was a reasonably foreseeable consequence of the failure of D to report L's dishonesty. The court agreed with Steyn J that the correct test was whether, as a result of the non-disclosure, there was a 'manifest and obvious risk' of financial loss from L's future dishonesty and that this test was satisfied. The second relevant issue was whether Hodge owed the banks a duty under the common law of negligence not to cause them the type of damage suffered by them. The essence of the banks' case was that they were seeking to recover damages resulting from a mere failure to speak. The court held that, on *Hedley Byrne* principles, there can be liability for such an omission only if there is a voluntary assumption of responsibility and a reliance on that assumption. On the facts, there had been no assumption by D and no reliance by the banks. An alternative submission for the banks was that even without an assumption and reliance there could be a duty of care not to cause economic loss. Unlike the differently constituted court in *Caparo*, the court in *Keyser Ullman* (in a single judgment delivered by Slade LJ on behalf of the whole court) thought that such a duty could arise only in rare cases. Even assuming, for purposes of the judgment, that such a duty was possible in respect of positive acts and statements, the court held that it could not arise from a mere failure by the insurers to disclose L's dishonesty. To impose such a duty in tort would contradict the basic principle of the law of contract that there is no obligation to disclose a material fact during pre-contractual negotiations before entering into an ordinary commercial contract. Interestingly, the existence of an established business relationship between the parties was not enough to turn the insurers' omission into a misrepresentation in tort any more than it could do so in contract. The judgment offers yet another warning that it is 'no part of the general function of the law of tort to fill in contractual gaps' (at 1011), even if 'the legal obligation falls short of the moral imperatives' (at 1013).

The unwillingness of the courts to superimpose a duty in tort upon a carefully structured tripartite relationship is shown by the decision in *Pacific Associates Inc v Baxter* [1989] 2 All ER 159, CA. A contractor successfully tendered for dredging and reclamation work for the employer, the ruler of Dubai. The contractor knew that the work would be supervised by a consultant engineer retained by the employer and that the contractor would only be paid sums on account when they were certified by the engineer, but there was no direct contractual relationship between the contractor and the engineer. The contract with the employer provided that the contractor was entitled to additional payment if it encountered hard material in the course of dredging which could not have been reasonably foreseen. The contractor's repeated claims for such payments were rejected by the engineer on the ground that the hard materials should have been foreseen. The contractor brought an action for £45m damages against the engineer alleging negligence or breach of a duty to act fairly and impartially in administering the contract by failing to certify and rejecting the claims for payment for hard materials. The duty was said to arise either from a voluntary assumption of responsibility under *Hedley Byrne* principles or from the close and direct proximity between the contractor and engineer. Both these arguments were rejected by the Court of Appeal which held that the engineer did not owe a duty in tort to act with due care to avoid economic loss to the contractor under the contract with the employer. As regards the alleged assumption of responsibility, there was no request to the engineer by or on behalf of the contractor for the engineer to render any service to the contractor. The relationship between engineer and contractor was the result of a contract between the contractor and the employer and of the engineer having agreed with the employer to perform the functions of engineer under the contract. The engineer was not employed to exercise due care in the interest of the contractor, and so could not be regarded as having assumed responsibility to do so. This kind of tripartite relationship is different from the direct assumption of responsibility in *Hedley Byrne*. Various reasons were given for rejecting the second basis of argument. Either economic loss to the contractor was not reasonably contemplated, in part because the contract provided for the correction of mistakes by the engineer by process of arbitration (Ralph Gibson LJ at 186, but Russell LJ at 190 had reservations); or there was insufficient proximity (Ralph Gibson LJ at 186, but Russell LJ considered that the proximity test was satisfied at 190, and Purchas LJ thought there was a degree of proximity in the sense that the contractor relied on the contractor, but regarded this as 'not the same quality of proximity' as required to establish a duty of care in the *Hedley Byrne* sense); or it was not 'just and reasonable' to impose a duty given that the parties had chosen to structure their relationships so that there was no contract between contractor and engineer (Russell LJ at 189–192, regarded this as the 'heart of the appeal'; see to like effect Ralph Gibson LJ at 186–187; Purchas LJ at 170).

A solicitor's immunity from actions for damages for alleged negligent advice was one of the issues considered in *Somasundaram v M Julius Melchior & Co (a firm)* [1989] 1 All ER 129. The Court of Appeal applied the test approved by the House of Lords in *Saif Ali v Sydney Mitchell & Co (a firm)* [1978] 3 All ER 1033, in relation to pre-trial work, by holding that advice as to a plea in criminal proceedings is something which is so intimately connected with the conduct of the cause in court that it is covered by the public policy immunity. This immunity extends not only to barristers but also to solicitors when acting as advocates. However, the court was not persuaded that the immunity applied to solicitors when a barrister had also been engaged to advise. It was said that the solicitor would enjoy the immunity only in one of the following situations: (1) the solicitor's advice on plea had subsequently been confirmed by counsel, counsel's intervention either negativing any evidence of negligence on the solicitor's part or breaking the causal link between the solicitor's advice and the eventual plea; or (2) the plea had resulted in a decision of the court, the action being contrary to public policy because it would involve an impermissible collateral attack on the decision of a court of competent jurisdiction.

The existence of a statutory right of appeal in respect of an erroneous opinion or advice given by the Charity Commissioners, led Knox J in *Mills v Winchester Diocesan Board of Finance* [1989] 2 All ER 317 to strike out a negligence action against the Commissioners proceeding concurrently with charity proceedings under s 28 of the Charities Act 1960. In any event Knox J doubted whether there was sufficient proximity between a potential object of a charity and the Commissioners to give rise to a common law duty of care.

Defective premises

Department of the Environment v Thomas Bates & Son Ltd [1989] 1 All ER 1075, CA, raised 'yet another variant of a vexed question: what is the liability of a builder in tort for economic loss?' (at 1077). The plaintiffs, underlessees of a building complex, sued the defendant builders alleging negligence concerning weakness of the concrete used to construct supporting pillars, and claiming the cost of carrying out remedial work. The judge found that the weakness in the concrete did not cause any imminent danger to the health and safety of persons using the building and that the remedial work had been carried out to restore the building to the full loading capacity for which the plaintiffs had bargained in taking their underlease. The judge dismissed the claim in respect of the remedial costs and his decision was upheld by the Court of Appeal, applying the decision of the House of Lords in *D & F Estates Ltd v Church Comrs for England* [1988] 2 All ER 992, All ER Rev 1988, p 323. It is difficult to distinguish the facts of this case from *Batty v Metropolitan Property Realizations Ltd* [1978] 2 All ER 445, which had been questioned (but not overruled) by Lords Bridge and Oliver in the *Church Commissioners* case. However, the Court of Appeal did not decide the present status of *Batty*, but simply considered whether the remedial works were 'to avert imminent risk of physical injury to persons'. On the judge's findings, once the weakness was detected in the pillars and warning was given there was no longer a danger, imminent or at all. The remedial works were done, not to avert inevitable danger, but to restore to the plaintiffs the full capacity of the building for which they bargained. An action in tort could not be used to recover these remedial costs, for this would be 'equivalent to the enforcement in contract of a warranty of fitness' (at 1085).

In *Robertson v Ridley* [1989] 2 All ER 474, the Court of Appeal held that an individual member could not sue the members' club to which he belonged in respect of injuries he had sustained by reason of the condition of the club's premises. The rules of the club did not give rise to a duty of care towards individual members to maintain the club premises in a reasonable state of safety.

Exercise of statutory powers

The House of Lords, in *Calveley v Chief Constable of the Merseyside Police* [1989] 1 All ER 1025, has upheld the decision of the Court of Appeal, [1988] 3 All ER 385, All ER Rev 1988 at 326. Lord Bridge, delivering the only speech, rejected the existence of a duty of care owed by a police officer investigating a suspected offence against a fellow officer, on the grounds that the way the investigation was carried out did not involve any foreseeable injury of a kind capable of sustaining a cause of action in negligence. Anxiety, vexation and injury to reputation were insufficient. Any duty in respect of economic loss would have run up against the general principle of non-liability for such loss, and would have eroded, if not destroyed the requirements of the tort of misfeasance in public office. It was held that for the latter tort to be proved, it had to be shown that a public officer had done an act in bad faith or, possibly, without reasonable cause.

The duty to prevent suicide

In *Kirkham v Chief Constable of the Greater Manchester Police* [1989] 3 All ER 882, an alcoholic with a long criminal record and suicidal tendencies was transferred, on remand by magistrates, from police detention to a remand centre. The police failed to follow the procedure for informing the prison authorities of the prisoner's suicidal tendencies. He was treated as a normal prisoner at the remand centre and placed in a cell alone where he committed suicide. His widow brought an action on behalf of the dependants and the estate claiming damages against the police for negligence. Tudor Evans J held that the police were not in the position of a 'mere bystander'. By taking the deceased into custody and detaining him at the police station they came under a duty to take reasonable care for his safety which was not discharged simply by passing him over to the prison authorities on remand by the magistrates. The discharge of the duty required them to pass on the information about his being a suicide risk. This breach of duty was an effective cause of his death because had the prison authorities known they would probably have been able to prevent him committing suicide. The most interesting parts of the judgment relate to the defences of contributory negligence and ex turpi causa. As regards the first, in finding that there was no 'fault' on the part of the deceased, Tudor Evans J was plainly applying a subjective test (although no authorities were considered), thus lending weight to the view that the usual objective and impersonal test is inappropriate in the case of persons suffering from some disability or, as in this case, 'diminished responsibility' (at 894). The defence of ex turpi causa was ruled out because of the absence of any 'causally related criminal activity' (suicide not being a criminal act). A wider ground of public policy, that suicide involves an act of moral turpitude and that the law should accordingly refuse to award damages in such a case, was also rejected on the ground that the 'moral turpitude, if any, involved in the act of suicide must depend on the circumstances in which it occurred' (at 893). In the present case of suicide in custody by a person who was at high risk and whose suicide could probably have been prevented by the exercise of reasonable care, the defence could not succeed.

Contributory negligence

Capps v Miller [1989] 2 All ER 333 adds a refinement to the tariff for contributory negligence in cases where a plaintiff on a motor cycle or moped suffers more severe injuries than he would otherwise have done because of a failure to fasten the chin strap of his crash helmet securely or at all. Glidewell and May LJJ held that a reduction of 10% should be made in the plaintiff's damages, rather than the 15% usually applied where there is a failure to wear a crash helmet (or seat belt in a car) at all. Where a crash helmet is worn but not properly fastened there is still a breach of traffic regulations, but according to these judges a lesser degree of blameworthiness. Croom-Johnson LJ, although preferring the figure of 15%, was willing to fall in line with his brethren. The court made it clear that the extent to which the damages should be reduced has to be assessed even though it is not possible to establish the extent to which the plaintiff's injuries have been increased by his blameworthiness.

Consent

The case of *F v West Berkshire Health Authority* [1989] 2 All ER 545, HL, is considered in the chapter on Medical Law, above.

Vicarious liability

The question whether a wrongful act by an employee arises within the course of his employment is ultimately a question of fact. But one may be certain that the 'prima facie propositions' by Lord Lowry in *Smith v Stages* [1989] 1 All ER 833, HL at 851, as to when an employee travelling to or from work can be regarded as within the course of his employment, will be used as guidelines in future cases of this kind. These lean heavily on Glidewell LJ's statement of principle in the Court of Appeal, [1988] ICR 201 at 211, but with some enlargement. The employers were held liable for damages in respect of injuries sustained by one of their employees in an accident which occurred while he was being driven home on a rest day by another employee after working away from their base. The negligent fellow-employee was 'going about his employer's business' when driving home in the employer's time. The essential point seems to be that the employee was 'on duty' (per Lord Lowry at 851) or 'employed to make the journey' (per Lord Goff at 838), because for the purpose of moving base a normal working day was set aside for the journey, for which he received a day's pay as well as a travel and lodgings allowance. The fact that he was not required to make the journey by any particular means, nor even on a particular working day, did not prevent the conclusion that he was employed to make the journey. As Lord Lowry said (at 851) 'one must not confuse the duty to turn up for one's work with the concept of already being "on duty" while travelling to it.' In the former situation the employee is not acting in the course of his employment; in the latter he is.

Economic torts

Conspiracy

In *Metall und Rohstoff AG v Donaldson Lufkin & Jenrette Inc* [1989] 3 All ER 14, the Court of Appeal had an opportunity, after extensive argument, to resolve the conflict between first instance judges, described in All ER Rev 1988 at 332, as to the scope of unlawful means conspiracy. The court (in a single judgment delivered by Slade LJ) reversed in part the decision of Gatehouse J, [1988] 3 All ER 116, and held that, even if unlawful means are involved, an essential ingredient of the tort of conspiracy is that the sole or predominant purpose of the conspirators' agreement was to injure the plaintiff's interests. An English company (AML) and its officers, who acted as brokers for the Swiss plaintiffs (M & R), were alleged to have traded fraudulently in the London Metal Exchange. To protect their position AML and its American parent companies (the first and second defendants) had seized metal warrants and closed accounts owned by M & R, who obtained a judgment against AML which remained largely unsatisfied. In an attempt to recover the outstanding damages and costs M & R issued a writ against the American parent companies alleging a conspiracy, not with a sole or predominant purpose to injure M & R, but 'as a conspiracy in effect to steal their warrants.' The Court of Appeal held that an alleged agreement in this form did not amount to a tortious conspiracy, even if the means used were unlawful, because the defendants had acted to protect their own commercial interests rather than to injure the plaintiffs. Leave to serve a writ in this form out of the jurisdiction was set aside.

Since leave to appeal was granted, the House of Lords itself may soon say whether this is the correct interpretation of Lord Diplock's controversial speech in *Lonrho Ltd v Shell Petroleum Co Ltd* [1981] 2 All ER 456 and, indeed, whether that decision should be followed in future. This possibility was enough for Vinelott J in *Derby & Co Ltd v Weldon (No 3)* [1989] 3 All ER 118, to refuse to strike out a conspiracy claim which did not allege that the sole or predominant purpose was to injure the plaintiffs. On the other hand, in *Lonrho plc v Fayed* [1989] 2 All ER 65, CA, counsel for the plaintiffs accepted that the Court of Appeal's decision in *Metall und Rohstoff* precluded a challenge to Pill J's decision to strike out the conspiracy claim, [1988] 3 All ER at 471, All ER Rev 1988 at 332. Clarification of the law by the highest court is thus eagerly awaited.

Interference with trade or business by unlawful means

The appeal in *Lonrho plc v Fayed* (above) was directed against the striking out of the plaintiff's claim based on the alleged unlawful interference with their trade or business (see All ER Rev 1988 at 330). This appeal was upheld. The first issue was whether or not a 'predominant purpose' to injure the plaintiff, rather than to further the defendant's own interests, is a necessary ingredient of this tort. The court held that it is not, given Lord Diplock's different treatment of this tort and the tort of conspiracy (in which such a 'predominant purpose' is needed) in *Lonrho Ltd v Shell Petroleum Co Ltd* (above) and in *Hadmor Productions Ltd v Hamilton* [1982] 1 All ER 1042 at 1052–1053. All that is necessary is that the act should be 'directed against' the plaintiff or intended to harm him. To this Dillon LJ (with whom Ralph Gibson and Woolf LJJ agreed) added (at 69) that the 'mere fact' that a person has suffered injury by an act of the defendant which is illegal does not automatically entitle him to bring an action: 'the complainant still has to show that on its true construction the statute which imposed the prohibition gave rise to a civil remedy.'

However, in the subsequent docks strike case of *Associated British Ports v TGWU* [1989] 3 All ER 796, Butler-Sloss LJ (at 813) and Stuart-Smith LJ (at 818) treated the 'intent to injure' as the essence of this tort, apparently equating the 'intent' with a desire to harm. This made it possible for them to distinguish this tort from the tort of inducing breach of a statutory duty which they (together with Neill LJ) held to be actionable only where the plaintiff has the right to claim damages for the breach of statutory duty in question. According to Butler-Sloss and Stuart-Smith LJJ, if an intention to injure is the essence of the tort of interference with business by unlawful means, then it matters not that the 'unlawful means' is the non-actionable breach of a statutory requirement. The statements to the contrary in *Lonrho v Fayed* were regarded as obiter and inconclusive. Neill LJ (at 808), on the other hand, saw great force in the argument that a breach of statutory duty cannot be relied upon as unlawful means for purposes of this tort unless it is actionable. The House of Lords' reversal of the docks strike decision on a different point, [1989] 3 All ER 822, leaves wide open the question which of these approaches to intention and to unlawful means expresses the correct principle.

The second issue in *Lonrho v Fayed* was whether the unlawful means (in this case alleged fraudulent misrepresentations to the Secretary of State by take-over bidders for the House of Fraser) must itself be actionable as a complete tort as between the alleged wrongdoer and the third party against whom the wrong was practised to the detriment of the plaintiff (in this case it was said that the Secretary of State had suffered no damage). The court held that it was not necessary to prove this. The court decided that it would not be right to strike out the cause of action because complicated issues of intention and causation and whether there had been conduct 'directed against' a business interest of the plaintiffs, could only be determined on the actual facts as they emerged at the trial.

Defamation

Two cases this year raised technical points about the pleading of the defence of justification: *Bookbinder v Tebbit* [1989] 1 All ER 1169, CA and *Morrell v International Thomson Publishing Ltd* [1989] 3 All ER 733, CA. A third related to the pleading of fair comment: *Control Risks Ltd v New English Library Ltd* [1989] 3 All ER 577, CA.

Damages

Fatal Accidents

In *Pidduck v Eastern Scottish Omnibuses Ltd* [1989] 2 All ER 261, Sheen J held that for the purposes of s 4 of the Fatal Accidents Act 1976 a pension and a widow's allowance received from an employers pension fund were 'benefits' and were therefore to be disregarded in assessing damages for the deceased's death. This decision has been affirmed: [1990] 2 All ER 69, CA.

Provisional damages

In *Hurditch v Sheffield Health Authority* [1989] 2 All ER 869, CA consideration was given to what constitutes a sufficient agreement that the case is one in which an award of provisional damages is appropriate, so as to place the plaintiff under a duty to apply for an order under RSC Ord 37, r 9.

Town and Country Planning

PAUL B FAIREST, MA, LLM
Professor of Law, University of Hull

After the number of cases in recent years, 1989 proved to be something of a lean year. Only two major cases were reported, one dealing with an issue of principle concerning the consideration of planning applications by a local planning authority, the other (a decision of the House of Lords) concerning a relatively narrow point about listed buildings.

Planning permission—material considerations

Section 29(1) of the Town and Country Planning Act 1971, as is well known, provides that

> 'in dealing with [an application for planning permission, the local planning authority] shall have regard to the provisions of the development plan, so far as material to the application, and to any other material considerations . . .'

An important decision in the year under review is concerned with the interpretation of this provision, and, in particular, the relevance of 'financial considerations' to planning decisions.

The case in question is *R v Westminster City Council, ex p Monahan* [1989] 2 All ER 74 (Webster J, QBD, and CA (Kerr, Nicholls, and Staughton LJJ)). The issue arose in connection with plans to modernise and improve the Royal Opera House, Covent Garden, which, it was proposed, would be substantially funded by a projected office development in the area. The applicants, members of the Covent Garden Community Association, sought judicial review by way of certiorari to quash a resolution of the planning and development committee of the Westminster City Council agreeing in principle to the grant of planning permission and listed building consents to the Royal Opera House for redevelopment of land in Covent Garden. At first instance and in the Court of Appeal, the applicants contended that the resolution of the planning committee was vitiated because the committee had improperly taken into account the Royal Opera House's financial reasons for seeking to carry out commercial development in the area, which was not in accordance with the development plan. The applicants' challenge failed, both at first instance and in the Court of Appeal. On 19 December 1988, the Appeal Committee of the House of Lords refused leave for a further appeal.

The facts of the case are complex, but the issue of law a relatively simple one. The Royal Opera House desired to undertake a programme of modernisation and reconstruction to ensure its future as a major international house. The cost of these improvements was estimated, in 1986, to be £56m. No grant aid from Government was likely to be forthcoming, and so the Royal Opera House sought to recover a substantial element of this cost by building office accommodation which could be sold or let at a profit. The council's attitude, as expressed in its development plan, was in general terms discouraging about further office development in the area (a conservation area), but supportive of the policy of developing and enhancing the Royal Opera House, in view of its importance for cultural and tourist interests.

The planning and development committee of the council, recognising the gravity of the issues involved, at first deferred a decision, and then, after consideration of further reports, became convinced that there was no possible alternative way of financing the improvements and extension to the Royal Opera House.

Their decision was challenged by the applicants. In essence, their challenge was based on two grounds:

(i) the provision of finance to maintain the international status of the Opera House was not a 'material planning consideration' which could lawfully justify development regarded by the Committee as involving a major departure from the development plan;

(ii) in the alternative, if financial matters could constitute a 'material planning consideration', the council had failed adequately to investigate the financial aspects sufficiently to entitle it rationally to conclude that the provision of office accommodation, by way of departure from the development plan, was in fact necessary to achieve the objectives relating to the Opera House.

Ground (ii) can be dealt with fairly briefly, as it was by both Webster J (at first instance) and Kerr LJ , with whose remarks the other members of the court concurred (on appeal). They both found that the committee had considered the matter fully and had applied itself conscientiously to the issues;

> 'To suggest that the conclusion which was then reached was irrational or manifestly unreasonable, or based on information which was, or should reasonably have been regarded as, inadequate, is in my view untenable' (per Kerr LJ at 102a)

It is ground (i) which presents the most controversial point. Both Webster J and the Court of Appeal were at pains to point out the nature of the question which fell to be considered, namely whether, as a matter of law, financial considerations could amount to 'material considerations' in the context of s 29 of the Town and Country Planning Act 1971.

> 'The courts are not concerned, in the sense of having no right to concern themselves, with the planning merits or demerits of the development in any respect. It is important to emphasise this, because many controversial views are held about the scheme, and a number of press comments have referred to these proceedings in ways which might well give the false impression that the courts are somehow involved in taking sides in the discussions' (per Kerr LJ at 91e–f).

In *Stringer v Minster of Housing and Local Government* [1971] 1 All ER 65 (the Jodrell Bank case), Cooke J had held that, while 'material considerations' must be considerations of a planning nature, they were not limited to matters of amenity. In that case it was said that the likelihood of interference with the radio–astronomical work of the telescope was a 'material consideration' to which regard might be had.

Later cases, especially *Newbury DC v Secretary of State for the Environment* [1980] 1 All ER 731 (a case concerning planning conditions) were not thought to have materially changed the test laid down in *Stringer*.

The Court of Appeal stressed that—

> 'planning authorities must be particularly careful not to give way too readily to assertions of financial constraints as a ground for relaxing policies which have been formulated in the public interest . . . Suppose that an urban authority had a policy of requiring the use of green tiles, which are substantially more expensive than others, in areas of residential developments bordering on the countryside, If a developer who wished to erect an otherwise highly desirable housing estate claimed that this would be uneconomic if green tiles had to be used, then the authority would clearly not be bound to reject his application out of hand. It would be bound to consider it on its merits, although it might well be highly sceptical about the assertion that the economic viability of the project would founder if green tiles had to be used, But if, after proper consideration, this were indeed the conclusion reached on a basis which would not admit of a charge of irrationality, then there could be no question about the validity of a decision which permitted the use of red or black tiles in the circumstances' (per Kerr LJ at 97f–h).

In the earlier case of *Bradford City Metropolitan Council v Secretary of State for the Environment* [1986] 1 EGLR 199, Lloyd LJ had regarded it as 'axiomatic' that planning consent cannot be bought and sold. The Court of Appeal accepted this dictum, but, on analysing the earlier cases, found them largely to be cases where planning or other consents had been granted for ulterior, and therefore impermissible motives (as in, for example, *Hall & Co Ltd v Shoreham-by-Sea UDC* [1964] 1 All ER 1). The present case, unlike *Hall's* case, did not involve an issue of a condition to serve the purposes of the local authority. Cases like the present

> 'involve the acceptance, faute de mieux, of a relatively undesirable feature of a development as a compromise or sacrifice in order to ensure the viability of the main project which is judged to be sufficiently desirable to warrant a partial relaxation of policy' (per Kerr LJ at 98d).

The Court of Appeal followed earlier dicta in the cases of *Sosmo Trust Ltd v Secretary of State for the Environment* [1983] JPL 806 and *Sovmots Investments Ltd v Secretary of State for the Environment* [1976] 1 All ER 178 at 186, to the effect that 'cost can be a relevant consideration.'

An interesting sidelight in the judgment is the approval of the approach of Lloyd LJ in the *Bradford* case quoted above, where he rejected the contention that the powers of a planning authority under a s 52 planning agreement were in some way wider that they were when determining an application for planning permission under s 29 of the Act,

> '. . . if a particular condition would be illegal, on the ground of manifest unreasonableness or otherwise, if it were imposed on an applicant for planning permission then it cannot acquire validity if it is embodied in a s 52 agreement, whether at the instance of the applicant himself or not' (at 100d).

Nicholls LJ, who concurred in the decision, based his decision much more closely on the 'package' nature of the proposals.

> 'If the purpose of granting permission for development A is to finance development B, that purpose can equally exist and be fulfilled if the two developments have no physical contiguity at all, They can be miles apart. A hypothetical example mentioned in argument was of the ROH owning land elsewhere in London, in Victoria for instance. Could permission for a

commercial development of land in Victoria have been properly granted solely to finance alterations to the Opera House situated in Covent Garden? . . . I am not persuaded by this reductio ad absurdum argument. Circumstances vary so widely that it may be unsatisfactory and unwise to attempt to state a formula which is intended to provide a definitive answer in all types of case. All that need be said to decide this appeal is that the sites of the commercial development approved in principle are sufficiently close to the Opera House for it to have been proper for the local planning authority to treat the proposed development of the office sites, in Russell Street and elsewhere, and the proposed improvements to the Opera House as forming part of one composite development project. As such it was open to the planning authority to balance the pros and cons of the various features of the scheme. It was open to the authority to treat the consequence, for the Opera House works, of granting or withholding permission for offices as a material consideration in considering the part of the application which related to offices' (at 103d–j).

Preservation of listed buildings

An important point concerning the preservation of listed buildings was considered by the House of Lords in *Robbins v Secretary of State for the Environment* [1989] 1 All ER 878.

Robbins was the owner of a windmill which had been built in 1868 and included in a list of buildings of special architectural or historic interest in 1951. Robbins had acquired the windmill in 1969 and had converted it into a dwellinghouse. Over the years, the condition of the windmill deteriorated, and the local planning authority, Ashford Borough Council, served a repairs notice on Robbins, with which he failed to comply. This led to the local planning authority taking steps for the compulsory acquisition of the property, to which Robbins objected.

Put at its simplest, Robbins' contention was that the compulsory purchase procedure could not validly be used, because a condition precedent to recourse to the compulsory purchase procedure was the service of a valid repairs notice. The repairs notice was, he maintained, invalid because it was excessive in its scope; thus, he contended, the ensuing compulsory purchase procedure was vitiated.

The point at issue was basically one of statutory construction, and thus it may be helpful to set out the relevant statutory provisions at the outset. The relevant sections are ss 114 and 115 of the Town and Country Planning Act 1971, as amended.

'114—(1) Where it appears to the Secretary of State, in the case of a building to which this section applies, that reasonable steps are not being taken for properly preserving it, the Secretary of State may authorise the council of the county or county district in which the building is situated . . . to acquire compulsorily under this section the building and any land comprising or contiguous or adjacent to it which appears to the Secretary of State to be required for preserving the building or its amenities, or for affording access to it, or for its proper control or management . . .
(3) This section applies to any listed building . . .
(4) The Secretary of State shall not make or confirm a compulsory purchase order for the acquisition of any building by virtue of this section unless he is satisfied that it is expedient to make provision for the preservation of the building and to authorise its compulsory acquisition for that purpose.

(5) The Acquisition of Land Act 1981 shall apply to the compulsory acquisition of land under this section.

(6) Any person having an interest in a building which it is proposed to acquire compulsorily under this section may, within twenty-eight days after the service of the notice required by section 12 of the Acquisition of Land Act 1981, apply to a magistrates' court acting for the petty sessions area within which the building is situated for an order staying further proceedings on the compulsory purchase order; and, if the court is satisfied that reasonable steps have been taken for properly preserving the building, the court shall make an order accordingly.

(7) Any person aggrieved by the decision of a magistrates' court on an application under subsection (6) of this section may appeal against the decision to the Crown Court,

115—(1) The compulsory purchase of a building under section 114 of this Act shall not be started by a council . . . unless at least two months previously they have served on the owner of the building, and not withdrawn, a notice under this section (in this section referred to as a "repairs notice")—(a) specifying the works which they consider reasonably necessary for the proper preservation of the building; and (b) explaining the effect of sections 114 to 117 of this Act . . .

(4) For the purposes of this section a compulsory acquisition is started when the council . . . serve the notice required by section 12 of the Acquisition of Land Act 1981.'

There was no doubt that the council had served on Robbins a notice which they believed to be a valid notice under s 115; however, Robbins claimed that the notice was invalid in that it purported to require him to carry out works which went beyond those required for the 'proper preservation' of the building (the term used in s 115(1)). On the contrary, he claimed, the works required would amount to a *restoration* of the building. The Act drew a distinction between *restoration* and *preservation*, as there were other sections of the Act (especially ss 96–100) which dealt with the issue of restoration.

The notice served on Robbins specified 20 items of works, 14 of which were conceded, on any definition, to be works of preservation. They related to works of an emergency nature (for instance, dismantling the dangerous remains of the fantail) or were works needed to prevent further deterioration of parts of the mill which were subsisting at the date of service of the notice. Thus, at least so far as these works were concerned, it was clear that they were properly characterised as works of preservation.

The other items gave rise to the trouble. Essentially, the following issues were considered:

(i) Does preservation relate to the preservation of the building
  (a) *as it was when it was listed* (the submission of counsel for the respondent)
    or
  (b) *as it was when the repairs notice was served* (the submission of counsel for the appellant)?

(ii) Independently of the answer to question (i), does the inclusion in the repairs notice of 'non-preservation' items render the whole notice, and thus the consequent compulsory purchase procedure, invalid?

These two questions will now be considered separately.

(i) To what date does 'preservation' relate?

This issue was considered extensively in the speeches delivered by Lord

Bridge and Lord Ackner, In the event they held that the question was irrelevant to the proceedings before the House, as some of the works specified in the notice referred to some parts of the mill which had already disappeared at the time of the listing of the mill in 1951. For example, one of the items in the list of works contained in the council's notice called for the full restoration of the fantail and the partial restoration of the sweeps of the mill. When the mill was listed in 1951 it was recorded that the fantail and the sweeps were partly missing. These, said Lord Bridge (at 885d) 'must be taken to be works for the restoration of the building to the condition that it was in before it was listed', Having heard full argument on the point, however, and bearing in mind that it might prove to be of major significance in later cases, the House of Lords addressed itself to the main question. Noting that the language of the sections is 'capable of either construction' (at 884a), Lord Bridge was of the view that the question 'is to be resolved purposively by considering the underlying policy of the legislation'. Holding that the policy of the legislation was the public interest in the preservation of buildings of special architectural or historic interest, he had 'no hesitation in concluding that the date of listing construction [was] to be preferred' (at 885a). These remarks were supported by Lord Ackner, who said that—

> 'the submissions of counsel for the appellant would clearly produce results contrary to the underlying policy of the Act, which is to preserve the building, ie to keep it and its features as they existed at the date of listing in sound condition' (at 889c).

(ii) Effect of the inclusion of 'restoration' works
Some of the items in the notice (for instance the restoration of the fantail and sweeps) clearly went beyond the scope of 'preservation' on either test. Did that mean that the whole repair notice was invalid? Counsel for the appellant contended that it did, notwithstanding the fact that his client had failed to carry out some items of work properly characterised as 'preservation'. The House of Lords, holding this to be 'a pure question of the construction of the section [where no] assistance is to be derived from authorities on severance in very different legal contexts' (at 885j) rejected this argument, saying that:

> 'Provided that the list of valid items is sufficiently substantial to support a conclusion by the Secretary of State, in the event that the specified works are not carried out, that reasonable steps are not being taken for properly preserving the building, it is difficult to see why the invalid items should not simply be disregarded' (at 886a)

The apparent dilemma in which the owner of a listed building might be placed by the inclusion in a repairs notice of 'excessive' items could be solved by recourse to s 114(6).

> 'This unusual provision empowers the magistrates' court to override the opinion of the acquiring authority and to pre-empt the decision of the Secretary of State in determining what works are reasonably necessary for the proper preservation of the listed building. The procedure will operate in the following way. The owner who wishes to retain his property in the listed building will put in hand the works specified in the repairs notice which he admits to be necessary for its proper preservation, but not the works specified in the items listed which he wishes to dispute. On receipt of notice under s 12 of the 1981 Act initiating

the compulsory purchase proceedings, he will then apply to the magistrates' court under s 114 for an order staying those proceedings. If the magistrates' court is satisfied that he has taken reasonable steps for properly preserving the listed building by the works he has already put in hand and that the disputed items are excessive, the owner will be entitled to an order staying further proceedings on the compulsory purchase order . . . If at the conclusion of the proceedings it is held against the owner that some of the disputed items are reasonably necessary for the proper preservation of the listed building, he will then be able to put in hand the works specified in relation to those items, and it is inconceivable that the acquiring authority would proceed with the acquisition. If they were to do so, the owner could make a fresh application to the magistrates' courts under s 114(6) which would be bound to succeed.'

(At 886d–h, per Lord Bridge, and see also 890a–e, per Lord Ackner.)